The Guide to

UK Company

Giving

6th edition

John Smyth & Denise Lillya & Tom Traynor

*Additional research by:*

**Alan French, Sarah Johnston** & Tom Traynor

*Contributions from:*

**Del Redvers**,
'Charity of the Year' and Smaller Organisations

# DIRECTORY OF SOCIAL CHANGE

Published by
Directory of Social Change
24 Stephenson Way
London NW1 2DP
Tel. 08450 77 77 07; Fax 020 7391 4808
e-mail publications@dsc.org.uk
www.dsc.org.uk
www.companygiving.org.uk
from whom further copies and a full publications list are available.

Directory of Social Change is a Registered Charity no. 800517

First published 1998
Second edition 1999
Third edition 2000
Fourth edition 2002
Fifth edition 2004
Sixth edition 2007

ISBN 978 1 903991 76 3

**British Library Cataloguing in Publication Data**
A catalogue record for this book is available from the British Library

Cover design by Gabriele Kern
Text designed by Gabriele Kern
Typeset by CPI Tradespools, Chippenham
Printed and bound by Page Bros, Norwich

Other Directory of Social Change departments in London:
General enquiries 08450 77 77 07

Directory of Social Change Northern Office:
Federation House, Hope Street, Liverpool L1 9BW
Research 0151 708 0136

# Contents

Welcome to the 6th edition of *The Guide to UK Company Giving* which continues to provide relevant, updated policy information and commentary on the current state of corporate community involvement in the UK.

This edition features nearly 500 companies, which together gave around £730 million in community support (including £365 million in cash donations) in 2005/06. We continue with the familiar layout format to help make the task of identifying potential new sources of corporate support both easier and, ultimately, more fruitful.

As ever, the majority of the guide consists of the individual company entries, but it also contains additional sections offering advice and information for fundraisers, voluntary organisations, community groups, companies and individuals.

## Company information

Our basic criterion for inclusion is that the company must have made cash donations of £20,000 or more in support of the community in its latest financial year. A few companies gave less than this, but have been included either because they give substantial help in other ways (at least £100,000 of in-kind support) or, because in previous years they have met our criteria and there is no obvious reason for suspecting the recent decrease to be the start of a downward trend.

Wherever possible, we have quoted the UK charitable donations figure declared by the company in its annual report and accounts as it continues to provide a tangible and unambiguous indicator of its commitment to the community. Failing this, we quote the worldwide donations figure whilst making it clear that this is the case. As acknowledged above, however, cash donations are not the only way in which a company can provide support for charities and community groups.

Where made available to us, we have included an additional figure for total community contributions. However, the means of measuring the cost of these, and even what should be included under this heading, are open to debate. In our view, the term should cover a company's charitable donations, plus support such as good-cause sponsorship and the value of gifts in kind, secondments and employee volunteering during company time.

If calculated by the company, we quote management costs separately as we do not consider it valid to include this as part of total community contributions.

Finally, if possible, we give a figure for any cause-related marketing initiatives a company may have undertaken. Again, we do not include this in the total community contributions figure because of its obvious commercial benefit to the company concerned.

## Entry layout

The layout used for the entries in this guide is described in the breakdown of the 'Fictitious Company' entry on pages 38 & 39. We hope that this will enable users to more readily access the information they require on the various types of support that each company may offer.

## Geographical and activity indexes

Most companies state that a link must exist for any appeal to be considered – the most obvious of these being geographical, business activity or employee involvement. To help you prepare a preliminary list of companies to look at further (not to immediately write to!), we have included an index to head office location (page 25) and an index to business activity (page 31). Whilst the head office index is geographically biased towards London, it provides a useful starting point.

Comprehensive search facilities are available at the subscription based website: www.companygiving.org.uk, which also lists the directors, brands, and subsidiaries of each company.

## Company listings

Our research probably accounts for 80–90% of all giving by companies. However, there are companies, which, by virtue of membership of one or more specific organisations, have declared an interest in supporting the community. We have therefore listed all current corporate members of Arts & Business, Business in the Community, London Benchmarking Group and the PerCent Club, even though the companies concerned do not necessarily have an entry in this guide.

We have also included details of ProHelp (formerly, the Professional Firms Group), potentially a very useful source of support for charities. ProHelp is made up of a group of professional practices (including surveyors, architects, accountants and solicitors), each of which has offered to provide their professional services free of charge (or at minimal cost) to voluntary and community groups in their locality. Rather than provide a list of ProHelp members, we have given the regional office contacts, as they are best able to provide up to date information on what is happening in their area and explain how you can access their services.

A brief explanation of each of these organisations is given at the start of the relevant section.

## Company comparisons

The level of giving by companies in this guide varies greatly (from around £20,000 to over £50 million). Perhaps because of this, we tend to equate 'big giver' with 'most generous', but this may not actually be the case. Whilst very large companies are applauded for giving say £4 million in donations, smaller companies giving a few hundred thousand pounds may actually be contributing a far greater proportion of their profits to charity.

To give an example: though HBOS plc and Richer Sounds plc appear towards opposite ends of the cash donations scale (£10.5 million compared with £217,000 in 2005/06), when this is expressed as a percentage of pre-tax profits their positions are reversed, giving 0.22% and 6%, respectively. Although the usefulness of comparisons made in this way is a matter for dispute (profits can go down as well as up), it does show how taken at face value figures can be misleading as far as who is making the greater gift to the community.

## Corporate social responsibility

Corporate social responsibility (CSR) continues to be the focus of much debate. Some people simply don't like the concept, believing that to put it into effect will have damaging consequences for business. Others dislike the term, which they see as confusing and limited in scope, excluding other important factors beyond the social (hence, the increasing use of the wider reaching 'corporate responsibility').

Our research deals with one aspect of CSR which, broadly speaking, is the philanthropic. However,

usage of the term will no doubt continue to develop until it either establishes itself with a generally accepted meaning, or is replaced by a newer form of words.

Nevertheless, our concern is not so much with the label, but whether there is any substance to back it up. Examples abound of company annual reports that glibly trot out statements of ethical intent or concern for the local community. More often than not, however, such statements fail to be substantiated with examples. For a number of companies the right to count themselves amongst established good corporate citizens appears to have been earned not through positive community action, but by signing up to any one of a number of 'me too' CSR membership bodies, such as the Global Reporting Initiative, FTSE4Good or AA1000. In fact, there are so many standards and institutions which companies can adopt or join in order to present themselves as socially responsible that there is a danger of their credibility being undermined.

## Measuring corporate support

The methods we use to gather information on companies' charitable support are relatively straightforward. Basic financial details and the level of cash donations for a particular year are obtained from annual reports or details lodged at Companies House. For other support in addition to cash donations (gifts in-kind, employee volunteering and so on) and the specifics of a company's charitable support policy, we use a questionnaire and/or speak to the relevant person. (With the larger companies such information is increasingly to be found on their websites, sometimes at great length.)

The inclusion of policy details within a company entry is a very important aspect of our work as it provides fundraisers with the information necessary to make an informed decision about which companies to target. As ever, we do not sanction the 'scatter-gun' approach, believing this to be not particularly successful, a waste of time for the parties concerned and potentially damaging to other, more qualified applicants.

Our ability to provide this service is, of course, reliant to a large extent on the cooperation of the companies whose details we intend publishing. It is regrettable, therefore, that this is not always forthcoming. In researching this edition we experienced one of the lowest return rates ever for our initial questionnaire. Whilst we can only speculate as to why this was the case ('Questionnaire Fatigue Syndrome'?), it is clear that some companies are failing to engage with at least one of their stakeholders.

In previous editions of this guide we have explained at some length the differences that exist between ourselves and organisations such as the London Benchmarking Group (LBG) and Business in the Community (via the PerCent Club) when it comes down to publishing figures on companies' support for the voluntary and community sectors. We will not repeat this, other than to say that, primarily through the efforts of the LBG, which was established in 1995 and now consists of over a hundred members, some agreement has been reached concerning what actually constitutes Corporate Community Involvement (CCI) and how its value should be measured.

Our main point of difference with these groups remains the inclusion of management costs as part of a company's total community contributions. The justification is that if community staff were not employed specifically to run the company's programme it would not happen, or at least would not be as effective. Reference is made to the fact that charities also have to employ administrative staff to run efficiently, and declare such costs in their annual report. This is so, but they don't then include such costs in their annual grant total! Furthermore, when in some cases management costs constitute a significant proportion of a company's total 'support', something isn't quite right.

Of these two relatively high profile organisations, only the LBG appears to be willing to ask the difficult questions of business. As a result, the continual monitoring and fine tuning of its measurement techniques and push to standardise the way in which companies calculate total community contributions is enabling us to present a more accurate and comprehensive picture of corporate support.

## Trends in corporate support

Companies, especially the larger ones, continue to seek out partners proactively, with some even requiring organisations to 'pitch' for the privilege. We have also seen an increase in the number of companies adopting a 'charity of the year', quite often chosen by the employees, who are then allowed to volunteer on company time for their chosen cause. This appears to have a number of benefits for the company beyond being seen as a good citizen. Not only is the adoption of a charity of the year often administratively more straightforward than dealing with numerous separate appeals, but it also induces a 'feel good' factor amongst employees and a sense of loyalty to their socially responsible employer.

In an interesting 'twist' on this process, Epilepsy Action launched a brand new initiative in 2006 inviting companies to apply to be its 'Company of the Year'!

Cause-related marketing (CRM) continues to be a popular form of fundraising, although we think it important that charitable organisations are aware that CRM is not purely philanthropic in nature and that companies will expect a decent business payback.

Because of this, CRM appears to be an area where a company can exploit the opportunity to improve its return on charitable donations through what has been termed 'strategic giving'. As a result partners are carefully selected for their popularity and profile raising potential, rather than the worthiness of their cause. This would seem to potentially exclude a significant portion of charities that are deemed either too small, too controversial or do not have the right image from the company's perspective.

Those organisations that do enter into a CRM promotion may find things are not quite as they expected. They may be expected to sign an agreement which prevents them from accepting funding from a company's competitors, or there may be some form of cap on the amount the charity can receive or the need for a specified 'trigger' to be set off. For example, it may not be enough for a linked product to be bought for the charity to benefit; the purchaser may have to complete a second stage, such as returning a coupon, before money is released. Perhaps in future some social objectives and evaluation criteria need to be incorporated into such partnerships.

Recent research conducted by the Smart Company towards the end of 2006, noted an increasing trend for companies in the UK to demonstrate their caring nature by establishing a corporate foundation. Nearly half of the foundations they looked at (52) were established in the last fifteen years, with the overall concern expressed being whether they are truly independent of their corporate founders.

This is an issue Directory of Social Change has raised in the past, with our concerns then still holding true now. Basically, it seems that many corporate trusts whilst being created with a stated purpose that is charitable, and thus securing the benefit of such status, have an unstated purpose that is concerned with giving effect to the wishes and policies of the company. Not surprising to the more cynically-minded of us, perhaps, but something nevertheless that needs to be monitored closely.

## Warning!

We are told that companies continue to receive many unsolicited or inappropriate appeals for support. Whilst many bring this upon themselves due to a lack of clear guidelines for potential applicants, this should not be seen as an excuse to conduct blanket mailings.

One of the findings of the December 2006 report 'An Evaluation of Corporate Community Investment in the UK' published by the Charities Aid Foundation, was that companies support a relatively narrow set of causes and issues that have not particularly changed over time. This, coupled with a survey which found the biggest frustration charities face in attempting to work with companies to be limited access to decision makers, means it is vitally important to do your research thoroughly.

Further information on how to successfully approach businesses for support is given in the 'Applying to companies' section. In general, however, before approaching any company in this guide its entry should be read carefully. As we have stated previously, unless there is some clear link with a company, or your project is clearly within its defined areas of support, you should NOT be applying.

We would also recommend that you download a copy of 'Charities Working with Business', published by the Institute of Fundraising. This gives a good overview of the issues involved in undertaking a relationship with a company and is available at: www.institute-of-fundraising.org.uk

## Acknowledgements

We would like to thank all the companies who have helped to compile this guide. Each was sent a questionnaire and a draft entry, following the return of which corrections were noted and incorporated. Failing any cooperation in this respect, information was gathered from sources in the public domain. Notwithstanding this, the text and any mistakes within it, remain ours rather than theirs.

And finally ...

If you have any comments about the guide, positive or negative, please get in touch with us at the Research Department of the Directory of Social Change, Federation House, Hope Street, Liverpool L1 9BW; tel: 0151 708 0136; fax: 0151 708 0139; e-mail: research@dsc.org.uk

# 'Charity of the Year' and Smaller Organisations

*Del Redvers*

Charity of the Year is a label increasingly applied to all manner of partnerships, but what does it really mean? Business Community Connections (BCConnections) researched how different charities and businesses use the Charity of the Year concept and in doing so identified several critical factors for success.

There are many forms of Charity of the Year partnership but with certain common themes. Most obviously and significantly they are time limited relationships although certainly not always one year in duration. The most widespread understanding of the term is a partnership in which the staff from a business undertake a range of activities to raise money for the identified charity. At the end of the year businesses often feel the need to replace the charity they support in order to prevent fundraising fatigue, and to ensure wider appeal to staff and customers as no one charity will be relevant to all stakeholders. This also gives the business the opportunity to support another charity.

Increasingly, however, other elements are added to the staff fundraising concept, such as cash donations, employee volunteering or other in-kind donations, sponsorship, cause related marketing or lobbying and campaigning. Sometimes these partnerships involve very little or no staff fundraising at all. Many businesses involved in these other types of Charity of the Year relationship would not be able to support a staff fundraising partnership, perhaps because they have smaller numbers of higher paid staff with less free time. Similarly, it makes sense for companies with relevant goods or services to donate them in-kind to the charity as part of their contribution. The term Charity of the Year is used to brand a relationship, because although it can be misleading, it is a widely understood and accepted term.

## For smaller organisations

Traditionally Charity of the Year relationships have been the preserve of large charities, frequently those able to offer national exposure to large corporate partners. There is, however, evidence to suggest a growing trend in the number of smaller charities seeking and successfully establishing Charity of the Year partnerships. The BCConnections research shows no reason why Charity of the Year should be out of bounds to small or medium sized charities and by the same token to Small and Medium Enterprises (SMEs). There are however a number of risks which can offset the many benefits available to both charities and businesses and which need to be weighed very carefully irrespective of the size of the organisation.

## The advantages ...

The research suggests that in general Charity of the Year partnerships do work for both partners. On the whole charities tend to put a financial value on the relationship of 6 or 7 times the cost of establishing and managing the partnership. Whilst larger charities frequently net income in excess of £100,000 through these relationships, smaller charities also tend to consider them worthwhile activities even if they are very unlikely to achieve a 6 figure financial contribution. A Charity of the Year partnership can ...

1. Provide a reasonably predictable and often large income stream over a fixed period of time.
2. Provide an excellent opportunity to significantly increase the profile and reputation of the charity.
3. Create a track record of working with the corporate sector.
4. Lever support from other businesses and customers.
5. Increase fundraising activity from existing supporters.
6. Educate the workforce and customers of the business about the charity or its cause.
7. Offer access to employees as a new market of potential supporters.
8. Last longer than 1 year. There is a growing trend towards the "Charity of 2 or 3 years" giving the security of a longer-term income stream.
9. Generate unrestricted income, although there is a developing trend towards restricted funds in these relationships.
10. Increase the morale at the charity, especially amongst the fundraising team.

## And Pitfalls ...

There are many issues for a charity to consider before deciding whether or not to pursue a Charity of the Year relationship.

These partnerships can be resource intensive to manage, most significantly in terms of staff time. The cost benefit analysis section of the BCConnections research reveals that managing a small Charity of the Year partnership often takes at least 10% of one person's time. A large partnership can occupy from 1 to 3 employees on a full time basis. There may also be costs associated with legal agreements for joint promotions, licencing and sponsorship arrangements.

Pitching for major Charity of the Year partnerships can be a significant undertaking in itself, requiring the investment of resources at an early stage, with no promise of a return. Once a partnership is agreed there is often a lengthy planning period before it is launched. Consequently, there exists a time lag between investing resources to develop the partnership and receiving the support. This can create a cashflow problem, particularly for smaller charities but also where a charity is expected to cover early costs such as producing badges and promotional material. Despite what can amount to considerable set up costs, these partnerships will always be time limited and therefore, for most charities, cannot be considered a sustainable source of income.

Frequently, businesses use voting schemes to engage staff in selecting the Charity of the Year. This often results in the exclusion of many types of charities from the selection process as in an unrestricted ballot, staff have a tendency to vote for charities such as children, cancer and other health related charities with poignant issues.

There is always an element of risk on both sides in any corporate community relationship as a link is forged between the reputations of the two partners. With Charity of the Year this link is likely to be well publicised and consequently the relationship can backfire if it is considered to be unethical.

## Getting a Charity of the Year partnership

If your organisation is seeking a Charity of the Year partnership, there are some things you should bear in mind ...

1. Be strategic in your approach. Focus on the good fit between your charity and your target companies. Start building relationships with these businesses and try to grow the company contacts you already have. Think ahead and plan which

business may adopt you next year or the year after that.

2. Decide on the cost benefit ratio you are prepared to accept. This is usually not just a financial exercise as it may involve judgements about intangible benefits and the potential worth of a partnership with the company in the longer term.

3. Be prepared to walk away. One of the most important messages to come out of the research is that charities need to assess at an early stage the potential value of the partnership, and then negotiate and decide whether or not it is worthwhile pursuing.

4. Consider approaching new businesses not previously involved in Charity of the Year partnerships.

5. Consider the benefits and drawbacks of a Charity of the Year partnership from the business point of view. Try to gain an understanding of why your target business might want a Charity of the Year partnership and more specifically with your organisation. This can help you to value your charity's worth and feel more confident about negotiating with the business.

6. If possible seek advice from a previous Charity of the Year of your target business. This should increase your understanding of the company, how they work and what they may want out of the partnership. This should be supplemented by in-depth research on the company from published sources.

7. Ask the business for a meeting at an early stage. This will give you more guidance about what they want from the partnership, before you invest significant resources. It will also help start to develop a relationship.

8. Be flexible about including other types of involvement for the partnership, apart from staff fundraising.

9. Consider at the outset how you could monitor the impact of your proposed Charity of the Year partnership on the wider community.

## The Pitch

When pitching for a Charity of the Year partnership, a key consideration is how the charity will be selected. If it is a management decision, there needs to be a focus on benefits to the business whilst for a staff ballot the proposal should be more emotive. Where possible engage the beneficiaries of the charity in the process.

Proposals should be tailored specifically to the business you are approaching and stick to any brief given. Should the pitch fail, always ask for feedback and if appropriate a contribution; it is worth asking if the business can compensate you in any way for the time and resources invested. However, always be mindful of possible future relationships with that business.

For smaller Charity of the Year partnerships there is often no formal pitch process. Businesses that already engage in small scale Charity of the Year partnerships are more likely to use existing contacts or staff recommendations to identify future partners. Smaller businesses that have never had a Charity of the Year may need some guidance from the charity to help them appreciate the potential of the relationship.

## Setting up the Partnership

### Planning

The importance of development time prior to publicising the partnership cannot be underestimated. In the BCConnections research over a quarter of the organisations did not plan the partnerships. Many larger businesses now select their Charity of the Year 6 months to 1 year before the publicised partnership year begins. For smaller partnerships however, 1 or 2 months can provide ample planning time.

### Agreement

A written agreement outlining the parameters of the relationships (objectives, targets, timeframes and budgets) plays an important role in managing the expectations of your partner. Clearly allocate responsibility for tasks and costs.

Seek to maximise the mutual benefit of the partnership. The greater the benefit for your business partner, the more seriously they will take the relationship and the greater the likelihood they will invest in Charity of the Year partnerships in the future.

Develop a plan of events, and a process for regular communication and review. Use the expertise of charity fundraisers to generate ideas for activities. Most charities find it easier to have a phased programme of fundraising events rather than doing everything at once.

### Financial Return

Consider whether there should be a minimum guaranteed return to the charity from the partnership. Some charities recommended including minimum guarantees in any documentation to protect against risk such as a minimum amount of cash to be raised. In addition agree what percentage of money raised will be restricted. Some charities will ask for a percentage of funding to be unrestricted to cover the costs of running the partnership. Also establish the timings of payments to the charity

throughout the year and consider the impact on cashflow. Whilst a single large cheque handed over at the end of the year may look impressive, it is often not a practical option, particularly for smaller charities.

### Communications

Establish who will be responsible for the overall publicity of the partnership. If a logo is to be designed for the new partnership who will pay for it? Ensure that use of logos is agreed in advance.

There is also the issue of internal communication with the company's employees. Several charities have commented that it takes time to motivate and inspire staff to get involved in a programme of fundraising or other activities and the timetable should allow for this. The appointment of charity champions amongst the staff of the business can help to co-ordinate activity and provides a communication channel, particularly for multi-site operations.

### Thinking Ahead

Discuss the sustainability of the partnership and develop an exit strategy early on in the relationship. During review meetings consider whether it is beneficial to both partners to keep the relationship going beyond the year. Even if the charity is not designated Charity of the Year going forward, it may be possible to maintain and develop specific elements of the relationship, such as relationships with suppliers and payroll giving.

## Measuring and Monitoring

There has been an increasing emphasis on measuring the impact and benefits of Charity of the Year partnerships as with all other aspects of corporate community involvement. Like other types of relationship, there need to be mechanisms for measuring the social impact, benefits to the business and benefits to the charity. Significantly, Charity of the Year partnerships require careful measurement of the relationship itself as it is often more involved than other types of corporate community partnership.

Critically both parties need to know if there was a positive benefit compared to the cost of their involvement. Effective measurement of the partnership enables both parties to decide whether to undertake similar ventures in the future and identifies areas for improvement. Knowing what you want to measure at the outset allows for the correct accounting procedures to be put in place. For instance, without prior planning it may be easy for a company to breakdown staff fundraising by office or team but not by individual activities. This would make it impossible to measure the effectiveness of each activity.

The following represent some of the measures used by the businesses and charities we interviewed during the course of the research to assess the success of the partnership.

- Targets met or exceeded in planning and preparation.
- Financial target met or exceeded.
- % of company branches involved.
- Outcome of the partnership for charity beneficiaries; e.g. number of individuals helped as a result, or number of pieces of equipment purchased, amount of research time enabled etc.
- Positive PR; e.g. the number of articles/column cms or amount of television time.
- Number of contacts the charity has developed.
- Staff and customer surveys; e.g. awareness and perceptions of business and charity.
- Feel good factor; e.g. for business – number of letters, comments received in chat room etc.
- Number of charity champions that come forward in the business.

## Conclusions

Charity of the Year relationships are a popular and highly visible way for charities and businesses to work together for mutual benefit and to target the social impact of corporate support for the voluntary sector. Whilst there are no hard and fast rules about establishing and managing Charity of the Year partnerships, a considered and strategic approach will help to maximise the many advantages offered by this type of relationship whilst minimising the risk.

Smaller charities should be encouraged to consider how they can adapt the models developed by larger organisations. Although there is definitely the opportunity for charities of all sizes to benefit from Charity of the Year relationships, they are not necessarily appropriate for all organisations and represent just one of several types of relationship that can form between the voluntary and corporate sectors.

The Charity of the Year research conducted by BCConnections is available in full with the cost-benefit analysis template and case studies at www.bcconnections.org.uk. The BCConnections website also has information to help charities or community organisations considering any form of partnership working with the corporate sector.

BCConnections would like to gratefully acknowledge the help of all the charities and businesses that participated in the Charity of the Year research.

Del Redvers is the Joint Chief Executive at Business Community Connections.

## How much do companies give?

Given that there is a statutory obligation for companies to declare their charitable donations where the total exceeds £200 in any one year, getting a figure is relatively easy. You just ask a company for a copy of its annual report or download it from the company website and look in the Directors' Report section. The figure for community contributions, however, is more difficult to obtain and less precisely calculated, if at all. The work of the London Benchmarking Group (LBG) and the PerCent Club, however, does appear to be having some success in addressing this.

Whilst many companies' level of donations remains fairly constant year on year, others fluctuate significantly, and for no apparent reason, which can make accurately predicting trends in company giving difficult. As if to confirm this, whilst we can normally say that each year, with a few exceptions, the top 25 companies by charitable donation and community contribution will remain the same, this is definitely not so for this edition.

The total cash donations made in 2005/06 by the 495 companies in this guide amount to £367 million, compared to £291 million in 2003/04. With a further £367 million declared for other forms of in-kind support, this gives a total community contributions figure of £734 million compared to £580 million in 2003/04. Whilst these figures obviously indicate that in monetary terms both cash and in-kind support continue to rise (with the greater increase being in in-kind giving), in percentage terms the increase is actually equal at 26% for each.

Furthermore, the percentage increase in cash donations has risen more sharply than that for total community contributions in the period since 2001. Between 2001/02 and 2003/04, cash donations rose by a mere 0.7% and total community contributions by 15%, compared with the 26% rises witnessed above.

This appears to go against the previously indicated trend that companies were moving away from straightforward cash donations towards in-kind giving in its various forms. We believe, however, the greater increase in cash donations is due to the number of natural disasters that have recently taken place around the world and the subsequent high level of financial support they drew.

In truth, the figures quoted above are probably a little way short of what is actually given, but even so, it may be useful to try and put this into perspective. Recent polls have shown that in general the public tends to overestimate the level of support received by the voluntary sector from big business (around one-quarter of total income in one case). In fact, it is calculated by organisations such as NCVO and CAF that just 3–4% is contributed by companies. Out of a total voluntary sector income of £26.3 billion in 2003/04, this equates to around £920 million which is somewhat closer to our total figure than other published estimates.

## Community contributions
### Total amount given

Of the £734 million given in total by all the companies in the guide, over 99% was donated by the top 400, and 46% (£338.2 million) by the 'Top 25' (see Table 1). The minimum figure required to gain entry to this illustrious group rose to £4.4 million. This follows the drop in entry requirements of £0.2 million to £3.4 million in the last edition.

As mentioned above, obtaining a figure for total community contributions (as opposed to purely cash donations) can be difficult. If the trend towards giving in-kind support in preference to cash donations continues once again, then this figure becomes increasingly important in order to gain an accurate picture of the levels of company support. It will be interesting to see, therefore, what affect the recently passed Companies Act 2006 will have on reporting levels. (The Act strengthens the requirements in the legislation on social and environmental reporting so that the 1,300 companies quoted on the UK stock market must report on environmental matters, employees, social and community issues and risks down company supply chains where they are necessary to understanding the company's business.)

### Changes in giving

For the top 400 companies contributions continue to rise (up by over 26%) although this covers the three-year period from 2003/04. However, with businesses

Table 1

## Top 25 by UK community contribution

2005/06

| | | |
|---|---|---|
| (1) | The Royal Bank of Scotland Group plc | £53.8 million |
| (2) | Lloyds TSB Group plc | £36.0 million |
| (3) | Barclays PLC | £35.3 million |
| (4) | Northern Rock plc | £24.8 million |
| (5) | BT Group plc | £20.0 million |
| (6) | ITV plc | £19.6 million |
| (7) | HSBC Holdings plc | £15.8 million |
| (8) | Fidelity Investment Management Limited | £13.7 million |
| (9) | GlaxoSmithKline | £12.0 million |
| (10) | Diageo plc | £11.8 million |
| (11) | HBOS plc | £10.5 million |
| (12) | Marks and Spencer Group plc | £9.3 million |
| (13) | Centrica plc | £8.1 million |
| (14) | Shell | £7.7 million |
| (15) | The Co-operative Group | £7.2 million |
| (16) | Unilever UK | £6.7 million |
| (=17) | J Sainsbury plc | £5.6 million |
| (=17) | Euro Packaging Limited | £5.6 million |
| (=19) | National Grid plc | £5.4 million |
| (=19) | Vodafone Group | £5.4 million |
| (=19) | Ecclesiastical Insurance Group plcl | £5.4 million |
| (22) | British Sky Broadcasting Group plc | £5.0 million |
| (23) | KPMG | £4.6 million |
| (24) | Deutsche Bank | £4.5 million |
| (25) | British Nuclear Fuels plc | £4.4 million |

more accurately calculating their in-kind support than in earlier editions of the guide, it is difficult to know with any certainty how much of this has previously been provided but not declared.

For the second edition running the Royal Bank of Scotland Group plc (1) has maintained pole position following a 25% increase in its community contributions (up from £40.1 million in 2003/04 to £53.8 million). Other companies increasing their total contributions substantially include Diageo plc (10) – up from £7.3 million to £11.8 million and the Co-operative Group (15) which more than doubled its level of contributions.

Nearly one-quarter of companies are new to the 'Top 25', including ITV plc (6) and Deutsche Bank (24). Of particular note, however, are Fidelity Investment Management Limited (8) and Euro Packaging Limited (17), both of which gave substantial funds to the foundations they have established.

Notable omissions from last time include bp plc (global community contributions figure available only) and Zurich Financial Services (decrease in community contributions).

## Contributions as a percentage of profit

Even with a significant increase in reported cash and in-kind support (up by £154 million for the top 400 companies), total community contributions only rose slightly as a percentage of pre-tax profits (up from 0.47% to 0.49%).This figure is still, therefore, a long way short of the PerCent Club guideline of 1% which, disappointingly, only 78 companies in the guide met.

# Charitable donations
## Total amount given

Of the £367 million given in cash by the companies in the guide, over 99% was donated by the top 400, and a staggering 64% (£233.9 million) by the 'Top 25' (see Table 2). The minimum figure required to gain entry to this illustrious group rose to £2.6 million, nearly double the figure (£1.4 million) required in the last edition.

## Changes in giving

For the first time since we have been producing this guide, Lloyds TSB Group plc (2) has been overtaken as the largest corporate donor by the Royal Bank of Scotland Group plc (1). The latter made cash donations of £39.0 million in 2005/06, compared to the former's £31.7 million.

Table 2

## Top 25 by UK charitable donation

2005/06

| | | |
|---|---|---|
| (1) | The Royal Bank of Scotland Group plc | £39.0 million |
| (2) | Lloyds TSB Group plc | £31.7 million |
| (3) | Northern Rock plc | £24.7 million |
| (4) | Barclays PLC | £16.7 million |
| (5) | HSBC Holdings plc | £15.8 million |
| (6) | Fidelity Investment Management Limited | £13.7 million |
| (7) | Diageo plc | £11.8 million |
| (8) | HBOS plc | £10.5 million |
| (9) | Shell | £7.7 million |
| (10) | Centrica | £6.7 million |
| (11) | Euro Packaging Limited | £5.6 million |
| (=12) | Vodafone Group | £5.4 million |
| (=12) | Ecclesiastical Insurance group plc | £5.4 million |
| (14) | Deutsche Bank | £4.5 million |
| (15) | GlaxoSmithKline plc | £4.0 million |
| (16) | British Sky Broadcasting Group plc | £3.8 million |
| (=17) | British American Tobacco plc | £3.5 million |
| (=17) | Prudential plc | £3.5 million |
| (19) | Marks and Spencer Group plc | £3.4 million |
| (=20) | British Nuclear Fuels plc | £2.9 million |
| (=20) | Dyson Limited | £2.9 million |
| (22) | Unilever UK | £2.8 million |
| (23) | Rio Tinto plc | £2.7 million |
| (=24) | Morgan Stanley International Limited | £2.6 million |
| (=24) | ScottishPower plc | £2.6 million |

*Note: These 2005/06 figures are for statutorily declared UK charitable donations only. This can understate total community contributions, particularly for the largest companies.*

Over half the companies listed in the 'Top 25' are new to it; something unprecedented in our experience. Some of these are familiar names that have re-entered after an absence, e.g. Centrica plc (10), whilst others have already been referred to in the context of Table 1, covering total community contributions. Those companies not seen here before include Dyson Limited (20) and Morgan Stanley International Limited (24), both of whom made large donations to the foundations they have established.

## Donations as a percentage of profit

For the top 400 companies the level of cash donations expressed as a percentage of pre-tax profit has stayed within a fairly narrow range from the early 1990s through to the present. From a low of 0.21% in 1995/96 to a high of 0.28% in 1992/93, this year's drop to 0.25% from 0.27% in 2003/04, represents only the second such decrease in the period.

## The potential for company giving

We believe companies have the capacity, if not the will, to put a whole lot more back into society. Normally, when asked what the total contributions figure is for all companies in the UK (on top of that given by those in the guide), we estimate there to be around a further £100 million available. (This would come from the numerous small/medium-sized enterprises whose level of giving is too low to be included, and from professional firms who are not obliged to publish such information.)

However, even £830 million doesn't sound particularly impressive when you consider that if every company in the current guide met the PerCent Club's standard of donating 1% of pre-tax profits to charity, contributions could be nearly double this amount.

This section gives basic information on identifying potential companies to approach, how to establish contact with them and how to put together a proposal for them to consider.

## Corporate social responsibility

Corporate social responsibility (CSR) is a much bandied about phrase which seeks to define what an increasing number of people and groups believe the wider role of business in society should be. This guide deals with one aspect of CSR which, broadly speaking, is the philanthropic. The term, however, is also current in the context of respect for human rights and the environment, for example. Despite the increasing interest in the issue of CSR (as witnessed by the number of articles, journals and conferences appearing around the topic), it should be remembered that company giving is way below that of the general public and, to a lesser extent, charitable trusts. Out of a total voluntary sector income in 2003 of £20.8 billion, government contracts contributed 37.0 per cent, the general public 36.6 per cent, charitable trusts 6.6 per cent, and business 4.3 per cent. Nevertheless, ethical issues aside, companies remain an important target for both national and local fundraising.

To make an effective appeal to industry you must have a basic understanding of why firms give. This will enable you to put forward good reasons why they should support your work. Many companies, especially the larger, higher profile ones, receive hundreds, if not thousands, of requests for support from charities, voluntary sector organisations and local community groups each year. For your appeal to be successful it needs to be more than a general plea to 'put something back into the community'. You can help a company justify its charitable support by telling them not just why you want the money, but why giving you support should be of interest to them. You can also tell them about any benefits they will get in return for their money and about the impact their donation will have on your work. At the very least you should be able to demonstrate a clear link with the company, for example, geographically, through your product or an employee contact, or some other connection.

## Why companies give

Most companies give out of *enlightened self-interest* rather than for pure altruistic or philanthropic

---

### Some basic don'ts when applying to companies

✗ Don't write indiscriminate 'Dear Sir/Madam' circular letters to any company you come across.

✗ Don't use any guide you may have access to as a simple mailing list.

✗ Don't write to a company that specifically says it does not support your kind of work.

✗ Don't write to a company unless *at least one* of the following applies:

▶ The company has a declared policy indicating a specific interest in your group's area of work.

▶ The company operates in the same locality as your group and a clear product link exists between your needs and its supplies.

▶ You have a strong personal link with a senior company officer, or a member of staff is actively involved in your work.

▶ There is some good reason to write to that particular company. The fact that the company makes a profit and your group needs money is not a sufficiently strong link.

---

reasons, and see their giving in terms of 'community involvement' or 'community investment'. The main reasons why companies give are:

▶ To *create goodwill*. Companies like to be seen as good citizens in the communities in which they operate and as a caring company by society at large.

▶ To *be associated with causes that relate to their business*. Mining or extraction companies often like to support environmental projects, for example.

▶ To *build good relations with employees*. Support for employee volunteering is a growing area of company giving, creating a 'feel good' factor amongst employees and a sense of loyalty to their socially responsible employer. Increasingly, some preference is given to those charities for which staff are raising money or for whom staff members are doing volunteer work. Funds raised may be matched (usually up to a set limit) and/or employees given work time off in which to volunteer.

▶ Because they are asked or *it is expected of them*. They also don't want to be seen as mean in relation to other rival companies in their particular business sector. They are concerned that the quantity and quality of their giving is appropriate to their status as a company.

▪ Because the *chairman/senior directors are interested in a particular cause* (and perhaps support it personally). This is quite often the case with smaller companies where, as a result, it can be difficult to get a donation for causes outside of this criteria. Unless you know a friend of the managing director to plead your case, success is unlikely.

▪ Because *they have always given*. Some companies never review their donation policy. They see their donations more as an annual subscription to a list of charities they wish to support each year. Your aim should be to get your charity's name on to such a list, where it exists.

It is worth pointing out that a certain amount of chaos exists in company giving. Outside of the largest givers, few companies have any real policy for their charitable giving. Mostly they cover a wide range of causes, or attempt to deal with each appeal on its merits. For privately-owned or family-controlled companies their giving is often little different from personal giving. For public companies, where it is the shareholder's funds that are being given away, there is pressure to dress up what they are doing, perhaps by claiming to give according to some well-defined criteria.

However, some companies do have clear policies. **Where such policies are printed, please respect them.** Dealing with a mass of clearly inappropriate applications is the single biggest headache in corporate giving and has caused some to consider winding-up their charitable support programme all together. Don't jeopardize someone else's chance of success by your own indiscriminate applications.

## What companies give

Many charities are unrealistic about what they might obtain from companies as, to use an oft-quoted phrase, 'the business of business is business'. In other words, corporate charitable support is often only a sideline, accounting for around four percent of the voluntary sector's income.

However, much company support lies outside of cash donations. In fact, many of the larger donors' cash donations are a decreasing percentage of their total giving. For smaller givers, however, cash will continue to remain their most common form of support for charities. Here, then, are a variety of ways in which companies can support charities:

▪ Support in kind, which includes giving company products or surplus office equipment; providing use of company facilities, including meeting rooms, printing or design facilities, help with mailings.

▪ 'Secondment' of a member of staff to work with the charity, where a member of the company's staff helps on an agreed basis whilst remaining employed (and paid) by the company.

▪ Providing expertise and advice, whether by contributing a senior member of staff to the charity's management board, or over the telephone on a one-off basis.

▪ Encouraging employees to volunteer, undertake fundraising drives, or support a payroll giving scheme.

▪ Sponsorship of an event, activity or award scheme.

▪ Sponsorship of promotional or educational activities. **Note:** Some companies handle sponsorship through their community affairs department, whilst other do so through the marketing department. In smaller firms donations and sponsorship are usually handled by the managing director.

▪ Cause-related marketing, where, to encourage sales of a particular product, the company contributes a donation to a specified charity in return for each linked product sold. This is becoming an increasingly common form of support, but not usually to the benefit of smaller, less attractive charities.

▪ Advertising in charity brochures, newsletters, annual reports and so on. Smaller companies are often prepared to give in this way, if asked. For larger companies, however, it is usually something they exclude as standard as the initial approach is often made by a third-party who would also receive a share of the donation.

## The types of companies that give

*Multinational companies* – Most multinational companies have global giving programmes, generally tied to areas where they have or are developing business interests. Some multinational companies have an international structure for managing their giving, with budgets set for each area and a common policy regarding what they wish to support. With others, community investment remains at the discretion of local company management in the country concerned.

Geographically speaking, the further out from the centre (i.e. the company's headquarters) you are, the less you can expect to get. This can be broken down as follows: (i) most money is spent in the headquarter's town or region; (ii) most money is spent in the home country of the company; (iii) more money is spent in developed countries than developing ones.

*Leading national companies* – These will usually: support large national charities; have their own sponsorship schemes; make smaller donations to local charities in the area in which they are headquartered or have a major business presence. Numerous national companies will make grants through regional offices, whilst retail stores such as B&Q will use the local store manager to give advice on a local application. Such stores may also provide the manager with a small budget to spend at their discretion.

*Larger local companies* – In any city or region there will be large companies who are important to the local economy. They will often feel a responsibility to support voluntary action and community initiatives in those areas, and value the good publicity this provides.

There are also companies with a regional remit. The water, electricity and independent television companies all have a specific geographical area within which they operate, even if they are part of a multinational company.

*Smaller local companies* – There are a myriad of companies that make up the local business community. Referred to as Small and Medium Enterprises (SMEs), they are often overlooked in the rush to target the large companies on which good information is generally available. However, from manufacturers on trading estates to accountants and solicitors in the high street, the majority of SMEs claim to be involved with their local community. A MORI poll in 2000 surveyed 200 managing directors of firms ranging in size from 20 to 1,000 employees. 16% said they are involved 'a great deal' with their local community and 45% said they are involved 'a fair amount'. Many of these companies are privately owned, so the best approach will often be through the managing director or senior partner.

## Key factors in approaching companies
### Research

Research is very important, not just into companies, but also into personal contacts. When planning an appeal, an important first step is to find which of the people associated with your charity have influence or know people who have. If you can find a link between one of your supporters and a particular company – use it.

- One of your trustees/members may be on the board of directors or have contacts there – it will prove useful for them to write or sign the appeal letter.

- One of your volunteers or supporters may be an employee of the company.

- Your clients/users (or their parents) may work for the company.

Alternatively, you might be able to tie your appeal in to a known personal interest of a director.

## Getting in touch

Generally an appeal through a personal contact will work the best. But if you haven't got a contact and can see no way of developing one, then you will have to come up with another link.

As a first step you might contact the company to find out the following:

- who is responsible for dealing with charitable appeals

- their name and job title

- what information they can send regarding their company

- any procedure or timetable for submitting applications

- whether they might be interested in coming to see your organisation at work.

Visits are useful when discussing bigger donations with the larger companies, but are difficult to arrange for anything small.

Almost certainly your appeal will be in the form of a letter. Make this as personal as you can. Circular letters tend to end up in the bin. Make the letter short and to the point.

### Be specific in your approach

Rather than sending out a circular mailing to 100 or 1,000 companies, you will be more successful if you select a few companies you believe will be particularly interested in your project, and target your application to them and their policy. (Many companies will not consider circular appeals as a point of policy.)

Find a good reason why you believe the company should support you and include this prominently in your letter. You may be able to relate what you are doing as a charity to companies which have some relevance to your work: for example, a children's charity can appeal to companies making children's products; a housing charity to construction companies, building societies, etc. Any relationship, however tenuous, creates a point of contact on which you can build a good case for obtaining the company's support. If there is no relationship, should you be approaching that company at all?

There may be occasions where a charity will not want to accept money from a company in a related industry. A health education charity may not want to accept money from a tobacco company or brewery or from the confectionery industry, or similarly an environmental group may not wish to accept a donation from a nuclear power company. Such charities may feel that if they did so they would be seen to be compromised. Similarly, a local charity might not want money from a company who has made people in the area redundant. Each charity has to judge where it draws the line.

## Be clear about why you need the money

You must be clear about the objectives of the work you are raising money for, particularly its time-scale and how it relates to your overall programme of work. Try to think in project terms rather than seeking money to cover basic administration costs. This can be difficult, because most people spend most of their money on administration in one form or another, so you need to conjure up projects out of your current activities to present to potential donors. You can build a percentage of administration costs into the costs of a project. If you relate what you are doing to a specific time-scale, this again makes what you are applying for appear more of a project than a contribution to your year-on-year core costs.

## Be persistent

Do not underestimate the persistence factor. If you do not receive a donation in the first year, do not assume that the company will never support you. Go back a second and even a third time.

If you are going back, mention the fact that you have applied to the company previously, perhaps saying that you are now presenting something different which may be (you hope) of more interest.

If the company gives you reasons for refusing support, use these to help you put in more appropriate applications in the future. If the response is that the company does not give to your particular type of activity, then you know that it is absolutely no use your going back. If the company said its funds were fully committed, you can try to find out when would be a better time to apply (although this might only have been a convenient excuse because the company did not want to give to you).

Note the response to your appeal and use any information you can glean to improve your chances the next time. People respect persistence, so it really is important to go back again and again.

# Identifying which firms to approach

The firms to approach will depend on what sort of organisation you are. If you are a national organisation then an appeal to the country's leading companies is appropriate. Local groups should approach local firms and local branches of national companies which have a presence in their area. All organisations can approach companies in allied fields: for example, theatres can appeal to fabric companies.

You will find the names and other details of companies in a whole series of useful directories.

## Sources of information

*The Kompass Register of British Industry and Commerce* (available in regional sections)
*Key British Enterprises*
*The Waterlow Stock Exchange Year Book*
*Major Unquoted Companies*

Individual company websites

To find key contacts in companies:
*The Directory of Directors* and *Who's Who* are useful for finding out more about company directors.
*Corporate Register* – updated quarterly – a guide to decision makers in UK Stockmarket companies.

The best sources of information on what companies exist in your area are:

▶ The local Chamber of Commerce, where most of the more prominent local companies will be members

▶ *The Kompass Register* (available at main libraries), in which companies are organised regionally

▶ The local council: the Rating Department might produce a list of major business ratepayers. The Economic Development section may have a list of major employers.

▶ The local newspaper(s), which will carry stories from time to time that mention the success or expansion of existing firms, or details of new ones planning to set up in the area

▶ The Confederation Of British Industry regional office

▶ Companies you have existing contact with. This could include those companies that supply you with goods, your bank, solicitors and/or accountants. Emphasize your organisation's value as a good customer. Ask them if they can provide any useful contacts.

Don't forget, most of these local companies have no donations policy and give to projects which catch the fancy of the managing director or senior partner. Some may never have given anything before, and may not know it is possible to give charitable gifts tax-effectively (via Gift Aid, for example), so you may need to try and persuade them to give. Alternatively, it might be easier to approach these companies for in kind support in the first instance, and later on, once they have given something, ask them to make a cash donation.

Lastly, one big problem you may face involves the ownership of seemingly independent companies. Many companies are in fact part of much larger concerns. In recent years there has been a substantial number of mergers and take-overs, plus the buying and selling of business between corporations. A useful source of information is the directory *Who Owns Whom*, which has a subsidiary index listing most subsidiaries of companies included in this guide. You can also use company annual reports, which (for most companies) can be obtained on request. These reports provide good background information on the company concerned, and occasionally information on its corporate support programme. Some private (and occasionally public) companies will not send out annual reports except to shareholders; in such cases you can go to Companies House to get hold of a copy. The main offices are situated in Cardiff, Edinburgh, Belfast and London, with satellite offices in Birmingham, Glasgow, Leeds and Manchester.

## Before writing a letter of appeal ...

You obviously should try to find out as much as you can about the companies you have identified as potential donors. But, remember that:

▷ Companies generally have less well defined policies than trusts, although you can often determine a pattern in their giving

▷ The chance of an application made 'out of the blue' getting substantial support is low. Appeals made towards the end of a company's financial year are also less likely to succeed.

▷ Companies are more conservative in their giving and are less likely to support innovative projects (at least until they have got established) or anything that is risky or controversial

▷ Companies policies change more frequently than those of trusts, because of mergers, take-overs, or a fall or rise in profits. So ensure your research is bang up-to-date. Consulting one of the above mentioned directories, or even a copy of the companies latest annual report and accounts is not necessarily enough; they may have been taken over since then. Check the financial press on a regular basis, or make a quick telephone call to see if

anything has changed, i.e. company name, address (they may have kept the same telephone number, but moved), your contact, and so on.

## Writing a letter of appeal

Firstly, put yourself in the position of the company. Why should they want to give their shareholders' funds to you? Why should they choose your charity's appeal ahead of any others they might receive? Think about the benefits they will get from supporting you and mention these in your letter (for sponsorship proposals these benefits will be central to your success or failure). Then consider the following important points:

▷ Think up a project or aspect of your work that the business sector might like to support. Generally, do not appeal for administration costs or a contribution to an endowment fund (although there will be cases where this approach will succeed). Recognise that companies are likely to be interested in some ideas and not others. For example, a drugs charity would be more likely to get money for education than rehabilitation. An appreciation of the kind of projects that companies like to support will be very helpful to you.

▷ Your letter should be as short as possible. Try to get it all on one side of A4. You can always supply other information as attachments. Company people are busy. You can help them by making your appeal letter short and to the point. It should be written clearly and concisely and be free from jargon. Someone not acquainted with what you are doing should be able to read and understand it and be persuaded to act on it. Give your letter in draft to someone outside your charity to read and comment on before finalising it and sending it out.

▷ You should state why you need the money and exactly how it will be spent. The letter itself should be straightforward. It should include the following information (not necessarily in this order): what the organisation does and some background on how it was set up; whom the organisation serves; why the organisation needs funds; how the donation would be spent if it were to be forthcoming; and why you think the company might be interested in supporting you.

▷ You should attempt to communicate the urgency of your appeal. Fundraising is an intensively competitive business; there is a limited amount of money to give away, and you have to ensure that some of it comes your way. If it appears that although you would like the money now it would not matter terribly much if you got it next year, this will put people off. But don't give the impression you are fundraising at the last minute. Show them you are professional and you have carefully planned your fundraising appeal. You should also try to show that your charity is well-run, efficient and cost-effective in how it operates.

▶ You should mention why you think the company should support your cause. This could range from rather generalised notions of corporate responsibility and the creation of goodwill in the local community, to much more specific advantages such as preventing children painting graffiti on its factory walls or the good publicity companies will get from supporting your cause. If the firm's generosity is to be made public, for example through advertising or any publicity arising from the gift, then emphasise the goodwill which will accrue to the company. Most companies would say that they do not require any public acknowledgement for the contributions they make, but most will appreciate and welcome this.

▶ Ask for something specific. It is all too easy to make a good case and then to mumble something about needing money. Many companies, having been persuaded to give, are not sure how much to give. You can ask a firm to give a donation of a specific amount (matched to what you believe its ability to contribute to be), or to contribute the cost of a particular item. You can suggest a figure by mentioning what other companies are giving. You can mention a total and say how many donations you will need to achieve this. Don't be unreasonable in your expectations. Just because a company is large and rich, it doesn't mean that it makes big grants.

▶ If you can demonstrate some form of 'leverage' this will be an added attraction. Company donations on the whole are quite modest, but companies like to feel they are having a substantial impact with the money they spend. If you can show that a small amount of money will enable a much larger project to go ahead, or will release further funds, say, on a matching basis from another source, this will definitely be an advantage.

▶ Having written a very short appeal letter, you can append some background support literature. This should not be a 50-page treatise outlining your latest policies but, like your letter, it should be crisp and to the point: a record of your achievements, your latest annual report, press cuttings, or even a specially produced brochure to accompany your appeal.

▶ Make sure that the letter is addressed to the correct person at the correct address. It pays to do this

background research. Keep all the information on file as it will make your job much easier next time.

▶ If you are successful, remember to say thank you; this is an elementary courtesy which is too often forgotten. If the company gives you any substantial amount of money, then you should probably try to keep it in touch with the achievements related to its donation (such as a brief progress report or copies of your annual report or latest publications).

▶ If you do not succeed, go back again next year (unless the company says that it is not its policy to support your type of organisation or to give to charity at all). Persistence can pay. If you have received a donation, go back again next year. The company has demonstrated that it is interested in what you are doing and in supporting you. It may well do it again next year, especially if you have thanked it for the donation and kept it in touch with how the 'project' developed.

## How companies reply to you

Many companies will not even reply to your appeal. A few may acknowledge receipt of your letter, and occasionally you will get thanked for your request and be told that it is being considered and you will only hear the outcome if you are successful. Up to half of the companies you approach will write back, depending on the spread of the companies you approach. Larger companies have a system for dealing with charity mail, and most will see it as good PR to give a reply. Smaller companies which are not giving much charitable support will not have the time or the resources to do anything but scan the mail and throw most of it in the bin.

What sort of reply should you expect? If you do an extensive appeal, you will inevitably get a lot of refusals. These will normally be in the form of a pre-printed or word-processed letter or a postcard. Occasionally you will get an individually typed letter

---

### The application letter – checklist

▶ Is it only one side of A4?

▶ Does it state what your link is with the company?

▶ Does it stress the benefits to the company?

▶ Is it clear why you need the money?

▶ Is it clear what you are asking for?

▶ Is it addressed to the correct contact?

▶ Is it attractive to the company?

▶ Is it endorsed?

of reply. If the company says yes, you will get a cheque or a Charities Aid Foundation or Charities Trust voucher. But more often companies will say no.

There may be various reasons given or phrases used by a company which refuses your request. The company may not mean what it says. Funds may still be available for those appeals it wishes to support; it may be able to give support and just not want to; or it may not want to now or in the future. You should try to read between the lines. Companies in trying to be polite may in fact be misleading you if you take what they say at face value.

## Sponsorship

Sponsorship is a term that fundraisers sometimes incorrectly use when making what essentially is a request for cash. 'Will you sponsor me in the London Marathon' is actually asking for a donation. 'Will you sponsor a page in our programme' is usually a request for advertising. Sponsorship is not a glorified donation, and the fact that you are a charity is largely irrelevant. It is a business arrangement. The charity is looking to raise funds for its work and the company wants to improve its image, promote and sell its products or entertain its customers. True commercial sponsorship is a partnership between the donor and the recipient, for *mutual benefit*.

The bulk of corporate sponsorship money goes to sport. As a charity, however, you will not be competing for a share of the same budget. Rather, you will be concerned with a smaller, but growing 'market', covering social sponsorship. Achieving success here will be no easier a task than if you were competing in the bigger league, but you can increase your chances by doing the following:

▶ *Identifying possible donors* – opportunities can arise not just because of the *nature* of the sponsorship (access to a target audience or public personalities), but also because the timing is appropriate (A building company is shortly to open a new shopping complex in your town)

▶ *Preparing a sponsorship package* – a written proposal outlining the project and highlighting all the benefits to be gained by the company. This should also include a price for the sponsorship which will reflect as much the benefits to the company as to yourselves.

▶ *Determining the budget head* – this will identify where the money is coming from, who is responsible for it, and what return is expected. The main possible sources are marketing, corporate image and employee relations (human resources department).

▶ *Making the approach* – arrange a face to face meeting with the person who will make the decision (based on the source above) to give a presentation and discuss the sponsorship opportunities. Only then will you be in a position to find out about the companies needs and how you can meet them.

▶ *Contractual issues* – once you have been successful in gaining sponsorship you will need to agree terms through a contract. This sets out a legal agreement about which you will need to be clear in order to avoid possible problems at a later date.

The above is but an outline of some of the major points you will need to consider before seeking out and obtaining a sponsorship deal. For more in-depth advice regarding this see *Finding Company Sponsors for Good Causes* (Chris Wells), published by the Directory of Social Change.

# Geographical index of head offices

This geographical index is based purely on the head office address given at the start of each company entry. While it is generally the case that companies give some preference to charities local to their operating sites, including the head office, this is not always so. Once this index has been used to produce a preliminary list of potential companies to approach, the individual entries for each company should be read carefully to determine whether or not your particular project falls within the company's criteria.

## Bath
Wessex Water plc

## Bedfordshire
### Luton
Huntleigh Technology plc
TUI UK Ltd
Vauxhall Motors Ltd
Whitbread Group plc

## Berkshire
### Bracknell
3M UK Holdings plc
BMW UK Ltd
Hewlett-Packard Ltd
Panasonic UK Ltd
Siemens plc

### Maidenhead
Alcatel Telecom Ltd
Costain Group plc

### Newbury
Baxter Healthcare Ltd
Bayer plc
Vodafone Group

### Reading
Foster Wheeler Ltd
Microsoft Ltd
Oracle UK
PepsiCo Holdings
Xansa Group plc

### Slough
BPB
Citroën UK Ltd
Computer Associates plc
Fiat Auto (UK) Ltd
Fujitsu Services Holdings plc
Honda Motor Europe Ltd
O2
Reckitt Benckiser plc
Sara Lee UK Holdings Ltd
Slough Estates plc

### Windsor
Centrica plc
HFC Bank Ltd
Intercontinental Hotels Group plc
Morgan Crucible Company plc

### Yattendon
Yattendon Investment Trust plc

## Bristol
Bristol & West plc
Imperial Tobacco Group plc
Orange
Western Power Distribution

## Buckinghamshire
### Chalfont St Giles
GE Healthcare

### Gerrards Cross
Uniq plc

### Iver
Cummins Engine Company Ltd

### Milton Keynes
Abbey
Luminar Leisure Ltd

## Cambridgeshire
### Cambridge
Marshall of Cambridge (Holdings) Ltd

### Peterborough
Anglia Regional Co-operative Society Ltd
awg plc
British Sugar plc
EMAP plc
Norwich & Peterborough Building Society

## Cheshire
### Cheadle Hulme
BASF plc

### Chester
MBNA Europe Bank Ltd

### Crewe
Focus (DIY) Ltd

### Hartford
AMEC plc

### Macclesfield
Cheshire Building Society
Ciba Speciality Chemicals plc

### Warrington
British Nuclear Fuels plc
De Vere Group plc
United Utilities plc

### Wilmslow
Topps Tiles plc

## Cumbria
### Carlisle
J Stobart and Sons Ltd

## Derbyshire
### Burnaston
Toyota Motor Manufacturing (UK) Ltd

### Derby
Egg plc
Nottingham East Midlands Airport
Thorntons plc

### Duffield
Derbyshire Building Society

## Devon
### Exeter
Pennon Group plc

## Dorset
### Bournemouth
Liverpool Victoria Friendly Society
Portman Building Society

### Wimborne
Cobham plc

## Durham
### Durham
Northumbrian Water

## East Sussex
### Brighton
Family Assurance Friendly Society

### Hove
Palmer & Harvey McLane Ltd

## East Yorkshire

### Hull
Northern Foods plc

## Essex

### Brentwood
Ford Motor Company Ltd

### Harlow
Yule Catto & Co plc

### Loughton
Clinton Cards plc

## Gloucestershire

### Barnwood
British Energy Group plc
Lincoln Financial Group

### Cheltenham
ADC Krone (UK)
Chelsea Building Society
Kraft Foods UK Ltd
Spirax Sarco Engineering plc

### Gloucester
Ecclesiastical Insurance Group plc

### Wotton-under-Edge
Renishaw plc

## Greater Manchester

### Manchester
Addleshaw Goddard
British Vita plc
Co-operative Group
Guardian Media Group plc
Kellogg's
Manchester Airport plc
My Travel Group plc

### Stockport
adidas (UK) Ltd
P Z Cussons plc

## Hampshire

### Basingstoke
De La Rue plc
Eli Lilly Group Ltd
MEPC Ltd
Shire Pharmaceuticals

### Eastleigh
Fortis Insurance Ltd

### Farnborough
BAE Systems
QinetiQ Group plc

### Hook
NTL UK Ltd
Serco Group plc

### Southampton
VT Group plc

## Hereford & Worcester

### Hereford
H P Bulmer Holdings plc
Wyevale Garden Centres Ltd

## Hertfordshire

### Cheshunt
Tesco plc

### Hemel Hempstead
Danka UK plc
DSG International plc
Kodak Ltd
Robert McAlpine Ltd

### Hoddesdon
Merck Sharp & Dohme Ltd

### Letchworth
Willmott Dixon Ltd

### Stevenage
Du Pont (UK) Ltd
UIA (Insurance) Ltd

### Watford
Camelot Group plc
Ladbrokes plc
Medtronic Ltd
Mothercare plc
TK Maxx

### Welwyn Garden City
Roche Products Ltd

## Kent

### Folkestone
Saga Leisure Ltd

### Hildenborough
Fidelity Investment Management Ltd

### West Malling
GKN plc
Kimberley Clark Europe Ltd

## Lancashire

### Blackburn
Daniel Thwaites plc

### Blackpool
In the Pink Leisure Group

### Bolton
Warburtons Ltd

### Chorley
Northern Trust Group Ltd

### Fleetwood
Lofthouse of Fleetwood Ltd

### Wigan
JJB Sports plc

## Leicestershire

### Coalville
Aggregate Industries plc

### Ibstock
Wilson Bowden plc

### Leicester
Alliance & Leicester plc
Lafarge Aggregates Ltd
Next plc

## London

3i Group plc
Abbott Mead Vickers – BBDO Ltd
Accenture
Aegis Group plc
Akzo Nobel Holdings plc
Allen & Overy
Allied London Properties plc
AMVESCAP plc
Anglo American plc
AOL UK
ARAMARK Ltd
Arup Group Ltd
Associated British Foods plc
Associated British Ports Holdings plc
AstraZeneca plc
AT&T (UK) Ltd
Aviva plc
BAA plc
Bain & Company Inc. UK
Bank of England
Barclays plc
Barloworld plc
BBA Group plc
Bestway (Holdings) Ltd
BHP Billiton plc
bp plc
British American Tobacco plc
British Land Company plc
Brixton plc
BT Group plc
Bunzl plc
BUPA Ltd
Cable & Wireless plc
Cadbury Schweppes plc
Cadogan Estates Ltd
Caledonia Investments
Canary Wharf Group plc
Caparo Group Ltd
Capita Group plc
Cazenove Group plc
Charter plc
Chevron Texaco UK Ltd
CIBC World Markets
Citigroup Global Markets Europe Ltd
Close Brothers Group plc
Coca Cola Great Britain
Cookson Group plc
Cooper Gay (Holdings) Ltd
Corus Group plc
Coutts & Co
Credit Suisse
Daejan Holdings plc
Daily Mail and General Trust plc
DDB London Ltd
De Beers
Deloitte
Deutsche Bank
Diageo plc
Dresdner Kleinwort

Economist Newspaper Ltd
EDF Energy
Eidos plc
EMI Group plc
Ernst & Young
F&C Asset Management plc
Financial Services Authority
FKI plc
Freshfields Bruuckhaus Deringer
Galiform plc
Glencore UK Ltd
Goldman Sachs International
Great Portland Estates plc
S G Hambros Bank & Trust Ltd
Hammerson plc
Hanson plc
Hays plc
Henderson Group plc
Herbert Smith
Hess Ltd
House of Fraser plc
HSBC Holdings plc
Hunting plc
IBM United Kingdom Ltd
ICAP plc
Imperial Chemical Industries plc
Informa plc
Innocent Drinks
Invensys plc
IPC Media Ltd
ITV plc
Jardine Lloyd Thompson Group Services
Johnson Matthey plc
Jones Lang LaSalle UK
Kaupthing Singer & Friedlander Ltd
Kingfisher plc
KPMG
Ladbrokes plc (formerly Hilton Group plc)
Laird Group plc
Land Securities Group plc
Lazard
Legal & General plc
John Lewis Partnership plc
Liberty International Holdings plc
Limit Underwriting plc
Linklaters
Lloyd's of London
Lloyds TSB Group plc
Lockheed Martin
London Stock Exchange
Lowe & Partners Ltd
Man Group plc
Marks and Spencer Group plc
Marsh Ltd
Mazars LLP
MEPC plc
McDonald's UK
Misys plc
J P Morgan Chase
Morgan Stanley International Ltd
National Express Group plc
National Grid plc
National Magazine Co Ltd
NEC (UK) Ltd
News International plc
Old Mutual plc
Osborne & Little plc

Otis Ltd
Pearson plc
Pentland Group plc
Philips Electronics UK Ltd
PricewaterhouseCoopers
Prudential plc
Psion plc
Rank Group plc
Ravensale Ltd
Resolution plc
Reuters Ltd
Rexam plc
Richer Sounds plc
Rio Tinto plc
Rolls-Royce plc
N M Rothschild & Sons Ltd
Royal London Mutual Insurance Society Ltd
Royal Mail Group plc
J Sainsbury plc
Savills plc
Schroders plc
Shell
Simmons & Simmons
D S Smith Holdings plc
W H Smith plc
Smith & Nephew plc
Smiths Group plc
Sodexho Ltd
Spar (UK) Ltd
SSL International plc
St James's Place plc
Standard Chartered plc
Starbucks Coffee Company
J Swire & Sons Ltd
Tate & Lyle plc
Taylor Woodrow plc
TDG plc
Telegraph Group Ltd
Thomson Corporation plc
Tomkins plc
Total Holdings UK Ltd
Travelex Holdings Ltd
Trinity Mirror plc
UBS
United Business Media
Wellington Underwriting
Whittard of Chelsea
Woolworths Group plc
WPP Group plc
WSP Group plc

## Merseyside

### Liverpool
Johnson Service Group plc
Littlewoods Shop Direct Group Ltd
Port of Liverpool
Stanley Leisure plc

### St Helens
Pilkington plc

## Middlesex

### Brentford
GlaxoSmithKline plc

### Enfield
Data Connection Ltd

### Feltham
UPS

### Hayes
H J Heinz Company Ltd
United Biscuits Ltd

### Harmondsworth
British Airways plc

### Hounslow
Bristol-Myers Squibb Pharmaceuticals Ltd
DHL International (UK) Ltd
United Airlines

### Isleworth
British Sky Broadcasting Group plc

### Stanmore
Dhamecha Group Ltd

### Uxbridge
Adobe Systems UK
Robert Bosch Ltd
Coats plc
Compass Group plc
EDS UK Ltd
Hasbro UK Ltd
Unisys Ltd
Xerox (UK) Ltd

## Norfolk

### King's Lynn
Dow Chemical Company Ltd

### Norwich
Archant
Bernard Matthews Ltd

## North Yorkshire

### Scarborough
Broadland Properties Ltd
McCain Foods (GB) Ltd

### York
Jarvis plc
Nestlé UK Ltd
Persimmon plc
Shepherd Building Group Ltd

## Northamptonshire

### Irthlingborough
R Griggs Group Ltd

### Islip
Inchcape plc

### Kettering
Weetabix Ltd

### Northampton
Avon Cosmetics Ltd
Levi Strauss (UK) Ltd
Christian Salvesen plc
Travis Perkins plc

**Wellingborough**
Scott Bader Company Ltd

**Worksop**
Wilkinson Hardware Stores Ltd

## Nottinghamshire

**Nottingham**
Alliance Boots
Capital One Holdings Ltd
Cooper-Parry
Nottingham Building Society

## Oxfordshire

**Abingdon**
RM plc

**Didcot**
AEA Technology plc

**Eynsham**
Oxford Instruments plc

**Oxford**
Amey plc
Midcounties Co-operative
UGC Ltd Unipart Group of Companies

## South Yorkshire

**Harworth**
UK Coal plc

**Kiverton**
Greencore Group plc

**Sheffield**
SIG plc

## Staffordshire

**Leek**
Britannia Building Society

**Rocester**
J C Bamford Excavators Ltd

**Stoke-on-Trent**
Caudwell Holdings Ltd
Michelin Tyre Public Ltd Company
Josiah Wedgwood & Sons Ltd

## Suffolk

**Southwold**
Adnams plc

## Surrey

**Addlestone**
Thales UK Ltd

**Camberley**
S C Johnson Ltd

**Chertsey**
Samsung Electronics (UK) Ltd

**Cobham**
Berkeley Group plc
Cargill plc

**Dorking**
Biwater plc
Friends Provident plc
UnumProvident

**Egham**
CEMEX UK Operations

**Epsom**
W S Atkins plc

**Guildford**
Allianz Cornhill Insurance plc
Colgate-Palmolive (UK) Ltd
PKF

**Leatherhead**
ExxonMobil

**Reigate**
Canon (UK) Ltd

**Tadworth**
Pfizer Ltd

**Walton-on-Thames**
Air Products Group plc
Unilever UK

**Weybridge**
Crest Nicholson plc
Gallaher Group plc
Procter & Gamble UK
Sony United Kingdom Ltd
Toshiba Information Systems (UK) Ltd
TT Electronics plc

## Tyne & Wear

**Billingham**
Huntsman Tioxide

**Gosforth**
Northern Rock plc

**Newcastle upon Tyne**
Bellway plc
Fenwick Ltd
The Go Ahead Group plc
Greggs plc
Newcastle Building Society

**Sunderland**
Arriva plc
Nike Inc
Reg Vardy plc

## Warwickshire

**Atherstone**
TNT UK Ltd

**Kenilworth**
CEF Holdings Ltd

**Nuneaton**
Adams Childrenswear Ltd

**Rugby**
GAP (UK) Ltd

**Warwick**
Calor Gas Ltd

McKesson Information Solutions UK Ltd

## West Midlands

**Birmingham**
Aga Foodservice Group plc
Birmingham International Airport Ltd
Bradford & Bingley
Euro Packaging Ltd
IMI plc
LINPAC Group Ltd
Mitchells & Butlers plc
Severn Trent plc
Wragge & Co LLP

**Coventry**
Coventry Building Society
E.ON UK plc
Jaguar Cars Ltd
Peugeot Motor Company plc

**West Bromwich**
West Bromwich Building Society

**Wolverhampton**
Carillion plc

## West Sussex

**Crawley**
Group 4 Securicor plc
Spirent plc

**East Grinstead**
Rentokil Initial plc

**Horsham**
Royal & Sun Alliance Insurance Group plc

**Littlehampton**
Body Shop International plc

## West Yorkshire

**Batley**
Cattles plc
SigmaKalon UK & Ireland

**Bradford**
Congregational & General Insurance plc
Kelda Group plc
Wm Morrison Supermarkets plc
Provident Financial plc
Yorkshire Building Society

**Burley-in-Wharfedale**
Findel plc

**Keighley**
Peter Black Holdings plc

**Leeds**
Alcoa UK Holdings Ltd
Arla Foods UK plc
ASDA Stored Ltd
Clariant UK Ltd
Communisis plc
Evans Property Group
Leeds Building Society
Thistle Hotels plc

Yorkshire Bank plc

*Saltaire*
Filtronic plc

## Wiltshire

*Bradford-on-Avon*
Avon Rubber plc

*Malmesbury*
Dyson Ltd

*Swindon*
Nationwide Building Society
RWE npower
Zurich Financial Services (UKISA) Ltd

## Worcestershire

*Redditch*
Halfords Group plc

## Ireland

*Belfast*
Bombardier Aerospace Europe Ltd
First Trust Bank

*Portadown*
Ulster Carpet Mills Ltd

## Scotland

*Aberdeen*
First plc
John Wood Group plc

*Dundee*
Low & Bonar plc

*Edinburgh*
AEGON Scottish Equitable plc
Agilent Technologies UK Ltd
HBOS plc
Kwik-Fit Holdings plc
John Menzies plc
The Royal Bank of Scotland Group plc
Scottish & Newcastle plc
Standard Life

*Glasgow*
Clydesdale Bank plc
Scottish Media Group plc
ScottishPower plc
Weir Group plc
Robert Wiseman Dairies plc

*Glenrothes*
Tullis Russell Group Ltd

*Perth*
Scottish & Southern Energy plc
Stagecoach Holdings plc

## Wales

*Aberdare*
Celtic Energy Ltd

*Cardiff*
Admiral Group plc
Dwr Cymru Welsh Water
First Plus Financial Group plc
Julian Hodge Bank Ltd
The Peacock Group
Principality Building Society

*Ewloe*
Redrow Group plc

*Llantrisant*
Buy as you View Ltd

*Merthyr Tydfil*
GE Aircraft Engine Services Ltd
Hoover Candy Group Ltd

*Rhondda Cynon Taff*
Celtic Energy Ltd

*Vale of Glamorgan*
Dow Corning Ltd

*Wrexham*
Tetra Pak Ltd

This section classifies the companies included in the guide according to their main activities. It should enable charities to target companies for specific appeals or services. Companies which fall into two or more categories are listed under each one, except in the more obvious cases, for example building companies and property companies, where the categories have been cross-referenced. Retailers have been split into further separate categories due to the diversity covered.

## Accountants

Accenture
Cooper-Parry
Deloitte
KPMG
Mazars LLP
PKF
PricewaterhouseCoopers

## Advertising/marketing

Abbott Mead Vickers – BBDO Ltd
DDB London Ltd
Lowe & Partners Ltd
WPP Group plc

## Aerospace

BAE Systems
Bombardier Aerospace Europe Ltd
Cobham plc
GE Aircraft Engine Services Ltd
QinetiQ Group plc
Smiths Group plc

## Agriculture

Man Group plc
Pfizer Ltd

## Airport operators

BAA plc
Birmingham International Airport Ltd
Manchester Airport plc
Nottingham East Midlands Airport

## Aviation

British Airways plc
J Swire & Sons Ltd
United Airlines

## Banking

Abbey
Alliance & Leicester plc
Bank of England
Barclays plc
Bristol & West plc
Cazenove Group plc
CIBC World Markets plc
Close Brothers Group plc
Clydesdale Bank plc
Co-operative Bank plc
Coutts & Co
Credit Suisse
Deutsche Bank
Dresdner Kleinwort
First Trust Bank
Goldman Sachs International
HBOS plc
HFC Bank Ltd
Julian Hodge Bank Ltd
HSBC Holdings plc
Kaupthing Singer & Friedlander Ltd
Lazard
Lloyds TSB Group plc
N M Rothschild & Sons Ltd
The Royal Bank of Scotland Group plc
S G Hambros Bank & Trust Ltd
Standard Chartered plc
Standard Life
UBS
Yorkshire Bank plc

## Brewers/distillers

Adnams plc
Diageo plc
Scottish & Newcastle plc
Daniel Thwaites plc

## Building/construction
### (see also Property)

AMEC plc
Bellway plc
Berkeley Group plc
Carillion plc
CEMEX UK Operations
Costain Group plc
Jarvis plc
Persimmon plc
Robert McAlpine Ltd
Redrow Group plc
Rexam plc
Shepherd Building Group Ltd
Taylor Woodrow plc
Travis Perkins plc
Willmott Dixon Ltd
Wilson Bowden plc
Yule Catto & Co plc

## Building materials

Aggregate Industries plc
BPB
Hanson plc

## Building merchants

Focus (DIY) Ltd

## Building societies

Bradford & Bingley
Britannia Building Society
Chelsea Building Society
Cheshire Building Society
Coventry Building Society
Derbyshire Building Society
Leeds Building Society
Nationwide Building Society
Newcastle Building Society
Norwich & Peterborough Building Society
Nottingham Building Society
Portman Building Society
Principality Building Society
West Bromwich Building Society
Yorkshire Building Society

## Business equipment

Danka UK plc
Xerox (UK) Ltd

## Business services

Bain & Company Inc. UK
Canon (UK) Ltd
Economist Newspaper Ltd
Hays plc
Informa plc
Rentokil Initial plc
Serco Group plc
The Thomson Corporation

## Cash & Carry

Bestway (Holdings) Ltd
Dhamecha Foods Ltd

## Catalogue shopping

Findel plc
Littlewoods Shop Direct Group Ltd
Mothercare plc

## Catering services

ARAMARK Ltd
Sodexho Ltd

## Chemicals & plastics

3M UK Holdings plc
Akzo Nobel UK Ltd
Scott Bader Company Ltd
BASF plc
Bayer plc
British Vita plc
Ciba Specialty Chemicals plc
Clariant UK Ltd
Dow Chemical Company Ltd
Dow Corning Ltd
Huntsman Tioxide
Imperial Chemical Industries plc
Kodak Ltd
Low & Bonar plc
Pfizer Ltd
Yule Catto & Co plc

## Clothing manufacture

GAP (UK) Ltd
Levi Strauss (UK) Ltd
Nike (UK) Ltd
Pentland Group plc

## Commodity traders

Cargill plc
Glencore UK Ltd

## Computer software

Adobe Systems UK
Computer Associates plc
Microsoft Ltd
Misys plc
Oracle UK
RM plc
Xansa Group plc

## Confectionery

Cadbury Schweppes plc
Lofthouse of Fleetwood Ltd
Thorntons plc

## Consulting engineers

Arup Group Ltd

## Defence

BAE Systems
QinetiQ Group plc

## Distribution

Bunzl plc
Cargill plc
DHL Express (UK) Ltd
John Menzies plc
Palmer & Harvey McLane Ltd

## Domestic appliances

Aga Foodservice Group plc
Dyson Ltd
Hoover Candy Group Ltd

## Drinks manufacture

H P Bulmer Holdings plc
Innocent Drinks
Cadbury Schweppes plc
Coca-Cola Great Britain
Intercontinental Hotels Group plc
Nestle UK Ltd

## Electricity

British Energy plc
British Nuclear Fuels plc
C E Electric UK Ltd
E.ON UK plc
EDF Energy
National Grid plc
RWE npower
Scottish and Southern Energy plc
ScottishPower plc
United Utilities plc
Western Power Distribution

## Electronics/computers

CEF Holdings Ltd
Cobham plc
Filtronic plc
Hewlett-Packard Ltd
IBM United Kingdom Ltd
Panasonic UK Ltd
Philips Electronics UK Ltd
Psion plc
RM plc
Samsung Electronics (UK) Ltd
Siemens plc
Sony United Kingdom Ltd
Spirent plc
Toshiba Information Systems (UK) Ltd
Unisys Ltd

## Engineering

AEA Technology plc
AMEC plc
BBA Group plc
Biwater plc
Charter plc
Cummins Engine Company Ltd
Dyson Ltd
FKI plc
GKN plc
IMI plc
The Laird Group plc
Marshall of Cambridge (Holdings) Ltd
Mott MacDonald Group Ltd
Rexam plc
Renishaw plc
Rolls-Royce plc
Smiths Group plc
Spirax Sarco Engineering plc
TT Electronics plc
The Weir Group plc
John Wood Group plc

## Financial services

3i Group plc
AMVESCAP plc
British Land Company plc
N Brown Group plc
Caledonia Investments
Capital One Holdings Ltd
Cattles plc
Citigroup Global Markets Europe Ltd
Egg plc
Ernst & Young
Family Assurance Friendly Society Ltd
F&C Asset Management plc
Fidelity Investment Management Ltd
First Plus Financial Group plc
Henderson Group plc
Julian Hodge Bank Ltd
HSBC Holdings plc
ICAP plc
Legal & General plc
Liberty International Holdings plc
Lincoln Financial Group
Liverpool Victoria Friendly Society
Lloyds TSB Group plc
Man Group plc
Manchester Unity Friendly Society
Marks and Spencer Group plc
MBNA Europe Bank Ltd
The Midcounties Co-operative
J P Morgan Chase
Morgan Stanley International Ltd
Northern Rock plc
Old Mutual plc
Principality Building Society
Prudential plc
The Royal Bank of Scotland Group plc
Saga Leisure Ltd
Schroders plc
St James's Place plc
Standard Chartered plc
Travelex Holdings Ltd
Wilson Bowden plc

## Food manufacture

Arla Foods UK plc
Associated British Foods plc
Diageo plc
Greencore Group plc
Greggs plc
H J Heinz Company Ltd
Jacob's Bakery Ltd
Kellogg's
Kraft Foods UK Ltd
Sara Lee UK Ltd
Bernard Matthews Ltd
McCain Foods (GB) Ltd
Nestle UK Ltd
Northern Foods plc
PepsiCo Holdings
Unilever UK
Uniq plc
United Biscuits (UK) Ltd
Warburtons Ltd
Weetabix Ltd

## Food services

Christian Salvesen plc

## Furniture manufacture

Cadogan Group Ltd
Galiform plc

## Gaming

Camelot Group plc
William Hill plc
Ladbrokes plc (formerly Hilton Group plc)
Littlewoods Shop Direct Group Ltd
Stanley Leisure plc

## Garden centres

Wyevale Garden Centres Ltd

## Glass

Pilkington plc

## Health – beauty products

Avon Cosmetics Ltd

## Healthcare

Alliance Boots
Baxter Healthcare Ltd
BUPA Ltd
GE Healthcare
Medtronic Ltd
Pfizer Ltd
Procter & Gamble UK
Smith & Nephew plc
SSL International plc

## Hotels

Adnams plc
De Vere Group plc
Intercontinental Hotels Group plc
Ladbrokes plc (formerly Hilton Group plc)
Daniel Thwaites plc
Whitbread Group plc

## Household/personal care

Peter Black Holdings plc
Colgate-Palmolive (UK) Ltd
P Z Cussons plc
S C Johnson Ltd
Kimberly-Clark Europe Ltd
Sara Lee UK Ltd
Osborne & Little
Procter & Gamble UK
Reckitt Benckiser plc
SigmaKalon UK & Ireland
Unilever UK
Josiah Wedgwood & Sons Ltd
Wilkinson Hardware Stores Ltd

## Industrial products/services

Du Pont (UK) Ltd
Foster Wheeler Ltd

## Information management

Communisis plc
Informa plc

## Information technology

Agilent Technologies UK Ltd
AOL UK
W S Atkins plc
Computer Associates

Data Connections Ltd
EDS UK Ltd
Fujitsu Services Holdings plc
Lockheed Martin
McKesson Information Solutions UK Ltd
Medtronic Ltd
NEC (UK) Ltd
Oracle UK

## Instrumentation

Huntleigh Technology plc
Invensys plc
Oxford Instruments plc
UGC Ltd Unipart Group of Companies

## Insurance

Admiral Group plc
AEGON Scottish Equitable plc
Allianz Cornhill Insurance plc
Aviva plc
BUPA Ltd
Co-operative Insurance Society Ltd
Congregational & General Insurance plc
Cooper Gay (Holdings) Ltd
Ecclesiastical Insurance Group plc
Fortis Insurance Ltd
Friends Provident plc
HFC Bank Ltd
Jardine Lloyd Thompson Group Services
Limit Underwriting plc
Liverpool Victoria Friendly Society
Lloyd's of London
Marsh Ltd
Provident Financial plc
Prudential plc
The Royal Bank of Scotland Group plc
The Royal London Mutual Insurance
Society Ltd
Royal & Sun Alliance Insurance Group plc
UIA (Insurance) Ltd
UnumProvident
Wellington Underwriting

## Legal

Addleshaw Goddard
Allen & Overy
Freshfields Bruuckhaus Deringer
Herbert Smith
Linklaters
Simmons & Simmons
Wragge & Co LLP

## Leisure

Caledonia Investments
De Vere Group plc
William Hill plc
In the Pink Leisure Group
Ladbrokes plc (formerly Hilton Group plc)
Luminar Leisure Ltd
MyTravel Group plc
Northern Trust Group Ltd
The Rank Group plc
Saga Leisure Ltd
Scottish & Newcastle plc
Thistle Hotels Ltd
TUI UK Ltd

Whitbread Group plc

## Life assurance

Resolution plc
Zurich Financial Services (UKISA) Ltd

## Logistics

John Menzies plc
Christian Salvesen plc
TDG plc
TNT UK Ltd
Uniq plc
UPS

## Manufacturing

Robert Bosch Ltd
Caparo Group Ltd
Cookson Group plc
Euro Packaging Ltd
FKI plc
Morgan Crucible Company plc
Tomkins plc
Ulster Carpet Mills Ltd

## Marine

QinetiQ Group plc
J Swire & Sons Ltd
VT Group plc

## Media

Aegis Group plc
Archant
British Sky Broadcasting Group plc
Daily Mail and General Trust plc
Economist Newspaper Ltd
EMAP plc
Guardian Media Group plc
IPC Media Ltd
ITV plc
National Magazine Co Ltd
News International plc
Pearson plc
Reuters Ltd
Scottish Media Group plc
Telegraph Group Ltd
Trinity Mirror plc
United Business Media
Yattendon Investment Trust plc

## Metals

Alcoa Manufacturing (GB) Ltd
Corus Group plc
Johnson Matthey plc

## Mining

Anglo American plc
BHP Billiton plc
Celtic Energy Ltd
De Beers
Rio Tinto plc
UK Coal plc

## Miscellaneous

Amey plc
Financial Services Authority

Johnson Service Group plc
Royal Mail Group plc

## Motors & accessories

Arriva plc
Avon Rubber plc
BMW UK Ltd
Citroen UK Ltd
Fiat Auto (UK) Ltd
Ford Motor Company Ltd
Honda Motor Europe Ltd
Inchcape plc
Jaguar Cars Ltd
Kwik-Fit Holdings plc
Michelin Tyre Public Ltd Company
Peugeot Motor Company plc
Toyota Motor Manufacturing (UK) Ltd
UGC Ltd Unipart Group of Companies
Reg Vardy plc
Vauxhall Motors Ltd

## Music

EMI Group plc

## Oil & gas/fuel

Air Products Group Ltd
bp plc
British Nuclear Fuels plc
Calor Gas Ltd
Centrica plc
Chevron Texaco UK Ltd
E.ON UK plc
ExxonMobil
Hess Ltd
Hunting plc
Shell
Total Holdings UK Ltd
United Utilities plc

## Pharmaceuticals

Alliance Boots
AstraZeneca plc
BASF plc
Bayer plc
Bristol-Myers Squibb Pharmaceuticals Ltd
P Z Cussons plc
GlaxoSmithKline plc
Eli Lilly Group Ltd
Merck Sharp & Dohme Ltd
Reckitt Benckiser plc
Roche Products Ltd
Shire Pharmaceuticals
Yule Catto & Co plc

## Plant equipment

J C Bamford Excavators Ltd
Barloworld plc

## Print/paper/packaging

Barloworld plc
Bunzl plc
De La Rue plc
LINPAC Group Ltd
Low & Bonar plc
Rexam plc

D S Smith Holdings plc
Tetra Pak Ltd
Tullis Russell Group Ltd

## Professional support services

Capita Group plc
Tullis Russell Group Ltd
WSP Group plc

## Property

Allied London Properties Ltd
AMEC plc
Berkeley Group plc
British Land Company plc
Brixton plc
Broadland Properties Ltd
Cadogan Group Ltd
Caledonia Investments
Canary Wharf Group plc
Crest Nicholson plc
Daejan Holdings plc
Dhamecha Group Ltd
Evans Property Group
Great Portland Estates plc
Hammerson plc
Jarvis plc
Jones Lang LaSalle UK
Kaupthing Singer & Friedlander Ltd
Kingfisher plc
Land Securities Group plc
Robert McAlpine Ltd
MEPC Ltd
Northern Trust Group Ltd
Ravensale Ltd
Redrow Group plc
Savills plc
Slough Estates plc
J Swire & Sons Ltd
Taylor Woodrow plc
Wilson Bowden plc

## Quarrying

Aggregate Industries plc
Lafarge Aggregates Ltd

## Retail – Clothing & footware

Adams Childrenswear Ltd
adidas (UK) Ltd
GAP (UK) Ltd
JJB Sports plc
Marks and Spencer Group plc
Next plc
TK Maxx

## Retail – Department & variety stores

Anglia Regional Co-operative Society Ltd
The Co-operative Group
Fenwick Ltd
House of Fraser plc
John Lewis Partnership plc
Littlewoods Shop Direct Group Ltd
Mothercare plc
The Peacock Group

Woolworths Group plc

## Retail – DIY/furniture

Galiform plc
Kingfisher plc
Wilkinson Hardware Stores Ltd

## Retail – Electrical

Buy As You View Ltd
DSG International plc
Richer Sounds plc

## Retail – Miscellaneous

The Body Shop International plc
Clinton Cards plc
Greggs plc
Halfords Group plc
WH Smith plc
Starbucks Coffee Company
Thorntons plc
Topps Tiles plc
Whittard of Chelsea plc

## Retail – Restaurants/fast food

Compass Group plc
Diageo plc
McDonald's UK
Mitchells & Butlers plc
Whitbread Group plc

## Retail – Supermarkets

Anglia Regional Co-operative Society Ltd
ASDA Stores Ltd
The Co-operative Group
John Lewis Partnership plc
The Midcounties Co-operative
Wm Morrison Supermarkets plc
J Sainsbury plc
Spar (UK) Ltd
Tesco plc

## Securities/shares

Goldman Sachs International
London Stock Exchange

## Shipping

Associated British Ports Holdings plc
Cargill plc

## Sugar refiners

British Sugar plc
Tate & Lyle plc

## Telecommunications

ADC Krone (UK)
Alcatel Telecom Ltd
AT&T (UK) Ltd
BT Group plc
Cable and Wireless plc
Caudwell Holdings Ltd
NTL UK Ltd
O2 plc
Orange

QinetiQ Group plc
Thales UK Ltd
Toshiba Information Systems (UK) Ltd
Vodafone Group

## Textiles

Coats plc
Osborne & Little
Sara Lee UK Holdings Ltd

## Tobacco

British American Tobacco plc
Gallaher Group plc
Imperial Tobacco Group plc

## Toy manufacture

Hasbro UK Ltd

## Transport & communications

Arriva plc
BBA Group plc
First plc
The Go Ahead Group plc
Group 4 Securicor plc
National Express Group plc
The Port of Liverpool
Stagecoach Group plc
J Stobart and Sons Ltd
TDG plc
VT Group plc

## Transportation

Otis Ltd
TNT UK Ltd

## Waste management

Biwater Ltd
Severn Trent plc

## Water

awg plc
Dwr Cymru Welsh Water
Kelda Group plc
Northumbrian Water
Pennon Group plc
Severn Trent plc
United Utilities plc
Wessex Water plc

# Alphabetical listing of companies

This section gives information on almost 500 companies from all sectors of industry, gathered from a combination of annual reports and company websites, and supplemented by our own research. The general layout showing the information on each company is on pages 38–39.

## Types of company

A company may be a public limited company (designated plc), normally a company with shares quoted on the stock exchange; a privately owned company; or a subsidiary company. If it is a subsidiary it may have retained its own identity for charitable donations and we would include an entry in this guide. Other subsidiaries included are British-based subsidiaries of an overseas-based company.

Where a company has been recently acquired it may not yet have decided whether it will continue to manage its own donations budget.

Through acquisitions and mergers, companies may now be owned by a holding company, a conglomerate, or a transnational company. We usually only give the name of the holding company. You may have to do your own research to link local companies and plants with the head office that may have ultimate control over their donations. The company annual report, usually available free on request, lists subsidiary and associate (less than 50% owned) companies and reports on the activity of the company during the year. We have included the main subsidiaries of each company within the entry. However, for many companies this is taken from the latest annual report, which can be several months out of date. The *Who Owns Whom* directory also lists subsidiaries of UK companies, and more up-to-date information can often be found on company websites.

## Interpreting financial information

The charitable donations figure given is that published by the company in the 'Director's Report' section of its annual report and accounts. As far as we know this legally should relate only to cash donations. However, we have noticed an increasing trend for companies to include the value of secondments, gifts in kind, advertising or sponsorship which, customarily, are included in the total contributions figure. Furthermore, a company's present level of donations does not necessarily indicate future commitments. Sending an appeal to less generous companies may actually persuade them to increase their donations. Certainly if they never receive appeals there will be no outside pressure on them to change their policy, although in general if a company is only giving a little your chances of success are reduced.

Normally a co-ordinated company donor will budget a certain sum for its charitable donations and stick within this amount. Some allocate all their budget at an annual meeting; others spread donations throughout the year. Some give to causes they wish to support until the budget is used up and then stop; others continue to give even after the budget is spent if an appeal takes their fancy. If they reply to your appeal, many will write and say that their budget is 'fully committed'. Often this is simply a polite way of refusing support.

The year-end is important in that if you get your appeal in soon afterwards the company will not have spent its charitable budget for the coming year. However, if a company allocates its budget evenly throughout the year and receives a flood of applications at the start of its new financial year, some which would have been supported later in the year now miss out. There is no fail-safe answer to this problem. However, your chances of success are usually improved by sending the application earlier rather than later in the company's financial year.

## How to interpret the donations policy

There are certain standard phrases that appear in the policy of the company entries.

*No response to circular appeals*
This means that 'Dear Sir/Madam' letters, whether they are hand-signed or use photocopied signatures, are probably not even read, let alone replied to.

*Preference for local charities in areas of company presence;*
*Preference for appeals relevant to company business;*
*Preference for charities where a member of staff is involved.*

These are self-explanatory. Local charities should check whether appeals can be made locally or must be sent to head office. Any link with the company should be highlighted.

*Preferred areas of support are ...*
We asked companies to tick preferred areas of support to indicate the sort of appeals most likely to interest them.

*Exclusions (No grants for ... )*
The same list was used as for the preferred areas, with common exclusions being: fundraising events, advertising in charity brochures, appeals from individuals, denominational (religious) appeals, political/campaigning activity, and bricks and mortar appeals.

**Before applying, potential applicants should always consider whether there is a particular reason why the company might want to support them.**

# Fictitious Productions plc

68 Nowhere Street, Anytown AN6 2LM
0151 000 0000; Fax: 0151 100 0000
**Website:** www.fictprod.co.uk

**Correspondent:** A Grant, CSR Manager

**Chief officer:** T Story
**Chief Executive:** S Yarn

| Year end | Turnover | Pre-tax profit |
|---|---|---|
| 31/12/2006 | £766,200,000 | £189,150,000 |

**Nature of company business**
The company is involved in production of fictitious information. Subsidiaries and locations include Cashflow Industries (Grimsby), False Publications (Liverpool), Sundry Matters (Bristol), and Wage Packet Co (Perth).
**UK employees:** 4,655

**Charitable donations**
2007: £196,000
2006: £250,000
2005: £225,000
2004: £184,000
2003: £243,000
Total community contributions: £475,000
Membership: BitC, L B Group, %Club

**Company name:** The full name of the company is given with the companies listed in alphabetical order.

**Address:** Head office, to which appeals should be sent unless otherwise stated.

**Telephone:** Appeals should be submitted *in writing*, but you may wish to ask for details of the appeals procedure, check the contact for charitable donations or request a copy of the latest annual report. The latter, along with community support information, may also be obtained via the quoted website address, if available.

**Contact for appeals:** Only the very large corporate donors have specialist staff dealing with appeals (a direct line number may be given in such instances). However, the company secretary or public relations department will deal with appeals to many companies.

**Officers:** We give the names of the *Chairman, Chief Executive* and/or *Managing Director*. There is not room to list all members of the main board.

**Financial statistics:** The *year end, turnover* and *pre-tax profit* (a figure in brackets denotes a loss). Most relate to 2005/06. The figures give an indication of the scale of the company's giving relative to its size.

**Nature of company business:** The main area of activity is given, together with subsidiaries and locations (where known). This can be useful if you are looking for a product or geographical link. We also state the number of UK employees, where available.

**Charitable donations:** Figures for the last five years are given, together with a figure for total community contributions (which includes the cost of in-kind giving, arts sponsorship, secondments, etc), where available. May state additional figures relating to management costs and cause-related marketing promotions.

**Membership:** Indicates whether the company is a member of the PerCent Club, Arts & Business, Business in the Community, and London Benchmarking Group.

## Community involvement

The company prefers to support local organisations in areas of company presence. It focuses its giving on sickness and disability, the arts, heritage, social welfare, education and youth, and environment.

**Community involvement:** This provides an overview of the company's community support policy (if one exists), detailing preferred causes and any geographical areas that are favoured.

### Exclusions

No response to circular appeals. No grants for fundraising events, purely denominational (religious appeals), local appeals not in areas of company presence, large national appeals, overseas projects, political activities or individuals. Non-commercial advertising is not supported. It does not sponsor individuals or travel.

**Exclusions:** Listing any areas, subjects or types of grants the company will not consider.

### Applications

In writing to the correspondent. Applications are considered by a donations committee which meets three times a year.

**Applications:** Including how to apply and when to submit an application. We also state whether there is further information available from the company.

## Corporate giving

The company's community contributions totalled £475,000 in 2006, including in-kind giving, cost of secondments and arts sponsorship as well as charitable donations. National grants range from £50 to £5,000. Local grants range from £25 to £500.
Major grant recipients in 2006 included Any Town Disability Network (for information leaflets), Perth Parent & Toddler Association (towards play equipment), and the local wildlife trust.

**Corporate giving:** Quotes total cash donations made and, if available, total community contributions.

Typical grants range, to indicate what a successful applicant can expect to receive.

Examples of grants, listing where possible the purpose and size of the grants. Large grants are often a good indicator of the company's priorities.

### In-kind support

The company donates surplus or used furniture/ equipment to local causes.
**Enterprise:** The company supports local enterprise agencies and considers secondment of employees to local economic development initiatives.

**In-kind support:** Some companies give gifts in kind, which can be anything from used stock to printing facilities.

### Employee-led support

A charity is selected each year to benefit from employee fundraising, with the company making a contribution.
**Payroll giving:** A scheme is operated by the company.

**Employee-led support:** Many company employees give time and money to local causes, including fundraising and expertise. If a payroll giving scheme is operated, we state so.

### Commercially-led support

**Sponsorship:** *The arts* – The typical sponsorship range is from £1,000 to £25,000. It sponsors Southport Sinfonietta and supported festivals in Grimsby and Perth.

**Commercially-led support:** Covers arts and good-cause sponsorship, if undertaken, together with a contact, if different from the main correspondent. Provides information on cause-related marketing promotions, if applicable.

# 3i Group plc

16 Palace Street, London SW1E 5JD

020 7928 3131; Fax: 020 7928 0058

Website: www.3igroup.com

Correspondent: Tony Brierley, Company Secretary

Chief officer: The Baroness Sarah Hogg

Chief Executive: Philip Yea

| Year end | Turnover | Pre-tax profit |
|---|---|---|
| 31/03/2006 | £1,053,000,000 | £855,000,000 |

Nature of company business
The group's principal activity is investment in a wide range of growing independent businesses.

Subsidiaries include: Garden Pensions Trustees Ltd

Main locations: Aberdeen, Manchester, London, Glasgow, Reading, Solihull, Leeds, Cambridge, Bristol, Birmingham

Total employees: 733

### Charitable donations

2006: £390,570
2004: £253,419

Management costs: £70,000

Membership: A & B, BitC

## Community involvement

The company continues to favour charitable initiatives with which members of staff are personally involved and local charities where 3i has an office. There is a preference for education, medical charities and organisations engaged in the relief of poverty and/or work of benefit to the community.

In addition to charitable donations, the company undertakes some arts sponsorship and occasional secondment to charities, as well as contributing through gifts in kind.

The company has offices in the UK in Aberdeen, Birmingham, Bristol, Cambridge, Glasgow, Leeds, London, Manchester, Reading, and Solihull. Each of these offices is allocated a tranche of the company's charitable budget which is administered centrally.

### Exclusions

No support for appeals from non-charities, advertising in charity brochures, animal welfare charities, appeals from individuals, children/youth, elderly people, enterprise and training, environment/heritage, fundraising events, overseas projects, political appeals, religious appeals, sickness/disability charities or sport.

### Applications

In writing to the correspondent.

Information available: The company produces a corporate social responsibility report.

## Corporate giving

In 2005/06, the company made charitable donations of £390,570 to a variety of charities. Approximately 26% of this figure was in matched donations of staff Give As You Earn contributions.

### In-kind support

In 2005/06, 3i continued to support the charity In Kind Direct, which distributes donated surplus products to other UK voluntary organisations.

### Employee-led support

3i supports the charitable activities of its staff by matching donations made under the Give As You Earn scheme and through their own fundraising efforts.

Payroll giving: The Give As You Earn scheme is operated by the company.

### Commercially-led support

Sponsorship: *The arts* – The company's major involvement continues to be sponsorship of the senior student orchestra of the Royal Academy of Music.

It has also supported the Young Vic Theatre scheme which enables children, otherwise denied the opportunity, to be inspired by theatre.

# 3M UK Holdings plc

3M Centre, Cain Road, Bracknell RG12 8HT

08705 360036; Fax: 01344 858278

Website: www.3M.com/uk

Correspondent: Corporate Communications Manager

Managing Director: Chuck Kummeth

| Year end | Turnover | Pre-tax profit |
|---|---|---|
| 31/12/2004 | £631,569,000 | £70,177,000 |

Nature of company business
Principal activity: manufacturing, marketing and distribution of a range of coated materials, pharmaceuticals and other related products and services. The ultimate parent company is Minnesota Mining & Manufacturing Company in the US.

Main locations: Bangor, Bedford, Aycliffe, Atherstone, Bracknell, Loughborough, Manchester, Abingdon, Clitheroe, Hillington, Gorseinon

UK employees: 3,330

### Charitable donations

2004: £338,491
2003: £267,938

Membership: BitC, %Club

## Community involvement

3M state that, 'Through a targeted contributions programme, we aim to help the communities closest to our UK and Ireland sites. We do this in a number of ways including:

- financial donations/grants
- in-kind gifts of 3M products and services
- volunteer services of our employees and retirees
- use of 3M facilities.

These resources are then focused on five key areas:

- education
- environment
- relief of suffering

- culture
- sport.'

## Exclusions

No support for advertising in charity brochures, appeals from individuals, purely denominational (religious) appeals, local appeals not in areas of company presence, large national appeals or overseas projects.

## Applications

In writing to the correspondent.

**Information available:** A Community Investment Report is downloadable from the company's website.

## Corporate giving

In 2004, the company made cash donations in the UK totalling £348,991. The purposes for which these donations were given were broken down as follows:

| Category | Grant total |
|---|---|
| Environment | £12,536 |
| Education | £105,163 |
| Relief of suffering | £89,763 |
| Culture | £47,499 |
| Sport | £9,630 |
| Other | £84,230 |

## In-kind support

The main areas of non-cash support are mentoring, gifts in kind of 3M products and services, and the use of 3M facilities.

## Employee-led support

Through the 3M 4Good employee volunteering programme, the company encourages employee volunteering by matching employee fundraising on a pound for pound basis and allowing company time off in which to volunteer.

**Payroll giving:** The Give As You Earn scheme is available to employees.

## Commercially-led support

**Sponsorship:** *Education-* 3M supports the Quantum Theatre of Science, which tours UK primary schools close to 3M sites, teaching pupils about science in an entertaining and engaging way.

**Cause-related marketing:** Following research commissioned in 2003 by The Guide Dogs for the Blind Association into Computer Vision Syndrome (CVS), 3M are offering schools the chance to receive one free anti-glare computer filter for every five purchased. The company will then donate £1 to the association for every filter sold.

# Abbey

PO Box 911, Milton Keynes MK9 1AD

0870 608 0104

Website: www.abbey.com

Correspondent: Alan Eagle, Trust Secretary, Abbey Charitable Trust 0870 608 0104; Fax: 01908 344257
E-mail: alan.eagle@abbey.com

Chief officer: Lord Burns

Chief Executive: Luqman Arnold

| Year end 31/12/2005 | Turnover | Pre-tax profit £596,000,000 |
|---|---|---|

**Nature of company business**
Provision of an extensive range of personal financial services.

**Subsidiaries include:** Scottish Mutual Assurance plc, Carfax Insurance Ltd, Cater Allen International Ltd, Scottish Mutual Investment Managers Ltd, Scottish Provident Ltd, Scottish Mutual Pension Funds Investments Ltd

**Main locations:** Glasgow, Milton Keynes, London, Sheffield, Bradford

**UK employees:** 32,364

### Charitable donations

2005: £1,556,947
2004: £1,672,493
2003: £1,500,000

Total community contributions: £1,632,176
Management costs: £145,914

Membership: A & B, BitC, L B Group

## Community involvement

The company's charitable support is given through The Abbey Charitable Trust. The trust (Charity Commission no. 803655) was set up with an initial donation from Abbey National plc (now simply 'Abbey') of £5 million following the sale of shares unclaimed since the company's flotation. This endowment fund received a further £750,000 from Abbey Housing Association Ltd, increasing the endowment fund to £5.75 million.

Further information about the trust is available at: www.abbey.com then go to Abbey corporate > Community involvement > Charitable trust.

The charitable trust is committed to supporting local communities and disadvantaged people, particularly in areas where Abbey has a significant presence. Its priorities currently are:

- education and training
- local regeneration projects which encourage cross-community partnerships
- financial advice to help with money management.

The trust, however, is looking to increase support through the Abbey Community Groups Programme, which aims to establish staff community partnership groups in areas with a branch presence.

Only organisations with charitable status will be supported. There is a preference to fund whole projects rather than make a partial donation.

## Exclusions

The company cannot make donations which:

- are for a specific individual
- support lobbying or political parties
- would benefit a single religious or ethnic group
- help causes outside the UK
- replace statutory funding
- last for more than one year
- help schools gain specialist schools status
- sponsor events, conferences or advertising
- fund salaries, core costs or holidays.

## Applications

In writing to the correspondent. There is no formal application form, nor closing date. Just write a letter of no more than two sides of A4. It should clearly state what the money will be spent on, how much is needed and how your request fits in with Abbey's stated priorities. If any further information is required, you will be contacted.

Remember, only registered charities or organisations with charitable status can be considered.

**Information available:** The company reports on its community involvement in its annual report and in the staff newsletter. It also produces a social responsibility report.

## Corporate giving

In 2005, total community contributions of £1,632,176 were made, of which £1,556,947 was in cash donations. Management costs totalled £145,914. Grants can range from £250 up to £20,000.

Please note that the total community contributions figure given above also includes the total of donations made by the trust (which receives some of its income from its own investments), not just the total made by the company. The value of support in the form of gifts in kind, good-cause sponsorship, training schemes and staff time is also included.

Abbey Community Groups currently exist in a number of areas around the country (Camden, Belfast, Glasgow, Bradford, Sheffield, Teeside and Milton Keynes) and have a budget allocation of around £40,000 each. Local level grants of up to £250 may be given by the groups to causes outside of those normally supported by the company.

Funds of up to £250 are also available for 'local civic responsibilities' for projects which will benefit the local community even if the recipient organisation does not have charitable status, e.g. towards a local agricultural show or villages' Christmas lights.

## In-kind support

Local charities organising fundraising events can apply through their local branch for prizes to raffle.

## Employee-led support

The increased importance of staff involvement in community matters is further shown through the existence of a matched time scheme for volunteering activities and a matched donation scheme.

The matched time scheme enables staff involved in out of working hours volunteering to have up to 35 hours a year of paid work time in which to volunteer. With the matched donation scheme an individual can claim up to a maximum of £500 and a group of four or more employees up to £2,500.

As with the Abbey Community Groups, categories outside of the trusts remit may be supported.

**Payroll giving:** The company operates the Charities Trust scheme.

# Abbott Mead Vickers – BBDO Ltd

151 Marylebone Road, London NW1 5QE

020 7616 3500; Fax: 020 7616 3600

Website: www.amvbbdo.com

Correspondent: Colin Fleming, Finance Director 0207 616 3909

| Year end | Turnover | Pre-tax profit |
|---|---|---|
| 31/12/2005 | £40,521,000 | £6,341,000 |

**Nature of company business**
Advertising agency and marketing services.

**Subsidiaries include:** Proximity, Drury Communications, Redwood Publishing, Electronic Solutions, Minerva, Hammond Communications, Fishburn Hedges, OMD, PHD, Rocket, Craik Jones Watson Mitchell Voelkel, Telecom Express Ltd, Aurelia Public Relations, Drum PHD

**Main locations:** London

**UK employees:** 291

### Charitable donations
2005: £60,000
2004: £90,000

## Community involvement

AMV is a leading advertising and marketing communications company employing nearly 300 staff.

BITC provide the following information from the case studies section of their website.

'AMV-BBDO has championed the creation of an innovative solution to London's homelessness: Big House; London's first residential facility helps the long-term homeless break away from street life – offering self-contained accommodation, tailored support and re-training. Over 300 AMV-BBDO staff participated at the idea-generating stage and over 100 employees were involved with fundraising or working directly with Big House. A March 2005 staff survey showed 91% agreement that 'AMV – BBDO's involvement with Big House makes me feel good about the wary we are contributing to the community.'

We understand the company supports both national and local charities, with a preference towards those based in London.

## Applications

In writing to the correspondent who can provide further information.

## Corporate giving

In 2005 AMV made cash donations totalling £64,000. It is not clear which organisations benefited from the donations.

## In-kind support

AMV encourages staff to involve themselves with community projects.

## Employee-led support

AMV employees have participated in schemes run by BITC (Business in the Community) which include reading with young children and providing mentoring support for young teenagers from less privileged backgrounds within London.

AMV committed substantial resources in the form of staff time to work with West London Mission/Big House in support of the creation of an innovative solution to London's homelessness – Big House.

**Payroll Giving:** The company operate the Give As You Earn scheme.

## Commercially-led support

**Sponsorship:** *The Arts* – Contact Colin Fleming, Finance Director.

# Accenture

60 Queen Victoria Street, London EC4N 4TW

020 7844 4000; Fax: 020 7844 4444

Website: www.accenture.com

Correspondent: Lucy Bloem, Corporate Citizenship Senior Exec. Sponsor

Managing Director: Lis Astall

| Year end 31/08/2005 | Turnover | Pre-tax profit |
|---|---|---|

**Nature of company business**
Management consulting and technology services organisation.

**Main locations:** Newcstle upon Tyne, Manchester, London, Leeds

---

### Charitable donations

2005: £484,000
2004: £573,989
2003: £584,265

Membership: BitC

---

## Community involvement

'Accenture is committed to being a good corporate citizen and playing its full part in society. This includes building mutually beneficial relationships with clients, employees and the broader community. Our aim is to integrate the principles of good corporate citizenship into everything that we do and make positive contributions to the communities in which we operate.'

Within the UK, Accenture have identified four main areas of focus for corporate citizenship:

- environment
- giving
- inclusion and diversity
- time and skills.

Donations in the UK are made through The Accenture Foundation (Charity Commission no. 1057696). In addition there is a UK Employee Charity Committee that gives out approximately a quarter of a million pounds a year based on employee proposals. There are also matching schemes and payroll schemes available for employees. Greatest support is via our time and skills offering where every Accenture employee is entitled to three days a year to spend on charitable activity of their choice.

## Exclusions

No support for advertising in charity brochures, individuals, fundraising events, medical research, overseas projects, political appeals or religious appeals.

## Applications

In writing to the correspondent. Proposals employee led.

## Corporate giving

Each identified area of focus for corporate citizenship – environment, giving, inclusion and diversity, time and skills – are explained on Accenture's website as follows:

**Giving:** As an organisation, Accenture make a number of grants to charities and other non-profit organisations. In addition, they offer their employees the chance to participate in tax effective giving through payroll schemes.

**Time and Skills:** Accenture enables employees to volunteer with local communities/charities using a three-day annual allowance. In addition, employees can work on a project with Accenture Development Partnerships or take a placement with Voluntary Service Overseas.

### The Accenture Foundation

In March 1996, the former Arthur Andersen & Co. Foundation in the UK split into two, which brought about the formation of The Andersen Consulting Foundation on 1 September 1996. The assets of the original foundation were divided between The Arthur Andersen Foundation (now defunct) and The Andersen Consulting Foundation, now renamed The Accenture Foundation.

The Accenture Foundation supports registered or exempt charities working in education and training and disadvantaged communities, especially when on behalf of children/young people and in areas local to Accenture offices. The trustees are listed on the Charity Commission's website as: Dr Julie Lamont; Kris Wadia; Nick Evans; Bill Crothers; Lucy Bloem and Stephen Adrian Walker.

In 2004/05, the Accenture Foundation made grants totalling £484,000. In 2003/04, The foundation had assets of £11 million, an income of £4.5 million and made grants to organisations totalling £952,000 of which £574,000 was provided by the Accenture firm. The foundation has instituted a focused programme of long-term donations to maximise the benefit to the recipients, with the charities appearing to be chosen based upon employees' suggestions (see below). Some ad hoc donations are, however, made to other charitable causes.

### UK Foundation

There is a further local giving budget which supports local corporate citizenship activities. In the UK, donations are distributed by the UK foundation based upon employee suggestions. These charities include: Links, Springboard, Kids Company, Weston Spirit, Fairbridge in Greater Manchester and the North East, The Prince's Trust, Princess Royal Trust for Carers, UK Youth, 100 Black Men of London and the UK Career Academy Foundation.

## In-kind support

Accenture actively seeks opportunities that will allow it to best utilise its key skills and so have the most beneficial impact on society and its people, e.g. education.

Ask Accenture is a charity initiative between Accenture and UK Youth. The idea is that Accenture provides advice on a variety of projects and schemes ranging from developing a business plan, to mentoring young people in the community. Accenture Development Partnerships (ADP) is a charitable organisation that makes high quality consulting services available to organisations working with developing economies.

Other organisations receiving support include Cares, Voluntary Service Overseas and the Prince's Trust Volunteer programme.

## Employee-led support

Accenture believe it is important for its staff to make a positive contribution to the communities in which it operates and, in so doing, develop new and valuable skills.

Support is given to local and national organisations whose activities benefit the communities in which it operates. Accenture offer support through either corporate or payroll giving, with the firm's staff collectively deciding to whom donations will be made.

**Payroll giving:** The employee run charity scheme donates money to charities nominated by employees. The money is collected through payroll giving and pooled together to make a difference. *Give As You Earn scheme:* Employees are able to sign up to donate to charities of their choice through tax effective payroll giving. *A Senior Executive Giving:* All UK senior executives give a portion of their salary to charity. The money is paid into the UK Accenture Foundation, and then is disbursed to charities at the request of the individual senior executive.

## Commercially-led support

**Sponsorship:** Accenture has sponsored numerous high profile community events and institutions over the past few years. The organisation claims that these associations help promote their business, while allowing them to enjoy the benefits of supporting worthwhile organisations that make a positive impact on local culture and community.

*The arts:* Accenture sponsors numerous arts organisations and initiatives including: Sponsorship of Innovation at the National Theatre which includes the provision of expertise and in-kind support for a number of innovative technology projects; a three-year corporate membership agreement with the Tate Britain and Tate Modern Galleries; Northern Ballet Theatre based in Leeds – this sponsorship aims to provide support to increasing business growth in the North of England and Scotland; Royal Shakespeare Company has been chosen as Accenture's latest global sponsorship initiative.

# Adams Childrenswear Limited

Attleborough House, Townsend Drive, Nuneaton, CV11 6RU

024 7635 1000; Fax: 024 7634 5583

Website: www.adams.co.uk

Correspondent: Georgina Kelly

Chief officer: Alan Smith

Chief Executive: Dean Murray

Nature of company business
Manufacturer and retailer of children's clothing.

Main locations: Nuneaton

## Community involvement

The company states on its website that: 'At adams kids, we work hard to support the community. As a brand, we aim to help improve the quality of life for children and their families'. This can be through corporate sponsorship or fundraising.

### Exclusions

No support for circular or general appeals, political or religious appeals.

### Applications

In writing to the correspondent.

## Corporate giving

Although no donations figure was available, Adams supports both Tommy's and WellChild (as a corporate sponsor). As part of its partnership with the latter various fundraising activities have been held.

## Commercially-led support

**Sponsorship:** The company undertakes good cause sponsorship (see 'WellChild', above).

# ADC Krone (UK)

Runnings Road, Kingsditch Trading Estate, Cheltenham, Gloucestershire GL 51 9NQ

01242 264400; Fax: 01242 264488

Website: www.adc.com

Correspondent: Community Connections Committee

Managing Director: M Barrett

| Year end | Turnover | Pre-tax profit |
|---|---|---|
| 31/10/2003 | £1,783,000 | (£44,000) |

Nature of company business
Telecommunications company.

Main locations: Glenrothes, Cheltenham

Total employees: 7,700

## Community involvement

Donations are made through the ADC Foundation (the charitable arm of ADC Telecommunications, Inc.) which was founded in 1999. The foundation's goal is to provide social and economic value by encouraging employee contributions and by making direct grants in two strategic focus areas: mathematics and science education, and non-profit access to technology.

Funding is available to groups in Glenrothes – Fife, and Cheltenham, with a preference for projects involving collaboration between more than one organisation. Areas of work which can be funded are:

- science, technology, engineering or mathematics education, at any level
- access to technology, where improved technology for an organisation will bring direct results to the beneficiaries of the group's work.

## Exclusions

The ADC Foundation will not consider requests for in-kind giving, general operating grants, capital grants or fundraisers including customer-sponsored charity benefit events. Nor does it make grants to individuals, for religious purposes, or to address generic quality of life issues.

## Applications

Having determined that your intended proposal fits with one of the foundation's focus areas (see 'Community Involvement' above), you should first fill out the online 'Letter of Inquiry'. These are accepted throughout the year with decisions being made quarterly. Details can be found at: http://www.adc.com/aboutadc/adcfoundation/howtoapply/index.jsp

Please note, however, that to gain input and ideas from every level and in all geographical locations, the foundation has established numerous advisory Community Connections Committees comprising of local ADC employees who make recommendations to the foundation regarding local grants that fit the foundation's chosen focus. It may, therefore, benefit your applications success if you have access to members of the said committee.

## Corporate giving

In 2005, worldwide community contributions totalled US$1,159,855. No breakdown figure covering the UK was available.

During 2005, the ADC Foundation established new ADC Cares 'local giving committees' at a number of sites worldwide, including Cheltenham, England (Glenrothes already has such a committee). Although not fully explained in the foundation's community report for the year, these appear to have the authority to make grant decisions at a local level without reference to the foundation. As such, the amounts involved are probably fairly small.

## Employee-led support

Employee giving is encouraged and supported via ADC Foundation programmes including employee 'Matching gifts'. The company will also help employee volunteer projects which support community needs, campaigns or foundation giving goals.

# Addleshaw Goddard

100 Barbirolli Square, Manchester M2 3AB

0161 934 6000; Fax: 0161 934 6060

Website: www.addleshawgoddard.com

Correspondent: The Trustees, Addleshaw Goddard Charitable Trust

| Year end | Turnover | Pre-tax profit |
|---|---|---|
| 30/04/2006 | £161,200,000 | |

Nature of company business
Legal firm.

Main locations: Leeds, London, Manchester

UK employees: 1,220

Charitable donations
2005: £66,491
Membership: A & B

## Community involvement

Addleshaw Goddard is a legal firm with offices in Manchester, Leeds and London. Support is given through various pro-bono activities. Financial help is given via the Addleshaw Goddard Charitable Trust (Charity Commission no. 286887), which aims to promote any charitable purpose on behalf of the communities in the City of London, Manchester and Leeds.

### Addleshaw Goddard Charitable Trust

In particular the trust seeks to support, 'the advancement of education, the furtherance of health and the relief of poverty, stress and sickness'.

It also promotes 'any charitable object connected with the legal profession, including persons engaged in the profession and their dependants'.

## Exclusions

No support for general or circular appeals, local appeals not in areas of company presence, individuals, or political/religious appeals.

## Applications

In writing to the correspondent.

## Corporate giving

In 2005, the firm donated nearly £65,000 to its associated trust. During the year the trust in turn made donations totalling £72,000 of which £60,000 went to the Tsunami Appeal.

The firm does not appear to attribute any value to its in-kind support and, as such, the figure quoted above significantly underestimates this.

## In-kind support

The firm's pro-bono work currently involves providing legal advice and assistance to the Springfield Legal Advice Centre and the National Autistic Society. Help is also given through the London referred charitable legal work.

## Employee-led support

Staff are encouraged to become involved with their local communities through fundraising activities and volunteer work.

Recent examples of organisations benefiting from this include: Read-It – a schools literacy programme in Leeds; the Leeds Law Mentoring scheme; St George's Crypt, Leeds; and, the Leeds Cares programme.

Staff in the Manchester office have been heavily involved in fundraising and volunteering on behalf of the Prince's Trust, with the aim of raising £100,000 on its behalf. Up to £20,000 of this total will be matched by the firm.

# adidas (UK) Limited

The adidas Centre, Pepper Road, Hazel Grove, Stockport SK7 5SD

0161 419 2500; Fax: 0161 419 2603

**Website:** www.adidas-group.com

**Correspondent:** Customer Care Department

**E-mail:** customercare@adidas.co.uk

**Managing Director:** Gil Steyaert

| Year end | Turnover | Pre-tax profit |
|----------|----------|----------------|
| 31/12/2005 | £341,889,000 | £53,528,000 |

**Nature of company business**
The distribution and retail of sports goods to the sports trade in the UK.

**UK employees:** 785

> ## Charitable donations
>
> 2005: £42,235
> 2004: £14,201

## Community involvement

At group level adidas publish a set of comprehensive corporate giving guidelines from which we have quoted.

Cash, in-kind donations (products, equipment, services, know how) and corporate volunteering form an important part of the company's support. These are provided selectively and focus on the following areas:

- sports within a social context or linked to another area of charitable engagement
- kids and youth associations which focus on the self-development and character building of youngsters
- preventative health projects – preferably sports related
- relief efforts.

In considering potential partners, adidas takes the following requirements into account:

- partners need to complement the core values of the adidas Group
- partners must clearly describe the intended use
- partners must acknowledge in writing that products donated by adidas are used only for the intended purpose
- projects to be supported must be limited in time with the content being clearly defined. As a rule, support is not given to recurring projects
- partners must organise and conduct the collection of product donations themselves and guarantee to bear the costs involved
- recipients of cash grants must clearly state how this has been allocated and be able to provide proof that it has been used for this purpose
- the organisation must provide adidas with post-documentation (progress report, photographs, CD, video) within 4 weeks of the project closing.

## Exclusions

No support for individuals; political parties or advocacy groups; discriminatory groups (race, creed, gender, sexual orientation, or age); religious causes; cultural festivals or projects in association with film, music or theatre sponsoring; research projects of any kind; or, advertising and promotion.

In addition, no grants will be made if there is a relevant risk that products will be perceived as bribery, or if the brand name or image could be jeopardised or misused.

## Applications

Requests must be submitted in writing and are accepted throughout the year. The request should be sent to the company's closest subsidiary or Liaison Office.

Project proposals should be no longer that two pages and the following information needs to be included:

- a brief description of the organisation and its goals
- a description of the project, target group, related time frame and possible project partners
- the amount required
- confirmation that the donation is tax-deductible
- the specific purpose for which the donation is to be used
- proof of the impact and results of the project
- brief information indicating the stability of the organisation – trustees, accounts, and other funding sources for the financial year
- format of reporting and documentation for the adidas Group.

All applications are reviewed on an individual basis. A decision is normally sent within four weeks of submitting a proposal.

## Corporate giving

In 2005, the company made donations to UK charities totalling £42,235 (2004: £14,201). We have no details of the beneficiaries, but as an indication of the possibility of success, we quote the following information provided by adidas.

'Globally, in 2005, the adidas Group received 13,153 donation requests and supported 40 requests with a cash grant and 1,243 with a product donation.'

### In-kind support

Donations in kind may be given in the form of products, equipment, services or know how.

### Employee-led support

Company staff are are encouraged to carry out voluntary work where aligned with the group's aims.

### Commercially-led support

**Cause-related marketing:** The adidas Group joins with charities or good causes to market products that make a positive impact on social issues, whilst achieving business objectives. We have no examples from the UK.

# Admiral Group plc

Capital Towers, Greyfriars Road, Cardiff, CF10 3AZ

0870 243 2431; Fax: 0870 243 2171

**Website:** www.admiralgroup.co.uk

**Correspondent:** Justin Beddows, Assistant Communications Manager

**Chief officer:** Alastair Lyons

**Chief Executive:** Henry Engelhardt

| Year end | Turnover | Pre-tax profit |
|---|---|---|
| 31/12/2005 | £638,000,000 | £119,494,000 |

**Nature of company business**
The company is the holding company for the Admiral Group of companies. The group's principal activity continues to be the selling and administration of private motor insurance and related products.

**Subsidiaries include:** EUI Limited, Able Insurance Services, Inspop.com Limited

**Main locations:** Swansea, Cardiff

**UK employees:** 1716

---

### Charitable donations

2005: £108,000
2004: £75,000

Membership: A & B

---

## Community involvement

The company's charitable donations are directed into two main areas: sponsorship of national charities and support of local community-based organisations.

There is some preference for helping organisations based in South Wales and groups involved with arts and culture, animal welfare, sport/recreation and women's issues. Support is also considered for general charitable purposes.

## Exclusions

No support for local appeals not in areas of company presence.

## Applications

In writing to the correspondent. Please note, however, that local support tends to be directed towards organisations involved with Admiral employees or their immediate family.

## Corporate giving

In 2005, the company made cash donations of £108,000 (2004: £75,000). Nationally, a number of charities were supported, the main ones being the Born Free Foundation, Tusk, Steve Redgrave Charitable Trust, Well Being of Women, and the South Wales-based Ty Hafan Children's Hospice.

## Employee-led support

The group encourages its employees to become involved with their local communities. In support of this, it launched 'Harry's Pot' in 1999, a fund to which staff can apply for a donation or sponsorship toward an organisation of their choice. In 2005, over 100 organisations received help through the scheme including: Sketty Primary; Circus Eruption; WISP Judo; and, Ebbw Vale Cricket Club.

## Commercially-led support

**Sponsorship:** *The arts* – Some recent events sponsored by the company include: National Waterfront Museum, Swansea; Cardiff Lesbian & Gay Mardi Gras; Swansea Jazz Festival; 2005 Cardiff Marathon and, Welsh National Opera.

# Adnams plc

Sole Bay Brewery, Southwold, Suffolk IP18 6JW

01502 727200; Fax: 01502 727201

Website: www.adnams.co.uk

Correspondent: Emma Hibbert, The Adnams Charity

Chief officer: Simon Loftus

Managing Director: Jonathan Adnams

| Year end | Turnover | Pre-tax profit |
|---|---|---|
| 31/12/2005 | £45,488,000 | £4,883,000 |

**Nature of company business**
The principal activities of the company are brewing, retailing and wholesaling beer, wines, spirits and minerals, property ownership and hotel management.

**UK employees:** 286

---

### Charitable donations

2005: £30,000
2004: £35,000

Membership: %Club

---

## Community involvement

Adnams plc is committed to giving not less than 1% of its annual profits to charitable causes and is a member of the 2006 PerCent Club. The company is also accredited with the SEE Stamp for socially, environmentally and ethically responsible businesses. It distinguishes companies that actually are responsible from those that merely claim to be.

In addition to providing in-kind support to local organisations, cash donations are made through The Adnams Charity (Charity Commission no. 1000203) which supports worthwhile causes within a 25-mile radius of St Edmund's Church in Southwold, Suffolk.

## Exclusions

No grants to individuals, although public bodies and charities may apply on behalf of individuals. Private members clubs are not eligible per se, but if the clear purpose is educational or for children, then the application may be considered.

## Applications

In writing to the correspondent. Applications must be for charitable causes within the above stated catchment area. Applications from national charities which operate within this area may be considered if assurances can be given that the money will be used for a specific purpose and to the benefit of the local community.

Before applying, please note the following:

- the trustees prefer applications for specific items
- grants are generally of a one-off nature
- grants are not made in successive years
- the trustees are reluctant to give grants to cover ongoing running costs, however, in very exceptional circumstances they may do so
- the Adnams Charity does not provide sponsorship of any kind
- the Adnams Charity does not provide raffle prizes

⬧ the Adnams Charity does not give funds indirectly to charities

⬧ the Adnams Charity does not give grants towards the cost of church bell repairs.

## Corporate giving

In 2005, the company made total community contributions of £117,295 of which £30,000 was in cash donations through The Adnams Charity.

### The Adnams Charity

Primarily funded by the company, from which it receives an annual income, in 2004/05 the charity made grants totalling just under £50,000. The grants are broken down in the accounts under five categories – education, health and social welfare, the arts, recreation, and community facilities. Besides stating the amount given to each beneficiary, a brief outline of the purpose for which the grant was given is included. Some examples are given below.

*Education:* Kessingland VCP School – The nursery unit was seeking support to buy outdoor play equipment. The trustees awarded £177.22 to purchase outdoor snakes and ladders, a gymnastics activity ball set, a small swing set and a garden bench.

*Health and social welfare:* Waveney Rape & Abuse Centre – Waveney Rape & Abuse Centre is run entirely by volunteers. It provides a free service to women and men who have been physically, sexually or, emotionally abused. It offers Alternative Therapies and self-confidence courses as part of the healing' process. The courses have been a huge success so far. The trustees awarded a grant of £1,000 for fifty alternative-therapy sessions for the coming year.

*The arts:* Sound o f Wangford – The Sound of Wangford is a community arts group which provides accessible arts education through practical activities to children in rural areas. Workshops on music, dance, costume-making and filming will take place during February half-term. Thirty-three children aged between eight and sixteen will take part. The end result will be a live performance for families and friends. A grant of £300 was awarded to purchase a sewing machine.

*Recreation:* Lowestoft Kuk Sool Won Club – Sixty children (some with learning difficulties) attend Lowestoft Kuk Sool Won Club. The children learn many things including self-defence, fitness and self-confidence. The trustees awarded a grant of £1,000 towards the cost of new safety mats.

*Community facilities:* Waldringfield Church Field Trust – Established in November 2003 following a gift of land, the Trust is developing the site to include recreational areas for sports such as football and cricket, all-weather walkways, conservation and car parking. The Trustees awarded a grant of £500 to provide fencing to the site, which will be installed by local volunteers.

### In-kind support

*Education/enterprise* – To help re-engage students disaffected by school life, Adnams has been inviting a group of 14–15 year olds from Kirkley High School in Lowestoft to the company every Friday. Working with volunteers in teams across the company, the special 'entrepreneurial spirit' curriculum has proven to be highly successful in lifting students' confidence and self belief.

# Adobe Systems UK

3 Roundwood Avenue, Stockley Park, Uxbridge UB11 1AY

020 8606 1100; Fax: 020 8606 4004

**Website:** www.adobe.co.uk

**Correspondent:** Marketing Department

**Managing Director:** Michael Higgins

| Year end | Turnover | Pre-tax profit |
|---|---|---|
| 30/11/2003 | £17,582,000 | £1,164,000 |

**Nature of company business**
Software producer.

**Main locations:** Uxbridge, London, Edinburgh

## Community involvement

Adobe supports non-profit organisations and projects located in Adobe communities that address community-specific needs, with an emphasis on the following criteria:

⬧ arts and cultural organisations with the mission or principal focus on the creation, promotion and exhibition of visual arts, multimedia or video

⬧ providing services to reduce hunger and homelessness and provide affordable housing

⬧ protecting the natural environment and improving public spaces for the enjoyment of the community

⬧ improving access to electronic information for people with disabilities.

Adobe's community support programme comprises:

⬧ Adobe Action Grants which provide one-time cash only grants for general operating and programme support through a competitive, quarterly online application process. Grant amounts range from $5,000–$20,000 (£2,700–£10,800) and are for one year only.

⬧ Adobe Community Investment Grants which provide multi-year (with annual review), comprehensive support, including cash, software, volunteers, and facilities use through an Adobe-initiated, RFP application process. Grant amounts are at least $20,000 (£10,800) and can be for up to three years.

⬧ employee volunteering.

⬧ software donation and training.

### Applications

In writing to the correspondent. Adobe Action Grants can be applied for online via the company's website.

## Corporate giving

In 2005, global community contributions totalled over $18 million (nearly £10 million) the majority of which was given in the USA; a figure for UK giving was not available.

However, the company reported in 'Adobe in the Community 2005', that: 'This year we made a significant philanthropic investment in international geographies by opening our giving and grants programme to non-profit organisations in regions like … the United Kingdom'. To this effect, support was given to the following organisations through the Adobe Action Grants scheme: AbilityNet; Depaul Trust; FareShare; Feltham Arts Association Ltd; Green Corridor; Groundwork Thames Valley; Notting Hill Housing Trust; and, Richmond Advice and Information on Disability.

Adobe lists the Charities Aid Foundation (CAF) as an international investment partner. Although they don't expand on what this entails, it may well be that CAF administer part of Adobe's charitable giving in the UK via a CAF Company Account.

In June 2006, Adobe launched its new global philanthropy programme, 'Adobe Youth Voices'. This is described as being designed to help underserved middle and high school aged youth develop the critical skills necessary to become active and engaged members of their communities. The programme will provide young people with access to multimedia tools and training, so enabling them to explore and communicate their ideas, concerns and aspirations. By engaging with their communities in this way, young people can further develop the critical skills needed for success in school, career and life.

By the end of the year the programme will have been introduced at 36 sites worldwide, including London. No further details were available as at July 2006, but we will be contacting Adobe for further information, following which we hope to be able to provide an update.

### In-kind support

**Software donation programme:** Adobe offers its latest version software to eligible schools and charities in partnership with Gifts in Kind International. As Adobe only has a limited amount of software to donate, preference is given to those qualifying organisations that are most closely aligned with the company's giving focus.

Please note that a process and shipping fee will be charged for all software donations. Details of these and a downloadable application form are currently available at: https://adobeprograms.giftsinkind.org/default1.htm

Software training in the use of Adobe products is available to teachers and not-for-profit staff in the United States, but it is not clear whether this extends to the UK.

Further in-kind support such as the provision of meeting space and other facilities in its offices can also be made available to voluntary groups where appropriate. Surplus office equipment can also be donated.

### Employee-led support

Employees are encouraged to volunteer for non-profit organisations and educational establishments whose aim's closely mirror those of the company's community support programme.

**Payroll giving:** Schemes exist in the offices in Edinburgh, London and Norwich, with employee's contributions being matched by the company.

### Commercially-led support

**Sponsorship:** *Education* – It sponsors an Institute of International Education centre in London, providing scholarships to people who are nearing the end of their courses and about to move into higher education.

# AEA Technology plc

Harwell Business Centre, Didcot, Oxfordshire OX11 0QJ

0870 190 1900; Fax: 0870 190 8261

Website: www.aeat.co.uk

Correspondent: Martin Millson

**Chief officer:** Dr Bernard Bulkin

**Chief Executive:** Andrew McCree

| Year end | Turnover | Pre-tax profit |
|---|---|---|
| 31/03/2006 | £147,800,000 | (£3,100,000) |

**Nature of company business**
AEA Technology plc and its subsidiaries offer a range of advanced technology products and services, and expert consultancy, based on deep industry understanding and close customer relationships.

**Subsidiaries include:** AGM Batteries Ltd, Waste Management Technology Limited

**Main locations:** Derby, Harlow, Harwell, Glengarnock, Risley, London, Winfrith, Barnsley

**UK employees:** 2,175

### Charitable donations
2006: £28,380
2005: £48,942
2004: £18,422
2003: £13,075

## Community involvement

The group's policy is to focus its corporate community involvement on promoting science and technology, for example in local schools.

### Exclusions

Previously no support for advertising in charity brochures, animal welfare, appeals from individuals, elderly people, fundraising events, medical research, overseas projects, political appeals, religious appeals, sickness/disability, social welfare or sport.

### Applications

In writing to the correspondent.

## Corporate giving

In 2005/06, the company made UK charitable donations of £28,380 (2004/05: £48,942). No further information was available.

Previous beneficiaries have included: Young Foresight; Junior Research Fellow, Cambridge University; a Research Professor in micro-analytical techniques at Oxford University; and ICRS-6 Conference.

### In-kind support

Previously the three main areas of non-cash support were gifts in kind, staff secondments and training schemes.

### Employee-led support

In the past the company has operated a staff volunteering scheme. Employees' volunteering/charitable activities have been supported by the company through financial help and by allowing time off to volunteer.

**Payroll giving:** The company has been involved with the Give As You Earn scheme.

### Commercially-led support

**Sponsorship:** Local schools close to company locations in the UK have received sponsorship through a 'school link'

programme and School Governor Award scheme. The Salters Institute A-level Physics project also received support.

# Aegis Group plc

43–45 Portman Square, London W1H 6LY

020 7070 7700; Fax: 020 7070 7800

Website: www.aegisplc.com

Chief officer: Lord Sharman of Redlynch

| Year end | Turnover | Pre-tax profit |
|---|---|---|
| 31/12/2005 | £8,079,100,000 | £94,000,000 |

**Nature of company business**
The principal activity of the group is the provision of a wide range of services in the areas of media communications and market research.

**Subsidiaries include:** Carat International, Synovate Europe, Vizeum, Isobar Communications

**Main locations:** London

**Total employees:** 12,205

> **Charitable donations**
> 2005: £400,000
> 2004: £200,000

## Community involvement

Aegis declined to participate in our survey, stating that, 'At present, we do not wish to be included in your publication'. However, we maintain our policy of including all relevant companies.

In the main, support is given at local operating company level to a range of charities and community projects. At group level, both local and national charities are given help. There is some preference for supporting children with particular needs.

Staff are also encouraged to engage with their local communities.

### Exclusions

No support for local appeals not in areas of company presence.

### Applications

We were unable to obtain the name of the person responsible for considering requests for support. Unless you have personal knowledge of a company employee willing to speak on your behalf, success is unlikely.

## Corporate giving

In 2005, the company made charitable donations of £400,000. Whilst this excludes fundraising by staff, the figure may well be a global one. No details of the beneficiaries were available.

## Employee-led support

Staff are allowed company time off in which to carry out volunteer work on behalf of charities and community projects.

# AEGON Scottish Equitable plc

AEGON, Scottish Equitable House, Edinburgh Park, Edinburgh EH12 9SE

0131 339 9191; Fax: 0131 339 9191

Website: www.aegonse.co.uk

**Correspondent:** Ian Young, Director & Group Secretary
E-mail: enqiries@aegon.co.uk

Chief officer: Otto Thoresen

Managing Director: Graham Dumble

| Year end | Turnover | Pre-tax profit |
|---|---|---|
| 30/12/2004 | | £79,700,000 |

**Nature of company business**
Insurance. Became part of the AEGON Group in 1994; now AEGON Scottish Equitable.

**Subsidiaries include:** Guardian Financial Services

**Main locations:** Lytham St Annes, Edinburgh

**Total employees:** 3,135

> **Charitable donations**
> 2004: £81,208
> 2003: £61,665

## Community involvement

The following extract is taken from the company's website: 'We may be a global company but we like to get involved locally too. And that includes taking part in community projects all over the country. After all, the people who work here aren't just part of a company, they're part of a local community too.

'For example, Park View Road playing fields are right next door to our Lytham office but they've been badly neglected. So when the Park View 4U community regeneration scheme was looking for support, we wanted to help out. Now Park View is well on the way to building a toddler playground, with plenty of play equipment to keep the local nursery children healthy and happy.'

We do not have any further information on what kind of support the company gives but it would seem that local initiatives benefiting children and young people are currently favoured in the UK.

Worldwide, the group have given long standing support to, among others, oncology research, Habitat for Humanity, the War Trauma Foundation, and the Alzheimer Center VU and their website states: 'We invest not just money, but time, thought, care and effort into the projects and charities we support. We choose them to reflect our ethos of business efficiency, increasing economic prosperity and our ultimate business aim – a better quality of life for everyone.'

### Exclusions

No support for circular appeals, fundraising events, advertising in charity brochures, appeals from individuals, purely denominational (religious) appeals, local appeals not in areas of company presence or overseas projects.

### Applications

In writing to the correspondent.

## Corporate giving

In 2004 the company donated £81,208 (2003: £61,665) to 'insurance and other charities'. Unfortunately, we have no specific information concerning the beneficiaries.

## Employee-led support

Staff from the company's training department in Edinburgh have been working with local school children on projects and courses designed to help them develop important skills such as team building, clear communication, problem solving and presentation skills.

## Commercially-led support

**Sponsorship:** In Lytham, AEGON is a sponsor of the Young Enterprise Programme where employees act as advisers to the children on the programme, aimed at giving young people a taste of life in the business world.

# Aga Foodservice Group plc

4 Arleston Way, Shirley, Solihull B90 4LH

0121 711 6000; Fax: 0121 711 6001

Website: www.agafoodservice.com

Correspondent: Shaun Smith, Financial Director
E-mail: info@agafoodservice.com

Chief officer: Victor Cocker

Chief Executive: William McGrath

| Year end | Turnover | Pre-tax profit |
|---|---|---|
| 31/12/2005 | £501,800,000 | £43,000,000 |

Nature of company business
Producer of cookers and refrigerators for the domestic, commercial and bakery markets and a home interiors retailer.

Subsidiaries include: Fired Earth, Divertimenti, Rangemaster

Main locations: Solihull, Nottingham, Telford, Banbury

Total employees: 5,641

### Charitable donations

2005: £18,637
2004: £26,422
2003: £21,112

## Community involvement

The 2005 accounts stated:

'Each operating company and its employees are encouraged to become involved with and to support local community projects, educational establishments, charities and other causes. This support may be via donations, fundraising or personal time and commitment. Our retail businesses have organised events and allowed charities to hold meetings in the group's outlets. Charitable initiatives can include financial and product donations, equipment maintenance and employee involvement.'

## Exclusions

No political donations.

## Applications

In writing to the correspondent.

### Information available

The company produces a social responsibility report within its annual report and accounts.

## Corporate giving

In 2005 the company donated £18,637 to charitable organisations. The principle beneficiaries were organisations concerned with medical research, palliative care, children and local community initiatives.

During 2005, Aga and its retail operations supported the CLIC-Sargent Appeal with the Chocolate Aga Campaign. A life-size edible chocolate Aga, created by artist Prudence Emma Staite, was placed on display in the window of one of the company's stores in London. It was then transported to Soho Square where it was smashed to pieces and auctioned off, raising £1,023. AFE, Divertimenti and Fired Earth worked with CRISIS supplying catering equipment to the Skylight Cafe project and Crash provided catering equipment and paint which was distributed to homelessness charities around the UK.

## In-kind support

The company supplied catering equipment to CRISIS's Skylight Cafe in London which has enabled them to increase their range of food by over 40%.

## Employee-led support

In 2005, employees raised over £2,200 for Children in Crisis through donations, raffles and charity auctions.

# Aggregate Industries Ltd

Bardon Hall, Copt Oak Road, Markfield, Leicestershire, United Kingdom, LE67 9PJ

01530 816600; Fax: 01530 816666

Website: www.aggregate.com

Correspondent: Mrs Mary Ford, Company Secretary
01530 816600; Fax: 01530 816666

Chief officer: Lord Norman Fowler

Chief Executive: Peter Tom

| Year end | Turnover | Pre-tax profit |
|---|---|---|
| 31/12/2004 | £1,514,100,000 | £147,600,000 |

Nature of company business
Aggregate Industries and its subsidiaries are engaged in the exploitation of land and mineral reserves principally for the supply of heavy building materials for construction activities.

The company became part of the Holcim Group in 2005.

Subsidiaries include: Supreme Concrete, Brown & Potter Ltd, Stoneflair Ltd, Three Counties Concrete Ltd, Ronez Ltd, Paragon Materials Ltd, London Concrete Ltd

Main locations: Coalville

UK employees: 5,430

Total employees: 10,520

---

Charitable donations

2004: £269,000
2003: £323,000

Membership: BitC

---

## Community involvement

The company's policy is to provide financial support to national charities which benefit the local areas and communities of Leicestershire and within the aggregates/construction industry.

In addition, the company has sites all over the UK, particularly in the East and West Midlands, London, the South West, Scotland and northern England. It supports charities local to those sites, especially those involved with children/youth, education, older people, enterprise/training, environment/heritage, or allied to the construction industry, medical research, science/technology, sickness/disability and social welfare.

### Exclusions

No support for advertising in charity brochures, animal welfare, appeals from individuals, the arts, fundraising events, overseas appeals, political appeals or religious appeals.

### Applications

In writing to the correspondent.

## Corporate giving

In 2004, the company made charitable donations amounting to £269,000. No information on how this was distributed was made available.

### Commercially-led support

**Sponsorship:** The company undertakes good-cause sponsorship.

---

# Agilent Technologies UK Ltd

South Queensferry, West Lothian EH30 9TG

0131 331 1000; Fax: 0131 331 3000

**Website:** www.agilent.com

**Correspondent:** James Wood

**E-mail:** james_wood@agilent.com

**Chief officer:** Tom White – VP

| Year end | Turnover | Pre-tax profit |
|---|---|---|
| 31/10/2003 | £79,347,000 | |

**Nature of company business**
Provision of information technologies, solutions and services.

**Main locations:** Winnersh, Queensferry

**Total employees:** 21,000

## Community involvement

The company supports projects to increase student interest and achievement in science education, with an emphasis on women and groups under-represented in the technology industry. Agilent also aims to increase the ability of communities to effectively address local health and human services needs, and environmental issues.

### Applications

In writing to the correspondent. The equipment donations to universities have a separate application policy, which runs from September to November each year and is processed on-line.

## Corporate giving

In 2005, Agilent made worldwide community contributions of $12.2 million (around £6.6 million). Of this, the largest proportion ($10 million) went to the Aligent Technologies Foundation, with the balance going to education ($1.7 million), health and human services ($0.3 million), and environment ($0.2 million).

In line with the company's overall objectives concerning science and mathematics, grants have been provided for the purchase of laboratory equipment and towards curriculum support for pre-university education development. Awards have also gone to a number of institutions including Beaumont School in St Albans and Queensferry Primary Scotland in West Lothian.

### Aligent Technologies Foundation

The Agilent Technologies Foundation is a separate, non-profit organization funded by Agilent Technologies which focuses on advancing pre-university science education around the world. The foundation makes pre-selected, foundation-initiated grants in countries where Agilent is located.

The foundation supports:

▸ programmes for strategic initiatives linked to change and improvement in student learning and engagement

▸ events and initiatives that strengthen the science education process

▸ programmes that include diversities of race, gender, class and ethnicity and support underrepresented segments of the population.

For more information, please contact:

Agilent Technologies Foundation, Grants Administrator, 1666 K Street, NW, Suite 420, Washington, DC, 20006, USA.

### Employee-led support

Employees are encouraged to volunteer, especially on Earth Day (1 December) when activities have included cleaning-up wildlife gardens and local beach clean-up. Employees may use up to four hours of company time per month, with manager approval, to work on community-supported education or community programmes. The 2005 Agilent Environment and Social Responsibility Report states that approximately 20% of Agilent employees worldwide donated close to 30,000 hours of volunteer community service.

---

# Air Products Group Ltd

Hersham Place, Molesey Road, Walton-on-Thames, Surrey KT12 4RZ

01932 249 200; Fax: 01932 258 502

**Website:** www.airproducts.co.uk/

Correspondent: Nicola Wilson, Corporate Communications Associate.

| Year end | Turnover | Pre-tax profit |
|---|---|---|
| 30/09/2005 | £4,475,955,000 | £551,250,000 |

**Nature of company business**
The manufacture and sale of industrial gases and related products for their production and use.

**Subsidiaries include:** Anchor Chemical (UK) Ltd, Ancomer Ltd, Magictalk Ltd, The Oxygen Therapy Company Ltd, Prodair Services Ltd, On-site Engineering Services Ltd, Rimer-Alco International Ltd, Unoco (UK) Ltd, Gardner Cryogenics Ltd

**Main locations:** Crewe, Walton-on-Thames

**UK employees:** 2,000

### Charitable donations

2005: £100,000

## Community involvement

Although Air Product's American parent company devotes an area of its website to corporate social responsibility, and even gives some outdated examples of support it has given in the UK, the local website has no such information.

However, although in the past we have had difficulty in obtaining information, the company has belatedly confirmed that it continues to support the following:

- higher education institutions, where there is some relevance to the company's broad areas of interest
- organisations in the locality of its operations (Surrey, Crewe, Manchester, Basingstoke, Didcot, Sandwell, Gateshead and North Wales) concerned with health and welfare, local community and arts.

The company gives preference to charities in which a member of staff is involved.

### Exclusions

No support is given to circular appeals, fundraising events, third parties, appeals from individuals, purely denominational (religious) appeals, local appeals not in areas of company presence, large national appeals, overseas projects, political parties or organisations, or for advertising in charity brochures.

### Applications

In writing to the correspondent. The contributions committee meets every two months and reviews all appeals.

**Information available:** On request the company can supply further information for those considering applying for support.

The parent company produces an n annual corporate social responsibility report.

## Corporate giving

In 2005, the company's charitable donations amounted to £100,000. We have no details of the beneficiaries.

Grants are occasionally given to the local branch of national organisations and range from £250 to £6,000. Grants are more commonly given to local organisations and are for £50 to £5,000.

## In-kind support

**Education:** The company provides work experience schemes for pupils and educational materials for schools. Used equipment is passed on to schools, as are products with the company logo for use as raffle prizes.

**Enterprise:** The company supports local enterprise agencies.

Discounts on balloon gas are occasionally offered to charities.

## Employee-led support

Employees who are active in charitable fundraising frequently have funds matched (50% of the amount raised up to a maximum of £500) by the company, primarily in the health and welfare fields. Staff are encouraged to become volunteers in their own time and to become school governors. Staff are also seconded to voluntary organisations such as Home-Start.

**Payroll giving:** The company operates a payroll giving scheme for employees.

## Commercially-led support

**Sponsorship:** The company will consider undertaking arts and good cause sponsorship.

# Akzo Nobel UK Limited

Oriel House, 16 Connaught Place, London W2 2ZB

020 7479 6125; Fax: 020 7479 6525

Website: www.akzonobel.uk.com

Correspondent: Company Secretary

Chief Executive: Hans Wijers

| Year end | Turnover | Pre-tax profit |
|---|---|---|
| 31/12/2005 | | |

**Nature of company business**
The group is an industrial materials company involved in polymer technology and surface science. Business areas are: pharmaceuticals; coatings; and chemicals.

**Subsidiaries include:** Akcros Chemicals Ltd, Diosynth Ltd, Organon Laboratories Ltd, Eka Chemicals Ltd, Mason Vehicle Graphics, Nobilas UK Limited, International Paint Ltd, Biosynth Ltd, Intervet UK Ltd, Organon Laboratories Ltd, Eka Chemicals, Intervet UK Ltd

**Main locations:** London, Newhouse, Gateshead, Southampton, Plymouth, Brentwood, Buckhaven, Milton Keynes, Cambridge, Beith, Henley-on-Thames, Congresbury, Blackburn

**UK employees:** 4,100

**Total employees:** 61,300

## Community involvement

From the contents of the company's website it is clear that Akzo Nobel acknowledges its wider responsibilities to society, though there is little specific reference to its UK programme.

The focus of the company's community programme for sponsorship and donations is to stimulate young talent, while the corporate projects the company is involved in are mainly international in character. The local units, meanwhile, have adopted a more regional approach.

Support through sponsorship and donations is given to selected activities in fields such as education, sports, science, healthcare, culture and the arts.

### Exclusions

The company provides no support for political parties, their institutions, agencies or representatives.

### Applications

In writing to the correspondent.

**Information available:** The organisation produced its first CSR Report in 2005.

## Corporate giving

We have not been able to obtain financial information for this company, or figures for its level of charitable giving.

**Education:** The company started its Education-Industry Partnership Programme in 1991. This aims to interest young students in science and technology through a closer collaboration between the company's sites and the educational system. There are about 60 projects in countries such as Italy, France, Ireland, UK, Sweden, Belgium and the Netherlands.

The company's education fund was founded in 1994 and uses corporate funds and employee contributions to support educational development projects in Brazil, Bolivia, Kenya, Burkina Faso, Ecuador, India, the Philippines and Vietnam. The funds are mainly used for building and equipping schools, helping to develop curricula and providing books.

### Employee-led support

The company's website states that in June 2005 the Akzo Nobel Community Programme was launched. 'This is a unique worldwide initiative designed to encourage employees to become actively involved in the local communities in which they live and work. The programme makes funding available to people on all sites giving them the opportunity to become engaged in worthwhile projects in their own communities. It was launched in tandem with a partnership between Akzo Nobel and the Red Cross which will focus on projects in China and Indonesia and will also give employees the chance to get involved.'

### Commercially-led support

**Sponsorship:** Beneficiaries have included The Coulthard Institute of Art, Museum of the Chemical Industry, The Royal Society, The National Museum of Science & Industry, The Museum of Film, Photography & Television and The National Railway Museum.

# Alcatel Telecom Limited

Voyager Place, Shoppenhangers Road, Maidenhead, Berkshire S16 2PJ

01628 42 8115

Website: www.alcatel.co.uk

Correspondent: Helen Simpson, Corporate Communications
E-mail: helen.j.simpson@alcatel.co.uk

| Year end | Turnover | Pre-tax profit |
|---|---|---|
| 31/12/2003 | £139,573,000 | |

**Nature of company business**
Alcatel provide products and services in virtually every sector of the telecommunications industry – broadband access, metro and core optical networking, 3G mobile infrastructure, carrier networking and enterprise solutions.

**Main locations:** Wokingham, London, Newport

## Community involvement

Alcatel in the UK claim to have 'always looked to have a strong involvement in sponsorship and community activities'. To this end it particularly seeks to support projects within the area local to each of the company's UK business sites; although UK-wide activities have also received help.

### Exclusions

No support for local appeals outside of areas of company presence.

### Applications

Enquiries should be directed to the appropriate person at the nearest Alcatel site/office. However, appeals made through employee connections may be more successful.

## Corporate giving

Although Alcatel were not prepared to put any figures on the value of its community support programme in the UK, with substantial interests worldwide we believe it warrants inclusion.

In 2003/04, support has been given to Sparkle – a local charity established to help disabled children in South Wales, The Anthony Nolan Trust – the UK's largest stem cell register, and JENOMA Cancer Charity.

### Employee-led support

Staff are encouraged to take part in fundraising and volunteering activities on behalf of local causes.

# Alcoa UK Holdings Limited

1 Park Row, Leeds LS1 5AB

Website: www.alcoa.com/united_kingdom/en/home.asp

Correspondent: (See 'Applications')

| Year end | Turnover | Pre-tax profit |
|---|---|---|
| 31/12/2005 | £539,522,000 | (£15,877,000) |

**Nature of company business**
Alcoa is a world leading producer of primary aluminium, fabricated aluminium, and alumina. Active in all major aspects of the industry.

**Subsidiaries include:** Reynolds Food Packaging, AFL Automotive, Howmet Ltd, AFL Telecommunications, ASA, Kawneer UK

**Main locations:** Co Down, West Bromwich, Sedgefield, Swansea, Telford, Tyldesley, Runcorn, London, Laindon, Durham, Exeter, Coalville, sedgefield, Preston, Amersham, Banbury, Birmingham, Biggleswade

**UK employees:** 3,102

**Total employees:** 129,000

## Charitable donations

2005: £39,000
2004: £32,000

## Community involvement

The company's support for local voluntary and community groups in England and Wales is funded by the Alcoa Foundation, based in the United States. Its website provides a comprehensive breakdown of its grant making worldwide.

Alcoa's grant making appears to be categorised into what are termed 'Areas of Excellence', i.e. global education and workplace skills, safe & healthy children and families, conservation and sustainability and business and community partnerships.

Priority is given to projects and organisations in or near communities where Alcoa offices or plants are located, currently: Amersham, Banbury, Biggleswade, Birmingham, Coalville, Dolgarrog, Durham, Exeter, Laindon. London, Newtownards, Preston, Runcorn, Sedgefield, Swansea, Telford, Tyldesley, and West Bromwich.

### Exclusions

Generally, no support for individuals, political or religious organisations, local appeals not in areas of company presence, capital campaigns, endowment funds or funds directed towards deficit reduction or operating reserves, advertising, fundraising events, trips, documentaries, videos, conferences or sponsorships, indirect or overhead costs, multi-year grants.

### Applications

In writing to your local foundation contact (situated at each Alcoa site), who will then make recommendations to the Alcoa Foundation for grant awards.

## Corporate giving

The Alcoa Foundation made donations in the UK totalling £275,570. Beneficiaries included the South Ribble Arts Forum, the Depaul Trust, (for computer and job training programmes for young people), the Devon Wildlife Trust, Groundwork Birmingham, Restore Hope Latimer, (for a youth programme for at risk teenagers), the Charities Aid Foundation (for the purpose of purchasing an ambulance in Belaya Kalitva in Russia and the renovation of apartments of WWII veterans) and various projects at local schools.

In 2005 the foundation made over £12.5m in grants around the world.

In the same year, Alcoa UK Holdings Limited made charitable donations of £39,000. We do not have a breakdown of the recipient organisation/s.

## Employee-led support

As part of the company's 'Week of Service' 2005, a number of events in support of the communities local to Alcoa sites were scheduled. These included: working with 'Restore Hope Latimer', staff were involved in clearing debris from Latimer Park's farm grounds and Chess river bank; painting and redecorating a cancer centre; helping local scouts complete essential repairs to their building including repainting the entire facility; working in partnership with The Boys and Girls Clubs of Wales to organise first-aid training for local youth sports teams.

# Allen & Overy

One Bishops Square, London, E1 6AO

020 7330 3000

Website: www.allenovery.com

Correspondent: The Pro Bono & Community Affairs Manager

| Year end | Turnover | Pre-tax profit |
|---|---|---|
| 30/04/2006 | £736,474,000 | £291,775,000 |

**Nature of company business**
International law firm.

**Main locations:** London

## Charitable donations

Total community contributions: £12,000,000
Membership: BitC, %Club

## Community involvement

Allen & Overy are an international law firm with an extensive pro bono community affairs programme – 'Values into Community Action' – which supports a broad range of initiatives. The firm states: 'The programme provides a valuable opportunity for personal and professional development. It responds to the desire of many individuals to use their skills and expertise to help others and to put something back into society.'

To oversee its pro bono work, Allen & Overy has appointed a Pro Bono and Community Work Committee. In each of the offices outside London, it has a Programme Contact and partner responsible for local programmes.

### Applications

Each Allen & Overy office has a community programme contact and partner who are responsible for their local initiatives.

## Corporate giving

Allen & Overy's lawyers regularly undertake pro bono (i.e. free) work on behalf of those needing legal advice and assistance, but who are unable to afford a solicitor and do not qualify for legal aid. The firm also encourages staff who are non-lawyers to involve themselves in community volunteering.

In 2005, 24 out of 25 Allen & Overy's offices worldwide undertook pro bono work on behalf of the communities in which they operate. Volunteers gave 50,000 hours of service which is estimated to be equivalent to £12 million in billings. We do not know what proportion of this is attributable to its UK offices.

Rising out of its longstanding relationship with Battersea Legal Advice Centre, in May 2005, Allen & Overy pioneered a scheme with the London Legal Support Trust. The firm now donates an amount equivalent to the interest it normally earns from consolidated client accounts (some £70,000 a year), to help sustain law centres and other not-for-profit providers of legal aid and social welfare work.

## In-kind support

Through the 'Values into Community Action' programme, a broad range of initiatives are supported.

A trainee secondment programme is in operation with Battersea Legal Advice Centre, enabling four trainees per year to work at the Centre, providing support services and additional casework resources for staff solicitors.

# Alliance & Leicester plc

Carlton Park, Narborough, Leicester LE19 0AL

0116 201 1000

Website: www.alliance-leicester-group.co.uk

Correspondent: Lisa Hallam, Corporate Social Responsibility Assistant
E-mail: csr@alliance-leicester.co.uk

Chief officer: Sir Derek Higgs

Chief Executive: R Pym

| Year end | Turnover | Pre-tax profit |
|---|---|---|
| 31/12/2005 | | 547,100,000 |

Nature of company business
Principal activity: provision of a range of personal financial services.

Main locations: Bootle, Leicester

UK employees: 7,296

### Charitable donations

2005: £1,020,000
2003: £512,000

Total community contributions: £1,285,000
Management costs: £40,000

Membership: BitC, %Club

## Community involvement

Alliance & Leicester's community investment and charitable donations programme are focused on five key areas:

- supporting its staff's efforts in raising money for charity through the group's matched donation scheme
- supporting initiatives aimed at improving both local and national education
- supporting organisations that help those who are experiencing financial difficulties
- supporting charities and organisations within the local communities in which its staff live and work
- supporting organisations who aim to improve the links between businesses and the communities in which they operate.

In applying these criteria, Alliance & Leicester state that they will:

- support selected charitable causes which are in line with the group's aims. These are likely to include housing, education, families, and financial inclusion as well as, other projects which impact on the group's customer or employee base
- encourage volunteering efforts in the communities in

which it operates, linking with organisations that promote partnerships between businesses and the community (e.g. Business in the Community and Cares Incorporated)

- consider sympathetically requests for its branches and cash handling services to be made available for collecting donations destined for national and regional appeals
- support educational initiatives and in particular look to support those with an emphasis on financial literacy.

**Charity of the Year:** Marie Curie Cancer Care and Pilgrim's Hospice (2006).

### Exclusions

No support for circular appeals, advertising in charity brochures, animal welfare, appeals from individuals, the arts, education, older people, environment/heritage, fundraising events, medical research, overseas projects, political appeals, religious appeals, science/technology, sickness/disability, sport or local appeals not in areas of company presence.

### Applications

In writing to the correspondent, who has stated that the charities committee selects charities to support and, as such, is unable to encourage other appeals. Unsolicited applications will not be acknowledged.

## Corporate giving

In 2005, community contributions amounted to £1,285,000. This was broken down as follows: £710,000 in charitable donations; £365,000 invested in the community; and, £210,000 in staff time/gifts in-kind. A further £40,000 was spent in managing the company's community investment programmes.

As an example of the group's support for local charities and communities, it significantly increased its investment in Merseyside. In 2005, over £365,000 was given to local community events and programmes in addition to its commercial sponsorship of the European Capital of Culture celebrations in Liverpool.

### In-kind support

As part of Business in the Community's 'Cares' scheme, the company is active in encouraging and supporting staff engaged in volunteering activities. Staff at the Leicester, Liverpool, Leeds and Manchester operations participate in the Right to Read scheme which aims to improve literacy standards by volunteers listening to primary school children read.

Management secondments, organising fundraising events, and the use of office space were also part of the in kind support provided by the company.

### Employee-led support

The company matches staff fundraising efforts. In 2005, the group donated £110,000 to charities through this scheme.

**Payroll giving:** A payroll giving scheme is in operation, through which £35,000 was donated to various charities.

### Commercially-led support

**Sponsorship:** This is always seen as a marketing activity, not patronage or as a charitable donation, and therefore must have some direct relevance to the company's business plan. Ideally it should give a return to the company equal to that which is produced by conventional advertising.

# Alliance Boots

Boots plc, D90 Building West G14, Nottingham, NG90 1BS

0845 070 5015

Website: www.boots-csr.com/

Correspondent: Rachel McGuire, Boots Charitable Trust Appeals Officer
E-mail: rachel.mcguire@boots.co.uk

Chief officer: Sir Nigel Rudd

Chief Executive: Richard Baker

| Year end | Turnover | Pre-tax profit |
|---|---|---|
| 31/03/2006 | | |

**Nature of company business**
The group's principal activities are: retailing of chemists' merchandise; the development, manufacture and marketing of healthcare and consumer products; the provision of opticians' and other healthcare services.

Main locations: Nottingham

Total employees: 63,000

### Charitable donations

2006: £1,420,000
2004: £2,360,000
2003: £3,100,000

Total community contributions: £2,670,000
Management costs: £280,000

Membership: BitC, L B Group, %Club

## Community involvement

In July 2006, Boots Group plc and Alliance UniChem plc merged to create Alliance Boots. At the end of 2006 the company's website stated its intention to introduce changes to its Corporate Social Responsibility management structure to reflect the composition of the new business. The following relates to The Boots Group plc.

The company's Community Investment programme – Healthy Communities – focuses on building active partnerships that will produce projects and initiatives with real health benefits. Partners have included NHS Hospital Trusts, Primary Care Trusts and other health organisations.

The company's resources are used to develop and support programmes that align with the direction of the business. The majority of the activities it supports are within Nottinghamshire where Boots has its headquarters.

Nationally its stores are involved in two key cause related marketing campaigns which support the national charities Tommy's and Breast Cancer Care. Links with schools outside Nottinghamshire, such as work experience placements, or support for very small local charitable appeals, are at the discretion of the local store manager. Any such requests should be made direct to the local store.

The company is proactive in developing partnerships and continues its strategy of building on existing partnerships with the voluntary and public sector.

## Exclusions

No support is given to the following: individuals; third parties – individuals or groups – raising funds on behalf of charities; expeditions or overseas travel; overseas charities or projects; political or campaigning groups; sport, leisure and entertainment; music and the arts; animal welfare; advertising; school capital projects and specialist college status.

## Applications

Appeals to Boots Charitable Trust should be sent to the correspondent. All applicants must complete an application form and send it, along with its annual report, accounts and any supporting documentation such as letters of support, by post to the trust.

The application is available in electronic format on the website or by post upon request in writing.

There are no deadlines for applications. Trustees meet regularly during the year, but a grant will take anything from 4 weeks (grants of less than £1,000) to 6 months (grants of £1,000+). All applications will be acknowledged.

Boots publishes information on its community investment in its annual report and on its website.

## Corporate giving

In 2005/06, the company's total community contributions were £2.67 million, including cash donations of £1.42 million

The company only responds to appeals made through the Boots Charitable Trust, an independent registered charity wholly funded by the Boots Company (Charity Commission no.: 1045927). Boots was founded in Nottingham over 150 years ago and still has its headquarters there. Therefore priority is given to charities benefiting Nottingham, Nottinghamshire and Erewash. Appeals may be considered from organisations located in other areas within the UK where The Boots Company plc has a significant representation and when the appeal is supported by a strong recommendation from that Boots business unit.

The trust's funding priorities are as follows:

### Health

This includes: community healthcare such as community healthcare services, home care, after care, relief of people who are disabled or have a medical condition and continuing care; and health education and prevention by promoting knowledge and awareness of specific diseases and medical conditions.

### Lifelong learning

Helping people of any age to achieve their educational potential, supporting supplementary schools, literacy and numeracy projects, community education, vocational/restart education for the unemployed and alternative education for excluded school pupils.

### Community development

Helping groups to organise and respond to problems and needs in their communities or networks. This could include groups such as Councils for Voluntary Services and self-help groups.

### Social care

This includes: personal social services – organisations assisting individuals or families to overcome social deprivation, such as people who are homeless or disabled and their carers, lone parent and childcare groups and other family support groups; social prevention schemes – activities preventing crime, dropping out and general delinquency and providing other social care, outreach work, social health and safety awareness schemes etc.; and community social activity – activities to promote social engagement for vulnerable people, mitigating against isolation and loneliness.

Projects are excluded for which there is a clear statutory obligation. The company is especially interested in approaches with the capacity to influence a wide audience within its area of support.

Additional information can be found on the company's website.

## In-kind support

In 2005 Boots worked in partnership with Cancer Research UK to support their national SunSmart Campaign, raising awareness of sun safety and Action for Sick Children – Dental Playbox Project, tackling dental diseases among children.

Boots has supported a number of Datalink schemes by donating unwanted film containers.

## Employee-led support

Volunteering programmes offers Boots employees the chance to participate in a wide range of community activities in company time, sharing their expertise and knowledge with local schools, hospitals and voluntary organisations.

Employees planning to raise money for charity can apply for matched funding to a maximum of £500.

**Payroll giving:** The company offers the Give As You Earn payroll giving facility.

## Commercially-led support

**Sponsorship:** Boots continued its programme of support in other areas of education as a key sponsor of both the Boots Science Building at the University of Nottingham and the Nottingham Trent University Boots Library.

# Allianz Cornhill Insurance plc

57 Ladymead, Guildford, Surrey GU1 1DB

01483 552349; Fax: 01483 552782

Website: www.allianzcornhill.co.uk

Correspondent: Vicky Flynn 01483 552349; Fax: 01483 552782 E-mail: vicky.flynn@allianzcornhill.co.uk

Chief officer: Clem Booth

Chief Executive: Andrew Torrance

| Year end | Turnover | Pre–tax profit |
|---|---|---|
| 31/12/2005 | | £206,400,000 |

Nature of company business
The group undertakes all classes of insurance business. It has 13 UK branches.

Subsidiaries include: Trafalgar Insurance plc, British Reserve Insurance Co Ltd, Pet Plan Ltd, Domestic Insurance Services Ltd, DBI Insurance Co Ltd

Main locations: Guildford, Bristol, Tunbridge Wells

UK employees: 4,300

## Charitable donations

2005: £89,314
2004: £153,498
2003: £102,852

Total community contributions: £89,314

Membership: A & B

## Community involvement

The company makes most of its donations to registered charities through the Charities Aid Foundation. It aims to be a good corporate citizen through a programme of support for charitable, cultural, educational and recreational projects. There is a preference for charities where the business is located (Guildford, Tunbridge Wells and Bristol), and in which a member of staff is involved and for charities working in the fields of children and youth, education, older people, enterprise/training, environment/heritage, fundraising events, science/technology, sickness/disability charities and social welfare.

Pet Plan Ltd, a subsidiary company, has an associated charitable trust – the Pet Plan Charitable Trust (Charity Commission no. 1032907). Some details are given below.

**Charity of the Year:** Association of Children's Hospices (2006).

## Exclusions

No response to circular appeals. No support for advertising in charity brochures, appeals from individuals, the arts, medical research, overseas projects, political appeals, religious appeals, sport or local appeals not in areas of company presence.

## Applications

For further details please contact the correspondent.

**Information Available:** Further tailored advice for applicants is available from the company on request.

## Corporate giving

In 2005, the company made donations of just over £89,314. Other than Childline, the company's charity of the year for 2005, we have no details of the beneficiaries.

The company has close links with the Surrey Community Foundation (Charity Commission no. 1111600).

## In-kind support

Non-cash support is given in the form of gifts in-kind, staff secondments and training schemes.

## Employee-led support

Employee fundraising is matched by the company to a maximum of £25,000 a year.

**Payroll giving:** The company operates the Give As You Earn scheme to which the company adds 10%.

## Commercially-led support

**Sponsorship:** The company occasionally undertakes good-cause sponsorship. Recent examples include mentoring and developmental sponsorships of the Jubilee Sailing Trust and the Prince's Trust.

Contact: Vicky Flynn, as above.

# Allied London Properties Ltd

1 Cavendish Place, London W1G 0QD

020 7291 7970; Fax: 020 7291 7971

Website: www.alliedlondon.com

Correspondent: John Ashurst, Company Secretary
E-mail: info@alliedlondon.com

Chief Executive: M J Ingall

| Year end | Turnover | Pre-tax profit |
|---|---|---|
| 31/12/2003 | £7,260,000 | £5,515,000 |

Nature of company business
Principal activity: property investors.

Subsidiaries include: Pellam Homes Ltd, Gough Cooper Properties Ltd, Hamiltonhill Estates Ltd

Main locations: London

UK employees: 38

## Community involvement

Previous information suggested that support is given to a wide range of charitable organisations, especially in the fields of education, health and community affairs.

## Exclusions

No support for appeals from individuals or overseas projects.

## Applications

The company stated that it does not wish to receive unsolicited requests for donations.

## Corporate giving

Recent information on the company's community involvement was not available.

In 1998, the company donated £47,000 to charitable organisations. Grants to national organisations ranged from £100 to £10,000. Grants to local organisations ranged from £50 to £500.

Support has been given to Industry in Education, Prince's Youth Business Trust, Action on Addiction, WellBeing, British Red Cross, Variety Club and NSPCC.

## In-kind support

In May 2005, Allied London's Spinningfields development in Manchester (close to the site of the city's first ever children's hospital) was used as the launch site for fundraising 'Balloon Race' on behalf of children's hospitals.

# AMEC plc

Head Office, 65 Carter Lane, London, EC4V 5HF

020 7634 0000; Fax: 020 7634 0001

Website: www.amec.com

Correspondent: Laura O'Neill

Chief officer: Jock Green-Armytage

Chief Executive: Sir Peter Mason

| Year end | Turnover | Pre-tax profit |
|---|---|---|
| 31/12/2005 | £4,942,500,000 | £25,400,000 |

Nature of company business
AMEC's provides a broad range of services to the oil and gas industry worldwide.

Subsidiaries include: CV Buchan

Main locations: Aberdeen, Ashford, London, Birchwood, Birmingham, Manchester

Total employees: 44,710

### Charitable donations

2005: £108,000
2003: £69,000

Membership: BitC

## Community involvement

AMEC states on its website that: 'Investing in our communities involves more than making charitable donations, but requires taking an active interest and making a positive contribution, whether it is in time, materials, or another form of giving. Our approach is based on providing support for the communities in which we live and work, leaving benefits in project locations long after we leave.

'We have established a good practice Community Investment Guideline, which gives our businesses a framework to assess how to help local communities in practical ways.' Unfortunately, copies of the guidelines are available for internal purposes only.

To help implement these 'good practices', regional committees have been established with each providing funds for charitable giving, matched funding and community involvement.

## Exclusions

Non-charitable grants cannot be considered.

## Applications

In writing to the correspondent.

**Information available:** The company's latest sustainability report, for 2005, is available online at www.amec.com.

## Corporate giving

In 2005, the company made cash donations in the UK of £108,000. We have no details of the beneficiaries.

In the past, grants to national organisations have ranged from £500 to £2,500, and to local organisations from £50 to £250. Examples of beneficiaries in the UK during 2003 include Engineers Against Poverty (EAP), an initiative promoted by the UK's Institution of Civil Engineers, the Institution of Mechanical Engineers and the Department for International Development. The company stated at that time that it was committed to support EAP with 'in kind' contributions of £100,000.

## In-kind support

The group tries to ensure that many of its waste products, such as toner cartridges and inkjets, are re-used to the advantage of worthwhile causes. There has also been a pledge of in kind support to Engineers Against Poverty (see above).

## Employee-led support

'The AMEC plc Board Charities Committee and our regional charities committees pledge to support, up to a capped amount, charity fundraising undertaken by groups of employees through fund matching grants. In 2003 the total amount of matched funding was £26,049, compared with a figure of £22,405 in 2002.'

## Commercially-led support

**Sponsorship:** *Education* – AMEC sponsors students at selected universities throughout their academic careers before they take up permanent positions in group companies. It is also funding the first Chair in Engineering Project Management at University of Manchester Institute of Science and Technology (UMIST).

# Amey plc

Sherard Building, Edmund Halley Road, Oxford OX4 4DQ

01865 713 100

Website: www.amey.co.uk

Correspondent: Communications Department

E-mail: group.hse@amey.co.uk

Chief officer: Sir Patrick Brown

Chief Executive: Mel Ewell

| Year end | Turnover | Pre-tax profit |
|---|---|---|
| 31/12/2005 | £1,200,000,000 | £52,000,000 |

Nature of company business
A leading provider of support services in the UK, ranging from transportation and education, to defence and health.

Main locations: Birmingham, Belfast, Preston, Middlesbrough, Manchester, Newport, Leeds, Holyhead, Glasgow, Edinburgh, Bristol

UK employees: 7,500

Total employees: 7,500

### Charitable donations

Membership: BitC

## Community involvement

In July 2005, Amey published its 'Community Involvement Policy' in which it stated that its express policy was:

- to seek to explain its objectives and business practices to communities in which it works and, where appropriate, to consult with representatives of those communities to establish their needs and priorities
- that the contribution to communities will be made both by the company itself and by the enthusiasm, creativity, skills and personal time of its employees and, in some instances, those of our business partners
- to encourage employees to be active in the community and to be involved with relevant charitable organisations. Amey will, wherever practical, support such endeavours
- to focus corporate charitable support primarily on a charity chosen by its staff, with the selection reviewed every two years, where Amey undertakes to match funds

raised by employees. The support for a nominated charity does not preclude fundraising at a more local level in support of any communities in which Amey is active as a business, or for charities clearly of relevance to the business.

**Charity of the year:** NSPCC (2004/05)

## Exclusions

No provision for funding or other support to political organisations of any sort, and only exceptionally to provide funding or support to religious organisations as part of an initiative to the general benefit of a community. No funding or support will be given to individuals outside the business.

## Applications

In writing to the correspondent.

## Corporate giving

In 2005, the company gave £38,000 in grants to organisations, which matched the amount which was raised by employees. Previous beneficiaries have included Unity City Academy in Middlesbrough which received over £2 million and the Duke of Edinburgh's Award was given £160,000 over a five year period.

## Employee-led support

Employees are encouraged to be active in the community. The company's charitable support is focused on a charity chosen by its staff, with the selection reviewed every two years. Amey matches funds raised by its employees.

Since 2002, Amey has raised over £100,000 for the NSPCC.

## Commercially-led support

**Sponsorship:** *Health* – Amey paid £5,000 to sponsor the provision of 3,000 water bottles for primary school pupils in Edinburgh.

# AMVESCAP plc

30 Finsbury Square, London EC2A 1AG

020 7638 0731; Fax: 020 7065 3962

Website: www.amvescap.com

Correspondent: Bob Duthie, Head of HR

Chief officer: Charles W Brady

| Year end | Turnover | Pre-tax profit |
|---|---|---|
| 31/12/2005 | £1,194,400,000 | £197,900,000 |

Nature of company business
Global investment management company.

Subsidiaries include: Perpetual Portfolio Management Ltd, INVESCO Asset Management Ltd, Perpetual Unit Trust Management Ltd, Perpetual Investment Management Services Ltd, INVESCO Private Portfolio Management Ltd, AIM, Atlantic Trust, Perpetual Investments Ltd, INVESCO UK Ltd, INVESCO Fund Managers Ltd

Main locations: London

Total employees: 6,261

## Charitable donations

2005: £110,000

2003: £52,000

## Community involvement

AMVESCAP seeks to support communities worldwide that are local to where its employees live and work. Help is given to various causes connected with the arts, education, the environment and sport, and may take the form of cash donations, in kind support or the provision of other resources.

In the UK, there appears to be particular emphasis on working to support children.

### Exclusions

No support for appeals from individuals or local appeals not in areas of company presence.

### Applications

In writing to the correspondent.

## Corporate giving

In 2005, the company made global donations of just under £1 million, of which £110,000 was given in the UK. We have no details of the beneficiaries.

### In-kind support

The company may provide unspecified resources to organisations.

### Employee-led support

Employees are encouraged to become involved with communities local to sites of company presence. In line with some other financial and professional companies, staff donate their time and skills to local schools through reading and mentoring schemes.

# Anglia Regional Co-operative Society Limited

Westgate House, Park Road, Peterborough PE1 2TA

01733 563151; Fax: 01733 313078

Website: www.arcs.co.uk

Correspondent: Ron Douglas, Secretary
E-mail: executive.officer@arcs.co.uk

Chief officer: Jean Humphreys

Chief Executive: Neil Double

| Year end | Turnover | Pre-tax profit |
|----------|----------|----------------|
| 03/09/2005 | £322,846,000 | £2,147,000 |

Nature of company business
Co-operative society trading in food, household goods, furniture and funerals.

Main locations: Peterborough

UK employees: 3,464

Total employees: 3,464

## Charitable donations

2005: £75,000

Total community contributions: £75,000

## Community involvement

The mutual society supports national and local charities at a regional level, and has an effective policy of soliciting charitable donations from its customers via its dividend scheme.

### Exclusions

No grants for: running costs; causes deemed to promote a particular religious viewpoint; statutory services, such as schools, libraries, hospitals and so on; improvements to property not owned by the applicant charity; party political causes; or causes they believe conflict with the ethos of the co-operative movement. No support for the arts, science/technology, social welfare or sport.

The society does not consider 'charity of the year' applications.

### Applications

In writing to the correspondent.

## Corporate giving

In 2004/05 the company donated £75,000 to charitable causes.

Beneficiaries were Macmillan Cancer Relief in Cambridgeshire and Oxfordshire, Help the Aged in Norfolk and Suffolk, Mencap in Cambridgeshire and Suffolk, Sense in Lincolnshire and Norfolk and The Meningitis Trust in Cambridgeshire and Norfolk.

The report and accounts for the year stated: 'The society was pleased to support a number of other local organisations in our trading areas by matching funds raised in our stores. Including those to benefit were, the East Anglian, Norfolk and East Suffolk branches of the Air Ambulance Service. The society was also pleased to help charities based in our new trading areas at Ilkey and Skipton.' A donation was also sent to the Tsunami Appeal in Asia.

In February 2006, members' donations to the share account, Share 600, were donated to the following organisations throughout the company's trading areas:

| | |
|---|---|
| Cerebral Palsy – Norfolk | £6,000 |
| Cerebral Palsy – Oxfordshire | £6,000 |
| Hospital At Home – Peterborough | £9,000 |
| National Autistic Society – Cambridgeshire and Norfolk | £3,000 |
| National Autistic Society – Suffolk | £6,000 |

### Employee-led support

The society will match the total amount raised by employees in any one year up to a maximum of £20,000.

### Commercially-led support

**Sponsorship:** – *Good-cause sponsorship* may be considered.

The co-operative runs a dividend scheme, which sees the trading profit of the organisation shared between its customers who have enrolled in a membership scheme.

Members have an opportunity at the point of sale to donate their dividend to share account number 600 (Share 600), the proceeds of which are presented each year to three or four charities, which are agreed by the board of Directors.

A sub-committee of the board meets quarterly to consider charitable claims and to recommend those worthy of Share 600 funds to the full board. In addition to the three or four main charities supported each year, consideration is given to other claims, which may be met by Share 600 funds. The main recipients are often national charities, but the donations are made to branches in its trading areas as the society looks to support the local community where it can.

The society has donated in excess of £500,000 from Share 600 since it was introduced in 1985.

# Anglo American plc

20 Carlton House Terrace, London SW1Y 5AN

020 7968 8888

Website: www.angloamerican.co.uk

Correspondent: Edward Bickham, Executive Vice President
E-mail: ebickham@angloamerican.co.uk

Chief officer: Sir Mark Moody-Stuart

Chief Executive: A J Trahar

| Year end | Turnover | Pre-tax profit |
|---|---|---|
| 31/12/2003 | £16,176,970,000 | £2,862,324,600 |

Nature of company business
The company, and its subsidiaries, joint ventures and associates, is a worldwide group in gold, platinum group metals and diamonds, with significant interests in coal, base and ferrous metals, industrial minerals and forest products.

Subsidiaries include: Mondi Packaging (UK) Ltd, Cleveland Potash Limited, Tarmac Group Ltd

Main locations: London

UK employees: 10,576

Total employees: 132,000

## Charitable donations

2005: £824,402

Membership: BitC, L B Group, %Club

## Community involvement

Charitable donations in the UK are mainly in the areas of education, sport and youth, health and HIV/AIDS, the environment, the arts, culture and heritage and housing and the homeless.

Within the United Kingdom, Anglo American with Tarmac have supported the staging of a major exhibition of British archaeological artefacts 'Buried Treasure' which started at the British Museum before moving to four (Cardiff, Manchester, Tyneside and Norwich) provincial centres and the establishment of the Merensky Room at the Natural History Museum. The company also supports work with homelessness charities (Centrepoint and the London Connection) and the refurbishment of St. Martin in the Fields, all of which are local to the UK head office.

In South Africa, through the Anglo Chairman's Fund, Anglo American Group companies channel their 'social investment giving'. Education receives the largest share of financial support. The Chairman's Fund assists schools, often in remote rural areas, to secure basic facilities. It supports projects for learners with special needs, pioneering new forms of learning for individuals of all ages and abilities for whom formal schooling has not traditionally catered. The Fund also promotes structured programmes for improved performance at schools in the key disciplines of mathematics, science and English.

'At an international corporate level, our priorities mostly relate to projects involved with international development objectives. Our central corporate donations fund also supports education, health (with priority given to HIV/AIDS) and environmental programmes and community development projects in central London.

'Amongst international projects supported in the past two years are Projects with CARE in Brazil and Zimbabwe; making Bees for Development's materials available to support sustainable livelihoods projects in South America; Starfish's work with AIDS affected families in South Africa; SightSavers International's projects in Mali and Tanzania; and in community projects with Transparency International and the Commonwealth Business Council as well as Leonard Cheshire's work with disabled people in Tanzania.'

Other areas attracting the Fund's support include community health (with a special concern for HIV/AIDS), skills training and income generation, environmental stewardship and care for the elderly, the very young and others isolated from established support and relief networks.

### Exclusions

No support for appeals from individuals, medical research, political appeals, religious appeals or sport.

### Applications

In writing to the correspondent.

## Corporate giving

The following information is taken from the company's website: During the year Anglo American and its subsidiaries made donations for charitable purposes or wider social purposes amounting to $56.7m, (1% of pre-tax profit). This excludes core business activities such as work on local business development, workplace HIV programmes.

Charitable donations of $1.5m (£824,402) were made in the UK consisting of payments in respect of education, sport and youth (16%), community development 1%, health and HIV/AIDS (14%), environment (20%), the arts, culture and heritage (14%), housing and the homeless (21%) and other charitable causes (14%).

### In-kind support

The company may, from time to time, provide additional support through gifts in kind. We have no details of the form this may take.

### Employee-led support

The company has an employee volunteering scheme and allows company time off for community support activities to take place. Employee fundraising is matched by the company up to a maximum of £500 per employee.

**Payroll giving:** A scheme is operated by the company on behalf of its employees.

## Commercially-led support

**Sponsorship:** Arts and good-cause sponsorship is undertaken.

Contact: Pamela Bell, at the above address.

# AOL UK

80 Hammersmith Road, London W14 8UD

020 7348 8000; Fax: 020 7348 8002

Website: www.aol.co.uk

Correspondent: Katrina Keeling, Head of Corporate
Responsibility
E-mail: ukcharity@aol.com

| Year end | Turnover | Pre-tax profit |
|---|---|---|
| 31/12/2004 | £162,700,000 | £3,200,000 |

**Nature of company business**
Launched in the UK in 1996, AOL UK is an interactive service
company and a division of AOL Europe – the internet, online
and e-commerce services company.

Main locations: London

UK employees: 456

### Charitable donations

2006: £60,000
2005: £60,000

Membership: L B Group

## Community involvement

'The community investment programme at AOL seeks to
extend the benefits of the internet to those who would most
benefit from the medium but are often the least likely to
obtain access through traditional means. This is often
addressed by providing direct funding, advice and support in
kind to charities and community groups going online to
demonstrate innovative use of the medium.'

'AOL UK currently focuses on funding online projects which
address the issues of the digital divide regarding the following
groups: the disabled, children outside of mainstream learning,
online safety and socially excluded young people. AOL UK
supports UK registered charities or recognised organisations
through local authorities and boroughs.'

## Exclusions

No funding or support for individuals (including, for
example, overseas events and marathons), advertising or
sponsorship in charity brochures (including calendars and ball
programmes).

## Applications

AOL UK does not accept unsolicited applications.

## Corporate giving

AOL gives at least £60,000 in cash donations in the UK (see
'Community Awards' below). Although no figures for total
community contributions were available, it is evident from
the examples of support given on the company's website that
it is quite substantial.

AOL UK has strong emphasis on assisting youth and disability
related charities as reflected in its relationships with the
following organisations:

Fairbridge is a youth development charity that offers long
term personal development programmes for young people
aged between 13 and 25. The relationship with Fairbridge
enables AOL UK to work with disenfranchised young people
who may benefit from having access to the online medium,
particularly with online learning.

 AOL is the official online media partner for 'Give it up for
the Children!' an NCH initiative AOL UK has raised
awareness of through providing information on how members
can get involved.

AOL UK has close ties with Centrepoint, a charity which helps
homeless and socially excluded young people to rebuild their
lives, the initiative has led to the use of the Internet in the
training, education and empowerment of disadvantaged
young people.

In 2000 AOL UK began working with John Grooms, a charity
which provides services to people with disabilities and their
families in the provision of funding, training and specialist
equipment. The objective is that with AOL UK's help the
beneficiaries will be able to make the most of being online.

**Community Awards**

In 2003 AOL in conjunction with Citizens Online launched
the AOL Innovation in the Community Awards with the aim
of encouraging community groups and charities across the
UK to conduct innovative use of the Internet. The awards are
open to community groups and registered charities that are
seeking funding for Internet-related projects with £2,000
available for the 90 successful organisations. The deadline for
the 2006 awards was 10 May with shortlisted organisations to
be informed by 16 June. More information regarding this is
available on the AOL company website.

Beneficiaries of the AOL's Innovation in the Community
Awards 2005 award included Alzheimer's Society, West Kent –
to develop an online forum for Alzheimer's sufferers; Grief
Encounter, North London – to develop an online interactive
workbook encouraging people to deal with bereavement;
Savile Town Community Association, West Yorkshire – to
launch an online loan scheme of sensory equipment for
children with disabilities.

## In-kind support

AOL supports GiveNow.org which is hosted by CAF
(Charities Aid Foundation) and the Time Warner Foundation.
GivenNow.org is the UK's first website to enable donors to
give both their time and money to the charities of their
choice. It has generated over £230,000 in donations since its
launch in 2002.

## Employee-led support

AOL's efforts to encourage employees to make a difference
include: Employee Volunteer Days allowing employees to
serve the community where they live and work.

## Commercially-led support

**Sponsorship:** *Disability* – A joint marketing initiative was
undertaken in association with the RNID, focusing on
marginalised groups who would most benefit from online
access. 'AOL Keyword: RNID' is a pioneering microsite on the
AOL UK service, bringing together a community of people
united by a common issue.

# ARAMARK Limited

Millbank Tower, 21–24 Millbank, London SW1P 4QP

020 7963 0000; Fax: 0207963 0500

Website: www.aramark.co.uk

Correspondent: Hannah Martin

Chief Executive: Andrew Main

| Year end | Turnover | Pre-tax profit |
|----------|----------|----------------|
| 30/09/2005 | £352,950,000 | (£4,873,000) |

**Nature of company business**
The management and provision of a range of food, vending and refreshment services to industry and commerce.

Main locations: Leeds, Aberdeen

UK employees: 11,988

## Community involvement

ARAMARK UK supports initiatives linked to the hospitality industry as well as selected organisations concerning children and the disabled.

The company also supports its employees in their charitable giving.

**Charity of the year:** Hospitality Action.

## Applications

In writing to the correspondent.

## Corporate giving

Unfortunately, we were unable to obtain a community contributions figure for 2005, whilst no cash donations were declared in the annual report and accounts for that year. From the information that is available, it appears that most of the company's support is in-kind in nature and/or directed through its employees.

Besides the support given to Hospitality Action, for which it has helped raise over £250,000, ARAMARK has assisted KidsOut in its fundraising through involvement in various events.

Springboard UK is a national organisation promoting careers in the hospitality industry and is another of ARAMARK's chosen charities. Springboard is actively involved in programmes for disabled people, the unemployed and adult learners, and is supported by the company through fundraising and events.

## Employee-led support

**Payroll giving:** Through the 'Pennies From Heaven' scheme employees are able to donate to the company's chosen charities by giving the odd pennies from their monthly pay.

Under an initiative with Hospitality Action help is being given to the NSPCC via this scheme.

# Archant

Prospect House, Rouen Road, Norwich NR1 1RE

01603 628311

Website: www.archant.co.uk

Correspondent: Keith Morris, Communications Manager
E-mail: keith.morris@archant.co.uk

Chief officer: Richard Jewson

Chief Executive: John Fry

| Year end | Turnover | Pre-tax profit |
|----------|----------|----------------|
| 31/12/2005 | £195,128,000 | £22,391,000 |

**Nature of company business**
Publisher of local, regional and national magazines, newspapers and websites.

Main locations: Ayr, Barnstaple, Dereham, Diss, Exeter, Ely, Felixstowe, Glasgow, Harlow, Hitchin, Huntingdon, Ipswich, Sudbury, Weston-super-Mare, Welwyn Garden City, Buryt St Edmunds, Colchester, Cheltenham, Cromer, Motherwell, Maidstone, Lowestoft, London, Norwich, Wimbledon, Preston, Reigate, St Albans, Southampton

UK employees: 2,800

### Charitable donations

2005: £103,000
2003: £73,000

Membership: BitC

## Community involvement

The company provides grants in the areas in which it operates, which is across most of England and parts of Scotland.

## Applications

In writing to the correspondent.

## Corporate giving

In 2005, charitable donations by the company totalled £103,000. No further information was available.

## In-kind support

The group's magazines and newspapers help raise funds through running local campaigns in their pages. This support generated over £1.73 million in donations from the public in 2005.

## Employee-led support

The Archant Gold Scheme matches the fundraising efforts of employees, to a maximum of £3,000 each.

**Payroll giving:** The company is part of the CAF payroll giving scheme and matches up to 50% of the donations, up to a maximum of £40,000 in total for all employees.

## Commercially-led support

**Sponsorship:** A wide variety of good causes and arts projects are sponsored by the group.

# Arla Foods UK plc

Arla House, 4 Savannah Way, Leeds Valley Park, Leeds LE3 2TP

0113 382 7000; Fax: 0113 382 7030

Website: www.arlafoodsuk.com

Correspondent: Adrian Thompson, Director of Human Resources
0113 382 7323
E-mail: adrian.thompson@arlafoods.com

Chief officer: Sir David Naish

Chief Executive: Tim Smith

| Year end | Turnover | Pre-tax profit |
|---|---|---|
| 30/09/2005 | £1,374,100,000 | £14,700,000 |

Nature of company business
Arla Foods UK plc, through its subsidiary companies, is a leading supplier of milk and dairy products in the UK market. The group supplies liquid milk, cream, butter, spreads, cheeses, fresh dairy products, yoghurts and desserts to the major supermarkets.

Subsidiaries include: Claymore Dairies Ltd, Blakes Chilled Distribution Ltd

Main locations: Liverpool, Manchester, Nairn, Norhallerton, Newcastle, Nottingham, Oakthorpe, Ruislip, Sheffield, Settle, Hatfield Peverel, Leeds, Ashby de la Zouch

UK employees: 6,035

---

### Charitable donations

2005: £100,000
2004: £100,000
2003: £100,000

Membership: BitC

---

## Community involvement

The company have produced a corporate social responsibility leaflet in which it outlines its policy regarding community/charitable support. The following is an extract from that leaflet.

'The company wants to contribute to the communities in which it operates. We also recognise our wider responsibility as corporate citizens to enable others to benefit from the prosperity of our business, when this is appropriate.

'We encourage and support employee and franchisee involvement in projects that have a direct impact on the local community.

'We will offer financial support to projects, within the areas in which we operate, that are supported by our employees and franchisees.'

Financial support is only available in two forms, both of which relate to the fundraising and volunteering activities of Arla employees (see below).

## Exclusions

The following will not normally be supported: animal welfare; individuals; medical research charities; sport; heritage appeals; science and technology; charitable advertising; political or religious organisations; or pressure groups.

## Applications

In writing to the correspondent.

## Corporate giving

In 2004/05, the company made cash donations to charitable organisations of £100,000. A donation was pledged to the Outward Bound charity to help send under-privileged on outdoor training schemes.

### In-kind support

Education: Employees are encouraged to work within the local community, through, for example, the 'Right to Read' scheme in Leicestershire and 'Reading Matters' in Leeds. Both of these involve staff in supporting school children with their reading development.

Employees have also worked closely with Education Leeds, organising one-day school conferences

### Employee-led support

The company provide matched funding of sums raised by its employees/franchisees. If a charity or community group requires other technical or professional skills, the local depot or area will endeavour to find someone from within the business with the appropriate skills.

Funding is also given to projects in which employees/franchisees already provide non-fundraising help. To receive funding employees/franchisees must work a minimum of ten community hours a month in the project. An example of this is support provided for employees who visited Romania to deliver aid to orphanages, hospitals and old people's homes.

---

# Arriva plc

Admiral Way, Doxford International Business Park, Sunderland SR3 3XP

0191 520 4000; Fax: 0191 520 4001

Website: www.arriva.co.uk

Correspondent: Karen Thornton, Administrator, Corporate Communications

Fax: 0191 520 4115
E-mail: info@arriva.co.uk

Chief officer: Sir Richard Broadbent

Chief Executive: David Martin

| Year end | Turnover | Pre-tax profit |
|---|---|---|
| 31/12/2005 | £1,626,800,000 | £107,900,000 |

Nature of company business
Bus operators (London and provincial bus services, coach commuter services, private hire, the operation of rail franchise); motor (sale, service and repair of motor vehicles, supply of parts, self-drive hire); bus and coach distribution (distribution, rental and finance).

Subsidiaries include: The Original London Sightseeing Tour Ltd, London Pride Sightseeing Tour Ltd, Londonlinks Buses Ltd, Stevensons of Uttoxeter Ltd

Main locations: Sunderland

Total employees: 32,404

---

**Charitable donations**

2005: £201,426

2004: £157,515

2003: £122,346

Membership: BitC

---

## Community involvement

In recent years the company has reviewed its 'Community Relations' policy, which now 'focuses both financial and practical support towards charities and projects that help people with disabilities, the elderly, the young, including education, and the environment'. The company has a Community Relations Committee which reviews community activities and support, policy and approves its budget.

### Exclusions

The company does not advertise in charity brochures or support political parties or religious movements.

### Applications

In writing to the correspondent.

## Corporate giving

In 2003 the company made cash donations of £122,346 to charity, with a further £173,574 given in in-kind support. Cash donations included those to Macmillan Cancer Relief, Business in the Community, RNIB, Foundation for Citizenship, Changing Faces and ENCAMS.

The Community Relation Committee has established partnerships with organisations including Age Concern and Age Concern Scotland, Common Purpose, the Foundation for Citizenship at Liverpool John Moores University and Leicester Racial Equality Council.

**Charity of the Year:** Cancer Research UK (2004).

### In-kind support

The company offers practical support, expertise and resources to community partners through gifts in kind, training schemes and employee volunteering.

### Employee-led support

The company provides employees with financial support and time off to carry out their charitable activities.

### Commercially-led support

**Sponsorship:** *The Arts* – Arts and good cause sponsorship are undertaken

Contact: Rebecca Miller (0191 520 4000).

**Cause-related Marketing:** £2,000 was raised in 2003 through the Going Your Way – Car Amnesty.

---

# Arup Group Limited

13 Fitzroy Street, London W1P 4BQ

020 7636 1531; Fax: 020 7580 3924

Website: www.arup.com

Correspondent: Keith Dawson

Chief officer: Terry Hill

| Year end | Turnover | Pre-tax profit |
|---|---|---|
| 31/03/2005 | £430,300,000 | |

**Nature of company business**

The company and its subsidiaries practice in the field of consulting engineering services, in architecture and other related professional skills. The group has 17 offices in the UK in addition to its head office in London.

**Main locations:** Edinburgh, Dundee, Douglas, Glasgow, Bristol, Cardiff, Cambridge, Newcastle upon Tyne, Liverpool, London, Manchester, Nottingham, Leeds, Solihull, Sheffield, Wrexham, Winchester, Belfast

**UK employees:** 5,008

**Total employees:** 7,000

---

**Charitable donations**

2005: £40,000

2004: £33,550

---

## Community involvement

Established to commemorate the life of the late Sir Ove Arup, The Ove Arup Foundation (Charity Commission no. 328138) is an educational trust supporting initiatives related to the built environment.

Endowed by the partnership for the first seven years of its existence (1989–1995) through an annual gift, the trustees decided in 2000 to provide further funding over the next five years and to increase the scope of the foundation internationally.

Around one-third of the foundation's funds are available each year for major projects. It gives grants for research and projects, including start-up and feasibility costs. Further information is available on the foundation's website (www.theovearupfoundation.org).

### Applications

In writing to the correspondent, with brief supporting financial information. Trustees meet quarterly to consider applications (March, June, September and December).

## Corporate giving

### The Ove Arup Foundation

In 2004/05, the foundation had an income of £41,716 of which £40,000 was derived via a donation from the Arup Group Ltd. Grants were made to 17 organisations totalling £56,200.

The largest grants were: Imperial College (£16,000); University of Cambridge (£12,500); and, London School of Economics (£10,000).

Other recipients included: Forum for the Future (£5,000); Architecture Centre Network (£4,700); XL Wales (£4,000); Herriot-Watt University and Architectural Association Foundation (£2,000 each); and, Anglo-Danish Society (£1,600).

# ASDA Stores Limited

ASDA House, Southbank, Great Wilson Street, Leeds LS11 5AD

0113 243 5435; Fax: 0113 241 8666

Website: www.asda.co.uk

Correspondent: Julie Ward, Foundation Administrator
0113 241 7253; Fax: 0113 241 8666

| Year end | Turnover | Pre-tax profit |
|---|---|---|
| 31/12/2005 | £14,786,193,000 | £388,183,000 |

**Nature of company business**
Principal activities: retailing of fresh food and clothing.

**Subsidiaries include:** Gazeley Holdings Ltd, The Burwood House Group plc, McLagan Investments Ltd, Gazeley Properties Ltd

**Main locations:** Leeds

**Total employees:** 145,235

### Charitable donations

2005: £300,000
2004: £559,996

Membership: L B Group

## Community involvement

The company stated that it does not make 'head office' donations, but that donations are given through the ASDA Foundation (Charity Commission no. 800382). Funded primarily by the profit made by ASDA Stores Ltd on its midweek lottery and through monies raised at charitable events organised by colleagues (staff), it focuses on: children and education, women's health issues, people with disabilities and victims of crime.

ASDA has a specialist environment team that is looking at innovative ways to reduce its impact on the environment in areas as diverse as packaging, recycling, waste management, energy and water use, transport and store development.

'At ASDA we believe we have an important part to play in every community we serve, so we have a Community Programme that supports local charities and good causes. That's as well as our national events, Tickled Pink and BBC Children In Need, which together have seen us raise more than £16.9 million over the last few years.

'We let each store and depot choose which local charities to support. After all, they work hard to really understand the issues that concern local people. Because of this, we have developed a huge range of programmes across the country, all designed to make lasting improvements to communities.

'We've found that getting involved is what makes a difference ... Whilst we know that money is the lifeblood of charities, we always try to do more than just write a cheque and move on to the next good cause. By throwing our hearts and souls into all our fundraising activities, people see that we genuinely care about the fantastic work they do – and that we go the extra mile to support them.

'Since becoming part of Wal-mart in 1999 we have raised over £14 million for charities across the UK.'

## Exclusions

No response to circular appeals. No support for advertising in charity brochures, appeals from individuals, medical research, overseas projects, political appeals, or local appeals not in areas of company presence.

## Applications

The first contact should be made with the local store. For the foundation, contact the correspondent named above.

## Corporate giving

### The ASDA Foundation

Funded primarily by profit made by ASDA Stores Ltd on its midweek lottery and funds raised at charitable events organised by colleagues (staff), it focuses on:

- the provision of facilities for recreation or other leisure time occupations in the interest of social welfare
- making donations or providing assistance for the relief of poverty, the advancement of education or the advancement of education, or religion
- making donations to any registered charity in the UK.

Since 1996, the charity's income has increased from £64,500 to £6.7m in 2005. Its expenditure in the same period rose from £145,000 to £6.2 million. Some of the donations had been to the Foundation for specific appeals/charities, e.g. the Tsunami Appeal, Children in Need, Breast Cancer Care, Tommy's Campaign. Other grants were made by the foundation to various charities for which we have no specific details. The company, ASDA Stores Ltd donated £300,000 to the foundation in 2005. however, it is clear that the company has provided much more in the way of in kind support, staff time, etc., which it has not been possible to put a figure on.

## In-kind support

In-kind help is given through the Stores of the Community programme. Every store supports a number of local charities and voluntary groups which are given some space in-store to advertise the services they provide or to look for support by being allowed to fundraise in stores.

ASDA also focuses on supporting local schools through its educational initiatives 'The Big' – Sum (2000), Eat (2001), Science (2002) Healthy Body (2003) and Healthy Eat (2005). The latter encourages primary school pupils to have a healthier diet via in-store tours and workshops. In total 360,000 school children have taken part in these activities.

An educational website has also been established so that work on The Big Healthy Body can continue in the classroom or at home.

In 2005, the company supplied 3,500 tents to the Kashmiri earthquake appeal.

## Employee-led support

Employees' volunteering/charitable activities are supported by the company financially, and by allowing staff time off to volunteer.

## Commercially-led support

**Cause-related marketing:** For over 9 years in succession, the company has run a joint promotional campaign with Breast Cancer Care (Tickled Pink for Breast Cancer Care), with colleagues (staff), customers and suppliers. In 2005, £3.5 million was raised.

# Associated British Foods plc

Weston Centre, 10 Grosvenor Street, London W1K 4QY

020 7399 6500; Fax: 020 7399 6580

Website: www.abfoods.com

Correspondent: Fiona Hare, Foundation Administrator
020 7399 6565; Fax: 020 7399 6584

Chief officer: Martin G Adamson

Chief Executive: Peter Jackson

| Year end | Turnover | Pre-tax profit |
|---|---|---|
| 17/09/2005 | £5,622,000,000 | £479,000,000 |

Nature of company business
The activities of the group primarily concern the processing and manufacture of food. The ultimate holding company is Wittington Investments Ltd.

Subsidiaries include: Food Investments, The Ryvita Co Ltd, British Sugar plc, Jacksons of Piccadilly Ltd, AB Technology Ltd, ABNA Ltd, Jordan's (NI) Ltd, R Twining & Co Ltd, Allied Techhnical Centre Ltd, Fishers Agricultural Holdings Ltd, Primark Stores Ltd, Nambarrie Tea Co Ltd, Allied Grain Ltd, British Sugar (overseas) Ltd

Main locations: London

UK employees: 20,996

Total employees: 35,416

## Charitable donations

2005: £300,000
2004: £400,000
2003: £200,000

## Community involvement

We have previously been advised that the company does not of itself make charitable donations. This despite its report and accounts regularly declaring annual charitable contributions of around £200,000. Although we have never been able to find out to whom this is given, we suspect it may cover small local level donations made by subsidiary companies.

We do know, however, that all charitable requests sent to Associated British Foods are passed on to the Garfield Weston Foundation which, although operated entirely independently of the company, is administered from the same address.

Given this link, and the fact that the trust receives its income from its almost 80% holding of Wittington Investments Ltd, which is the holding company of Associated British Foods plc, we feel it appropriate to draw readers attention to this.

This trust is one of the largest UK grant-making trusts, having made grants of £38,000,000 in 2005/06. Further information can be found in *A Guide to the Major Trusts Volume 1*, published by the Directory of Social Change.

### Exclusions

No sponsorship is undertaken.

### Applications

There is no one at head office who deals with charitable donations made directly by the company, rather than by the Garfield Weston Foundation. Applications should therefore be made directly to the subsidiary companies.

## Corporate giving

We have no further information on the £200,000 declared in the company's annual report as its charitable donations in 2003, other than that subsidiaries control a large part of the group's donations programme, and policies are therefore determined largely at local level.

# Associated British Ports Holdings plc

150 Holborn, London EC1N 2LR

020 7430 1177; Fax: 020 7430 1384

Website: www.abports.co.uk

Correspondent: Mrs Margie Collins, Corporate Communications Manager
E-mail: mcollins@abports.co.uk

Chief officer: Chris Clark

Chief Executive: Bo Lerenius

| Year end | Turnover | Pre-tax profit |
|---|---|---|
| 31/12/2005 | £434,900,000 | £167,600,000 |

Nature of company business
The provision of port and transport-related services to ship and cargo owners, and the ownership and development of properties at port locations.

Subsidiaries include: Grosvenor Waterside (Holdings) Ltd, Grosvenor Waterside Investments Ltd, Amports Vehicle Terminals Ltd, Amports Cargo Services Ltd, Grosvenor Waterside Developments Ltd, Southampton Free Trade Zone Ltd, Northern Cargo Services Ltd, The Teighmouth Quay Co Ltd, ABP Marine Environmental Research Ltd

Main locations: Barrow, Barry, Ayr, Swansea, Teignmouth, Troon, Southampton, Plymouth, Port Talbot, Silloth, Newport, Lowestoft, Ipswich, King's Lynn, Immingham, Hull, Fleetwood, Garston, Grimsby, Goole, Cardiff

UK employees: 2400

## Charitable donations

2005: £123,000
2004: £74,000
2003: £78,000

Total community contributions: £421,000

Membership: BitC

## Community involvement

The company states that it supports maritime charities – given the nature of its business – and major medical research charities, particularly those which are of relevance to the company's employees. Within these categories support is given to a range of charitable activity, including advertising in charity brochures, appeals from individuals, the arts, children/youth, education, the elderly, enterprise/training, environment/heritage, fundraising events, medical research, science/technology, sickness/disability charities, social welfare and sport.

It also supports organisations which are based in the areas where its ports are located, namely East Anglia, the Humber region, the South Coast, South Wales and the North West.

### Exclusions

There are no definite exclusions, instead the company will consider all appeals individually.

### Applications

In writing to the correspondent. Applications are sorted and likely candidates referred to the Group Chief Executive.

**Information available:** The company produces a corporate social responsibility report.

## Corporate giving

In 2005, the company made total community contributions of £421,000 including cash donations to charity of £123,000. In the main, cash donations were made to charities within the maritime, medical and medical research sectors. Major beneficiaries during the year included: The British Heart Foundation; Cancer Research UK; Dr Mack's Cancer Equipment Fund; Naomi House Children's Hospice; National Society for the Prevention of Cruelty to Children; and, Ty Hafan Children's Hospice.

Besides donations towards causes of long-standing, one-off donations were made to the Tsunami Appeal (£30,000), London Bombings Relief Charitable Fund (£5,000), and UNICEF's South East Asia Earthquake Children's Appeal (£3,000).

### In-kind support

To assist with the development of the local skills base, the company continues to concentrate a great deal of community-based projects on giving assistance to improve the educational facilities near their ports. As well as financial support, the company supports competitions and learning initiatives.

The company also hosts port visits and tours for local schoolchildren. A number of their ports also offer work experience to local schoolchildren and students, apprenticeships, work placements and graduate work experience programmes.

### Employee-led support

The company will consider sponsoring employees in their fundraising activities and provides support through staff secondments.

ABP encourage staff to sit as school governors and/ or give talks and presentations on ports and the economy, the environment and careers in transport, general business advice and other advice on working life.

Donations made by staff through fundraising and giving are matched by the company.

### Commercially-led support

**Sponsorship:** *The arts* – the company sponsors one large project annually, usually with an opera or ballet company. In 2005, arts sponsorship rose to £152,000 (up from £35,000 in 2004) mainly as a result of payment of £144,000 to the Welsh National Opera as part of a £277,000 four-year deal.

In Southampton, the port continued its support of the English National Ballet by sponsoring its performance of 'Giselle' at the Mayflower Theatre.

Contact: Proposals should be addressed to Mrs M Collins, Corporate Communications Manager.

# AstraZeneca plc

15 Stanhope Gate, London W1K 1LN

020 7304 5000; Fax: 020 7304 5151

**Website:** www.astrazeneca.com

**Correspondent:** Justin Hoskins, Assistant Company Secretary, Charitable Appeals Department

**Chief officer:** Louis Schweitzer

**Chief Executive:** David Brennan

| Year end 31/12/2005 | Turnover £13,162,955,000 | Pre-tax profit £3,664,193,200 |
|---|---|---|

**Nature of company business**
The group's principal activities are the research, development and marketing of medicines for serious health conditions.

The group operates in the United Kingdom, Belgium, France, Germany, Italy, Spain, Sweden, the Netherlands, Canada, Puerto Rico, United States of America and Japan.

**Main locations:** Alderley Edge, Bedford, Macclesfield, Loughborough, Luton, London, Stonehouse, Tytherington, Wilmslow, Chorlton-cum-Hardy, Brixham, Bristol, Edinburgh

**UK employees:** 11,600

**Total employees:** 64,900

### Charitable donations

Membership: BitC, L B Group, %Club

## Community involvement

The following extract is taken from AstraZeneca's website at www.astrazeneca.com: 'We aim to make a positive contribution to our local communities through charitable donations, sponsorships and other initiatives that help to make a difference. Our commitment is reflected in our Community Support Policy, which aims to ensure that our community activities focus on bringing benefit in ways that are consistent with our business of improving health and quality of life, and on promoting the value of science among young people.

'We have a dedicated community support database which gathers global information centrally, enabling the sharing of information and best practice across the organisation and supporting accurate financial reporting of our overall spend in this area. The database also helps us to ensure that all our efforts are aligned with our commitment to bring benefit mainly through healthcare and science education initiatives. We also contribute where possible to disaster relief efforts and during 2005 we donated money and medicines to help the victims of the earthquake in Pakistan, and those who were affected by Hurricane Katrina in the US.'

Support from the corporate office in London is only given to UK-based charities and charities local to the office or to manufacturing sites around the UK. Overseas aid is given by the overseas branches/companies.

## Exclusions

No support for circulars, advertising in charity brochures, individuals, older people, fundraising events, political/ discriminatory groups, religious appeals, sport, anything contrary to company business or, with very limited exceptions, capital projects.

## Applications

In writing to the correspondent at the head office address.

# Corporate giving

In 2005, AstraZeneca provided community support totalling $34 million (£18,686,451) worldwide. Of this, 45% was in charitable contributions.

Regrettably, no indication was given as to how much of this support went to UK charities, although some examples of beneficiaries were provided.

The group supports the work of the Brightside Trust, a charity that aims to help underprivileged young people to enter the medical and healthcare professions. Support included a two year secondment to the charity as well as an ongoing contribution in cash ($160,000 in three years).

Through its 'Inspiring Science' programme, run in conjunction with the CREST awards scheme in the UK, a programme of project work relevant to the secondary education science curriculum is undertaken. Schools of the students judged to have delivered the best projects receive a cash prize.

Further information is available at: www.inspiringscience.co.uk

### Zeneca Science Teaching Trust

Zeneca established this trust, (Charity Commission no. 1064864) to provide financial assistance to support a programme of projects designed to help build the knowledge skills and understanding required to teach science effectively and confidently at primary school level. The trust currently has a fund of $19 million which was provided by the company.

Further information on the trust is available at: www.astrateachscience.co.uk

### The Astra Foundation

We were advised previously that the Astra Foundation (Charity Commission no. 1014774) was in the process of being wound down. Although the trust's record at the Charity Commission is still active, no accounts have been provided since 2001.

## In-kind support

**Education:** AstraZeneca runs a UK-wide bursary scheme to help secure the future of chemistry. Launched in 2003, the programme includes awards of £1,000 up to 4 years to 50 students studying chemistry at 23 UK universities. The scheme aims to encourage A level students to study chemistry and university and first year students to pursue a career in chemistry on graduation.

The group also supports a Diversity Mentoring programme managed between the University of Manchester and the UMIST Careers Service. Aimed at establishing links between black and Asian students and employers, staff from various departments within the company help students learn a variety of personal and professional skills. Staff also contribute to a number of employability workshops.

A Partnering Schools scheme links employees and staff from local community secondary schools on a one to one basis. The main focus is the support of industry/work related aspects of the school curriculum, particularly in science/technology.

At primary school level support is given through activities which include the provision of science clubs and science workshops for teachers and pupils. The group has a network of over 40 employees with science backgrounds who work with over 80 partners primary schools n East Cheshire.

## Employee-led support

Employees are encouraged to become involved in community-based charitable activities through a matched funding scheme, whereby individuals' efforts in fundraising may be matched by a company donation.

## Commercially-led support

The group's product donation and patient assistance programmes make medicines available free of charge or at reduced prices.

# AT&T (UK) Ltd

Highfield House, Headless Cross Drive, Redditch B97 5EQ

01527 518 181

**Website:** www.att.com

**Correspondent:** Phil Coathup, Media Relations Director

**Nature of company business**
Telecommunications and networking company.

**Main locations:** London

**Total employees:** 70,000

# Community involvement

Previously, we were advised that the company's UK donations were channelled through its US foundation. Whilst there has been evidence of this in the past on the foundation's website, this no longer appears to be the case. In fact, the website now has little in the way of financial or grant information (you used to be able to search by country) and makes no reference to a willingness to fund organisations outside of the USA.

Irrespective of this, the company has always taken a proactive approach when it comes to funding and we have no reason to believe this has changed. Areas of interest include education, underserved communities and arts and culture, especially where these are linked to broadening access to technology.

## Exclusions

The foundation does not support the following categories:

- individuals
- organisations whose chief purpose is to influence legislation or to participate or intervene in political campaigns on behalf of or against any candidate for public office
- endowments or memorials
- construction or renovation projects
- sports teams or any sports-related activity or competition, even if it addresses our program interests
- fundraising events or advertising.

## Applications

In writing to the correspondent.

As far as the foundation is concerned, as there is no longer any encouragement or evidence of applications from outside of the USA being accepted directly, please refer to AT&T (UK) Ltd for the latest advice.

## Corporate giving

The company are involved with The Prince's Trust Technology Leadership Group and raised funds for Cancer Research UK in 2006 through the 'Tee It Up with AT&T' Global Charity Golf Tour.

The last grant information we have concerning the AT&T Foundation relates to 2004, when the only grant paid in the UK was $50,000 to the Charities Aid Foundation (CAF also received support every year from 1999 to 2002). Other beneficiaries since the foundation was established in 1996 are Almeida Theatre Company, Edinburgh International Festival, Royal Court Theatre, Royal National Theatre and Tate Gallery.

will not preclude staff or local businesses from organising local events in support of other charities or good causes.

**Charity of the Year:** RedR, WaterAid and Progressive Supranuclear Palsy (PSP) Association (2006).

### Exclusions

No support for appeals from individuals.

### Applications

In writing to the correspondent.

## Corporate giving

In 2006, the group donated £97,534 (2005: £85,000) to principally local charitable organisations in areas of company presence.

### Employee-led support

Employees are encouraged to volunteer and fundraise on behalf of local good causes.

**Payroll giving:** A scheme is in operation.

# W S Atkins plc

Woodcote Grove, Ashley Road, Epsom, Surrey KT18 5BW

01372 726140; Fax: 01372 740055

Website: www.atkinsglobal.com

Correspondent: Keith Clarke, Chief Executive

Chief officer: Ed Wallis

Chief Executive: Keith Clarke

| Year end | Turnover | Pre-tax profit |
|---|---|---|
| 31/03/2006 | £1,052,500,000 | £74,800,000 |

Nature of company business
The group operates primarily as a multi-discipline design and engineering consultants with a focus on engineering and appropriate building design. The company's operations are based in over 70 offices throughout the UK.

Main locations: Epsom

UK employees: 13,300

### Charitable donations

2006: £97,534
2005: £85,000
2004: £101,000
2003: £115,000

Membership: BitC

## Community involvement

The company's 2006 Corporate Responsibility Report states that group businesses are formally involved in community charitable, educational and environmental initiatives, including numerous voluntary community and fundraising activities undertaken by their staff.

It was decided that in future the group will focus on three charities each year, with at least one relating to the company's professional work and one other to a specific good cause. This

# Aviva plc

St Helen's, 1 Undershaft, London EC3P 3DQ

020 7283 2000; Fax: 020 7662 8182

Website: www.aviva.com

Correspondent: Kate Hughes, Consultant - Corporate Social Responsibility 01904 452385

Chief officer: Lord Sharman of Redlynch

Chief Executive: Richard Harvey

| Year end | Turnover | Pre-tax profit |
|---|---|---|
| 31/12/2005 | £50,939,000,000 | £3,450,000,000 |

Nature of company business
The company transacts life assurance and long-term savings business, fund management, and all classes of general insurance through its subsidiaries, associates and branches in the UK, Continental Europe, North America, Asia, Australia and other countries throughout the world.

Subsidiaries include: Norwich Union Wealth Management Limited, Norwich Union Trust Managers Limited, CGU Bonus Ltd, Commercial Union Life Assurance Co Ltd, Norwich Union Life Holdings Limited, London & Edinburgh Insurance Group Ltd, Norwich Union Annuity Limited, CGU Insurance plc, General Accident plc, Norwich Union Healthcare Limited, CGU Underwriting Ltd, Norwich Union Life & Pensions Limited, Morley Properties Ltd, Morley Fund Management Ltd, Morley Pooled Pensions Ltd, CGNU Life Assurance Ltd, Northern Assurance Co Ltd, Norwich Union Insurance Limited, CGU International Insurance Ltd, Norwich Union Portfolio Services Limited, your-move.co.uk Ltd, Norwich Union Investment Funds Limited, Norwich Union Linked Life Assurance Limited

Main locations: Croydon, Bristol, Cheadle, Eastleigh, Exeter, Glasgow, York, Southampton, Sheffield, Romford, Stevenage, Norwich, Newcastle

Total employees: 54,791

## Charitable donations

2005: £1,700,000
2004: £1,300,000
2003: £1,300,000

Management costs: £500,000

Membership: A & B, BitC, %Club

## Community involvement

Aviva were formerly known as CGNU which itself was formed following the merger in 2000 of CGU with Norwich Union.

The company's policy on charitable giving is to support local charities and community organisations particularly in those areas where the company has a major presence. In addition, it provides a significant level of support to a small number of national charities.

Morley Fund Management is a wholly owned, independently managed asset management business of Aviva plc. There is significant charitable activity/giving/staff volunteering/ sponsorship/partnerships and match funding within the Morley company and detailed information of this is given on the Aviva website under Morley Fund Management/ community.

Norwich Union Central Services is the internal service provider to the Aviva business units. Norwich Union Insurance is the largest insurer in the UK and Norwich Union Life is a leading provider of life, pensions and investment products and one of the largest Financial Adviser providers. As with the Morley Fund, these businesses publish their own separate CSR reports and undertake significant charitable activity and giving. We would again advise that the Aviva website is visited where the Norwich Union businesses have separate 'community' sites detailing their charitable/ community contribution.

## Exclusions

At group level, Aviva will not normally consider supporting:

- individuals looking for sponsorship or charity fundraising donations either on their own behalf or that of a charity (staff excluded)
- political organisations
- extreme 'high risk' or 'free sports'
- organisations or issues already supported by Norwich Union in the UK
- charities already receiving long-term support around the world, either from Norwich Union or an Aviva company
- a staff charity of the year (on a separate basis)
- paid advertisements in charity brochures or events programmes.

## Applications

When we spoke to Aviva's Consultant for Corporate Social Responsibility she suggested that Norwich Union details should be given in relation to the Aviva group's charitable giving, applications, etc. However, there is detailed information on the Aviva website and we would suggest this website is visited when considering an application. Written applications should be sent to the contact.

## Corporate giving

In 2005, the group made total community contributions of £5.7 million of which £3.9 million was invested in the UK. Of this, £1.7 million was in direct donations to charitable causes.

Some of the charitable organisations supported during the year included:

- Breakthrough Breast Cancer
- Wheelpower
- The Princess Royal Trust for Carers.

In addition, the group supported the Make a Wish Foundation UK, which was chosen by staff in the UK as their 'charity of the year', and National Children's Homes.

### In-kind support

Support is also given through the donation of items such as IT equipment, furniture, company branded materials and the use of office space free of charge.

### Employee-led support

Staff are encouraged to take part in community-related projects through various initiatives, such as, staff volunteering, mentoring and fundraising activities, which the company matches.

The Make a Wish Foundation was the staff chosen charity.

**Payroll giving:** The Give As You Earn scheme is in operation.

### Commercially-led support

**Sponsorship:** Group sponsorship criteria is as follows:

Aviva plc and BUs will actively select organisations to which they may offer support.

Aviva will consider supporting organisations which are considered to be, or have the potential to be, a leader in their respective fields, and have earned a world-wide reputation for excellence.

Aviva will consider supporting centres of excellence in a variety of fields but primarily the arts, education, social responsibility and the environment.

At group level, when considering support, Aviva will look for organisations or initiatives which are, or have the potential to be international in focus and reach, considered to be a "Centre of Excellence".

# Avon Cosmetics Ltd

Nunn Mills Road, Northampton NN1 5PA

01604 232425; Fax: 01604 232444

**Website:** www.avon.uk.com

**Correspondent:** Natalie Deacon, Corporate Public Relations Officer

| Year end | Turnover | Pre-tax profit |
|---|---|---|
| 31/12/2004 | £281,757,000 | £23,508,000 |

**Nature of company business**
The principal activities of the company are the distribution and sale of beauty products and the sale and distribution of gift and decorative products.

**Main locations:** Northampton

**Total employees:** 1,795

## Charitable donations

Membership: BitC

## Community involvement

Avon Breast Cancer Crusade raises money for UK breast cancer charities. Early Crusade funding was used as the deposit to secure the space for the Breakthrough Toby Robins Breast Cancer Research Centre – the first dedicated breast cancer research facility in the UK. The Centre aims to eradicate breast cancer by discovering the causes of the disease, finding methods of prevention and developing new treatments and more effective diagnosis. The money raised by the Crusade continues to make a major contribution to the ongoing work at the Centre.

Globally primarily concentrating its support on raising awareness and funds for the fight against breast cancer and domestic violence.

Outside of this, support is limited to local causes, especially in Northamptonshire, and again with particular relevance to women's issues.

### Exclusions

No support for advertising in charity brochures, animal welfare charities, appeals from individuals, the arts, overseas projects, political appeals, religious appeals, science/ technology or sport.

### Applications

In writing to the correspondent.

## Corporate giving

In 2005 £1.2 million was raised in the UK by staff and customers for the Avon Breast Cancer Crusade. Whilst it is clear that the company is heavily engaged in facilitating this fundraising, we have been unable to obtain any figures giving a breakdown of its financial contribution towards this.

Since 1992 £12 million has been raised for UK breast cancer charities, with Breakthrough Breast Cancer being a major partner.

The Avon Foundation (a registered US charity) was established in 1955 to improve the lives of women. Over the period of 50 years that the Foundation has been established it has raised and awarded over $450 million.

### Employee-led support

Support is also given to employees' volunteering /charitable activities through financial help, matching employee fundraising and giving, and allowing company time off to volunteer.

**Payroll giving:** Avon operate the Give As You Earn scheme.

### Commercially-led support

**Cause-related marketing:**Avon Breast Cancer Crusade and Breakthrough Breast Cancer have worked in partnership since 1992 during which time Avon has raised over £10 million for Breakthrough.

Those wishing to get involved in fundraising for breast cancer research can do so by ordering online the Avon Breast Cancer Crusade Fundraising Pack.

# Avon Rubber plc

Hampton Park West, Melksham, Wiltshire, SN12 6NB

01225 896800; Fax: 01225 896899

Website: www.avon-rubber.com

Correspondent: Peter Slabbert, Finance Director 01225 861100; Fax: 01225 861199
E-mail: enquiries@avon-rubber.com

Chief officer: Trevor Bonner

Chief Executive: Terry Stead

| Year end | Turnover | Pre-tax profit |
|---|---|---|
| 30/09/2005 | £239,735,000 | (£2,825,000) |

**Nature of company business**
Principal activities: design and manufacture of components for the automotive industries; design and manufacture of other polymer based products.

Main locations: Westbury, Trowbridge, Melksham

UK employees: 4,363

### Charitable donations
2005: £26,000
2004: £31,000

## Community involvement

The company supports local charities in areas of operation via the Community Foundation for Wiltshire & Swindon which administers the donor advised Avon Rubber Fund.

Support is given to education, medical research and religious appeals, as well as through advertising in charity brochures and support for fundraising events.

### Exclusions

No support for animal welfare charities, circular appeals, appeals from individuals, local appeals not in areas of company presence, large national appeals or overseas projects.

### Applications

All applications are dealt with by the Wiltshire and Swindon Community Foundation, 48 New Park Street, Devizes, Wiltshire SN10 1DS (Tel: 01380 729284. Fax: 01380 729772; website: www.wscf.org.uk; e-mail: info@wscf.org.uk).

Further details of the foundation can be found in *A Guide to Local Trusts in the South of England* published by the Directory of Social Change.

## Corporate giving

In 2005, the company made cash donations in the UK of £26,000. Beneficiaries included the Inspire Foundation.

# awg plc

Anglian House, Ambury Road, Huntingdon, Cambridgeshire PE29 3NZ

01480 323000; Fax: 01480 323115

Website: www.awg.com

Correspondent: Tony Field, Secretary to the Company Collective

Chief officer: Peter Hickson

Chief Executive: Jonson Cox

| Year end | Turnover | Pre-tax profit |
|---|---|---|
| 31/03/2006 | £1,552,200,000 | £108,800,000 |

Nature of company business
Water supply and distribution, waste water collection and treatment, and process engineering.

Subsidiaries include: Maintenance & Property Care Ltd, Power Services HVDE Ltd, Ambury Developments Ltd, PURAC Ltd, Rutland Insurance Ltd, Alpheus Environmental Ltd, Morrison International Ltd, MVM Holdings Ltd

Main locations: Peterborough, Huntingdon

UK employees: 9,042

Total employees: 9,042

---

### Charitable donations

2005: £1,000,000
2004: £1,180,000
2003: £1,100,000

Membership: BitC

---

## Community involvement

AWG is owned by a private consortium, Osprey, comprising of Canada Pension Plan Investment Board, Colonial First State Global Asset Management, Industry Funds Management and 3i Group plc. Following the acquisition of AWG by Osprey, the company was officially delisted from the stock exchange on 21 December 2006. We do not know if this will affect AWG's charitable giving in the future.

The company states that it is the group's policy that its community investment should be based predominantly on the practical involvement of employees in community activities.

AWG's community policy is that support is given in three key areas in counties where its principal businesses are located:

- youth education
- social regeneration
- environment.

It aims to do this by: (i) adopting a coordinated approach to employee involvement in community activities; (ii) charitable giving in support of the three key areas above; and (iii) recycling of equipment and materials to community projects.

It also operates a charitable trust: The Anglian Water Trust Fund (Charity Commission no. 1054026). This trust aims to help people in conditions of need in the area it operates. The grants to individuals are in the form of paying household bills or purchasing essential household items, with many grants being made to pay the water/sewage bills issued by Anglian Water. Grants are also made to organisations which can help such people move out of debt, such as those wishing to install

or improve money advice services. Further information can be found in *A Guide to Local Trusts in the Midlands*, also published by DSC, or on the trust's website (www.awtf.org.uk).

### Applications

In writing to: The Trustees, PO Box 42, Peterborough PE3 8XH (01733 331177; Fax: 01733 334344; e-mail: admin@awtf.org.uk).

### Exclusions

No support for advertising in charity brochures, appeals from individuals, political appeals or sport (unless at educational level), animal welfare, medical research or religious appeals.

### Applications

Please see above for details.

## Corporate giving

In 2004/05 the company made its usual donation of £1 million to The Anglian Water Trust Fund and also supplied £210,000 in cash and in-kind support.

In the same period the Trust Fund made £157,295 available to organisations for debt advice and debt prevention. Some of the organisations benefiting from grants were:

County Court Help Desks

Buckingham Citizens Advice Bureau

Northampton Welfare Rights Advice Service

Cambridge Independent Advice Centre

Lowestoft County Court

Basildon Citizens Advice Bureau

Partnership Innovation Budget Projects

Basildon Citizens Advice Bureau

Northampton Welfare Rights Advice Service

Youth Debt Project

Dough UK Project (previously Mancroft Advice Project)

NCH Project

### In-kind support

This is provided through the recycling of redundant office equipment and materials, i.e. computers, office furniture and left-over building materials. Offers may also be made to do work at cost or, where appropriate, no cost, i.e. road building, construction work, plumbing or electrical work. Procurement through AWG's supply chain may also be possible, enabling materials and equipment to be bought at a lower price.

Support may also be given through talks/lectures to schools/colleges/universities, mentoring or supporting reading in schools.

### Employee-led support

The company operates a ' give me five' scheme which allows employees to take up to 30 work time hours to get involved in community activities. Designed with personal development at the heart, any new skills, competencies and relevant experience gained can be linked with the employee's annual appraisal and personal development plan. Employees give their time, skills and expertise to many organisations including: The Prince's Trust, Young Enterprise, Education Business Link organisations, mentoring programmes, CITB, Special Constables, Age Concern, WaterAid and many more

This year nearly 100 'give me five' volunteers supported the Community Service Volunteer's Make A Difference Day campaign across the UK. A total of ten AWG Community projects were registered across the divisions. In addition to the financial support for materials etc., employees gave their time, skills and expertise in all sorts of ways including designing and building a sensory garden for a special needs school, transforming a disused piece of land into a road safety / play area for a nursery school and making over a reception area for a local hospice.

**Payroll giving:** The company operates the Give As You Earn scheme.

# BAA plc

130 Wilton Road, London SW1V 1LQ

020 7834 9449; Fax: 020 7932 6699

Website: www.baa.co.uk

Correspondent: Mrs Maria Bernadette Lewis

Chief officer: Marcus Agius

Chief Executive: Mike Clasper

| Year end | Turnover | Pre-tax profit |
|---|---|---|
| 31/03/2006 | £2,275,000,000 | £757,000,000 |

**Nature of company business**
BAA plc owns and operates seven UK airports: Heathrow, Gatwick, Stansted, Aberdeen, Edinburgh, Glasgow and Southampton. Each airport is run by a separate operating company.

**Subsidiaries include:** Aberdeen Airport Limited, Edinburgh Airport Limited, World Duty Free plc, Southampton International Airport Limited, Heathrow Airport Limited, Gatwick Airport Limited, Glasgow Airport Limited, Stanstead Airport Limited

**Main locations:** Heathrow, Gatwick, Edinburgh, Glasgow, Southampton, Stansted, Aberdeen

**UK employees:** 10,307

**Total employees:** 12,724

---

### Charitable donations
2006: £1,313,000
2005: £1,446,000
2004: £1,088,000
2003: £736,000

Membership: BitC, L B Group, %Club

---

## Community involvement

The company has its own charitable trust, The BAA 21st Century Communities Trust: (Charity Commission no. 1058617). This provides grants in the areas surrounding its airports. Support is concentrated on projects which will be of community benefit in the areas of education, environment and economic regeneration. Applications should be made to the airport near the project.

There are also a couple of charitable trusts connected to Gatwick Airport. Gatwick Airport Community Trust (Charity Commission no. 1089683) which supports welfare causes, community facilities and development, the arts, cultural, sports and environmental and conservation schemes.

Applications should be made to: The Trustees, PO Box 102, Crawley, West Sussex RH10 9WX (01892 826088).

Gatwick Airport Pantomine Society (Charity Commission no. 1090214) supports a wide range of causes in West Sussex, including help for people who are sick, have disabilities, need medical treatment or have housing difficulties, community development and animal charities. Applications should be made to: Barry Charles Lloyd, 14 Lambourn Close, East Grinstead, West Sussex RH19 2DP (01342 315991).

### Exclusions
No support is given to circular appeals, advertising in charity brochures, animal welfare, appeals from individuals, children/youth, elderly people, fundraising events, medical research, overseas projects, political appeals, religious appeals, science/technology, or sickness/disability.

### Applications
Applicants are advised to contact the community relations manager at their local airport.

*BAA Aberdeen*: Aberdeen Airport, Dyce, Aberdeen AB21 7DU (0870 040 0006; Fax: 01224 775845).

*BAA Edinburgh*: Edinburgh Airport, Scotland EH12 9DN (0870 040 0007; Fax: 0131 344 3470).

*BAA Gatwick*: Gatwick Airport, West Sussex RH6 0NP (0870 000 2468).

*BAA Heathrow*: Heathrow Airport, 234 Bath Road, Hayes, Middlesex UB3 5AP (0870 000 0123; Fax: 020 8745 4290).

*BAA Southampton*: Southampton Airport, Hampshire SO18 2NL (0870 040 0009; Fax: 023 8062 7193).

*BAA Stansted*: Stansted Airport, Enterprise House, Bassingbourne Road, Stansted, Essex CM24 1QW (0870 000 0303; Fax: 01279 662066).

**Information available:** Written guidance is provided in letter form in response to requests. The company also produces a social responsibility report.

## Corporate giving

In 2005/06, cash contributions from the company totalled £1,313,000. Of this, 0.15% went to the BAA Communities Trust.

The BAA 21st Century Communities Trust gave a total of £867,000 in grants in 2004/05. Grants were generally in the range of £5,000 to £10,000 each, although some of larger amounts were made. Recipients included: Limelight Projects (£98,800); Sportscotland (£76,375); Hayes Skill Centre (£50,000); Barnardos (£10,000); Grampian Autistic Society (£5,000); and, Jubilee Sailing Trust (£2,000).

Gatwick Airport Community Trust gave £145,900 in 141 grants in 2005. This was broken down as follows: Young people £27,700); Elderly (£3,100); Disabled/disadvantaged (£23,350); Community facilities/environment (£39,100); Sport and recreation (£27,000); Arts, theatre and music (£25,650).

According to the accounts for the Gatwick Airport Pantomime Society no donations have been made in the last two years (2004/2005).

### In-kind support
Redundant IT equipment is supplied to local schools through the 'Tools for Schools' initiative, along with decoration and refurbishment projects.

## Employee-led support

The company matches both employee giving and fundraising on a pound for pound basis, although this varies. Staff are also given time off to volunteer.

**Payroll giving:** The company operates the Give As You Earn scheme.

# Scott Bader Company Ltd

Wollaston Hall, Wollaston, Wellingborough, Northamptonshire NN29 7RL

01933 663100; Fax: 01933 666608

Website: www.scottbader.com

Correspondent: Sue Carter, Commonwealth Secretary

Chief officer: Bob Coxon

| Year end | Turnover | Pre-tax profit |
|----------|----------|----------------|
| 31/12/2005 | £129,078,000 | |

**Nature of company business**
The company manufactures and distributes synthetic resins and chemical intermediates.

**Main locations:** Fareham, Brierley Hill, Leeds, Stockport, Plymouth, Wollaston

Total employees: 598

### Charitable donations

2005: £163,022
2004: £104,691
2003: £122,826

Membership: %Club

## Community involvement

The company was given into common ownership by its founder Ernest Bader in 1951 and is now a leading member of the common ownership movement. Its large philanthropic expenditure reflects the ethos of the company. The Scott Bader Company is wholly owned by the Scott Bader Commonwealth Ltd, a company limited by guarantee and a registered charity (Charity Commission no. 206391). The Commonwealth's income comes almost exclusively from distributions of profit made to it by the Scott Bader Company.

The company supports projects which respond to the needs of those who are most underprivileged. They aim to help people to help themselves based on community based projects. National and local charities are supported, with preference being given to those within a 25-mile radius of Scott Bader locations in the UK.

### Criteria

The board is guided by the following criteria in determining whether to recommend a project to members of the community:

- Is the project within the commonwealth's specified areas of focus?
- Does the project enable people to help themselves?
- Does the amount of money and assistance given by the Commonwealth make a significant difference?

- Are others involved in the project by way of contributing funds or in other ways?
- Is the project adopted by a member of the Commonwealth who will stay in contact with the project and keep members informed on progress?

In trying to decide rationally where to offer support, board members will look for evidence of:

1. clear, relevant and realistic objectives

2. the competence to achieve them

3. potential for replication of the innovative aspects of a project

4. the effect that a Commonwealth grant is likely to have on other potential funding sources

5. where necessary, a medium/long-term funding strategy

6. projects, activities or charities which find difficulty raising funds

7. projects, activities or charities which are innovative, imaginative or pioneering

8. projects which are initiated and/or supported by local people and which will improve the self-respect and self-reliance of those involved.

There were no geographical restrictions put upon the international funds during the year 2005 and the overall policy continued to focus on those groups of people, or communities, to which an injection of finance would give an opportunity to become self sufficient in the long term. The board also gave priority to those organisations that have found it difficult to raise money from other sources and in particular for pump priming projects.

At an Extraordinary General meeting held on 17 March 2005 members agreed to the introduction of a Group Charitable Fund, whereby 50% of the fund made available by Scott Bader Company Limited will be available to fund projects sourced and supported by the Commonwealth Board of Management. The remaining 50% will be made available to companies within the Group of Scott Bader Co. Ltd, to fund charities that they wish to support, subject to approval of the Directors/Trustees of the Commonwealth Board of Management. This is to encourage greater involvement by members worldwide in the charitable work and to ensure that donations made have an impact in all the countries where Scott Bader has a presence, UK, France, South Africa, Dubai, USA, Czech Republic, Sweden, Germany, Croatia and Spain.

### Exclusions

There is no support available for individuals in need, animal welfare, travel & adventure schemes, construction, renovation or maintenance of buildings, arts projects or sports. Political, religious appeals or sponsorship proposals will not be considered.

### Applications

In writing to the correspondent. Applications for donations can be made at any time.

There is no application form, but the following points should be taken into account in applying for a grant:

- applications should be no longer than four A4 sides
- supporting material may be sent, but is unlikely to be seen by board members.

The following should be included:

- a short general description of the project and its aims

- a budget broken down under different expenditure headings, indicating what part of the budget is requested from the trust and if the grant is for more than one year
- the names of any other agencies likely to contribute to the cost, and an indication of where money will come from when any funding from the Commonwealth runs out
- information on how the project is to be monitored and, if possible, evaluated and made known to others
- for on-going projects a set of audited accounts.

All applications received are reviewed by the Commonwealth Secretary and, if the criteria are met, the application will be considered at quarterly meetings of the Commonwealth Board of Management. Members in a general meeting have the final decision on grants of over £5,000.

General meetings are held in February, May, August and November each year. Only those who work within the Scott Bader Company Ltd are able to become members of The Scott Bader Commonwealth, and to participate in the charitable and philanthropic work of the Commonwealth.

## Corporate giving

The company made a donation to the charitable company of £163,022 (2004: £104,691). The Trust made 281 donations during 2005 and these can be split into three categories, local, national (UK), and international. A good proportion of the donations to local charities tended to be small but greater in number. The local charities also benefited from a Charity Nomination Scheme, whereby each UK based Commonwealth member can nominate a charity, or charities, of their choice to receive up to a maximum of £120. A total of £25,990 was distributed through this scheme in 2005.

Larger donations made by the Commonwealth are as follows:

*International*

Scott Bader Company Limited – tsunami, Dubai Round Table £5,000

Scott Bader Company Ltd (payment for Save A Child) £3,400

Abaseen Foundation (Pakistan Earthquake Disaster) £3,000

InterAct £3,000

SBCL – Payment for Fulton School for the Deaf £2,500

June & Brian Cox Educational Trust £1,350

Tigre Trust £1,000

*UK General*

Hope Project £10,000

Kettering Centre for the Unemployed £6,000

St Mary's Parochial Church Council £5,000

The Hope Project £5,000

KIDS £260

A sum of £5,000 was made available for distribution to charities chosen by the Life President, Mr Godric Bader and listed in the 2005 Accounts as the President's Fund. The following list details how this fund was distributed:

Forum for the Future £1,500

Quaker Peace & Social Witness £750

Peace Child International £500

The Lansbury House Trust Fund £500

Oxford Research Group £500

Victoria Centre £500

Global Net £250

TREAT £250

Seekers Library £250

### Employee-led support

Scott Bader matches employees' fundraising to a maximum of £5,000. Groups of members raised £7,789 for a charity of their choice and this was matched by the company. Volunteering is encouraged and examples of staff support are:

- employees arranged for a Fun Fair to be opened for special needs children and then acted as helpers
- local children were invited to enjoy the use of the swimming pool at the Head Office of Scott Bader
- a group of employees designed and constructed a Christmas grotto for the enjoyment of local children
- volunteers helped at a youth project which teaches them to recycle and maintain bicycles.

### Commercially-led support

Sponsorship is not undertaken.

# BAE Systems

Warwick House, PO Box 87, Farnborough Aerospace Centre, Farnborough, Hampshire GU14 6YU

01252 373232

Website: www.baesystems.com

Correspondent: The Subscriptions & Donations Committee

Chief officer: Dick Olver

Chief Executive: Mike Turner

| Year end | Turnover | Pre-tax profit |
|---|---|---|
| 31/12/2005 | £15,411,000,000 | £696,000,000 |

**Nature of company business**
The main activity of the Group is Defence – comprising the design and manufacture of civil and military aircraft, surface ships, submarines, space systems, radar, avionics, communications, electronics and guided weapon systems.

**Subsidiaries include:** Spectrum Technologies plc, Future Naval Systems, IFS Defence Ltd, Innovation Partnerships Worldwide Ltd, Gripen International, RG Ammunition, Airbus UK, Avionics Group, AMS Integrated Systems

**Main locations:** Srathclyde, Prestwick, Somerset, London, Northamptonshire, Wiltshire, Yorkshire, Surrey, Cumbria, Cwymbran, County Durham, Cheshire, Buckinghamshire, Bristol, Cambridgeshire, Bridgend, Lancashire, Leicestershire, Kent, Isle of Wight, Hertfordshire, Hampshire, Greater Manchester, Gloucestershire, Glascoed, Glasgow, Essex, Edinburgh, Dunfermline, Dorset

**Total employees:** 74,000

### Charitable donations

2005: £1,200,000
2004: £1,100,000

Total community contributions: £10,500,000

Membership: BitC, L B Group

## Community involvement

'BAE Systems takes an active role in community and educational activities, supporting charities and working directly with those communities close to our facilities worldwide.'

### Exclusions

No support for circular appeals, animal welfare, appeals from individuals, the arts, political appeals, religious appeals, or local appeals not in areas of company presence.

### Applications

In writing to the correspondent. The committee meets quarterly. Local appeals are handled by the regional site managers. Letters should at least be 'topped and tailed'.

## Corporate giving

In 2005 total community investment was £10.5 million. This figure included cash and in-kind donations to charity as well as direct support for education. The annual report put the cash figure at £1.2 million donated for charitable purposes in the UK.

### In-kind support

The company has provided equipment and materials, professional services and the use of in-house facilities either free of charge or with a discount.

### Employee-led support

Charity Challenge was launched in 1989, to challenge young employees to invent imaginative ways of raising funds for charities. In response, BAE matches pound for pound up to a ceiling of £100,000 any monies raised. A total of £2.7 million and 4,200 volunteer days were given through the scheme in 2005.

A number of staff give time and energy to support local community programmes involving education and training (such as job shadowing/work experience and mentoring schemes), and the development of local business enterprise initiatives. Staff are also seconded to charities and enterprise projects, through the individual business units rather than head office. The company matches employee fundraising and has a matching scheme for hours spent by employees volunteering (up to an allocated amount).

**Education:** The company is involved in a range of projects to promote better understanding between industry and education at national and local level. It aims to strengthen its links with a number of schools, technology colleges and universities.

**Payroll giving:** A payroll deduction scheme is operated in some parts of the business.

### Commercially-led support

**Sponsorship:** *Education and sport* – The group sponsors events benefiting young people.

# Bain & Company Inc. UK

40 Strand, London WC2N 5RW

020 7969 6000; Fax: 020 7969 6666

Website: www.bain.com

Correspondent: Graham Elton, Partner 020 7969 6050; Fax: 020 7969 6666
E-mail: graham.elton@bain.com

**Chief officer:** Orit Gadiesh

**Nature of company business**
Bain & Company is one of the world's leading global strategy consulting firms, serving clients across six continents.

**Main locations:** London

**UK employees:** 328

### Charitable donations

Management costs: £25,000

Membership: BitC

## Community involvement

The following information is taken from the company's website. Bain's London office encourages and facilitates its employees to contribute their time and skills to community work through the 'Bain Cares' community involvement programme. This has three key areas:

- education
- homelessness
- high impact volunteering

Further significant in-kind investment is made through pro bono consulting on important social issues. Over 70% of the employees in Bain's London office are included in the community programme.

### Exclusions

Bain do not make grants. All support is given in-kind.

### Applications

In writing to the correspondent.

## Corporate giving

Although Bain do not give grants, the level of in-kind support is significant and warrents inclusion here.

### In-kind support

**Education:** This involves employees in a variety of programmes including in-depth mentoring of secondary students, and one-on-one reading programmes with primary schoolchildren and mentoring through the Prince's Youth Trust.

**Homelessness:** The company has had an ongoing working relationship with Business Action on Homelessness for a number of years. A recent example of this involved small teams of Bain volunteers creating a website.

**London Cares:** Bain is a founder member of the organisation which aims 'to create a step change in quantity and quality of employee volunteering in the UK'. This initiative has enabled employees to volunteer to undertake activities such as cleaning up the Thames or gardening at homeless shelters.

**Pro bono consulting:** Bain aims to make a significant case team investment (on average every two years) on important social issues. Work has recently been carried out alongside Business Action on Homelessness, and the World Faiths Development Dialogue.

Bain also provides support – financial, marketing, advisory – to foundations such as Fulbright, the Voices Foundation and the Wellbeing Trust.

## Employee-led support

An Employee Challenge Fund has been established to enable one-off activities to be sponsored through the participation of London 'Bainies' in team-based challenges.

**Payroll giving:** The firm operate a payroll giving scheme.

# J C Bamford Excavators Ltd

Lakeside Works, Denstone Road, Rocester, Uttoxeter, Staffordshire ST14 5JP

01889 590312

Website: www.jcb.com

Correspondent: Steve Owens, Administrator, Bamford Charitable Foundation

Chief officer: Sir A P Bamford

Chief Executive: John Patterson

| Year end | Turnover | Pre-tax profit |
|---|---|---|
| 31/03/2006 | | |

Nature of company business
The company manufactures heavy construction and agricultural equipment.

Main locations: Wrexham, Uttoxeter, Stoke-on-Trent, Rocester, Rugeley

Total employees: 6,300

### Charitable donations
2006: £200,000
2005: £200,000
2004: £200,000

## Community involvement

The company channels its community support through the Bamford Charitable Foundation (Charity Commission no. 279848). Grants are made to support welfare purposes within a 40-mile radius of Rocester.

Beneficiaries have included schools, hospices, hospitals, language centres, medical welfare associations and catholic organisations.

## Exclusions

No support for advertising in brochures, animal welfare charities, appeals from individuals, enterprise/training, overseas projects, political appeals, sport, small purely local appeals not in areas of company presence, larger national appeals, or circulars. The company does not welcome proposals for arts sponsorship.

## Applications

In writing to the correspondent. A donations committee meets quarterly. Local branches do not have an independent grant-making policy and local appeals should be addressed to head office. The company welcomes relevant appeals from charities, but the guidelines above should be carefully considered, as appeal mail is becoming too large to handle.

## Corporate giving

### The Bamford Charitable Foundation

In 2004/05, the foundation had an income of nearly £58,000 and made donations and commitments totalling £285,000. This overspend has been a feature of the trust's finances in recent years and is met from an expendable endowment, the initial amount of which was £2 million.

The foundation gives around £200,000 a year in grants, mostly of £1,000 or more. Major beneficiaries in 2005 were: Denstone Foundation (£180,000); Cancer Research Fund and Alton Castle (£15,000 each); and, Elton John AIDS Foundation, Elm Farm Research Centre and The Stroke Association (£10,000 each).

Other smaller grants were paid to: Russian National Orchestra Trust (£5,000); The Bethel Project (£4,000); Great Wood Community Primary School (£3,000); Uttoxeter Methodist Church (£2,500); U Can Do I.T. (£1,500); and, British Mexican Society (£1,000).

## In-kind support

The company regularly assists disaster relief programmes by donating equipment. Following the Asian earthquake of October 2005, JCB gave £500,000 of equipment.

## Employee-led support

Preference is given to projects in which a member of staff is involved, for which the company will provide financial support and/or match the employee's fundraising.

# Bank of England

Threadneedle Street, London EC2R 8AH

020 7601 4444

Website: www.bankofengland.co.uk

Correspondent: Mrs Linda Barnard, Community Relations Unit
020 7601 4239; Fax: 020 7601 4553
E-mail: linda.barnard@bankofengland.co.uk

Chief officer: Mervyn King, Governor

| Year end | Turnover | Pre-tax profit |
|---|---|---|
| 28/02/2006 | | £80,000,000 |

Nature of company business
The Bank of England is the central bank of the United Kingdom and aims to maintain a stable and efficient monetary and financial framework in pursuance of a healthy economy.

The bank is based in London and has agencies in Belfast, Birmingham, Bristol, Cambridge, Exeter, Glasgow, Leeds, Liverpool, Manchester, Newcastle, Nottingham, Southampton, and Greater London. It operates a printing works in Loughton, Essex, in addition to its Registrar's Department in Gloucester. Subsidiaries include companies purchased in the course of its function of regulating the financial markets such as Minories Finance (formerly Johnson Matthey Bankers following the sale of that company's principal business).

Main locations: Belfast, Birmingham, Leeds, Cardiff, Cambridge, Bristol, Exeter, Gloucester, Glasgow, Southampton, Newcastle-on-Tyne, Loughton, Manchester, Liverpool, London, Nottingham

UK employees: 1,908

## Charitable donations

2006: £389,000
2005: £409,000
2004: £521,000
2003: £495,000

Total community contributions: £617,000

Membership: BitC

## Community involvement

Support is given throughout the UK to local, regional and national organisations. Donations are made from its head office, its 12 agencies across the UK, its Registrar's Department in Gloucester and its printing works in Essex. Between 500 and 600 grants are made each year, from over 3,000 applications.

The main focus is on supporting initiatives which enable people from disadvantaged backgrounds to access training or education opportunities which lead to worthwhile employment or further learning. Support is given towards:

- medical research and health
- children and youth
- social and moral welfare
- disasters
- people with disabilities
- older people
- environmental causes.

### Exclusions

No support is given towards: expeditions; holidays; orchestras; conferences; overseas work; organisations of a political nature; religious activities (unless they benefit the wider community); appeals from individuals; choirs; theatres; churches; animals; or third-party fundraising.

### Applications

Donations can be made locally at the discretion of the branch agent and subject to a limited budget. Otherwise, appeals should be addressed to the correspondent.

**Information available:** The bank produces a social responsibility report.

## Corporate giving

In 2003/04 cash donations totalled £521,000. Other community involvement, including staff time, totalled £236,000. A further £80,000 was given towards academic research, with an exceptional donation of £500,000 going to the Houblon-Norman-George Fund for economic studies.

Beneficiaries have included British Heart Foundation, Cleveland Community Foundation, Get it While You Can to help people with housing, drug and alcohol problems, Gloucester Kidney Patients Association, Jericho Community Project – Birmingham, Rose Road Children's Appeal – Southampton and Spring Centre for Disabled Children.

## In-kind support

As part of the bank's Education Business Partnership activities in Tower Hamlets and Hackney, work experience placements are arranged for local people, while staff are encouraged to take part in various school initiatives.

The bank also donates gifts in kind of surplus goods, computers and furniture.

## Employee-led support

The bank supports employees' volunteering/charitable activities through giving time off to volunteer, financial support, matching employee fundraising to a maximum of £250, and matching employee giving pound for pound. Staff are also encouraged to take up community positions, such as trustees, board members and magistrates.

# Barclays plc

Community Affairs, 8th Floor, 1 Churchill Place, Canary Wharf, London E14 5HP

020 7116 1000

Website: www.barclays.co.uk

Correspondent: The Head of Community Affairs

Chief officer: Matthew W Barrett

Chief Executive: John Varley

| Year end | Turnover | Pre-tax profit |
|---|---|---|
| 31/12/2005 | | £5,280,000,000 |

**Nature of company business**
Barclays plc is a UK-based financial services group engaged primarily in the banking and investment banking businesses. In terms of assets employed, Barclays is one of the biggest financial service groups in the UK. The group also operates in many other countries around the world.

**Subsidiaries include:** FIRSTPLUS Financial Group plc, Charles Schwab Europe, Woolwich plc, Gerrard Management Services Ltd

**Main locations:** London

**UK employees:** 62,682

## Charitable donations

2005: £16,700,000
2004: £11,200,000
2003: £9,900,000

Total community contributions: £35,300,000
Management costs: £2,840,000

Membership: A & B, BitC, L B Group, %Club

## Community involvement

'A large part of the UK community budget is administered by our regional community mangers who support initiatives that meet the needs of local communities – everything from sea safety programmes with the RNLI in the south west to the establishment of an Asian community radio station – Spice FM – in Tyne and Wear. In 2005 the themes we focused on were arts, education, disability, the environment, and social inclusion.'

## Exclusions

No support for animal welfare, appeal from individuals, circular appeals, fundraising events, medical research, political appeals, religious appeals, sport or intermediate fundraising bodies.

## Applications

Appeals to head office should be sent to the correspondent above. Local appeals should be sent to the relevant community manager.

**North West (region includes Scotland):** North West Community Relations Team, 1st Floor East Wing, Octagon House, Gadbrook Park, Northwich, Cheshire CW9 7RB

**North East:** North East Community Relations Team, Sycamore House, Meadow Court, 124 Millshaw, Leeds LS11 8LZ

**Eastern:** Eastern Community Relations Team, Church Street, Peterborough PE1 1XE

**Central:** Central Community Relations Team, North Wing, Avon House, Longwood Close, Westwood Business Park, Coventry CV4 8JN

**Wales & West:** Wales & West Community Relations Team, 2nd Floor, Windsor Court, 3 Windsor Place, Cardiff CF10 3BT

**London & Southern:** London & Southern Community Relations Team, Level 8, 1 Churchill Place, London E14 5HP

**South West:** South West Community Relations Team, Monmouth House, Blackbrook Park Avenue, Taunton TA1 2YY

## Corporate giving

Barclays, a founder member of the PerCent Club, made UK contributions totalling £35.3 million in 2005. Of this, £16.7 million was in charitable donations, with £2.84 million being accounted for in management costs. A further £3.8 million was invested in international support.

## In-kind support

**Community Placements:** This scheme introduces former Barclay employees (who have recently left the bank either through retirement or a redundancy package) to voluntary organisations which would benefit from the individuals financial skills and knowledge, and which fit within the focus of the bank's community programme.

## Employee-led support

**Volunteers & fundraising:** Barclays state that because of the wide range of organisations (national and local) its employees want to support, its approach has always been not to limit help to a single 'adopted' charity. Employees are therefore supported in their choices in a variety of ways.

Staff wishing to provide practical help to charities and community groups can apply for grants through its employee volunteering scheme. Additionally, the 'Volunteer 2day scheme' allows staff at least 2 days of Barclays time each year in which to volunteer.

Charities or community groups which think they would benefit from Barclay volunteer support through the 'Make a Difference Day' are encourage to e-mail the bank's local community team. Contact details and a template to help you with applying are available on its website.

Employees' fundraising efforts are matched up to a set maximum. Employees can apply for matched funding a maximum of three times a year.

**Payroll giving:** Barclays operates the Pennies from Heaven payroll giving scheme. It also offers Give As You Earn for employees. Around 10,000 staff give through one or both of these schemes. 2004 saw matched-funding support extended to the Give As You Earn scheme.

## Commercially-led support

**Sponsorship:** Arts and good-cause sponsorship is ONLY undertaken at regional level.

*Sport* – Barclays Spaces for Sports scheme focuses on regeneration and sports, creating sustainable sports sites for people to engage in sport and physical activities in areas without such facilities (www.barclays.co.uk/spacesforsports).

# Barloworld plc

3rd Floor, Medici Court, 67–69 New Bond Street, London W1S 1DF

020 7629 6243; Fax: 020 7495 5898

Website: www.barloworld.com

Correspondent: Carolyn Munro, Joint Secretary to the Charities Committee
E-mail: cmunro@barloworld.co.uk

Chief officer: W A M Clewlow

Chief Executive: A J Phillips

| Year end | Turnover | Pre-tax profit |
|---|---|---|
| 30/09/2003 | £1,315,956,000 | £62,504,000 |

**Nature of company business**
Barloworld plc is a wholly owned subsidiary of Barlow Ltd of South Africa. The company is an international group of manufacturing and distribution companies. Activities comprise the distribution and servicing of materials, handling equipment, earth-moving equipment and other capital equipment; paper making and converting; and the manufacture of laboratory, optical and scientific equipment.

Main locations: Stone, London

UK employees: 2,500

Total employees: 25,963

### Charitable donations
2003: £34,715

## Community involvement

Support is given to 'traditional charities', particularly those concerned with elderly, young, sick and disabled people, education, the arts, environment and heritage, medical research, and social welfare on both a national and local basis. Preference is given to projects in areas where the company has a presence and to appeals where a member of staff is involved.

### Exclusions

The company does not support appeals from non-charities, and rarely advertises in charity brochures for fundraising events. No support for animal welfare, appeals from individuals, fundraising events, overseas projects, political appeals, religious appeals, science/technology or sport.

### Applications

Written applications should be sent to Carolyn Munro or Ruth Pollard, Joint Secretaries to the Charities Committee which meets three times a year to consider appeals.

## Corporate giving

In 2005 the company spent £1.7 million (£1.1 million in 2004) directly on community projects. This amounted to 1% of profit after tax.

Grants normally range from £250 to £1,000, with most being for £250 or £500.

Grants have previously been made to: Against Breast Cancer, British Heart Foundation, Help the Aged, Prostate Cancer Charity and Cruse Bereavement Care.

**The arts:** Appeals for donations are considered selectively.

## Employee-led support

The company encourages staff to become volunteers in their own time. The company matches employee fundraising to a max of £500.

**Payroll giving:** The company operates a payroll deduction scheme for employee contributions which it occasionally matches.

# BASF plc

PO Box 4, Earl Road, Cheadle Hulme, Cheshire SK8 6QG

0161 485 6222; Fax: 0161 486 0891

Website: www.basf.de/uk/

Correspondent: Director of Corporate Services

Chief officer: Barry Stickings

Managing Director: Fried-Walter Munstermann

| Year end 31/12/2005 | Turnover | Pre-tax profit |
|---|---|---|

Nature of company business
Chemicals, paints, plastics, pharmaceuticals.

Subsidiaries include: Basell UK Ltd, Elastogram UK Ltd, Hydrowingas Ltd, Basell Polyolefins UK Ltd, BTC Speciality Chemical Distribution Ltd, Frank Wright Ltd

Main locations: Didcot, Cheadle, Deeside, Wilmslow, Woolpit, Richmond, Ruddington, Seal Sands, London, Nottingham, Alfreton, Ashbourne

UK employees: 814

## Charitable donations

2005: £39,000,000

Total community contributions: £39,000,000 (global)

## Community involvement

BASF chose not to provide any updated information for this guide and requested its details be removed. However, we maintain our policy of including all relevant companies. The following information is therefore mainly drawn from the company's website and 2005 corporate report.

The company prefers to support local charities in areas where the company operates (mainly in the North West, North East and East Midlands) working in the fields of: the arts and culture; education and training; employment promotion; science/technology; and sport.

## Exclusions

No grants for purely denominational (religious) appeals or local appeals not in areas of company presence.

## Applications

In writing to the correspondent for national appeals. For local appeals contact the nearest relevant site.

## Corporate giving

BASF state that: 'The communities in which our sites are located play an important role in our success. We can only be successful if we enjoy the trust and support of our neighbours. This is why we work at all sites to be recognised as a dependable partner and an attractive employer that takes its social responsibility seriously. In this way, we add to each region's competitiveness as well as our own.'

The BASF Group worldwide made total community contributions of €56.8 million (£39 million) in 2005 on the 'specific sponsorship of humanitarian, cultural and social issues'. This was broken down as follows: charities €4.6 million (£3.15 million); arts & culture €6.7 million (£4.6 million); education and training, and employment promotion €37 million (£25.3 million); science/technology €2.5 million (£1.7 million); sports €2.7 million (£1.85 million); and, other €3.3 million (£2.25 million). We do not know what proportion of the total was in cash donations.

Although no separate figures were available for the UK, some examples of the types of projects supported were given.

**Education:** The Catalyst Museum in Widnes, Cheshire is solely devoted to chemistry and provides over 100 different exhibits through which children and adults can discover how products of the science are used in everyday life.

Operated by a charitable trust, the board of trustees includes a representative from BASF which provides support through direct funding for school visits and grants to the museum.

The company also sponsor various teaching packs for schools connected with the science and technology curricula through, for example, working with the Chemical Industry Education Centre.

## In-kind support

**Training:** In 2002, the company ran a successful 'Stress Awareness' course at its Seal Sands site for employees and their families. It also provided check-ups on weight and body fat, and gave advice and leaflets on a variety of health issues to staff at its Cramlington works as part of Men's Health Week.

## Employee-led support

Most of BASF's sites work with local schools by providing school visits, work experience placements and practical help with school projects.

## Commercially-led support

**Sponsorship:** *The arts* – The company continues to sponsor the Hallé Orchestra, having done so since 1970.

*Science/technology* – BASF continue to sponsor The Daily Telegraph BASF Science Writer Awards. It has also sponsored a number of chemistry workshops and seminars organised by the Royal Society of Chemistry and The British Association and Salters' Chemistry.

# Baxter Healthcare Limited

Wallington, Compton, Newbury, Berkshire RG20 7QW

01635 206000; Fax: 01635 206115

Website: www.baxterhealthcare.co.uk

Correspondent: Office Services (Sponsorship)
E-mail: cfob@baxter.com

| Year end | Turnover | Pre-tax profit |
|----------|----------|----------------|
| 31/12/2003 | £200,127,000 | £1,453,000 |

**Nature of company business**
Technologies related to the blood and circulatory system.

**Main locations:** Thetford, Stockport, Merthyr Tydfil, Liverpool, Newport, Northampton, Newbury, Northwood, Oxford, Glasgow, Harlow, Ipswich, Kidderminster, Cardiff, Bristol, Belfast, Bangor

**Charitable donations**

2006: £37,000
2005: £41,000

## Community involvement

This international group operates the Baxter International Foundation which supports the health and well-being of communities worldwide where Baxter employees live and work. Since 2002, the foundation has focused exclusively on increasing access to healthcare, particularly for the disadvantaged and underserved.

Support is only given to registered charities. These must be nominated by a Baxter employee and operate in an area where there is a Baxter facility, or where a large number of Baxter employees live. Whilst the charities supported do not have to be health-focused, the projects supported must improve access to healthcare.

In the UK, assistance is only given in the areas where the company operates. Currently, these are Bangor, Belfast, Bristol, Cardiff, Glasgow, Harlow, Ipswich, Kidderminster, Liverpool, Merthyr Tydfil, Newbury, Newport, Northampton, Northwood, Oxford, Stockport, and Thetford.

### Exclusions

No grants are made to: capital or endowment campaigns; disease-specific organisations; educational institutions (unless to increase the skills and availability of health-care providers); hospitals; individuals; organisations which benefit a restricted part of the community, such as service or religious charities; or fundraising events.

### Applications

To be considered for support from the foundation, registered charities must be nominated by a Baxter employee, not via unsolicited applications, and be eligible under the foundations guidelines. Details of the latter can be found at www.baxter.com

Any queries about the foundation, your organisation's eligibility and so on, can be addressed via e-mail to: fdninfo@baxter.com

Applications are considered quarterly, usually in January, April, July and September.

## Corporate giving

In 2005, the foundation awarded over US$4.2 million (£2.3 million) in grants to support the health and well-being of communities worldwide. Whilst the company gave support totalling US$14 million (£7.7 million) 'to address critical local needs'. We do not know exactly how much of this went to organisations in the UK, but understand there to have been two beneficiaries in 2005/06. These were Changing Faces (US$74,828/£41,000 awarded over three years, to help support its expansion into Wales), and the NSPCC (US$67,401/£37,000 for increased therapeutic services for abused children in Hampshire).

In 2002, grants to six UK organisations were made totalling $110,721. Princess Royal Trust for Carers received $144,000 for a nationwide project to improve the quality of carers' centres. Amber Foundation was given $66,416 for a comprehensive healthy living programme, to help unemployed young people living in its Tottenham House centre gain self-respect and find the confidence to enter the workplace. Rural Needs Initiative received $20,105 for a support worker assisting new and expectant mothers in Kennet and North Wiltshire. Thetford Counselling Service was awarded $9,432 to train counsellors in relationship problems, family difficulties, personal crises, depression, stress, bereavement and childhood abuse. Child Victims of Crime, a Warrington based charity, received $8,000 to provide professional counselling services for nominated individuals at a multi-activity centre in Eastling, near Faversham in Kent. A total of $6,768 went to Northampton Emergency Aid Team for volunteer training on first aid courses run by St John Ambulance and British Cross, ambulance aid training run by Two Shires Ambulance NHS Trust, and basic driving training with police and ambulance driving instructors.

In addition to the above, Baxter Healthcare Limited have given grants to a number of patient groups to aid their partner support activities (Tony Ward Adventures, National Kidney Foundation, Kidney Research UK and Haemophilia Society).

### In-kind support

Product donations are made in support of disaster relief programmes, underdeveloped nations and countries in crisis.

### Employee-led support

Although a 'matching gifts' programme for employees' fundraising efforts exists in the States, we are unsure if this extends to the UK.

# Bayer plc

Bayer House, Strawberry Hill, Newbury, Berkshire RG14 1JA

01635 563000; Fax: 01635 563513

Website: www.bayer.co.uk

Correspondent: Steve Painter, Head of Corporate Communications 01635 563522

Chief officer: Werner Wenning

| Year end 31/12/2005 | Turnover | Pre-tax profit |
|---|---|---|

**Nature of company business**
Marketing of around 2,000 pharmaceutical, chemical and agro-chemical products of Bayer AG.

**Subsidiaries include:** H C Starck, W Hawley & son, pbi Home & Garden

**Main locations:** Sheffield, Sudbury, Waltham Cross, Newbury, Bridgend, Hauxton, Branston

**Total employees:** 93,000

## Community involvement

The company supports charities that have a business link, a staff link or a geographical link. The company's main sites are Newbury, Branston, Bridgend, Hauxton, Sheffield, Sudbury and Waltham Cross.

The following information was provided by the company.

'It is Bayer's aim to give support:

*Professionally* – employing as much information as possible to ensure funds are put to best use.

*Sympathetically* – so that recipients of our support understand our philosophy.

*Impartially* – remaining unaffected by unhelpful emotional appeals from otherwise needy initiatives.

*Systematically* – to create a greater understanding of Bayer's overall contribution to society, and to build on our reputation as a company that cares for its people, its customers and the community, and to reflect accurately the company's business interests.

'Our criteria for giving are that the activity must be:
- local to one or more of our UK facilities
- linked to our employees' own community activities
- linked to one of Bayer's 10,000 products or services
- genuinely and specifically benefiting from Bayer's involvement
- beneficial to numbers or groups of people.

'We will also favour activities which enhance people's general quality of life in areas local to Bayer's facilities, through:
- cultural activities
- environmental improvement
- community work
- educational enrichment.

'While activities meeting the above criteria will be considered, they do not automatically qualify for support, as other factors (such as budget already committed) must be taken into account.'

The company places almost all Bayer Foundation monies with two throughway organisations – Berkshire Community Trust and West Berkshire Education Business Partnership.

### Exclusions

No support for national initiatives, individuals, religious, political or racial movements, sporting or recreational activities unless closely associated to Bayer, entries in log books, year books or support for advertising or to make up for a lack of government or local authority funding.

### Applications

Charities wishing to be considered for funding should apply in the first instance to one of the following organisations:

Berkshire Community Trust (for community initiatives in Berkshire) or West Berkshire Education Business Partnership (for educational initiatives in Berkshire).

Then, exceptionally, in writing to the correspondent.

## Corporate giving

All community support is given through the Bayer Foundation

### In-kind support

The company supports education, particularly science projects for young people.

### Employee-led support

Employee fundraising is matched by the company.

### Commercially-led support

**Sponsorship:** The company undertakes arts and good-cause sponsorship. Examples include: The youth programme at the Corn Exchange, Newbury; Newbury & Royal County of Berkshire Show; Newbury Spring Festival; Riding for the Disabled; Speenhamland School Millennium Play Area Project, and The Watermill Theatre youth group.

# BBA Group plc

20 Balderton Street, London W1K 6TL

020 7514 3999; Fax: 020 7408 2318

Website: www.bbagroup.com

Correspondent: Sarah Shaw, Group Secretary

Chief officer: Roberto Quarta

Chief Executive: Michael Harper

| Year end 31/12/2005 | Turnover £1,510,800,000 | Pre-tax profit £59,900,000 |
|---|---|---|

**Nature of company business**
An international group of aviation services and materials technology businesses.

**Subsidiaries include:** Lynton Group Ltd, H+S Aviation Ltd, APPH Aviation Services Ltd, ASIG Ltd, APPH Ltd, Oxford Aviation Services Ltd

**Main locations:** London

**UK employees:** 2,239

**Total employees:** 13,318

### Charitable donations
2005: £4,000
2004: £15,000
2003: £20,000

## Community involvement

The company's 2005 Corporate Social Responsibility Report states: 'While BBA Group does not dictate specific group-wide community goals or programmes, we do require that each business identify and embrace meaningful programmes that meet the needs of the community. Management at each facility must specify their chosen community projects and charities in the strategic planning process – the decision to invest in local concerns is at the discretion of each facility, but meaningful participation in some form is mandatory.

'Each community that the BBA companies are a part of has different needs and priorities. That is why we empower local management to determine the most appropriate ways to get involved in and interact with their surrounding communities and local charities. As a result, the connections that the individual BBA companies make in their respective communities is quite varied.'

### Exclusions

Previous information provided stated that there is no support available for advertising in charity brochures, appeals from individuals, political appeals, or religious appeals.

### Applications

In writing to the correspondent.

## Corporate giving

In 2005, the company made global cash donations totalling £143,000 (2004: £182,000) of which only £4,000 was given in the UK. Although this amount is below our threshold for inclusion, it may be a one-off fall in donations. We shall therefore monitor the situation over the coming year before deciding whether or not to continue including BBA.

UK beneficiaries included Marie Curie Cancer Care and Childline.

## Bellway plc

Seaton Burn House, Dudley Lane, Seaton Burn, Newcastle upon Tyne NE13 6BE

0191 217 0717; Fax: 0191 236 6230

Website: www.bellway.co.uk

Correspondent: G K Wrightson, Group Company Secretary

Chief officer: H C Dawe

Chief Executive: J K Watson

| Year end | Turnover | Pre-tax profit |
|---|---|---|
| 31/07/2006 | £1,240,193,000 | £220,709,000 |

**Nature of company business**
The company's main activity is house building.

**Subsidiaries include:** Litrose Investments Ltd, The Victoria Dock Company Ltd

**Main locations:** Bedworth, Altrincham, Wetherby, Tamworth, Uxbridge, Wakefield, Ringwood, Merstham, Newcastle upon Tyne, Glasgow, Eastcote, Chadderton, Chelmsford, Cardiff

**UK employees:** 2,446

---

### Charitable donations

2006: £87,291
2005: £85,290
2004: £97,786
2003: £89,197

---

## Community involvement

Past information provided suggests that the company supports a wide range of national charities and local charities near to main office locations.

The company has established the Bellway Fund within the Community Foundation (Tyne & Wear/Northumberland) in order for it to support charitable initiatives outside of the sphere of its core operations.

### Exclusions

Previous information suggested the company provides no support for advertising in charity brochures, appeals from individuals, animal welfare, fundraising events, overseas projects, political appeals, or religious appeals.

### Applications

In writing to the correspondent.

## Corporate giving

In 2005/06, the company's support for charitable causes totalled £87,291 (2004/05: £85,290). No further information on how this was distributed was made available.

We do know, however, that the following organisations received support via the Bellway Fund: Delaval Community Primary School, Hadrian School, Christ Church School (Feng Shui Community Garden) and Fairbridge in Tyne & Wear (£500 each); and, Jesmond Dene Real Tennis Club and Friends of Hedworthfield School (£300 each).

### In-kind support

In addition to cash donations the company provides in kind support. For the first time this year [2005] its divisions supported Community Service Volunteers' initiative, 'Make a Difference Day', a day of national volunteering which provided the opportunity for Bellway employees to support worthwhile causes in their own locality and in some instances introduce people to volunteering.

---

## Berkeley Group plc

Berkeley House, 19 Portsmouth Road, Cobham, Surrey KT11 1GD

01932 868555; Fax: 01932 868667

Website: www.berkeleygroup.com

Correspondent: Charity Committee

Chief officer: Roger Lewis

Managing Director: Tony Pidgley

| Year end | Turnover | Pre-tax profit |
|---|---|---|
| 30/04/2005 | £917,900,000 | £165,100,000 |

**Nature of company business**
Principal activity: residential housebuilding and commercial property investment and development.

**Subsidiaries include:** St James Group Ltd, Exchange Place No. 2 Ltd, St John Homes Ltd, Thirlstone Homes Ltd, The Crosby Group plc, West Kent Cold Storage Ltd, St George plc, The Beaufort Home Development Group Ltd, St David Ltd

**Main locations:** Edgbaston, Twickenham, Cobham, Potters Bar, Portsmouth

**UK employees:** 766

## Community involvement

We were unable to obtain any information about the company's current support. The following is therefore a repeat of the last information the company provided. Berkeley continues to support a wide range of local and national charities as long as they are based near to offices of operation. Preferred areas of support are: children/youth, elderly people, environment/heritage and sickness/disability charities.

### Exclusions

No support for: animal welfare; appeals from individuals; the arts; education; enterprise/training; fundraising events; local appeals not in areas of company presence; medical research; overseas projects; political appeals; religious appeals; science/technology; social welfare; or sport.

### Applications

In writing to the correspondent. However, we understand the company has a charity committee which tends to plan its giving in advance.

## Corporate giving

In 2005, the company's charitable donations totalled £190,977 (£440,957 in the previous year).

Past beneficiaries have included: Princess Alice Hospice (Esher, Surrey), St John Ambulance (Surrey), Paishill Park (Cobham, Surrey) and various cancer charities and children's hospitals.

# Bestway (Holdings) Ltd

Abbey Road, Park Royal, London NW10 7BW

020 8453 1234; Fax: 020 8965 0359

Website: www.bestway.co.uk

Correspondent: Zulfikaur Wajid-Hasan, Bestway Foundation, Bestway Head Office

Chief officer: Sir Anwar Pervez

| Year end | Turnover | Pre-tax profit |
|---|---|---|
| 30/06/2005 | £996,209,000 | £48,262,000 |

Nature of company business
The subsidiaries of the holding company are involved in the operation of cash and carry warehouses supplying groceries, tobacco, wines and spirits, beers and other household goods.

Subsidiaries include: Icecross, Map (UK)

Main locations: Bolton, Birmingham, Oldbury, Luton, London, Liverpool, Manchester, Northampton, Newcastle-under-Lyme, Peterborough, Plymouth, Romford, Swansea, Croydon, Bristol, Cardiff, Gateshead, Exeter, Leicester, Leeds

Total employees: 2,831

## Community involvement

The group donates 2.5% of its annual profits to the registered charity, The Bestway Foundation (Charity Commission no. 297178), established by the group in 1987. The Foundation's objects are:

The advancement of education for the public benefit both in the UK and overseas by providing assistance by way of grants, endowments, scholarships, loans or otherwise.

The Bestway Foundation has continued to provide scholarships to students and sponsor the Government's Specialist Schools and Academies Programme. The Foundation has also continued to fund the development of village schools and rural Basic Health Care Units in Pakistan.

In the year 2005 the group's annual charity fundraiser was held Paris. The main beneficiary was the Crimestoppers Trust.

In the UK, the group is a supporter of Age Concern, The Prince's Trust, John Kelly Technology College, The National Grocers Benevolent Fund, The Duke of Edinburgh's Award Scheme, The Specialist Schools Trust, The NSPCC, Save the Children and others.

### Exclusions

No grants for trips or travel abroad.

### Applications

In writing to the correspondent, enclosing an sae. Applications are considered in March/April. Telephone calls are not welcome.

## Corporate giving

In the year ended 30th June 2005 the group made charitable donations of £684,000 (2004: £610,000) to the Bestway Foundation.

In the same financial year, The Bestway Foundation awarded grants to a total value of £202,636 (2004: £841,922). The amounts paid were as follows: £117,413 (2004: £194,188) to registered UK charities, £85,223 (2004: £74,364) to foreign charities – individuals, £0.00 to non-registered UK charities (2004: £573,100).

## Employee-led support

The company is actively involved in fundraising to raise extra funds for distribution.

# BHP Billiton plc

Neathouse Place, London SW1V 1BH

020 7802 7000; Fax: 020 7802 3177

Website: www.bhpbilliton.com

Correspondent: Naomi Korolew

| Year end | Turnover | Pre-tax profit |
|---|---|---|
| 30/06/2006 | | |

**Nature of company business**

BHP Billiton plc operated solely as a holding company for the BHP Billiton Group plc. The principal activities of the group are mineral and hydrocarbon exploration and production, metals production, marketing, and research and development.

**Main locations:** Liverpool, London

### Charitable donations

2006: £632,772
2005: £577,235

Membership: BitC, %Club

## Community involvement

Support is given to community groups around its sites, which are in Westminster, London and North Wales (Liverpool Bay).

### Applications

In writing to the correspondent.

Applications to the Lennox First Oil Fund (beneficial area: North Wales, Wirral, Sefton and Fylde) should be addressed to the External Affairs Officer, BHP Billiton Petroleum Ltd, Llaneurgain House, Northop Country Park, Northop, Flintshire CH7 6WD.

## Corporate giving

In 2005/06, the company made cash donations in the UK of £632,772 (2004: £577,235). We have no details of the beneficiaries.

The company's Liverpool Bay Asset (LBA) provides support in North Wales, through increased economic opportunities, environmental improvements and positive community initiatives. Grants are available through the Lennox First Oil Fund. Grants range from £500 to a maximum of £2,000 and total around £30,000 a year.

During 2005/06, the company received Business in the Community's 'Big Tick Award' as winners of the Post Office Rural action award – Awards for Excellence.

### Employee-led support

BHP Billiton has established a Matched Giving Programme through which the company will match the community contributions made by employees. Every employee (including full and part time) is entitled each year to match their contributions to not-for-profit organisations that benefit the community. These contributions can be employee volunteering, fundraising or cash donations (including pay-roll donations).

# Birmingham International Airport Limited

Birmingham, B26 3QJ

08707 335511

Website: www.bhx.co.uk

Correspondent: Andy Holding, Birmingham Airport Community Affairs and Environment Unit 0121 767 7448; Fax: 0121 767 7359

E-mail: andyh@bhx.co.uk

| Year end | Turnover | Pre-tax profit |
|---|---|---|
| 31/03/2005 | £110,195,000 | £29,085,000 |

**Nature of company business**

The principal activity is the operation and management of Birmingham International Airport and the provision of associated facilities and services.

**Main locations:** Birmingham

**UK employees:** 730

**Total employees:** n/a

### Charitable donations

2005: £50,000
2004: £50,000
2003: £50,000

Membership: A & B, BitC

## Community involvement

The company set up a trust to fund a wide range of community-based projects which will benefit the community and environment around Birmingham Airport. The Community Trust Fund (Charity Commission no. 1071176) receives £50,000 each year from the airport, topped up by fines imposed on airlines for exceeding the airport's noise violation levels. Geographically, the trust supports a very defined area which, broadly speaking, is that bounded by Grove End, Berkswell, Honiley and Washwood Heath. Projects outside of this region cannot be funded, even if the communities feel they are affected by the disruption caused by the airport. The trust acts independently of the airport management, with nine representatives of the following bodies making up the trustees: The Airport Consultative Committee (3), Birmingham City Council (2), Birmingham International Airport (2) and Solihull Council (2).

Areas of work the trust supports are:

> environment improvement and heritage conservation
> bringing the community closer together through facilities for sport, recreation and other leisure-time activities
> improving awareness of environmental issues or environmental education and training activities
> encouraging and protecting wildlife

It describes the types of projects it wishes to support as including community centres, community groups, sports, playgroups, schools, youth clubs, scouts, gardens/parks, environment, music and churches. Work should benefit a substantial section of the community rather than less inclusive groups, although work with older people or people with special needs is positively encouraged.

The maximum grant made is for £3,000, and grants tend to go to community groups with low incomes; organisations with large turnovers are rarely supported. Grants may be for capital or revenue projects, although the trust will not commit to recurrent or running costs, such as salaries.

### Exclusions

No grants to: individuals, sports kits, trips or projects resulting in short term benefit e.g. events, performances or visits, commercial organisations, or those working for profit, projects which have already been carried out or paid for; organisations which have statutory responsibilities such as hospitals or schools, unless the project is clearly not a statutory responsibility. Grants are not normally given towards the purchase of land or buildings or general repair and maintenance; requests for equipment, fixtures and fittings may be supported. Grants will also not normally be recurrent.

Support will not be considered for advertising in charity brochures, animal welfare, overseas projects, political or religious appeals, medical purposes, or science/technology.

### Applications

On a form available from the correspondent. When the form is sent, applicants will be advised when the next grant allocation meeting is being held. The trust may want to visit the project. All applications will be acknowledged.

Applications can be submitted at any time, with grants awarded twice a year in April and October. Successful applicants are required to submit a progress report after six months, and again after 12 for longer projects.

Grants will not be awarded to the same organisation in consecutive years. Applicants must wait at least two years before applying for another grant.

Information Available: The company produces further information in its application guidelines.

## Corporate giving

The company makes an annual contribution of £50,000 to the trust, with money from fines increasing the fund to over £160,000. In 2005/06 it had an income of £63,000 and made grants totalling £67,000.

### In-kind support

In addition to cash donations made via the Community Trust, the company provides non-cash support through gifts in kind. The value of these has not been costed.

### Employee-led support

The company has an employee volunteering scheme and provides support by allowing company time off in which to volunteer.

### Commercially-led support

**Sponsorship:** The company undertakes arts and good-cause sponsorship.

## Biwater Limited

Biwater House, Station Approach, Dorking RH4 1TZ

01306 740740; Fax: 01306 885233

Website: www.biwater.com

Correspondent: Richard Bourton, Director of Business
E-mail: corporate.communications@biwater.com

Chief officer: D F W White

Chief Executive: D L Magor

| Year end | Turnover | Pre-tax profit |
|---|---|---|
| 31/03/2005 | £192,400,000 | £5,600,000 |

Nature of company business
Principal activities: contracting, manufacturing and the provision of services to the water industry worldwide.

Main locations: Dorking

UK employees: 660

Total employees: 1,271

### Charitable donations
2005: £36,568

## Community involvement

The company supports Dorking charities. This is all the information we have been able to confirm about the company's community involvement.

### Exclusions

No support is given to individual appeals, purely denominational (religious) appeals or overseas projects. No sponsorship or advertising in charity brochures is undertaken.

### Applications

In writing to the correspondent.

## Corporate giving

In 2005, the company and its subsidiary undertakings made donations for charitable purposes of £44,497 (2004: £25,766) of which £36,568 (2004: £22,836) was in the United Kingdom mainly for education, community support and medical purposes.

### Employee-led support

**Payroll giving:** The company operates a scheme.

## Peter Black Holdings plc

Airedale Mill, Lawkholme Lane, Keighley, West Yorkshire BD21 3BB

01535 661131; Fax: 01535 609973

Website: www.peterblack.co.uk

Correspondent: Katy Bell, Charities Coordinator

Chief officer: Gordon L Black

Chief Executive: Stephen Lister

| Year end | Turnover | Pre-tax profit |
|---|---|---|
| 31/01/2001 | £253,445,000 | £14,574,000 |

Nature of company business
The company's main activities are in personal care products, footwear and accessories.

Subsidiaries include: Hexel International Ltd

Main locations: Leicester, Keighley, Westbury, Tunbridge Wells, Trowbridge, Wakefield, Swadlincote, Marlow, London

UK employees: 1,538

## Community involvement

The company appears to route its charitable support through the Peter Black Charitable Trust (Charity Commission no. 264279). There is some preference for supporting appeals from groups in the West Yorkshire area working in arts and culture, and health and welfare.

## Exclusions

No grants to individuals.

## Applications

In writing to the correspondent.

## Corporate giving

**Peter Black Charitable Trust**

In 2003/04, the trust had assets of £280,000 and an income of £56,000. Grants totalled £31,000. Grants of £1,000 or over included Yorkshire Ballet Seminars (£2,000) and Leeds International Pianoforte Competition and The Ilkley Players – Lightning Appeal (£1,000). Other grants included Yorkshire Cancer Research (£300 in two grants), Leeds Jewish Welfare Board (£200 in two grants), Bradford WIZO, Ilkley Summer Festival Ltd, Leeds Teaching Hospitals Fund, Sport on Saturday Club – Ilkley and Yorkshire Wildlife Trust (£100 each), Ilkley Literature Festival (£50), Bradford Jewish Benevolent Society (£25).

# BMW UK Ltd

Ellesfield Avenue, Bracknell, Berkshire RG12 8TA

01344 426565; Fax: 01344 480203

Website: www.bmw.co.uk

Correspondent: Rosemary Davies, Public Relations Manager 01344 480102; Fax: 01344 480306 E-mail: rosemary.davies@bmw.co.uk

Chief Executive: Patrick O'Donnell

| Year end | Turnover | Pre-tax profit |
|---|---|---|
| 31/12/2005 | £3,439,064,064 | £184,697,463 |

**Nature of company business**
The principal activity is the importation, storage and distribution of BMW products in the UK.

Subsidiaries include: Park Lane Ltd

Main locations: Bracknell

UK employees: 454

> **Charitable donations**
>
> 2005: £25,000
>
> Total community contributions: £85,998

## Community involvement

Major donations are given to two or three national charities selected by the company, preferably related to the motor industry (BEN is the favoured charity), children or a charity in which a member of staff has a particular interest.

## Exclusions

No response to circular appeals.

## Applications

The policy outlined above means that BMW UK are unable to respond positively to letters requesting support/sponsorship.

## Corporate giving

In 2005, the company made total UK community contributions of just over £110,000 of which £25,000 was in cash donations to charity. Smaller donations are made to local charities through the Berkshire Community Trust. Grants to national organisations range from £250 to £3,000 and to local organisations from £50 to £1,000.

## In-kind support

In addition to cash donations, BMW gave other support through gifts in kind. We have no information on the form this may take.

**Education:** The company has a separate education programme which is designed to respond to student enquiries and provide resource materials for schools, rather than giving money to projects/schools.

## Employee-led support

**Payroll giving:** The company operates the BEN scheme.

# The Body Shop International plc

Watersmead, Littlehampton, West Sussex BN17 6LS

01903 731500; Fax: 01903 726250

Website: www.thebodyshopinternational.com

Correspondent: Lisa Jackson, Principal – Body Shop Foundation 01903 844039; Fax: 01903 844202

Chief officer: Adrian D P Bellamy

Chief Executive: Peter Saunders

| Year end | Turnover | Pre-tax profit |
|---|---|---|
| 25/02/2006 | £485,800,000 | £37,600,000 |

**Nature of company business**
The Body Shop is a multi-local, values-led, global retailer. The group sells skin and hair care products through its own shops and franchised outlets in 47 markets worldwide.

Subsidiaries include: Soapworks Ltd

Main locations: Glasgow, Littlehampton

UK employees: 3,091

Total employees: 7,534

> **Charitable donations**
>
> 2006: £1,000,000
> 2005: £1,300,000
> 2004: £1,000,000
> 2003: £900,000
>
> Total community contributions: £1,180,090
>
> Membership: L B Group, %Club

## Community involvement

The Body Shop mission statement states that: 'We will operate our business with a strong commitment to the well being of our fellow humans and the preservation of the planet.

'The Body Shop Values Principles set out our commitments and the actions we will take to further these commitments. Charitable contributions in cash or kind must always support the aims of these principles, and no donations can be made to organisations or causes which conflict with these aims.

'The Body Shop International will channel all its central donations through our Foundation and its regional grant making committees.'

With respect to the above, The Body Shop Foundation (Charity Commission no. 802757) is funded by annual donations from the company and through various fundraising initiatives. Its aim is to:

- support organisations at the forefront of social & environmental change
- support groups with little hope of conventional funding
- support projects working to increase public awareness.

The foundation is currently running the following grants programmes:

- global main grants programme
- regional funding panels: Asia Pacific; UK & Republic of Ireland; Europe, Middle East & Africa; and, The Americas
- global small grants programme
- West Sussex grants programme.

In the UK & Republic of Ireland (RoI) region, the grants panel has representatives from all areas of the business. Presently, funding in the region is for: Human rights – child trafficking; Environmental protection – youth education on recycling issues; Animal protection – wildlife protection.

## Exclusions

The foundation does not:

- sponsor individuals
- fund sporting activities or the arts
- sponsor or support fundraising events, receptions or conferences.

In addition, no donations can be made to promote religious causes or political campaign causes, although the foundation may work with religious or political organisations on partnership projects and fund raise with organisations that have a political or religious foundation for causes that support its values and principles.

No donations can be made to, nor funds raised for organisations linked to animal testing, organisations advocating violence or discrimination or in other ways promoting behaviour inconstant with the foundation's principles.

## Applications

The Body Shop International and The Body Shop Foundation no longer accept unsolicited applications for funding.

However, in exceptional circumstances the company may respond to a humanitarian emergency and make a special donation to a public appeal, but such a donation must have the approval of the CEO.

**Information available:** The company produce an annual 'Body Shop Values Report', which is available online.

## Corporate giving

### The Body Shop Foundation

An annual donation is made from the company to the foundation. The total company donations in 2003/04 of £1,000,000 included £600,000 to the foundation. Other donations are made to the foundation by franchisees, employees and friends of The Body Shop. Grants in the UK in 2001 included £20,000 to Black Liners for a youth magazine for Black and Asian Londoners, Emmaus Project for work with homeless people and National Missing Persons Helpline for running costs, £15,000 to Undercurrents and £10,000 each to Genetics Forum for a magazine to stimulate debate on genetic research and ISEC for a conference on anti-globalisation and Soil Association for sustainable organic farming.

**Campaigns:** During 2003/04 the theme of its campaign was Help Stop Violence in the Home. Funds were raised for Refuge, consisting of selling campaigning pin badges and providing freepost envelopes for customers to use in donating old mobile phones. A total of £90,000 was raised for the charity.

**Enterprise:** Soapworks in Glasgow's Easterhouse district, a poor area blighted by unemployment, was opened by The Body Shop in 1988 and now employs over 120 local people and produces the majority of soap sold in the company's retail outlets worldwide. A commitment was given to donate the equivalent to 25% of Soapworks' cumulative after-tax profits to local community projects. Between 1989 and 2001, £349,896 has been donated.

## In-kind support

**Gifts in kind club:** As a way of managing the large number of requests that the company receive for end of line or 'seconds quality' product by The Body Shop, it established a club.

For a small administration fee, it supplies mixed products (mostly shower gels and hair products) to charitable projects and organisations in the UK.

The groups supported by the 'Gifts in Kind' club must work to provide direct benefit – including groups like women's refuges, homeless & refugee centres.

This scheme currently operates in the UK with 150 members receiving a box of product every 2 months. Unfortunately, there is a waiting list of groups wishing to join this scheme.

However, should you require more details about this programme, please contact Sue Allen in the foundation office.

## Employee-led support

Employees are encouraged to take an active role in their local communities. At the UK global head office, employees were entitled to six days of volunteer time in the last financial year, with 38% supporting local projects and causes as individuals and as business teams (2005: 23%).

For example, the global product team undertook a day of conservation work to support a conservation group based near the head office in West Sussex, whilst the global marketing team spent a day creating a play area for children at an inner city farm close to the London head office.

## Commercially-led support

**Cause-related marketing:** The company's 2006 Stop Violence in the Home campaign seeks to raise awareness of the problem of domestic violence and its effect upon children through the purchase of a campaign-linked product (Daisy Soap and Mint Lip Care Stick).

# Bombardier Aerospace Europe Limited

Airport Road, Belfast BT3 9DZ

028 9045 8444; Fax: 028 9073 3396

Website: www.bombardier.com

Correspondent: Alan McKnight, Corporate Community Involvement Manager 028 9073 3538

| Year end | Turnover | Pre-tax profit |
|---|---|---|
| 31/01/2006 | £470,217,440 | £40,893,940 |

**Nature of company business**
The principal activities of the company are the design, development and manufacture of aircraft components and the provision of related products and services.

Main locations: Belfast

Total employees: 5,358

### Charitable donations

2005: £214,835

Membership: A & B, BitC

## Community involvement

As a founding member of the Northern Ireland PerCent Club, Bombardier Aerospace is an active participant in the economic, cultural and social development of the communities in which it operates. It strives to achieve this through a number of means:

- encouraging and enabling employees to become involved in volunteering and fundraising
- supporting cross-community, educational and other community investment initiatives
- match funding for donations from the Employees Charities Society.

It would seem that company donations are made to the Bombardier Aerospace (NI) Foundation which then allocates the funding and match funds donations made by the Employees Charities Society. We do not have specific details of the organisations benefiting from the Foundation.

Bombardier is a member of Business in the Community's Opportunity Now campaign and works to ensure inclusiveness and equality for women in the workplace.

As part of its community outreach, and as a direct result of the West Belfast/Greater Shankill Task Force recommendations, Bombardier plays a major role in the Employers' Forum, aimed at addressing long-term unemployment in those areas. In conjunction with Belfast Institute for Further and Higher Education and community training organisations the company established a 19 week training programme to provide long-term unemployed people with foundation engineering skills. More than 90% of those who have completed the programme have gained full-time employment in local companies.

To date, the Employers' Forum, which is funded by the Foundation, has helped 190 formerly long-term unemployed individuals into employment across the Greater Belfast area.

### Exclusions

No support for projects outside Northern Ireland, individuals, travel, sports, arts, well-funded national organisations, large medical charities, capital projects, projects normally funded by statutory bodies, third party fundraising, i.e. advertising in charity programmes or at charitable social events.

### Applications

By completion of an application form which should be requested either by telephone or in writing to the correspondent.

## Corporate giving

The Directors' Report for 2005/06 states that the group made donations for charitable purposes totalling $386,140 (£214,835).

Bombardier Aerospace meets Business in the Community's PerCent Standard by committing to invest 1% or more of its pre-tax profit in the community, focusing on projects relating to education, economic development/community regeneration, equal opportunities, environment and employee volunteering. It would appear that the 1% of pre-tax profits is allocated to the Bombardier Aerospace Shorts Foundation for the purposes outlined above.

### In-kind support

The company provides materials for employee led community projects.

### Employee-led support

Bombardier employees and apprentices are actively encouraged to fundraise for charity and to take on volunteering projects. From running marathons to building playgrounds, thousands have benefited from donations and time given by employees.

Supported by the company, employee volunteers have organised a Charities Society in which deductions from salary for charitable donations can be made, where requested by an employee. The Employees' Charities Society meets quarterly to decide which registered charities to support through such contributions. The foundation matches pound for pound donations to charities approved by the society.

### Commercially-led support

**Sponsorship:** The foundation has forged close links with all levels of education in Northern Ireland. Bombardier has sponsored a chair in aerospace engineering at Queen's University of Belfast and has supported other projects at local universities. The company has also undertaken good-cause sponsorship.

# Robert Bosch Limited

Communications (RBGB/COM), Broadwater Park, Denham, Uxbridge, Middlesex UB9 5HJ

01895 834 466

Website: www.bosch.co.uk

Correspondent: Communications

| Year end | Turnover | Pre-tax profit |
|---|---|---|
| 31/12/2005 | £1,380,000,000 | |

**Nature of company business**
Bosch is a leading global manufacturer of automotive and industrial technology, consumer goods and building technology.

**Main locations:** Denham, St Neots, Worcester, Stowmarket, Milton Keynes

**UK employees:** 4,920

## Community involvement

The Bosch Group in the UK is a subsidiary of Robert Bosch GmbH. The group is made up of a number of organisations, each of which has a separate responsibility for supporting their local communities.

There is a charitable foundation in Germany – The Robert Bosch Foundation – which we were advised considers appropriate applications from the UK. A website exists (www.bosch-stiftung.de) but, not in English!

### Exclusions

No support for local appeals not in areas of company presence.

### Applications

Due to the non-centralised nature of support, please refer to your nearest Bosch facility.

## Corporate giving

The company stated that it regularly provides support to charitable projects and local community groups within its catchment area. Support can be either in the form of cash donations or in kind. Cash donations vary in size, with decisions made on merit.

Bosch declined to provide any figures quantifying its level of support, as they prefer 'not to seek any recognition for this'.

### In-kind support

In-kind support can include the provision of products, e.g. power tools, for raffle prizes.

### Employee-led support

Employees are encouraged to undertake voluntary work and fundraising activities. The company matches employee fundraising up to a maximum of £100.

# bp plc

1 St James's Square, London SW1Y 4PD

020 7496 4000; Fax: 020 7920 8263

Website: www.bp.com

Correspondent: Manager of Social & Global Investment

Chief officer: Peter D Sutherland

Chief Executive: The Lord Brown of Madingley

| Year end | Turnover | Pre-tax profit |
|---|---|---|
| 31/12/2005 | £141,000,000,000 | £17,543,829,000 |

**Nature of company business**
The group's principal activities comprise of exploration and production of crude oil and natural gas; refining, marketing, supply and transportation; and the manufacturing and marketing of petrochemicals. BP has major operations in Europe, North and South America, Asia, Australasia and parts of Africa.

**Subsidiaries include:** Britoil, Burmah Castrol

**Main locations:** London

**Total employees:** 96,200

---

**Charitable donations**

2005: £439,700

Membership: A & B, BitC

---

## Community involvement

### Education

The company states: 'We believe that a more educated society is a more sustainable society, so naturally we treat education as a priority. Since 1968, our UK Schools Link programme has put members of staff into primary and secondary schools to support subjects such as energy, environment, leadership and business skills. Our BP Educational Service provides exciting, energy-related teaching resources for the UK primary and secondary education curricula.

'We also take education out of the classroom. With sponsorship and practical support from our energy experts, we helped to produce a new gallery at London's Science Museum. It helps young people explore the different ways in which energy powers every aspect of our lives – and encourages them to think about how we can all play a part in meeting the planet's growing energy demands in the years ahead.

'Some of the capital's most celebrated cultural institutions depend on BP for sponsorship and support. The BP Portrait Award at the National Portrait Gallery, free outdoor screenings of Royal Opera House productions and award-winning exhibitions at the British Museum are all part of our commitment to a vibrant society.'

### Arts and Culture

'We believe that, wherever we operate, our activities should generate economic benefits and opportunities for an enhanced quality of life for those affected by our business. Our Arts and Culture programme is a key aspect of an overall commitment to the community in London and the city's most outstanding arts and cultural institutions.'

### Applications

In writing to the correspondent.

## Corporate giving

In 2005, the company's total community contributions in the UK amounted to $79.7 million, [£43,803,200] of which $0.8 million [£439,700] was made in cash donations to UK charities. Two areas supported in the UK by BP are:

**Education:** BP supports a range of educational activities, from primary and secondary schooling through to higher education and workplace learning.

The company's main educational activity for UK schools and colleges is the BP Schools Link Scheme. This supports the partnership between members of the workforce and teachers to enhance the education of young people both in and out of the classroom. The objectives of the scheme are to:

⬧ enhance the education of young people in the communities where BP operates

- provide opportunities for BP employees to get involved in the community
- enhance the reputation of BP
- provide BP with a vehicle for listening to local communities
- increase local understanding of BP – including policies on health, safety and environment, communication and business philosophy.

Contact details for local Schools Link coordinators are listed on the website, along with various web-based educational resources.

Through BP Educational Services, which has worked closely with practicing teachers and experts for nearly 40 years, BP produce and distribute educational resource packs about the company and its industry. For further information see the company's website.

## Employee-led support

The following extract is taken from the company's website: 'We do encourage our employees to become involved in community and charitable activities and we support their contributions through our BP Employee Matching Fund. As a result of this employee match-giving programme, charitable organisations in the UK benefited from more than US$6 million [£3,275,000] and over 34,000 hours of volunteering time in 2004.' BP employees choose to support charitable activities. We also wish to play our part and believe the best way to support charitable causes chosen by our employees is to provide matched giving.

'Any BP employee can apply for up to $5,000 a year of matched giving through the BP Employee Matching Fund. The BP Employee Matching Fund enables personal donations, volunteer time or funds raised by employees to be matched by BP. In 2005 BP employees gave around $9.6 million to charitable organizations worldwide, including funds raised for humanitarian relief. BP provided matching grants totalling around $9.8 million to these charities.'

## Commercially-led support

**Sponsorship:** *The arts* – BP states that it focuses its support on providing 'Access to Arts & Culture', access to opportunities, performances, or art that would otherwise not be exhibited and thus reach new and wider audiences.

BP has a number of partnerships within the field of arts and culture including those with British Museum, Royal Opera House, National Portrait Gallery, Tate Britain, National Theatre, Almeida Theatre and The National Art Collections Fund.

An example of benefit to the arts world is the BP Summer Big Screen series, which is 'an exciting programme of live outdoor screenings of Royal Opera and Royal Ballet evening performances. These performances are relayed onto huge screens in the Covent Garden Piazza and other locations across the UK, where thousands of people are able to enjoy for free some of the Royal Opera House's best loved repertory performed by world famous artists. This is now a major strand of the Royal Opera House's growing education, outreach and access programme which concentrates on providing accessible, low cost opportunities for people to experience opera and ballet, often for the first time'.

One of BP's major sponsorship programmes is the Energy Gallery at The Science Museum in London. Supported by BP Education it aims to give young people a better understanding of what energy is and the issues surrounding it.

'During 2005, BP worked with The Eden Project, an environmental education charity and visitor attraction in Cornwall, UK, to find out what would motivate consumers to reduce and offset the GHG emissions generated by their vehicles. We announced an $8-million project at Imperial College, London, to research the use of energy in cities.

'With sponsorship and practical support from BP energy experts, Energy – fuelling the future, a recent gallery at London's Science Museum, helps young people explore the different ways in which energy powers every aspect of our lives – and encourages them to think about how we can all play a part in meeting the planet's growing energy demands in the years ahead.'

# BPB

Sefton Park, Stoke Poges, Slough SL2 4JS

01753 668 800; Fax: 01753 668 888

Website: www.bpb.com

Correspondent: Robert Heard, Group Secretary

Chief officer: Sir Ian Gibson

Chief Executive: Richard Cousins

| Year end | Turnover | Pre-tax profit |
|---|---|---|
| 31/03/2005 | £2,316,800,000 | £258,700,000 |

**Nature of company business**
The principal activities of the company are making gypsum products, and supplying plasters and plasterboard; and with investments in the manufacture of complementary building materials and paperboard products.

**Subsidiaries include:** British Gypsum Ltd, Artex-Rawplug Ltd, Commatone Ltd

**Main locations:** Loughborough, Newark, Ruddington, Slough

Total employees: 12,689

### Charitable donations
2005: £216,500
2004: £128,000
2003: £159,000

## Community involvement

BPB only gives to registered charities. A very limited number of grants are available to local charities close to group operations.

### Exclusions

No support for non-charities, overseas projects, sponsorship or local appeals not in areas of company presence.

### Applications

In writing to the correspondent.

## Corporate giving

In 2004/05, the company's charitable donations amounted to £216,500 (2004: £128,000) including support for organisations providing shelter for the homeless and low-cost accommodation for young people linked to skills training and job opportunities.

## Employee-led support

The company reports that it encourages the involvement of its employees in local community projects, but does not state what form this takes.

# Bradford & Bingley

Bradford & Bingley plc, PO Box 88, Croft Road, Crossflatts, Bingley, BD16 2UA

01274 555555

Website: www.bbg.co.uk

Correspondent: Michael Hammond, Community Affairs Manager 0121 633 8143; Fax: 0121 643 6396
E-mail: community.affairs@bbg.co.uk

Chief officer: Rod Kent

| Year end | Turnover | Pre-tax profit |
|---|---|---|
| 31/12/2005 | | £263,500,000 |

Nature of company business
Building society. Its main activities include: lending money towards residential and commercial property and offering a range of retail savings services; operating as an independent retailer of mortgage, investment, and insurance products; offering residential estate agency and selected other property related services.

Subsidiaries include: Mortgage Express, The MarketPlace

Main locations: Birmingham

Total employees: 3,000

### Charitable donations

2005: £443,250
2004: £876,933
2003: £732,637

Total community contributions: £1,320,612

Membership: A & B, BitC, L B Group, %Club

## Community involvement

Preventing and alleviating the causes of homelessness continues to be our main corporate area of support. However, in 2005 a larger focus was given to the support of charities and organisations throughout West Yorkshire, specifically in Bradford and the Aire Valley where the Head Office is based.

### Exclusions

No support for advertising in charity brochures, animal welfare, appeals from individuals, medical research, overseas projects, political appeals, religious appeals, or science/technology.

### Applications

In writing to the correspondent. Please ensure that your application falls into one of the areas Bradford & Bingley supports. Unfortunately, applications outside of those areas will not be considered. They are also unable to support individual requests for sponsorship even if the charity being fundraised for falls into its areas of support.

Applications are accepted by post or e-mail, and Bradford & Bingley are happy to have an initial discussion on the telephone if you are uncertain if your project is eligible for an application.

Although there is no specific application form, please include in your proposal specific details of the project you are requesting support for, costings and any publicity opportunities associated with your project.

Please do not send valuable documents or any artwork with your initial application as they will request these at a later date, if proceeding with your application. Applications are normally replied to within 21 days.

## Corporate giving

During 2005 the group allocated £1,320,612 to its programme of community investment, including payments to charitable organisations of £443,250.

### In-kind support

This included secondments, gifts in kind and support for a school reading scheme.

### Employee-led support

The company has established a charity matching scheme under which staff fundraising efforts for a charity of their choice are matched pound for pound up to £250. During 2005, 85 employees received matching totalling £19,151. Staff Give As You Earn payments are also matched (£74,628 of employee donations were matched in the year). A target to have 10% of the workforce donating via this method was set for 2006.

The company teamed up with Shelter and provided 70 runners for the London Marathon, which raised over £150,000.

Staff are supported who are involved as school governors.

### Commercially-led support

**Cause-related marketing:** For every new FirstSave and SmartSave account opened, Bradford & Bingley made a £1 donation to the Wallace & Gromit's Children's Foundation. In 2005 over £11,000 was donated. In addition, the branch network sold a range of pin badges provided by the foundation which raised a further £27,700.

**Sponsorship:** Support is given to the National Museum of Photography, Film & Television in Bradford. Community and grass roots support is given sports organisations including Bradford Bulls.

# Bristol & West plc

PO Box 27, Temple Quay, Bristol BS99 7AX

0117 979 2222; Fax: 0117 929 3787

Website: www.bristol-west.co.uk

Correspondent: Kelly Cutler, Corporate Responsibility Officer
E-mail: kelly.cutler@bristol-west.co.uk

Chief officer: Brain J Goggin

| Year end | Turnover | Pre-tax profit |
|---|---|---|
| 31/03/2006 | £1,051,000,000 | £94,500,000 |

Nature of company business
The company provides a range of financial services. It is now part of the Bank of Ireland.

Main locations: Bristol

UK employees: 1,662

---

### Charitable donations

2006: £106,596
2005: £105,347
2004: £179,156
2003: £89,583

---

## Community involvement

As the Bristol & West Building Society, the company's annual report fully disclosed its charitable donations by providing a full list of grant recipients. Following the merger with the Bank of Ireland, however, this is no longer the case and the donations policy of the company may well have changed. The only comment in the 2006 annual report was that charitable donations went to a wide range of beneficiaries.

### Exclusions

No support is given to appeals from individuals, purely denominational (religious) appeals, overseas projects or for advertising in charity brochures.

### Applications

In writing to the correspondent.

## Corporate giving

**Quartet Community Foundation (Charity Commission no. 1080418) (formerly Greater Bristol Foundation)**

Support is given to a variety of charities through its charitable fund, which is administered by quartet Community Foundation.

Applications are welcomed from projects in the south west of England (website: www.gbf.org.uk).

During 2006 the group made charitable donations of £106,596 (2005: £105,347).

## Employee-led support

**Payroll giving:** The Give As You Earn scheme is operated.

In 2005/06 the company's employees raised over £103,000 for their chosen 'Charity of the Year' – Childline.

Staff have voted for two charities for 2006/2007 – The Association of Children's Hospices (ACH) and Starlight Children's Foundation. 'The Association of Children's Hospices support children and young people who are expected to die before, or shortly after, reaching adulthood. Through the provision of help at home, or in a purpose built building, highly trained staff help the children and their whole family with the medical and emotional challenges that having a life-limiting or life threatening illness or condition brings, and help them to make the most of life.

'Starlight is a children's foundation that brightens the lives of seriously and terminally ill children by granting their wishes and providing hospital entertainment to help take their minds off the pain, fear and isolation caused by their illness. When Starlight began in 1987, they helped just 4 children; this year, they will help over 500,000 children all over the UK including Northern Ireland. Where possible, mums, dads, brothers and sisters are involved to strengthen family bonds at what is often a time of great stress, and give everyone happy memories to share, no matter what the future may hold.'

## Commercially-led support

Support is given to CLIC (Cancer and Leukaemia in Childhood). Bristol and West also run two savings accounts (CLIC Direct and CLIC Kids) which generate funds for the charity. Savings accounts are also offered supporting Bristol City Football Club, Bristol Rovers Football Club and Bristol Shoguns Rugby Club.

---

# Bristol-Myers Squibb Pharmaceuticals Limited

BMS House, Uxbridge Business Park, Sanderson Road, Uxbridge UB8 1DH

01895 5230000; Fax: 01895 523010

Website: www.b-ms.co.uk/

Correspondent: Facilities Manager

| Year end | Turnover | Pre-tax profit |
|---|---|---|
| 31/12/2003 | £174,423,000 | £15,962,000 |

**Nature of company business**
Pharmaceutical and health care company.

**Subsidiaries include:** ConvaTec Limited

**Main locations:** Moreton, Rhymney, Deeside, Uxbridge, Chester, Ickenham

UK employees: 2,000

## Community involvement

'Bristol-Myers Squibb's mission is to extend and enhance human life. To help achieve that mission, Bristol-Myers Squibb has established a grants and charitable contributions programme to support medical, educational, and treatment-related philanthropic initiatives.

'Grants may be available to support medical education programs, scientific conferences, development of health care publications and other educational and scientific activities. Grants may also be available to support programs involving patient education and community-related activities, such as health fairs and screening programmes. Grants may be awarded for the funding of specific projects or activities, or a series of programmes that occur over a specified period of time.'

Funding is also available to research institutions in the UK through the Unrestricted Biomedical Research Grants Programme, which is concerned with medical research into nutrition, neuro-science, metabolism, infectious diseases, cardiovascular illness or cancer.

Locally, grants may also be given for community projects around the company's main sites, which are in Chester, Deeside, Ickenham, Moreton (Wirral), Rhymney and Uxbridge.

### Exclusions

Bristol-Myers Squibb does not make grants in support of non-scientific or non-educational programs.

No support for individuals, political appeals, religious appeals, local appeals not in areas of company presence, fundraising events or advertising in charity brochures

## Applications

In writing to the correspondent.

## Corporate giving

No current information regarding the size of Bristol-Myers Squibb's community investment budget was available. However, given the global nature of the company and the existence of a philanthropic foundation, it is fair to assume that it qualifies for inclusion here.

## In-kind support

Products are only donated for disaster relief purposes.

## Employee-led support

Employees are encouraged to support their local communities.

In January 2005 the Moreton facility was named overall winners of the Wirral Investment Network Making a Difference Award 2005. The Making a Difference Award recognises companies that have demonstrated excellent support for their local communities in areas of health, education, charities, volunteer groups and community engagement. Bristol-Myers Squibb was selected because of its outstanding civic involvement through encouragement of employee volunteerism and a clear strategy between philanthropic donations and the development of ongoing community relationships.

## Commercially-led support

**Sponsorship:** *Health education* – Bristol-Myers Squibb sponsors 'One Vision', a European photographic competition which encourage new and positive ways of looking at the life of people with HIV and AIDS. Through this competition, Bristol-Myers Squibb also contributes essential funds to community HIV and AIDS groups, including UK organisations.

# Britannia Building Society

Britannia House, Leek, Staffordshire ST13 5RG

01538 399399; Fax: 01538 393337

Website: www.britannia.co.uk

Correspondent: Christine Massey, Secretary to the Trusttees
E-mail: christine.massey@britannia.co.uk

Chief officer: Ian Adam

Chief Executive: Neville Richardson

| Year end | Turnover | Pre-tax profit |
|---|---|---|
| 31/12/2005 | | £120,500,000 |

Nature of company business
Building society.

Subsidiaries include: Mortgage Agency Services Ltd, Western Mortgage Services Ltd, Verso Ltd

Main locations: Leek

UK employees: 2,339

---

### Charitable donations

2005: £558,000
2003: £500,000

Membership: BitC

## Community involvement

The society makes the majority of its donations through the Britannia Building Society Foundation (Charity Commission no. 1069081) which supports projects that address issues such as homelessness, education, debt and community safety, together with encouraging prudent money management and improving money advice services.

Support is only given to organisations within 25 miles of Leek, where the society is based, in the counties of Staffordshire, Cheshire and Derbyshire. This area covers the city of Stoke on Trent, and the towns of Stafford, Stone, Uttoxeter, Ashbourne, Buxton, Macclesfield, Congleton and Crewe and the rural communities between.

Every two years, Britannia employees nominate a charity to raise money for. In 2006 the charity was CLIC Sargent.

### Exclusions

Generally no support for circular appeals, advertising in charity brochures, fundraising events, medical research, overseas projects, political appeals, religious appeals, sport, or local appeals not in areas of company presence.

### Applications

Applications to the foundation should be made on a form available form Christine Massey, Secretary at the above address. Before making an application, a copy of the grants and donations policy should be obtained from the foundation to check eligibility. The trustees meet quarterly.

## Corporate giving

**Britannia Building Society Foundation:** The foundation was set up by the society in 1997 and receives a cash donation from the society of £300,000 a year.

Grants range from £250 to £25,000, with preference for specific items and not for large appeals. Capital projects and running costs will be supported, however – there are limited funds for this type of application. Grants for running costs will normally be restricted to three years, with a maximum of five years. Any non-profit organisation can be supported and applicants need not be registered charities, so long as a registered organisation is supporting them and will accept the grant on their behalf.

### In-kind support

**The Community Fund:** supports non-profit events and voluntary groups. It is primarily used to make one-off, smaller value donations of equipment or help in kind to projects that will be of direct and immediate benefit to Britannia's home communities.

### Employee-led support

The company is involved with a national volunteering scheme, Number Partners that brings together business volunteers and schools.

**Payroll giving:** The company operates the Give As You Earn scheme.

## Commercially-led support

**Sponsorship:** *The arts* – The society supports the arts and recently entered into a ten-year agreement with the Regent Theatre in Hanley, Stoke-on-Trent.

# British Airways plc

Waterside (HBBG), PO Box 365, Harmondsworth, Middlesex UB7 0GB

0845 779 9977

Website: www.ba.com

Correspondent: Community Relations Department

Chief officer: Martin Broughton

Chief Executive: Willie Walsh

| Year end | Turnover | Pre-tax profit |
| --- | --- | --- |
| 31/03/2006 | £8,515,000,000 | £620,000,000 |

**Nature of company business**
Principal activities: the operation of international and domestic scheduled and charter air services for the carriage of passengers, freight and mail and the provision of ancillary airline and travel services.

**Subsidiaries include:** Air Miles Travel Promotions Ltd, CityFlyer Express Ltd, Travel Automation Services Ltd, The Plimsoll Line Ltd, Go Fly Ltd

**Main locations:** Harmondsworth

**Total employees:** 47,012

### Charitable donations

2006: £898,081
2005: £830,000
2004: £396,398
2003: £237,804

Total community contributions: £5,430,000 (global)
Management costs: £100,000

Membership: A & B, BitC, L B Group, %Club

## Community involvement

British Airways Community Relations department is responsible for all community investment activity in the UK and abroad. The community investment programme is closely aligned to the company's business priorities and focuses on five main areas: Education and youth development; sustainable tourism; environment; heritage; and the support of staff.

Support is concentrated on appeals in areas in which the company operates and which provide the opportunity for substantial staff involvement. Other causes may be supported if they fit within the priorities listed above.

### Exclusions

No support for appeals from individuals, political appeals or religious appeals. Advertising in charity brochures is rarely undertaken.

### Applications

In writing to the Community Relations Department. However, please note that the company states it does not wish to generate a significant number of additional requests as most resources are already allocated to long-term sustainable projects within the established programme.

## Corporate giving

In 2005/06, the company's total community contributions worldwide were £5.4 million of which cash donations direct to charitable causes totalled £898,081. It is not clear whether the charitable donations were restricted to the UK or worldwide.

In December 2005 the company held two Community and Conservation Days. Around 70 employee-supported charities attended. The company presented staff volunteers with cash awards for charity projects which totalled £55,000.

Through the British Airways Environmental Awards Scheme, 27 schools in London received financial support and expertise from the airline to create wildlife gardens and re-cycling projects. The grants totalled £60,000.

### In-kind support

A highlight of the company's support for education and youth development is its Community Learning Centre. This showcases how British Airway's uses IT, language, customer service, design and branding skills, and has programmes linked directly to the school curriculum. Support has been given to groups such as women returning to work, although the centre is open to people of all ages. In 2005/06 the company developed an on-line heritage programme for schools which takes pupils through the history and development of the airline. There were also themed weeks for local schools involving activities linked to citizenship, geography and education for sustainable development. An example of this was 'China Week', when the centre was transformed into a Chinese landscape. It involved ten year old students from a local school in Hounslow in environment workshops where they learned about the endangered giant panda, the importance of bamboo and some basic language.

Computer Clubs for Girls (CC4G) has been set up to address the issue of the low number of girls taking IT as a career choice. These are out of hours clubs set up within schools, where the girls are able to learn new skills using IT applications and tools such as digital photography, graphic design, sound recording and editing. All the courseware and activities are set in themes such as dance, music, fashion, games and sport. Employers are encouraged to engage in this initiative by allowing employees who are IT professionals to volunteer to partner a CC4G school. There is at present 12 BA staff volunteering for this initiative.

British Airway's continues to support the UNICEF Change for Good programme and has raised over £21 million through passenger and staff donations. During the year more than 50 projects were supported by these donations.

### Employee-led support

Numerous charities are supported by employee fundraising, including causes run by the staff themselves, such as Happy Child and Dreamflight, for underprivileged and sick children. The company operates an employee volunteering scheme. Other support for staff involvement includes tickets to assist employees supporting overseas projects, merchandise for raffles and consultancy support to staff charities.

Over the past three years over £230,000 has been awarded to charities supported by staff in their volunteering activities through the 'Community Volunteering Awards'.

**Payroll giving:** The British Airways Giving Scheme was launched in December 2003.

# British American Tobacco plc

Globe House, 4 Temple Place, London WC2R 2PG

020 7845 1000; Fax: 020 7240 0555

Website: www.bat.com

Correspondent: Jennie Gibbons, UK Social Reporting Mananger

Chief officer: Jan du Plessis

Managing Director: Paul N Adams

| Year end | Turnover | Pre-tax profit |
|---|---|---|
| 31/12/2005 | £23,984,000,000 | £2,588,000,000 |

Nature of company business
Principal activities: the manufacture, market and sale of cigarettes and other tobacco products.

Subsidiaries include: Rothmans Finance plc, Tobacco Insurance Co Ltd, Weston Investment Co Ltd, Rothmans International Tobacco (UK) Ltd

Main locations: Corby, Darlington, London, Southampton, Aylesbury

Total employees: 55,000

### Charitable donations

2005: £3,500,000
2003: £2,400,000

Total community contributions: £15,200,000 (global)

Membership: BitC, L B Group, %Club

## Community involvement

Generally speaking the group's community and charitable activities involve the environment, employment and education, arts and cultural activities, disaster relief and primary healthcare.

In the UK, the focus is currently on the environment, tertiary education and the arts. A response is also made to natural disasters in conjunction with the group company concerned.

### Exclusions

No support for causes outside the company's areas of focus.

### Applications

In writing to the correspondent.

**Information available:** The company produce a social responsibility report which can be downloaded from its website.

## Corporate giving

In 2005, total community contributions amounted to £15,200,000 worldwide. Charitable donations in the UK accounted for £3,500,000. One of the beneficiaries was the British American Tobacco Biodiversity Partnership, which received £1,000,000 each year between 2001 and 2005. For the five-year period 2006 to 2010, the partnership will receive £1,500,000 each year.

# British Energy Group plc

Systems House, Alba Campus, Livingston EH54 7EG

01506 408700; Fax: 01506 408888

Website: www.british-energy.com

Chief officer: Adrian Montague

Chief Executive: Bill Coley

| Year end | Turnover | Pre-tax profit |
|---|---|---|
| 31/03/2006 | £2,593,000,000 | £599,000,000 |

Nature of company business
The group's principal activity is the generation and sale of electricity.

Main locations: Bridgwater, Leiston, Hunterston, Heysham, Hartlepool, Eggborough, East Kilbride, Dungeness, Torness, Barnwood

UK employees: 5,500

### Charitable donations

2006: £178,864
2005: £58,583
2004: £93,535
2003: £43,512

Membership: BitC

## Community involvement

The company states in its annual report that it continues to work with a number of charities on a local basis, with employees nominating potential charities to be chosen as British Energy's charity of the year (see below).

Individual power stations operate community programmes and sponsorships on behalf of local good causes.

The company is a member of Scottish Business in the Community.

**Charity of the Year:** Help the Hospices (2006/07).

### Exclusions

No support for circular appeals, fundraising events, appeals from individuals, purely denominational (religious) appeals or local appeals not in areas of company presence.

### Applications

Applications should be addressed to: Julie Bennett, PR Services Manager, British Energy, Barnett Way, Barnwood, Gloucester GL4 3RS.

## Corporate giving

In 2006, the company made cash donations totalling £178,864 (2005: £58,583). The majority of this went to the 2005/06 'Charity of the Year' – The Prince's Trust – on behalf of which £350,000 was raised.

### Charity of the Year

To be considered for British Energy's charity of the year, the criteria charities need to meet are that they are:

▶ a national charity with a strong presence in both Scotland and England

▶ a charity that contributes to community life and can work with the company at a local level

▶ a charity that has the creativity and enthusiasm to maintain fundraising

▶ a charity that celebrates the company's values of safety, openness, and respect and recognition.

Selection for the next charity of the year will begin in spring 2007.

## In-kind support

The company provides in kind support by, for example, using landfill tax credits to fund refurbishment of nature reserves within the vicinity of its power stations.

## Employee-led support

The company has promised to match funds raised by staff on behalf of their chosen charity of the year up to a maximum of £100,000.

**Payroll giving:** The company operates a scheme.

## Commercially-led support

**Sponsorship:** Arts and good-cause sponsorship are undertaken. Past examples include Edinburgh's Christmas Lights, St Andrew's Ambulance organisation's mobile first-aid unit for major events, children's fire safety and library learning projects around the country, Suffolk Police's air support and traffic accident helicopter, the UK Scouts PR badge and Northern Ballet's innovative theatrical programme.

British Energy has recently provided a £10,000 mentoring sponsorship and practical support to Leiston High School in Suffolk, to help it develop an engineering course.

# British Land Company plc

10 Cornwall Terrace, Regent's Park, London NW1 4QP

020 7486 4466; Fax: 020 7935 5552

Website: www.britishland.com

Correspondent: Claudine Blarney, Corporate Responsibility Executive 020 7486 4466; Fax: 020 7467 2869
E-mail: claudine.blarney@britishland.com

Chief officer: Sir John Ritblat

Chief Executive: Stephen Hester

| Year end | Turnover | Pre-tax profit |
|---|---|---|
| 31/03/2006 | | £1,590,000,000 |

Nature of company business
Property investment and development, finance and investment.

Subsidiaries include: London & Henley Ltd, 135 Bishopsgate Financing, Union Property Corporation Ltd, Broadgate Property Holdings Ltd, Exchange House Holdings Ltd, Derby Investment Holdings Ltd, Sealhurst Properties Ltd, Peacocks Centre Ltd, Adamant Investment Corporation Ltd, MSC Funding Ltd, Meadowhall Shoping Centre Ltd

Main locations: London

UK employees: 718

Total employees: 718

## Community involvement

The company states that: 'British Land builds constructive relationships with the communities in which it operates. It does this by supporting selected local initiatives through staff volunteering, skills mentoring and financial assistance. Larger national programmes may also be supported where they benefit communities neighbouring British Land's investments.

'British Land is strongly committed to investing in the future by providing facilities for young people and children through sponsorship of the arts, sport and education, and funding and fostering support for improvement of the environment.'

The company supports Arts & Business, Business in the Community and the Carbon Trust.

### Exclusions

The company will not provide support for political purposes.

### Applications

In writing to the correspondent.

**Information available:** The company's 2005 Corporate Social Responsibility Report is online.

## Corporate giving

In 2005/06, the company made cash donations totalling £67,640 (2004: £92,467).

Particular support was given to charities involving young people, especially in activity based projects. This included £50,000 donated to the National Literacy Trust's 'Reading is Fundamental' initiative, and £10,000 to the Capital Kids Cricket programme.

### In-kind support

'British Land is partnering with the East London Business Alliance to help find job opportunities for long-term unemployed people in East London. The Company is investigating work placements and apprenticeship opportunities at Broadgate and in British Land developments.

'The Company wants to increase the scale of this activity, and is working with the charitable housing association London & Quadrant to encourage all construction contractors to achieve a set percentage of apprentices in their workforce.

'British Land's property managers at Meadowhall in Sheffield are investigating a community support policy for the shopping centre. In 2006, British Land aims to partner Barclays Sitesavers and the local council in funding a multi-use games park in the disadvantaged area of Thorntree, Middlesbrough, near the company's Teesside Shopping Park. The games park will have playing areas, an assault course and tree planting.'

### Employee-led support

'British Land staff, working through the Education Business Partnership in Camden London, NW1, provide reading support to children at Netley Primary School. 20 employees are taking part in the scheme, with teams of readers visiting the school every week. This activity dovetails with the Company's commitment to reading being a fundamental skill for all children.

At head office, a Corporate Responsibility Award Scheme exists for all British Land employees. The award scheme encourages employees to become involved in local activities, projects and events, such as sports for children and wildlife projects with local schools.

## Commercially-led support

**Sponsorship:** British Land undertakes extensive sponsorship of organisations involved in arts, education and sport. Below are some examples:

*The arts* – The company is a founding exhibition patron of The Royal Academy of Arts. Support has also been given to the British Museum, The Royal Ballet School, the Royal Opera House, English National Opera, the National Theatre, Wigmore Hall, National Gallery of Scotland, and the Regent's Park Open Air Theatre.

*Education* – British Land is an active supporter of the Architecture Foundation and the London Biennial. It also supports a project, working with architects and students at South Camden Community School, to prepare a plan to improve the pedestrian close to Warren Street Underground Station. The results will be displayed at an exhibition at the British Library.

*Sport* – British Land has been the sole sponsor of The British Land National Ski Championships for 28 years and also supports The British Land Alpine Ski Team.

# British Nuclear Fuels plc

H440, Hinton House, Risley, Warrington, Cheshire WA3 6AS

01925 832000; Fax: 01925 822711

Website: www.bnfl.com

Correspondent: Robert Jarvis, Head of Corporate Community Involvement

Chief officer: Gordon Campbell

Chief Executive: Michael Parker

| Year end | Turnover | Pre-tax profit |
|---|---|---|
| 31/03/2006 | £1,417,000,000 | £4,520,000,000 |

### Nature of company business
The principal activity is expertise across the whole range of the nuclear fuel business.

**Subsidiaries include:** International Nuclear Fuels Ltd, Deva Manufacturing Services Ltd, Magnox Electric plc, Direct Rail Services Ltd

**Main locations:** Bradwell, Calder Hall, Berkeley, Trasfyndd, Maentwrog, London, Oldbury, Wylfa, Dungeness, Risley, Sizewell, Sellafield, Hinkley Point, Hunterston, Littlebrook, Capenhurst, Chapelcross, Daresbury

UK employees: 13,093

Total employees: 22,287

## Charitable donations

2006: £2,900,000
2005: £3,100,000
2004: £3,300,000
2003: £3,200,000

Total community contributions: £4,380,308

Membership: A & B, BitC, L B Group, %Club

## Community involvement

The company states on its website that: 'Our community programme aims to be mutually beneficial for the communities in which we operate and our employees. We support areas most in need of our help – taking action now to improve the quality of life in the future. Our initiatives cover environmental, economic and social issues such as:

▸ health, drugs, the elderly and the disabled

▸ social exclusion, crime prevention, the homeless and the disadvantaged

▸ environmental restoration

▸ regeneration

▸ arts, music and sport.

'In line with our overall policy and the Government's initiative to reduce social exclusion, our charitable support strategy is mainly centred on areas of deprivation and social exclusion.'

BNFL are also committed to supporting and developing its education programme at local, national and international levels, actively encouraging an interest in science and technology at all ages.

**Charity of the Year:** Some of the company's sites choose a charity of the year for which to raise money.

### Exclusions
No support for circular appeals, large national appeals (except North West based), small purely local appeals not in areas of company presence, advertising in charity brochures, animal welfare charities, medical research, overseas projects, political appeals, or religious appeals.

### Applications
In writing either to the correspondent above, or to the general manager of the nearest factory. A donations committee meets monthly.

## Corporate giving

In 2005/06, the company made total community contributions of £4.38 million of which £2.9 million was in cash donations. Typical national grants range from £100 to £15,000. Local grants range from £25 to £1,000.

The contributions figure includes £2.1 million to support West Cumbrian economic regeneration initiatives. BNFL has given support for over ten years to the West Cumbria Development Fund as well as various development companies, investment and enterprise agencies.

£55,000 was given in community support around the Capenhurst site for initiatives including the refurbishment of the local village hall, repair work to the local parish church and the development of a youth shelter in a deprived area of Chester.

The company continues with its longstanding support for the work of The Prince's Trust in Cumbria.

## In-kind support

**Education:** BNFL is involved in schemes such as Teachers from Industry and courses run in the North West by businessdynamics. It provides educational materials for schools and work experience schemes for pupils and teachers. Some of the latest resources include: a suite of CD-ROMs developed for the teaching of maths, chemistry and physics.

You can visit the company's education website at: www.bnfleducation.com

## Employee-led support

Staff are encouraged to become volunteers in their own time. The company provides match funding for employee fundraising up to a maximum of £100 per employee.

**Payroll giving:** The Give As You Earn scheme is in operation.

## Commercially-led support

**Sponsorship:** *The arts* – Appeals for arts sponsorship are welcomed.

# British Sky Broadcasting Group plc

Grant Way, Isleworth, Middlesex TW7 5QD

020 7705 3000

Website: www.sky.com

Correspondent: The Head of Corporate Responsibility

E-mail: corp.responsibility@bskyb.com

Chief officer: Rupert Murdoch

Chief Executive: James Murdoch

| Year end | Turnover | Pre-tax profit |
|---|---|---|
| 30/06/2006 | £4,148,000,000 | £798,000,000 |

**Nature of company business**
The leading satellite pay television operator, BSkyB launched its digital television services in the UK on 1 October 1998 offering 300 channels including sport, news, films and general entertainment.

**Subsidiaries include:** BSkyB Finance Ltd, Sky Subscribers Services Ltd, Sky Ventures Ltd, Sky In-Home Service Ltd, Sky Television Ltd

**Main locations:** Livingstone, Dunfermline, Isleworth

**UK employees:** 11,216

### Charitable donations

2006: £3,825,000
2004: £1,050,061
2003: £678,000

Total community contributions: £5,071,350
Management costs: £30,000

Membership: A & B, BitC, L B Group, %Club

## Community involvement

The 2005/06 annual reports states: 'The Group continues to align its community investment activities to the wider goals of the business and its customers and utilises its brand, platform and technology in community investment. Current initiatives include Living for Sport; Make a Difference, the staff community involvement scheme; and the three year charity partnership with the Chicken Shed Theatre Company.'

Much of the community involvement is taken by its Reach for the Sky project which aims to increase the motivation of disaffected young people.

### Exclusions

No support for animal welfare charities, appeals from individuals, elderly people, environment/heritage, medical research, overseas projects, political or religious appeals.

### Applications

All formal requests for support must be made in writing. Funding decisions are made in two ways: nationally, the Head of Corporate Affairs and the Community Affairs Manager meet regularly to discuss proposals and requests; locally, each site has its own committee which decides on funding for local projects.

The company endeavours to respond in writing to every written request within 21 days of receipt.

## Corporate giving

In 2005/06 community contributions by the company totalled £5,101,350. This was broken down as follows:
- cash 75%
- in-kind 15%
- management costs 6%
- time 4%

The following areas were supported:
- young people 48%
- disability, community, broadcasting and other issues 30%
- art and culture 22%

### In-kind support

Non-cash support includes the provision of training, and scholarships for conferences run by the Media Trust.

BSkyB also provides free satellite space for the Community Channel, a resource available to all charities who wish to use digital television to raise funds and/or awareness.

**Education:** Schools local to BSkyB's main sites enjoy a close working relationship with the company, in particular, with regard to the development of curriculum resource material.

### Employee-led support

Employees are encouraged to take part in fundraising activities and are allowed two days paid leave in which to do so. They can also apply for match funding

**Payroll giving:** Employees can participate in a Give As You Earn scheme.

# British Sugar plc

Sugar Way, Peterborough, PE2 9AY

01733 563171; Fax: 01733 563068

Website: www.britishsugar.co.uk

Correspondent: John Smith, Charity Coordinator
E-mail: jbsmith@britishsugar.co.uk

Chief officer: G H Weston

Chief Executive: Mark Carr

| Year end | Turnover | Pre-tax profit |
|---|---|---|
| 13/09/2005 | | |

**Nature of company business**
British Sugar is a wholly-owned subsidiary of Associated British Foods (see separate entry). It operates from locations in East Anglia, the North East and the East and West Midlands (Bardney, Bury St Edmunds, Cantley, Newark, Peterborough, Telford and Wissington).

Main locations: Bardney, Telford, Wissington, Newark, Peterborough, Bury St Edmunds, Cantley

UK employees: 600

### Charitable donations
2005: £55,000
2004: £85,450

## Community involvement

We were advised in August 2006 that the company no longer makes charitable donations and, as such, should not be included in the guide.

Whilst it is true that the focus of the company's charitable support appears to have changed, the fact remains that it still has a charity budget administered by the British Sugar Foundation (Charity Commission no. 290966). We believe, therefore, its continued inclusion to be justified in order to help give a full picture of UK corporate community support, whilst accepting the need to make clear the restrictions that now exist for organisations seeking funding from the company/foundation.

Following a review of its charitable giving policy, the foundation, and by extension the company, allocates all of its charitable and sponsorship funds, including the cost of product donations, to its employee matching scheme. Confusingly, this is not fully reflected in the objectives stated in the foundation's 2005 annual report and accounts, although it does make reference to the 'Money Match' scheme. Furthermore, email contact links from the company's website under headings such as 'Charity' and 'Charity donations' imply that requests for donations outside of employees community activities will still be considered, despite having been told that they are not.

In general terms, support is focussed on the communities in which British Sugar plc operates. Of particular interest are local organisations involving health, education and the environment.

### Exclusions

General and national appeals are not supported. No support for circular appeals, advertising in charity brochures, animal welfare, appeals from individuals, the arts, enterprise/training, fundraising events, overseas projects, political appeals, religious appeals, science/technology or sport.

### Applications

In view of the fact that the company, through its foundation, no longer gives direct support to charities, speculative applications would seem pointless.

## Corporate giving

In 2004/05, the British Sugar Foundation had a total income of £62,399 of which £55,000 came from the company and £1,800 from the employees' payroll giving scheme. Charitable donations made during the period amounted to nearly £56,000. Beneficiaries included: British Heart Foundation (£6,971); Association of Children with ME (£4,158); Beaumond House (£3,000); Acle High School Association (£2,000); Blofield Pre-school Playgroup (£1,500); and, Medehamstede Explorer Scouts (£1,406).

### In-kind support

The company makes product donations.

### Employee-led support

Through its charitable foundation, the company makes every effort to encourage participation in community fundraising projects among its employees. It operates a 'Money Match' scheme, which effectively doubles the amount of money reaching the nominated charitable organisation.

**Payroll giving:** An employee scheme is operation (for which the foundation is the approved charity agency). In 2005, £1,800 was received from employees under the scheme.

# British Vita plc

Oldham Road, Middleton, Manchester M24 2DB

0161 643 1133; Fax: 0161 653 5411

Website: www.britishvita.com

Correspondent: Mrs Alison Vesey, Public Relations Manager
0161 655 2661
E-mail: avesey@britishvita.com

Chief Executive: Howard Harris

| Year end | Turnover | Pre-tax profit |
|---|---|---|
| 31/12/2004 | £959,000,000 | £52,600,000 |

**Nature of company business**
The manufacture and processing of polymers, including cellular foams, plastics and non-woven materials.

Subsidiaries include: Hyperlast Ltd, The Rossendale Combining Co Ltd, Caligen Foam Ltd, Kay-Metzeler Ltd, H E Mowbray & Co Ltd

Main locations: Manchester

UK employees: 2776

Total employees: 7,839

### Charitable donations
2004: £63,490
2003: £57,460

## Community involvement

The company stated that they have no policy for charitable giving and that there is no specific budget for this activity.

### Applications

In writing to the correspondent.

## Corporate giving

In 2004, the group as a whole donated a total of £63,490 to charitable causes. A breakdown of this amount was not available.

# Brixton plc

50 Berkeley Street, London W1J 8BX

020 7399 4500

Website: www.brixton.plc.uk

Correspondent: Simon Wilbraham, Company Secretary

Chief Executive: Timothy C Wheeler

| Year end 31/12/2005 | Turnover | Pre-tax profit £288,900,000 |
|---|---|---|

**Nature of company business**
Principal activities: property investment and development and some property dealing.

Subsidiaries include: B-Serv Ltd, Equiton Management Ltd, Premier Greeford Management Ltd

Main locations: London

UK employees: 98

Total employees: 98

### Charitable donations
2005: £65,000
2004: £55,000
2003: £60,000

## Community involvement

In 2005, the company adopted a new community investment policy. This sets out its commitment to support community organisations local to its property portfolio as well as charities for the homeless. The policy also covers company support for employees involved in volunteering and fundraising activities.

Brixton are patrons of CRASH, the construction and property industry charity for the homeless.

### Exclusions

Support for registered charities only. No support for individuals, students, fundraising events, local appeals not in areas of company presence, local branches of national charities and charities whose main aim is to support other charities. Brixton Estate undertakes no secondment or sponsorship of the arts.

### Applications

In writing to the correspondent. Grant decisions are made by the board which meets six-monthly.

## Corporate giving

In 2005, the company donated £65,000 to around 30 charitable organisations. We have no details of the beneficiaries.

### In-kind support

Brixton was a founder guardian of the Thames Valley Adventure Playground in Taplow, which provides recreational facilities for children with special needs. It has also supported London Youth, a charity which helps to train youth workers and organises sports, arts and cultural events across London.

At Christmas, the company donate money to the homeless charity Crisis, rather than sending Christmas cards.

### Employee-led support

The company set itself a number of 'community' targets for 2006, one of which was to encourage staff to get involved in community projects. Staff can take time off work for volunteering (one day per year) and the company matches funds they raise (up to an agreed maximum).

### Commercially-led support

**Sponsorship:** *Education* – Brixton is a corporate sponsor of the Reading Real Estate Foundation, which supports real estate education at the University of Reading.

# Broadland Properties Ltd

137 Scalby Road, Scarborough, North Yorkshire YO12 6TB

01723 373461; Fax: 01723 500021

Correspondent: Tessa Hazlewood, PA to the Chairman

Chief officer: John Guthrie

| Year end 31/12/2005 | Turnover | Pre-tax profit |
|---|---|---|

**Nature of company business**
Property dealers.

Main locations: Scarborough

## Community involvement

We were advised by the contact that as 'an extremely private company we have no wish to be part of the guide'. This statement may be due to the fact that the company is wholly owned by the chairman (either directly or through family trusts) and, as such, it is difficult to tell whether donations made under the company's name are in fact those of the individual.

Our policy, however, remains to include all relevant companies in this guide.

Although all applications are considered, there is a preference for certain causes, with support generally only being given to charities with a Scarborough postcode.

### Exclusions

Generally no support for local appeals outside of the Scarborough area. No support for advertising in charity brochures, animal welfare, appeals from individuals, overseas projects, political appeals or religious appeals.

### Applications

In writing to the correspondent.

## Corporate giving

Although no figures for community contributions were forthcoming, we do know that recent donations include

£150,000 to the Scarborough Museums Trust towards the redevelopment of the Rotunda Museum and £12,500 to the Cairngorm Biathlon and Nordic Ski Club under the sports sponsorship scheme, SPORTSMATCH.

# N Brown Group plc

Griffin House, 40 Lever Street, Manchester M60 6ES

0161 238 2000; Fax: 0161 238 2020

Website: www.nbrown.co.uk

Correspondent: Steve Smith, Head of HR
E-mail: enquiries@nbrown.co.uk

Chief officer: Lord Alliance of Manchester

Chief Executive: Alan White

| Year end | Turnover | Pre-tax profit |
|---|---|---|
| 26/02/2005 | £460,300,000 | £18,600,000 |

Nature of company business
Provider of direct home shopping and financial services.

Main locations: Manchester

UK employees: 4,430

Total employees: 4,430

## Charitable donations

2005: £37,433
2004: £35,426
2003: £39,145

## Community involvement

The company's website states:

'The board of directors of N Brown Group plc recognises the importance of supporting the community in which it operates and supports a number of local concerns, such as hospices, a hospital, children's trusts and charities for older people.'

### Exclusions

No support for local appeals not in area of company presence.

### Applications

In writing to the correspondent.

## Corporate giving

In 2004/05, grants totalled £37,433. Examples of beneficiaries were not available.

## In-kind support

In support of Red Nose Day in 2005, the company made its national call centre in Manchester available to assist in taking pledges. This service was provided free of charge and pledges amounting to more than £200,000 were taken by over 200 of the company's staff.

The company maintains close links with the Christie Hospital in Manchester and regularly assists in fundraising for that organisation.

The group has also recently started to donate redundant IT equipment to charities operating in developing countries.

## Employee-led support

'The company also supports the fundraising activities of its own employees and considers requests for charitable donations or support on their merit.'

# BT Group plc

BT Group Communications, PP A5F, 81 Newgate Street, London EC1A 7AJ

020 7356 5000; Fax: 020 7356 5520

Website: www.bt.com

Correspondent: Steve Kelly 020 7356 6678

Chief officer: Sir Christopher Bland

Chief Executive: Ben Verwaayen

| Year end | Turnover | Pre-tax profit |
|---|---|---|
| 31/03/2006 | £19,514,000,000 | £2,177,000,000 |

Nature of company business
The group's principal activity is the supply of communications services and equipment

Subsidiaries include: Cellnet Group Ltd, Martin Dawes Telecommunications Ltd, Telecom Securicor Cellular Radio Ltd

Main locations: London

UK employees: 91,600

Total employees: 99,900

## Charitable donations

2006: £2,500,000
2004: £1,200,000

Total community contributions: £19,970,000
Management costs: £1,330,000

Membership: A & B, BitC, L B Group, %Club

## Community involvement

Through its Corporate Responsibility Programme BT continues to support a variety of organisations and good causes at local and national level. The central theme of its community activities is improved communications.

BT concentrates its support in the areas of:
- charities and fundraising
- education – from primary schools to universities
- volunteering – BT encourages its staff to volunteer for community activities
- arts and heritage.

### Exclusions

No response to circular appeals. No denominational appeals, political appeals, appeals from individuals or brochure advertising.

### Applications

Decisions on major grants are made at head office by the Board Community Support Committee which meets quarterly. Smaller grants can be made by staff of the relevant Community Unit at their discretion. Local appeals should be sent to the appropriate BT local office. (Each BT zone has its own community affairs staff operating a programme which reflects the needs of that area.)

**Contacts:** BT Community Helpline (0845 723 1013)

Voluntary Sector Programmes – Beth Courtier (023 8082 3340)

Education and Employment Partnerships – Dave Hancock (0121 230 7855).

# Corporate giving

Much of the following was taken from BT's website which contains a wealth of information and advice; far more than we could do justice to within the limitations of this guide. What follows, therefore, is a summary of BT's community support and readers are advised to visit the relevant part of BT's website if further details are required.

BT believe that it can make the biggest impact from its charitable giving by focusing resources on the causes that will benefit most from its communications technology and expertise.

BT state that: 'As a member of the Per Cent Club, we are committed to give a minimum of 0.5% of our UK pre-tax profits (before exceptional items) to direct activities in support of society. Our provision was £5.6 million [£1.2 million of which was donated directly to charities] in the 2004 financial year. BT operations provided a further £12.4 million in funding and support-in-kind.'

BT's community activities are in four main categories:

**Charities and fundraising:** *Charities* – A wide range of initiatives are supported with a special focus on a campaign with the UK children charity, ChildLine. Through the 'Am I Listening' campaign, BT want to highlight the benefits of listening to children and young people – with events like the Big Listen – whilst raising significant funds to enable ChildLine to continue to provide counselling and advice to more young people.

Help has also been given to the charity Community Network, which provides teleconferencing facilities for the voluntary sector. For example, FaithLink which allows people to partake in church services by 'phone.

The Telephone Helplines Association also received support from BT in the development of paper and internet versions of the Telephone Helpline Directory which lists over 900 national, regional and local helplines throughout the UK.

*Fundraising* – BT's ability to co-ordinate major UK charity telethons through the management of the entire telephone network and the provision of call centres to take donations over the 'phone, has benefited numerous charities. Examples include Children in Need, Comic Relief and Disasters Emergency Committee.

*Awards* – BT Community Connections is a UK-wide award programme providing local community groups with access to the internet. Since 2000, when the scheme started, over 3,400 internet-ready PCs have been given to a diverse range of groups. Two recent beneficiaries are Croham Hurst Good Neighbours in Croydon and Exmouth and District Youth Action Group. BT have invested a further £1.3 million in the scheme in 2004.

Applications are open to individuals and groups who can show that the provision of an internet-ready PC will be of benefit to the local community. Those interested in applying should visit www.btcommunityconnections.com or send

contact details to BT Community Connections, PO Box 4500, London W1A 7LF.

**Education:** 'The BT Education Programme is backing the drive to better communication in a number of key areas:

- by providing primary and secondary schools with a unique range of free educational resources, dedicated to supporting the teaching of speaking and listening skills. All have been developed in consultation with teachers and are strongly linked to curriculum requirements.

- by encouraging schools to become more active at promoting better communication. One way is through the Communication Skills Roadshow, which visits schools around the country, using a mixture of drama and classroom workshops to stimulate interest in getting more out of life through better communication. Another way is through the BT Volunteers scheme, which enables schools to draw on the support of nearly four thousand volunteers, taken mainly from BT's own staff.

- by offering funds to school projects that demonstrate novel ways for students to improve their communication skills and become more active and effective young citizens. Through the BT Schools Awards scheme, the Education Programme backs financial backing for hundreds of such projects a year.'

Details of all BT's education activities can be found at www.bt.com/education

**Employee involvement:** See below.

**Arts and heritage:** See below.

BT have also launched a digital inclusion campaign to support the UK government's aim to give all citizens internet access by 2005. For more information, see the 'Digital inclusion' section of the company's website.

## In-kind support

BT gives in-kind support to ChildLine, such as strategic and technical advice. Its support has included the donation of premises for several years, large-scale promotions and staff fundraising initiatives, and sponsoring the annual BT ChildLine Awards for Services to Children.

## Employee-led support

**Employee involvement:** Through the BT Volunteers programme, BT encourage staff to volunteer and spend time for community activities. It also helps others (companies, schools) to organise volunteering programmes. As a result over 150 Volunteer Clubs have been established across the UK and is available to BT retirees and employees' family and friends.

**Payroll giving:** BT's commitment to Give As You Earn enables employees to donate to the charity of their choice. In 2004 financial year over £1.7 million was given by employees. This sum was matched to the tune of £1 million by BT.

## Commercially-led support

**Sponsorship:** *The arts* – Through a pioneering partnership with the UK's leading modern art gallery, Tate, BT sponsors its website Tate Online. Support is also given to the preservation of the UK's telecommunications heritage.

# H P Bulmer Holdings plc

The Cider Mills, Plough Lane, Hereford HR4 0LE

01432 352000; Fax: 01432 352084

Website: www.bulmers.com

Correspondent: Alistair Cormie, Company Secretary

Chief officer: W M Samuel

Chief Executive: M J Hughes

Managing Director: T M Furse

| Year end | Turnover | Pre-tax profit |
|---|---|---|
| 31/12/2003 | £136,011,000 | £908,000 |

Nature of company business
The principal activities of the group are the manufacture and sale of cider, and the wholesale distribution of alcoholic and non-alcoholic drinks, including the distribution of premium beers.

Subsidiaries include: The Beer Seller Ltd, Symonds Cider & English Wine Company Ltd, Inch's Cider Ltd

Main locations: Hereford

UK employees: 1,637

Total employees: 2,070

## Charitable donations

2005: £365,077
2004: £358,459

## Community involvement

This once family-owned cider producer, although now part of Scottish & Newcastle, still make charitable donations to a variety of Hereford-based projects via The Bulmer Foundation (Charity Commission no. 1093558). The foundation relies heavily upon donations from H P Bulmer Holdings plc / Scottish & Newcastle plc for its income.

The primary objectives of the foundation are to:

▶ advance the education of the public in the principles of sustainable development

▶ to conduct research into the social, economic and environmental effects of land and estate management

▶ the promotion for the benefit of the public of urban or rural regeneration in areas of social and economic deprivation, particularly in Herefordshire.

### Exclusions

No response to circular appeals. No support for advertising in charity brochures, local appeals not in areas of company presence, large national appeals or overseas projects.

### Applications

In writing to the correspondent. Charities are advised to approach the Bulmer's community support budget for funds, rather than any of its brands, which include Strongbow.

## Corporate giving

In 2005, the foundation received donations from H P Bulmer Holdings plc / Scottish & Newcastle plc of £365,077 (2004: £358,459). We have no details of the recipients.

### In-kind support

In addition to making cash donations, support is provided through gifts in kind.

### Employee-led support

Employees are encouraged to become actively involved in the community and, amongst other things, a number of employees are school governors, sports club officials and participate in the Young Enterprise Scheme in local schools.

We understand that in addition to the charitable donations figure above, the company provides match funding of employees' weekly contributions to an employee community fund. This fund donates around £10,000 a year to local causes chosen by employees.

# Bunzl plc

110 Park Street, London W1K 6NX

020 7495 4950; Fax: 020 7495 4953

Website: www.bunzl.com

Correspondent: Julia Battyll, Independent Consultant

Chief officer: A Habgood

Chief Executive: Michael Roney

| Year end | Turnover | Pre-tax profit |
|---|---|---|
| 31/12/2005 | £2,808,300,000 | £176,700,000 |

Nature of company business
Providing outsourcing solutions and customer service orientated distribution and light manufacture, primarily of plastic and paper based products.

Subsidiaries include: Filtrona United Kingdom Ltd

Main locations: London

UK employees: 6,000

Total employees: 12,000

## Charitable donations

2005: £201,000
2004: £200,000
2003: £193,000

Membership: BitC, %Club

## Community involvement

The company stated that: 'At the group level a cross section of projects within registered charities are sponsored predominantly in the fields of healthcare, education, disability, children and the arts.

'Each business area is encouraged to develop their own local charitable giving programmes in line with the group guidelines but taking into account local company requirements including marketing initiatives and budgetary considerations.

'All employees are encouraged to act as responsible and responsive citizens of their communities and to support projects, organisations and services that work towards the common good and improvement of their community and society.'

## Exclusions

The group will not support appeals from individuals, advertising in charity brochures, political or religious appeals.

## Applications

In writing to the correspondent. Subsidiaries have a donations budget independent of head office and should be contacted directly.

**Other Information:** The group produce a social responsibility report which is available in their annual report.

## Corporate giving

In 2005, the company made cash donations totalling £201,000 (2004: £200,000). The company's 2005 Corporate Social Responsibility Report gave the following information concerning its charitable activities:

'In the UK and at group level (Bunzl) has continued to support a cross section of projects within registered charities in the fields of healthcare, education and disability. In 2005 Bunzl and its employees across the world made significant donations to various disaster funds including tsunami support via UNICEF, the Red Cross and a special fund set up by one of Bunzl's UK employees, as well as support to Hurricane Katrina victims via the American Red Cross and Salvation Army.

'Bunzl continued to sponsor projects relating to prostate/breast cancer research through Imperial College London. Queen Elizabeth's Training College was supported to set up a painting and decorating course and for a Job Club with the aim of training disabled people to return to or start work. Support was also given to Leonard Cheshire's Workability programme, which provides computers and training for disabled people to obtain a recognised computer/IT qualification in their own homes, as well as part sponsoring two Discover IT centres which enable disabled people to learn about computers in a friendly and informal training centre. In addition, Group companies and individual employees worldwide continue to support local charitable initiatives.'

## In-kind support

In addition to cash donations, the company provides support through gifts in kind.

## Employee-led support

All employees are encouraged to support projects, organisations and services that work towards the improvement of their community.

**Payroll Giving:** The company operates the Charity Direct payroll giving scheme and will match employee fundraising.

# BUPA Ltd

BUPA House, 15–19 Bloomsbury Way, London WC1A 2BA

020 7656 2000

Website: www.bupa.co.uk

Correspondent: Mrs Lee Saunders, BUPA Foundation Administrator 020 7656 2591; Fax: 020 7656 2708
E-mail: saunderl@bupa.com

| Year end | Turnover | Pre-tax profit |
|---|---|---|
| 31/12/2003 | £3,368,000,000 | £134,500,000 |

**Nature of company business**
Principal activities: operation of health insurance funds and the provision of healthcare facilities and services, including ownership and management of hospitals, care homes, children's nurseries, homecare health screening services and occupational health services.

Subsidiaries include: Care First Group plc

Main locations: London

UK employees: 40,000

Total employees: 4,000

### Charitable donations
2003: £2,500,000
Membership: BitC, L B Group, %Club

## Community involvement

BUPA's donations are made through The BUPA Foundation (Charity Commission no. 277598) which was set up to prevent, relieve and cure, sickness, ill-health and infirmity and to safeguard health by way of research. It aims to produce long-term benefits that will have an impact on health of both individuals and the whole country. The charity currently invites applications for medical research grants in the following areas:
- Medical research grants
- Specialist themed research grants
- BUPA Foundation Awards

Unfortunately we do not have details of the company's current financial position.

## Exclusions

The company does not support appeals from individuals, political appeals or religious appeals.

## Applications

The foundation's website provides detailed information regarding applications, eligibility and closing dates for each of the three fields in which awards are made. Applications for Medical Research grants can be downloaded from the website. Applications for Specialist Themed grants and BUPA Foundation awards should be made in writing to the contact.

## Corporate giving

**BUPA Foundation**

In 2004, the foundation's income was £2,897,182, the vast majority of this (£2,578,500) was Gift Aid donation made by the company.

The BUPA Foundation supports a number of annual awards to recognise and promote excellence in healthcare. The foundation continued its policy of donating grants to relevant research bodies, and during 2004 granted £3,051,606 to 31 different projects (2003: £1,222,220 to 12 projects. Some of those in receipt of grants awarded during 2004 were: University of Bristol (£295,568), St George's Hospital Medical School (£187,442), Institute of Child Health (£180,492), University of Aberdeen (£179,857), University of Oxford (£161,544), University of Manchester £153,040), Sheffield Children's Hospital NHS Trust (£146,563).

In October 2002 the foundation received a written commitment from the company stating it will continue to make an annual Gift Aid payment of at least £1,500,000 up to and including 2005.

## In-kind support

**BUPA Community Connections:** Set up to assist and support BUPA staff in their voluntary community work, help can range from the provision of manpower, training, publicity and supplies, to practical advice on fundraising and volunteering activities. Financial support may also be given.

## Employee-led support

Through BUPA Community Connections staff have supported a range of causes from the RNIB and 'Can You Be A Buddy?' a scheme which offers friendship to people with learning disabilities, to raising funds for UNICEF in its fight against child exploitation and sky diving for Action Research.

Other employee volunteering schemes have focused on education, the environment, the elderly, community mediation and homelessness. Further details on each of these is given on the company's website where volunteering by staff is actively encouraged by providing a wide range of volunteering opportunities in over ten specialist areas such as children and young people, families, the arts and animal welfare.

**Payroll giving:** The company operates the Give As You Earn Scheme.

## Commercially-led support

**Sponsorship:** *Health* – BUPA continues to support the Great Run series because of its relation to health issues.

---

# Buy As You View Ltd

Ty Rhondda, Forest View Business Park, Llantrisant CF72 8LX

0800 138 7788; Fax: 01443 445004

Website: www.buyasyouview.co.uk

Correspondent: Community Affairs Director 0800 138 7788; Fax: 01443 445004

| Year end | Turnover | Pre-tax profit |
|----------|----------|----------------|
| 31/03/2005 | £29,856,702 | £5,755,953 |

Nature of company business
Retailers of electrical household goods.

Main locations: Warrington, Sunderland, Rotherham, Collshill

UK employees: 689

### Charitable donations

2005: £36,331
2004: £450,000

## Community involvement

The company focuses its support in areas where it has a presence (South Wales, Midlands, Yorkshire and the North East), and has recently targeted projects linked to education, health, sport, and crime prevention. A wide range of smaller community-related projects is also supported, subject to strict funding criteria.

## Exclusions

No support for local appeals not in areas of company presence.

## Applications

In writing to the correspondent.

## Corporate giving

In 2004/05, the company made charitable donations totalling £36,331. This is a significant reduction on donations in the previous year, which totalled £472,468. No information was available in the company's accounts on any further charitable activities, or why there has been such a dramatic reduction in charitable giving compared to previous years.

---

# C E Electric UK Ltd

Manor House, Station Road, New Penshaw, Houghton-le-Spring, DH4 7LA.

0800 668877

Website: www.ce-electricuk.com

Correspondent: Jon Bird, Director, External Affairs 0191 387 7310

Chief officer: David Sokol

Chief Executive: Greg Abel

| Year end | Turnover | Pre-tax profit |
|----------|----------|----------------|
| 31/12/2005 | £501,200,000 | £147,600,000 |

Nature of company business
CE Electric UK is the parent company of Northern Electric Distribution and Yorkshire Electricity Distribution, the electricity distribution businesses for the North East, Yorkshire and North Lincolnshire.

Subsidiaries include: Yorkshire Power Group Ltd, Northern Electric plc, Integrated Utility Services

Main locations: Leeds, Newcastle upon Tyne

UK employees: 2,534

### Charitable donations

2005: £54,568
2004: £91,625
2003: £38,000

Total community contributions: £114,568

Membership: BitC

## Community involvement

The company has produced detailed and clear information on its community programme and policies. It states: 'As the monopoly distributor of electricity throughout the region, we recognise that our customers and the community in which they live are the same. Our community involvement is thus an extension of our customer service programme and is aimed at making a visible difference to the life of those communities.'

CE Electric UK advised that it has an ongoing community investment strategy. Decisions on expenditure are made on a one-off basis, usually in response to requests from outside the company. The criteria used are:

- will the expenditure benefit a locality as opposed to a national cause?
- is the location one where we are working with the community on quality of supply or other issues?
- will we be a sole funder as opposed to one of a large number?
- is the expenditure on one of our preferred areas (environment, young people, rural affairs)?
- is there a reasonable opportunity for gaining positive PR commensurate with the level of expenditure?

There is a preference for supporting local charities in the North East, Yorkshire and north Lincolnshire areas.

### Exclusions

No support for circular appeals, advertising in national charity brochures, animal welfare, appeals from individuals, the arts, fundraising events, heritage, medical research, overseas projects, political or religious appeals, science/technology, sickness/disability, or a 'charity of the year'.

### Applications

In writing to the correspondent.

**Information available:** The company produce a social responsibility report.

## Corporate giving

In 2004, the group made charitable donations of £91,625, principally to local charities serving the communities in which the group operates. This included 16 donations totalling £6,700 to projects or charities supported by employees through volunteering or fundraising activities and 29 donations totalling over £44,000 to community projects, half of which were in market towns that were part of the Government's Market Towns Initiative.

Looking towards the future and the London 2012 Olympics, CE Electric UK has launched a long-term initiative to find and develop local athletic talent within its operating area. The scheme will fund the employment of Community and Performance Sports Coaches to help work with local athletic stars of the future over the next five years and beyond. Run in conjunction with Sportsmatch and England Athletics, the programme will also support athletics clubs and 'untapped' talent at schools across Yorkshire. CE Electric UK and the Community Coaches will be visiting local schools in the Autumn to spread the word about healthy living and getting fit for the future.

The company also has money invested in the Community Foundations for the Tyne & Wear, County Durham and Tees Valley. The income from these investments goes to fund community projects in the respective areas. In 2004, nine projects were funded at a total cost of around £15,000.

## In-kind support

The company has made donations of office furniture and equipment, including computers, when they are surplus to requirements.

CE Electric undertakes an education programme in schools and via the web to educate children in the need to avoid contact with electrical wires and equipment. In 2004 the company employed a full time member of staff who gave 227 talks at 119 schools to more than 20,000 children. The overall cost to the company for several initiatives to promote safety, excluding staff time, was more than £60,000. The programmes will have contributed to the reduction in incidents involving unauthorised interference with the company's equipment from 35 in 2001 to 23 in 2004.

### Employee-led support

Employees are encouraged to volunteer for community-based and charitable activities. The company matches employees fundraising efforts up to a maximum of £200 per employee.

Under the Global Days of Service programme operated by the company's parent company, MidAmerican Energy Holdings Company, organisations for which employees volunteer can gain a financial contribution depending on the number of hours volunteered. In 2004 the contribution was £12,000.

**Payroll giving:** The company provides employees with the opportunity to make charitable donations through a payroll giving scheme.

# Cable and Wireless plc

Lakeside House, Cain Road, Bracknell, Berkshire RG12 1XL

020 7315 4000

Website: www.cw.com

Correspondent: Paul James, Head of Public Affairs

Chief officer: Richard Lapthorne

Managing Director: John Pluthero

| Year end | Turnover | Pre-tax profit |
|---|---|---|
| 31/03/2006 | £3,230,000,000 | £112,000,000 |

Nature of company business
The group's principal activity is the provision of telecommunication services.

Main locations: Coventry, London, Swindon, Southampton, Wokingham, Birmingham, Bracknell

UK employees: 267

Total employees: 17,430

### Charitable donations
2006: £200,000
2005: £1,700,000
2004: £1,100,000

## Community involvement

Cable & Wireless provided the following information on its community investment policy:

'Cable & Wireless has a long-standing tradition of good corporate citizenship and is committed to making a positive social contribution to the communities in which we operate.

'Cable & Wireless has therefore developed a community investment programme designed to support local communities and respond to their needs.

'We recognise the positive role that the internet and ICT can play in supporting learning and in facilitating personal, social and economic development.

'In line with our core business, the Cable & Wireless community investment programme focuses social investment in three key areas – allowing us to make a real and substantial impact:

- addressing the 'Digital Divide' – enabling people from disadvantaged backgrounds to access the benefits of the Internet and Information and Communications Technology (ICT).
- Internet safety and security – raising awareness and understanding of internet safety issues and encouraging individuals to stay safe on-line.
- encouraging positive use of the Internet – encouraging individuals, charities and not-for-profit organisations to develop creative and innovative internet content and to use the Internet as a tool for education, learning and for positive social purposes.

'Preference is given to projects which:
- focus on education and training
- have an international focus, reflecting the global nature of Cable & Wireless
- provide opportunities for Cable & Wireless employees to make an active contribution
- demonstrate substantial grass roots impact.

'Cable & Wireless is committed to developing projects in partnership with charitable, not-for-profit and community-based organisations and welcomes the opportunity to jointly discuss ideas and project proposals.'

### Exclusions

The company only supports proposals that match its policy and does not offer support for advertising. No support for individuals other than employees. Proposals must relate to locations where the company does business or potentially has global scope. No support for political or religious causes or UK-centric projects.

### Applications

In writing to the correspondent or e-mail community@cw.com

**Information available:** Cable & Wireless produced its second community report in January 2004 entitled: 'Making the Difference: Cable & Wireless in the Community'. Copies can be downloaded from its website.

## Corporate giving

In 2006, the company made worldwide community contributions of £2.5 million. Of this, £200,000 was donated in the UK for charitable purposes. These figures represent a considerable drop on the previous years, which were £7.7 million and £1.7 million respectively. No explanation for the fall was given.

Within the three key areas mentioned above, Cable & Wireless have supported the following groups/organisations:

*Addressing the 'Digital Divide'* – Young people/Bracknell Forest Borough Council; children with learning difficulties/ NCH; older people/Age Concern & Microsoft; disabled people/U Can Do IT; unemployed people/London Borough of Camden ITEC.

*Internet safety and security* – Schoolchildren/Childnet International; website owners and parents/Internet Content Rating Association; law enforcement/Internet Watch Foundation.

*Encouraging positive use of the internet* – School arts ICT/ WebPlay; young people/Childnet International; dyslexic learners/Dyslexia International Tools & Technologies; deaf children/Deafchild International; disabled people/Employers Forum on Disability.

Comprehensive information on all of these initiatives is available on the company's website.

### Employee-led support

The company actively encourages employees to support the work of the charities or voluntary organisations in their own local community.

In support of this a matched giving scheme has been established. This 'fixed pool of funds' is used to match money raised for charitable causes by UK employees up to a maximum of £1,000 per employee in any one financial year.

**Payroll giving:** The company operates the Give As You Earn scheme. In 2002/03, over £102,000 was donated to a range of UK charities through the scheme.

### Commercially-led support

**Sponsorship:** The company undertakes arts and good-cause sponsorship.

# Cadbury Schweppes plc

25 Berkeley Square, London W1X 6HT

Website: www.cadburyschweppes.com

Correspondent: CSR Manager

Chief officer: John Sunderland

Chief Executive: Todd Stitzer

| Year end | Turnover | Pre-tax profit |
|---|---|---|
| 01/01/2006 | £6,508,000,000 | £843,000,000 |

**Nature of company business**
Principal activities: the manufacture and marketing of confectionery and soft drinks.

**Subsidiaries include:** Reading Scientific Services Ltd, Connaught Investments plc, Berkeley Square Investments Ltd, Trebor Bassett Ltd

**Main locations:** Bournville, Maple Cross, Hertfordshire

**UK employees:** 7,409

**Total employees:** 55,799

### Charitable donations

2005: £750,000
2004: £700,000
2003: £650,000

Total community contributions: £3,200,000
Management costs: £630,000

Membership: BitC, L B Group, %Club

## Community involvement

Cadbury believe that gone are the days when a company's guilty social conscience could be absolved through charitable handouts and philanthropy. Instead, it sees 'community investment [as] a business imperative' and, as such, it applies business techniques to its community programme in order to maximise benefit to those communities identified as most in need.

Most requests for charitable donations are channelled through the Cadbury Schweppes Foundation (Charity Commission no.

1050482) – the company's charitable trust in the UK. This has no endowment but is funded by grants from the company each year.

Grants are given mainly in support of organisations working with education and enterprise, health, welfare or the environment. National charities and local groups around its sites (in Birmingham, Bristol, London and Sheffield) can be assisted.

### Exclusions

In view of the policy of concentrating grants behind selected projects, most ad hoc appeals have to be declined and are therefore not encouraged.

The foundation does not support: requests for commercial sponsorship, help with funding of individuals' education and training programmes, purchase of advertising space, involvement in fundraising projects, travel or leisure projects, donation of gifts in kind (including company products), regional projects unless in the locality of company operations.

Normally support has not been given for projects outside the UK since it is policy to provide support through local businesses in the many countries around the world where Cadbury Schweppes has operations.

### Applications

As indicated above, appeals outside the criteria defined are not encouraged, as most grants are committed in advance on an ongoing basis. Any correspondence should be addressed to The Cadbury Schweppes Foundation at the above address.

## Corporate giving

In 2005, global donations, in kind support and staff time totalled £9,800,000. In previous years, about one third of this total figure was given in the UK, making a total contribution of about £3,200,000 here.

### Cadbury Schweppes Foundation

In 2005 the foundation received a donation of £750,000 from the company. The foundation in turn made grants totalling just over £1,000,000, with beneficiaries in the UK including the Prince's Trust, the Confectioners' Benevolent Trust, Business in the Community, oneLondon Limited, St Mungo's, UK Career Academy Foundation and Young Enterprise.

### In-kind support

**Education:** Regular links are maintained with schools through work experience, work shadowing, collaborative projects and provision of school packs. A number of schools are now assigned a 'Links Manager' in order that the business can support their work.

### Employee-led support

The company seeks to increase employee participation in community activities. Team Challenges are effectively team-building and personal development activities which are performed by staff for the benefit of good causes. Various opportunities have been offered for staff to get involved, including: mentoring individual pupils, coaching and organising team sports, providing business and management advice and support to head teachers and community managers.

Employees' fundraising efforts are acknowledged through a 'Cash-Match' scheme up to a usual limit of £200, although exceptions can be made in response to team events or those raising over £1,000. Employees have been cash-matched for activities ranging from raffles to sponsored show jumping.

Rather than sending corporate Christmas cards, the company donates the money it would have spent (around £10,000) to Crisis at Christmas. Christmas trees in offices (with room for messages) encouraged staff not to send cards to colleagues and make donations to local charities of their choosing.

**Payroll giving:** A scheme is available to employees wishing to make tax-effective donations to a charity of their choice.

### Commercially-led support

The company has previously run a 'Get Active' token collection scheme which provided sports equipment in schools. However, following negative feedback the company has decided to cease customer reward schemes.

## Cadogan Group Ltd

18 Cadogan Gardens, London SW3 2RP

020 7730 4567; Fax: 020 7881 2300

Website: www.cadogan.co.uk

Correspondent: Sue Wizard, Personal Assistant to Lord Cadogan

Chief officer: The Earl Cadogan D.L.

Chief Executive: Stuart Corbyn

| Year end | Turnover | Pre-tax profit |
|---|---|---|
| 31/12/2005 | | £51,000,000 |

**Nature of company business**
The principal activity of the group is property investment. Subsidiaries are involved in the manufacture and distribution of menswear, upholstered furniture and protective workplace clothing, and the retailing of furniture.

**Subsidiaries include:** Multifabs Ltd, Chelsea Land Ltd, Holliday & Brown Ltd, Christy & Co Ltd, Oakley Leisure Parks Ltd, Furniture Village plc, Oakley Investment Ltd, Michelsons Ltd

**Main locations:** London

**UK employees:** 50

## Community involvement

The company has stated in the past that: 'One of our shareholders has a charitable trust and the bulk of our donations are now made that way'.

We believe this to be The Cadogan Charity (Charity Commission no. 247773) which holds 4.2% of the allotted ordinary shares in the Cadogan Group Limited, and from which it derives the majority of its income.

### Exclusions

No grants to individuals.

### Applications

In writing to the correspondent.

## Corporate giving

Previously we were told that the company made its own charitable donations of around £50,000 a year. We have been unable to confirm if this is still the case.

## The Cadogan Charity

In 2005, the charity had an income of £975,000 of which £963,000 was investment income received from the shares it has in the company. Donations totalled £1,022,028 and were broken down as follows:

| Category | Grant total |
| --- | --- |
| Community and social welfare | £560,300 |
| Medical research | £288,500 |
| Military charities | £79,000 |
| Conservation and environment | £61,000 |
| Education | £26,000 |
| Animal welfare | £8,000 |

Beneficiaries included: Migratory Salmon Foundation (£50,000); Inventure Trust and U Can Do I.T. (£10,000 each); Dockland Settlements and Colon Cancer Concern (£5,000 each); St Luke's Hospital for the Clergy (£2,500); and, King George's Fund for Sailors and Dogs' Home Battersea (£2,000 each).

# Caledonia Investments

Cayzer House, 30 Buckingham Gate, London SW1E 6NN

020 7802 8080; Fax: 020 7802 8090

Website: www.caledonia.com

Correspondent: Major M G Wyatt, Director
E-mail: enquiries@caledonia.com

Chief officer: Peter N Buckley

Chief Executive: Tim Ingram

| Year end | Turnover | Pre-tax profit |
| --- | --- | --- |
| 31/03/2006 | | £3,480,000 |

Nature of company business
Caledonia is a UK investment trust company, listed on the London Stock Exchange.

Subsidiaries include: The Sloane Club Group Ltd, Edinmore Holdings Ltd, Edinburgh Crystal Glass Co Ltd, Amber Industrial Holdings plc, St Lawrence Properties Ltd, Sterling Industries plc

Main locations: London

UK employees: 40

Total employees: 1,148

### Charitable donations
2006: £110,000
2004: £102,000

## Community involvement

The company has a preference for appeals relevant to company business and charities in which a member of company staff is involved. There is also a preference for education, environment/heritage, arts and enterprise/training.

### Exclusions

No grants for fundraising events, advertising in charity brochures, religious appeals, local appeals not in areas of company presence, large national appeals, overseas projects or circular appeals, and absolutely no individual sponsorship of college/university students.

### Applications
In writing to the correspondent.

## Corporate giving

In 2005/06, the company donated a total of £110,000 to charities. Grants to national organisations ranged from £200 to £2,000. We have no details of the beneficiaries.

# Calor Gas Limited

Athena Drive, Tachbrook Park, Warwick CV34 6RL

01926 330088

Website: www.calorgas.co.uk

Correspondent: Suzanne Weir, Community & Events Manager
01926 318634
E-mail: sweir@calor.co.uk

Managing Director: Howard Kerr

| Year end | Turnover | Pre-tax profit |
| --- | --- | --- |
| 31/12/2005 | | |

Nature of company business
Bottled gas supplier.

Main locations: Warwick

### Charitable donations
2005: £50,000

Membership: BitC, %Club

## Community involvement

Calor Gas supports a wide range of community initiatives from charity work to education, rural and environmental projects. The company's website now provides comprehensive information about its community work, as the following quote shows:

'Calor is committed to contributing to the communities we serve. We are focused on building long standing relationships with relevant organisations and providing real support to make a difference. Initiatives such as Calor Village of the Year, Calor Scottish Community of the Year and our work with BITC, Rural Revival, The Fairyland Trust and Childline, have boosted communities and local businesses and contributed hundreds of thousands of pounds to local projects.'

### Applications
In writing to the correspondent.

## Corporate giving

Although a member of Business in the Community and the Per Cent Club (by virtue of contributing 1.1% of pre-tax profits to the community in 2005), complete figures were not available. However, based on figures that have been published in relation to 'Calor Village of the Year' and the 'Gift of the Gas' campaign (see below), cash donations for 2005 were at least £50,000 with substantial in-kind support on top of this for specific educational projects.

In 2005, Calor launched its 'Gift of the Gas' campaign to benefit those who need support from ChildLine, the UK's free, 24-hour helpline for children in danger or distress. The company has pledged to contribute £5 to the charity for every redundant Calor cylinder returned to the company's local sites. By the end of 2005, over £50,000 had been raised from returned gas cylinders and fundraising barbecue events held during the summer season.

## In-kind support

Calor's support of the Fairyland Trust has provided the trust with a Mongolian Yurt that is used as a travelling 'Fairy Café' as well as publication of its annual report and help at numerous Fairy Fairs.

## Employee-led support

**Education:** Calor operates a mentoring programme where staff are encouraged to support and guide students in their coursework at local schools during lunch breaks. The company also operates Business Days for local schools, designed to give students an insight into business areas such as advertising, marketing, customer care and production.

These programmes have so far involved over 300 students in over ten schools.

## Commercially-led support

**Sponsorship:** The Calor Village of the Year competition for England and Wales provides a national prize of £42,000 with additional prizes being given in over 43 counties.

The company state that the competition is: 'Calor's way of supporting customers in rural communities and encouraging rural sustainability.

'The competition is not about pretty window boxes and the village green. It is based upon six major aspects of village life – community, business, young people, older people, environment and information technology.'

To mark the 10th anniversary of the competition in 2006, a special 'best of the best' competition was held featuring past regional winners. The outcome was £20,000 being awarded to the winning village of St Neot's.

Calor also now run similar competitions in Scotland and Wales.

# Camelot Group plc

Tolpits Lane, Watford, Herts WD18 9RN

01923 425000; Fax: 01923 425050

Website: www.camelotgroup.co.uk

Correspondent: Dianne Thompson, Chief Executive

Chief officer: Gerry Archer

Chief Executive: Dianne Thompson

| Year end | Turnover | Pre-tax profit |
|---|---|---|
| 31/03/2005 | £4,194,000,000 | £47,200,000 |

## Nature of company business
The principal activity of the company is the operation and promotion of the National Lottery in the United Kingdom.

The shareholders of the company are Cadbury Schweppes plc, De La Rue plc, International Computers Ltd, Thales Electronics plc (formerly Racal) and Consignia Enterprises Limited (formerly Post Office Enterprises).

**Main locations:** Reigate, Sunderland, Leeds, Northampton, London, Liverpool, Cardiff, Glasgow, Exeter, Birmingham, Belfast

**Total employees:** 913

### Charitable donations
2005: £2,000,000
2004: £2,500,000
2003: £2,700,000

Total community contributions: £3,100,000

Membership: BitC, L B Group, %Club

## Community involvement

The company concentrates its community support on combating disadvantage in areas close to its business. There are four main themes: developing skills, creating new opportunities, enhancing communities and encouraging social responsibility in the industry. The company's community investment programme is built around three main elements: community partnerships, employee involvement and the Camelot Foundation.

The geographical areas given preference are near to the company's headquarters in Watford, its call centre in Aintree – Liverpool, Glasgow, Cardiff and Belfast.

### Exclusions

Activity outside of the community involvement policy; overseas appeals/sponsorship; individuals; advertisements in charity brochures/programmes; general appeals.

### Applications

In writing to the correspondent.

## Corporate giving

The group made charitable contributions of £3.1 million of which £2 million was paid to the Camelot Foundation (Charity Commission no. 1060606). Further, unspecified, in-kind support was also made during the year. Since its inception in 1993, Camelot has invested, on average, 5% of its pre-tax profits each year in the community.

### The Camelot Foundation

The Camelot Group launched The Camelot Foundation in November 1996 and donates £2 million of funding to it each year.

The foundation concentrates on helping marginalised and vulnerable young people by bringing them into the mainstream of life. New funding programmes were launched in 2002 to bring this about:

### Transforming Lives:

Around £1 million a year will be disbursed through this programme to organisations working with the foundations target groups.

### Annual Strategic Grants Programme:

These grants will be used to focus each year on a specific aspect of the foundation's programme and may, for example, be used to bring attention to an important but under recognised issue. About £400,000 will spent each in achieving this.

### Annual Events

£175,000 will be committed each year to raising the profile of the foundation by highlighting two key issues in its area of interest.

**Employee Participation Programme**

Each year £300,000 will be allocated to match the fundraising activities of Camelot employees.

During 2005 grants included the following:
Transforming Lives Programme:
- After Adoption
- The Holocaust Memorial and Education Centre
- Changing Faces
- Youth at Risk
- Young People Now
- Youth Enquiry Service
- The FAW Football in the Community Ltd

4front Awards Programme (including Fast 4ward Awards):
- Fun for all in Cornwall
- Giving hope to street children in Thika
- Performance based application for Asylum Seekers
- Platform of Creativity
- Music Matters
- There's No Sound Underground
- Think Positive, Work Positive

Self Harm Awards Programme:
- Bristol Crisis Service for Women
- Colchester Rape Crisis
- Islington Mind
- Newham Asian Women's Project
- Off Centre Hackney
- Penumbra
- Scottish Development Centre for Mental Health
- The WISH Centre
- Trust for the Study of Adolescence

Further details on each of these programmes can be obtained by contacting the foundation on 020 7828 6085 or e-mailing: info@camelotfoundation.org.uk

Grant guidelines and an application form for the 'Transforming Lives' programme are available by sending an A4 self-addressed envelope, with a first class stamp to: Camelot Foundation, University House, 11–13 Lower Grosvenor Place, London SW1W 0EX.

**The Company**

The 'Community Partnership' element of its support sees Camelot working closely with many charitable and commercial organisations to the benefit of the community. According to the company these include:
- supporting business/school partnerships
- offering business skills for practical or teaching purposes to tertiary colleges
- supporting programmes aimed at creating skills and opportunities for young, disadvantaged, unemployed people
- funding strategic initiatives that focus on the infrastructure of community development and citizenship
- supporting research, education, and treatment regarding gambling addiction and responsible gambling.

Organisations that Camelot has worked with include: Media Trust, Common Purpose, Education Extra and GamCare.

## In-kind support

This is provided through gifts in kind and staff secondments.

## Employee-led support

Camelot Group employees are encouraged and assisted to support the causes they choose through match funding and volunteering. This is made possible through Camelot's Employee Community Involvement programme. Camelot has also made direct contributions to their communities with 7% of Camelot employees contributing nearly 1,000 volunteer hours to assist local projects.

Employees can apply for match funding for charitable activities and events that they are actively involved in, staff are encouraged to raise funds for charities large and small across the UK.

Camelot employees are also offered half a day a month for volunteering activities. To further encourage employees to give their professional skills to organisations as well as to fundraise for charities of their choice, the company developed a 'time-bank' for matched funding purposes with a common value of £16 per hour.

## Commercially-led support

**Sponsorship** Camelot is Lead Sponsor of the GB Rowing Team which includes the lead men's sweep crew and the lead women's crew for competition and training.

The sponsorship began in May 2005 when both crews competed – with Camelot-branded kit and equipment – at Dorney Lake, near Windsor, in the first World Cup held in the UK for almost 20 years.

The agreement between Camelot and the Amateur Rowing Association (ARA – the national governing body for the sport) is scheduled to last through four full seasons from 2005 – including the Beijing Olympiad – and concludes in January 2009, when Camelot's current licence to operate The National Lottery expires.

# Canary Wharf Group plc

One Canada Square, Canary Wharf, London E14 5AB

020 7418 2000; Fax: 020 7418 2222

Website: www.canarywharf.com

Correspondent: Lynne McVay

Chief officer: Sir Martin Jacomb

Chief Executive: George Lacobescu

| Year end | Turnover | Pre-tax profit |
|----------|----------|----------------|
| 31/12/2005 | £30,500,000 | (£1,600,000) |

Nature of company business
Property development, investment, and management.

Subsidiaries include: CW Lending Ltd, CW Lending II plc, Heron Quays Properties Ltd

Main locations: London

### Charitable donations

2005: £284,317
2004: £96,763

Membership: BitC

## Community involvement

The company has 'a continued commitment to supporting the local community'.

### Exclusions

No support for local appeals not in areas of company presence.

### Applications

In writing to the correspondent.

## Corporate giving

In 2005, the company made charitable donations of £284,317 (six months ended 31 December 2004 – £96,763). We have no details of the beneficiaries.

# Canon (UK) Ltd

Cockshott Hill, Woodhatch, Reigate, Surrey RH2 8BF

01737 220000; Fax: 01737 220022

Website: www.canon.co.uk

Correspondent: Lisa Attfield, Public Relations Corporate Executive
E-mail: lisa.attfield@cuk.canon.co.uk

Managing Director: Lars-Erik Kennbert

| Year end | Turnover | Pre-tax profit |
|---|---|---|
| 31/12/2004 | £303,617,000 | £6,600,000 |

### Nature of company business
The principal activity of the company is the provision and support of information and communications technology solutions to business and the sales and servicing of consumer electronic products.

Subsidiaries include: Joe Walker Ltd, Libra Business Services Ltd

Main locations: Reigate

UK employees: 2,032

### Charitable donations
2004: £35,287
2003: £15,751

## Community involvement

Canon state that in the course of an average week they receive around 50–60 proposals from charitable or community organisations requesting support in either cash or product donation form.

Through its CARE (Community Action Review Enterprise) committee Canon will consider supporting national and local charities in the UK, especially those connected with one of the following six categories:

- business & community – aimed at building relationships with local businesses thus encouraging job creation and community interaction
- education – designed to support schools, colleges and extra-curricular activity
- art & culture – to benefit creative events and programmes which encourage community interest and participation
- humanitarian – designed to provide assistance and support for a variety of health related causes
- environment – aimed at supporting community and environmental organisations to help improve their surroundings
- employee matching – matching of Canon employee charitable fundraising efforts.

### Exclusions

No support for overseas projects, religious or political appeals.

### Applications

In writing to the correspondent who is a member of the CARE Committee. The committee meets quarterly to assess requests for support.

## Corporate giving

In 2004, Canon made cash donations in the UK totalling £35,287. We have no information regarding the beneficiaries.

### In-kind support

The company's main form of non-cash support is through gifts in kind, such as the donation of equipment/consumables.

### Employee-led support

Canon have an employee volunteering scheme and match employee fundraising up to a maximum of £500.

**Payroll giving:** The company has a scheme in operation.

### Commercially-led support

**Cause-related marketing:** 'The Other Side of Fashion' was conceived by Canon as a way of raising funds for the work carried out by Red Cross Societies across Europe.

Over 100 of the fashion industry's style icons were asked to take a photograph, or series of photographs, which captured their relationship with fashion. The results were then reproduced in a magazine showcasing the 'Other Side of Fashion' Collection. On sale across Europe, all profits will go to European Red Cross Societies.

Although no figures are available regarding how much this has raised, two previous projects 'On the Other Side of the Lens' and 'On the Other Side of Football', raised 'hundreds of thousands of euros for the Red Cross'.

# Caparo Group Ltd

Caparo House, 103 Baker Street, London W1U 6L

020 7486 1417; Fax: 020 7224 4109

Website: www.caparo.co.uk

Correspondent: The Lord Paul of Marylebone

Chief officer: The Lord Paul of Marylebone

| Year end | Turnover | Pre-tax profit |
|---|---|---|
| 31/12/2003 | £321,000,000 | £4,900,000 |

### Nature of company business
Specialists in the manufacture and supply of steel and engineering products.

Subsidiaries include: Nupac Ltd, Osborne Hotel Torquay Ltd

Main locations: London

UK employees: 2,259

Total employees: 4,200

## Charitable donations

2005: £500,000
2004: £400,000
2003: £400,000

## Community involvement

The company makes its charitable donations through the Ambika Paul Foundation (Charity Commission no. 276127). The trust continues to support the education and training of young people and to apply income for the benefit of any charitable organisation or purposes as the trustees consider appropriate.

## Exclusions

No support for: advertising in charity brochures; animal welfare; appeals from individuals; elderly people; environment/heritage; fundraising events; overseas projects; political appeals; religious appeals or sickness/disability charities.

## Applications

In writing to: Trustees of The Ambika Paul Foundation, at the above address

## Corporate giving

The company previously made donations to the foundation of around £400,000 a year, but in 2005, this increased to £500,000.

### Ambika Paul Foundation

In 2005, the foundation had an income of £723,211 of which £500,000 was donated by the Caparo Group Ltd. During the year 27 grants totalling £105,511 were made. Major UK beneficiaries included: Shine (£20,000); Zoological Society of London (£10,500); PiggyBankKids (£2,675); and, Women's India Association (£1,000). A donation of £60,000 was made to the Prime Minister's National Relief – India in aid of the Asian Tsunami.

## Employee-led support

Employees' volunteering/charitable activities are supported financially and by giving company time off to volunteer.

## Commercially-led support

**Sponsorship:** At London Zoo it sponsors the Ambika Paul Children's Zoo and the Pygmy Hippo project.

# Capita Group plc

71 Victoria Street, Westminster, London SW1H 0XA

020 7799 1525; Fax: 020 7799 1526

Website: www.capita.co.uk

Correspondent: Anna Prudente, Marketing Administrator

Chief officer: Rodney Aldridge

Chief Executive: Paul Pindar

| Year end 31/12/2005 | Turnover £1,435,500,000 | Pre-tax profit £153,100,000 |
|---|---|---|

**Nature of company business**

The group provides a range of white-collar integrated professional support services to clients in local and central government, education, and the private sector. Services include: administrative services; consultancy; IT and software services; and human resource provision.

Main locations: London

Total employees: 23,431

## Charitable donations

2005: £400,000
2003: £200,000

Management costs: £10,000

Membership: L B Group, %Club

## Community involvement

Support is currently directed mainly towards two national charities as stated below. The company's charitable programme is managed by a central charity team. Additionally, a large degree of fundraising takes place at a local level and is supported by individual businesses and encouraged by a network of 'Charity Champions'.

A proportion of all money raised for the NSPCC goes to their affiliates in Scotland and Ireland, reflecting the contributions that are made by Capita businesses in those countries.

**Charity of the Year:** NSPCC, Prince's Trust and Macmillan Cancer Relief.

## Exclusions

No support outside that being given to Capita's chosen charities.

## Applications

In writing to the correspondent, but note that corporate support appears limited to the charities already mentioned.

## Corporate giving

In 2005, the company made charitable donations of £400,000. Support in this year was given to the Prince's Trust and the NSPCC.

A third charity, Macmillan Cancer Relief, was chosen by staff for support and benefited from the company's annual Christmas card donation, payroll giving and locally run fundraising events.

## Employee-led support

The company states that it fully supports the individual charity work and fundraising activities of its staff. During 2005 staff raised money for its chosen charity, Macmillan Cancer Relief.

Unfortunately, we do not know if this includes matched funding or time off for volunteering.

In 2006, the Capita Challenge, an outdoor activity race bringing together teams of Capita staff from across the UK raised £28,000 on behalf of the NSPCC.

## Commercially-led support

**Sponsorship:** Capita undertake good-cause sponsorship. This is currently directed in support of the NSPCC and the Prince's Trust.

# Capital One Holdings Ltd

Trent House, Station Street, Nottingham NG2 3HX

Website: www.capitalone.co.uk

Correspondent: Community Relations

Chief officer: Richard D Fairbank

| Year end | Turnover | Pre-tax profit |
|---|---|---|
| 31/12/2003 | | £17,084,000 |

Nature of company business
Credit card provider.

Main locations: Nottingham, London

UK employees: 2,000

### Charitable donations

Membership: BitC, %Club

## Community involvement

The company's website states: 'Capital One is dedicated to sharing our success with the communities in which we operate. We've built the foundation for a strategic community relations program by forming long-term, collaborative alliances with agencies that are dedicated to revitalising communities and helping youths at-risk. We offer leadership grants to non-profit organisations, volunteer community outreach programs and donations to help underprivileged children.'

Capital One therefore focuses it community activities around issues affecting children and young people in Nottingham. As the company works proactively with community partners and agencies, the majority of funding is already allocated to key projects that have been identified in consultation with these groups.

Support is also available to groups through the volunteering activities of the company's staff.

### Exclusions

The company does not support individuals or advertise in publications.

### Applications

In writing to the correspondent. Please be aware, however, that each year most funding is already allocated and that consideration will only be given to requests that closely fit the company's strategy.

## Corporate giving

No overall figure for the company's community contributions was available. We do know, however, that it continues to provide £10,000 a year to Money Advice Team, which is dedicated to improving debt management services in the UK. Other beneficiaries have included Notts County Football in the Community, Teach First and Young Potential.

## Employee-led support

Employees who volunteer for 50 hours or more in their own time can receive up to £250 for their organisation. Teams of between five and 20 employees can be seconded for a day to undertake a one-day community challenge. Activities performed in the past have included helping create a sensory garden at Nottingham Royal Society for the Blind, conservation work in Bestwood Country Park and painting murals in schools and community groups. The business skills of employees can also be utilised, with projects including the design of marketing material to encourage people to adopt or foster children with special needs and the installation of computer equipment at after-school support centres in Nottingham.

## Commercially-led support

**Sponsorship**

Events are only sponsored which are concerned with children's causes and would raise at least three times the amount of money requested for the sponsorship.

# Cargill plc

Knowle Hill Park, Fairmile Lane, Cobham, Surrey KT11 2PD

01932 861000; Fax: 01932 861200

Website: cargill.com

Correspondent: Jo Cooper, Secretary, Cargill Cares Council

Managing Director: Graham Secker

| Year end | Turnover | Pre-tax profit |
|---|---|---|
| 31/05/2006 | | |

Nature of company business
Cargill is an international provider of food, agricultural and risk management products and services.

Subsidiaries include: Cerestar, The Duckworth Group, First4Farming, Sun Valley

Main locations: Newbury, Wolverhampton, York, Worksop, Tilbury, Runcorn, Manchester, Liverpool, Hereford, Hull, Cobham, Within St Hughes

Total employees: 1,100

## Community involvement

Cargill states on its website that: 'To organise community involvement activities, many of our locations have established Cargill Cares Councils, formalised groups of employees that coordinate volunteer programs and direct resources to meet community needs. With enriched communities" as one of Cargill's four measures of performance, Cargill businesses are also including community involvement as part of their annual business plans.'

At corporate level support is focused on the following three main areas: nutrition and health, education and environmental stewardship. Through the Cargill Citizenship Fund, strategic grants are provided to regional, national or global non-profit or non-governmental organisations that provide programmes and services to multiple Cargill communities. The company provides direct grants for regional, national and global partnerships and provides matching funds for selected local projects supported by its businesses.

Local community organisations must request funding from the Cargill Cares Council (if established) at their nearest facility.

The company also supports staff volunteerism.

### Exclusions

Grants are not given to:

- organisations that do not serve communities where Cargill has a business presence
- individuals or groups seeking support for research, planning, personal needs or travel
- public service or political campaigns
- lobbying, political or fraternal activities
- benefit dinners, fundraising events or tickets to the same
- fundraising campaigns, walk-a-thons, or promotions to eliminate or control specific diseases
- athletic scholarships
- advertising sponsorships
- religious groups for religious purposes
- publications, audio-visual productions or special broadcasts
- endowment campaigns.

### Applications

Local organisations seeking support should contact their nearest Cargill Cares Council.

Regional, national or global non-profit or non-governmental organisations meeting Cargill's criteria for support should to submit a 2-3 page letter of inquiry via mail, fax or e-mail. The letter should include the following:

- Name of organization and mission
- Description of project for which funds are requested
- How the project/program fits within Cargill's focus areas
- Amount requested

The mailing address is: Cargill Citizenship Committee, PO. Box 5650, Minneapolis, MN 55440-5650, U.S.A.

Cargill will review the letter of inquiry and determine whether the organisation will be invited to submit a complete proposal. All letters will receive a response. Those organisations invited to submit a proposal must complete the Cargill Citizenship Fund Guidelines and Application Form. Cargill may request additional information or a site visit. The committee reviews applications on an ongoing basis. Decisions concerning applications are generally made within 90 days of receipt.

## Corporate giving

Cargill contributes more than US $36 million annually to charitable and non-profit organisations around the world. We were unable to obtain any figures for the UK.

## In-kind support

The company's main area of non-cash support is gifts in kind.

## Employee-led support

Cargill encourages all employees to share their time and talent to enrich its communities. Its corporate employee volunteerism policy allows employees to take up to two hours per month from work to participate in Cargill-sponsored community service or volunteer opportunities.

# Carillion plc

24 Birch Street, Wolverhampton WV1 4HY

01902 422431; Fax: 01902 316165

Website: www.carillionplc.com

Correspondent: Richard Tapp, Director of Legal Services, Chairman to the Appeals Committee

Chief officer: Philipn Rogerson

Chief Executive: John McDonough

| Year end | Turnover | Pre-tax profit |
|---|---|---|
| 31/12/2005 | £2,025,500,000 | £51,900,000 |

**Nature of company business**
Providing expertise in commercial and industrial building, refurbishment, civil engineering, road and rail construction and maintenance, mechanical and electrical services, facilities management and PFI Solutions

Main locations: Wolverhampton, Leeds, Manchester, Liverpool, London, Bristol, Brentford, Glasgow

UK employees: 11,867

Total employees: 15,268

### Charitable donations

2005: £84,000
2004: £76,000
2003: £67,000

Membership: BitC, %Club

## Community involvement

Formerly the construction services division of Tarmac, Carillion was formed in 1999. In order to guide the company's approach to supporting good causes through financial or in kind contributions the following charities policy was adopted:

- the charitable objective should be close to or have some connection with the group and its objectives
- the subject matter should be tangible and be able to reflect the support given by the group, i.e. the group should receive some public recognition
- there should be a balance between the following charitable objectives – health, community, environment, education and arts.

**Charity of the Year:** The Wildlife Trust.

### Applications

In writing to the correspondent.

**Information available:** The company produces a social responsibility report. Its website contains comprehensive details of its community activities.

## Corporate giving

In 2005 the company made cash donations totalling £84,000. Main beneficiaries included: The Wildlife Trust; Business in the Community; The British Heart Foundation; and, CRASH.

## In-kind support

The company gave gifts in kind in the form of staff secondments and its participation in the New Deal Scheme for

Construction which aims to provide young, unemployed people with the opportunity to enter the construction industry. The scheme is an attempt to solve the skills crisis the UK construction industry is currently experiencing.

## Employee-led support

The company operate an employee volunteering scheme and allow staff time off to carry out charitable work.

---

# Cattles plc

Kingston House, Centre 27 Business Park, Woodhead Road, Birstall, Batley WF17 9TD

01924 444466; Fax: 01924 448324

Website: www.cattles.co.uk

Correspondent: JayneJohnson, CSR Manager
E-mail: jaynejohnson@cattles.co.uk

Chief officer: Norman Broadhurst

Chief Executive: Seán P Mahon

| Year end | Turnover | Pre-tax profit |
|---|---|---|
| 31/12/2005 | £705,210,000 | £115,134,000 |

Nature of company business
Provision of financial services such as secured and unsecured personal loans, hire purchase credit facilities and merchandise.

Subsidiaries include: Dial 4 A Loan, Welcome Financial Services Ltd, Shopacheck Financial Services, The Lewis Group, Welcome Car Insurance

Main locations: Oxford, Manchester, Leeds, Hull, Glasgow, Nottingham

UK employees: 4,866

### Charitable donations

2005: £422,180
2004: £262,727
2003: £93,480

Membership: BitC

## Community involvement

Cattles primarily targets its support towards three key areas:

▷ raising standards in financial education

▷ improving the welfare of young people

▷ addressing the issues of social disadvantage.

Community investment in these areas is achieved in three ways:

▷ developing partnerships with a small number of key charities or community organisations whose work relates to our business activities and which follows its key areas of activity

▷ involving employees in our community and charity work and favouring projects where our employees have a particular interest

▷ contributing to charitable initiatives, through cash donation and gifts in kind (including time and resources), which relate to the activities of the business and reflect the three elements of our community investment policy.

## Exclusions

No support for general appeals, fundraising events or individuals.

## Applications

In writing to the correspondent.

## Corporate giving

Over the last few years, Cattles standard of reporting on its community investment has improved significantly, which we applaud. In 2005, community contributions in the UK totalled £422,180 (2004: £262,727) which comprised cash donations, gifts in-kind and employee volunteering time. No further breakdown of this figure was given. An additional £127,929 was expended on managing the company's community investments.

Beneficiaries included: Outward Bound; The Variety Club; Duke of York Community Initiative Programme; NSPCC; The National Deaf Children's Society; KidsOut; Action for Blind People; and, Cancer Research UK.

During 2005, Cattles also continued its support for the promotion of financial education. Over £160,000 in cash, time and resources was donated to two organisations working in this area – Credit Action and DebtCred.

## In-kind support

The company may occasionally provide support through gifts in-kind.

## Employee-led support

The company supports Business in the Community's employee volunteering programme through membership of the *Cares* initiative at its main operating locations (Leeds, Nottingham, Hull and Bradford).

Through this, it has developed the 'Hands Up' volunteering scheme. Cattles provides tools, materials and eight hours of paid time for teams of employees to complete different challenges designed to improve the quality of life for people living in local communities. During 2005, Cattles donated 1,717 hours of time (2004: 491) to community initiatives.

Outside of this scheme, employees can, subject to certain criteria being met, have their own fundraising efforts matched by the company via 'CashMatch'.

**Payroll giving:** A scheme is operated by the company.

---

# Caudwell Holdings Limited

Minton Hollings, Shelton Old Road, Stoke-on-Trent, Staffordshire, ST4 7RY

Website: www.caudwell.com

Correspondent: (see applications section)

| Year end | Turnover | Pre-tax profit |
|---|---|---|
| 31/12/2005 | £2,120,999,000 | £91,968,000 |

Nature of company business
Supply of communications products and services.

UK employees: 8,248

## Community involvement

The Caudwell Group is perhaps better known through its high street presence in the form of 'phones 4 u'. The related Caudwell Charitable Trust (Charity Commission no. 1079770), has all its administration and management costs covered by the company. It is not clear however, whether it makes any direct cash donations to the trust.

The aims of the Caudwell Charitable Trust are:

- to make donations to specific child cases of sickness, specialised medical requirements and dying wish holidays, applicants must be under the age of 18
- to buy or build a property to aid children/children's charities
- to continue to fulfil its half a million pound pledge to the NSPCC Full Stop Campaign.

In September 2006, the Caudwell Group announced that it had completed the sale agreement with Doughty Hanson & Co and Providence Equity Partners, under which the private equity firms have acquired the entire group for a total of £1.46 billion. It is uncertain what affect this will have on the company's giving policy.

### Exclusions

The Charity does not give to other charities or trusts, with the exception of the NSPCC.

Funding currently unavailable for:

- building works or fixtures and fittings
- gardening, fencing or hard surfacing
- domestic appliances, decorating, clothing or bedding
- respite care/childcare/residential holidays
- dolphin therapy/faith healing
- PCs or laptops, unless specifically designed for those with special needs
- motor vehicle purchase/lease/adaptations/accessories
- equipment repair, maintenance or adaptations
- holidays (excluding holidays for terminally ill children)
- lifts (internal or external)
- play equipment (not including therapy tricycles).

### Applications

All applications must be made on one of the charity's application forms. This can be downloaded from its website, along with full guidelines (www.caudwellcharity.co.uk). Alternatively send a request by e-mail (charity@caudwell.com) or telephone 0845 3001348 and leave your name and address, spelling out any difficult words on the charity's answering machine.

## Corporate giving

**The Caudwell Charitable Trust**

In 2005, grants to 954 children totalling £1,797,500 were made.

## Employee-led support

The Caudwell Group's first fundraising campaign 'Raise the Roof' was funded by a weekly jeans day, where company employees donated £1 to come to work in their jeans every Friday.

# Cazenove Group plc

20 Moorgate, London EC2R 6DA

020 7155 5000; Fax: 020 7155 9800

Website: www.cazenove.com

Correspondent: Bernard Cazenove, Trustee
E-mail: bernard.cazenove@cazenove.com

Chief officer: David Mayhew

Chief Executive: Robert Pickering

| Year end | Turnover | Pre-tax profit |
|---|---|---|
| 31/12/2005 | £66,500,000 | £48,100,000 |

Nature of company business
Investment bank.

Main locations: Salisbury, London, Oxford, Chester

UK employees: 1,154

### Charitable donations

2005: £0
2004: £260,644
2003: £259,058

Total community contributions: £0

## Community involvement

Following an announcement in late 2004 that Cazenove would combine its investment banking business with JPMorgan's to form a new jointly-owned company called JPMorgan Cazenove, and the subsequent demerger of Cazenove Capital Management, the situation regarding its future level of community support has become a little unclear.

In previous years, the closely associated Cazenove Charitable Trust (Charity Commission no. 1086899), has received a number of substantial donations from the Cazenove Group. A number of major projects identified during this period subsequently had the responsibility for the large grants they were to receive taken on by the Cazenove Group. As a result, the company did not provide the trust with any substantial donations for the period May 2004 to December 2005.

Until it becomes clearer as to how the relationship between the new joint-venture and the charitable trust is to proceed, the information given here relates to the trust.

The main areas of its work are homelessness, unemployment and children who are disadvantaged, although any charities that Cazenove employees are involved in may also be eligible. It is likely that preference is given to organisations around its offices, which are in Chester, London (Southwark), Oxford and Salisbury.

### Applications

Applications to the trust should be made in writing and sent to: Bernard Cazenove, Trustee, Cazenove Charitable Trust at the above address.

## Corporate giving

Cazenove Group Limited made no charitable donations during 2005.

**Cazenove Charitable Trust**

According to the Cazenove Group's annual report and accounts for the year, the trust made donations totalling £153,500. No details of the beneficiaries were available.

## Employee-led support

Previously, staff were available for volunteering and secondments, with fundraising efforts of staff are matched to a maximum of £1,000. We do not know if this is still the case.

**Payroll giving:** The company is involved in the payroll giving scheme organised by CAF.

# CEF Holdings Ltd

141 Farmer Ward Road, Kenilworth, Warwickshire CV8 2SU

01926 514380

Website: www.cef.co.uk

Correspondent: (See below.)

Managing Director: Roger Thorn

| Year end | Turnover | Pre-tax profit |
|---|---|---|
| 30/04/2004 | £459,000,000 | £31,000,000 |

**Nature of company business**
Principal activity: electrical wholesalers and manufacturers.

**Subsidiaries include:** Dennis Vanguard International Ltd, City Electrical Factors Ltd

**Main locations:** Kenilworth

**UK employees:** 4,083

## Community involvement

The company covenants its donations to the Janet Nash Charitable Trust (Charity Commission no. 326880). The trust usually prefers to support a number of the same organisations each year, particularly children's and sickness/disability charities. In previous years some preference has been shown for causes in the West Midlands and Warwickshire where the company is based.

## Exclusions

No support for advertising in charity brochures, animal welfare, appeals from individuals, fundraising events, overseas projects, political appeals, religious appeals or local appeals not in areas of company presence.

## Applications

We have recently been informed by The Janet Nash Charitable Trust that: 'The charity does not, repeat not, ever, consider any applications for benefit from the public'.

All potential beneficiaries are identified personally by the trustees. Unsolicited applications are not, therefore, acknowledged.

## Corporate giving

**The Janet Nash Charitable Trust**

In 2005/06, the trust had an income of £421,283. In previous years almost all of the trust's income was derived in donations from CEF. However, on this occasion we have been unable to confirm this.

The trust made grants to organisations totalling £200,891 and to individuals totalling £202,211 (£403,102 in all). Major beneficiaries included: Shirley Medical Centre (£51,000); Royal Air Force Museum – Hendon (£25,000); SENSE (£5,000); Dyslexia Institute (£4,000); Bobath Children's Therapy Centre, Wales (£3,000); and Crimestoppers Trust (£2,000).

## In-kind support

The company has given gifts in kind and rewired charities' properties on certain occasions.

# Celtic Energy Ltd

Heol Ty Aberaman, Aberdare, Rhondda Cynon Taff, CF44 6RF

01685 874201; Fax: 01685 878105

Website: www.coal.com

Correspondent: Richard Walters, Chief Executive

Chief Executive: Richard Walters

Managing Director: Richard Walters

| Year end | Turnover | Pre-tax profit |
|---|---|---|
| 30/03/2001 | £60,000,000 | £7,000,000 |

**Nature of company business**
The main activities are opencast coal mining, land redevelopment and associated activities.

**Main locations:** Aberdare

**UK employees:** 400

**Total employees:** 400

## Charitable donations

Total community contributions: £55,000

## Community involvement

Celtic Energy Limited is the successor in South Wales to the former British Coal Corporation that was privatised by the government in 1994 and was responsible for all of British Coal's opencast mining activities in South Wales. Celtic Energy's community programme is mainly focused on the local communities around the company's sites.

Previous information provided suggested that support is given in three ways (see below). For all three categories, the company tends to support local schools, youth groups and disability organisations. National charities are only ever supported where they are working specifically in the area of the company's sites.

The three categories supported are:
- encouraging communication and education
- setting up site liaison committees to ensure community involvement
- providing support to local schools, charities, sporting groups and local organisation.

## Exclusions

No support for political or religious appeals.

## Applications

In writing to the correspondent.

## Corporate giving

We have been unable to obtain an up to date figure for the company's level of community support. We therefore repeat the previous information published regarding this.

Each site has a local liaison fund which is used to distribute money in support of local voluntary organisations. There also exists a central community budget. Donations from this are used to support organisations that fall outside the remit of the local liaison funds. This allows the company to respond to more general appeals, although still with a South Wales bias.

About £50,000 is available for distribution in total each year. Grants typically range from £50 to £500.

### In-kind support

The company has an educational programme, distributing information packs to schools on opencast mining, and encourages pupils to visit its operations. Support is also given through gifts in kind.

# CEMEX UK Operations

CEMEX House, Coldharbour Lane, Thorpe, Egham, Surrey TW20 8TD

01932 568833; Fax: 01932 568933

Website: www.cemex.co.uk

Correspondent: Chief Administrator for Charities

Chief officer: Lorenzo Zambrano

| Year end | Turnover | Pre-tax profit |
|---|---|---|
| 31/12/2003 | £4,873,100,000 | £133,000,000 |

Nature of company business
Principal activities: production and supply of materials for use in the construction industry.

Main locations: Rugby, Barrington, South Ferriby, Egham

UK employees: 12,563

Total employees: 34,815

Charitable donations
2003: £186,000

## Community involvement

Formerly RMC Group plc the company was taken over by CEMEX in 2005. It states on its UK website that: 'CEMEX takes its role as a good neighbour very seriously. The company operates an open door policy and welcomes visitors and comments to company operations. CEMEX strives to maintain and enhance strong links with community groups, local authorities, business partners, environmental organisations and other community partners to strike a balance between the operations and the environment.'

The company's website makes reference to a CEMEX UK Foundation, but this does not appear to be registered at the Charity Commission, whilst attempts to elicit further information were unsuccessful.

CEMEX's website provides community news relating to its major sites at Rugby, Barrington and South Ferriby. The emphasis appears to be on supporting local causes/projects along with nationwide support for initiatives involving community safety.

Grants are also available under the Landfill Tax Credit scheme.

### Exclusions

No support for circular appeals, animal welfare, appeals from individuals or advertising in charity brochures.

### Applications

In writing to the correspondent. All appeals are considered by a monthly committee which decides what to support.

## Corporate giving

Currently we have no figures regarding the level of CEMEX's community investment. Previously, the RMC Group made charitable donations totalling £186,000 in 2003, through its support of various local and national appeals.

However, we do know that at the South Ferriby plant substantial donations have been made through the long established Rugby Benevolent Fund (the name refers to the brand of cement). For example, over the past two years, besides supporting charities and other needy causes, £95,000 was donated to Saxby All Saints Village Hall for refurbishment and £40,000 to the new South Ferriby village school for the construction of a children's play area, environmental garden and woodland walk. It is not clear, however, what percentage of this came from the company and what came from employees' fundraising efforts.

The company also supports the Quarry Products Associations 'Play Safe, Stay Safe' campaign which helps raise awareness amongst younger people of the risks associated with playing in quarries.

As part of CEMEX's commitment to reducing accidents a scheme has been running for more than 15 years which rewards sites where employees have achieved targets without lost time injuries (LTIs) with donations to local charities. As part of this the company recently gave £1,000 to Keech Cottage Children's Hospice.

Under the Landfill Tax Credit scheme donations totalling £64,000 were made in 2004/05. The recipients were: Lincolnshire Wildlife Trust (£33,500); Lancashire Wildlife Trust (£15,000); and, Bonby Playing Filed Association (£15,500).

### In-kind support

Environment: CEMEX has worked with the Wildlife Trust and Suffolk Wildlife Trust in restoring quarry sites it is no longer extracting aggregates from. These provide both nature reserves and leisure facilities for the local community.

# Centrica plc

Millstream, Maidenhead Road, Windsor, Berkshire SL4 5GD

01753 494000; Fax: 01753 494001

Website: www.centrica.com

Correspondent: The Community Relations Adviser

E-mail: community@centrica.co.uk

Chief officer: Roger Carr

**Chief Executive:** Sir Roy Gardner

| Year end | Turnover | Pre-tax profit |
|---|---|---|
| 31/12/2005 | £13,448,000,000 | £1,368,000,000 |

**Nature of company business**

Centrica's principal activities are the provision of gas electricity and energy related products and services. The group also operates gas fields and power stations and provides roadside assistance and other motoring services.

**Subsidiaries include:** AA Corporation Limited, British Gas Trading Ltd, Automobile Association Developments Limited, Accord Energy Ltd, British Gas Services Ltd, Automobile Association Underwriting Services Limited, Automobile Association Insurance Services Limited, GB Gas Holdings Limited, Hydrocarbon Resources Ltd, Goldfish Guides On-line Limited

**Main locations:** Windsor

**UK employees:** 29,948

**Total employees:** 35,410

---

### Charitable donations

2005: £6,700,000
2004: £5,800,000

Total community contributions: £8,146,000
Management costs: £540,000

Membership: BitC, L B Group, %Club

---

## Community involvement

'Over and above the impact of our day-to-day operations, we seek to address issues of wider social concern that are relevant to our business. We focus our resources where we can make an effective contribution and enable our employees to get involved in community activities. To make a real difference, we must focus on those social issues that are most closely aligned with our business.

'Our approach is characterised by:

- systematic management based on clearly identified objectives
- long-term partnerships with community organisations and charities
- ongoing evaluation of our contributions and the impacts they achieve.'

### Exclusions

Due to key areas of project focus it is not usually possible to consider requests relating to individuals, animal welfare organisations, building projects or research. This also applies to requests for support from political or denominational groups, the arts or sports organisations.

### Applications

In writing to the correspondent.

## Corporate giving

In 2005 the company made contributions of £8.2 million in the UK, including £6.7 million in cash donations.

### In-kind support

Centrica provides in-kind support from computers and IT equipment to office furniture and stationary.

Centrica works with a range of charities and community organisations to support vulnerable customers and tackle fuel poverty. It is also involved in educational initiatives to raise awareness of energy efficiency and work with partners to support skills development.

### Employee-led support

Employees are encouraged and enabled to 'make a positive impact' on their local communities. In 2005 staff were involved in more than 15,000 hours of volunteering activities. This equated to around £420,000 in cash terms.

In 2005 the 'Helping Children Shine' partnership with NCH raised more than £250,000.

### Commercially-led support

**Sponsorship:** This form of support is only considered if it forms part of a specific project with which the company is already involved.

---

# Charter plc

52 Grosvenor Gardens, London SW1W 0AU

020 7881 7800; Fax: 020 7259 9338

**Website:** www.charterplc.com

**Correspondent:** James Deeley, Company Secretary

**Chief officer:** David Gawler

**Chief Executive:** Michael Foster

| Year end | Turnover | Pre-tax profit |
|---|---|---|
| 31/12/2005 | £1,065,700,000 | £103,500,000 |

**Nature of company business**

The company is an international engineering company. The group's activities are concerned with welding and cutting, air and gas handling and specialised engineering. Products are manufactured internationally to meet customer requirements across a wide range of industries around the world.

**Subsidiaries include:** Howden Compressors Ltd, ESAB, Howden Sirocco Ltd

**Main locations:** London

**UK employees:** 9,362

---

### Charitable donations

2005: £84,000
2004: £50,000
2003: £100,000

---

## Community involvement

The company's 2005 annual report states that through its subsidiaries it is 'involved in number of social, community and sponsoring activities. Individual businesses may contribute to specific activities in their location'.

### Exclusions

No support for circular appeals, advertising in charity brochures, appeals from individuals or local appeals not in areas of company presence.

## Applications

In writing to the correspondent. Many more applications are received than can be supported, and applicants are advised to consider if there is any particular reason why their appeal should be supported by the company. All applications will be answered.

## Corporate giving

In 2005, donations totalled £84,000 (2004: £50,000). Charities given support included, St Margaret of Scotland Hospice and Belfast Children in Need.

# Chelsea Building Society

Administrative Headquarters, Thirlestaine Hall, Thirlestaine Road, Cheltenham, Gloucestershire GL53 7AL

01242 271526; Fax: 01242 271222

Website: www.thechelsea.co.uk

Correspondent: Gill Greenwell, Secretary
E-mail: charitablefoundation@thechelsea.co.uk

Chief officer: T Harrison

Chief Executive: R Hornbrook

| Year end | Turnover | Pre-tax profit |
|---|---|---|
| 31/12/2005 | | 45,600,000 |

Nature of company business
Building society providing low cost retail savings and mortgages.

Main locations: Bournemouth, Reading, Worthing, London, Maidstone, Oxford, Paignton, Norwich, Chatham, Cheltenham, Brighton, Bristol, Watford, Ipswich, Leicester, Guildford, Birmingham, Exeter, Plymouth, Southampton

UK employees: 957

Total employees: 957

## Charitable donations

2005: £73,000
2004: £75,000
2003: £50,000

Membership: A & B

## Community involvement

The society gives its contributions to charity through the Chelsea Building Society Charitable Foundation (Charity Commission no. 1079292).

The primary focus of the foundation is to help relieve suffering and disadvantage and to benefit local communities. The foundation's priorities for the allocation of funds are:
- homelessness
- the disadvantaged, vulnerable or socially excluded
- all forms of disability
- health – self help and voluntary groups
- encouraging prudent money management for example money advice services
- security and community safety.

## Exclusions

The trustees will not usually consider grants for the following:
- activities which are mainly/usually the statutory responsibility of central or local government, or some other responsible body (except proposals for added support service)
- schools, universities and colleges (except for projects which will specifically benefit disabled students and are additional to statutory responsibilities)
- hospitals, medical centres, medical treatment research (except projects extra to statutory responsibilities)
- collecting funds for later distribution to other charities or individuals
- political or pressure groups
- profit distributing organisations
- individuals or individual fundraising efforts, including expeditions or overseas travel
- general fundraising events, activities or appeals
- fabric appeals for places of worship and the promotion of religion
- animal welfare or wildlife
- charities which have substantial reserves (in excess of 12 months expenditure) or in serious deficit
- the purchase of minibuses or other vehicles
- the acquisition, renovation and refurbishment of buildings.

No support for applications from outside of the society's areas of operation within the UK.

## Applications

Applications can only be considered if made in writing on the foundation's application form, which can be downloaded from the foundation's website. The completed application form should be forwarded together with any supporting or background material together with a copy of the signed financial reports and accounts to the correspondent. All applications will be acknowledged and applicants will be notified of the result of their application as soon as possible, although this could take up to six months.

Normally only applications from registered charities will be considered. Exceptionally, applications from self-help groups, voluntary organisations, projects with charitable aims/for charitable activities will be considered if the application is supported by a registered charity.

Information available: An introductory leaflet *Lending a Helping Hand* can be provided on request.

## Corporate giving

In 2004/05 the foundation had an income of £76,000, all of which came from the society.

Grants normally range from between £250 and £5,000, depending upon the number of requests received.

Donations are only made to charities operating within the society's area of operations in the UK.

In November 2005, donations were distributed as follows:

| | |
|---|---|
| Mental Health/Learning Difficulties | 30% |
| Housing/Homelessness | 8% |
| Children/Young People | 17% |
| The Disabled | 25% |
| Older People | 18% |
| Advice/Service Help | 12% |

In 2005/06 beneficiaries included Gloucestershire Dance and Prospect Housing & Support Services (£3,000 each), House of St Barnabas-in-Soho, Gloucester City Dial-A-Ride, 870 House, Mutley Greenbank Trust and TACT (£2,000 each), Cricklewood Homeless Concern, AGE-LINK and Discover (£1,500 each) and Off the Fence Trust, FACT, Generate Opportunities Ltd, Richmond Borough Association for Mental Health and Volunteer Reading Help (£1,000).

### In-kind support

'The society continues to support community projects through the provision, not only of sponsorship, but also of advice and expertise to charities and local community groups which enables them to raise funds for themselves. This contribution was recognised in the year through receipt of a number of awards for services to the community.'

# Cheshire Building Society

Castle Street, Macclesfield, Cheshire SK11 6AF

01625 613612; Fax: 01625 617246

Website: www.cheshirebs.co.uk

Correspondent: Kathy Cowell, Senior CSR Manager
01625 613612; Fax: 01625 617246

Chief officer: Tom Marshall

Chief Executive: Colin Whittle

| Year end | Turnover | Pre-tax profit |
|---|---|---|
| 31/03/2005 | | 6,600,000 |

Nature of company business
Building society provider of competitive investments, mortgages, and complementary financial services.

Main locations: Bolton, Maccelesfield, Mold, Wigan, Stockport, Warrington, Chester, Crewe, Buxton, Accrington

UK employees: 780

### Charitable donations

2005: £268,000
2004: £700,000

Membership: L B Group

## Community involvement

A community support programme was launched by the society in 1997 to support less well-known causes in the North West or within its brand operating regions. The society supports mainly small, local medical charities and those that work with disabled people, the environment, children, elderly people and homeless people. Support is also given to sporting, educational and special schools projects in branch areas.

The society has also established the Cheshire Foundation whose aim is to 'improve the way we offer support to our local community, making it more transparent and sustainable and easier to apply'.

### Exclusions

No support for political, religious or military organisations, overseas charities, appeals from individuals, arts sponsorship, third-party funding or NHS funding

### Applications

Application forms can be requested from the Corporate Affairs team on 01625 613612, who will also be able to offer help and guidance.

The Foundation meets on a quarterly basis in January, April, July and October and the society states that no funding decisions will be made outside of these dates.

**Information available:** A set of guidelines are available for applicants as well as a schedule of the society's funding commitments for the year.

## Corporate giving

The support of the society falls into five areas:

- educational projects – working together with organisations to develop understanding and value of education at all levels
- community support – encompasses a wide range of activities
- social inclusion – projects that aim to ensure everyone, regardless of background, experience and circumstances have access to services
- grass roots sport – encourages young people to become involved in sporting projects
- financial education – support to projects that encourage financial awareness or alleviate problems associated with debt.

The Cheshire Foundation meets quarterly to consider applications for funding above £150 and a Community Contribution Award has been introduced to support smaller projects.

During 2005, the society committed £268,000 to the development of its Corporate Social Responsibility agenda. Projects and organisations supported included Cerebral Palsy Sport, Headstrings, the Cheshire Show, Anthony Nolan Trust Garden, and Henshaws Society for Blind People.

### Employee-led support

Staff members took part in 19 fundraising initiatives, including the British Red Cross Dragon Boat Race.

### Commercially-led support

**Sponsorship:** Current partners are:

- Granada Action – sponsors Granada Television's Community Action Programme
- Careline – support to help meet operating costs
- UK Villages – sponsors parts of the UK Villages website that have a Cheshire branch on their high street.

# Chevron Texaco UK Limited

1 Westferry Circus, Canary Wharf, London E14 4HA

020 7719 3000

Website: www.chevron.com

Correspondent: Public Affairs (Sponsorship) 01224 334000

Managing Director: R B Brown

| Year end | Turnover | Pre-tax profit |
|---|---|---|
| 31/12/2005 | £9,604,400,000 | £222,200,000 |

Nature of company business
Principal activity: oil and gas exploration and production on the UK Continental Shelf. The company is part of the Chevron Corporation based in San Francisco.

Subsidiaries include: Gulf Oil Refining Ltd, Gulf Oil Ltd, Pelmans Petrolium Ltd, Telegraph Service Stations Ltd, De La Pena Lubricants Ltd, Gulf Service Stations Ltd, Curran Petrolium Ltd

Main locations: Pembroke, Aberdeen

UK employees: 1,102

## Charitable donations

2005: £459,000

## Community involvement

Chevron Texaco in the UK provide 'sponsorship' for projects involving the arts, education and the environment in, or near, to one of its four operating sites – Aberdeen, Pembroke, Swindon and East London.

### Exclusions

No support for circular appeals, individuals, local appeals not in areas of company presence, large national appeals or overseas projects.

### Applications

In writing to the correspondent. Normally a decision will be made within 3 weeks of receiving an application. Decisions cannot be discussed over the telephone.

## Corporate giving

In 2005, the company declared in its 'Annual Report of Contributions', charitable donations of US $800,000 (around £440,000) in Europe. Further in-kind support is also provided, but no figure was available for this.

As far as the UK is concerned, declared charitable donations in 2005 totalled at least £459,000, based on the annual returns of Chevron Limited and Chevron North Sea Limited. We have no information regarding the beneficiaries other than that they fell within the general categories for support mentioned above.

### Commercially-led support

**Sponsorship:** *The arts* – The company annually commissions promising young British and Norwegian artists to produce paintings of environmental subjects for inclusion in a full-colour calendar.

The Young Musician of Wales competition and the Highland Festival in Scotland are also sponsored by the company.

*Environment* – The Pembroke Refinery in Wales sponsors environmental education in local schools.

# Christian Salvesen plc

500 Pavilion Drive, Brackmills, Northampton NN4 7YJ

01604 662600; Fax: 01604 622605

Website: www.salvesen.com

Correspondent: Tom Salvesen, Marketing and Communications Manager

Chief officer: David Fish

Chief Executive: Stewart Oades

| Year end | Turnover | Pre-tax profit |
|---|---|---|
| 31/03/2006 | £820,700,000 | £15,600,000 |

Nature of company business
Principal activities: logistics and food services.

Subsidiaries include: Inverleith Insurance Co Ltd, Inveralmond Insurancce Ltd

Main locations: Northampton, Edinburgh

UK employees: 8,540

Total employees: 13,245

## Charitable donations

2006: £30,551
2005: £23,649
2004: £22,000
2003: £45,000

## Community involvement

The company is committed to supporting projects that involve the community.

### Exclusions

The company does not make political donations.

### Applications

Apply in writing to the contact. The Group Charities Committee meets quarterly.

## Corporate giving

In 2006 the company made cash donations totalling £30,551 to a variety of registered UK charities including SPARKS and TransAid.

We do not have a definite breakdown of the cash donations.

### In-kind support

The company works closely with Remploy in promoting economic independence for disabled people through helping them back into work and has won awards for the work done in this area at its Motherwell depot. As a result of this partnership, the company has succeeded in employing over fifty registered disabled people in a variety of roles.

Company staff are occasionally seconded to the community.

## Employee-led support

The company supports projects that involve the community through both financial aid and by in kind support such as employee involvement. A wide range of events and activities is organised and takes place at individual sites to support local and national charities and community based projects. In some instances the company will match the funds raised locally.

## Commercially-led support

**Sponsorship:** *Education* – The company sponsors an MSc student each year on the Logistics and Supply Chain Management course at the Heriot-Watt University School of Management. The student is given the opportunity to complete their MSc projects within the company and will also be considered for the Group's Graduate Management Development Programme.

*Medical Research* – The company also supports SPARKS (Sport Aiding medical Research for Kids) during each year by sponsoring a celebrity golf challenge.

The company is a founder member of TransAid, the leading charity specialising in effective transport solutions in the developing world and continues to have an active involvement with the charity.

# Ciba Specialty Chemicals plc

Charter Way, Macclesfield, Cheshire SK10 2NX

01625 421933; Fax: 01625 619637

Website: www.cibasc.com

Correspondent: Patrick Gorman, Head of Communications Northern Europe

| Year end | Turnover | Pre-tax profit |
|----------|----------|----------------|
| 31/12/2005 | | |

**Nature of company business**
Ciba is a global speciality chemicals company developing and supplying materials and processes that provide colour, care, durability and performance for a wide range of consumer and industrial products.

**Main locations:** Grimsby, Blackburn, Leatherhead, Paisley, Macclesfield, Clayton, Bradford

**UK employees:** 2,400

**Total employees:** 19,000

## Community involvement

Support is given to local communities in the areas in which the company is located. Its approach is to adapt community relations programmes so that they meet local neighbourhood needs. Initiatives include the encouragement of dialogue with its local communities through local community newspapers and the provision of feedback to enable the creation of appropriate activities. Charitable focus is placed upon issues including science and technology, and the environment.

## Exclusions

Past information provided suggested that there is no support available for appeals from areas that are not located near to a Ciba Specialty Chemicals site. No support for political or religious appeals or requests for individual aid/sponsorship.

## Applications

In writing to the correspondent.

## Corporate giving

No information was publicly available to indicate the size of the company's charitable budget, nor was any indication given on the returned draft entry. As a major company in the chemical world, however, it is assumed its cash and in-kind support are sufficient to warrant inclusion here.

## In-kind support

**Science and Education:** Ciba Specialty Chemicals is especially interested in programs that help children, young people and families and that foster understanding and respect between community members. In particular, activities and programs that improve science education will not only contribute to the creation of new generations of innovative scientists but will also improve the broader public understanding of our products and our industry.

**Environmental Excellence:** The company website states: 'The nature of our business means that responsible behaviour in all aspects of environment, health and safety (EHS) is essential. Ciba Specialty Chemicals seeks to use its expertise in this area and reinforce its reputation by supporting community initiatives that improve the natural environment and that encourage efficient use of resources.'

## Employee-led support

'Ciba Specialty Chemicals encourages employee outreach, fundraising and involvement in local communities and recognizes the benefits for the individual, for the community and for the company. We will continue to support our employees in endeavours that improve the quality of life where they live and work.'

Some examples of this have involved employees volunteering to help local causes including creating and maintaining a garden for The Harbourne Resource Centre, a specialist residential unit and day care centre for people with Alzheimer's disease and functional mental health needs; funding Netherlands Special School Christmas party and organising community challenges at Woodlands Cricket Club and Netherlands Scout Hut.

# CIBC World Markets plc

Cottons Centre, Cottons Lane, London SE1 2QL

020 7234 6000; Fax: 020 7234 6691

Website: www.cibcwm.com

Correspondent: Angela Carter, Children's Miracle Selection Committee 020 7234 6403
E-mail: angela.carter@cibc.co.uk

| Year end | Turnover | Pre-tax profit |
|----------|----------|----------------|
| 31/10/2004 | | 17,311,000 |

**Nature of company business**
Investment bank.

**Main locations:** London

## Community involvement

The company's support is all channelled through Miracle Day, which occurs on the first Wednesday of December each year with all commission generated on that day donated to children's charities. Further funds are raised at a number of events hosted by CIBC World Markets for clients and staff.

The key objectives of Miracle Day include:

- to raise the quality of life for children in the communities served by CIBC World Markets
- to demonstrate our dedication in helping to prepare children for future success
- to encourage volunteerism and foster community involvement on the part of our employees.

To be eligible to apply for funds groups must be UK/ European registered charities which are well-administered, with a record of achievement and the potential for success which will bring a tangible benefit to children in the communities where they live within Europe.

### Exclusions

No grants are made to individuals, political or advocacy groups, private schools, endowment funds, grantmaking trusts or groups that limit their activities to a specified ethnic or religious group. Grants are for one year only and cannot be recurrent. Organisations which have applied unsuccessfully in each of the three previous years may not apply (although these prior applications do not affect any applications made after the one year break).

### Applications

In the first instance, eligible charities should apply using the online application form.

The selection process begins in January with a review of the charities that have been nominated by clients, suppliers, professional affiliates or CIBC World Markets' employees. Charities who have applied independently via the Children's Miracle website are also considered. Any charities that do not comply with the specific Eligibility Guidelines are discarded. Charities that have been declined for more than three concurrent years are also removed, but can reapply a year later. The remaining charities are then invited to submit a proposal to the Children's Miracle Selection Committee, detailing their support for children's needs and their specific donation requests.

Full details of how to complete this stage of the application are given on the company's Children's Miracle Day website at: www.cibcmiracleday.com

Up to 14 charities may be selected to receive a donation from the forthcoming year's fundraising efforts. The selection process is usually completed by mid-May.

## Corporate giving

### CIBC World Markets Children's Miracle Foundation

In 2004/05, the foundation had an income of £396,000 of which £192,500 came from fees and commission earned by employees on Miracle Day (2004) and £36,500 from other donations and fundraising events. A further £165,500 was transferred from CIBC upon the formation of the foundation. Grants totalling £249,000 were made during the year to the following ten charities: Brainwave (£30,759); Chernobyl Children Lifeline (£20,600); Children with AIDS Charity (£17,500); Debra (£38,959); Down Syndrome Educational Trust (£20,000); Evelina Children's Hospital Appeal (£28,259);

Hope (£17,500); The Pace Centre (£15,000); Rainbow Trust (£20,350); and, SNAP (£20,000).

The foundation's annual report and accounts usefully gives information on the background of each of the beneficiaries, the projects supported and the impact of the funding.

Beneficiaries of the 2006 Miracle Day were: Children's Heart Foundation; CHICKS; Evelina Children's Hospital Appeal; The Hope Centre; Naomi House Children's Hospice; The Promise; The Rainbow Trust Children's Charity; and, SNAP.

### In-kind support

CIBC World Markets recognise that there are many essential regulatory requirements that charities are now expected to fulfil. To assist those charities it already works with via the foundation, in-kind support is given in helping them deal with the practicalities of, for example:

- risk and health and safety assessments
- IT security policies
- business recovery planning
- money laundering.

CIBC has also provided meeting and training facilities and associated catering for meetings and seminars held by the chosen charities at its offices.

### Employee-led support

In addition to the donation of commissions, staff are encouraged to take part in sponsored activities, which have included runs, bungee jumps and slimming programmes.

# Citigroup Global Markets Europe Limited

Citigroup Centre, 33 Canada Street, Canary Wharf, London E14 5LB

020 7986 4000; Fax: 020 7986 2266

**Website:** www.citigroup.com

**Correspondent:** Daniel Noonan

| Year end 31/12/2005 | Turnover | Pre-tax profit |
|---|---|---|

**Nature of company business**
Provider of financial services.

**Main locations:** London

### Charitable donations

2005: £964,000
2004: £895,000
2003: £880,000

Membership: BitC, L B Group

## Community involvement

The company has three areas of giving:

- financial education – such as educational projects, encouraging improved consumer habits and the creation of wealth in a community
- educating the next generation – such as literacy development, technology-based curriculum resources,

career and education preparation activities, teacher training and access to arts and culture

- building communities and entrepreneurs – such as affordable housing, economic development, welfare-to-work schemes, community infrastructure, sustainable development, disaster appeals and community-based health and welfare services.

### Exclusions

It is the foundation's policy not to make grants to:

- individuals for educational or other purposes
- political causes or candidates
- religious, veteran or fraternal organizations, unless they are engaged in a significant project benefiting the entire community
- fundraising events, telethons, marathons, races or benefits
- courtesy advertising.

### Applications

In writing to the correspondent.

## Corporate giving

#### Citigroup Foundation

Outside of the United States, cash donations appear to be made through the foundation rather than directly from the company. In 2005, over 3,075 grants were made totalling more than US$85 million (nearly £47 million). Of this, US$1,753,500 (£964,000) was given in the UK in 22 grants. Major beneficiaries included: Charities Aid Foundation (CAF) which received ten grants totalling US$611,000 (£336,000) for various programmes; Habitat for Humanity – Great Britain, Friends of the Prince's Trust and the National Academy Foundation (US$ 200,000/£110,000 each); Young Enterprise (US$134,000/£74,000 in two grants); and, Teachers Network (US$40,000/£22,000).

It should be noted that the grants to CAF benefited the following organisations: Langton Park School; Count the Beat; Centre for Innovation in Voluntary Action; Bygrove Primary School; African-Caribbean Diversity; UK Career Academy Foundation; Tower Hamlets Education Business Partnership; Aldeburgh Productions; Specialist Schools Trust; and, Teach First.

### Employee-led support

The Citigroup Volunteer Incentive Programme is designed to recognise employees who devote their personal time to community service and to support the organisations for which they volunteer. To qualify for a grant, employees must complete 50 hours of service with an approved organisation during a 12-month period or less. The Citigroup Foundation will award a US$500 grant to the organisation that benefits from the employee's service. Individual employees may only request one grant per calendar year.

If you wish your group to be added to the approved list of recognised organisations, it is necessary for at least five or more Citigroup employees to put your name forward.

Further details regarding the procedure for doing this are given at www.easymatch.com/citi

## Citroën UK Ltd

221 Bath Road, Slough SL1 4BA

0870 606 9099

Website: www.citroen.co.uk

Correspondent: Julian Leyton, Public Relations

Fax: 01753 812120

Chief officer: C Satinet

| Year end | Turnover | Pre-tax profit |
|---|---|---|
| 31/12/2003 | £1,199,864,000 | £14,758,000 |

Nature of company business
The main activity of the company is the importing and the sale of Citroën cars, vans and replacement parts.

Main locations: Slough

UK employees: 553

## Community involvement

Despite attaining membership standard for the 2005 Per Cent Club (the company apparently gave 1.4% of its pre-tax profits to charitable causes), Citroen UK Ltd have not been very forthcoming regarding its community support policy. Furthermore, although part of the Peugeot Citroen Group it is unclear whether donations are made through the PSA Peugeot Citroen Charity Trust (Charity Commission no. 266182) as is the case with Peugeot Motors.

In the past we have been advised that the company only accepts applications through other agencies such as The Sponsorship Bureau International. Any queries regarding this, or related charitable matters, should be addressed, in writing, to the correspondent given below.

As a general rule, we were told it is better to apply for support through the individual dealerships.

### Applications

In writing to the correspondent.

## Corporate giving

Unfortunately, the only information we have concerning charities the company has supported dates from 1999 when BEN (the industry charity) and WOMAC (Women on the Move Against Cancer) were beneficiaries. Just over £41,000 was given in total in that year.

### In-kind support

Support is given to local charities in the form of gifts and time.

**Education:** Local schools pupils are offered work placements, with specific students receiving mentoring.

## Clariant UK Ltd

Calverley Lane, Horsforth, Leeds LS18 4RP

0113 258 4646; Fax: 0113 239 8473

Website: www.clariant.co.uk

Correspondent: Company Secretary

Chief officer: J H B Ketteley

| Year end | Turnover | Pre-tax profit |
|---|---|---|
| 31/03/1999 | £374,200,000 | £100,000,000 |

**Nature of company business**
The principal activities are the manufacture and distribution of speciality chemical products and the manufacture, assembly and distribution of technical safety systems.

**Subsidiaries include:** Lancaster Synthesis Ltd, A P Chemicals Ltd

**Main locations:** Aberdeen, Ruabon, Leeds, North Allerton, Pontypridd, Wigan, Selby

**Total employees:** 2,963

## Community involvement

Formerly BTP plc, the company was taken over in March 2000 by Swiss-based Clariant. As it is 'not company policy to complete questionnaires', we have been unable to update the information we hold. We therefore repeat the information previously published.

Donations are given to local charities in areas of company presence.

### Exclusions

No support for advertising in charity brochures, animal welfare, appeals from individuals, overseas projects, political appeals, religious appeals or local appeals not in areas of company presence.

### Applications

Appeals should be addressed to the appropriate company or branch manager.

## Corporate giving

In 1999, the company donated £46,000 to charity. No further information was provided.

# Clinton Cards plc

The Crystal Building, Langston Road, Loughton, Essex IG10 3TH

020 8502 3711; Fax: 020 8502 0295

Website: www.clintoncards.co.uk

Correspondent: Secretary to the Chairman

Chief officer: Don Lewin

Chief Executive: Don Lewin

Managing Director: Clinton Lewin

| Year end | Turnover | Pre-tax profit |
|---|---|---|
| 30/01/2005 | £336,735,000 | £27,007,000 |

**Nature of company business**
The main activity is the specialist retailing of greeting cards and associated products. The group has 730 stores nationwide.

**Subsidiaries include:** Strand Cards Ltd, The Greeting Store Group Ltd, Macnoll Ltd, Papertree Ltd, Plumbell Ltd, GSG Holdings Ltd

**Main locations:** Loughton

**UK employees:** 7,932

---

**Charitable donations**

2005: £300,719
2004: £188,670

## Community involvement

Donations are principally made to national charities.

### Applications

In writing to the correspondent.

## Corporate giving

The company's charitable donations have continued to increase, and in 2005 reached £300,719 (2004: £188,670). No information was available on beneficiaries, although the company states that donations are mainly to national charities.

# Close Brothers Group plc

10 Crown Place, London EC2A 4FT

020 7426 4000

Website: www.closebrothers.co.uk

Correspondent: R D Sellers, Company Secretary

Chief officer: Sir David Scholey

Chief Executive: Colin D Keogh

| Year end | Turnover | Pre-tax profit |
|---|---|---|
| 31/07/2005 | | 131,739,000 |

**Nature of company business**
Close Brothers is the parent company of a group of companies involved in merchant banking.

**Subsidiaries include:** Air & General Finanace Ltd, Reabourne Technology Investment Management Ltd, Kingston Asset Finance Ltd, OLIM Ltd, Braemar Finance Ltd, Eidos Partners, Winterflood Investment Trust, Surrey Asset Finanace Ltd, Armed Services Finance Ltd, Winterflood Securities Ltd, Commercial Finance Credit Ltd, Mortgage Intelligence Ltd

**Main locations:** London

**UK employees:** 1,648

---

**Charitable donations**

2005: £323,000
2004: £46,000

Membership: BitC

---

## Community involvement

We were advised that the company does not participate in surveys. We understand from its annual report, however, that it provides two types of charitable donation. One through which it encourages and supports its staff in their own charitable fundraising efforts, and the other in response to major humanitarian and environmental incidents.

### Exclusions

No support for appeals from individuals.

## Applications

In writing, in the first instance, to the correspondent.

## Corporate giving

In 2005, the company's charitable donations increased significantly from £46,000 to £323,000 reflecting the consistent rise and fall in its donations that has taken place over the years. Of this amount, over £100,000 was donated to the Tsunami Earthquake Appeal.

## Employee-led support

Staff are encouraged in their charitable fundraising activities and receive matched funding from the group.

---

# Clydesdale Bank plc

30 St Vincent Place, Glasgow G1 2HL

0141 248 7070; Fax: 0141 204 0828

**Website:** www.cbonline.co.uk

**Correspondent:** Irene Swankie, Community Affairs Manager, Corporate Affairs Department 0141 242 4359; Fax: 0141 242 4100
E-mail: irene.swankie@eu.nabgroup.com

**Chief officer:** Malcolm Williamson

**Chief Executive:** Lynne Peacock

| Year end | Turnover | Pre-tax profit |
|---|---|---|
| 30/09/2005 | £936,766,000 | £185,190,000 |

**Nature of company business**
The company is a wholly owned subsidiary of National Australia Bank Ltd. It offers a full range of banking services through 230 branches in Scotland, England and the Isle of Man. In addition to general banking business, these services include investment management, executor and trustee work, insurance broking, debtor finance, corporate finance, corporate trusteeship, registration and global custody.

**Subsidiaries include:** Edinburgh

**Main locations:** Glasgow

**UK employees:** 2,803

**Total employees:** 6,176

---

**Charitable donations**

2004: £84,000
2003: £100,000

Membership: A & B, BitC

---

## Community involvement

The bank currently has community investment priorities in numeracy, financial literacy, enterprise, and volunteer development and promotion. Through its Community Partnerships programme, the bank actively seeks out suitable groups with which to work. However, it also welcomes approaches from charities and not-for-profit organisations that can demonstrate their ability to manage a community programme and evaluate its success objectively.

In October 2004, the entire business and undertakings of Yorkshire Bank plc were transferred to Clydesdale Bank plc by their parent company, the National Bank Australia. The year end financial figures for 30 September 2005 refer, therefore, to those for the 'Group', i.e. Clydesdale and Yorkshire Banks. The donation figures, however, refer solely to Clydesdale Bank plc. Details of donations made by Yorkshire Bank plc can be found in a separate entry.

**Charity of the Year:** British Heart Foundation.

## Exclusions

No response to circular appeals. No support for advertising in charity brochures, animal welfare, appeals from individuals, overseas projects, political appeals, religious appeals, capital projects or salary expenses, or local appeals not in areas of company presence.

Please note that due to the volume of partnership proposals received the company is unable to discuss these by telephone, or to meet with organisations prior to receiving a written proposal.

## Applications

In writing to the correspondent at: Clydesdale Bank Exchange, Level 7, 20 Waterloo Street, Glasgow G2 6DB.

Please include a short letter setting out the following: a brief description and history of your organisation, your latest annual report and accounts, confirmation of its charitable or not-for-profit status, how it is funded and how you plan to use the funds for which you are applying.

Applications are considered by a charitable donations committee.

**Information available:** Clydesdale's parent company (National Australia Bank) published its second corporate social responsibility report in 2005.

## Corporate giving

In 2003/04, Clydesdale Bank made charitable donations of £84,000. National grants range from £100 to £10,000. Local grants range from £50 to £500.

Major grant recipients in 2005/06, included: The British Heart Foundation; Leukaemia Research; Macmillan Cancer Support; The Prince and Princess of Wales Hospice, Glasgow; and, Princess Royal Trust for Carers.

In January 2005, Clydesdale and Yorkshire Banks joined forces to launch a new charity partnership initiative with the British Heart Foundation. As part of this each bank donated £20,000 and agreed to match employee fundraising on behalf of the charity on a pound for pound basis.

## In-kind support

The company provides additional support through gifts in kind, e.g. the provision rent free premises to the British Heart Foundation and of rooms for meetings held by local community groups and charities.

## Employee-led support

An employee volunteering scheme is supported by the company financially and through the provision of company time off for fundraising activities. Initiatives benefiting from this include the Financial Education Partnership, Partners in Leadership, Arts & Business Skills Bank and Numbers Partners.

In addition to this, the bank's Staff Volunteer Grants Programme rewards and recognises the personal contribution of staff by providing grants to charitable organisations which they work with in their own time. Grants of up to £500 are awarded quarterly.

Employee fundraising and giving on behalf of the bank's charity of the year (British Heart Foundation) are matched.

**Payroll giving:** The Give As You Earn scheme is operated by the company.

## Commercially-led support

**Sponsorship:** The bank sponsors the arts, sport and business-related organisations/events.

Contact: Helen Everett (Tel. 0113 247 2400).

---

# Coats plc

1 The Square, Stockley Park, Uxbridge, Middlesex UB11 1TD

020 8210 5000; Fax: 020 8210 5030

Website: www.coatsplc.co.uk

Correspondent: Carolyn Gibson, Secretary

Chief officer: Gary Weiss

Chief Executive: Michael Smithyman

| Year end | Turnover | Pre-tax profit |
|---|---|---|
| 31/12/2004 | £1,711,900,000 | (£4,100,000) |

Nature of company business
Principal activities: manufacture, processing and distribution of sewing thread for industrial and domestic use, homewares and fashionwares.

Subsidiaries include: William Hollins & Co Ltd, Jaeger Holdings Ltd, The British Van Heusen Co Ltd, CV Home Furnishings Ltd, Hicking Pentecost Ltd, The Jaeger Co Ltd, Pasolds Ltd, The Jaeger Company's Shops Ltd, Tootal Group Ltd, Tootal Thread Ltd

Main locations: Uxbridge, Glasgow

UK employees: 1,865

Total employees: 30,498

> **Charitable donations**
> 2004: £66,055
> 2003: £38,500

## Community involvement

Previous information suggested charities which the appeals committee would ordinarily support come under the following headings: education, the community, the arts, medical research and healthcare, and the environment. Beneficiaries are almost invariably closely associated with the company and its associates.

## Applications

In writing to the correspondent.

## Corporate giving

In 2004 charitable donations totalled £66,055.

### The Coats Foundation Trust

Though this trust (Charity Commission no. 268735) has the company name and strong links with the company, it had assets of £1.8 million (2004/05) with no investments in the company. In 2004/05 it received £66,805 from Coats plc. £20,588 of this amount was sent to the Tsunami Relief Fund to aid Coats employees in Sri Lanka and £46,217 was invested by Deutsche Asset Management on their behalf.

Other grants were distributed by the foundation as follows:

| | Organisations | Individuals | Total |
|---|---|---|---|
| Relief of older, impotent and poor people | £23,588 | £13,200 | £36,788 |
| Education | £1,765 | £41,585 | £43,350 |
| Total | £25,353 | £54,785 | £80,138 |

## In-kind support

**Enterprise:** In the past, the company has seconded staff to local enterprise agencies and initiatives dealing with youth employment.

## Employee-led support

Previous information stated monies raised by employee fundraising are matched by the company for certain selected charities. It is unknown whether this is still the case.

## Commercially-led support

**Sponsorship:** *Education* – The company supports several academic appointments in a number of educational centres.

---

# Cobham plc

Brook Road, Wimborne, Dorset BH21 2BJ

01202 882020; Fax: 01202 840523

Website: www.cobham.com

Correspondent: Pauline Howell, H R Director

Chief officer: G F Page

Chief Executive: A E Cook

| Year end | Turnover | Pre-tax profit |
|---|---|---|
| 31/12/2005 | £970,300,000 | £126,000,000 |

Nature of company business
Design and manufacture of equipment, specialised systems and components used primarily in the aerospace, defence, energy and electronics industries and the operation and maintenance of aircraft, particularly in relation to special mission flight operations.

Subsidiaries include: FR Aviation Group Ltd, European Antennas, Precision Antennas, Chelton (Electrostatics) Ltd, Flight Precision Ltd, Micromill Electronics Ltd, Flight Refuelling Ltd, Chelton Radomes, Wallop Defence Systems, Chelton Ltd, Slingsby Aviation Ltd, Racal Antennas, FR Aviation Services Ltd, Chelto Radomes Whitney, Slingsby Engineering Ltd, ERA Technology, FR Aviation Ltd

Main locations: Almondbank, Bournmouth, Southampton, Nottingham, Wimbourne, Teeside, Kinloss

UK employees: 4,348

Total employees: 10,715

> **Charitable donations**
> 2005: £51,469
> 2003: £36,324

## Community involvement

The company restricts its charitable support to causes in the Dorset area where it is based and to business-related national organisations. Within this area it will consider charities in the fields of children/youth, education, enterprise/training, fundraising events, medical research, science/technology and sickness/disability. Advertising in charity brochures will also be considered, again if Dorset-based.

### Exclusions

No support for animal welfare, individuals, the arts, elderly people, environment/heritage, overseas projects, political appeals, religious appeals, social welfare or sport.

### Applications

In writing to the correspondent.

## Corporate giving

In 2005, the company made charitable donations totalling £51,469. The following breakdown was provided:

- disaster relief £14,400
- business enterprise charities £9,000
- rescue and armed service charities £6,000
- health charities £3,000.

Note: The above totals only cover grants in excess of £200.

Organisations in the UK receiving support included: the Royal Aeronautical Society; RAF Museum; and, the Institution of Mechanical Engineers School s Aerospace Challenge.

### In-kind support

In-kind support can be provided to local initiatives in the form of the free use of meeting rooms and premises, the donation of surplus computer equipment and furniture, and the offer of places on in-house training courses.

The company also states that it has supported disaster relief programmes through the provision of aircraft, supplies and mobile communications equipment. It is not clear, however, whether this means equipment donated by the company specifically in response to these disasters, or that some of its equipment happened to be used by the rescue services.

# Coca-Cola Great Britain

1 Queen Caroline Street, Hammersmith, London W6 9HQ

020 8237 3000; Fax: 020 8237 3700

Correspondent: The Secretary, The Consumer Information Centre

| Year end | Turnover | Pre-tax profit |
|---|---|---|
| 31/12/2005 | £131,450,000 | £12,296,000 |

Nature of company business
Principal activity: production of soft drinks.

Main locations: London, Lisburn

### Charitable donations

2005: £937,000
2004: £851,000
Membership: A & B, BitC, %Club

### Applications

In writing to the Consumer Information Centre at the above address.

## Corporate giving

The year 2006 PerCent Club Report stated that total community contributions in the UK amounted to £1.73 million. The annual report for Coca-Cola Holdings (UK) Ltd put the donations figure at £937,000.

'In Great Britain, Coca-Cola is committed to being an active member of our local community that aims to make a positive difference, particularly by helping young people to achieve their personal best. As part of this commitment we take into account the unique needs and requirements of our local community in line with our two key areas of focus:

- encouraging active lifestyles
- supporting young people through education.

'We care about the communities where we live and work and encourage our employees to get involved in our Citizenship programmes and play an active role in supporting their own local community.

'Coca-Cola Great Britain also directs charitable donations through the Coca-Cola Youth Foundation, which aims to provide a positive contribution to the development of young people, mainly teenagers, through physical, cultural, artistic or other educational pursuits.'

### In-kind support

Employees at our Coca-Cola head office in the London Borough of Hammersmith and Fulham, volunteer their time to act as business mentors to young people and Head Teachers from the local schools in the borough.

### Employee-led support

Active Citizen Fund: each year, the company helps local community groups through the donation of drinks as well as Coca-Cola branded merchandise. In order to encourage employees to play an active role in their local communities Coca-Cola Great Britain has created the Active Citizen Fund.

In support of the national Valued Youth programme, Coca-Cola Great Britain launched its first employee mentoring scheme in 2002/3. Through the scheme, each year approximately 10% of employees act as business mentors to the secondary school students participating in the Valued Youth programme within the London Borough of Hammersmith and Fulham.

**Payroll giving:** A scheme is operated by the company.

### Commercially-led support

Much of Coca-Cola's community support is classified under 'cause-related marketing' and thus does not feature in any donations account.

# Colgate-Palmolive (UK) Limited

Guildford Business Park, Middleton Road, Guildford GU2 8JZ

01483 302222; Fax: 01483 303003

Website: www.colgate.co.uk

Correspondent: Sally Brown

| Year end | Turnover | Pre-tax profit |
|---|---|---|
| 31/12/2003 | £226,336,000 | £49,594,000 |

**Nature of company business**
Producer of toothpastes, soaps, toiletries, detergents and similar products.

Main locations: Guildford

UK employees: 643

## Community involvement

The parent company supports children's causes across the world concerned with promoting the importance of oral health through education and prevention. The primary focus is to reach children in schools through videos, storybooks, songs, CD-ROMs and interactive activities. This information refers to the global grants programme of its US parent company; there was no indication available as to whether the UK division is grant making.

### Applications

In writing to the correspondent. The global grants programme address is:

Colgate-Palmolive Company
Contributions Department
300 Park Avenue
New York, NY 10022
USA

## Corporate giving

Very little information is available about the company's support in the UK. The last details we were given quoted cash donations of around £44,000. Given the size of the company, we assume this still to be the case.

# Communisis plc

Wakefield Road, Leeds LS10 1DU

0113 277 0202; Fax: 0113 271 3503

Website: www.communisis.com

Correspondent: Martin Young, Company Secretary

Chief officer: Michael Smith

Chief Executive: Steve Vaughan

| Year end | Turnover | Pre-tax profit |
|---|---|---|
| 31/12/2005 | £264,785,000 | £4,099,000 |

**Nature of company business**
An information management and communications business.

Subsidiaries include: Waddington Labels Ltd

Main locations: Liverpool, Leicester, Stamford, Newcastle-upon-Tyne, Rickmansworth, Leeds

UK employees: 2,016

Total employees: 2,065

### Charitable donations
2005: £34,250
2003: £24,245

## Community involvement

Communisis provides support for various local charities sited all over the UK; however it does give preference to those in areas of company presence.

The company prefers to support charities concerned with animal welfare, children/youth, education, the elderly, enterprise/training, environment/heritage, fundraising events, medical research, overseas projects, science/technology, sickness/disability, social welfare and sport.

### Exclusions

Sports sponsorship for individuals.

### Applications

The company does not provide support for advertising in charity brochures, the arts and political or religious appeals. No support is given towards appeals from individuals.

Information Available: The company produces a social responsibility report which is contained within its annual report.

## Corporate giving

In 2005, the company made cash donations totalling £34,250. Past beneficiaries have included Cancer Research UK, Children With Leukaemia, Meningitis Trust, Mental Health Foundation, and Lineham Farm, Leeds.

### Employee-led support

Company support for employees' volunteering/charitable activities is determined on each individual case.

# Compass Group plc

Rivermead, Oxford Road, Denham, Uxbridge UB9 4BF

01895 554554; Fax: 01895 554555

Website: www.compass-group.com

Correspondent: Mike Stapleton, Director Corporate Affiars

Chief officer: Francis H Mackay

Chief Executive: Michael J Bailey

| Year end | Turnover | Pre-tax profit |
|---|---|---|
| 30/09/2005 | £12,704,000,000 | £171,000,000 |

**Nature of company business**
The principal activity is the provision of food services to business and industrial organisations.

Subsidiaries include: Eurest, Select Service Partner Ltd, National Leisure Catering Ltd, Payne & Gunter Ltd, Select Service Partner Airport Restaurants Ltd, Letheby & Christopher Ltd

Main locations: Uxbridge

UK employees: 87,804

Total employees: 410,074

### Charitable donations
2005: £1,340,000
2003: £1,157,000

Management costs: £710,000

Membership: BitC, %Club

## Community involvement

Compass states on its website that: 'We have a strong track record in community engagement. Compass in the Community established in 1996 recognises the best community based initiatives across the world that tackle social exclusion, improve employability and promote sustainability and diversity and rewards successful teams with a donation to support their project.'

Unfortunately, only limited information concerning its UK operations was available.

### Exclusions

The company does not support advertising in charity brochures, animal welfare, individuals, the arts, elderly people, heritage, medical research, overseas projects, political or religious appeals and science/technology.

### Applications

In writing to the correspondent.

## Corporate giving

In 2005, the company made worldwide community contributions of £1,340,000. We do not know what proportion of this was given in the UK or who the beneficiaries were.

### In-kind support

Compass have been working with the charity Training for Life which assists people from a socially excluded or long term unemployed background re-establish their self-esteem.

The company also support the Hoxton Apprentice in London's Shoreditch. At the 100-seater Restaurant for Life, a team of apprentices, who were previously unemployed or homeless are trained and mentored by a complement of professionally qualified and experienced personnel over a six-month period. Following this, many move onto work placements or full-time employment with companies such as Whitbread or Compass.

### Employee-led support

Employees undertaking voluntary work in the community are recognised by the company through the presentation of awards and donations to their nominated charities.

# Computer Associates plc

Ditton Park, Riding Court Road, Dachet, Slough, Berkshire SL3 9LL

01753 577733

Website: www.ca.com/community

Correspondent: Tina Leach, Community Relations Specialist 01753 242860; Fax: 01753 241160 E-mail: christina.leach@ca.com

Year end        Turnover        Pre-tax profit
31/03/2006

### Nature of company business
The group is one of the world's largest management software companies, delivering software and services across operations, security, storage, and life cycle management for performance and reliability of IT environments.

Main locations: Edinburgh, Taunton, Nottingham, Datchet, London, Altrincham

UK employees: 900

### Charitable donations
2006: £500,000
2005: £500,000
2004: £500,000

Membership: BitC

## Community involvement

The company has a preference for UK-wide or European charities. It prefers to support charities concerned with children/youth, education, science/technology and health.

### Exclusions

The company does not provide support for individual appeals or charities concerned with any form of discrimination and will only review grants that apply as above under 'Community involvement'.

### Applications

Grant applications are only accepted via an online form at: www.ca.com/community/grants.htm (see 'Grant Guidelines and Application').

Please note that the majority of grants are initiated by CA and do not stem from unsolicited proposals. Unsolicited proposals are reviewed on an ongoing basis.

## Corporate giving

In 2006, the company made charitable donations totalling £500,000. Beneficiaries included: National Centre for Missing & Exploited Children, Starlight, National Space Centre, Young Enterprise, Education Business Partnership, The Outward Bound Trust, Staywise (Royal Berkshire Fire & Rescue Service), Marie Curie Cancer Care, Thames Hospice Care, Guide Dogs for the Blind, World Food Programme, Children in Need, The Prince's Trust, and the National Children's Home.

In 2005, the company established the Computer Associates Digital School House Foundation (Charity Commission no. 1107476) in order to 'advance education of the public in computer software and other technologies'.

### In-kind support

In addition to cash donations, the company provides support through gifts in kind and staff secondments.

### Employee-led support

The company encourages staff to volunteer by allowing an unlimited time off.

**Payroll Giving Scheme:** The Give As You Earn payroll giving scheme is in operation. The company then matches employee contributions by 200% (up to £14,000 per employee).

### Commercially-led support

**Sponsorship:** The company does not undertake any form of sponsorship.

# Congregational & General Insurance plc

Currer House, Currer Street, Bradford BD1 5BA

01274 700700; Fax: 01274 370 754

Website: www.congregational.co.uk

Correspondent: Margaret Slater, Marketing Manager

Chief officer: Robert B Copleton

Managing Director: Carlo Cavaliere

| Year end | Turnover | Pre-tax profit |
|----------|----------|----------------|
| 31/03/2005 | £188,300,000 | £2,540,000 |

Nature of company business
The transaction of general insurance business, in the form of the insurance for fire and other damage to property.

Main locations: Bradford

UK employees: 59

### Charitable donations

2005: £260,000
2004: £120,000

## Community involvement

The company is a wholly-owned subsidiary of The Congregational & General Charitable Trust (Charity Commission no. 297013). The trust was established to 'promote the Christian religion and in particular United Reformed Church and Congregational denominations and other churches which are of the protestant tradition'. It supports a wide range of churches, educational establishments, charitable organisations and community projects. There is a preference for West Yorkshire.

## Exclusions

The company does not make political donations. No support for medical research, overseas projects, or science/technology. Sponsorship is not undertaken.

## Applications

Applications to the associated trust should be made in writing to: David Collett, Secretary of the Trustees, Currer House, Currer Street, Bradford, West Yorkshire, BD1 5BA.

The closing dates for applications to be considered are 31 January and 31 July each year.

## Corporate giving

The company make an annual Gift Aid contribution to the trust. In 2005, this amounted to £260,000.

### Congregational & General Charitable Trust

In 2004/05, the trust had an income of £314,071 and made 60 grants totalling £67,705. In line with the trusts constitution, the beneficiaries were mainly churches and other religious organisations. However, around £3,000 was donated to 'Other charities', i.e. Newham Community Renewal Programme (£1,000) and Mission Aviation Fellowship (£2,000).

In June 2006, the trust also committed itself to supporting 'set all free'. Established by Churches Together in England, the project aims to raise awareness about the role of the church in the abolition of the slave trade and ensure that churches continue to end its modern day equivalent.

Currently the minimum grant given is £500 and the maximum £7,500 to any one cause. The amount of money given to the trust from the insurance company is dependent upon the profits the company makes and will vary from year to year.

### Employee-led support

Employees have supported various charities during the past 12 months via raffles and fundraising. Depending upon the activity, the sum raised may receive match funding from the company.

# Cookson Group plc

165 Fleet Street, London, EC4A 2AE

020 7822 0000; Fax: 020 7822 0100

Website: www.cooksongroup.co.uk

Correspondent: Mrs Pat Dowton, Appeals Administrator

Chief officer: Robert Beeston

Chief Executive: Nick Salmon

| Year end | Turnover | Pre-tax profit |
|----------|----------|----------------|
| 31/12/2005 | £1,634,600,000 | £81,400,000 |

Nature of company business
The Cookson Group is a holding company for an internationally-based group of companies principally engaged in the manufacture of specialist industrial materials, equipment, processes and services for use in industry. The group is divided into three divisions: electronics, ceramics and precious metals.

The group is located mainly in the UK, North America and Western Europe.

Subsidiaries include: Wilkes Lucas Ltd

Main locations: London

Total employees: 15,774

### Charitable donations

2005: £100,000
2004: £100,000
2003: £300,000

Membership: BitC

## Community involvement

The company supports both national and local charities, with a preference for those based in the City or its environs. Preferred areas of support include: homelessness (especially regarding young people), advertising in charity brochures, animal welfare charities, children/youth, education, elderly people, environment/heritage, medical research, overseas projects, and sickness/disability charities.

## Exclusions

No support for appeals from individuals; the arts; enterprise/training; fundraising events; political appeals; religious appeals; science/technology; social welfare; or sport.

## Applications

In writing to the correspondent. Telephone approaches are not welcomed.

## Corporate giving

In 2003 community contributions totalled £300,000. Previous beneficiaries have included Sight Savers International, The Bede Foundation, CBI Education Foundation, Council for Industry & Higher Education and Crisis.

# Cooper Gay (Holdings) Ltd

52 Leadenhall Street, London EC3A 2EB

020 7480 7322; Fax: 020 7481 4695

Website: www.coopergay.com

Correspondent: A A Mason, Secretary to the Cooper Gay Charitable Trust

Chief officer: Martin Shaw

Chief Executive: Toby Esser

| Year end | Turnover | Pre-tax profit |
|---|---|---|
| 30/09/2005 | £58,400,000 | £9,000,000 |

Nature of company business
Insurance brokers.

Subsidiaries include: James Steele Insurance

Main locations: London

## Community involvement

The company appears to make donations through the Cooper Gay Charitable Trust (Charity Commission no. 327514). This trust has the following objects:

- to make grants/donations for provision or maintenance of facilities in hospitals, homes or other bodies/organisations
- to promote research and results of research to the public.

The trustees in 2005 were: A A Mason; K G Turner; D A Allen; J C Begbie; M D Conway.

The trust also encourages staff of the company and its subsidiaries to submit applications for charities in which they have a particular interest.

## Exclusions

Only registered charities are supported. No support for students.

## Applications

In writing to the correspondent. Applications are considered twice a year.

## Corporate giving

### Cooper Gay Charitable Trust

In 2004/05, the trust had an income of £8,252 (2004: £221,665) and a total expenditure of £93,832 (2004: £316,000). No information regarding the beneficiaries was included with the accounts at the Charity Commission.

# The Co-operative Group

PO Box 53, New Century House, Manchester M60 4ES

0161 834 1212; Fax: 0161 833 1383

Website: www.co-op.co.uk

Correspondent: SarahLees, Campaigns Manager 0161 834 1212; Fax: 0161 833 1383

Chief officer: Bob Burlton

Chief Executive: Martin Beaumont

| Year end | Turnover | Pre-tax profit |
|---|---|---|
| 14/01/2006 | £7,397,000,000 | £258,400,000 |

Nature of company business
The major activities of the Co-operative Group include food retailing, funerals, travel agents, pharmacies and farming. It is the parent organisation of Co-operative Financial Services, whose operating subsidiaries, the Co-operative Bank plc, smile and Co-operative Insurance Society, provide an extensive range of banking and insurance products. Within these financial statements, results are allocated into three key segments - Trading, Banking and Insurance.

Subsidiaries include: CIS Mortgage Maker Ltd, Millgate Insurance Brokers Ltd, Syncro Ltd, Farmcare Ltd, Hornby Road Investments Ltd, Goliath Footwear Ltd, CIS Policyholder Services Ltd, CRS (Properties) Ltd, Herbert Robinson Ltd, CIS Unit Managers Ltd

Main locations: Manchester

UK employees: 69,974

### Charitable donations

2005: £4,400,000
2004: £3,900,000
2003: £1,350,000

Total community contributions: £7,200,000

Membership: BitC, L B Group, %Club

## Community involvement

Previously, details of the community support given by this Manchester headquartered co-operative was covered by three separate entries. One for the Co-operative Group (formed in 2001 following the earlier merger of CWS and CRS), the Co-operative Bank and the Co-operative Insurance Society (the latter two comprising Co-operative Financial Services which was formed in 2002). Now, however, this information has been brought together under the name of the Co-operative Group, the parent company of Co-operative Financial Services and various retail, travel, funeral and property businesses.

As there are a variety of community initiatives in place and various sources of funding available, we have tried to locate information about these under the business unit to which they relate. However, within the confines of our work we cannot cover all of these in depth and therefore refer you to the appropriate website (if applicable) for fuller details.

In general, the group's community investment strategy targets support at co-operative, self-help and community groups in the areas in which it trades. This support is measured using the London Benchmarking Group model, which includes both cash and in-kind donations. The figure quoted includes all

Co-operative Group units across the UK, but excludes commercial and arts sponsorship with direct commercial benefits as well as support for the wider co-operative movement (unless this has clear charitable purposes).

## Exclusions

Generally, no grants are made towards: projects which are in conflict with the group's ethical policy; funding political parties; religious appeals; the costs of individuals or groups to travel overseas for charitable purposes or fundraising; funding for individuals, including school fees; sports and arts initiatives (unless it is a project which benefits disadvantaged groups and sports or arts is a means to these ends); equipment for hospitals and schools which would normally be funded by statutory sources, and salaries or running costs.

## Applications

Further information can be had by contacting the correspondent, or by visiting the websites mentioned herein.

Application forms and details on applying to the Community Dividend Fund can be found at:

www.co-operative.co.uk/en/communityfund/

# Corporate giving

In 2005/06, the group made total community contributions of nearly £7.2 million (2004/05: £7.3 million) in the UK. Unfortunately, no further breakdown for this was available, although we suspect it to be similar to that for 2004/05 when the figures were as follows:

Financial support £4,400,000

Employee time £1,300,000

Gifts in Kind £600,000

Management costs £1,000,000.

Some examples of the various initiatives the group have in place as part of its overall community investment strategy, and of grant making funds available to community groups, are given below.

### CIS / the Co-operative Bank

The current community strategy takes the form of a five-year plan and covers three key areas:

- financial education and capability
- crime reduction and supporting victims of crime
- diversity and inclusion.

Further information on each of these areas are available at: www.cis.co.uk >About us >CIS in the community and at: www.co-operativebank.co.uk >About us >Ethics in action >Community involvement.

Although the majority of CIS's and the bank's support is devoted to partnerships on projects supporting one of its key themes, a £250,000 endowment fund (The Co-operative Bank Community Fund) has been established with the Community Foundation for Greater Manchester to ensure local organisations will continue to benefit from the company's support.

CIS has also launched a Black & Minority Ethnic Fund with the foundation to encourage applications from grassroot groups in this sector.

In addition to the above, the Co-operative Bank also provides support through its 'Customers who Care' scheme and its various charity 'Affinity Cards' (see 'Commercially-led support', below).

### Co-operative Group

*Community Dividend Fund* – Co-operative Group dividend cardholders can donate the odd pence left over from each profit-share to the community dividend scheme, but may also choose to donate a percentage or all of their share of the profit. These donations then go to the Co-operative Community Investment Foundation (Charity Commission no. 1093028), or Community Dividend Fund, to give it its working title.

In 2005, £1.43 million was paid out to 2,016 community groups across the UK. Grants range from £100 to £5,000, with the average amount awarded for the year being £713.

*Co-operative Action Foundation* – The group also has another charitable fund: The Co-operative Action Foundation (Charity Commission no. 1098718). This offers both grants and loans, but the grants programme is currently undergoing a strategic review. Further information will be posted on the website at: www.cooperativeaction.coop

## In-kind support

In-kind donations are made by the group, but we have no further details regarding this.

## Employee-led support

*Volunteering* – Staff within the group are actively encouraged to volunteer – donating their time, expertise, energy and enthusiasm to their local communities.

Three categories of volunteering activities are available to staff: team challenges, individual volunteering (e.g. victim support volunteers, mentoring, reading or numeracy volunteering in schools) and specialist volunteering (e.g. Prince's Trust Business Mentoring, interview technique training for prisoners, financial education training).

*Matched giving* – The 'Charity Booster' scheme enables staff who fundraise for charity to apply for a boost to increase the amount of money they raise, and subject to certain conditions, individuals can apply for a £100 boost, and teams up to £400.

**Payroll giving:** Staff are able to contribute to their chosen charity through the provision of a payroll giving scheme.

## Commercially-led support

**Sponsorship:** *Sport* – CIS has a comprehensive programme of grassroots activities including the donation of kits and football equipment and the setting up of football coaching events around the UK. Through the 'Kits for kids' scheme, junior teams can receive a brand new football strip. The latest round of applications closed on 15 December 2006.

**Cause-related marketing:** *Affinity cards* – The bank has an affinity partnership, with partners receiving a donation for each new branded card and a margin on its use. The most recent figures we were able to obtain relate to 2003, when a total of £1,406,610 was distributed between RSPB, Oxfam, Amnesty International UK, Greenpeace, Tearfund, Save the Children, Help the Hospices, WaterAid, ActionAid, Barnardos, Help the Aged, Children's Aid Direct, Christian Aid and Ramblers Association.

*'Customers Who Care'* – This scheme donates 1.25 pence for every £100 spent on credit and debit cards. Charities to benefit were Pesticide Action Network UK (£43,000), Friends of the Earth (£37,000) and Surfers Against Sewage (£20,000). Funding was also given to two campaigning groups; £200,000 to a national advertising 'Safer Chemicals' campaign and

£76,000 towards the biomonitoring of 44 members of the European Parliament. Again these figures relate to 2003.

# Cooper-Parry

3 Centro Place, Pride Park, Derby DE24 8RF

01332 295 544; Fax: 01332 295 600

Website: www.cooperparry.com

Correspondent: Human Resources Department 01332 295544
E-mail: thought@cooperparry.com

Chief officer: Colin Shaw

Chief Executive: Jeremy Bowler

| Year end 31/12/2005 | Turnover £13,000,000 | Pre-tax profit £3,200,000 |
|---|---|---|

Nature of company business
Accountants and business advisors.

Main locations: Nottingham

UK employees: 220

### Charitable donations

Total community contributions: £100,000

Membership: BitC

## Community involvement

Cooper-Parry's community support is mainly given in the form of employees' time. A wide variety of community activities have been supported, ranging from charities dispensing relief to the needy to those providing help for the deaf, local arts and music groups, and schools and universities. Each year a charity is nominated to raise funds for through various events.

### Exclusions

No cash donations are made in support of charitable causes. No support for local appeals outside of Nottingham, Leicester and Derby, where the firm has offices.

### Applications

In writing to the correspondent.

## Corporate giving

The firm's community support, although in kind, has previously been valued at around £100,000 during one year.

The company also hosts the Cooper Parry Corporate Challenge, a half marathon which raises money for designated charities each year. In 2005, £30,000 was raised for the nominated charities.

### In-kind support

As a founder member of the local ProHelp Group, a regular and substantial commitment to larger community enterprises is made.

Time is normally provided free of charge, particularly to smaller groups and organisations, but more substantial bodies may be asked to contribute toward the costs involved.

# Corus Group plc

30 Millbank, London SW1P 4WY

020 7717 4444; Fax: 020 7717 4455

Website: www.corusgroup.com

Correspondent: Richard Shoylekov, Company Secretary
020 7717 4444; Fax: 020 7717 4455

Chief officer: Jim Leng

Chief Executive: Philippe Varin

| Year end 31/12/2005 | Turnover £10,140,000,000 | Pre-tax profit £580,000,000 |
|---|---|---|

Nature of company business
The manufacture and sale of steel and aluminium. Major manufacturing businesses are located in Port Talbot and Llanwern in South Wales, Scunthorpe and Teesside, Rotherham, Scunthorpe, Deeside and Ebbw Vale, with distribution outlets throughout the UK and Europe.

Subsidiaries include: Orb Electrical Steels Limited, Cogent Power Limited

Main locations: Corby, Deeside, York, Wolverhampton, Saltburn-by-the-Sea, Scunthorpe, Rotherham, Port Talbot, Newport

Total employees: 50,300

### Charitable donations

2005: £394,019
2004: £340,358
2003: £283,341

## Community involvement

Formerly trading as British Steel, Corus was formed following the merger with Dutch steel company, Koninklijke Hoogovens in 1999. We were advised at the time that the company had not yet formulated a community support policy, but hoped to have done so before the end of 2000. However, as we did not receive a reply to our 2001 survey, we do not know if a new policy is in place, or whether the group continues with the policy established by British Steel.

As British Steel, the company made grants centrally, mainly to national appeals. It also had a preference for local charities in areas of company presence, appeals relevant to company business and charities in which a member of staff was involved. It also supported the arts, environmental projects and educational activities. Other areas of support were children/youth, elderly people, enterprise/training, social welfare (if related to the NHS), religious appeals and sport.

### Exclusions

No support for purely denominational appeals, small purely local appeals not in areas of company presence, appeals from individuals, fundraising events or circulars.

### Applications

Applications (including sponsorship) should be in writing to the correspondent, although local appeals should be made through local offices of Corus.

## Corporate giving

In 2005, Corus made charitable donations totalling £394,019.

Through its Corus Community Awards scheme, the company seeks to support a wide range of charitable causes in the communities where it has manufacturing and distribution premises.

Awards are made for: the provision of facilities for recreation and other leisure time activities; the relief of the aged, poor, sick, disabled or others in special need; the understanding and appreciation of the arts; the preservation and improvement of features of historic or public interest or natural beauty; the advancement of education.

## Employee-led support

As British Steel, employee volunteering was encouraged by giving financial support and matching employee fundraising.

# Costain Group plc

Costain House, Nicholson Walk, Maidenhead SL6 1LN

01628 842444; Fax: 01628 674477

Website: www.costain.com

Correspondent: Maggie Evans

Chief officer: David Jefferies

Chief Executive: Andrew Wyllie

| Year end | Turnover | Pre-tax profit |
|----------|----------|----------------|
| 23/12/2005 | £678,100,000 | £25,000 |

UK employees: 3,186

> ## Charitable donations
> 2005: £21,121

## Community involvement

The company states: 'The autonomous nature of Costain Group companies and sites means that most [community] activity is identified resourced and supported through local management.

'The Costain approach to community involvement depends on location, resources and the company's positioning in the community [sites can come and go in a matter of weeks, or can be part of the area for several years]. Broadly, there are three categories: the site-based approach; divisional or company approach; and, the head office approach.'

Divisions generally have a nationwide or regional commitment, often focusing on areas in which their offices and employees are based, whereas the commuter nature of staff at group head office means they tend not to live in the immediate area. In the latter case Costain has developed relationships with a few carefully selected community projects.

In view of the above variation in approach, the company has recently established a 'Community Chest'. Rather than simply giving to needy causes, employees are invited to bid for small sums on behalf of the community project they are involved in. However, only if certain criteria are met will the community chest pay out.

## Exclusions

No support for local appeals not in areas of company presence.

## Applications

In writing to the correspondent, or by contacting your nearest Costain site/office.

## Corporate giving

In 2005, the group made cash donations in the UK of £21,121. No details of the beneficiaries were available.

A fair amount of in-kind support is given by the group, although, perhaps due to its autonomous nature, this appears not to have been costed.

## In-kind support

At divisional level the group has undertaken refurbishment projects. For example, in updating a 6th form centre for pupils at Altwood School in Maidenhead, and refurbishing a derelict building on behalf of the Gatehouse scheme in London, to provide sales space for products produced by the mentally disabled.

At head office, staff are involved in a lunchtime reading scheme with a local primary school. Whilst accounting and public relations expertise is provided to the local parish church for their 'Breakaway' project for homeless people. The church has also had its roof replaced at cost.

## Employee-led support

Staff are encouraged to become involved in local community projects and may receive financial support on behalf of their chosen project through the 'Community Chest' fund.

# Coutts & Co

440 Strand, London WC2R 0QS

020 7753 1000; Fax: 020 7753 1028

Website: www.coutts.com

Correspondent: Mrs C L Attwater, Administrator, The Coutts Charitable Trust

Chief officer: The Earl of Home

| Year end | Turnover | Pre-tax profit |
|----------|----------|----------------|
| 31/12/2005 | | |

**Nature of company business**
Banking and allied financial services. Coutts is the private banking arm of the Royal Bank of Scotland Group. The bank's main location is London, but there are 17 regional offices.

**Main locations:** Liverpool, Manchester, Newcastle upon Tyne, Oxford, Nottingham, Winchester, Tunbridge Wells, Bristol, Cardiff, Cambridge, Isle of Man, Jersey, Leeds, Eton, Guildford, Bath, Birmingham, Bournemouth

> ## Charitable donations
> 2005: £257,000
> 2004: £116,000

## Community involvement

The Coutts Charitable Trust (Charity Commission no. 1000135) was set up in 1987 to formalise Coutts's charitable giving and makes a large number of small donations to a wide range of charities each year. In 2004/05, the trust made 513 donations totalling £315,000 to charities with an emphasis on the homeless, rehabilitation and self-help (drugs, alcohol, young offenders), disadvantaged adults and children, youth organisations and the relief of poverty.

## Exclusions

No response to circular appeals. No support for appeals from individuals or overseas projects.

## Applications

Applications to the Coutts Charitable Trust should be addressed to the correspondent above, at any time. Applications should include clear details of the purpose for which the grant is required. Grants are made regularly where amounts of £500 or less are felt to be appropriate. The trustees meet quarterly to consider larger donations.

## Corporate giving

### Coutts Charitable Trust

The trust is funded by the bank under a deed of covenant equivalent to one half of 1% of the bank's pre-tax profit with a minimum of £50,000. In 2004/05 the company donated £257,000.

Grants are given by the trust to UK organisations only and it prefers to support organisations in areas where the bank has a presence, mainly London.

## In-kind support

Coutts & Co works with the Prince's Trust to help young entrepreneurs in England and Wales. As part of its support, Coutts hosts a series of lunches and dinners to introduce its clients and guests to the work of the Prince's Trust.

## Employee-led support

**Payroll giving:** The company operates the Give As You Earn scheme.

## Commercially-led support

### Sponsorship:

Coutts also has a history of supporting the arts, including sponsorship for Welsh National Opera and the Royal Opera House. In-kind support is also given.

# Coventry Building Society

Oakfield House, PO Box 600, Binley Business Park, Coventry CV3 9YR

024 7665 3615

Website: www.thecoventry.co.uk

Correspondent: Melanie Eales, Company Secretary

Chief officer: David Harding

Chief Executive: David Stewart

| Year end | Turnover | Pre-tax profit |
|---|---|---|
| 31/12/2005 | £114,700,000 | £53,700,000 |

Nature of company business
Building society.

Main locations: Coventry

UK employees: 854

Total employees: 854

### Charitable donations
2005: £54,044
2004: £50,000
2003: £54,758

## Community involvement

The society has two methods of supporting the community. Firstly, support is channelled through the Coventry Building Society Charitable Foundation (Charity Commission no. 1072244) which receives an annual donation from the society.

The society only makes donations to registered charities that are based or active within the region covered by Coventry Building Society's branch network. Its priority is to give to groups, or activities, aimed at improving the quality of life and opportunity among groups who are disadvantaged or deprived, the consequence of which may lead to social exclusion.

They welcome applications that focus on:

- young people, particularly those who are disadvantaged
- vulnerable groups such as the frail and the elderly, people with physical disability, people with learning disabilities or those who are mentally ill
- small neighbourhood groups in areas where they are experiencing the greatest disadvantage
- supporting communities and voluntary organisations through assisting them in the achievement of social and community development.

Secondly, the society has a 'TLC in the Community' programme, the aim of which is to support and enhance the work of the charitable foundation.

The TLC in the Community Programme will support initiatives and activities:

- that actively involve Society staff who volunteer their support or raise funds to benefit charities or causes within the community
- that aim to improve the quality of life and opportunity amongst those who are disadvantaged
- that benefit the community by improving local services or facilities
- by organising and/or supporting charitable promotions/ events within the local community area served by the Society's branch network.

The TLC programme will support national charities, but wherever possible, would prefer to benefit to be for local projects within the branch operating area. An organisation does not need to be registered to receive support from TLC.

## Exclusions

The society will not consider grants for the following:

- large charities which enjoy national coverage
- charities with no base within the branch area
- charities with an annual donated income in excess of £250,000
- charities with assets over £500,000

- projects requiring an ongoing commitment
- large capital projects
- maintenance or building works for buildings, gardens or playgrounds
- major fundraising
- projects which are normally the responsibility of other organisations (such as the NHS, Education Department and local authorities)
- sponsorship of individuals
- requests from individuals
- replacing funds that were the responsibility of another body
- educational institutions unless for the relief of disadvantage
- sporting clubs or organisations unless for the relief of disadvantage
- medical research and equipment
- more than one donation for the same organisation in any one year – further applications will be considered after three years
- animal welfare
- promotion of religious political or military causes.

### Applications

To apply for a grant print off and fill in the application form from the company website listed below. Send the completed application form accompanied with a copy of recent report and accounts to: The Trustees, Coventry Building Society Charitable Foundation, PO Box 600, Oakfield House, Binley Business Park, Coventry CV3 9YR for consideration.

In some circumstances the society may request further information before considering the application. The trustees meet in February, May, August and November.

The society states: 'it may not be always be possible to support all applications even if they fully meet the foundation's criteria. We reserve the right to support those charities we believe to be worthy of our support'.

**Information available:** Further information regarding the application form and policy guidelines is available at the society's website: www.thecoventry.co.uk

## Corporate giving

In 2005, the society made cash donations of £54,044 of which £50,000 went to its charitable foundation.

### Coventry Building Society Charitable Foundation

Since the foundation's launch in 1998 over £475,000 has been donated to various charitable organisations. As it wishes to support as many good causes as possible the maximum single donation will normally be £3,000. As a general rule, donations are normally between £500 and £2,000.

In 2005, the foundation had an income of £52,073 and made donations totalling £44,429. Examples of beneficiaries include: Kairos Women Working Together (£3,000); The Castle Toy Library (£2,000); The What? Centre Ltd, Sound It Out Community Music (£1,500 each); and, Rev and Go, and Brittle Bone Society (£1,000 each).

### In-kind support

The society provides fundraising assistance to a number of major charitable appeals by allowing the use of its branches as collection points for public donations.

TLC provides in kind support by donating gifts and prizes for fundraising events which include items such as balloons, goodie bags, teddy bears, clocks, book tokens, champagne and books. They will also place community advertisements in programmes for local fundraising events such as fetes, carnivals and concerts. TLC also provides large publicity cheques to anyone who wishes to publicise the amount they have raised for a charity or other organisation.

### Employee-led support

The society also supports staff involvement in local community initiatives through the TLC in the Community Programme. The 2003 Annual Report states that a third of the company's employees were involved in or associated with a community activity.

Donations made by staff through fundraising are matched by the foundation to a maximum of £250.

# Credit Suisse

One Cabot Square, London EC14 4QJ

020 7888 8888; Fax: 020 7888 1600

Website: www.credit-suisse.com/uk/en/

Correspondent: Marie Burke, Vice President Corporate Social Responsibility

Chief officer: Jonathan Davie (Vice)

| Year end 31/12/2005 | Turnover | Pre-tax profit £4,000,000 |
|---|---|---|

Nature of company business
Global investment bank.

Main locations: London

### Charitable donations

Membership: BitC, L B Group

## Community involvement

Unfortunately, we have been unable to update the information previously provided under the Credit Suisse First Boston name (now simply, Credit Suisse). We can confirm, however, the contact name to be correct. Previously, we were advised that:

Support is given to towards the education of inner-city youth, such as after-school educational programmes and arts, music and sports groups. Other types of beneficiaries have included older people's homes, schools, public parks and homelessness causes. Much of the UK support is centred around its head office in Tower Hamlets. It has a transatlantic partnership with Habitat for Humanity, involving itself with building houses in Southwark, Tower Hamlets and New York.

**Charity of the year:** Richard House Children's Hospice (2004).

### Applications

In writing to the correspondent. All European donations are processed centrally from London.

## Corporate giving

Of the US$4,725,109 donated worldwide in 2003, US$836,024 was given in 57 grants in Europe. The worldwide figure was broken down as follows: education 53%; human services 24%; youth development 17%; arts 3%; health 2%; and sports and recreation 1%. It regularly supports Isle of Dogs Community Foundation.

## Employee-led support

Staff are encouraged to take part and establish fundraising events for the charity of the year. In 2002 a total of £338,000 was raised for NCH Action for Children through this. Staff have volunteered with Tower Hamlets Education Business Partnership (THEBP) to work with children aged 7 to 13 to improve their reading, maths and IT skills. Employees who are involved with voluntary groups can apply for 'mini-grants' for those groups.

## Commercially-led support

**Sponsorship:**

It is a corporate sponsor of SS Robin Trust, which has transformed the world's oldest complete steamship into a photo gallery and interactive learning resource for children.

# Crest Nicholson plc

Crest House, 39 Thames Street, Weybridge, Surrey KT13 8JL

01932 580555; Fax: 01932 858217

Website: www.crestnicholson.com

Correspondent: MargaretBrown, Secretary to the Company Secretary

Chief officer: J W Matthews

Chief Executive: S Stone

| Year end | Turnover | Pre-tax profit |
|---|---|---|
| 31/10/2005 | £714,300,000 | £79,200,000 |

**Nature of company business**
Property developer.

**Main locations:** Cardiff, Brentwood, Bristol, Hemel Hempstead, Weybridge, Tamworth, Westerham

UK employees: 860

Total employees: 860

> ### Charitable donations
>
> 2005: £48,000
> 2004: £36,000
> 2003: £15,000
>
> Membership: A & B

## Community involvement

Following a three-year partnership with Shelter which ended in 2005, the company has embarked upon a two-year fundraising partnership with the Variety Club. It supplements this financial commitment with in-kind support for a number of environmental/conservation initiatives.

## Applications

In writing to the correspondent.

The company produces a social responsibility report.

## Corporate giving

In 2004/05, the company made cash donations in the UK totalling £48,000. We assume this was mainly given in support of Shelter, its then charity partner.

For its new charity partner (the Variety Club) the company aim to raise £60,000 over two years.

## In-kind support

The company has worked in partnership with the Surrey Wildlife Trust and The Woodland Trust to raise public awareness about important conservation issues and to protect rural habitats.

## Employee-led support

Employees are encouraged to take part in fundraising activities and participate in sponsored events on behalf of the company's nominated charity partner.

# Cummins Engine Company Ltd

Yarm Road, Darlington DL1 4PW

01325 556000; Fax: 01325 368040

Website: www.cummins.com

Correspondent: Christine Davies, Trustee, Human Resources

Chief officer: Tim Solso

Chief Executive: Tim Solso

Managing Director: J Edwards

| Year end | Turnover | Pre-tax profit |
|---|---|---|
| 31/12/2003 | £449,140,000 | (£45,191,000) |

**Nature of company business**
The principal activity is the manufacture, sale, distribution and servicing of diesel engines and components. The company is a subsidiary of Cummins Engine Company, Inc (US).

**Subsidiaries include:** Holset Engineering Co Ltd, Newage International Ltd

**Main locations:** Ramsgate, Huddersfield, Daventry, Darlington, Stamford, Hinckley, Oakham, Wellingborough, Cumbernauld

> ### Charitable donations
>
> 2006: £45,000
>
> Membership: BitC

## Community involvement

The company's global website states that: 'Community Involvement Teams (CITs) are employee-driven committees that represent the diversity of the workforce and all levels of management. They are driven by the philosophy that a company cannot function without a healthy community.

'Each team establishes a work plan, a budget and a focus area for community service. Every two years, these teams are audited against a set of functional excellence criteria. The audit process ensures that corporate responsibility remains an important business objective across all business units, provides a measurement and recognition process and identifies areas for development over the next two-year cycle.

'Community involvement teams have the responsibility of developing an annual plan, organizing volunteer activities, responding to community requests for donations and developing proposals for the Cummins Foundation.'

Within the UK, the company prefers to support projects local to its manufacturing plants and offices (north east England, Northamptonshire, West Yorkshire, Lincolnshire and Kent). Organisations concerned with youth, education, the environment, and disadvantaged people are favoured.

### Exclusions

No support for appeals from individuals, or local appeals not in areas of company presence.

### Applications

In writing to the correspondent.

## Corporate giving

Total cash donations vary between £40,000 and £50,000 a year. We were previously advised that grants to national organisations range from £500 to £3,000. Grants to local organisations can be for up to £10,000.

In 2005, Cummins in Darlington, donated nearly £6,000 for DASH (Darlington After School and Holiday) for disabled children as well as had employees directly engaged in support.

### In-kind support

The main areas of non-cash support are secondments, gifts in kinds and training schemes.

### Employee-led support

To encourage employee volunteering and involvement, each plant has a Community Involvement Team which coordinates community activities based on local needs. These can include mentoring schemes with local schools and fundraising events on behalf of local good causes. The latter may receive additional money from the Cummins Foundation.

Recently, employees at the Darlington site have supported Young Enterprise North East (YENE), part of the UK business-education charity Young Enterprise.

# P Z Cussons plc

PZ Cussons House, Bird Hall Lane, Stockport SK3 0XN

0161 491 8000; Fax: 0161 491 8191

Website: www.cussons.com

Correspondent: Marie Gallagher, Secretary

Chief officer: A J Green

Chief Executive: G A Kanellis

| Year end | Turnover | Pre-tax profit |
|---|---|---|
| 31/05/2006 | £539,900,000 | £61,200,000 |

### Nature of company business
Principal activities: manufacture and distribution of soaps, toiletries, cleaning agents, pharmaceuticals, refrigerators and air conditioners.

Subsidiaries include: Cussons Group Ltd, Cussons (UK) Ltd, PC Products (1001) Ltd, Cussons (International) Ltd, Parnon Ltd, Fragrance Chemicals Ltd

Main locations: Stockport

Total employees: 10,377

### Charitable donations
2006: £50,000
2005: £53,000
2004: £50,000

## Community involvement

Within the corporate social responsibility section of its 2005 Annual Report and Accounts, the company states: 'We support a range of charitable causes, both in the UK and overseas, mainly through a UK-based shareholding trust (The Zochonis Charitable Trust, Charity Commission no. 274769)] and additional contributions made through staff time and gifts in-kind.'

Past information has suggested the company has a preference for local charities in areas of company presence, particularly projects involving children and youth, social welfare, medical, education, recreation and people with disabilities.

### Exclusions

The company will not make any form of political contribution.

Past information has suggested that generally, the company will give no support for circular appeals, fundraising events, advertising in charity brochures, individuals, denominational appeals, large national appeals or overseas projects.

### Applications

The charities committee only meets once a year in May. Appeals should be addressed to the correspondent at head office.

## Corporate giving

The company donates around £50,000 each year to charities. We have no details of the beneficiaries.

Despite encouraging staff volunteering and providing gifts in-kind, it does not appear to calculate the value of these forms of support to the community.

The associated Zochonis Charitable Trust made grants of nearly £1.5 million in 2004/05, for general charitable purposes. Its income is derived almost exclusively from share holdings in the company, but acts independently. Further details can be found in *A Guide to the Major Trusts Volume 1* published by the Directory of Social Change.

### In-kind support

In addition to cash donations the company provides support by providing gifts in kind.

### Employee-led support

The company allows employees time off to volunteer.

# Daejan Holdings plc

Freshwater House, 158–162 Shaftesbury Avenue,
London WC2H 8HR

020 7836 1555; Fax: 020 7497 8941

**Website:** www.daejanholdings.com

**Correspondent:** BFreshwater, Chairman

**Chief officer:** B S E Freshwater

| Year end | Turnover | Pre-tax profit |
|---|---|---|
| 31/03/2006 | £95,689,000 | £162,659,000 |

**Nature of company business**
Property investment and trading, with some development. The major part of the group's property portfolio comprises commercial, industrial and residential premises throughout the UK and in the US.

**Subsidiaries include:** Astral Estates (London) Ltd, The Cromlech Property Co Ltd, Bampton Holdings Ltd, St Leonards Properties Ltd, InputStripe Ltd, The Halliard Property Co Ltd, City and Country Properties (Midlands) Ltd, Hampstead Way Investments Ltd, Seaglen Investments Ltd, Pegasus Investment Co Ltd, Brickfield Properties Ltd, Limebridge Co Ltd, Rosebel Holdings Ltd, City and Country Properties (Camberley) Ltd, Bampton (B&B) Ltd, Inputstock Ltd, Bampton (Redbridge) Ltd, City and Country Properties (Birmingham) Ltd, The Bampton Property Group Ltd

**Main locations:** London

**Total employees:** 145

> ### Charitable donations
> 2006: £120,000
> 2005: £120,000
> 2003: £120,000

## Community involvement

Part of The Freshwater Group of companies, Daejan mainly supports orthodox Jewish charities, especially in the educational and medical fields, in the USA, Britain and Israel. Support is also given to organisations concerned with the relief of poverty. The company channels its giving through the Charities Aid Foundation.

The Freshwater Group is also associated with two or three other substantial private charitable companies, whose policy is similar to that of Daejan Holdings.

## Exclusions

Organisations dealing with professional fundraisers, large overhead expenses and expensive fundraising campaigns are avoided. Support is not given to the arts, enterprise or conservation.

## Applications

In writing to the correspondent (who is also the correspondent for the payroll giving scheme). There is no donations committee.

## Corporate giving

The company maintained its level of charitable support at £120,000 in 2006. No further information was available.

## Employee-led support
**Payroll giving:** The company operates the Give As You Earn Scheme.

# Daily Mail and General Trust plc

Northcliffe House, 2 Derry Street, London W8 5TT

020 7938 6000; Fax: 020 7937 3745

**Website:** www.dmgt.co.uk

**Correspondent:** Charities Committee

**Chief officer:** Rt Hon. Viscount Rothermere

**Chief Executive:** C J F Sinclair

| Year end | Turnover | Pre-tax profit |
|---|---|---|
| 28/09/2005 | £2,138,000,000 | £253,400,000 |

**Nature of company business**
Principal activity: publication and printing of newspapers and periodicals.

**Subsidiaries include:** Staffordshire Sentinel Newspapers Ltd, DMG Pinnacle Ltd, Northcliffe New Media Holdings plc, Euromoney Publications plc, The Publishing Co Ltd, Hull Daily Mail Publications Ltd, W.H.Y Publications limited, Northcliffe Newspapers Group Ltd, Cornwall & Devon Media Limited, Herald Express Ltd, Derby Daily Telegraph Ltd, Harmsworth Quays Printing Ltd, Leicester Mercury Group Ltd, DMG Trinity Ltd, The Journal Co Ltd, Aberdeen Journals Ltd, DMG Home Interest Magazines Ltd, DMG Angex Ltd, Lincolnshire Publishing Co Ltd, Bristol United Press plc, Armdag Newspapers Limited, Northcliffe Retail Ltd, Gloucestershire Newspapers Ltd, Nottingham Post Group Ltd, Essex Chronicle Series Ltd, Metropress Ltd, Harmsworth Quays Ltd, DMG Exhibition Group Ltd, The Western Morning News Co Ltd, Express & Echo Publications Ltd, Alderton Limited, DMG Business Media Ltd, Arts and Entertainment Programming Ltd, Grimsy & Scunthorpe Newspaper Ltd, Associated Newspapers Ltd, South West Wales Publications Ltd, New Era Television Ltd, DMG Antique Fairs Ltd, Central Independent Newspapers Limited, Teletex Ltd, British Pathe plc, DMG Radio Ltd, Westcountry Publications Ltd, The Cheltenham Newspaper Co Ltd, DMG Regional Radio Pty Ltd, The Printworks Ltd, The Courier Printing & Publishing Co Ltd, Publications Ltd

**Main locations:** London

**Total employees:** 18,000

> ### Charitable donations
> 2005: £880,000
> 2003: £548,000
> Total community contributions: £880,000

## Community involvement

Daily Mail & General Trust (DMGT) donate money, time and in-kind donations informed by 'the communities we serve and the concerns and contributions of our readers and listeners'.

## Exclusions

No support for circular appeals, appeals from individuals, older people, enterprise/training, environment/heritage, fundraising events, overseas projects, political/religious appeals, sickness/disability charities, social welfare, or sport.

## Applications

In writing to the correspondent.

## Corporate giving

In 2005, the company donated a total of £880,000, including £264,000 in cash to the London Bombings Relief Fund.

### In-kind support

The company's publications lend support to charitable and community causes through their editorial pages. Teletext Holidays supports the Family Holiday Association through involvement on its committee and sponsored events. The charity focuses on providing much needed holidays to families who would otherwise not be able to afford one.

### Commercially-led support

**Sponsorship:** *The arts* – the company undertakes arts sponsorship (local to company headquarters).

---

# Daniel Thwaites plc

PO Box 50, Star Brewery, Blackburn, Lancashire BB1 5BU

01254 686868; Fax: 01254 263590

Website: www.thwaites.co.uk

Correspondent: Mrs Joan Halse, Secretary and Trustee
01254 686803
E-mail: joanhalse@thwaites.co.uk

Chief officer: Mrs Ann Yerburgh

Managing Director: P A Baker and I A M Harkness

| Year end | Turnover | Pre-tax profit |
|---|---|---|
| 31/03/2005 | £159,600,000 | £12,800,000 |

**Nature of company business**
Principal activities are the brewing and canning of beer, the distribution of wines and spirits and the operation of hotels and public houses.

Main locations: Blackburn

UK employees: 2,479

Total employees: 2,479

> ### Charitable donations
>
> 2005: £28,000
> 2004: £25,893

## Community involvement

The company operates The Daniel Thwaites Charitable Trust (Charity Commission no. 1038097). The trust states that 'emphasis is placed on giving tangible, physical help, be that wheelchairs, computers, musical instruments, beds or other specialist equipment for helping improve interaction, or items such as bingo machines and televisions that improve the quality of life for groups of people'. Support is given across the UK, although there is a preference for appeals from within a 50 mile radius of Blackburn.

## Applications

In writing to the correspondent.

## Corporate giving

In 2004/05, the company made charitable donations of £28,000 through its charitable trust.

Beneficiaries have included: Blackburn and Darwen Churches Action; Lancashire Neighbourhood Watch Forum; Barnardos Family Action Group; Samaritans – Blackburn; and, Bowland Pennine Mountain Rescue Team.

### Commercially-led support
#### Sponsorship

A wide range of sports sponsorship is provided, from test match cricket and Formula One racing, right through to grassroots sponsorship of clubs and competitions. Hundreds of sports clubs across the North West and Yorkshire are sponsored each year, with an interest in North West county associations and leagues. Over £500,000 is spent on sponsorship each year, although it was unclear whether this all went to grassroots organisations or included the major corporate sponsorship of high profile sporting events.

---

# Danka UK plc

1230 Arlington Business Park, Theale, Berkshire RG7 4TX

0118 928 4900; Fax: 0118 928 4901

Website: www.danka.co.uk

Correspondent: Human Resource Department

Chief officer: Lang Lowery III

Chief Executive: Todd L Mavis

| Year end | Turnover | Pre-tax profit |
|---|---|---|
| 31/03/2005 | £668,216,000 | (£45,526,000) |

**Nature of company business**
The principal operating subsidiary, Danka Industries Inc, and its subsidiary undertakings are engaged in the supply and servicing of business equipment in the USA. Danka International markets the products of Canon, Heidelberg, Ricoh and Toshiba throughout the European and Australasian markets.

Main locations: Hertfordshire, London, Birmingham, Cheshire, Belfast, Berkshire

UK employees: 2,637

Total employees: 7,355

## Community involvement

Danka supports programmes that improve the social and educational well-being of communities where it operates.

### Exclusions

Local appeals not in areas of company presence.

### Applications

In writing to the correspondent. The request should contain:
- name and address of organisation requesting assistance
- if applicable, the name of the Danka employee who is acting as internal advocate for the organisation
- the purpose of the organisation
- description of specific activities/services for which support is requested

▶ income and expense statements for the current and prior year.

## Corporate giving

The company donated £30,000 to charitable causes in 2000, continuing the downward trend evident since the 1997 high of £185,000. It may be, however, that in the past we have unknowingly quoted worldwide donations as UK ones. This has not been confirmed by the company.

### In-kind support

Donations of copiers, faxes, printing services etc. are evaluated based on the organisations' programme needs and Danka's equipment availability.

### Employee-led support

Employees are encouraged to spend time working in the community if it is based on the Community Relations Committee's goals and objectives. Primary consideration is given for situations that allow large numbers of Danka employees to participate.

# Data Connection Limited

100 Church Street, Enfield, Middlesex EN2 6BQ

020 8366 1177; Fax: 020 8363 1468

Website: www.dataconnections.com

Correspondent: Doreen Willis, Office Services Manager
E-mail: info@dataconnections.com

| Year end | Turnover | Pre-tax profit |
|---|---|---|
| 31/08/2005 | £38,061,041 | £264,598 |

Nature of company business
Providers of information technology.

Main locations: Enfield

Total employees: 294

### Charitable donations
2005: £18,124
2004: £7,573
2003: £258,360

## Community involvement

An IT company based in Enfield, we understood that in 2003 the company allocated around 90% of their donations budget to causes in the borough, the remaining 10% being spent on national programmes. We do not know if this is still the case.

There is a preference for causes supported by employees.

### Applications

In writing to the correspondent.

## Corporate giving

The Annual Report for the year 31st August 2005 states that during the year the company made charitable donations of £18,124 (2004: £7,573). Unfortunately we have no information as to the organisations benefiting from the donations.

# DDB London Ltd

12 Bishops Bridge Road, London W2 6AA

020 7258 3979; Fax: 020 7402 4871

Website: www.ddblondon.com

Correspondent: Mrs FionaShafran, Head of Human Resources

Chief officer: P Hammersley

Chief Executive: Michael Bray

Managing Director: J Murray

| Year end | Turnover | Pre-tax profit |
|---|---|---|
| 31/12/2005 | £98,651,000 | £5,111,000 |

Nature of company business
The principal activity of the company is advertising and marketing services.

Subsidiaries include: Smythe Dorward Lambert Ltd, Alcone Marketing Group Ltd, Omnicom Finance Ltd, The Computing Group Ltd, Scope Ketchum Sponsorship Ltd, Market Access Ltd, Markforce Associates Ltd, Paling Walters Targis Ltd, Premier Magazines Ltd, Prism International Ltd, TBWA Simons Palmer Ltd, Omnicom UK Ltd, Solutions in Media Ltd, TISSA Ltd, Countrywide Communications Ltd, The Anvil Consultancy Ltd, WWAV Rapp Collins Group Ltd, Colour Solutions Ltd, First City/ BBDO Ltd, Gavin Anderson Ltd, Macmillan Davies Hodes Consultants Ltd, Scope Communications Group Ltd, Doremus & Co Ltd, Specialist Publications Ltd, Alcone/Europe Ltd, Floral Street Holdings Ltd, Porter Novelli Ltd, Medi Cine International plc, WWAV Rapp Collins Ltd, Macmillan Davies Hodes Advertising Ltd, DAS Financial Services Ltd, Interbrand UK Ltd, Ketchum Public Relations plc, BMP Countrywide Ltd, Griffin Bacal Ltd, Billco Ltd, CPM International Group Ltd, Genesis Digital Creation Ltd, Countrywide Porter Novelli Ltd, Perception Design Ltd, Interbrand Group Ltd, BBDO Europe Ltd, BMP DDB Ltd, Data Warehouse Ltd

Main locations: London

UK employees: 360

### Charitable donations
2005: £29,000
2004: £40,000

## Community involvement

DDB London Ltd is one of the companies in the Omnicom Group and is the trading name of BMP DDB Limited.

We were previously advised that the company supports national and international charities with direct donations and also gives support via gifts in kind. It normally supports the arts, children/youth, education, the elderly, enterprise/ training, environment/heritage, fundraising events, medical research, political and religious appeals, science/technology, sickness/disability, social welfare, sport and advertising in charity brochures.

The company's charity of the year is chosen through staff nomination of a charity which is directly involved with any of the issues stated above.

### Exclusions

No support for animal welfare.

## Applications

In writing to the correspondent.

## Corporate giving

In 2005, cash donations to charity totalled £29,000 (2004: £40,000). We have no details of the beneficiaries.

## Employee-led support

Employee fundraising and giving both receive matched support from the company.

**Payroll giving:** The Give As You Earn and NABS schemes are in operation.

# De Beers

17 Charterhouse Street, London EC1N 6RA

020 7404 4444; Fax: 020 7430 1821

Website: www.debeersgroup.com

Correspondent: Mr Robert Barltrop, Secretary to the Oppenheimer Charitable Trust

Chief officer: Nicky F Oppenheimer

Managing Director: David Noko

| Year end | Turnover | Pre-tax profit |
|---|---|---|
| 31/10/2005 | £4,373,728,700 | £585,875,190 |

**Nature of company business**
Principal activities: mining of gem and industrial diamonds; marketing through the Central Selling Organisation of diamonds produced by the group and other producers; manufacture and marketing of synthetic diamond and related hard materials for use in industry; management of a portfolio of international investments in mining, industrial and finance companies.

Main locations: London

### Charitable donations

2005: £60,000
2003: £69,753

## Community involvement

In 1961, the Oppenheimer Charitable Trust (Charity Commission no. 200395) was established to channel the donations of the Diamond Trading Companies of the De Beers Group. De Beers Consolidated Mines Ltd, which does not operate in this country, channels its donations through the De Beers Fund. The Fund makes grants predominantly in South Africa, Botswana and Namibia, where the company has large mining interests, although help is also given worldwide.

Social investment is focused on projects initiated and driven by communities, with key requirements being sustainability and impact.

## Exclusions

The company does not provide support for appeals from individuals, animal welfare, overseas projects, fundraising events or political appeals.

## Applications

Grants are made in three ways: by application to the trustees; by recommendation to the trustees; and on the initiative of the trustees themselves.

## Corporate giving

In 2005 the Oppenheimer Charitable Trust made grants in the UK totalling £60,400. In the main, grants were of a very small amount, the majority being for £350 p.a. Details of the recipient organisations are listed in the Trustees Annual Report for the year ending 31st October 2005.

## Employee-led support

The company supports employees' volunteering/charitable activities by allowing them company time off and by providing financial support.

# De La Rue plc

De La Rue House, Jays Close, Viables, Basingstoke, Hampshire RG22 4BS

01256 605000; Fax: 01256 605004

Website: www.delarue.com

Correspondent: Mrs Teresa Kerr, PA to Chair and Chief Executive

Chief officer: Nicholas Brookes

Chief Executive: Leo Quinn

| Year end | Turnover | Pre-tax profit |
|---|---|---|
| 25/03/2006 | £610,800,000 | £73,700,000 |

**Nature of company business**
The company is a commercial security printer and papermaker, involved in the production of over 150 national currencies and a wide range of security documents. The company is also a leading provider of cash handling equipment and solutions to banks and retailers as well as a range of identity systems to governments worldwide.

**Subsidiaries include:** Royal Mint Services Ltd, Camelot Group plc, Portals Group, Portals Property Ltd

**Main locations:** Byfleet, Knutsford, Lisburn, Peterborough, Portsmouth, Dunstable, Gateshhead, Loughton, Overton, Westhoughton, Bath, Basingstoke

UK employees: 2,302

Total employees: 6,022

### Charitable donations

2006: £97,000
2005: £205,000
2003: £198,610

## Community involvement

Previously it was believed that donations by the company were made through the De La Rue Charitable Trust (Charity Commission no. 274052), when in fact they are made in addition to those of the trust.

Unfortunately, we have no information concerning the type of project the company is likely to support. We do know, however, that the trust aims to direct funds to causes around the world in countries where De La Rue operates.

Emphasis is given to educational projects which promote relevant skills, international understanding and bring relief from suffering.

### Exclusions

Generally no support for circular appeals, fundraising events, brochure advertising, individuals, purely denominational (religious) or political appeals, local appeals not in areas of company presence or large national appeals. No telephoned applications can be considered.

Applications that do not fall within the above categories will not be considered unless there are extenuating or emergency circumstances. Grant applications made by individuals either in the UK or abroad cannot be considered.

All circular appeals will be rejected.

### Applications

In writing to the correspondent. Registered charities only can apply.

Applications are considered at trustees meetings held in February and July.

## Corporate giving

In 2005, contributions by the company totalled £97,000, down from £205,000 in 2004. We have no details of the beneficiaries.

### The De La Rue Charitable Trust

The trusts income is generated from dividends received from investment fund holdings. In 2004/05, this amounted to £50,700 of which just under £17,000 was paid out in grants.

Funds are allocated to charitable and good causes that fall within policy categories, for example, education, international understanding, relief of suffering, the hospice movement and for special community projects and institutions close to De La Rue locations and within its national and international markets.

### In-kind support

De La Rue, through the Police Community Clubs of Great Britain, helped promote citizen education in schools. In support of a bullying and vandalism awareness programme, it provided booklets to sixty pupils at The Alderton School in Loughton, Essex, near to the Debden Banknote printing site.

### Employee-led support

The company matches employee fundraising. Each company location is encouraged to sponsor a different local cause on an annual basis with employees donating time and commitment as well as funds.

**Payroll giving:** The company operates the Give As You Earn scheme.

### Commercially-led support

**Sponsorship:** De La Rue sponsor relevant and/or topical charitable projects which could inform a variety of people as to the activities, purpose and culture of De La Rue.

# De Vere Group plc

2100 Daresbury Park, Warrington WA4 4BP

01928 712111

Website: www.deveregroupplc.co.uk

Correspondent: D C Edwards, Company Secretary

Chief officer: Lord Daresbury

Chief Executive: Carl Leaver

| Year end | Turnover | Pre-tax profit |
|---|---|---|
| 25/09/2005 | £312,031,000 | £58,958,000 |

**Nature of company business**
The main activity is the operation of hotels and leisure facilities.

**Main locations:** Warrington, Leeds, Blackpool, Chester, Norwich, Cambridge, London, Loch Lomond

Total employees: 6,379

### Charitable donations
2004: £50,000
2003: £77,100

## Community involvement

As of 7 September 2006, the company was delisted from the London Stock Exchange following its acquisition by AHG Venice Ltd. At this stage we do not know how, if at all, this may affect the company's current community support policy detailed herein.

According to the company's 2005 annual report, due to the multiplicity of locations from which it operates the group's strategy is to encourage each business unit to develop its own social responsibility policies. As a result of this, the hotel and fitness club division, for example, supports over 30 national and international charities as well as local charities, hospices and hospitals.

In addition to this the group provides in-kind support and encourages its employees to become involved in local charity and community events.

### Exclusions

No support for local appeals not in areas of company presence.

### Applications

In writing to the correspondent.

## Corporate giving

In 2004/05, the company's charitable donations in the UK totalled £55,000 (2004: £50,000). Small donations of around £10 or a bottle for a fundraising event are distributed regularly. Larger donations are considered by a charitable appeals committee two/three times a year. Donations can be for £100 to £10,000 and may be given by deed of covenant.

Examples of national charities supported during the year include: Macmillan Nurses; British Heart Foundation and Save the Children.

### In-kind support

Many of the hotels and fitness clubs within the group provide free access to their facilities by, for example, allowing the use of swimming pools to teach under-privileged children to swim, or, by allowing the use of kitchens to teach teenagers from local youth centres how to prepare healthy food.

The company also provides training and work experience under several recognised programmes.

## Employee-led support

Employees provide career talks for teenagers who are about to leave school/college, whilst some hotels and clubs run schemes to allow qualifying employees paid time off to support chosen charities and community events.

**Payroll giving:** The Give As You Earn scheme is in operation.

# Deloitte

Stonecutter Court, 1 Stonecutter Street, London EC4A 4TR

020 7303 7149; Fax: 020 7583 8517

Website: www.deloitte.co.uk/community

Correspondent: Richard Stone, Director of Community Investment
E-mail: richardstone@deloitte.co.uk

Chief Executive: John Connolly

| Year end | Turnover | Pre-tax profit |
|---|---|---|
| 31/05/2005 | £1,355,500,000 | £418,500,000 |

Nature of company business
Audit, tax, corporate finance and management consultancy services.

Main locations: Bristol, Cardiff, Leeds, Southampton, Reading, London

UK employees: 8,567

## Charitable donations

2005: £400,000
2004: £400,000
2003: £250,000

Total community contributions: £28,700,000

Membership: A & B, BitC, L B Group, %Club

## Community involvement

The Deloitte Foundation supports a wide variety of charities, with a particular focus on causes supporting children and young people, health and the community. One-third of the foundation's budget is used to provide matched funding for staff contributions, to payroll giving and charity fundraising.

Deloitte commits in excess of 1% of UK pre-tax profit towards its community involvement. It is committed to supporting the community at a national and local level through its network of 20 offices throughout the UK. (Each region has a small budget for supporting local charities.)

**Charity of the Year:** British Heart Foundation and Leukaemia Research Fund (2005/06).

## Exclusions

No support for advertising in charity brochures, for animal welfare, appeals from individuals, the arts, overseas projects or political/religious appeals.

## Applications

In writing to the Deloitte Charity Committee. However, few ad hoc or unsolicited requests for funding are approved by the committee.

## Corporate giving

The Deloitte Foundation made donations of £400,000. Following the tsunami disaster on Boxing Day 2004 the UK firm made a donation of £1 million to the Disasters Emergency Committee appeal. Staff raised an additional £146,000. After the London bombings, the sum of £100,000 was donated to the London Bombings Relief Fund.

## In-kind support

In kind support is given through the provision of pro bono professional services. 15,000 hours of professional time is given through business mentoring and school mentoring projects across the UK.

## Employee-led support

Employee fundraising activities are matched by the company.

**Payroll giving:** the Give As You Earn scheme is in operation. The charitable fund also matches the contributions made by the staff fund through this. In 2004 a total of £500,000 was raised through payroll giving according to the firm's website.

## Commercially-led support

**Sponsorship:** Deloitte has a broad range of sponsorship programmes that include supporting the arts, culture and sport. A key partnership has been made with the National Portrait Gallery and Deloitte is the gallery's Contemporary Photography Displays partner.

# Derbyshire Building Society

PO Box 1, Duffield Hall, Duffield, Derby DE56 1AG

08456 004005

Website: www.thederbyshire.co.uk

Correspondent: Mrs Chris Butler, Community Develoment Officer 01332 844340

Chief officer: R Ian Menzies-Gow

Chief Executive: Peter Richardson

| Year end | Turnover | Pre-tax profit |
|---|---|---|
| 31/12/2005 | £258,000,000 | £17,700,000 |

Nature of company business
Core business activities are focused on: mortgage lending, personal savings and investment products, life and general insurance business, and personal financial advice.

Main locations: Derby

Total employees: 575

## Charitable donations

2005: £3,688
2003: £20,846

Membership: %Club

## Community involvement

The Derbyshire's website states: 'We are committed to making a positive difference to the quality of life in the communities in which we serve.

'We embrace the principle that corporate citizenship is vital to the long-term success of the Society and play an active role in tackling a whole range of issues- crime reduction, drug addiction, economic regeneration, social inclusion and breaking down the barriers of disability and discrimination.

'Although we provide financial support to community projects and charities every year, our work is not just about money. It's also about investing time, imagination, effort and expertise to support projects and stimulate new initiatives. Everyone at The Derbyshire is encouraged to take part in community and charity events and each year Peter Richardson, our Chief Executive, presents the 'Ambassador of the Year' award to colleagues whose contribution has been exceptional.'

In 2005 the society supported over 250 community groups, organisations and charities in their region and over 50% of employees are actively involved in the community, by offering their expertise and participating in fundraising events.

### Exclusions

No support for advertising in charity brochures, animal welfare, appeals from individuals, overseas projects or political or religious appeals.

### Applications

In writing to the correspondent.

## Corporate giving

Cash donations for 2005 were £3,688. Some 250 projects were supported during the year by the society and its community partners. Current community projects include Rainbows Children Hospice which provides palliative and terminal care to life limited children in Derbyshire, Leicestershire, Nottinghamshire, Lincolnshire and Northamptonshire, the hospice receives a range of support from the society, its staff and customers, including donations.

### In-kind support

Employees' expertise is sometimes provided to support projects and stimulate new initiatives.

### Employee-led support

Many branches of the Derbyshire have adopted Rainbows Children Hospice as their charity of the year. Staff participate in fundraising activities on its behalf, facilitate public giving, for example, by inviting members of the public to contribute to Rainbows 'Light of Hope Appeal' by purchasing a light in celebration of the life of someone special.

To help co-ordinate this and other, though not all, community initiatives supported by staff, a Community Development Team was established in 2000.

### Commercially-led support

**Sponsorship:** *Environment* – East Midlands in Bloom

'The Derbyshire recognises how important it is that our towns and villages are welcoming and environmentally friendly both to residents and visitors alike. This annual competition, sponsored by The Derbyshire, offers cities, towns and villages throughout the East Midlands the opportunity to showcase their commitment by improving and maintaining their immediate environment. These regional competitions feed into the National Britain in Bloom competition organised by the Royal Horticultural Society.'

*Sport* – Derbyshire Building Society 10k and Fun Run, Derby

Held in conjunction with Sporting Futures a Derby based charity that uses sport as a catalyst to engage with young people enabling them to build meaningful relationships with family, friends and the wider community in which they live. Now in its 6th year, this annual event attracted over 2,800 entrants in 2006. The 10k route follows a single lap through the heart of Derby. The 2 mile family fun run route is flat – a perfect challenge for shorter distance runners, families, children and wheelchair entrants.

The Derbyshire is the main sponsor of Derby County football team.

# Deutsche Bank

Winchester House, 1 Great Winchester Street, London EC2N 2DB

020 7545 8000

Website: www.deutsche-bank.com

Correspondent: Charity Committee

Chief officer: Dr Josef Ackermann

| Year end | Turnover | Pre-tax profit |
|---|---|---|
| 31/12/2005 | £18,314,000,000 | |

**Nature of company business**
Deutsche Bank is the holding company of a group providing international merchant banking and investment management services.

**Subsidiaries include:** Morgan Grenfell

**Main locations:** Edinburgh, London

**Total employees:** 67,474

### Charitable donations

2005: £4,500,000
2004: £3,500,000
2003: £3,400,000

Membership: A & B, BitC, L B Group, %Club

## Community involvement

Deutsche Bank's citizenship philosophy is to 'help people to help themselves'. It sets out to achieve this through a community development programme focusing on five areas: arts and culture, community development, science and society, sustainability, and sport. Within this, there is a preference for supporting low-income communities and projects which directly involve the bank's staff.

**Charity of the Year:** Each year Deutsche Bank adopts a corporate charity to support. Staff are encouraged to fundraise on its behalf.

### Exclusions

No support for advertising in charity brochures, enterprise/ training, small local appeals not in areas of company presence or appeals from individuals.

## Applications

In writing to the correspondent. All appeals are reviewed, and grants decisions made, by a charities committee which meets quarterly.

## Corporate giving

In 2005, the bank made donations in the UK totalling £4,500,000, through sponsorship and directly through various foundations.

## In-kind support

The bank, through a major employee volunteering programme called Initiative Plus, encourages its staff to provide their time, skills and energy on a voluntary basis to local education projects. Staff can apply for a grant of up to £300 from the bank to donate to the organisation with which they volunteer. Since its inception in 2001, almost £100,000 has been donated through the programme in the UK.

## Employee-led support

Volunteering activities undertaken by employees independently of the community development programme can result in grants of between £100 and £1,000 being given to the charity or good cause the employee is helping.

Employees' charitable donations are matched by the bank. We do not know if there is a cap on this.

## Commercially-led support

**Sponsorship:** *Sport-* Athletics and other sporting activities have been sponsored by the bank.

# Dhamecha Group Ltd

Wembley Stadium Industrial Estate, First Way, Wembley, Middlesex HA9 0TU

020 8903 8181; Fax: 020 8902 2620

Website: www.dhamecha.com

Correspondent: P K Dhamecha, Financial Director

| Year end | Turnover | Pre-tax profit |
|---|---|---|
| 31/03/2005 | £270,900,000 | £4,900,000 |

**Nature of company business**
The principal activities are wholesale food cash and carry, property dealings and the manufacture and sale of paper disposable products.

**Subsidiaries include:** London Paper Products Ltd

**Main locations:** Wembley, Barking, Croydon, Enfield, Watford

**UK employees:** 301

| Charitable donations |
|---|
| 2005: £200,000 |
| 2004: £200,000 |
| 2003: £180,000 |

## Community involvement

The company makes an annual charitable donation to the closely-linked Laduma Dhamecha Charitable Trust (Charity Commission no. 328678). The trust supports general charitable purposes in the UK and abroad, but primarily seeks to provide the following:

- relief for sickness by provision of medical equipment and/ or establishing or improving the facilities at hospitals as the trustees determine
- an educational establishment in rural areas to make children self sufficient in the longer term.

Only organisations can benefit.

## Applications

In writing to the correspondent, who is a trustee of the Laduma Dhamecha Charitable Trust.

## Corporate giving

In 2004/05, the Laduma Dhamecha Charitable Trust had an income of £249,000 of which £200,000 came from Dhamecha Group Ltd. The trust made charitable donations of £315,000. No list of beneficiaries was available.

# DHL Express (UK) Limited

Orbital Park, 178–188 Great South West Road, Hounslow, Middlesex TW4 6JS

020 8818 8000

Website: www.dhl.co.uk

Correspondent: KarenPiesley, PR Executive
E-mail: gb.community@dhl.com

Managing Director: C Muntwyler

| Year end | Turnover | Pre-tax profit |
|---|---|---|
| 31/12/2005 | £441,175,000 | (£72,113) |

**Nature of company business**
Global express distribution.

**Main locations:** Hounslow

**UK employees:** 8,517

| Charitable donations |
|---|
| 2004: £15,132 |
| 2003: £34,000 |
| Total community contributions: £452,870 |
| Membership: BitC |

## Community involvement

Every year DHL reviews its community investment programme and assess how they can align their approach with the interests of its employees and the changing needs within society. In 2006, DHL focused its efforts on two programmes, the DHL Matched Funding programme and introducing DHL Skills in Motion.

Please note that DHL has taken over Excel plc on whom we previously published information.

## Exclusions

At national level, support for animal welfare, and political or religious groups is excluded.

## Applications

Local requests for support should be addressed to the local DHL Service centre. Head office does not deal with local requests.

**Information available:** The company published its first UK community investment report in 2004

## Corporate giving

In 2004, the company launched the Yellow Wheel Appeal, a programme supporting children with disabilities. It combines fundraising with in-kind shipping and an employee skills sharing initiative. In 2004, in-kind shipping totalled £437,743 and matched funding totalled £15,132.

Support has also been given to children with disabilities (Whizz-Kidz), humanitarian assistance (IFRC – International Federation of Red Cross and Red Crescent Societies and Merlin), HIV/Aids awareness and prevention (TackleAfrica) and digital inclusion (Digital Links International).

Because of the introduction of the above programme, DHL no longer makes ad hoc donations or provides grants/sponsorships in response to speculative appeals or requests.

### In-kind support

In kind support is given to charities and community groups throughout the UK in the form of free express delivery. This amounts to tens of thousands of pounds.

In 2004, DHL supported a unique scheme that has turned old mobile phones into trees. Recycling bags were placed in 2,000 HSBC branches in the UK and Channel Islands. For every person that donated a phone, the environmental organisation Future Forests planted a tree. By November 2004 almost 17,000 phones had been recycled and an equivalent number of trees planted.

In 2004, DGL UK donated around 1,500 PCs, laptops and monitors to Digital Links with the aim of supporting education and increasing future employment opportunities for children in poorer regions of the world.

### Employee-led support

#### Matched Funding

The company matches pound-for-pound funds raised by their employees for charities of their choice. While the top ten charities supported by their staff over the past few years are well known national organisations, the full list includes many smaller community-based charities such as local hospices. In 2005 the main beneficiaries were organisations involved with cancer research and those that support children and youth.

#### Skills in Motion

This is a skill-sharing programme where employees are teamed up with staff from DHL's charity partners and work together to complete an agreed project that will be of long-term benefit for the community organisation.

# Diageo plc

8 Henrietta Place, London W1M 9AG

020 7927 5200; Fax: 020 7927 4600

Website: www.diageo.com

Correspondent: Geoffrey Bush, Director of Corporate Citizenship

**Chief officer:** Lord Blyth of Rowington

**Chief Executive:** P S Walsh

| Year end | Turnover | Pre-tax profit |
|---|---|---|
| 30/06/2006 | £9,704,000,000 | £214,600,000 |

**Nature of company business**
The group's principal activity is the manufacture and distribution of spirits, wines and beer.

**Subsidiaries include:** United Distillers & Vintners (HP) Ltd, Guinness Ltd, United Distillers & Vintners (ER) Ltd

**Main locations:** London

**Total employees:** 22,619

### Charitable donations
2006: £11,800,000
2005: £14,400,000
2004: £7,300,000
2003: £6,500,000

Membership: A & B, BitC, L B Group, %Club

## Community involvement

As well as the support given through the Diageo Foundation (see below), the company makes its own contributions to assist charitable and community activities in the communities it serves. Currently, besides its primary focus on responsible drinking, Diageo's other community activities fall into three further focus areas, chosen to reflect where it's businesses have the greatest impact and where the company can make the most difference. These are:

▹ skills for life – working with unemployed or disadvantage people to help them find worthwhile work or start new business ventures

▹ water of life – projects that protect the environment or improve access to safe drinking water in developing countries

▹ local citizens – supporting Diageo's businesses and employees in community activities and responding to disasters with emergency relief.

### The Diageo Foundation

The Diageo Foundation was established by Diageo plc to support its businesses around the world in their community involvement by providing kick-start funding and expertise.

To be eligible for funding from the Diageo Foundation projects must meet or be considered capable of meeting Diageo's community objectives. The Diageo Foundation supports applications which demonstrate the following:

▹ partnerships with community groups and charities rather than individuals

▹ excluded and disadvantaged people who, with support, can help themselves to transform their own lives

▹ where our involvement can make a significant measurable difference

▹ kick-start funding to get Diageo businesses and people involved locally.

There is normally a three-year limit to any funding commitment

The maximum funding available for any one project is £50,000. Payments are made normally over a maximum period of three years.

The Diageo Foundation encourages projects which obtain additional funding from external sources as this can lead to sustainability.

## Exclusions

The following are outside the foundation's guidelines:

- locations where Diageo does not have a business presence
- organisations which are not registered charities
- individuals
- loans or business finance
- medical charities or hospitals
- promotion of religion
- animal welfare
- expeditions or overseas travel
- political organisations
- advertising
- product donations
- capital projects (e.g. buildings).

## Applications

Applications to the Diageo Foundation should be addressed to the Administrator at the above address.

Please write providing details of the project, how it relates to the Diageo Foundation's focus areas and the amount of funding required – on no more than two sides of a sheet of paper. The foundation will contact you if it requires further details.

You will normally receive written notification of whether your application has been successful or not within 6–8 weeks.

## Corporate giving

The company commits approximately 1% of annual worldwide trading profit to support community activities – about £20.2 million in total in 2006. During the year, UK group companies made donations of £11.8 million to charitable organisations, including £700,000 to the Diageo Foundation and £6.5 million to the Thalidomide Trust. Group companies in the rest of the world made donations totalling £8.4 million.

The range of projects supported by Diageo is wide, from education and the environment to employability and homelessness. Its website provides a comprehensive list and outline of the organisations and people it has helped, an example of which are given below.

**Employment:** Tomorrow's People was set up by Diageo nearly 20 years ago and has become a specialist national charitable organisation helping people and communities. The company is supporting a new three-year pilot scheme launched by Tomorrow's People in July 2003 to help ex-offenders between the ages of 18 and 24 get back into work.

## In-kind support

The company acknowledges that whilst financial contributions are important, the giving of time and skill by its staff or surplus products and other in-kind donations can often achieve more.

## Employee-led support

Employee fundraising/giving receives match funding.

**Payroll giving:** The company operate the Give As You Earn scheme.

## Commercially-led support

**Sponsorship:** The company undertakes good-cause sponsorship.

# Dow Chemical Company Ltd

Estuary Road, King's Lynn, Norfolk PE30 2JD

01553 692100; Fax: 01553 694552

Website: www.dow.com

Correspondent: Carol Allen, UK Communications

Chief officer: William S Stavropoulos

Chief Executive: William S Stavropoulos

| Year end | Turnover | Pre-tax profit |
|---|---|---|
| 31/12/2005 | | |

### Nature of company business
The company is a worldwide manufacturer and supplier of chemicals and performance products, plastics, hydrocarbons and energy, and consumer specialities including agricultural products, and consumer products.

**Main locations:** King's Lynn, Wilton, Sandbach, Seal Sands, Heathrow Boulevard, Middlesbrough, Mirfield, Nuneaton, Billingham

**UK employees:** 1,000

**Total employees:** 55,000

## Community involvement

Dow states on its global website that: 'The challenge of becoming more transparent lies in part in the ability to provide information relevant to a wide variety of stakeholders. The communities in which we operate are an important stakeholder for Dow. In an effort to increase the relevancy of our public reporting efforts for this particular stakeholder, Dow – in addition to its global report web site – will publish to the Internet key data for its 20 major manufacturing locations.'

Whilst we whole heartedly commend Dow's efforts in this respect, it is unfortunate from a UK point of view that their facilities here do not rank amongst the top 20. The scant information we did receive only arrived after contacting their US office to point out the unwillingness of its UK subsidiary to cooperate with us.

The following information was provided by the UK Communication's at Dow Chemical: 'Our corporate donation policy is to support the communities in which we have a significant presence, which for us in the UK is primarily King's Lynn, Mirfield and the Teeside area.

'Specifically, we aim to support social needs, scientific education, or projects that improve the environment. In addition, projects should bring a real benefit and be supported by organisations in the local community.'

## Exclusions

No response to circular appeals. No support for advertising in charity brochures, appeals from individuals, local appeals not in areas of company presence, enterprise/training, overseas projects, political appeals, religious appeals or sport.

## Applications

According to Dow's Corporate Giving leaflet, 'Sharing Our Success', preferential consideration is given to requests for donations recommended by employees. Unsolicited applications/blanket appeal letters are not therefore considered.

## Corporate giving

In 2005, Dow made worldwide donations of $17.5 million (about £9.5 million) of which $2.3 million (about £1.25 million) was given in Europe. No further information was available.

## Employee-led support

Employees' volunteering/charitable activities are supported by the company. We were previously advised that Dow match employees' fundraising and giving to a maximum of £500 each, although we do not know if this is still so.

# Dow Corning Ltd

Cardiff Road, Barry, Vale of Glamorgan CF63 2YL

01446 732350; Fax: 01446 747944

Website: www.dowcorning.com/barry

Correspondent: Community Relations Co-ordinator 01446 732350; Fax: 01446 747944

**Nature of company business**
International provider of innovative silicone and silicon-based products, technologies, and services.

**Main locations:** Barry

**UK employees:** 600

### Charitable donations

Membership: BitC

## Community involvement

Each year Dow Corning receives many requests for support for local projects with help being given through donations of equipment, sponsorship or practical support from employees. The company stressed that though happy to listen to new requests for support, funds are limited. Moreover, in considering applications it looks at a number of factors.

A small team of employees meet monthly to discuss all the requests. Priority is given to requests from local groups and the team tries to make sure that any Dow Corning donation helps as many people as possible and has a long-term benefit.

Consideration is given to requests that meet the following criteria:

- projects that are local to the Barry, South Wales site and benefit people locally. Preference is given in order to Barry and Sully areas then Vale of Glamorgan. Requests from further a field cannot be considered
- activities that will help young people learn more about science, maths and technology, or skills that they will need in their future careers

- ideas that will help organizations or communities to improve safety or the local environment and that lead to better community vitality
- projects that promote good citizenship.

The company appears to take its responsibility towards the local community very seriously. Besides providing assistance in the forms mentioned above, regular communication with local people takes place through a number of channels. These include: the publication of a regular community newsletter – 'Dow Corning News'; the provision of a helpline for those concerned about environmental and health and safety issues; open house 'Forums for Neighbours'; and, a monthly Community Advisory Panel consisting of representatives from the Barry area – the panel even publishes minutes of its meetings on the company's website! Oh, for more companies to be so open.

## Exclusions

No support for raffle prizes, for individuals (such as sponsorship for overseas travel or individual fundraising), donations to central funds of charities, political or religious groups, one-off events such as fetes, parades, shows, tournaments, concerts, group travel expenses for excursions or overseas adventures, medical research, general fundraising appeals where Dow Corning funding is not used on specific projects or purchases, uniforms or sports strips for sports teams, national or international appeals, or advertising.

## Applications

In writing to the correspondent. Only written appeals will be considered.

## Corporate giving

The company's website gave the following examples of donations made in 2006:

'Members of the local sailing club can now sail with confidence with the aid of a donation by Dow Corning towards the purchase of a safety rescue boat. The new high speed boat is used to keep a watch on novice and expert sailors and will be able to reach those in difficulty quickly. A great example of improving the safety of water sports.

'A local nursery school received funding for the purchase of a climbing wall. The wall uses small foot and hand holds and encourages children as young as 4 to improve their eye/hand/leg/foot coordination as they traverse the wall.

'Occasionally, Dow Corning receives requests to help support large-scale projects. These are often multi-thousand dollar requests and are way beyond the site's own donations budget. A separate funding avenue has been set up whereby local organisations can apply for a corporate grant. Grant requests can be received from across Europe and are reviewed by European site managers. They are awarded once annually.

'A Barry woodland regeneration project has been awarded US$19,000 [around £10,300) from Dow Corning's Corporate Giving Fund in 2005.

'The project will be coordinated by the Woodland Trust, a UK woodland conservation organisation, which plans to plant and manage 40 acres of woodland and public open space. Currently, the proposed site is open fields and lies just a short distance from the Barry site. Designed to involve the local community, the area will be a focus for primary school children to plant a tree and others in the community to do similarly with the resulting woodland managed under the existing country park management structure.

'The new woodland will see 15,000 trees being planted over 3 years and will help improve the local biodiversity. It complements the Barry site's own pond project where a natural wetlands area is being preserved.'

## In-kind support

The company may occasionally make donations of equipment.

*Environment:* The company has recently received planning permission to build a 'green' nature centre at Cadoxtoin Ponds, next its site. To be built from sustainable resources, the building will feature solar panels, rainwater harvesting, and ground-sourced heating. Due to open in spring 2007, the building will be used, amongst other things, as a classroom for visiting school parties.

## Employee-led support

Employees are encouraged to become involved in supporting their local communities through practical help. A major part of this is the active programme the company has in supporting students and teachers in local schools with science, maths and technology.

# Dresdner Kleinwort

PO Box 52715, 30 Gresham Street, London EC2P 3XY

020 7623 8000; Fax: 020 7623 4069

Website: www.drkw.com

Correspondent: Bea Malleson or Karen Green, Community Investment Team

Chief officer: Dr Herbert Walter

| Year end | Turnover | Pre-tax profit |
|---|---|---|
| 31/12/2005 | | |

Nature of company business
Investment banking.

Main locations: London

### Charitable donations

Total community contributions: £1,000,000

Membership: BitC, L B Group

## Community involvement

The company concentrates its support on promoting regeneration in East London, supporting local charities, and local projects of national charities, which:

- encourage and promote new and young businesses
- enhance the skills and broaden the horizons of young people
- meet specific community needs.

Projects should be one-off or have the potential to become financially sustainable in future years. Preference is given to work which encourages collaboration between private, voluntary and public sector organisations, attract additional resources and seek to share best practice and experiences to a wider audience.

## Applications

In writing to the correspondent. The following information is known to have been applicable in previous years, so is repeated here with updates: Applications for funding in 2008 must be submitted by June 2007, with a final decision made by the end of November 2007 and payment made, where appropriate, in 2008.

## Corporate giving

Up-to-date financial information was not available. Details of recently supported organisations were previously available on its website. They have included: Apna Ghar for an emergency line for Asian women and young people experiencing domestic violence; E-Skills 4 Industry to provide work experience at Tower Hamlets College; Leyton Orient Community Sports Programme to broaden opportunities for schoolchildren; Teach First to attract more graduates into teaching in challenging schools and Treloar Trust to give greater independence to young people with physical disabilities.

In previous years donations have totalled about £1,000,000, with about one quarter of that amount being cash donations.

## Employee-led support

The company has a matching funds scheme for employee fundraising. Employees are also encouraged to volunteer.

**Payroll giving:** The company operates the Give As You Earn scheme

## Commercially-led support

**Sponsorship:** *The arts* – Sponsorship is mainly of events in the City of London, such as the City of London Festival and the Spitalfields Festival. A number of major arts organisations have also been supported. However, sponsorship is usually an exception rather than the norm.

# DSG International plc

Maylands Avenue, Hemel Hempstead, Hertfordshire HP2 7TG

0870 850 3333

Website: www.dsgiplc.com

Correspondent: Community Relations Manager 0870 850 3333 E-mail: communityrelations@dixons.co.uk

Chief officer: Sir John Collins

Chief Executive: John Clare

| Year end | Turnover | Pre-tax profit |
|---|---|---|
| 29/04/2006 | £7,403,400,000 | £302,900,000 |

Nature of company business
The company's main activity is the retailing of high technology consumer electronics, personal computers, domestic appliances, photographic equipment, communication products and related financial and after sales services.

Subsidiaries include: DSG Retail Ltd, PC World, Curry's, Coverplan Insurance Services Ltd, The Link, Partmaster, Mastercare Service and Distribution Ltd, PC World Business

Main locations: Nottingham, Sheffield, Bury, Hemel Hempstead

UK employees: 40,012

---

## Charitable donations

2006: £875,000
2005: £875,000
2004: £875,000
2003: £875,000

Total community contributions: £1,370,000
Management costs: £70,000

Membership: BitC, L B Group, %Club

---

# Community involvement

Areas of support are:

- crime – improving co-operation on crime prevention and in particular reducing retail crime or promoting community safety
- health – improving public education and understanding of health-related issues and, in certain circumstances, supporting families in need
- regeneration – improving local social, economic and environmental conditions in and around major company sites (such as Sheffield, Nottingham, Hertfordshire and Bury)
- education – helping to provide information technology to disadvantaged groups and support training initiatives to bridge the digital divide
- social inclusion – local projects to promote the inclusion of young people into mainstream education and society.

It also supports employees volunteering and the causes they support. Each year employees vote for a charity to support and raise funds through selling badges, recycling and other employee fundraising activities. The theme from October 2004 to February 2006 was *Young Futures* and the beneficiaries were ChildLine, NCH Action for Children and Teenage Cancer Trust.

DSG International Foundation is a registered charity (Charity Commission no. 1053215). Grants are available to both local and national charities, with a preference for those with employee's involvement. Grants range from £100 to £10,000, with most donations being of less than £2,000 or coming in the form of gift vouchers.

**Applications:** On a form available from the correspondent, or downloadable from the website. For donations of more than £2,000, contact the corporate affairs department before submitting an application.

## Exclusions

No grants are made towards: third party fundraising activities; political or religious organisations; projects that should be funded from statutory sources, overseas appeals; community sponsorship of any kind; or animal charities.

## Applications

On a form downloadable from the website. A response is usually given within six weeks. Applications made to group stores are referred to head office, rather than a decision being made locally.

# Corporate giving

### DSG International Foundation

In 2005/06, the group donated £875,000 to the foundation (formerly known as the Dixons Foundation), which gave over 350 grants.

Previous beneficiaries have included South Bradford Educational Action Zone (£100,000), Dixons CTC, London Business School, and London School of Economics. One organisation received a donation of £65,000, three of £25,000, nine of £10,000, a further nine of £5,000.

Grants tend to range from £100 to £10,000. Donations below £1,000 are often made in the form of gift vouchers to support the purchase of specific items of equipment.

Limited support has been given in the past to causes falling within what may be termed 'quality of life', including carers, disabled, advice lines, elderly, hospices, hospital units, medical conditions and related support groups, respite care and medical research. As this is not a prime area of support, donations tend to be up to £1,000. The company continues to support Kings College Hospital Islet Programme. The contribution is used to fund research into finding a cure for diabetes.

## In-kind support

The company also gives assistance through seconding staff to enterprise initiatives and gifts in kind. For example, it supports CREATE, a training project based in Liverpool and Tottenham for long-term unemployed people, by providing end-of-life white goods (washing machines, fridges etc.) which are refurbished by CREATE members.

## Employee-led support

Staff are allowed time off for activity of community benefit as well as being encouraged to become volunteers in their own time. The Switched on to Volunteering scheme rewards employees who volunteer by donating funds to the charity or group they volunteer for.

Stores can get involved in fundraising and awareness raising activities for local community groups. As well as in-store collections, staff can be involved in wearing fancy dress, carol singing or similar fundraising activities. For this type of support, apply to the local store manager for approval.

The company set up the Dixons Charity Fundraising Scheme in 1992, and in 2000/01, employees raised more than £140,000 for the NSPCC Full Stop campaign, through badge sales, recycling inkjet cartridges and employee fundraising. Employee fundraising for official charities is matched up to a maximum of £1,000 by the company.

**Payroll giving:** The Give As You Earn scheme is operated.

## Commercially-led support

The company states that its sponsorship programmes all come from the marketing, rather than community, budget, and decisions are made for purely commercial reasons. However, charitable programmes have been run in the past and will be considered for the benefits they can bring the company.

Ink for IT is a scheme run by PC World which supports the development of computer skills in schools and charities through the provision of free IT equipment in return for used recyclable inkjet cartridges. For further information see www.pcworld.co.uk.inkforit.

Community Fonebak is a scheme run by The Link in partnership with Shields Environmental which gives vouchers to schools, charities and community groups when unused mobile phones are returned for recycling. For further information, see www.communityfonebak.com

# Du Pont (UK) Limited

Wedgwood Way, Stevenage, Hertfordshire SG1 4QN

01438 734000; Fax: 01438 734836

Website: www2.dupont.com/Social_Commitment/en_US/

Chief officer: Charles O Holliday Jnr

### Nature of company business
Operating in more than 70 countries, DuPont offers a wide range of innovative products and services for markets including agriculture, nutrition, electronics, communications, safety and protection, home and construction, transportation and apparel.

Main locations: Londonderry, East Kilbride, Maydown, Ruabon, Corby, Stevenage, Sudbury, Bristol, Darlington, Romiley

## Community involvement

The company's website states that: 'DuPont is committed to improving the quality of life and enhancing the vitality of communities in which it operates throughout the world. Through financial contribution and the volunteer efforts of its employees, DuPont supports programmes that address social progress, economic success and environmental excellence – all vital components of community sustainability.

'Each year, DuPont contributes to numerous efforts that meet the needs of various groups and global communities where the company operates. Areas of support include:

- educational programmes
- culture and the arts
- environmental initiatives
- human and health service organisations
- civic and community activities.'

Within these criteria support may be available from three sources. Firstly, from the individual DuPont business units in the UK. Secondly, from the Corporate Contributions Office in the USA. Thirdly, from the DuPont Centre for Collaborative Research and Education, also in the USA.

## Exclusions

No grants are made to: non-registered charities; disease-specific organisations; endowment funds; service organisations; individuals; political causes; sectarian groups whose work is only available to members of one religious community; or organisations without good equal opportunity processes.

## Applications

As each DuPont site in the UK is responsible for its own community contributions, please contact the most appropriate one.

Applications are also considered centrally by its head office in the USA. The DuPont Contributions and Membership Team are responsible for non education-related monetary contributions. Most corporate grants involve programmes in the DuPont headquarters community of Wilmington, Delaware, and other communities where the company has a major presence.

Applications must be submitted in writing on a one to two-page letter defining who your organisation is, the project which requires funding and how this meets the aims of the company's corporate responsibility programme. An e-mail address should also be included, if possible. Applications are generally considered around May and September.

For non-education related appeals, the address is:

Corporate Contributions Office
DuPont Public Affairs
1007 Market Street
Wilmington, DE 19898
USA.

For educational appeals, the address is:

DuPont Center for Collaborative Research and Education
PO BOX 80030/1370
Wilmington, DE 19880–0030
USA.

## Corporate giving

As each DuPont site in the UK is responsible for its own community contributions, no community contributions figure was available. However, we believe the company's stated commitment to supporting community sustainability warrants its inclusion here.

### DuPont Community Fund

Since 1990, over 400 projects worldwide have received support from the fund. Company sites can nominate projects that enhance local community life for awards on an annual basis. The fund matches $ for $ up to $10,000 (around £5,400) any donation made to the project by the local DuPont site.

### DuPont Centre for Collaborative Research and Education

Unlike the above fund, it does not appear to be necessary for projects to be nominated by a DuPont site (although support from such may add weight to your application). However, in applying, it must be clearly shown how the project relates to DuPont's mission, operating philosophy, and areas of support of the company's community involvement programme. Grants are geared towards primary, secondary and higher education institutions and programmes.

## In-kind support

The company website suggests that in-kind support, e.g. the donation of land to a conservation group, may be made in cases where the organisations programmes and activities relate to the company's goals.

## Employee-led support

Through the DuPont Volunteer Recognition awards, the time and effort given by employees in support of their favoured charity or local community is acknowledged by the company. In addition to this, grants of $1,000 (around £540) are given to the organisation benefiting from the volunteering employees.

# Dwr Cymru Welsh Water

Pentwyn Road, Nelson, Treharris CF46 6LY

01443 452300; Fax: 01443 452323

Website: www.dwrcymru.com

Chief officer: Lord Burns

Managing Director: Nigel Annett

| Year end | Turnover | Pre-tax profit |
|---|---|---|
| 31/03/2005 | £494,100,000 | £75,200,000 |

**Nature of company business**
Provision of water services.

**Main locations:** Treharris

### Charitable donations

2005: £22,394
2004: £24,570

## Community involvement

Glas Cymru is a single purpose company formed to own, finance and manage Welsh Water (Dwr Cymru). It is a 'company limited by guarantee' and because it has no shareholders, any financial surpluses are retained for the benefit of Welsh Water's customers.

With respect to this, the 2005 annual report and accounts states: 'When Glas Cymru acquired Welsh Water, the board decided not to engage in major corporate sponsorship and donations, but to focus our effort on community engagement around the traditional strengths of Welsh water in the fields of education, conservation and recreation centred on the assets of the company'. This primarily takes the form of in-kind support.

### Applications

**Note:** As a not-for-profit company operating for the benefit of its customers, any donations that are made by Welsh Water are done so in support of employees fundraising efforts. Applications outside of this are not, therefore, accepted or acknowledged.

## Corporate giving

In 2004/05, the company made charitable cash donations totalling just over £22,000. Major beneficiaries included: Keep Wales Tidy (£10,000); Water Aid (£5,250); Hereford Waterworks Museum (£5,000); and, Handicapped Anglers Trust (£1,949). Although no figure for community contributions was available, this could be quite substantial based on the examples given below under 'In-kind support'.

### In-kind support

**Education:** Welsh Water has developed a programme of activities to educate children about their environment through, for example, the *Living and Learning with Water* interactive website. It also operates four education centres located across Wales staffed by full-time seconded teachers or environmental rangers and to which visits are free of charge. Finally, in partnership with the Welsh Assembly's Healthy Schools Initiative, *Think Water – Dewis Dwr*, it has supported the provision of water coolers to nearly 400 schools based in 'Communities First' areas across Wales.

**Recreation:** The company encourages visitors to share in the resources offered by its reservoirs. Facilities include fishing, sailing, canoeing, windsurfing and diving. Larger sites offer visitor centres, bird watching hides, picnic areas and marked pathways and nature trails.

**Community involvement:** *Crimestoppers* – Welsh Water works with the four Welsh Police Forces to prevent distraction burglaries often in the form of bogus callers. Customers concerned about the latter can register for the company's password scheme. This enables them to identify genuine company representatives by use of an agreed word or phrase.

### Employee-led support

The company stated that: 'We have continued to promote our community investment scheme to assist employees who wish to become involved in charitable or other projects within their local communities.' In other words, any donations the company makes are to support (match) the fundraising efforts of its employees.

# Dyson Limited

3–5 Ives Street, London  SW3 2ND

01666 827200

Website: www.dyson.co.uk

**Correspondent:** The James Dyson Foundation, Dyson Press Office
E-mail: jamesdysonfoundation@dyson.com

**Chief officer:** J Dyson

| Year end | Turnover | Pre-tax profit |
|---|---|---|
| 31/12/2005 | £151,315,000 | £26,988,000 |

**Nature of company business**
Manufacture of domestic appliances.

**Total employees:** 776

### Charitable donations

2005: £2,885,000
2004: £150,000

## Community involvement

The company's charitable giving is made through The James Dyson Foundation, (Charity Commission no. 1099709), which was established in November 2002. The foundation was set up for general charitable purposes including advancing education by the provision of grants, scholarships, prizes, to advance scientific or medical research and to promote the provision of facilities in the interest of social and community welfare.

Dyson's charity partnerships have raised £1.7m for Breakthrough Cancer, £1.5m for Meningitis Research Foundation and £448,000 for Cancer and Leukaemia in Childhood, (CLIC).

### Exclusions

The foundation does not provide support for political purposes and local appeals not in areas of company presence.

### Applications

In writing, by e:mail or post, to the correspondent.

## Corporate giving

#### The James Dyson Foundation

The foundation relies principally on funds received from Dyson Limited which, in 2005, donated £2,885,000 (2004: £150,000). During that year the foundation made a gift of £191,162 to CLIC. In the same year, the foundation donated £2,000 to the Science Museum which enabled it to hold a two-day educational open day at its venue in

Wroughton, Wiltshire. The foundation is exploring ways in which the two organisations might work together in the future in advancing education in the field of design and engineering.

The foundation also donated £50,000 to Winston's Wish, £25,000 to Malmesbury School, £12,000 to the Royal College of Art (in Bursaries), £4,000 to the Intellectual Property Institute, £1,600 to the Roundhouse Trust, £1,200 to the Malmesbury & Tetbury District Round Table, £1,000 to the Salvation Army in Catford and £2,000 each to Wiltshire Association for the Blind and Malmesbury Carnival. Over £20,000 was given in gifts of less than £1,000 each.

Additionally, the foundation donated £200,000 to the Disasters and Emergency Committee in January 2005 following the Asian Tsunami.

### In-kind support

Design engineers from Dyson host workshops at schools and universities throughout the country and the foundation provides free resources to Design and Technology teachers throughout the UK.

The company provide an information pack for teachers and lecturers which can be used in conjunction with the Dyson Education Box and both are free of charge.

Vacuum cleaners are available for donation to charitable fundraising each year.

### Employee-led support

Dyson workers in Malmesbury, Wiltshire, are currently involved in a range of fundraising activities in support of CLIC, including parachute jumps, French boules competitions and sponsored runs across the Sahara. Dyson's employees also contribute to the foundation and are encouraged to take an active role in selecting projects and fundraising, especially for Dyson's charity partnerships.

### Commercially-led support

The sale of a special edition Dyson vacuum cleaner is helping to raise money for Dyson/CLIC care grants. The vacuum cleaner was designed by four year old Megan, winner of the on-line 'Colour my Dyson' competition. £10 from every machine sold is donated directly to CLIC.

# E.ON UK plc

Westwood Way, Westwood Business Park, Coventry CV4 8LG

024 7642 4000; Fax: 024 7642 5432

Website: www.eon-uk.com

Correspondent: The Corporate Responsibility Manager

Chief officer: Dr Wulf Bernotat

Chief Executive: Dr Paul Golby

| Year end | Turnover | Pre-tax profit |
|---|---|---|
| 31/12/2005 | £6,928,000,000 | £869,000,000 |

Nature of company business
Principal activity: the trading of electricity and gas in UK markets. Through Central Networks E.ON UK runs the electricity distribution network for the Midlands, from the Lincolnshire coast to the Welsh borders.

Subsidiaries include: Ergon Insurance Ltd, Kinetica Ltd, East Midlands Electricity, Wavedriver Ltd, DR Investments

Main locations: Nottingham, Coventry

UK employees: 12,121

### Charitable donations
2005: £74,673

Total community contributions: £2,100,000

Membership: BitC, L B Group

## Community involvement

E.ON UK is a leading energy company in the UK. Community support is focused on areas relevant to the company's business activities – where it is based and where its employees live and work, i.e. predominantly in and around its offices, call centres and power station sites.

As well as a regional focus, community activities are targeted on areas relevant to the business and where maximum benefit can be brought. Community investment strategy is based on two main themes – the company aims to develop projects that fit into one of these: Education through Energy and Community Energy Solutions.

### Exclusions

No support for: advertising in charity brochures; animal welfare; appeals from individuals; enterprise/training; fundraising events; medical research; political appeals; religious appeals; or sickness/disability charities.

### Applications

In writing to the correspondent.

## Corporate giving

In 2005 donations to charitable organisations amounted to £74,673. Almost £170,000 went to over 400 charities through matched funding and matched time.

### Employee-led support

The company encourages its people to get involved in its employee volunteering programme – over 1,700 participated in 2005.

The company match funds employees fundraising efforts.

**Payroll giving:** The company have established an employee payroll giving scheme.

Other initiatives exist to support employee fundraising activities, such as providing maths and IT support for schoolchildren.

# Ecclesiastical Insurance Group plc

Allchurches Trust Ltd, Beaufort House, Brunswick Road, Gloucester GL1 1JZ

01452 528533; Fax: 01452 423557

Website: www.ecclesiastical.co.uk

Correspondent: Mrs R J Hall, Company Secretary

Chief officer: B J E Sealy

Chief Executive: G V Doswell

| Year end | Turnover | Pre-tax profit |
|---|---|---|
| 31/12/2005 | £359,913,000 | £71,491,000 |

**Nature of company business**
Principal activity: general and long-term insurance.

**Subsidiaries include:** Ecclesiastical Insurance Office Ltd, Crusade Services Ltd, Ansvar Insurance Co Ltd, Gerling Global London Market Ltd, Ansvar Conference Services Ltd, Hinton & Wild (Home Plans) Ltd, The Churches Purchasing Scheme Ltd, Blaisdon Properties Ltd, Ansvar Pensions Ltd, Allchurches Investment Management Services Ltd, Eccint Ltd, Allchurches Life Assurance Ltd

**Main locations:** Gloucester

**UK employees:** 784

**Total employees:** 970

### Charitable donations

2005: £5,350,000
2003: £4,300,000

## Community involvement

The company is owned by the Allchurches Trust (Charity Commission no. 263960) to which all charitable grants made by the company are given.

The object of the trust is to promote the Christian Religion and to contribute to the funds of any charitable institutions, associations, funds or objects and to carry out any charitable purpose.

The trust has adopted the following priorities:

▷ supporting the mission and work of the dioceses and cathedrals of the Church of England by the distribution of annual grants

▷ supporting requests for financial assistance from Anglican churches, Churches of other Denominations and Christian communities and organisations in accordance with its grant making policy

▷ maintaining a special project fund to support substantial projects which may have a broad impact on the Christian community in the UK

▷ establishing an overseas project fund to support the church and Christian community overseas in accordance with its grant making policy.

There is a preference for charities working within Gloucestershire.

The trustees regularly review the grant making policy of the trust 'to ensure it remains appropriate to the strategic direction of the Charity and its objects'. A copy of the grant making policy is available from the company secretary at the registered office.

Applicants are advised to visit the website: www.allchurches.co.uk

### Exclusions

The trustees do not make grants to charities with political associations. Support is not normally given for advertising in charity brochures, animal welfare charities, individuals, the arts, fundraising events, medical research, or sport.

### Applications

Applications are not considered by the company. Instead, applications should be submitted in writing in the form prescribed, detailing charity number, the objectives of the charity, the appeal target, how the funds are to be utilised, funds raised to date and previous support received from the trust. If available, the application should be accompanied by supporting literature and annual report.

Further details about the work of Allchurches Trust Ltd or advice on how to apply for financial assistance can be obtained by contacting the Company Secretary, Beaufort House, Brunswick Road, Gloucester, GL1 1JZ or e-mail: atl@eigmail.com

## Corporate giving

During 2005 the company donated £5.35 million to the trust (2004: £4.9 million). This amount includes a special donation of £650,000 (2004: £500,000) due to exceptional current year performance.

The trust has a general fund which responds to requests for financial assistance from Anglican churches, Churches of other Denominations and the Christian community in accordance with its grant making policy. In general, the trust supports appeals from churches for building and restoration projects, repair of church fabric, church community initiatives, religious charities and charities preserving the UK heritage. During the year the trust allocated £470,000 (2004: £440,000) to the general fund.

### Commercially-led support

**Cause-related marketing:** The company has launched an ISA charitable giving scheme; or the 'nicer ISA' as they have termed it!

Under the scheme, every Ecclesiastical ISA investor has the opportunity to select a charity from a carefully chosen list. If this option is taken up, the equivalent of 0.25% of an individual's savings will be donated to their selected charity on an annual basis.

# Economist Newspaper Ltd

25 St James's Street, London SW1A 1HG

020 7830 7000; Fax: 020 7839 2968/9

**Website:** www.economist.com

**Correspondent:** Sally Bibb, Charities Liaison Officer

**Chief officer:** Sir Robert Wilson

| Year end | Turnover | Pre-tax profit |
|---|---|---|
| 31/03/2006 | £218,000,000 | £31,000,000 |

**Nature of company business**
Principal activities: publication of The Economist and specialist publications including European Voice and, in the United States, CFO, Journal of Commerce, and Roll Call; supply of business information (Economist Intelligence Unit).

**Main locations:** London

### Charitable donations

2005: £105,000
2004: £200,000

## Community involvement

Donations are largely made through The Economist Charitable Trust (Charity Commission no. 293709). The principal activity of the trust is the disbursement of monies received from The Economist Newspaper Limited to various charities. 50–60% of the trust's donations go to charities in the fields of communication, education, literacy and retraining for individuals and groups who are disadvantaged in some way.

A match funding scheme is in operation for individual staff members' fundraising efforts.

## Exclusions

The Economist Charitable Trust does not support appeals from non-charities, circular appeals, applications of a chain-letter type, gala charity events, advertising in charity brochures, appeals from individuals, larger national appeals, church restoration appeals, politically sensitive organisations, organisations of a religious or denominational nature, single service (among forces) charities, arts sponsorship (see above) or appeals from ordinary educational establishments (e.g. schools, university building funds). *Special schools or projects for disabled students are the exception to this rule.*

Animal welfare appeals are supported via staff matching only. Fundraising events are only supported by gifts in kind, and these are usually bought from other (e.g. disabled) voluntary organisations. Sport appeals are only supported if for the disabled.

## Applications

In writing to the correspondent. A simple letter plus latest report & accounts is preferred – a phone call to clarify specific queries is welcomed.

The Economist Charitable Trust is run by a small team of staff volunteers. Applications can be made at any time.

**Advice to applicants:** The company states that multiple approaches are wasteful and counter-productive, particularly when they are addressed to directors who retired some time ago, indicating use of out-of-date lists. A few applications each year are rejected simply because they are badly presented. Many more fail because their deadlines for events are far too close when they apply. Applicants are also advised that if they are asked for additional information, this is a sign of interest in the project and not the opposite.

Unsigned, circular appeals will not receive a response.

## Corporate giving

In 2005 the company donated £105,000 to the trust.

Approximately 30–40% of funds are used to match donations made by employees of The Economist Group. Remaining funds are utilised to make small donations to small and local charities. The average donation disbursed in the year was £845 (2004: £701). The trust also receives smaller amounts from various other sources, which are disbursed.

## In-kind support

The company's main area of non-cash support is gifts in kind. For example, the Economist also supports the visual arts by allowing its premises to be used for exhibitions. There are frequent events throughout the year, allowing up and coming artists to display their work to the general public.

Secondments to charities have occurred in the past, but only for a short period and part-time. The company operates the Give As You Earn payroll giving scheme and matches employee fundraising.

## Employee-led support

A wide range of causes are supported via staff matched fundraising.

**Payroll giving:** The company operates the Give As You Earn scheme.

## Commercially-led support

**Sponsorship:** Arts sponsorship may be undertaken.

---

# EDF Energy

40 Grosvenor Place, Victoria, London SW1X 7EN

020 7242 9050

Website: www.edfenergy.com

Correspondent: Community Involvement Team

E-mail: corporate.responsibility@edfenergy.com

Chief officer: Daniel Camus

Year end 31/12/2005    Turnover    Pre-tax profit

**Nature of company business**
Operators of coal fired power stations. Suppliers of gas and electricity.

Main locations: Sunderland, London

UK employees: 11,519

Total employees: 11,519

### Charitable donations

2005: £2,270,000
2003: £1,655,431

Total community contributions: £2,840,000

Membership: A & B, BitC, L B Group, %Club

## Community involvement

The company is interested in causes concerned with education, youth, community development, environment and culture and the arts. Support is given in the area the company operates which covers London, the south east and the south west of England, as well as around its customer services centre in Sunderland. It has entered into a special partnership with Mencap, which it encourages all its staff to make monthly contributions to.

It also operates a charitable trust: EDF Energy Trust (Charity Commission no. 1099446). This trust aims to relieve fuel poverty in the UK and mostly supports customers of group companies. In other words, it donates a sum of money to individuals in order for them to be able to pay their domestic bills, which is effectively a tax-efficient way for the group to recover funds owed to it from non-payers without adding to the financial burden of the individuals involved.

Applications: In writing to Ms Susan Jordan, Charis Ltd, Hedley House, Rightwell, Bretton, Peterborough PE3 8DJ (tel: 01733 331177).

## Applications

See Community Involvement above.

## Corporate giving

In 2005, a total of £2,840,000 was donated, including £300,000 to the School Grounds Awards programme and £1,300,000 to the EDF Energy Trust.

### In-kind support

An educational website (www.electricityineducation.co.uk) has been set up to provide educational resources about electricity. It has also visited London schools to give talks and distributed a safety guide to children in Eastern England.

It has donated its used office furniture to Green-Works for distribution to voluntary groups.

### Employee-led support

The company has a Helping Hands scheme which allows all employees to spend two days performing voluntary work on normal pay if they match these two days of work in their own time. Around a quarter of its staff takes part in community work, with over 18,000 hours of community work being performed during working hours, as well as a further 24,000 hours of voluntary work by employees in their own time. It has also launched a similar scheme called Energetic Hands which uses the same concept to spread the specific message of saving energy.

Employees' donations and fundraising efforts are matched by the company.

In 2005, over £250,000 was raised for the company's charity partner, Mencap. This comprised £150,000 raised by employees and £100,000 matched by EDF Energy.

### Commercially-led support

#### Cause-related marketing:

The company allows customers to pay their bills at a premium rate (which includes a 'green tariff'), with the extra payments being matched by the company and donated to causes which promote renewable energy. Grants during 2005, as in previous years, included those to hydro and wind power schemes, a biomass project and photovoltaic (sunlight into electricity) schemes.

#### Sponsorship:

It sponsors the School's Herald, an occasional supplement in a daily Plymouth newspaper which is produced entirely by local schools in the area. Grants are provided to cover the additional newsprint and staff time, whilst employees can be seconded to help out with any aspect of the production.

It has sponsored Durham Wildlife Trust's educational programme, London Jazz Festival's New Audience scheme to allow schools, community and youth groups from disadvantaged areas to attend, and Southwark Aylesbury Estate Summer Festival to enable local community groups to promote their services, as well as sponsoring Tate Britain and Tate Modern.

# EDS UK Ltd

4 Roundwood Avenue, Stockley Park, Uxbridge, Middlesex UB11 1BQ

020 8848 8989; Fax: 020 8756 0130

Website: www.eds.com

Correspondent: Corporate Communications

| Year end | Turnover | Pre-tax profit |
|---|---|---|
| 31/12/2004 | £2,843,437,000 | £228,313,000 |

**Nature of company business**
The principal activity is information technology.

**Subsidiaries include:** Electronic Data Systems

**Main locations:** London, Luton, Uxbridge

**Total employees:** 22,352

### Charitable donations

2004: £49,805
2003: £54,540

Membership: A & B

## Community involvement

The company informed us that it no longer has a policy of making cash donations to charity, although it may still consider supporting charities suggested by employees. Instead, it runs programmes and events that raise money for selected charities.

### Applications

We have been informed that decisions regarding charitable giving are made principally by the US Foundation and we have been unable to obtain information showing any grants awarded by the foundation to UK organisations since it was established. However, there is the facility on the company's website for non-US organisations to apply. For further information on applications to the foundation visit the company's website: http://www.eds.com/about/community/foundation where full details are given. All applicants must complete the appropriate foundation application forms and submit all supplemental information requested. The application procedure for grants from the foundation appears to be fairly stringent. There is a separate form for non-US funding. Applications should be sent to EDS Foundation, 5400 Legacy Drive, H36 F47, Plano, TX 75024, USA. Occasionally UK site managers may make a small contribution to charities local to their particular site. Applicants should apply to the UK head office at 4 Roundwood Avenue, Stockley Park, Uxbridge, Middlesex UB11 1BQ.

## Corporate giving

#### The EDS Foundation

The EDS Foundation was created to support EDS's philanthropic efforts in communities where the company's employees live and work around the world. As of 31st December 2005, net assets of the Foundation were $6,274,698. Although the company has over 200 sites in the UK, we can find no information that the foundation has made any grants to UK organisations since its creation. This may not necessarily be the foundation's policy, and it may be worth making an initial approach.

### In-kind support

The company has an Education Outreach programme which offers creative learning experiences to students. For example, 'EDS and England's Worthing High School joined in partnership to create a six-week initiative that helps prepare students for careers. As part of this initiative, EDS employees help students create their first CVs, write cover letters, and complete applications. Students also practice for job interviews and participate in mock interviews at EDS offices.'

The company also runs the EDS Technology Grant Programme, which 'helps teachers of children ages 6 through 18 purchase information technology products and services that will improve their students' ability to learn. Each year, EDS offices worldwide sponsor and award $1,500 grants to teachers through a competitive application process. The grants are awarded to teachers through their schools, and schools applying for a grant must be located within 50 miles of a sponsoring EDS account.

'Grants must be used to pay for technology products, training and services. EDS encourages teachers to propose innovative classroom projects or student exercises. Teachers are asked to explain the innovative nature of their project, how they or their students will use the requested technology and how the technology will improve their students' ability to achieve curriculum objectives. Examples of qualified grant expenditures include computer software and hardware, multimedia equipment, Web-cams, CD-ROM libraries, scanners, modems, Internet access, technical training, specialized technology tools and equipment such as Robotics Kits and other classroom learning aides that are considered advanced in the area of technology.'

### Employee-led support

EDS organises Global Volunteer Day (GVD) each October. The following is an extract from the company's website. 'Since its inception in 1993, EDS colleagues have worked on more than 4,000 community projects, contributed more than 500,000 hours and touched the lives of more than 1 billion people in 32 countries.'

### Commercially-led support

**Sponsorship:** *Education* – EDS is a founding technology sponsor of the JASON Project, a worldwide distance learning programme through which 1.7 million students in the US and abroad are taught each year.

# Egg plc

Riverside Road, Derby DE99 3GG

01332 335236

Website: www.egg.com

Correspondent: James Bell, Head of Community Relations
E-mail: community@egg.com

Chief officer: Nick Prettejohn

Chief Executive: Mark Nancarrow

| Year end | Turnover | Pre-tax profit |
|---|---|---|
| 31/12/2005 | £497,600,000 | £106,700,000 |

Nature of company business
On-line financial institution.

Main locations: Derby

UK employees: 2,100

### Charitable donations

2004: £250,000
2003: £250,000

Total community contributions: £500,000

Membership: BitC

## Community involvement

The company's support is given through its Local Talent Fund, which aims to support local causes committed to developing local talent. The beneficial area is within 25 miles of any of its offices, which are in Derby, Dudley and London. Projects must involve Egg employees, either before an application is made or providing opportunities for staff to get involved. Areas of support are:

- Education – 'from primary all the way up to post graduate'
- Sport – 'table tennis to mountaineering, whatever your game is'
- The arts – 'including visual and performing arts'
- Regeneration – 'anything from fixing the local scout hut roof to painting a narrow boat'.

### Applications

On a form available from the correspondent, or downloadable from the website (www.egg.com). The guidelines state that:

- Your scheme must be located within 25 miles of one of Egg's sites based in Derby, Dudley or London.
- The purpose of your scheme must be the development of local talent.
- Your scheme must fall into one of the four key areas – education, sport, the arts or regeneration.
- Your request must involve the use of people who work for Egg.

## Corporate giving

In 2004 it gave £250,000 in cash grants. It appears that this is roughly the same each year. It also allowed staff to volunteer during work time, at a cost of the equivalent of £250,000 to the company. Beneficiaries included Derby County Football Club to launch a football skills challenge in a number of local schools, Derby Rugby Football Club to launch a rugby development programme, Derbyshire Community Foundation for a music competition and Derbyshire Local Education Authority for a creative thinking project with primary school headteachers.

### Employee-led support

All employees are encouraged to be active within the communities, which can take place during working hours. The guidelines state: 'keep in mind it's not just about money, you could ask for a bit of elbow grease from our people too'.

**Payroll giving:** The company participates in the GAYE scheme.

### Commercially-led support

Derby Playhouse has received support to create the Egg Theatre Academy.

# Eli Lilly Group Ltd

Lilly House, Priestley Road, Basingstoke RG24 9NL

01256 315000; Fax: 01256 315412

Website: www.lilly.co.uk

Correspondent: The Secretary, Lilly Grants Committee

| Year end | Turnover | Pre-tax profit |
|---|---|---|
| 28/12/2005 | | |

**Nature of company business**
Eli Lilly & Company Ltd is a research-based corporation that develops, manufactures and markets human medicines, medical instruments, diagnostic products and agricultural products. Corporate headquarters are located in Indianapolis, USA.

**Subsidiaries include:** Elanco Products Ltd

**Main locations:** Basingstoke, Windlesham, Speke

**UK employees:** 2,500

**Total employees:** 42,600

## Community involvement

The company's grant programme in the UK offers financial assistance to registered charities (national and local) and local community-based organisations close to its operating sites (Basingstoke, Speke and Windlesham). The company particularly supports activities working in the fields of healthcare, science education and children/youth development. Community contributions made by the company include charitable donations, good cause sponsorship, in-kind support and non-commercial advertising.

Support varies according to the needs of the local community, with each site having a grants committee that meets regularly to respond to requests for financial help. A total of up to 50 projects a year may receive support.

**Charity of the Year:** TB Alert (2006).

### Exclusions

The Lilly Foundation does not support individuals, endowments, debt reduction, religious or political appeals, fraternal or veteran organisations, beauty or talent contests, fundraising activities related to individual sponsorship, conferences or media productions, non-accredited educational groups, memorials and local appeals not in areas of company presence.

### Applications

Applications from national charities should be addressed to the correspondent. Applications from local charities should be addressed to 'The Secretary, Local Grants Committee', at the relevant operating unit (Basingstoke, Speke or Windlesham).

**Information available:** The company produce a downloadable pdf file entitled: 'Lilly in the Community'.

## Corporate giving

In 2004, Lilly's global philanthropy (directly from the company and via its foundation) totalled around £39 million in cash donations. Unfortunately, no foundation report or figure from the company was available showing how much of this went to organisations in the UK. However, it is fair to assume that it was sufficient to ensure the company's inclusion in our research findings.

In 2006, the company's charity of the year is TB Alert, the only British charity working solely on fighting TB in the UK and overseas. Employees will aim to raise a minimum of £20,000 to help support the charity's work which, we believe, will be match-funded by Lilly. This is the sixth year that Lilly has concentrated its employee fundraising efforts with one charity and follows successful partnerships with RNIB, Diabetes UK, CancerBACUP, National Osteoporosis Society and Carers UK.

**The Lilly Outstanding Achievement in Mental Health Awards**

Now in their eighth year, the awards are designed to recognise and reward those people who help to 'breakdown misunderstanding and stigma and reintegrate individuals with severe mental illness into the community'.

- The Lilly Reintegration Award: entries are judged on their simplicity, innovation and how easily they could be replicated. The winner wins a Certificate of Excellence and a grant of £5,000 to invest in their winning project. Two runner-up entries win a Certificate of Achievement and grant of £2,000.
- Lilly Moving Life Forward Award: any individual who has suffered from severe mental illness can enter. The winner received a Certificate of Excellence and vouchers of their choice worth £500.

### In-kind support

**Education:** Initiatives include involvement in local education/business partnerships and the provision of work experience schemes for pupils and teachers, and educational materials for schools. In Speke, for example, it worked with other local businesses to create the country's first Partnership for Learning Centre.

**Enterprise:** The company gives support to local enterprise agencies and was a founding supporter of the Basingstoke & Andover Enterprise Centre.

**Health:** The company donates pharmaceutical products to medical charities and causes around the world. In 2004, this was valued at £184 million (Note. This is most likely based on the wholesale rather than cost price).

### Employee-led support

Preference is given to charities in which a member of staff is involved. Staff are also encouraged to become school governors. Employees are encouraged to raise funds for the company's 'Charity of the Year' and are allowed to spend up to four hours of their working time per month helping a company-approved charity.

**Payroll giving:** The company operates a scheme for employees.

### Commercially-led support

**Sponsorship:** At national level this is very selective. At a local level some good cause sponsorship up to about £1,000 is undertaken, usually for health-related causes.

# EMAP plc

40 Bernard Street, London WC1N 1LW

**Website:** www.emap.com

**Chief officer:** Adam Cathcart

**Chief Executive:** Tom Moloney

| Year end | Turnover | Pre-tax profit |
|---|---|---|
| 31/03/2006 | £1,154,000,000 | £223,000,000 |

**Nature of company business**
Principal activities: publishing consumer magazines, providing business-to-business communications media, and operating radio and cable TV channels.

Subsidiaries include: Trade Promotion Services Ltd, Construction Research Communications Ltd, Box Television Ltd, Seymour International Ltd, Cap Motor Research Ltd, Glenigan Ltd, I&E Ltd

Main locations: London, Peterborough, Kettering

UK employees: 7,721

### Charitable donations

2006: £14,500
2004: £60,000

## Community involvement

Each Emap business division operates its own community support programme, reflecting the needs and preferences of a distinct community. This takes three main forms – giving money, giving time and raising awareness of good causes.

Generally, only charities in which a member of company staff is involved will be supported.

### Exclusions

If a member of company staff is not involved, no support will be given.

### Applications

As each division within the group operates its own community support programme, initial enquiries should be addressed to the appropriate human resource department. Please note, however, that current policy means unsolicited appeals are very unlikely to receive support.

## Corporate giving

Although the cash donation element of Emap's community support has declined in the new millennium (down from £115,000 in 2000/01, to £14,500 in 2005/06), it is clear that its level of facilitated giving and in-kind support is sufficiently high to warrant inclusion here.

Unfortunately, as the company does not cost the value of this form of support, we cannot give it its full credit.

### In-kind support

Donation of staff time is made primarily through the Media Trust, of which Emap has recently become a corporate member. In 2005, nearly £500,000 worth of advertising space was given in support of the trust.

In addition to the above, Emap brands work with individual organisations to help raise their profile and funds on their behalf, e.g. Kerrang! is helping to raise awareness of the Samaritans amongst 16 to 25 year olds.

### Employee-led support

Staff are encouraged to support good causes through match funding and payroll giving schemes. The first sees any sum raised by an individual or team matched by the company up to a maximum of £500, whilst under the second, the company will donate up to £50 a month to any charity or group of charities an employee chooses to support through payroll giving. In 2005/06, the amount donated by the company in support of this totalled £14,500.

**Payroll giving:** The Give As You Earn scheme is in operation.

# EMI Group plc

27 Wrights Lane, London W8 5SW

020 7795 7000; Fax: 020 7795 7296

Website: www.emigroup.com

Correspondent: Kate Dunning, VP Social Responsibility
E-mail: dunningk@emigroup.com

Chief officer: Eric Nicoli

| Year end | Turnover | Pre-tax profit |
|---|---|---|
| 31/03/2005 | £305,800,000 | £48,700,000 |

Nature of company business
EMI covers all aspects of the music industry from music recording and publishing through to manufacture, marketing and distribution.

Subsidiaries include: Virgin Records Ltd, Virgin Music Group Ltd

Main locations: London

UK employees: 1,156

Total employees: 6,672

### Charitable donations

2005: £300,000
2004: £300,000
2003: £400,000

Total community contributions: £1,045,679

Membership: A & B, BitC, L B Group, %Club

## Community involvement

The focus of the company's community investment programme is music education and access to music. The EMI Music Sound Foundation (Charity Commission no. 1104027), established by EMI in 1997 but independently governed, supports secondary schools seeking specialist performing arts or music status, provides grants to other schools, music teachers and music students, and offers a number of bursaries through colleges in the UK and Ireland.

EMI works with a number of other community partners (see below) and is closely involved in the development and implementation of the government's Music Manifesto, a collaborative strategy to enhance music provision in schools and the wider community.

### Exclusions

EMI Group will not fund secondments, individuals seeking sponsorship, expeditions, sporting activities or wildlife charities. No donations are made to political, sectarian, religious or racist organisations.

### Applications

Applications (including sponsorship proposals) should be made in writing to the correspondent. For grants for music students and teachers, EMI MSF trustees meet every six months, in March and September, to consider those applications most worthy of help. More information, and an application form, can be found at: www.musicsoundfoundation.com

## Corporate giving

In 2004/05, worldwide community contributions totalled £2 million including cash donations of £300,000 within the UK. One organisation to benefit from EMI's financial support has been the Music House for Children, with whom the company has a long-standing partnership. Providing music and arts education for children throughout London, EMI's annual donation funds places at Music House for children from low-income families.

Other community partners include: The Roundhouse in north London which, as part of its redevelopment as a state-of-the-art performing centre for young people, is being fitted out by EMI with professional music recording facilities and performance space; Teach First, an organisation that, in seeking to attract the most able UK graduates to teach in under-resourced secondary schools, is supported by EMI in the recruitment and training of music teachers; and, Creative Goals which receives support for its media, creative and design industries centred personal development training programme aimed at 18–30 year olds no longer in full-time work or education.

### Music Sound Foundation

Grants to date include £1.1 million to support specialist schools bids, £382,000 to individuals to help with instrument purchase, £165,000 for music bursaries and £120,000 to fund music in primary schools.

### In-kind support

The royalties-free performance of songs that EMI owns the copyright to has been approved for benefit concerts. Benefit CDs have been released, with all profits generated going to a particular cause.

### Employee-led support

The company aims to encourage and support the commitment, enthusiasm and participation of employees who are involved in voluntary activities within their local communities, and give consideration to projects which they put forward and in which they become involved. An employee-matching scheme exists for UK employees.

### Commercially-led support

**Sponsorship:**

The EMI Group is a corporate member of several arts organisations including the Roundhouse in London.

# Ernst & Young

1 More London Place, London SE1 2AF

020 7951 2000; Fax: 020 7951 1345

Website: www.ey.com

Correspondent: Nicky Majors, Director of Corporate Responsibility 020 7951 1132
E-mail: nmajor@uk.ey.com

Chief officer: Nick Land

| Year end | Turnover | Pre-tax profit |
|---|---|---|
| 30/06/2003 | £811,600,000 | £191,700,000 |

**Nature of company business**
Financial and professional services provider.

Main locations: Reading, Southampton, Liverpool, London, Luton, Manchester, Newcastle, Nottingham, Cambridge, Bristol, Hull, Inverness, Leeds, Glasgow, Edinburgh, Exeter, Birmingham, Belfast, Aberdeen

UK employees: 6,703

### Charitable donations

Total community contributions: £1,327,000 -2000
Management costs: £56,000

Membership: A & B, BitC, L B Group, %Club

## Community involvement

The firm's annual review for 2000/01 stated: 'Many of our people play a very active role in contributing their time and money to community activities and we are proud to have supported all our staff and partners in this. Our offices select their own charities and on a firm-wide basis we continued with a programme [of support for chosen charities].' More recent guidelines were not available, other than that the company is interested in sponsoring arts projects and organisations.

### Applications

In writing to the correspondent or contact your nearest regional office.

## Corporate giving

Up-to-date information on the size of donations made was not available. However, the 2002/03 annual report stated that recent beneficiaries have included Comic Relief, Mango, NCH Action for Children, Tax Aid and Unicorn.

According to the 2000 PerCent Club annual report, Ernst & Young made total community contributions of £1,327,000 of which £372,000 was in cash donations.

### In-kind support

The firm's commitment to supporting the non-profit sector saw the waiving of professional fees totalling over £800,000. This included the provision of accounting services to Comic Relief.

The British Dyslexia Association and NCH Action for Children, the leading children's charity with which the firm work on the joint arts initiative Life Matters, also received in kind support.

### Employee-led support

Employees are actively encouraged to play a role in supporting their local communities.

### Commercially-led support

**Sponsorship:** *The arts* – In 2003/04 Turner's Britain at Birmingham Museum and Art Gallery was supported. There appears to a different exhibition sponsored each year, with recent examples being Art Deco 1910–1923 at the Victoria and Albert Museum, Matisse Picasso at Tate Modern, Vermeer and the Delft School at the National Gallery and Monet in the 20th Century at the Royal Academy of Arts.

# Euro Packaging Limited

118 Amington Road, Yardley, Birmingham, B25 8JZ

**Correspondent:** The Trustees

| Year end | Turnover | Pre-tax profit |
|---|---|---|
| 31/12/2005 | £126,593,000 | £212,000 |

**Nature of company business**
Manufacturer and consolidator of packaging products.

UK employees: 274

### Charitable donations
2005: £3,852,804

## Community involvement

The company makes its charitable donations through the Euro Charity Trust (Charity Commission no.1058460). The objects of Euro Charity Trust are listed as 'the relief of poverty, to assist the vulnerable and to assist in the advancement of education in the UK and the rest of the world'. The trust receives all its income from the group headed by Euro Packaging Holdings Limited. Donations are made to both organisations and individuals worldwide.

In November 2006, MidOcean Partners announced the acquisition of various companies comprising the Euro Packaging Group. It was uncertain how, if at all, this would affect its giving policy.

### Applications
In writing to the trustees at 118 Amington Road, Yardley, Birmingham B25 8JZ.

## Corporate giving

In 2005, the trust had an income of £6.6 million of which £5.55 million (2004: £2.3 million) came from the company. Grants totalled £3.9 million. It is likely grants are made to organisations in the area local to Euro Packaging sites (Birmingham in the UK, and Malaysia) and Malawi, where the settlor is originally from.

# Evans Property Group

Millshaw, Ring Road, Beeston, Leeds LS11 8EG

0113 271 1888; Fax: 0113 271 8487

**Website:** www.evanspropertygroup.com

**Correspondent:** Claire White, Personal Assistant to the Managing Director
E-mail: clwhite@evanspropertygroup.com

**Chief officer:** M W Evans

**Managing Director:** J D Bell

| Year end | Turnover | Pre-tax profit |
|---|---|---|
| 31/03/2005 | £38,528,000 | £20,523,000 |

**Nature of company business**
Property investment and development.

**Subsidiaries include:** Marchington Properties, Millshaw Property Co Ltd, White Rose Property Investments Ltd, Mulgate Investments Ltd, Lichfield Securities Ltd, Furnival Estates Ltd, Astra House Ltd

**Main locations:** Leeds

**UK employees:** 57

### Charitable donations
2005: £123,605
2004: £188,272
2003: £58,013

## Community involvement

Charitable support is given to both local and national charities. The group has supported various charities on a long term basis.

### Exclusions
No support for local appeals not in areas of company presence, appeals from individuals, animal welfare, overseas projects, and political or religious appeals.

### Applications
In writing to the correspondent.

**Information available:** The company produces a social responsibility report.

## Corporate giving

In 2004/05, the group made cash donations totalling £123,605. During the year the group continued its support of a wide variety of local and national charities including the NSPCC, Gurkha Welfare Trust, the Variety Club, Barnardos, Yorkshire Cancer Research, and Yorkshire County Indoor Bowling.

### In-kind support
The company provides support through gifts in kind and joint promotions.

### Employee-led support
An employee volunteering scheme is in operation.

The company matches employee fundraising.

### Commercially-led support
**Sponsorship:** The company undertake arts and good-cause sponsorship. Please contact Claire White for further information.

# ExxonMobil

ExxonMobil House, Leatherhead, Surrey KT22 8UX

01372 222000

**Website:** www.esso.co.uk

**Correspondent:** The Community Affairs Adviser

| Year end | Turnover | Pre-tax profit |
|---|---|---|
| 31/12/2005 | | |

**Nature of company business**
Principal activities: the exploration for, production, transportation and sale of crude oil, natural gas and natural gas

liquids; the refining, distribution and marketing of petroleum products within the UK.

**Subsidiaries include:** Mainline Pipelines Ltd, Dart Oil Co Ltd, Retail Petroleum Services Ltd, Cleveland Petroleum Co Ltd, Comma Oil & Chemicals Ltd, ExxonMobil International Ltd, Redline Oil Services Ltd, Mode Wheel Property Ltd

**Main locations:** Leatherhead, Fawley, Fife, Aberdeen

**UK employees:** 5,200

### Charitable donations

2005: £2,600,000

Total community contributions: £2,600,000

Membership: BitC

## Community involvement

'It is ExxonMobil's policy to be a good corporate citizen wherever we do business. In the UK, we support the local communities around our key business locations. Our focus is on employee volunteering, education, environmental and neighbourhood projects.'

The company directs its support to the neighbourhoods around its key business locations. As a result its community programme is based on the needs and wants of the people in those areas. Emphasis is placed, therefore, on: education (particularly the teaching of science, technology, maths and environmental concerns), and the environment. ExxonMobil employees and their families are also encouraged to participate in community initiatives through the VIP (Volunteer Involvement Programme) scheme.

ExxonMobil proactively plans its programmes and likes to establish long-term working partnerships with the organisations it works with in the voluntary sector. Almost all funds are committed at the beginning of the year, therefore unsolicited requests are rarely supported. There is a preference for voluntary organisations working in the areas of Leatherhead, Fawley, Fife and Aberdeen.

### Exclusions

No response to circular appeals. No grant support for advertising in charity brochures, animal welfare, appeals from individuals, medical research, overseas projects, political appeals, religious appeals, or sport.

### Applications

The company responds to all appeals received, but in view of the policy outlined above unsolicited appeals are very rarely successful.

## Corporate giving

In 2005 ExxonMobil invested nearly £2.6 million in community projects and initiatives. Beneficiaries included the Countryside Education Trust, New Forest Ninth Centenary Trust and the Summer Street Centre.

**Education:** The Exxon/Mobil Growing School Links programme reaches out to about 50 schools around the company's main operating sites and helps promote greater understanding of science and technology in everyday life. Scholarships and grants for equipment, course and staff development are given in support of university teaching through the Exxon/Mobil Engineering Teaching Fellowships.

**Environment:** In Scotland, ExxonMobil are supporting the launch of two new British Trust for Conservation Volunteers 'Green Gym' initiatives. These provide local people to improve their fitness whilst involving themselves in practical conservation activities such as hedge planting and improving footpaths.

In support of energy efficiency, ExxonMobil are working with the charity Energy Action Scotland to tackle fuel poverty. Low income families are helped through the installation of efficient heating systems and other energy efficient measures.

### In-kind support

Locally, ExxonMobil offer resources and in-kind support to groups who are invited to run activities, training days and conferences at some of its sites.

### Employee-led support

Through the Volunteer Involvement Programme (VIP) employees and their families are encouraged to give support to local charities and non-profit organisations. Through the VIP scheme employees can apply for grants to support fundraising, individual volunteering or team volunteering activities. Awards can be given to a range of initiatives from medical welfare to recreation, conservation and education.

**Payroll giving:** The company operates the Payroll Giving in Action scheme.

### Commercially-led support

**Sponsorship:** *The arts:* – long-term support has been given to exhibitions at the National Gallery.

# F&C Asset Management plc

Exchange House, Primrose Street, London EC2A 2NY

020 7628 6000; Fax: 020 7628 8188

**Website:** fandc.com

**Correspondent:** Audrey Morrison, Company Secretary

**Chief officer:** Robert Jenkins

**Chief Executive:** Alain Grisay

| Year end | Turnover | Pre-tax profit |
|---|---|---|
| 31/12/2005 | £306,965,000 | (£106,324,000) |

**Nature of company business**
The group's business is asset management.

**Main locations:** London

**UK employees:** 713

**Total employees:** 713

### Charitable donations

2005: £75,000
2004: £85,000
2003: £58,000

Membership: BitC

## Community involvement

The following extracts are taken from F&C's 'Policies on the Community'.

'In line with good practice, F&C seeks to differentiate between community activities that are largely philanthropic in nature (charitable) and those that have a more direct business benefit (social investment and commercial initiatives in the community).

'In seeking to maximise its positive impact on society through active involvement with the communities in which it operates, F&C is committed to:

- focusing on activities which support and reinforce its social and environmental responsibility
- consulting key stakeholders about their expectations of F&C
- supporting selected charities
- encouraging employee involvement in community related initiatives
- encouraging employee donations and fundraising events by staff, and where appropriate, matching their contributions.

'F&C has a formally constituted Charities Committee, chaired by an executive director, which is responsible for the apportionment of donations within these policy guidelines.'

## Applications

In writing to the correspondent.

## Corporate giving

In 2005, the company made charitable donations of £75,000. We have no details of the beneficiaries.

## Employee-led support

**Payroll giving:** F&C has a policy of matching employee donations made through the tax efficient Give As You Earn (GAYE) scheme.

F&C set a budget of £25,000 to match employee GAYE contributions and has set itself the target of spending the full amount. In 2005, the matched figure was £17,000.

# Family Assurance Friendly Society Limited

16–17 West Street, Brighton, East Sussex BN1 2RL

01273 725272; Fax: 01273 736958

Website: www.family.co.uk

Correspondent: Tony Horton, Community Affairs Manager

Fax: 01273 776856
E-mail: t.horton@family.co.uk

Chief officer: Robert Doleman

Chief Executive: John Reeve

| Year end | Turnover | Pre-tax profit |
|---|---|---|
| 31/12/2005 | £268,899,000 | |

Nature of company business
Provision of financial services (life assurance, savings and protection schemes).

Main locations: Brighton

UK employees: 290

---

**Charitable donations**

2005: £7,000
2003: £6,480

Total community contributions: £115,000

---

## Community involvement

The company's support of charitable organisations is predominantly through non-cash assistance, i.e. arts sponsorship and gifts in kind.

There is a preference for charities local to Brighton & Hove and the East Sussex area, and for those in which a member of staff is involved.

Support is generally considered for organisations concerned with the arts, children/youth, education, older people, environment/heritage, fundraising events, medical research, and sport (where young people are involved).

### Exclusions

The society does not normally support advertising in charity brochures, the arts, enterprise/training, heritage, overseas projects, political/religious appeals, science/technology or social welfare.

### Applications

In writing to the correspondent. Further information and advice are available to applicants from the society.

**Information available:** The society comments on its social responsibilities with the annual report and accounts.

## Corporate giving

In 2005, community contributions totalled £115,000 of which £7,000 was donated in cash to support local charities and the local activities of national charities. Over the last few years the society has raised over £100,000 for local charities.

The company continues to support their core community projects: Blatchington Mill School, Middle Street Primary School, Brighton and Hove City College and in cooperation with Brighton & Hove City Council, the provision of music workshops to 12 nurseries. Support was also given to Tommy's.

### In-kind support

The society provides further charitable support through seconding staff and gifts in kind.

Under the auspices of the Professional Footballers' Association, the society, in partnership with Brighton and Hove Albion Football Club, provide the opportunity for over 600 boys and girls to receive coaching and play football during their school holidays.

### Employee-led support

Employees' volunteering/charitable activities are supported by the company. The society allows time off (four days a year) and matches employee fundraising and giving up to a maximum of £250 per person.

The society encourages its employees to volunteer for a range of activities which have a positive effect in one area of community life. In 2005, over 30 employees took part in staff development projects, whilst over 40 took part in challenges including fundraising days, assisting governors of local schools and community projects with the National Trust, the RSPCA and many others.

## Commercially-led support

**Sponsorship:** *The arts* – The society undertakes good-cause sponsorship.

---

# Fenwick Ltd

Elswick Court, 39 Northumberland Street, Newcastle upon Tyne NE99 1AR

0191 232 5100; Fax: 0191 222 0310

Website: www.fenwick.co.uk

Correspondent: Mrs A Moles, Secretary to the Company Secretary

Chief officer: M A Fenwick

| Year end | Turnover | Pre-tax profit |
|---|---|---|
| 28/01/2005 | £274,702,144 | £25,808,303 |

Nature of company business
Department stores.

Main locations: Bracknell, Canterbury, Brent Cross, Leicester, Kingston, Newcastle, London, York, Windsor, Tunbridge Wells

UK employees: 2,646

### Charitable donations

Total community contributions: £143,000 – 1999

## Community involvement

The company supports projects in areas where it has a presence (i.e. the North East, North Yorkshire, East Midlands and South East). There is a preference for: the arts; children/youth; education; elderly people; medical research; sickness/disability charities and social welfare.

## Exclusions

No support for circular appeals, advertising in charity brochures, political appeals, overseas projects or small purely local appeals not in areas of company presence.

## Applications

In writing to the correspondent. Local stores have an independent budget for appeals.

## Corporate giving

Repeated requests for information regarding the company's community investment policy have gone unanswered. We are, therefore, only able to give a now outdated figure regarding its level of support (see below) which may be doing a disservice to either Fenwick's or local organisations looking for support. We do know, however, that the company is a corporate member of the Northumberland Wildlife Trust, The Migraine Trust, The Bobath Centre and the Commonwealth Youth Exchange Council. What, if anything, this means beyond providing financial support we are unsure.

In 1999 the figure of £143,028 was declared as total community contributions. No indication was given as to how much of this was in cash donations.

Past grant beneficiaries have included: St Oswald's Hospice, Canterbury Festival, Northumberland Wildlife Trust, St Edmund's School – Canterbury, and St Andrew's Hospital – Northampton.

## In-kind support

Main areas of non-cash support are: gifts in kind and training schemes.

A survey conducted by The Guardian in November 2005 into the amount per pound given to good causes from the sale of charity Christmas cards, concluded that the company were 'easily the worst on our high-street test. Most card packs gave just 5–6% to charity. For example, a £3.95 pack of 16 cards gives 21p to Cancer Research, equal to 5.3% of the cost. A £4.99 pack of 16 "luxury" cards gives 28p to Oxfam equal to 5.6%.'

## Commercially-led support

**Sponsorship:** *The arts* – The company undertakes sponsorship. We have no information regarding current or past support.

---

# Fiat Auto (UK) Ltd

Fiat Auto (UK) Ltd, 240 Bath Road, SLOUGH, SL1 4DX

01753 786400; Fax: 01753 577710

Website: www.fiat.co.uk

Correspondent: Andrew Weller

| Year end | Turnover | Pre-tax profit |
|---|---|---|
| 31/12/2005 | £535,637,000 | (£21,092,000) |

Nature of company business
Principal activity: Fiat car distributors.

Main locations: Slough

UK employees: 158

### Charitable donations

2005: £27,941
2004: £72,000

## Community involvement

The company's donations are made through the Fiat Auto (UK) Charity (Charity Commission no. 1059498). There is a preference for organisations working with children/youth, education, and medical research.

## Exclusions

Generally no support for circular appeals, appeals from individuals, purely denominational (religious) appeals, or political appeals.

## Applications

In writing to the correspondent.

## Corporate giving

**Fiat Auto (UK) Charity**

In 2004, (the latest accounts available), this charity had an income of £138,045, most of which was given in grants. The income comes from the following:

*Fiat Dealers & Fiat Auto (UK) Ltd* – each pay £1 for every new Fiat sold through the Fiat Dealer Network

*Fiat Auto (UK) Ltd* pays 35p for every:

- new Fiat vehicle sold other than through the Fiat Dealer Network
- new Alfa Romeo car sold through any sales channel.

Beneficiaries for the year 2004 included Children's Society which received £84,883 with £31,566 given to BEN. Three other organisations each received £6,000: Sick Kids Friends Foundation, Macmillan Cancer Research and York Hill Royal Hospital for Sick Children.

## Employee-led support

The company has an employee volunteering scheme.

**Payroll giving:** The company operates a payroll giving scheme which makes contributions to the trade charity BEN.

## Commercially-led support

**Sponsorship:** Good-cause sponsorship is undertaken.

**Cause-related marketing:** Joint promotions are run on behalf of BEN.

# Fidelity Investment Management Limited

Oakhill House, 130 Tonbridge Road, Hildenborough, Kent TN11 9DZ

**Website:** fidelityukfoundation.org

**Correspondent:** Susan Platts-Martin, Fidelity UK Foundation 01732 777364

| Year end | Turnover | Pre-tax profit |
|---|---|---|
| 30/06/2005 | £566,235,000 | £193,000 |

**Nature of company business**
The management and distribution of unit trusts and the management of pension funds.

**UK employees:** 2,344

> ### Charitable donations
>
> 2005: £13,738,000
> 2004: £10,220,000

## Community involvement

Fidelity Investments community involvement and charitable giving falls into one of three categories:

- a community sponsorship programme (Fidelity Cares), which supports small fundraising and community events local to its offices
- employee activities, e.g. volunteering, charity days and a matched funding scheme
- the Fidelity UK Foundation (Charity Commission no. 327899).

The foundation currently directs the majority of its grants to locations where the company has an office, i.e. Kent, Surrey and London. Support is focused on arts and culture, community development, education, and health.

With a view to those charities receiving grants achieving long-term self-sufficiency, support is usually for projects such as capital improvements, technology upgrades, organisational development and planning initiatives.

### Exclusions

No support for non-registered charities (exempt charities excepted), sponsorships or benefit events, scholarships, corporate memberships, advertising and promotional projects, or exhibitions.

Grants are not generally made for: start-up, sectarian or political organisations; private schools, colleges or universities; individuals.

### Applications

In writing to the correspondent, including a copy of the foundation's summary form, downloadable from www.fidelityukfoundation.org/apply.html

The site includes full details of the application requirements.

Each application is considered on an individual basis against the foundation's criteria. Telephone meetings and/or visits are made by foundation staff to establish a fuller understanding of the applicant and their needs.

Although there are no deadlines for submitting grant proposals, final decisions can take between three and six months, with an initial response being given to all applicants within three months.

## Corporate giving

In 2005, the foundation received a donation of £13.7 million (2004: £10 million) from Fidelity Investment Management Limited, of which £12.2 million (2004: £9 million) was expendable endowment.

**Fidelity UK Foundation**

The foundation's assets in 2005 stood at £61.9 million. It had a total income of £14.4 million and made grants totalling £2.05 million (2004: £902,000). Increasingly, the foundation has made use of challenge and conditional grants. A total of £401,000 (2004: £291,500) was approved in the year where the conditions for payment had not been met by 31 December 2005. The actual total of approved grants given for the year was £1.7 million (2004: £990,500).

Grants were broken down by category as follows:

- community £490,000
- education £304,000
- arts and culture £759,000
- health £507,000.

Beneficiaries included: *Community* – Westminster Children's Society (£75,000) and Vauxhall City Farm (£5,370); *Education* – The Children's Trust (£95,000) and The PACE Centre (£7,500); *Arts and Culture* – The South Bank Centre (£150,000) and Sir John Scane's Museum (£47,000); and, *Health* – Moorfields Eye Hospital Development Fund (£150,000) and Chase Hospice Care for Children (£10,000).

We have no information regarding the beneficiaries of the 'Fidelity Cares' sponsorship programmes for small local fundraising and community events.

## Employee-led support

Employees are encouraged to volunteer and raise funds on behalf of charitable organisations.

A matched funding scheme is in placed which in 2005 saw £61,707 (2004: £123,590) donated to local children's charities, schools and hospitals, amongst others.

# Filtronic plc

The Waterfront, Salts Mill Road, Saltaire, Shipley, West Yorkshire BD18 3TT

01274 530622; Fax: 01274 531561

Website: www.filtronic.com

Correspondent: Helen Sharman, Human Resources Manager

Chief officer: Rhys Williams

Chief Executive: Professor J David Rhodes

| Year end | Turnover | Pre-tax profit |
|---|---|---|
| 31/05/2006 | | (£6,745,000) |

**Nature of company business**
The principal activity is the design and manufacture of microwave products and compound semi conductors for cellular and broadband telecommunications systems and military applications.

**Main locations:** Newton Aycliffe, Shipley, East Kilbride, Wolverhampton

**UK employees:** 991

**Total employees:** 2,953

> **Charitable donations**
>
> 2006: £27,000
> 2005: £26,000
> 2004: £25,000
> 2003: £24,000

## Community involvement

Past information suggested the company has two main charities which it supports and which are also supported by employee fundraising events. Any other support given to charities is likely to be local and small-scale. There are three manufacturing sites in the UK: Shipley, Wolverhampton and Stewarton.

## Exclusions

The company will not support any political purposes.

## Applications

In writing to the correspondent.

## Corporate giving

In 2005, the company made cash donations totalling £26,000. We do not have a breakdown of this amount.

## Employee-led support

The company encourages its staff to actively take part in fundraising events.

# Financial Services Authority

25 The North Colonnade, Canary Wharf, London E14 5HS

020 7066 1000

Website: www.fsa.gov.uk

Correspondent: Karen Gorman, Financial Capability
020 7066 1634; Fax: 020 7066 1635
E-mail: karen.gorman@fsa.gov.uk

Chief officer: Callum McCarthy

Chief Executive: John Tiner

| Year end | Turnover | Pre-tax profit |
|---|---|---|
| 31/03/2006 | £270,600,000 | £8,800,000 |

**Nature of company business**
Regulator for the financial services industry.

**Main locations:** London, Edinburgh

**UK employees:** 2,610

> **Charitable donations**
>
> 2006: £200,000
> 2005: £100,000
>
> Membership: BitC, L B Group, %Club

## Community involvement

The following is a summary of the FSA's Community Affairs Programme:

'As we are funded by a levy on the industry, it was decided that only staff volunteering and providing relevant in-kind resources (such as computer equipment) would be part of our programme.

'Our community affairs policy concentrates its efforts in the area around Canary Wharf – the boroughs adjoining Tower Hamlets. The Community Affairs Department develops and maintains partnerships with reputable, effective local organisations that are working to regenerate the area.

'The current programme focuses on education, regeneration and employability issues. This gives us helpful insights into community education. These insights are useful in our work to improve standards of personal finance education. The programme also helps regenerate the area through social inclusion initiatives.

'We are a founder member of the Heart of the City initiative, which aims to promote and encourage community involvement and charitable giving by City organisations, employees and individuals. We have produced a Good Practice Guide, which together with the Bank of England sponsored survey on corporate community involvement, is available on the Heart of the City website.'

## Exclusions

Local appeals not in areas of the authority's presence. Projects outside of the focus of the Financial Capability Innovation Fund

## Applications

For further information about the Financial Capability Innovation Fund and to download an application pack, please visit: www.fsa.gov.uk/financial_capability/. If you are unable to access the internet, telephone: 020 7066 0084, or write to the correspondent named above.

## Corporate giving

Although the authority state they are unable to help charitable bodies financially because of the way it is funded (through an industry levy), this is not strictly true.

As part of the National Strategy for Financial Capability, the Financial Services Authority (FSA) launched the Financial Capability Innovation Fund in June 2005. Through the provision of grants, the fund aims to encourage innovative projects run by voluntary organisations to help people become more financially capable.

From September 2006, the FSA is inviting applications for the second round of funding under this scheme. Applications are welcomed from across the UK, especially for those activities that: (i) involve giving information or advice which is consistent with the fund's objectives to promote public understanding of the financial system; (ii) provide people with the skills to make the best of such information and advice.

A minimum of £200,000 will be made available for funding projects running up until 31 March 2008. The majority of awards are likely to be for between £10,000 and £40,000, although larger awards will be considered too.

Examples of successful applicants from the first round of funding include: British Refugee Council, East Surrey Domestic Violence Forum, Omagh Independent Advice, Quaker Social Action – East London and Sacar – Bradford.

## In-kind support

The FSA offer the use of conference rooms free to all community partners, local charities and local schools (local being Tower Hamlets and surrounding boroughs). PC donations are made in the local community through the Tools for Schools scheme (www.tfs.org.uk). A free copying facility is also offered to all community partners.

No recent figures were available for the value of the FSA's staff volunteering and other resources provided to the community. Previous figures provided were in the region of £50,000 but we suspect the value of these forms of support may now be greater.

## Employee-led support

The authority state: 'We have an established and varied community affairs programme offering employees a wide range of volunteering opportunities.

'This programme has grown from its early focus on education and business link activities to innovative initiatives aimed at social inclusion issues and regeneration. These include various schemes such as: mentoring, work placements, school governors, board members and executive partnerships. We also offer staff the chance to participate in team challenges. Our schemes help the young, the homeless, the unemployed through to employees assisting in non-executive type roles.'

**Education:** Over 300 of the authorities' employees are actively involved in programmes delivered by Tower Hamlets Education Business Partnership. FSA staff provide help at four primary and secondary schools in reading, numeracy, science, sports and computing.

Following the success in Tower Hamlets, similar employee volunteering schemes now exist at schools in Greenwich, Hackney, Newham and Lewisham.

**Community:** In partnership with East London Business Alliance (ELBA), the authority provide volunteers for ELBA's wide range of community programmes. These include executive partnership mentoring, trustees for local charities, team challenges and support for local community organisations.

**Payroll giving:** The authority runs the Give As You Earn scheme.

# Findel plc

Burley House, Bradford Road, Burley-in-Wharfedale, West Yorkshire LS29 7DZ

01943 864686; Fax: 01943 864986

Website: www.findel.co.uk

Correspondent: Dr I Bolton, Company Secretary

Chief officer: Keith Chapman

Chief Executive: D A Johnson

| Year end | Turnover | Pre-tax profit |
|---|---|---|
| 31/03/2006 | £527,796,000 | £35,067,000 |

Nature of company business
Principal activities: the sale of greeting cards, paper products, gifts and educational supplies through mail order catalogues and the provision of e-commerce and mail order services to third parties.

Subsidiaries include: James Galt & Co Ltd, Home Farm Hampers, Express Gifts Ltd

Main locations: Ashby-de-la-Zouch, Accrington, Burley-in-Wharfedale, Swindon, Cheadle

UK employees: 2,868

Total employees: n/a

### Charitable donations

2006: £78,826
2005: £79,550
2004: £76,000

## Community involvement

The company supports local communities with a preference for local communities in the areas in which they operate (Yorkshire, Lancashire, Cheshire and the East Midlands).

Donations are made to organisations with particular emphasis on those working with children/youth, education, older people, medical research and sickness/disability, including many less well-known charities.

### Exclusions

The company does not normally support appeals from individuals, animal welfare, the arts, enterprise/training, environment/heritage, science/technology, social welfare, sport, political or religious appeals or overseas projects.

### Applications

In writing to the correspondent.

## Corporate giving

In 2003/04 the company made cash donations of £76,000. Beneficiaries included Abbeyfield Ilkley Society, Macmillan Cancer Relief, Meningitis Trust, Sir Leonard Hutton Foundation and The Hospital Heartbeat Appeal.

Cash donations have exceeded £1.25 million over the past ten years.

### In-kind support

The group provides support by frequently donating products from home shopping and educational supplies catalogues to schools, hospices and other establishments in the areas in which they are based.

# First plc

395 King Street, Aberdeen AB24 5RP

01224 650100; Fax: 01224 650140

Website: www.firstgroup.com

Correspondent: Avril Gill, Marketing Manager

Chief officer: Martin Gilbert

Chief Executive: Moir Lockhead

| Year end | Turnover | Pre-tax profit |
|---|---|---|
| 31/03/2005 | £2,693,400,000 | £128,900,000 |

Nature of company business
The provision of passenger transport services primarily through provision of local bus and coach services and passenger railways.

Subsidiaries include: CentreWest London Buses Ltd, Great Eastern Railway Ltd, Northampton Transport Ltd, North Western Trains Co Ltd, Leicester Cuty Bus Ltd, Hull Trains Company Ltd, Great Western Trains Co Ltd

Main locations: Aberdeen

Total employees: 67,500

### Charitable donations

2005: £40,000
2004: £34,000
2003: £69,000

Membership: BitC

## Community involvement

The company states in its latest annual report:
'Throughout 2005/06, the group and its staff have continued to give their support to a number of local and national charitable activities. All our operating companies support local events through donations, sponsorships or the use of resources and facilities made available to them by the group.'

Generally there is a preference for supporting the following: children/youth, education, older people, enterprise/training, fundraising events, medical research, sickness/disability charities, social welfare and sport.

### Applications

In writing to the correspondent.

**Information available:** Corporate Social Responsibility Report 2005.

## Corporate giving

In 2004/05, the company's charitable donations totalled £40,000. The company does not keep a record of the cash value of its in-kind support.

The following is taken from the company's website:

**National Charities**

'For the past three years First has sent an electronic Christmas card to all contacts. The money saved from this is donated to charities nominated by First employees.

'For the past eight years, First has had a bursary with the Outward Bound Trust. As part of this bursary we send a group of young people on a personal development and activity course. The young people who attend the course are selected by First from schools in areas where we operate bus and rail services.

'First also supports Save the Children, Macmillan Cancer Research and Barnardo's.

**Local charities**

Particularly close to First is the Archie Foundation, a charity established in June 2000 to raise money to provide child and family-centred facilities for the new children's hospital in Aberdeen. The appeal reached its goal of £3m in August 2003, and although the appeal ended proactive fundraising around this time, the list of pledges and additional events generated a further £2m. The appeal officially closed on 18th December with a total of just over £5m. First has also supported the Archie Foundation by making donations, some of which have gone to fund the Research Unit in the new children's hospital – a key aspect of its work.

'In addition to the Archie Foundation, there are many local charities and organisations which First support at a local level through sponsorship, donations in money or in kind and through providing transport to and from charitable events.

'Many of these are long established connections with charitable organisations. For example, First made its fourth annual donation to the Prince & Princess of Wales Hospice in Glasgow, which funded the transformation of the reception into a warm and welcoming environment for visitors and patients.'

Each year the company also asks employees to nominate local charities to support.

### In-kind support

First provided the Archie branded bus which was key in promoting the Archie Foundation's message and brand.

### Employee-led support

Employees' volunteering/charitable activities receive financial support from the company, which also matches their fundraising and giving.

Staff have also supported the Archie Foundation by nominating it as the beneficiary charity for the Centenary Fund, raising funds at dinner dances, taking part in the Great Scottish Run, selling Archie badges, taking tables at Archie organised balls and dinners and working free of charge to provide free transport to events.

# First Plus Financial Group plc

Croescadarn Close, The Avenue Business Park, Pentwyn, Cardiff, CF23 8FF

029 2030 3020; Fax: 029 2030 6265

Website: www.firstplus.co.uk

Correspondent: Natalie Manson, Head of Communication

Chief Executive: J Masding

| Year end | Turnover | Pre-tax profit |
|---|---|---|
| 31/12/2005 | | |

Nature of company business
Personal finance company.

Main locations: Cardiff

UK employees: 350

### Charitable donations

2005: £15,000
2004: £15,000

## Community involvement

In order to be seen as a responsible member of the community and to involve staff in a worthwhile project, FIRSTPLUS formed Putting Cardiff Kids FIRST when it was less than one year old. This continues to be the sole focal point of the company's charitable support.

### Exclusions

Appeals outside of the Cardiff postcode area and outside of the remit of Putting Cardiff Kids FIRST.

### Applications

FIRSTPLUS invites applications for grants from organisations that have a Cardiff postcode and benefit children in the area. Application forms can be downloaded from the company's website (see under 'Our Community'). A panel of staff considers each application and makes awards.

## Corporate giving

In 2005, over £15,000 was donated to charitable organisations and groups working on behalf of children in the Cardiff area. Recent beneficiaries have included: The Hollies Special School and Rubicon Dance.

## Employee-led support

Money raised by staff through events such as summer balls, sporting or social occasions in aid of 'Putting Cardiff Kids FIRST' is matched pound for pound by the company. Over £200,000 has been donated since 1998.

# First Trust Bank

First Trust Centre, 92 Ann Street, Belfast BT1 3AY

028 9032 5599

Website: www.ftbni.com

Correspondent: Better Ireland Coordinator

Chief officer: Dermot Gleeson

Chief Executive: Eugene Sheehy

| Year end | Turnover | Pre-tax profit |
|---|---|---|
| 31/12/2005 | £104,600,000 | |

Nature of company business
Banking.

Main locations: Belfast

Total employees: 24,403

### Charitable donations

Total community contributions: £1,052,724
Membership: A & B, BitC, %Club

## Community involvement

First Trust Bank is a subsidiary of the Allied Irish Bank (AIB) and is a member of both Business in the Community and the PerCent Club.

The company has a detailed community giving policy. Grants are available to organisations from Northern or Southern Ireland which have been established for at least 12 months. Under the AIB Better Ireland programme, projects addressing social exclusion within the community under the following specific areas are considered:

- drug and alcohol abuse and its effect on children
- lack of children's education through poverty
- supporting children who are homeless.

Within the above programme operates 'Schoolmate', a flagship project run in partnership with Barnardos, ISPCC and Focus Ireland.

### Exclusions

No grants are made towards: operating costs or salaries; international projects; third party fundraising activities; projects benefiting individuals rather than groups; private clubs; overseas travel; counter and public collections, or raffles; high-risk ventures, such as parachute or bungee jumping; or projects exclusively to a particular segment of society.

### Applications

Full information on eligibility and how to apply is given on the bank's website, from where an application form can be downloaded. Alternatively, these can be picked up and submitted at a local branch of First Trust or Allied Irish Bank.

Applications should include a covering letter marked for the attention of the Better Ireland Coordinator. There is no closing date as applications are accepted and reviewed on an ongoing basis.

Usefully, advice on preparing an application is provided, the bank having seen a number which do not 'do justice' for the group that has prepared it. There are also a number of 'case studies' detailing the types of organisations and work that have been supported in the recent past.

## Corporate giving

Although we were unable to obtain a cash donations figure for 2005, according to the PerCent Club Report for 2006, total community contributions amounted to £1,052,724. A recent beneficiary is the Colin Glen Trust, a commercially viable, cross-community organisation which is committed to the development and management of the Colin Glen River Valley, situated just outside Belfast. The project benefiting the community through conservation, education, training and provision of quality affordable leisure facilities.

Please note that the financial information quoted refers to First Trust Bank's income before taxes for 2005.

### Employee-led support

Employees are urged to become involved with the local community, so enabling many small projects to succeed.

In 2005, support given by the bank's staff to CLIC Sargent was recognised at the Northern Ireland Council for Voluntary Action Link Awards ceremony.

Through the Allied Irish Bank's Partnership Fund, money raised by staff is either matched or a donation made to the organisation in recognition of the personal time given by the employee.

### Commercially-led support

**Sponsorship:** *Sports* – Sport is sponsored at all levels, from grassroots golf, rugby and Gaelic sports, through to major events such as national rugby leagues and the Ryder Club.

# FKI plc

86 Fetter Lane, London EC4A 1EN

020 7832 0000; Fax: 020 7832 0001

Website: www.fki.co.uk

Correspondent: A Ventrella, Company Secretary

Chief officer: Gordon F Page

Chief Executive: Paul Heiden

| Year end | Turnover | Pre-tax profit |
|---|---|---|
| 31/03/2006 | £1,273,400,000 | £70,500,000 |

Nature of company business
FKI plc is a major international engineering group quoted on the London stock exchange. Its specialised business areas are Lifting Products and Services, Logistex, Hardware and Energy Technology products, with operations principally from Europe and North America, it sells to customers in most countries of the world.

Subsidiaries include: Whipp & Bourne, Hawker Siddeley Switchgear Ltd, Bridon International Ltd, Brush Transformers Ltd, Brush Traction, CERTEX UK, Froude Consine, Brush Electrical Machines Ltd, Parsons Chain Company

Main locations: London

Total employees: 12,407

### Charitable donations

2006: £100,000
2005: £100,000
2004: £100,000
2003: £100,000

## Community involvement

The company allocates its charitable budget in March each year. This is distributed in April. The following extract is taken from the group's website:

'FKI businesses are encouraged to support the local communities in which they operate. FKI also supports charitable activities and donations to both local and international good causes through its corporate donations policy, updated in 2004 to include the potential for funds raised by employees towards charitable causes to be matched by donations from the Group.'

### Applications

In writing to the correspondent.

## Corporate giving

In 2005/06, the company gave £100,000 in support of charities. This figure now appears to be the norm each year for donations.

In 2005/06 68% of FKI's businesses, representing 85% of employees, participated in local community activities, charitable events or made charitable donations to good causes, e.g. local charities, schools, hospitals and sports teams.

FKI also makes annual contributions to the Headstart scheme, part of The Engineering Development Trust which in turn is a component of The Royal Academy of Engineering's Best programme. The Headstart scheme promotes careers in science and engineering to 16–17 year olds through university-based, residential courses. The Group is also becoming more directly involved with Headstart through its graduate scheme, providing volunteer graduates to speak at a number of the residential courses. 'FKI embraces opportunities like this to re-invest in the engineering graduates of the future.'

A large percentage of FKI's US based businesses also support United Way, a charity which includes around 1,350 community-based organisations run by local volunteers. This support includes voluntary deductions from employee wages and locally organised fundraising events.

Other charities to which businesses have contributed include the Indian Ocean Earthquake appeal, Chinese Aid Development Council, American Cancer Society, Salvation Army and Cancer Research.

### Employee-led support

Funds raised by employees towards charitable funds are matched by donations from the group.

# Focus (DIY) Limited

Galsworth House, Westmere Drive, Crewe CW1 6XB

01270 501555; Fax: 01270 250507

Website: www.focusdiy.co.uk

Correspondent: Charities Administrator, Human Resources

Chief officer: W E Archer

| Year end | Turnover | Pre-tax profit |
|---|---|---|
| 30/10/2005 | £470,926,000 | £1,164,000 |

Nature of company business
The third largest DIY retailer in the UK.

Main locations: Crewe

UK employees: 5,271

## Charitable donations

2005: £29,960
2004: £35,255

## Community involvement

Focus's website states: 'Our charity initiative is not just about donating money, although this is certainly part of it! We are constantly seeking different and creative ways of doing our bit, be it offering DIY services, donating products or personnel.'

**Charity of the Year:** The Meningitis Trust

## Exclusions

No support for individuals.

## Applications

In writing to the correspondent.

## Corporate giving

In 2005, support was given to UK charities and a number of community projects by way of cash, gifts in kind and donations of human resources. The company estimate that this amounted to £29,960 (2004: £35,255). We have no details of the beneficiaries outside of the Meningitis Trust whom Focus have supported since 2001.

### In-kind support

In addition to cash donations, the company provides support through gifts in kind and donations of human resources. Previous support is outlined below:

**Education:** Initiatives supporting the curriculum to assist development and skill levels from nurseries to secondary schools, as well as special schools.

**Family:** Promoting the development of childcare services; assisting parents to combine work and family responsibilities.

**Healthcare:** Involvement with NHS Hospitals and health-related charities, including support for people with disabilities, learning difficulties, long-term and terminally-ill patients.

**Animals:** Support for local animal rescue services and national charitable organisations.

### Employee-led support

Staff are encouraged to become involved in local fundraising initiatives, as well as on behalf of the 'Charity of the Year'.

### Commercially-led support

**Sponsorship:** Previously we were informed that various projects are sponsored that benefit the wider communities and which often have a link to the environment. Projects that receive sponsorship should offer sustainability and regeneration, e.g. city and urban garden projects and redecoration of community centres.

# Ford Motor Company Ltd

Room 1/619, Eagle Way, Brentwood, Essex CM13 3BW

01277 252551; Fax: 01277 252429

Website: www.ford.co.uk

Correspondent: Phil Taylor, Director, Ford Britain Trust
01277 252551; Fax: 01277 252429

Chief officer: Roelant de Waard

| Year end | Turnover | Pre-tax profit |
|---|---|---|
| 31/12/2005 | £1,781,000,000 | |

### Nature of company business

The Ford Motor Company Ltd is a wholly owned subsidiary of the Ford Motor Company of Dearborn, Michigan, USA. Principal activity: the manufacture of motor cars and commercial vehicles, component manufacture and associated leasing and hire purchase activities.

The company and its subsidiaries operate principally in the UK and the Republic of Ireland. It is part of an integrated vehicle manufacturing group of Ford companies throughout Europe.

**Main locations:** Bridgend, Halewood, Dunton, Essex, Southampton

**UK employees:** 14,200

## Charitable donations

2006: £250,000
2004: £318,030

Membership: BitC, %Club

## Community involvement

The company funds the Ford Britain Trust (Charity Commission no. 269410), a charitable organisation wholly supported by company contributions. Recipient organisations should preferably be registered charities. The majority of donations are one-off grants to local charities in the areas where the company has a presence. There is also a preference for charities in which a member of staff is involved.

Within these guidelines preference is given to projects concerned with education, environment, children and youth, the disabled, and projects that will provide a clear benefit to local communities.

Note: National charities are rarely supported by the trust, and then only when the purpose of their application has specific benefits to communities in close proximity to Ford locations.

The objects of the trust are the 'advancement of education, and other charitable purposes beneficial to the community'. The trust pays particular attention to organisations located near to Ford Plants, or located where a substantial percentage of Ford employees reside. Currently these areas are: Dagenham/East London; Croydon, Essex; Merseyside; South Wales; Southampton; Daventry and Lemington Spa.

The salary of the Director and his assistants is paid for by Ford Motor Company. The trust's income consists of donations from the company, and interest earned on those donations.

## Exclusions

For the Ford Britain Trust: National charities are rarely supported, except for specific local projects in Ford areas.

Applications in respect of sponsorship, individuals, research, overseas projects, travel, religious or political projects are not eligible. Applications for core funding and/or salaries, revenue expenses, and major building projects are rarely considered.

Generally: no support for circulars, fundraising events, brochure advertising, individuals, purely denominational appeals, political appeals, local appeals not in areas of company presence or overseas projects.

### Applications

Applications to the Ford Britain Trust should be addressed to the Director. The trustees meet in March, July and November each year. Applications are considered in order of receipt and it may take several months, therefore, for an application to be considered.

Although each application is carefully considered, the number of applications the trust receives far outstrips its resources and regretfully, therefore, the number of applicants the trust is able to help is limited.

**Information available:** Guidelines for applicants are given on the company's website at www.ford.co.uk/ie/fobtrust

## Corporate giving

### Ford Britain Trust

The trust's income consists of donations from the company, and interest earned on these donations. In 2005/06 the trust received a donation of £250,000 from the company – no further information was available for this year at the time of writing. In 2004/05 the trust made grants totalling £318,000 in the following categories: schools and education (£111,000); community service (£70,000); youth (£64,000); disability (£46,000); and, special needs education (£27,000).

Applications in respect of new Ford vehicles are considered only when two-thirds of the purchase price is available from other sources. In such cases any resultant grant is unlikely to exceed £2,000, although registered charities may be eligible for a reduction on the recommended retail price.

Grants are not available for the purchase of second-hand vehicles.

### In-kind support

Examples include the loan of community buses and the donation of surplus PCs.

**Enterprise:** The company supports local enterprise agencies. Support is given in the form of youth training, resources, equipment or management expertise.

### Employee-led support

The company allows employees two days off per year for voluntary activities, gives financial support to employees' volunteering and gives contributions to employee fundraising.

### Commercially-led support

**Sponsorship:** *Education* – Ford has established a Professorship at the Loughborough University of Technology, concerned with advanced automatic engineering. The position is endowed at a cost of £50,000 a year. It also sponsors engineering professorships at the University of East London, Anglia Polytechnic University, Bradford University and Liverpool John Moores University. These posts are endowed with £20,000 each. The company sponsors undergraduates at universities and business schools, and supports the development of national schools programmes, Technical and

Vocational Educational Initiatives and the Certificate of Pre-Vocational Education.

*Environment* – Ford organises the Henry Ford European Conservation Awards which have a total prize fund of $500,000 and participants from 23 countries across Europe. It is operated in association with the Conservation Foundation, UNESCO and other leading conservation agencies in all participating countries.

# Fortis Insurance Ltd

Fortis House, Tollgate, Eastleigh, Hampshire SO53 3YA

023 8064 4455

**Website:** www.fortisinsurance.co.uk

**Correspondent:** Rosie Lawrence, HR Manager

**Chief Executive:** Barry Smith

| Year end | Turnover | Pre-tax profit |
|---|---|---|
| 31/12/2005 | £590,300,000 | £57,800,000 |

**Nature of company business**
Principally motor, travel and household insurance, and small commercial lines business.

**Main locations:** Eastleigh, Gloucester

**UK employees:** 1,052

### Charitable donations

2005: £36,878
2004: £39,542
2003: £49,205

## Community involvement

The company appears to support general charitable purposes. Although company foundations exist in the Netherlands and Belgium (the company's 'home' territories), support is limited to organisations within those countries.

### Exclusions

No support for local appeals not in areas of company presence, general/circular appeals.

### Applications

In writing to the correspondent.

## Corporate giving

In 2005, the company made charitable donations in the UK totalling nearly £37,000. No details of the beneficiaries were available.

### Employee-led support

Staff are encouraged to participate in volunteering and fundraising activities on behalf of charities and local community organisations.

# Foster Wheeler Ltd

Shinfield Park, Reading RG2 9FW

0118 913 1234; Fax: 0118 913 2333

Website: www.fcw.com

Correspondent: G J Rimer, Company Secretary 0118 913 2053

Chief officer: I M Bill

| Year end | Turnover | Pre-tax profit |
|---|---|---|
| 31/12/2005 | £292,793,000 | £19,591,000 |

Nature of company business
Principal activity: industrial services and equipment.

Main locations: Glasgow, Teeside, Reading

UK employees: 1880

### Charitable donations

2005: £12,000
2003: £46,462

Total community contributions: £14,217

## Community involvement

Although not explicitly stated in replying to our request for information, the company now appears to channel its community support through the Berkshire Community Foundation.

### Exclusions

No grants for advertising in charity brochures, animal welfare, appeals from individuals, elderly people, environment, fundraising events, heritage, overseas projects, religious or political appeals, social welfare, sport or local appeals not in areas of company presence.

### Applications

In writing to the correspondent.

## Corporate giving

The company's support for the community totalled £14,217 in 2005, of which £12,000 was given in cash donations through the Berkshire Community Foundation.

### In-kind support

The company donates gifts in kind. We have no information about the form this may take.

# Freshfields Bruuckhaus Deringer

65 Fleet Street, London EC4Y 1HS

020 7936 4000; Fax: 020 7832 7001

Website: www.freshfields.com

Correspondent: Michelle Milnes, Community Affairs Manager
020 7716 6616
E-mail: michelle.milnes@freshfields.com

| Year end | Turnover | Pre-tax profit |
|---|---|---|
| 27/03/2006 | | |

Nature of company business
International law firm.

Main locations: London

UK employees: 2,156

Total employees: 5,500

### Charitable donations

2006: £178,019
2005: £246,000

Total community contributions: £3,257,470
Management costs: £220,838

Membership: BitC, L B Group, %Club

## Community involvement

An Anglo-German international law firm created by a merger in August 2000, it has an established charities committee called the Freshfields in the Community group (FITC). This comprises of partners and staff and meets to present the views of the firm in the planning of staff charitable activities. The majority of the firm's 18 European offices are already participating in FITC and are involved in a range of activities including pro bono legal advice, fundraising, raising educational achievement in schools, mentoring, team challenges and involvement in regeneration programmes and projects.

### Applications

In writing to the correspondent.

**Information available:** In 2005, the firm produced its first corporate social responsibility report.

## Corporate giving

In 2005/06, the firm provided cash support totalling £178,019 and made total UK community contributions of over £3.25 million. It should be noted that cash support is ONLY given in relation to employees volunteering activities. A donations budget does not exist to provide support outside of this.

Charitable involvement includes:

**Education:** The local Redlands Primary School decided to give up its annual summer trip for pupils as the cost of tickets for parents with more than one child to consider was proving too great. Funding from the firm towards the cost of hiring buses enabled the outings to be reinstated.

**Homelessness:** The firm aims to help homeless people in London in two ways: by providing emergency one-off assistance to people sleeping rough, and by helping homeless people re-integrate into society through ongoing volunteering.

### In-kind support

Freshfields is involved in pro bono work, providing free legal advice and representation to clients who cannot afford to pay for it and where public funding is not available. The firm's lawyers act in a wide range of pro bono matters, including representing members of the public before the courts and employment tribunals, advising at law centres and providing legal advice to charities and local schools.

The firm also works with two London schools, Redlands Primary in Tower Hamlets and Haggerston, a secondary school in Hackney. Around 385 London staff are involved in a variety of activities to help these schools and their pupils including mentoring, development of reading and language skills.

As a member of the Business Action on Homelessness campaign, some 76 placements have been provided at the firms London office through the Ready to Work programme. Permanent full or part-time work has resulted for some of those taking part in the scheme.

## Employee-led support

Freshfields encourages every member of the firm to take part in an activity to help a charity or community-related project by providing time off to volunteer. In 2005 33% of staff in London took part in one or more community affairs programmes surpassing the annual target of 30% staff participation in each office set by the entire firm.

The firm's website states that its philosophy is to promote active employee participation, rather than simply fundraising.

**Payroll giving:** The form operate the Give As You Earn scheme.

## Commercially-led support

**Sponsorship:** Good-cause sponsorship is occasionally undertaken.

# Friends Provident plc

Pixham End, Dorking, Surrey RH4 1QA

0870 608 3678; Fax: 01306 654991

Website: www.friendsprovidentfoundation.org

Correspondent: Diana Monger, Secretary to the Trustees

Chief officer: Sir Adrian Montague

Chief Executive: Keith Satchell

| Year end | Turnover | Pre-tax profit |
|---|---|---|
| 31/12/2005 | £7,691,000,000 | £367,000,000 |

Nature of company business
Long-term insurance.

Subsidiaries include: Regional Properties Ltd, London Capital Holdings Ltd, Box Hill Investments Ltd, Preferred Assurance Co Ltd, Larpent Newton & Co Ltd

Main locations: Dorking, Exeter, Salisbury, Manchester

Total employees: 5,110

| Charitable donations |
|---|
| 2005: £151,476 |
| 2003: £324,337 |
| Membership: BitC, L B Group |

## Community involvement

Most of the company's charitable donations are channelled through the Friends Provident Foundation, although the company's 2005 annual report and accounts state that some charitable donation were 'paid by the group'.

The foundation operates independently of the company and its trustees plan to develop a proactive programmed funding approach, supporting charities operating in areas where the group has traditionally focused its charitable giving.

### Exclusions

No support is given to: individuals who are conducting their own fundraising for charity; personal appeals by, or on behalf of, individuals; applications for specialist school status or school building projects; local fundraising activities and events, except in the vicinities of its four main sites (Dorking, Salisbury, Exeter and Manchester); advertising, including goodwill messages, except selected opportunities with its community partners; overseas trips and travel expenses; political parties; or religious organisations, including local churches.

### Applications

In writing to the correspondent.

## Corporate giving

In 2005, the company's accounts stated that total charitable donations amounted to £1,954,539, including grants paid by the company and donations approved by the Friends Provident Foundation. The foundations accounts show donations from the company for the year to be £151,476, with the remainder paid by the foundation. (It should be reiterated from the previous edition that the foundation received over £20 million in shares from the company in 2004, making this level of charitable donation possible.)

## Employee-led support

Where appropriate, the company may match, pound for pound, employees' fundraising efforts.

**Payroll giving:** The company operates the Give As You Earn scheme and matches contributions by employees.

## Commercially-led support

**Sponsorship:** *The arts* – Friends Provident supports local (to company presence) events such as Salisbury Arts Festival.

# Fujitsu Services Holdings plc

Observatory House, Windsor Road, Slough, Berkshire SL1 2EY

0870 234 5555

Website: www.uk.fujitsu.com

Correspondent: Phillippa Holroyd, Head of Employee Policies and Procedures

Chief officer: Richard Christou

Chief Executive: David Courtley

| Year end | Turnover | Pre-tax profit |
|---|---|---|
| 18/05/2006 | £2,293,700,000 | £154,300,000 |

Nature of company business
Holding company of an IT services group.

Subsidiaries include: FDK Electronics UK Ltd, Glovia International, Teamware Group

Main locations: Slough

### Charitable donations

2006: £178,000
2005: £51,000
2004: £19,000
2003: £35,000

Total community contributions: £178,000

Membership: BitC

## Applications

In writing to the correspondent.

## Corporate giving

In 2006 donations totalled £178,000 (2005: £51,000), including £100,000 donated to the Tsunami Disaster Relief Fund in May 2005. No further details were available.

## Employee-led support

The company states: 'Our commitment to diversity extends into the communities in which we operate. Through our Charitable Support and Community Relations policy we encourage all our employees to become involved in helping to give something back to society.' We could not find a published copy of the policy on the website.

# Galiform plc

66 Chiltern Street, London, W1U 4JT

Website: www.mfigroup.co.uk

Correspondent: Jon Coulson, Head of Marketing & Advertising

Chief officer: Will Samuel

Chief Executive: Matthew Ingle

| Year end | Turnover | Pre-tax profit |
|---|---|---|
| 24/12/2005 | £1,552,200,000 | (£110,800,000) |

Nature of company business
Manufacture and retail sale of furniture.

Subsidiaries include: Howden Joinery Ltd, Sofa Worshop, Hygena Ltd

Main locations: London

Total employees: 12,879

### Charitable donations

2005: £515,000
2004: £400,000
2003: £300,000

## Community involvement

'It is our aim to contribute to the well-being of the communities within which we trade and where our colleagues live. Our policy is to support local charitable causes, colleagues who pursue good works within their local communities and, generally education and the arts.'

## Exclusions

No grants for overseas projects, political or religious appeals, science/technology or local appeals not in areas of company presence.

## Applications

In writing to the correspondent.

## Corporate giving

In 2005 the group made cash donations to community organisations and charities totalling £515,000.

### In-kind support

The company donates furniture to worthy causes. In 2003 the sum of these donations was £29,000.

### Employee-led support

The company financially assist employees' volunteering/ charitable activities.

**Payroll giving:** A scheme is in operation.

### Commercially-led support

**Sponsorship:** In 2003 the group continued its sponsorship of the London Chamber Orchestra's 'A Chance to Play' scheme which enables schoolchildren to start learning to play musical instruments. It is also sponsoring the English National Opera's 'The Ring Cycle', which will be performed during 2004 and 2005.

# Gallaher Group plc

Members Hill, Brooklands Road, Weybridge, Surrey KT13 0QU

01932 859777; Fax: 01932 832532

Website: www.gallaher-group.com

Correspondent: Ms Michelle McKeown, Group Corporate Affairs Manager
E-mail: info@gallaherltd.com

Chief officer: John Gildersleeve

Chief Executive: Nigel Northridge

| Year end | Turnover | Pre-tax profit |
|---|---|---|
| 31/12/2005 | £8,214,000,000 | £516,000,000 |

Nature of company business
The manufacture and marketing of a range of cigarettes, cigars and pipes and handrolling tobacco products for the UK, Republic of Ireland, mainland European, Russian and other markets.

Subsidiaries include: J R Freeman, Benson & Hedges Ltd

Main locations: Weybridge, Perivale, Lisnafillan (N Ireland), Crewe, Cardiff

UK employees: 1,761

Total employees: 11,100

## Charitable donations

2005: £451,747
2004: £624,358
2003: £393,250

Total community contributions: £814,236
Management costs: £10,000

Membership: BitC, L B Group

## Community involvement

The company gives mainly to large national charities, and to smaller organisations working in areas of company presence (Surrey, Wales, Northern Ireland, Crewe, and South London). Preference is given to organisations concerned with the arts, education, elderly people, enterprise/training, environment/ heritage, medical research, overseas projects, science/ technology, sickness/disability, social welfare, and charities where a member of staff is involved.

### Exclusions

No support for circular appeals, telephone appeals, fundraising appeals, purely denominational (religious) appeals, local appeals not in areas of company presence or for advertising in charity brochures.

### Applications

Appeals, relating to Gallaher Ltd only, should be addressed to the correspondent. Applications are considered by the appeals committee which meets occasionally, usually three or four times a year.

Regional contacts for local appeals only:

Jane Guttridge, J R Freeman & Son, PO Box 54, Freeman House, 236 Penarth Road, Cardiff CF1 1RF

Helen Hewitt, Virginia House, Weston Road, Crewe, Cheshire CW1 1GH

Catriona McBride, 201 Galgorm Road, Lisnafillan, Gracehill, Ballymena, Co Antrim, N Ireland BT24 1HS

Subsidiary companies have their own budgets for charities, and their charitable giving is autonomous, although budget levels are agreed with the parent company.

## Corporate giving

In 2005, the company made charitable donations of £814,236, which included £451,747 to projects and organisations in the UK. Donations in the UK are also made through the Charities Aid Foundation.

Typical grants to national organisations range from £1,000 to £10,000 and to local organisations from £500 to £1,000. Local branches are given guidelines and a budget for making their own donations.

### In-kind support

**Enterprise:** The company supports local enterprise agencies and initiatives.

### Employee-led support

**Payroll giving:** The company operates the Give As You Earn scheme, with employees' donations being matched by the company to a maximum of £100 per month, or up to £1,200 in any one year.

### Commercially-led support

**Sponsorship:** *The arts* – Gallaher sponsors the Ulster Orchestra and its recordings. Requests for sponsorship will not be considered.

# GAP (UK) Ltd

Castle Mound Way, Rugby, Warwickshire CV23 0WA

01788 818300

Website: www.gapinc.com

Managing Director: Bernadette Foster

| Year end | Turnover | Pre-tax profit |
|---|---|---|
| 28/01/2006 | | |

**Nature of company business**
Clothing supplier and manufacturer.

**Main locations:** London, Coventry, Rugby

## Charitable donations

2005: £575,100

## Community involvement

Whilst the company provides much information on its grant-making activities in the USA, little is available on its work in the UK except for a list of grant beneficiaries (see below). However, as all funding appears to come via the Gap Foundation, it can be assumed that the main areas of work supported here are as in the USA. These areas are: education, youth, health, welfare, arts and community work. The geographical focus of its UK work is Warwickshire, Leicestershire and the surrounding areas. There also appears to be some support for charities based in London, where the company has an office.

### Applications

Gap Foundation does not accept unsolicited proposals. Its strategy is to seek out and build strong partnerships with a limited number of national, regional and local community organisations.

## Corporate giving

In 2005, cash donations in the UK via the Gap Foundation totalled around £575,100. The ten organisations benefiting from this were: CLIC Sargent (£460,000); London Bombings Relief Charitable Fund (£48,000); Centrepoint (£48,000); Mercia MS Therapy Centre (£4,000); Cystic Fibrosis Trust, Brackley (£2,700); Warwickshire & Northamptonshire Air Ambulance (£2,700); Leicester & Rutland Headway (£2,700); Mary Ann Evans Hospice, Nuneaton (£2,700); Myton Hospice, Warwick(£2,700); and, Rugby Toy Library (£1,600).

Given that the foundation also matches funds raised by employees for qualifying charitable organisations, it is likely that the total cash donations made by Gap in the UK are somewhat higher than that quoted. In addition, there appears to be a fair degree of in-kind support (see below) for which, in relation to the UK, there is no value available.

## In-kind support

The company works with Gifts In Kind International and makes substantial product donations each year. In 2004, the company made product donations of over $25 million worldwide. (Note: We assume this figure to be at wholesale rather than cost price as is the norm in the US)

## Employee-led support

The company states that through its foundation it supports employee volunteerism, both in the US and internationally. So, for example, it matches employees' donations dollar for dollar. It also gives a $150 donation to any organisation an employee provides with over 15 hours of voluntary help.

## Commercially-led support

**Sponsorship:** GapKids UK has sponsored the launch of a book by a fashion photographer (Mario Testino) which was published for the benefit of Sargent Cancer Care for Children. This event marked the start of a two-year fundraising campaign by GapKids on behalf of the charity, which hoped to raise £100,000.

# GE Aircraft Engine Services Ltd

Caerphilly Road, Nantgarw, Merthyr Tydfil CF15 7YJ

01443 841041

Website: www.ge.com

Correspondent: Emma Barnsley, Head Receptionist
01443 841041

| Year end | Turnover | Pre-tax profit |
|---|---|---|
| 31/12/2005 | £530,899,000 | (£13,769,000) |

**Nature of company business**
The provision of aircraft engine and other aviation repair services.

Main locations: Bristol, Cardiff, Newcastle, London, Manchester, Leeds, Royal Tunbridge Wells, Prestwick

> ### Charitable donations
>
> 2005: £8,756
> 2004: £6,850

## Community involvement

The GE Foundation, the philanthropic foundation of GE, invests in improving educational quality and access, and in strengthening community organisations around the world.

Globally GE connects with thousands of local community projects each year. In the UK and Ireland, GE contributes hours through GE Volunteers, or with charitable support for local and national campaigns in the form of donations, collections or individual sponsorship.

## Exclusions

No support for individuals or local appeals not in areas of company presence.

## Applications

In writing to the correspondent.

## Corporate giving

The company has made charitable donations totalling £8,756 during the year 2005 (£6,850: 2004).

The GE Foundation has recently awarded over £307,777 in grants in the UK

## Employee-led support

GE Volunteers is a global organisation of employees and retirees who are committed to strengthening the communities where they live and work by partnership with local charitable organisations to address pressing needs and key opportunities.

Through active engagement in more than 50 countries, GE Volunteers makes significant impact in the areas of education, community development and the environment. Across the UK, the volunteers work in schools to improve reading and numeracy skills and support a wide range of community organisations including hospitals, homeless shelters, and children's homes. They help to build capacity, enhance living and working environments in disadvantaged communities and better equip young people for the world of work through partnerships with Young Enterprise and SETNET, among others.

In June 2006, during GE's global Volunteering Week, 1,050 GE Volunteers in the UK gave over 5,500 hours service in the Community. In September 2006, 42 of their sites took part in the World's Biggest Coffee morning fundraising for Macmillan.

Ongoing project highlights include:

The annual Welsh Three Peaks walking challenge organized by volunteers from Aircraft Engines. Around 75 teams of ten enter, raising £100,000 for Ty Hafan children's hospice.

Knitting programme at GE Money in Greater London, created to meet the needs of local hospitals and hospices.

# GE Healthcare

Pollard's Wood, Nightingale Lane, Chalfont St Giles, Buckinghamshire HP8 4SP

01494 545200

Website: www.gemedicalsystemseurope.com/uk

Correspondent: David Boyd, Public Affairs Manager
01494 545200

Chief officer: Joseph M Hogan (President)

Chief Executive: Joseph M Hogan

| Year end | Turnover | Pre-tax profit |
|---|---|---|
| 31/12/2005 | £1,000,000,000 | |

**Nature of company business**
Principal activities are the development, manufacture and sale of specialised products for research-based biotechnology supply and for the diagnosis and treatment of disease. Major UK locations are Slough, Amersham, Bedford and Hatfield.

Subsidiaries include: Amersham Pharmacia Biotech

Main locations: Amersham, Cardiff, Chalfont St Giles, Little Chalfont, Gloucester

## Community involvement

According to the parent company's website, GE and its philanthropic arm, the GE Foundation, develop and support various programmes in its communities around the world. It is likely that GE Healthcare directs its community support through the GE Foundation. (See below.)

### Exclusions

No support for advertising in charity brochures, animal welfare, appeals from individuals, the arts, fundraising events, overseas projects, political or religious appeals, sport or umbrella organisations raising monies for any such causes.

### Applications

The foundation states that it does not accept unsolicited applications.

## Corporate giving

In 2005, the GE Foundation donated around £40,000,000 to projects worldwide under headings including US Education, Non-US Education, Disaster Relief, Public Policy and Community Matching Gifts. Figures for the UK were not given.

### Employee-led support

Help is given via GE Elfun, a global organisation of GE volunteers, employees and retirees.

Examples of support includes improving literacy in schools, mentoring young people, providing work experience, teaching computer skills, building and repairing playgrounds and community buildings, and working with older people. Employees also update computer equipment no longer required by GE, for donation to charitable organisations or schools.

Nine Elfun branches currently exist in the UK.

# GKN plc

PO Box 55, Ipsley House, Ipsley Church Lane, Redditch, Worcestershire B98 0TL

01527 517715; Fax: 01527 517700

Website: www.gknplc.com

Correspondent: Grey Denham, Company Secretary

Chief officer: Roy Brown

Chief Executive: Kevin Smith

| Year end | Turnover | Pre-tax profit |
|---|---|---|
| 31/12/2005 | £3,648,000,000 | £73,000,000 |

Nature of company business
An international company involved in the automotive and aerospace industries.

Main locations: Birmingham, London, Weston super Mare, West Bromwich, Sutton Coalfield, Walsall, Telford, Portsmouth, Redditch, Yeovil, Edgware, Eastleigh, Chesterfield, Lichfield, Leek, Isle of Wight

UK employees: 5,400

Total employees: 37,047

---

**Charitable donations**
2005: £236,900
2003: £840,000

Membership: %Club

---

## Community involvement

The main emphasis of GKN's community involvement continues to be on education and community activities.

Preference is given to appeals from local and community organisations in areas where the company has a branch (particularly local to the Corporate Centre in Redditch, Worcestershire). Donations are made through the Charities Aid Foundation.

### Exclusions

No response to circular appeals. No support for animal welfare, political appeals, religious appeals, sport or local appeals not in areas of company presence.

### Applications

Appeals, in writing, should be addressed to the Company Secretary at the address shown above. Local appeals should be sent to local branches. Subsidiary companies make small grants independently of head office.

**Advice to applicants:** As a substantial proportion of the company's charitable budget is already committed to community projects/charities, only a small proportion remains for donations to individual appeals. Applicants should therefore ensure that they send only appropriate appeals.

## Corporate giving

In 2005, worldwide community contributions totalled £902,200. Of this, £236,900 was given in cash donations in the UK – £139,000 for educational purposes and £97,900 for community activities. We have no details of the beneficiaries.

In 2003, grants were made to 139 organisations, although it is not known how much these grants were for. Beneficiaries included: Access Partnership, Aldridge Cricket Club, Birmingham Association of Youth Clubs, Birmingham Settlement, Black Country Museum, Canford Magna, Cot Death Society, Disability Access Charter, Edwards Trust, Great Ormond Street Hospital, Help the Aged, Jubilee Sailing Trust, Midland Societies for the Blind, National Missing Person's Helpline, Outward Bound Trust, Prince's Trust, RNIB – New College Worcester, St Giles Hospice, Turning Point, West Mercia Scouts and Yellow Ribbon Foundation.

### Employee-led support

Employees are involved in community projects, notably through fundraising. Staff fundraising at Corporate Centre is matched pound for pound by the company. Preference is given to supporting charities in which a member of staff is involved. Staff are allowed time off during working hours to volunteer.

**Payroll giving:** The company operates the Give As You Earn scheme.

### Commercially-led support

**Sponsorship:** The company undertakes arts sponsorship.

# GlaxoSmithKline plc

GSK House, 980 Great West Road, Brentford,
Middlesex TW6 9GS

020 8047 5000

Website: www.gsk.com

Correspondent: Katie Pinnock, Corporate Donations Committee
020 8047 5000

Chief officer: Sir Christopher Gent

Chief Executive: Dr Jean-Pierre Garnier

| Year end | Turnover | Pre-tax profit |
|---|---|---|
| 31/12/2005 | £21,660,000,000 | £6,732,000,000 |

## Nature of company business

The group's principal activities are the creation and discovery, development, manufacture and marketing of pharmaceutical products, including vaccines, over-the-counter medicines and health-related consumer products.

Subsidiaries include: Wellcome Ltd, Stafford-Miller Ltd, The Wellcome Foundation Ltd

Main locations: Stevenage, Hertfordshire, Stockley Park, Middlesex, Ulverston, Cumbria, Ware, Hertfordshire, Montrose, Tayside, Greenford, Middlesex, Dartford, Kent, Barnard Castle, County Durham, Beckenham, Kent

Total employees: 103,166

## Charitable donations

2005: £4,000,000
2004: £4,000,000
2003: £4,000,000

Total community contributions: £12,000,000
Management costs: £21,000,000

Membership: A & B, BitC, L B Group, %Club

## Community involvement

Within the UK GlaxoSmithKline concentrates its corporate community support programme in the areas of health, medical research, science education, the arts and the environment.

The company state: 'We strive to be consistent in our selection of charities to support. We challenge them to be innovative, dynamic and cost effective with our donations. We expect to see something more – we try to see where we can add value in a creative way.'

All charitable donations made in the UK are agreed by the Corporate Donations Committee, which is a board-level committee. Support is considered in four headings: healthcare; scientific education and medical research; the arts; and the environment. A six page document outlining the selection criteria used for each of these four categories is downloadable from the company's website at: www.gsk.com/community/uk.htm

## Exclusions

No support for appeals from individuals. For example, the company is unable to provide support for individual students or Raleigh International applicants, but does support organisations such as the British Medical Association Charity Trust, which in turn provides financial assistance to medical students. No support for fundraising events, advertising in charity brochures, purely denominational (religious) appeals, political appeals or sport.

## Applications

Appeals for charitable support on a national scale should be addressed in writing to the correspondent.

Organisations seeking support for community projects within the locality or region of GSK sites should contact the relevant site to request the correct company contact.

Applicants are asked to supply a concise summary of their aims, objectives and funding requirements together with a copy of their most up-to-date audited accounts.

## Corporate giving

In 2005, GlaxoSmithKline's worldwide cash donations totalled £63 million, including £2 million of in-kind giving. The company also made product donations of £296 million, but as this was not at nominal value we believe its inclusion would seriously skew our overall findings concerning the level of corporate community support in general. Management cost stood at a hefty £21 million.

In the UK, GlaxoSmithKline made donations to charitable activities of £4 million, helping over 80 organisations in health, medical research, science education, the arts and the environment. In addition to this, group companies contributed a further £8 million of support for community purposes, bringing total UK community contributions for 2005 to £12 million.

Examples of some of the types of organisations and projects the company has supported in the UK in 2005, are given below. Fuller details on each of these are available on the company's website.

### Healthcare:

'*The 2007 GSK Community Health IMPACT Awards:* Working in partnership with the King's Fund, a leading independent health charity, GSK's annual IMPACT Awards programme recognises and promotes the work of small-to-medium-sized voluntary organisations in the UK, which have made a demonstrable impact on the health of their local communities. The awards give UK-registered charities the chance to win ten awards of £20,000, with one overall winner receiving an extra £10,000 on top. In addition, 10 highly commended organisations receive £5,000 each. The awards are open to charities that have been working in local community healthcare for at least three years with an annual budget of less than £1 million.'

Please note that the 2007 deadline for applications for this award has now passed.

*British Red Cross – Gateway options for independence:* 'GSK has supported The British Red Cross since 2001 to devise and trial a model of service, to help young adults with physical disabilities to transition from adolescence to independent living as an adult.

'Over the last three years, the Gateway Centre in Irvine, Scotland has made significant and permanent changes to the quality of young people's lives, developing individually tailored life plans to increase their self-confidence and independence. In addition to the residential aspect of the project, the Centre is also used as a day service by more than 150 young people each year, who benefit from the support of care professionals.

'These young people are gradually building the confidence and the skills to integrate successfully into the community and build new lives for themselves. Over the next three years, GSK is supporting The British Red Cross to expand the existing Gateway service beyond the base in Irvine and ultimately produce a model to introduce at a national level.

### Science education and medical research

'A strong science base, high quality science education and medical research are crucial to the pharmaceutical and life science sector. Working closely with the education, academic and research communities GlaxoSmithKline aims to support the advancement of knowledge and the education of the next generation of scientists.

'Current programmes include an annual scheme that has seen £6 million awarded to over 65 medical research projects in the last 13 years. Under the scheme, a small number of charities are invited to apply each year. In 2005 funding was awarded to the Alzheimer's Research Trust, British Liver Trust, Samantha Dickson Research Trust and Spencer Dayman Meningitis UK. The awards make a significant difference to the on-going work of vital projects and facilitate new medical advances into life threatening diseases.

'As part of its drive to equip and motivate young people to take up careers in science GSK has donated £1 million to a government, industry and higher education partnership. The four-year scheme is known as INSPIRE (INnovative Scheme for Post-docs in Research and Education) programme. Under the programme post-doctoral science researchers (post-docs) from Imperial College who have recently completed their PhDs spend around half their time in selected specialist science schools while at the same time studying towards a postgraduate teaching qualification.

'Through INSPIRE pupils and teachers have access to active, leading-edge scientists. Their involvement not only enriches the science curriculum but will also lead to improved achievement in science and an increase in the number of science teachers.

'GSK is also investing £780,000 over six years in support of Science Across The World, an international educational programme designed to promote discussion and awareness of scientific issues that affect people's lives around the world, and stimulate students' interest and confidence in science. Over 3,400 teachers and 100,000 students from 100 countries take part in the programme.

'Encouraging awareness and interest in science by a wider audience has seen GSK donate £1 million in support of Phase 2 of the Natural History Museum's Darwin Centre. The Darwin Centre is the most significant development that the Natural History Museum has undertaken since it moved to its present site in South Kensington in 1881. It is a new and unique Life Sciences complex providing world-class storage facilities for precious collections. Phase Two will house the Museum's botanical and entomological collections, laboratories and other working space for 125 scientists. Scheduled to open in 2007, it will be accessible to visitors in both a physical and virtual form, and will become an integral part of the visitor experience at the Museum.'

### The arts

*Gardens of Glass – Chihuly at Kew:* 'As part of our UK community investment programme, we sponsored 'Gardens of Glass: Chihuly at Kew', an innovative exhibition at the Royal Botanic Gardens of the work of Dale Chihuly, the internationally celebrated glass artist. The event ran from May 2005 until January 2006.

'Our global headquarters are in Brentford, close to the Royal Botanic Gardens, so we have worked in partnership with Kew, a UNSECO World Heritage Site on a number of projects.'

### The environment

'GSK has made a donation of £148,000 to fund a three-year programme aimed at increasing volunteering opportunities for participation in projects concerned with the conservation of the UK's natural resources. This donation will enable Earthwatch to increase the number of volunteer places for its 'Dyscovery Projects' from 150 to 500 and increase public understanding of science-based conservation.'

## Employee-led support

'The company also supports employees in the UK who are 'Making a Difference' in their own communities. Through the scheme staff are able to apply for funding for charity or community organisations that they are directly involved with.'

**Payroll giving:** The company operates the Give As You Earn scheme.

## Commercially-led support

**Sponsorship:** *The arts* – The company may undertake sponsorship to enable or facilitate the performance, display or establishment of worthy arts projects.

Contact: Proposals should be sent for the attention of the Corporate Events Manager, at the above address.

# Glencore UK Ltd

50 Berkley Street, London W1H 0LU

020 7629 3800; Fax: 020 7499 5555

Website: www.glencore.com

Correspondent: Colin Smith, Secretary to the Glencore Foundation

Chief officer: W Strothotte

| Year end 31/12/2004 | Turnover | Pre-tax profit |
|---|---|---|

Nature of company business
Commodity traders.

Subsidiaries include: Inomex Ltd

Main locations: London

Total employees: 259

### Charitable donations
2004: £54,000

## Community involvement

The company's donations are made through the Glencore Foundation (Charity Commission no. 1041859) which states its principal objectives are 'to contribute to the education and welfare needs of society, principally in Israel'. According to the trust's correspondent, it also gives grants to non-Jewish organisations.

The company itself only supports local charities in areas of company presence (it has regional offices at Strathro, Inverness, Thame and Wymondham). There is a preference for children and youth, medical, education and welfare.

Preference is also given for supporting charities in which a member of staff is involved.

## Exclusions

No support for circular appeals, fundraising events, advertising in charity brochures, appeals from individuals, culture and recreation, research, environment and heritage, local appeals not in areas of company presence or overseas projects.

## Applications

In writing to the correspondent.

## Corporate giving

### The Glencore Foundation

The charity derives its annual income from Glencore UK Ltd, Glencore Energy UK Ltd and Glencore Commodities Ltd which, in 2004, totalled $2.4 million (£1.4 million).

In practice, grants are given throughout the world to Jewish organisations. In 2004, the trust made grants totalling $1.56 million (£920,000). The vast majority of grants were to Jewish charities; however, the following non-Jewish UK charities also received support: KIDS ($45,815/£27,000) and CRISIS ($45,815/£27,000).

## Employee-led support

The company has a matching scheme for fundraising by employees.

**Payroll giving:** The company operates a scheme on behalf of its employees.

# The Go Ahead Group plc

3rd Floor, 41–55 Grey Street, Newcastle-upon-Tyne NE1 6EE

0191 232 3123; Fax: 0191 221 0315

Website: www.go-ahead.com

Correspondent: Keith Ludeman, Managing Director

Chief officer: Sir Patrick Brown

Chief Executive: Keith Ludeman

| Year end | Turnover | Pre-tax profit |
|---|---|---|
| 01/07/2005 | £1,463,600,000 | £83,600,000 |

Nature of company business
The principal activities of the group are the provision of integrated public transport - through its aviation, bus, parking and rail operations. Its subsidiaries provide transport solutions across London, the Home Counties, the North East and the South East of England.

Subsidiaries include: Tourist Coaches Ltd, MetroCity (Newcastle) Ltd, City of Oxford Motor Services Ltd, Aviance UK Ltd, Brighton & Hove Bus and Coach Company Ltd, Meteor parking Ltd, Thameslink Rail Ltd, Reed Aviation Ltd, Hants & Dorset Motor Services Ltd, Abingdon Bus Comoany Ltd, Metrobus Ltd, Chauffeured Parking Services Ltd, London General Transport Services Ltd, Govia Ltd, New Southern Railway Ltd, Victory Railway Holdings Ltd, Wilts & Dorset Bus Company Ltd, London Central Bus Company Ltd, Thames Trains Ltd

Main locations: Brighton & Hove, Newcastle upon Tyne, London, North Eastern England, Oxford, Wiltshire, Dorset

UK employees: 21,630

---

### Charitable donations

2006: £400,000
2005: £552,000
2004: £196,000
2003: £273,000

## Community involvement

The company states on its website: 'Go-Ahead Group plc makes various donations to charities throughout the year and is committed to making a positive impact on the local community, in the form of financial support. Our operating companies also provide "support in kind", including providing resources such as bus services to a charity.

'In line with our devolved structure, each of our operating companies sets its own corporate responsibility objectives and targets. To monitor our progress in all these areas, we publish an annual online group-wide environmental and social report. Each of our companies also publishes individual annual environmental and social reports [to report directly to local stakeholders]'.

## Exclusions

No support for advertising in charity brochures, animal welfare, appeals from individuals, environment/heritage, overseas projects, political appeals or religious appeals.

## Applications

In writing to the correspondent.

## Corporate giving

In 2005/06, the company provided charitable donations, sponsorship and community support in the UK totalling £400,000 (although the group summary report for the same period quotes a figure of £460,944).

No breakdown between cash and in-kind giving is provided, which we believe not to be in the spirit of the requirements of the Companies Act 1985.

## In-kind support

In kind support includes providing bus services to charities, the donation of advertising space, and the development and delivery of programmes on safer bus travel for schoolchildren.

**Education:** Since 2002, the company has offered education resource packs to help teachers introduce 'transport' into the national curriculum.

## Employee-led support

The company assists employees' volunteering/charitable activities through financial support.

## Commercially-led support

**Sponsorship:** The company undertakes arts sponsorship.

# Goldman Sachs International

Peterborough Court, 133 Fleet Street, London EC4A 2BB

020 7774 1000

Website: www.gs.com/uk/index.html

Correspondent: Charitable Services Group

**Nature of company business**
Provision of investment banking, trading, asset management and securities to corporations, financial institutions, governments and wealthy individuals.

Main locations: London

## Community involvement

The company stated that it 'supports charities that are local to its office in London'. This appears to be restricted to education and youth projects concerned with business and entrepreneurship.

### Exclusions

Grants will not be made to individuals; fraternal organisations; political causes, campaigns or candidates; or fundraising events.

### Applications

In 2004, the company stated: 'Please note that there are not, and never will be, donations or grants made to organisations not currently supported by the company and no correspondence will be entered into.'

This appears slightly at odds, however, with advice given in the foundation's grant guidelines. Whilst these clearly state that 'rarely will a grant be made in response to an unsolicited proposal', it does invite 'prospective applicants' to informally submit their ideas.

This should take the form of a short letter (of around two pages) describing the project or organisation for which the grant is sought, its mission, accomplishments, budget size and current funding needs. 'Documentation of results achieved to date is highly desirable', as are copies of published project descriptions or brochures. On receipt, staff will decide whether additional materials are required and contact prospective grantees accordingly.

Note: A 'Program Officer' has been added to the firm's London office to direct the foundation's international work.

## Corporate giving

Although the company were unwilling to provide financial information regarding its community involvement, we believe this to be mainly channelled through the Goldman Sachs Foundation. However, the grant guidelines for this (see website) state that: 'the firm also makes direct contributions via its Charitable Services Department'.

Since its establishment in 1999, the foundation has made over grants totalling around $72 million.

In the UK, a recent beneficiary has been the National Academy for Gifted and Talented Youth at the University of Warwick. This enables bright teenage students from disadvantaged groups to attend day courses, weekend residences, summer schools, on-line learning and mentoring in various subjects so they have a better chance of achieving their potential.

### In-kind support

As 'part of a long tradition of public service and socially responsible business practice', Goldman Sachs has established the Community Capital Group to promote public awareness and understanding of the role played by the modern market system in local communities around the world.

Through the sharing of its financial expertise and supporting innovative community projects it seeks to promote how use of efficient capital markets tools can increase local economic opportunity.

### Employee-led support

Launched in 1997, Community TeamWorks (CTW) is an annual, global volunteering initiative that gives each employee one day off from work each spring to volunteer in a team-based project organised with local charities. It also offers a range of mentoring programmes for employees. The lists for both of these programmes are now full.

---

# Great Portland Estates plc

33 Cavendish Square, London W1G 0PW

020 7647 3000; Fax: 020 7016 5500

Website: www.gpe.co.uk

Correspondent: Sally McLaren, Secretary to the Chairman

Chief officer: Richard Peskin

Chief Executive: Toby Courtauld

| Year end | Turnover | Pre-tax profit |
|---|---|---|
| 31/03/2006 | £41,000,000 | £188,000,000 |

**Nature of company business**
The main activity of the company is property development and investment.

**Subsidiaries include:** Collin Estates Ltd, 90 Fetter Lane Ltd, Jekyll Properties Ltd, Petra Investments Ltd, B & H S Management Ltd, Knighton Estates Ltd, Courtana Investments Ltd, Pontsarn Investments Ltd, J L P Investment Co Ltd, Ilex Ltd, 34/43 Russell Street Ltd

Main locations: London

UK employees: 65

### Charitable donations
2006: £98,650
2004: £78,700

Total community contributions: £101,678

## Community involvement

The company supports both national and local charities, especially those involved in medical research, the homeless and the community.

### Exclusions

No specific exclusions were indicated to us, although the preferences stated above should be noted.

### Applications

In writing to the correspondent.

## Corporate giving

In 2005/06, the company made total community contributions in the UK of nearly £102,000 of which £98,650 was in cash donations. We have no details of the beneficiaries. We were previously advised that donations are paid in CAF vouchers.

## In-kind support

The company provides additional support through gifts in kind, for example, the donation of old office equipment following the company's move to Cavendish Square.

## Employee-led support

The company has an employee volunteering scheme which involves staff mentoring pupils at St Vincent's School, Marylebone. Employees are also given company time off in which to carry out charitable activities.

## Commercially-led support

**Sponsorship:** The company undertake good-causer sponsorship.

# Greencore Group plc

UK Processes Office, Mansfield Road, Kiveton, Sheffield S26 5PF

01909 545900; Fax: 01909 545950

Website: www.greencore.com

Correspondent: (See 'Applications')

Chief officer: E F Sullivan

Chief Executive: D J Dilger

| Year end | Turnover | Pre-tax profit |
|---|---|---|
| 30/09/2005 | | |

**Nature of company business**
Manufacturer and supplier of convenience foods and ingredients to consumer, industrial and food service markets.

**Subsidiaries include:** The Roberts Group Ltd, W W Bellamy (Bakers) Ltd, Pauls Malt Limited, Hazlewood Foods Limited, Paramount Foods (UK) Ltd, Rathbones Bakeries Ltd, William McKinney (1975) Ltd, R & B (Bristol) Ltd

**Main locations:** Deeside, Hunslet, Kiveton, Lisburn, Runcorn, Worksop, Newmarket, Lydney

**UK employees:** 10,098

## Community involvement

Eire-based Greencore Group primarily operates in the UK with the companies it acquired from Hazlewood Foods in 2001. Greencore stated: 'As a policy, our corporate support is directed solely towards the charities we are asked to support by our major customers and our trade charity, Caravan.

'Our operating businesses are encouraged to support worthy projects in their immediate areas (circa 10 mile radius) and provide/raise money for local hospitals, scout groups, sporting clubs and so on, which are known to us because of their local connections.'

Support for staff fundraising initiatives is also considered.

## Exclusions

No support for worthy local causes/projects unless within the immediate area (circa 10 mile radius) of an operating site.

## Applications

Small local organisations seeking support will normally be aware of Greencore manufacturing facilities close to them. However, if you are unsure about this first check on the company's web site (www.greencore.com) to see if there is one close by. If so, there exists the means to log a request for support through the 'Contact Us' facility under 'Other Enquiries'.

Greencore asked it be made clear that: 'Requests that ignore our clearly stated guidelines will not receive a response, but those with genuine enquiries will be assisted to discuss their projects with the appropriate contact.'

## Corporate giving

We were advised that: 'Because of the decentralised nature of our [Greencore's] operations we do not account centrally for charitable donations or split out UK from elsewhere. UK charitable support is, however, likely to equal or exceed the £60,000 previously given by Hazlewood.'

No specific examples of support were available.

## In-kind support

The company provides access to its expertise to a limited number of small non-competing businesses and in support of undergraduate business-focused training in a number of universities.

## Employee-led support

Staff who set out individually to support a particular cause will be considered for 'sponsorship' by the company.

# Greggs plc

Fernwood House, Clayton Road, Jesmond, Newcastle upon Tyne NE2 1TL

0191 281 7721

Website: www.greggs.co.uk

Correspondent: Gillian Hansom, Trust Administrator

Chief officer: Derek Netherton

Managing Director: Sir Mike Darrington

| Year end | Turnover | Pre-tax profit |
|---|---|---|
| 31/12/2005 | £533,400,000 | £50,200,000 |

**Nature of company business**
The principal activity of the group is the retailing of sandwiches, savouries and other bakery related products with a particular focus on takeaway food and catering. The majority of products sold are manufactured in house.

**Main locations:** Newcastle upon Tyne

**UK employees:** 18,833

### Charitable donations

2005: £609,000
2004: £615,000
2003: £420,000

Membership: BitC, %Club

## Community involvement

The company gives 1% of pre-tax profits in charitable donations, mainly through the Greggs Trust (Charity Commission no. 296590). The main objective of the trust is the alleviation of the effects of poverty and social deprivation in the areas where the company trades. Projects in the fields of the arts, the environment, conservation, education and health will be considered, so long as they have a social welfare focus and/or are located in areas of deprivation.

The trustees have also decided to continue to allocate a proportion of the funds available for distribution, through a number of approved agencies, in grants to individuals experiencing hardship.

## Exclusions

Grants will not be made for the following purposes other than as specified:

▶ academic research

▶ animal welfare

▶ capital appeals or running costs of fee-charging residential homes and nurseries

▶ commercial charity reference books/directories

▶ conferences/seminars/exhibitions/publications

▶ festivals, performances and other arts and entertainment activity, unless of specifically educational value and involving groups from areas of greater social need or disadvantaged by low income or by disability

▶ foreign travel/expeditions/holidays and outings other than for disadvantaged groups

▶ fundraising organisations, general fundraising appeals, fundraising events and sponsorship

▶ hospitals, health service trusts, medically related appeals and medical equipment

▶ loans, repayment of loans or retrospective funding

▶ national appeals and general appeals of established regional organisations

▶ medical research

▶ minibuses and vehicles, other than community transport schemes which serve a combination of groups in a wide geographical area

▶ overseas projects or organisations working abroad

▶ purchase, conversion and restoration of buildings other than community-based projects serving areas of greater social need and/or particularly disadvantaged or at-risk groups

▶ religious advancement or religious buildings, community aspects of church-based or other religious projects may be considered if projects show outreach into the community and provide services of benefit to the community as a whole or to particularly disadvantaged or at-risk groups

▶ restoration and conservation of historic buildings and the purchase or conservation of furnishings, paintings, other artefacts or historic equipment

▶ school appeals, other than for projects at LEA schools in areas of greater social need, such as after school clubs and activities promoting parental and community involvement

▶ sports buildings, equipment and sporting activities other than where particularly disadvantaged groups are involved and where the activity is ongoing rather than one-off

▶ statutory agencies and activities that are primarily the responsibility of statutory agencies

▶ uniformed organisations such as scouts, guides, sea cadets and organisations associated with the armed services other than areas of greater social need where projects involve outreach into the community and wider community benefit.

## Applications

The trustees meet twice a year, usually in May and November. Applications for major grants may be submitted at any time, but if they are to be assessed in time for these meetings they should be sent no later than mid-March or mid-September. There are no application forms; applicants for small grants are asked to note the guidance relating to major grants and are advised to use their discretion in providing sufficient information to support their case.

Applicants for major grants are asked to set out their application briefly in a letter, giving full address, phone/fax number and a contact name, the purpose of the application, the amount requested, details of any other applications for the same purpose and responses if available. More information about the project or work proposed may be provided in supporting documents.

Applications must include the following:

▶ latest audited accounts or financial report required by the Charity Commission and, if a period of three months or more has passed since the year end, a certified statement of income and expenditure for the period

▶ latest annual report or, if not available, a summary of current work

▶ the applicant organisation's equal opportunities policy and practice

▶ details of constitutional status (actual documents need not be included); charity registration number if applicable; organisational structure; composition of management committee; management arrangements for the project for which the application has been made; details of staff and volunteers

▶ budget for the organisation as a whole for the current year and costings for the project for which the application is made

▶ if support for a salaried post or posts is requested, the job-description for the post(s)

▶ details of the organisation's policy and provision for training of management body, staff and volunteers

▶ details of how it is intended to evaluate the work for which a grant is requested.

The trust aims to respond to applications for small grants within about two months and to acknowledge applications for major grants in the same period. Applicants will be informed if their application has not been selected for further consideration. If an application has been selected for further assessment the administrator may be in touch to request further information or to arrange a visit.

## Corporate giving

In 2005, the company made charitable donations of £609,000, including £350,000 to the Greggs Trust.

### Greggs Trust

For 2005, the trust had an income of £914,978. This was derived from the company's donation, and also from employees under Give As You Earn, major shareholders and income from investments.

Previous beneficiaries of the trust include Escape Family support, West End Refuge, Workers Educational Trust – Hartlepool and Trinity Youth Association. Hardship payments are also made to individuals.

For more information on the Greggs Trust, see the Guide to the Major Trusts Volume 1, published by the Directory of Social Change.

### In-kind support

The company sponsors school Breakfast Clubs in deprived areas across the UK.

### Employee-led support

The company encourages its staff to work with local communities, and makes time available for them to do so.

**Payroll giving:** The company operates the Give As You Earn scheme, money from which is contributed to the Greggs Trust.

### Commercially-led support

Greggs North East division sponsors the Greggs Cancer Run, an annual event which has raised over £2 million since 1983 – the event is organised by a group of dedicated staff. Greggs North West Division has also sponsored a similar event in Manchester.

# R Griggs Group Ltd

Cobbs Lane, Wallaston, Northamptonshire NN29 7SW

01933 663281; Fax: 01933 662848

Correspondent: Sian Patchett, Company Services Administrator

| Year end | Turnover | Pre-tax profit |
|---|---|---|
| 31/03/2005 | £75,655,032 | £1,960,057 |

### Nature of company business
The group is principally engaged in manufacture, selling, distribution and marketing of footwear, distribution of clothing and related accessories, property investment and the sports and leisure industry.

**Subsidiaries include:** Wear:Aer International Ltd, Dr Martens Dpt Store Ltd, Ferrersmere Estates Ltd, Airwair Ltd

Main locations: Wallaston

Total employees: 284

### Exclusions

No support for advertising in charity brochures, animal welfare, appeals from individuals, elderly people, environment/heritage, medical research, overseas projects, political appeals, religious appeals, science/technology or sickness/disability charities.

### Applications

The company stated that requests can only come from employees to match their contributions and efforts. Unsolicited applications will be ignored.

## Corporate giving

We were unable to retrieve up-to-date information regarding the charitable donations/community involvement of this company. The most up-to-date information was that it gave nearly £46,000 in 2000. There appears to be no reference to charitable giving in the Annual Report of 2005.

# Group 4 Securicor plc

The Manor, Manor Royal, Crawley, West Sussex, RH10 9UN

01293 554 400

Website: www.securicor.com

Correspondent: Nigel Lockwood, Group Communications Executive

Chief officer: Jorgen Philip-Sorensen

Chief Executive: Nick Buckles

| Year end | Turnover | Pre-tax profit |
|---|---|---|
| 31/12/2005 | £4,129,900,000 | £254,000,000 |

### Nature of company business
Group 4 Securicor plc provides security services, cash services and justice services internationally.

Main locations: Sutton

Total employees: 395,771

### Charitable donations

2005: £300,000
2004: £328,000
2003: £121,000

## Community involvement

The following is an extract from the company's 2005 Annual Report: 'Prior to the merger, Securicor had a charitable trust which made numerous modest financial donations to charities supporting a wide range of causes. In 2006, Group 4 Securicor will focus on the support of child-related community projects around the world and the charitable trust has therefore been discontinued.'

Looking at the records at the Charity Commission for the Securicor Charitable Trust (no. 274637) we can confirm that the trust appears to be in the process of being wound down.

### Exclusions

The group will not give political contributions. It is not known if there are any other exclusions.

### Applications

Applications to the Group Communications Executive.

## Corporate giving

In 2005, the company declared charitable contributions by the group amounting to £300,000. It is not clear from the annual report whether the donations were made to UK charities/organisations or to projects internationally. We have no details of the beneficiaries.

### In-kind support

This can include the occasional provision of cash pick up services at events.

### Employee-led support

The company encourages its employees to get involved with their local community, although this appears to be in their own, rather than company, time. However, the company has introduced a matching programme for local projects in which business units are involved around the world. The programme allows any business unit providing funds (either corporately or raised by employees) for local community projects to seek matching funding from Group 4 Securicor plc. The scheme is subject to some simple criteria which ensure that the programme is focused on local community projects.

**Payroll giving:** The company operates the Give As You Earn scheme.

# Guardian Media Group plc

164 Deansgate, Manchester M60 2RR

0161 832 7200; Fax: 0161 832 0155

Website: www.gmgplc.co.uk

Correspondent: P E Boardman, Company Secretary

Chief officer: Paul Myners

Chief Executive: Sir Robert Phillis

| Year end | Turnover | Pre-tax profit |
|---|---|---|
| 02/04/2006 | £700,300,000 | £66,400,000 |

**Nature of company business**
Newspaper and magazine publishing. The group has national newspapers as well as regional evening and weekly papers in the North West, Berkshire and Surrey.

**Subsidiaries include:** Surrey and Berkshire Newspapers Ltd, Guardian Newspapers Ltd, Star Newspaper (Camberley) Ltd, GMG Radio Holdings Ltd, Workthing Ltd, Greater Manchester Newspapers Ltd

**Main locations:** Manchester, London

**UK employees:** 7,107

---

### Charitable donations

2006: £351,261
2005: £630,950
2004: £279,500
2003: £185,400

Membership: BitC

---

## Community involvement

The Guardian Media Group plc is wholly-owned by The Scott Trust. It has a board of ten members who are chosen from areas of the media industry that reflect GMG's business interests. Its main aim is to ensure the commercial success of the group and to uphold the trust's values.

While each division of Guardian Media Group chooses to support its own charitable ventures, a more strategic focus has been placed at the centre of the group with the creation of the Scott Trust Foundation (Charity Commission no. 1027893), formerly the Guardian Foundation. Its remit reflects one of the trust's key objectives of 'promoting the causes of freedom of the press and liberal journalism both in Britain and elsewhere'. (The foundation's main purpose, however, is the training of journalists primarily in Eastern Europe and Africa.)

In 2005, the Scott Trust Charitable Fund was set up to support projects associated with independent journalism, journalist ethics, media literacy and journalist training in the UK and abroad. The fund includes representatives from all GMG divisions.

## Exclusions

No support for animal welfare, environment/heritage, political or religious appeals.

## Applications

In writing to the correspondent. Appeals sent directly to individual papers are dealt with separately.

## Corporate giving

In 2005/06, the company made charitable donations totalling £351,261. No specific details of UK grant beneficiaries were available.

The Scott Trust is currently spending £56,000 supporting the development of talented journalists in this country, providing bursaries for six aspiring writers to study journalism at the City University, London, and Sheffield University.

The Scott Trust Appeals Meeting takes place quarterly to review requests for charitable donations. Charities receive a maximum donation of around £250 each.

## In-kind support

The company gives additional support to charities through gifts in kind and staff secondments.

## Employee-led support

Employees fundraising efforts are matched pound for pound up a maximum of £100 per employee.

**Payroll giving:** The Give As You Earn scheme is in operation. Over one-third of employees have signed up for the scheme, resulting in charities receiving over £100,000 in total in 2005/06.

## Commercially-led support

**Sponsorship:** *The arts* – The company also sponsors the arts, especially theatre, music, modern arts, film and dance. For example, the London Film Festival, National Film Festival and Serpentine Gallery have been supported recently.

---

# Halfords Group plc

Icknield Street Drive, Washford West, Redditch, Worcestershire, B98 0DE

01527 517601; Fax: 01527 513201

Website: www.halfordscompany.com

Correspondent: Nicola O'Neill, Public Relations Co-ordinator 01527 513315; Fax: 01527 504780

Chief officer: Richard Pym

Chief Executive: Ian Mcleod

| Year end | Turnover | Pre-tax profit |
|---|---|---|
| 31/03/2006 | £681,700,000 | £77,000,000 |

**Nature of company business**
The principal activity of the group is the retailing of auto, leisure and cycling products.

**Main locations:** Manchester, Brighton, London, Glasgow, Berwick on Tweed, Workington

**UK employees:** 10,069

## Community involvement

Halfords Group's cash donations to charity have taken just under a 45% drop during the last financial year. The company does however support the work of charities by encouraging staff to fundraise, providing sponsorship and providing in-kind support through providing free advice on and free fitting for child seats in cars.

Halfords is a member of the Employers' Forum on Disability, which is a not for profit employers' organisation having over 375 member organisations, who employ approximately 20% of the national workforce. The Forum acts as a 'self-help' club, bringing its members together to share best practice on disability. It provides events at both a regional and national level where members meet, share best practice and keep up to date with disability issues. Additionally, members benefit from a dedicated information line to help them understand and manage both the legislation and the best practice approach to disability.

**Charity of the Year:** The Meningitis Trust (2006).

### Exclusions

The group will not fund appeals from individuals, applicants on behalf of individuals, private fund raising groups or organisations not registered with the Charity Commission.

### Applications

To the contact in writing.

## Corporate giving

In 2006, the company contributed £20,000 (2005: £36,000) to charities in the UK, principally donating to BEN, the Motor and Allied Trades Benevolent Fund. The fund gives support and assistance to the employees and families of those working in the motor industry, including Halfords employees.

### In-kind support

Small donations in the form of raffle prizes may be given to local organisations holding fundraising events. In this instance "local" is defined as within a 20-mile radius of head office in Redditch. The organisation must pick up any item.
Halfords stores may also offer support to local charities/ fundraising initiatives outside the beneficial area defined, as long as the remaining criteria are met. In these cases, Halfords will only provide a raffle prize or product donation; no cash will be given.

The company has taken various actions in order to meet their responsibilities regarding disability issues including training store colleagues in disability awareness, responding to some of the physical obstacles in stores and other access issues, and auditing their website for ease of navigation.

It is estimated that around eight out of ten child seats in the UK are wrongly fitted in cars, sometimes leading to injury or death of young babies and toddlers. As a retailer of child seats, Halfords has invested in training around 1,600 store staff in the demonstration and free fitting of child seats. They have also run roadshows at Halfords stores across the UK,

working with road safety officers to give free advice and fitting services to parents and guardians.

The company also holds its own national child seat safety week at all superstores, to raise awareness of the issue.

### Employee-led support

Support for the 2006 'Charity of the Year', will involve all of Halfords employees in the UK and the Republic of Ireland in fundraising initiatives for the Trust. The Halfords partnership will focus on raising awareness amongst staff and customers and raising money to support the charity's campaigns

### Commercially-led support

**Sponsorship:** The Company is the technical sponsor of the British Heart Foundation London to Brighton cycle ride, providing 150 cycle mechanics from their stores to keep the fundraisers on the road and will provide help and service to the estimated 57,000 riders who take part. The British Heart Foundation is the UK's leading charity on heart disease and its prevention and this is the third year of sponsorship for Halfords.

# S G Hambros Bank & Trust Ltd

SG House, 41 Tower Hill, London EC3N 4SG

020 7597 3000; Fax: 020 7597 3056

**Website:** www.sghambros.com

**Correspondent:** Corporate Communications, Head Office

**Chief officer:** The Honourable Nicholas Assheton

**Chief Executive:** W J Newbury

| Year end | Turnover | Pre-tax profit |
|---|---|---|
| 31/12/2005 | £26,818,000 | £11,689,000 |

**Nature of company business**
Banking, retail financial services and direct investments, throughout the UK and in many parts of the world.

**Subsidiaries include:** Network Security Management, Cunningham, Hart & Co (Holdings), Berkeley (Insurance)

**Main locations:** London

**UK employees:** 118

**Total employees:** 118

## Community involvement

We were unable to find any current information regarding the company's charitable giving.

### Exclusions

No response to circular appeals. No support for appeals from individuals, purely denominational (religious) appeals or local appeals not in areas of company presence.

### Applications

Appeals to head office should be addressed to the correspondent. Grant decisions are made by the chairman or the whole board once a month. Local appeals should be sent to the appropriate regional office.

## Corporate giving

The Bank made charitable donations of £1,095 during the year (2004: £7,600). The last community contributions figure provided was for 1997 when just over £170,000 was donated. It is not clear why the donations made to charity have fallen to these levels.

## Employee-led support

**Payroll giving:** The company operates the Give As You Earn scheme.

# Hammerson plc

10 Grosvenor Street, London W1K 4BJ

020 7887 1000; Fax: 020 7887 1010

Website: www.hammerson.com

Correspondent: Stuart Haydon, Company Secretary
E-mail: stuart.haydon@hammerson.co.uk

Chief officer: J F Jelson

Chief Executive: J G Richards

| Year end | Turnover | Pre-tax profit |
|---|---|---|
| 31/12/2005 | £249,200,000 | £698,600,000 |

Nature of company business
Property investment and development. 70% of the company's property assets are in the UK, with the remainder in France and Germany. Within the UK, the office property portfolio is mainly in London, with retail interests in Birmingham, Brent Cross, Bristol, Leicester, Peterborough, Reading, Sheffield, Southampton and Stockport.

Main locations: London

UK employees: 226

### Charitable donations

2005: £112,670
2004: £103,385
2003: £109,000

## Community involvement

A brief comment in the company's annual report states that: 'donations are made to a variety of social, medical and arts charities and to charities in localities where the group owns property. In addition to these charitable donations, the company provides financial assistance to other projects of benefit to the community'.

## Exclusions

No support for political appeals.

## Applications

In writing to the correspondent. Each application is considered on its merits, but about 95% of applications will be unsuccessful.

**Information Available:** The company produces a corporate social responsibility report which can be accessed via their website www.hammerson.com

## Corporate giving

In 2005, the company made charitable donations totalling £112,670. A concise breakdown of this amount was unavailable. However, we do know that donations were made to a variety of medical, social and arts charities and to community projects in localities where Hammerson owns property.

## Employee-led support

The company encourages employees' volunteering/charitable activities.

# Hanson plc

1 Grosvenor Place, London SW1X 7JH

020 7245 1245; Fax: 020 7235 3455

Website: www.hansonplc.com

Correspondent: Paul Tunnacliffe, Company Secretary

Chief officer: Mike Welton

Chief Executive: Alan Murray

| Year end | Turnover | Pre-tax profit |
|---|---|---|
| 31/12/2005 | £3,715,700,000 | £429,300,000 |

Nature of company business
Hanson is a leading international building materials company. It operates in North America, the UK, Continental Europe, Australia and Asia Pacific.

Main locations: Bristol, Stewartby

Total employees: 24,300

### Charitable donations

2005: £93,000
2004: £183,000
2003: £152,000

## Community involvement

Hanson has a largely decentralised programme of charitable donations focused on the communities in and around its operational sites. Within this, it targets:

- community groups in the immediate vicinity, with the aim of building sustainable relationships with its neighbours
- support for employee volunteering and giving
- environmental organisations with an interest in habitat creation and management
- charities with links to the company's industry.

Hanson is often asked to support local projects by donating materials. There exists a general policy of supporting community projects in this way, particularly those close to its operations.

Local management teams have overall responsibility for engagement with the communities in which they are located. Where the local community wants to meet formally with staff on a regular basis, community liaison groups are held. These provide an opportunity to meet and address concerns with input from a broad range of interested parties.

## Exclusions

No support is given to circular appeals, fundraising events, appeals from individuals or for advertising in charity brochures.

## Applications

In writing to the correspondent.

## Corporate giving

In 2005, the group made charitable donations worldwide of £309,000, including £93,000 in the UK. The group also donated $100,000 to the Red Cross to help support those in New Orleans affected by Hurricane Katrina; a number of their employees had been affected by the catastrophe. In addition, employees of the company and suppliers established a relief fund for Hanson employees affected by the hurricane, with the company matching donations made.

At a corporate level Hanson is a patron of CRASH the construction and property industry charity for the homeless, contributing to their core funding. It recently made three-year commitments to the Royal Botanic Gardens at Kew and the Rotunda Museum of Geology in Scarborough.

**Environment:** Previously funds were available from the Hanson Environment Fund through landfill tax credits. However, as of 16 October 2006 the scheme has closed to new applicants.

## In-kind support

Goods and services are provided to local communities.

## Employee-led support

In the UK Hanson has a programme which matches the first £500 of an employee's fundraising with a contribution from the company.

---

# Hasbro UK Limited

2 Roundwood Avenue, Stockley Park, Uxbridge, Middlesex UB11 1AZ

020 8744 6458

Website: www.hasbro.co.uk

Correspondent: Head of Community Affairs, Community Affairs Department

| Year end | Turnover | Pre-tax profit |
|----------|----------|----------------|
| 25/12/2005 | £139,877,000 | £10,717,000 |

Nature of company business
Toy and game manufacturer.

Main locations: Uxbridge, Newport

Total employees: 289

### Charitable donations

2005: £37,764
2004: £39,735

## Community involvement

For a number of years Hasbro has helped local communities throughout the UK by donating toys and games. At its head office at Stockley Park it has a 'Hasbro in the Community' team.

Hasbro is keen to work with and help communities local to its operating sites (its Stockley Park offices, or its Newport warehouse). In particular it wishes to support children and families. Support given includes that to schools and playgroups.

All requests for donations must be made through a registered charity or community organisation.

## Exclusions

No grants to individual applicants. No grants to organisations concerned with animals.

The company does not undertake any form of advertising or souvenir brochures.

## Applications

In writing to the correspondent.

## Corporate giving

In 2005, the company made donations to charity amounting to £37,764 (2004: £39,735). We have no information regarding the specific beneficiary organisations.

The company's website states that cash donations and sponsorship are given to its nominated charities of the year.

## In-kind support

The company operates an employee volunteering scheme under which staff are allowed work time off to become involved with the local community. Help has been given to primary schoolchildren with their reading, and community organisations which received computer, marketing or public relations advice.

Hasbro regularly give donations of toys to schools, hospitals, day care centres, charity fundraising events and so on.

## Employee-led support

Since September 2002 Hasbro has raised over £64,000 for Debra.

**Payroll giving:** Hasbro has introduced a Give As You Earn scheme, both at Stockley Park and Newport at its warehouse.

Employees also have the opportunity to donate their last hour's salary of the year to charity.

## Commercially-led support

**Sponsorship:** Hasbro sponsor projects at local and national level. This year Hasbro's Play-Doh is supporting the 2006 Barnardo's Big Toddle. The funds raised from this sponsored event will be used towards helping children with disabilities, children with special needs and children in their development.

---

# Hays plc

141 Moorgate, London EC2M 6TX

020 7628 9999

Website: www.hays-plc.com

Correspondent: Poppy Penhallow, Human Resources Assistant
E-mail: enquiries@hays.com

Chief officer: Bob Lawson

Chief Executive: Denis Waxman

| Year end | Turnover | Pre-tax profit |
|---|---|---|
| 30/06/2006 | £1,826,600,000 | £192,500,000 |

**Nature of company business**
The company and its subsidiary undertakings form a business services group which provides a range of specialist services for commercial, industrial and professional customers. The group has three core activities: distribution; commercial (office support services); and personnel (specialist staff recruitment agencies).

**Main locations:** London

**Total employees:** 7,569

---

### Charitable donations

2006: £11,140
2005: £21,612
2004: £56,388
2003: £59,644

Membership: BitC

---

## Community involvement

The company has a Good Neighbour Policy, which seeks to ensure that Hays strongly supports the communities in which it operates, regularly communicating with key local stakeholders and becoming involved in local projects.

Generally, the company supports one national charity nominated by its employees, with other assistance going to small local charities which have no access to national funds. Particular emphasis is given to charities which provide for older people and the very young, especially disability charities.

**Charity of the year:** Marie Curie Cancer Care (2006/07).

### Exclusions

Generally no support for circular appeals, appeals from individuals, overseas projects, political appeals, sport, local appeals not in areas of company presence, or large national appeals.

### Applications

In writing to the correspondent.

## Corporate giving

In 2005/06, the company made donations to charity of just over £11,000. Although this is below our minimum level for inclusion, we believe this may be a one-off. However, as the company's level of cash donations has continued to decline over the past five years, we shall continue to monitor the situation.

For 2003/04, the company supported the NSPCC and its sister charity in Scotland, Children 1st. through charitable donations and activities over £75,000 was raised.

### In-kind support

The company recycles toner and printer cartridges and donates the proceeds to the Lighthouse Club, the construction industry charity. £21,500 was donated to the charity through this initiative. The recycling of old mobile phones also benefits this charity.

### Employee-led support

Across the UK staff support a wide range of regional and local charities with individual team and office-based activities. Funds raised used to be matched by the company, but we don't know if this is still the case.

---

# HBOS plc

Group Community Relations Department, PO Box 5, The Mound, Edinburgh EH1 1YZ

0870 600 5000; Fax: 0131 243 5437

Website: www.hbosplc.com

Correspondent: Joan Hemmery, HBOS Foundation Manager

Chief officer: DennisStevenson

Chief Executive: James Crosby

| Year end | Turnover | Pre-tax profit |
|---|---|---|
| 31/12/2005 | £23,617,000,000 | £4,808,000,000 |

**Nature of company business**
The group's principal activities are divided into five divisions, namely: retail banking, insurance and investment, business banking, corporate banking and treasury.

**Subsidiaries include:** St James's Place Capital plc, Insight Investment Management Ltd, Clerical Medical Investment Group Ltd, CAPITAL BANK plc, BM Solutions, Colley's, esure.com, Godfey Davis, Hill Hire plc, Intelligent Finance, St Andrew's Group, Halifax plc

**Main locations:** Edinburgh

**UK employees:** 17,040

**Total employees:** 71,885

---

### Charitable donations

2005: £10,470,000
2003: £5,800,000

Management costs: £930,000
CRM figure: £2,600,000

Membership: A & B, BitC, L B Group, %Club

---

## Community involvement

HBOS plc was formed following the merger of the Bank of Scotland and Halifax plc, all charitable donations are channelled through the HBOS Foundation (Registered Charity no. SCO32942) which was launched in 2002. Additional support is provided through in kind giving, affinity cards, and Halifax's extensive corporate sponsorship programme.

### HBOS Foundation

The foundation's activities are centered on three key areas:

▹ national grants and the regional Community Action programme – providing donations to charities and community groups across the UK

▹ colleague fundraising – via the Million £ Challenge and colleague matched funding

▶ HBOS volunteering – providing encouragement, opportunities and support to colleagues who are donating their time to support the community in which they live and work.

**Charity of the Year:** I CAN (2006).

## Exclusions

The HBOS Foundation will not provide support for: charitable advertising; sponsorship of fundraising events for registered charities; sponsorship of individuals or third party fundraising initiatives; any project or initiative which discriminate on the grounds of colour, race, sex or religious beliefs; political appeals; animal rights groups; overseas projects; or conferences.

## Applications

If you are applying for a grant of over £50,000, for further information please call the HBOS Foundation Helpline on 0845 673 2005. Alternatively, an HBOS Foundation funding application form can be downloaded from the company's website. Please complete the form and post it to HBOS Foundation, Po Box No 5, The Mound, Edinburgh, EH1 1YZ.

If you are applying for a grant of under £50,000, further information is available on the above mentioned helpline. An application form can be downloaded as above. However, completed forms should be posted to your nearest or most appropriate regional co-ordinator. HBOS Foundation Regional Co-ordinators are based across the UK and represent the majority of HBOS businesses, including subsidiaries. Download a PDF version of a map of the UK to find out where the regional co-ordinators are based.

## Corporate giving

The HBOS foundation works on a national and local level to support a wide range of charities. During 2005, the foundation made charitable donations of £10,470,000 of which £1.1 million went to the Tsunami Appeal. A further £2.6 million was donated to various charities as a result of their affinity to the Visa charity credit cards offered by Halifax plc and the Bank of Scotland.

*National grants* – The foundation's national programme supports a mix of one year and multi-year projects and initiatives across Scotland, England, Wales and Northern Ireland. Managed centrally, by the HBOS Foundation, there's a proactive approach to sourcing potential nationwide projects and initiatives that enable the foundation to benefit different parts of the community. Projects tend to be aligned towards the money advice and financial literacy theme, but support a diverse range of organisations, helping communities.

Examples of organisations supported during 2005 include: NCH (£100,000); Centrepoint (£280,000 over three years); Gingerbread (£100,000 over two years); The Alzheimer's Society (£51,700); MACA, Refugee Council (£50,000); and, Terrence Higgins Trust (£80,000 over two years).

*Regional grants* – As part of the foundation's commitment of supporting communities where HBOS plc does business, the foundation operate a structure of regional co-ordinators enabling it to work more closely with local communities and respond to local issues. Through the Community Action programme local grants of up to £10,000 to support a diverse range of projects can be provided – from funding equipment at a special needs school to supporting a debt advice service in an economically deprived area. The two key themes of the programme are money advice and financial literacy, and developing and improving local communities.

Examples of beneficiaries in 2005 include: £6,000 to the 'Safe Drive, Stay Alive' campaign, a road safety initiative aimed at young drivers across Surrey; £2,500 to Ravencliffe Special School in Halifax to enable the purchase of an adapted tricycle for use by pupils; and, £2,100 to Open Minds in Perth for the purchase of various items of equipment.

As part of the foundation's support for organisations promoting financial awareness and money advice, its focus has been on projects working with disadvantaged groups and communities. Organisations receiving support include RNID – 'Make It Count', St Vincent de Paul Society and Refuge. In May 2006, HBOS announced its support for two financial education programmes across the UK. Over £1 million will be provided for an initial period of three years for the two programmes – 'MoneyHelp', for adults who are financially excluded or have limited basic skills and 'MoneyHelp Schools', a pilot programme for pre and post-16 year olds.

## In-kind support

Each year the foundation supports twelve charities by offering pin badges each month for sale to customers and colleagues. A full list of those charities chosen for support in 2006 is given on the foundation's website.

Charities may also be offered collection account facilities in the company's branches enabling them to raise funds for major appeals at low cost.

## Employee-led support

Staff who regularly volunteer in their own time can apply to the foundation for an award of up to £250 on behalf of the organisation they volunteer with. Team challenge volunteering enables staff to apply for up to £250 per project.

The foundation also matches staff fundraising up to £500 per staff member per year and employee giving to a maximum of £500 per employee per year. In 2004, 1,423 colleagues donated £1,478,000 through the scheme.

Staff of HBOS are occasionally seconded to work in charities.

**Payroll giving:** The Give As You Earn scheme is in operation.

## Commercially-led support

**Sponsorship:** HBOS currently invests around £4 million a year in community sponsorship activity. Delivered under the Bank of Scotland name, it is targeted at supporting the promotion and development of sport and the arts in Scotland. Community sponsorship activity is delivered through partnership with the recognised national organising or governing body.

**Cause-related marketing:** A total of £2.6 million went to charities as a result of Bank of Scotland and Halifax plc affinity Visa credit card schemes.

Contact: Further information about some of the more significant sponsorships that are benefiting the community can be obtained by contacting the sponsorship team on 0131 243 7000.

# H J Heinz Company Ltd

Hayes Park South Building, Hayes, Middlesex UB4 8AL

020 8573 7757; Fax: 020 8848 2325

Website: www.heinz.co.uk

Correspondent: Ms Claire Small, Trust Administrator
E-mail: charitable.trust@uk.hjheinz.com

| Year end | Turnover | Pre-tax profit |
|---|---|---|
| 28/04/2004 | £562,391,000 | £80,366,000 |

**Nature of company business**
Principal activities: the manufacture, processing, growing and distribution of food.

**Main locations:** Chorley, Hayes, Kitt Green, Leamington, Kendal, Fakenham, Grimsby, Westwick, Okehampton, Liverpool, Luton, Telford

**UK employees:** 500

**Total employees:** 3,800

> **Charitable donations**
>
> 2004: £121,000

## Community involvement

The H.J. Heinz Company Limited established the H J Heinz Charitable Trust (Charity Commission no. 326254) in 1983 as a vehicle for its charitable in the UK. It is committed to providing funding and support to promote the improvement of health and nutrition within its local communities. Priority support is given to charitable programmes and organisations that operate in areas where Heinz has significant operations and interests. In particular, it helps charitable organisations dedicated to maintaining and improving nutrition and nutritional education, youth services and education.

The charitable trust confines its giving to purposes accepted in law as charitable in the following five key programme areas:

- nutrition – supporting improvements in, and a better understanding of, the medical aspects of nutrition and health in the community with a particular emphasis on paediatrics
- youth and education – supporting the positive development of youngsters in our communities by strengthening systems that affect learning and by sustaining programmes that supplement the formal education process
- local community – supporting and enhancing the local communities in which H.J. Heinz has significant operations
- quality of life – promoting programmes that support and add to the quality of life for residents in communities local to company operations, including support for the arts, as well as cultural and environmental programmes
- volunteerism – supporting charitable work of Heinz employees through a programme that provides funding to nationally recognised charitable organisations in recognition of volunteer service.

## Exclusions

No support is given to circular appeals, purely denominational (religious) appeals, political appeals, individuals undertaking educational or vocational studies, or individuals or groups for sponsored events.

The trust does not undertake commercial sponsorship or advertising in charity brochures.

### Applications

In writing to the correspondent. Applications should include a short general description of the society and/or project, with a statement of aims together with any supporting material.

The trustees meet once a year, usually in July or August to consider major appeals for donations. However, a sub-committee, which is authorised to make grants of up to £10,000, meets more frequently. This committee also selects applications to be considered by the trustees at their annual meeting.

## Corporate giving

In 2004, the trust had an income of £126,000 of which £121,000 came from the company. It made 50 donations ranging from £50 to £8,225 and totalling £64,000. Beneficiaries included a number of organisations to which there is an ongoing commitment. Some of those receiving grants of £1,000 or more during the year included: Royal Academy of Arts (£8,225); Muscular Dystrophy Campaign (£5,000); UNICEF (£3,453); The English Speaking Union (£2,500); Caravan (£1,600); and, CHICKS (£1,000).

### In-kind support

The company gives goods to raise money for local charities.

**Education:** The company is involved in local education/business partnerships and provides educational materials for schools.

### Commercially-led support

**Sponsorship:** *The arts* – The company undertakes arts sponsorship on a national and local level. For example it has sponsored the 'Orchestra of the Mill', a community orchestra in Wigan.

*Education* – The company has sponsored research at Surrey University into the cholesterol properties of certain fibre foods.

*Enterprise* – Heinz is one of the sponsors for Wigan New Enterprise Ltd, particularly the Youth Enterprise Centre.

Contact: Vicki Gregory, Marketing Manager.

# Henderson Group plc

4 Broadgate, London EC2M 2DA

020 7818 5310; Fax: 020 7818 6900

Website: www.hendersongroupplc.com

Correspondent: Director of Corporate Affairs

Chief officer: Rupert Pennant-Rea

Chief Executive: Roger Yates

| Year end | Turnover | Pre-tax profit |
|---|---|---|
| 31/12/2005 | £265,800,000 | £64,000,000 |

**Nature of company business**
The principal activities of the group are the provision of investment management services and the transaction of various

classes of insurance business. The group has businesses in the UK, Europe and the US.

**Subsidiaries include:** Pearl Assurance plc, Henderson Fund Manangement plc, National Provident Life Ltd, Towry Law plc, London Life Ltd

**Main locations:** Bristol, Peterborough, Tunbridge Wells, Bracknell

**Total employees:** 881

### Charitable donations

2005: £63,000
2004: £38,000
2003: £44,000

## Community involvement

Formerly trading as HHG plc, the company changed its name in 2005 to Henderson Group plc. Its preferred charity since 1987 is Community Links, the inner city charity running community-based projects in East London.

### Exclusions

No response to circular appeals or to sponsorship requests for individuals. No support for: fundraising events; advertising in charity brochures; religious appeals; or overseas projects.

### Applications

In writing to the correspondent.

## Corporate giving

During 2005, the group donated a total of £63,000 supporting charities. This was broken down into the following categories:

- social and welfare £26,000
- education and international £19,000
- medical and other £18,000.

### Employee-led support

Employees are encouraged to get involved in charitable activities with the group matching pound for pound any money raised. Included in the total amount supporting charities, is donated £35,000 in employee matching grants during 2005.

# Herbert Smith

Exchange House, Primrose Street, London EC2A 2HS

020 7374 8000

Website: www.herbertsmith.com

**Correspondent:** Elizabeth Sewell, Secretary to the Chairites Committee 0207 374 8000

| Year end | Turnover | Pre-tax profit |
|---|---|---|
| 31/12/2004 | | |

**Nature of company business**
International law firm.

**Main locations:** London

### Charitable donations

Membership: A & B, BitC, L B Group, %Club

## Community involvement

Herbert Smith was one of the first law firms to start an extensive Community Action Programme. The firm was a founding member of the UK-based charity, the Solicitors Pro Bono Group (Charity Commission no. 1064274). Besides pro bono work, the firm is involved in other community projects as well and encourages its staff to get involved with their local communities. In particular, it provides help with legal matters and works with nearby schools in raising educational standards through mentoring and learning support programmes.

### Exclusions

Donations are only made to UK registered charities.

### Applications

In writing to the correspondent.

## Corporate giving

Although we do not have a breakdown of the firm's community support, in cash, time or in-kind giving, it is fair to assume from the information given on its website that community support is substantial; hence its inclusion. In 2004, donations were made to 62 charities and beneficiaries included Alone in London, the Alzheimer's Research Trust, Women's Link and the World Wildlife Fund.

Below are some examples of the types of work the firm undertakes.

**Legal advice:** *Death Row Prisoners* – Herbert Smith is on the panel of London solicitors which deals with appeals for those facing the death penalty for murder in the Caribbean. Support is also given to Amicus, a UK charity working on behalf of death row prisoners in America.

*Royal Courts of Justice* – Herbert Smith is one of over 20 City firms which support the Citizen Advice Bureau located in the Royal Courts of Justice. The firm provides qualified solicitors on a rota basis who attend as honorary legal advisers to supplement the CABs full-time advisory staff.

**Education:** *The Thomas Buxton Junior School Project* – In conjunction with the Tower Hamlets Education Business Partnerships (THEBP) over 150 volunteers from the firm assist pupils at the school with their reading, writing and IT skills.

Also in partnership with the THEBP, the firm helps GCSE students studying foreign languages (French, German and Spanish) and, with the support of Herbert Smith's Charities Committee, sponsored a trip to Brussels for 21 language students.

### In-kind support

The firm have previously supplied and installed IT equipment for the pupils at Thomas Buxton Junior School in Whitechapel. On-going technical back-up is provided as part of the package.

### Employee-led support

Herbert Smith encourages staff to volunteer and in 2004, 33% of London based staff actively participated in the firm's pro bono and volunteering programme, contributing over 7,700 hours to 20 schemes. Volunteering schemes cover pupils from nursery through to university and homeless people. The following extract is taken from the company's website:

'We believe that Community Action and pro bono work should be voluntary, however, from the moment staff join the firm we encourage them to use 24 hours of working time a year on schemes facilitated by the programme, it is recognised in appraisals, and our lawyers record it as accountable time.'

The firm's Staff Social Committee supports and initiates fundraising activities for a variety of charities including the staff's chosen Charity of the Year, the Shooting Star Children's Hospice and the annual London to Brighton bike ride for the British Heart Foundation. Jeans for Genes day is also supported. In 2005 the committee increased the amount raised through the firm's matched funding programme. In addition the firm operates a payroll-giving scheme.

# Hess Limited

Level 9, The Adelphi Building, 1–11 John Adam Street, London EC2N 6AG

020 7331 3000

Website: www.hess.com

Correspondent: Andy Mitchell, Communications Manager - andy.mitchell@hess.com

| Year end | Turnover | Pre-tax profit |
|---|---|---|
| 31/12/2005 | £903,563,550 | £660,098,880 |

**Nature of company business**
The exploration and production of oil and gas. The ultimate holding company is the Hess Corporation based in the USA.

**Subsidiaries include:** Western Gas Limited

**Main locations:** London, Aberdeen

**Total employees:** 182

---

**Charitable donations**

2006: £5,496
2005: £5,496
2004: £30,228

---

## Community involvement

The Environment, Health, Safety and Social Responsibility Report for 2005 produced by the Hess Corporation states: 'We have a long tradition of investing in projects that improve health, education and quality of life in communities where we live and work. We support charitable and other non-profit organizations, community projects, scholarships and employee volunteerism.

'We work closely with the local communities to help us understand and evaluate specific needs. This collaboration ensures the sustainability of our social responsibility program.

'In 2005, we invested $7.7 million in cash and in-kind donations worldwide, including disaster relief contributions.'

The UK company prefers to support appeals relevant to company business and local charities in areas of company presence.

Preferred areas of support are the environment, medical research, science/technology and sickness/disability charities. Support tends to be given to specific projects.

### Exclusions

No support is given for advertising in charity brochures, animal welfare, appeals from individuals, purely denominational (religious) appeals, local appeals not in areas of company presence, overseas projects or political events.

### Applications

Appeals from national charities should be addressed in writing to the correspondent. The Aberdeen office (Scott House, Hareness Road, Altens, Aberdeen AB12 3LE, tel. 01224 243000) deals with appeals relevant to that region.

## Corporate giving

In 2005 the company made charitable contributions amounting to £5,459 (2004: £30,025). No recent information was available on the beneficiary organisations.

### In-kind support

In addition to charitable donations, the company also undertakes a range of activities in support of the community in which it operates. These include its partnership with the Lawn Tennis Association in funding the City Tennis Clubs programme and an ongoing relationship with the Restoration of Appearance and Function Trust.

### Employee-led support

Employee involvement is encouraged.

### Commercially-led support

**Sponsorship:** An agreement between Hess Gas Limited and Age Concern seeks to inform vulnerable older people at risk in cold weather on how best to keep warm and minimise their fuel bills.

---

# Hewlett-Packard Ltd

Cain Road, Bracknell RG12 1HN

Website: www.hp.com

Correspondent: Corporate Marketing Department

E-mail: hp.philanthropy@porternovelli.co.uk

Managing Director: Stephen Gill

| Year end | Turnover | Pre-tax profit |
|---|---|---|
| 31/10/2005 | £2,844,200,000 | |

**Nature of company business**
Hewlett-Packard Ltd is a subsidiary of the Hewlett-Packard Company incorporated in the USA. The principal activities of the group are the design, manufacture and marketing of measurement and computation products and systems.

**Main locations:** Bracknell, Bristol, Erskine (Glasgow)

---

**Charitable donations**

Membership: BitC

---

## Community involvement

Hewlett-Packard's (HP) community support programme in the UK is currently under review. As such, we have been asked by the company to publish the following interim information:

'HP's philanthropy programmes are described in some detail on the web-site http://grants.hp.com

'HP's philanthropy programmes all focus on providing IT for innovative uses. HP Ltd has no programme of direct cash support for charitable work.'

### Applications

UK registered charities and accredited educational institutions who wish to apply for a grant from Hewlett-Packard (HP) are invited to refer to the website http://grants.hp.com to position their proposal within one of HP's programmes.

Proposals should be sent for consideration to: HP Philanthropy Programme, c/o Sally Clift, Porter Novelli, 21 St Petersburgh Place, London W2 4LA.

# HFC Bank Limited

North Street, Winkfield, Windsor, Berkshire SL4 4TD

01344 890000; Fax: 01344 890014

Website: www.hfcbank.co.uk

Correspondent: Debbie McFadyen, PA to Head of Communications 01344 890000 ext 2559

Chief officer: David Keys

Managing Director: Gary Gilmer

| Year end | Turnover | Pre-tax profit |
|---|---|---|
| 31/12/2005 | £618,231,000 | (£52,982,000) |

Nature of company business
The principal activity of the company comprises banking services.

Subsidiaries include: Hamilton Financial Planning Services Ltd, Hamilton Life Assurance Co Ltd, HFC Bank plc, Hamilton Insurance Co Ltd, DLRS Ltd

Main locations: Winkfield, Birmingham, Bracknell

UK employees: 3,679

### Charitable donations

2005: £176,730
2004: £164,067
2003: £150,000

## Community involvement

The company supports national and local charities, with preference given to those operating in Berkshire and the Midlands. There is a preference for causes connected with youth, education and economic development. The national charity supported in 2005 was Macmillan Cancer Relief and the major regional charities supported were Berkshire Community Foundation and the Acorns Children's Hospice in Birmingham. A wide range of other charities were also supported with an emphasis on those serving the communities in which the company operates.

### Exclusions

No support for advertising in publications and associated materials, animal welfare, appeals from individuals, the arts, enterprise/training, fundraising events, medical research, overseas projects, political appeals, religious appeals, science/ technology or sport.

### Applications

In writing to the correspondent.

**Information available:** Potential applicants can obtain guidelines from the company.

## Corporate giving

In 2005, the company made charitable contributions of £176,730. (2004: £164,047).

### In-kind support

The company also provides support through a schools mentoring initiative.

### Employee-led support

Through the Give as You Earn payroll giving scheme, the company matches its employees' charitable contributions and fundraising activities up to a maximum of £250. Employees are actively involved in their own fundraising. The company also contribute to organisations with which staff are volunteers.

**Payroll giving:** The Give As You Earn scheme is in operation.

# William Hill plc

Greenside House, 50 Station Road, Wood Green, London N22 7TP

020 8918 3600

Website: www.williamhillplc.co.uk

Correspondent: Helen Grantham, Group Company Secretary

Chief officer: Charles Scott

| Year end | Turnover | Pre-tax profit |
|---|---|---|
| 27/12/2005 | £9,812,300,000 | £175,700,000 |

Nature of company business
A leading provider of bookmaking services in the UK through an estate of licensed betting offices, by telephone, online and via interactive television. The company also operates an online casino and two greyhound stadia.

Main locations: Haringey

UK employees: 10,699

### Charitable donations

2005: £351,000

## Community involvement

In March 2005, the company established a Corporate Responsibility Committee to monitor its corporate social responsibility activities.

The company's charitable donations are focused on organisations involved in areas of greatest relevance to its business and include contributions to those involved in:

- promoting a responsible approach to gambling; undertaking research into problem gambling; and providing information, advice and help to those who are at risk or are experiencing difficulties with their gambling
- greyhound and racehorse welfare
- support to disadvantaged individuals in horse and greyhound racing.

Support is also given, wherever possible, to company employees involved in their own fundraising efforts.

### Exclusions

No support for circular or general appeals, or to political or religious organisations.

### Applications

In writing to the correspondent.

## Corporate giving

In 2005, the company made charitable donations in the UK totalling £351,000 of which £200,000 went to the Responsibility in Gambling Trust. A contribution was also made to the British Greyhound Racing Fund.

### Employee-led support

A proportion of the group's charitable donations budget is set aside to match funds (up to a specified limit) raised by employees on local charitable projects which fall within the company's donations criteria.

## Julian Hodge Bank Ltd

30–31 Windsor Place, Cardiff CF10 3UR

029 2022 0800; Fax: 029 2023 0516

Website: www.jhb.co.uk

Chief officer: John Mitchell

Chief Executive: Jonathan Hodger

Managing Director: D M Austin

| Year end | Turnover | Pre-tax profit |
|---|---|---|
| 31/10/2005 | | £14,500,000 |

Nature of company business
Provision of a wide range of personal and business banking services and independent financial advice.

Main locations: Cardiff, Nantwich

## Community involvement

The Julian Hodge Group state that for many years, as part of its commitment to helping the community, it has provided charitable support through the Jane Hodge Foundation (Charity Commission no. 216053) and, to a lesser extent, the Sir Julian Hodge Charitable Trust (Charity Commission no. 234848).

Charities benefiting from the foundations help include those concerned with health, education, and social issues. The trust supports general charitable purposes, medical research,

medical and surgical science, education, religion, older people and the disabled.

### Applications

Please refer to the application criteria for the related trusts.

## Corporate giving

Although we have been unable to obtain a figure regarding the banks level of support via the above trusts, full details of the trusts support criteria and application procedure can be found in the Directory of Social Change publications 'A Guide to the Major Trusts Volumes 1 and 2'.

In 2002, the foundation sponsored the creation of the Julian Hodge Institute of Applied Macroeconomics at the Cardiff Business School. It has pledged funding over a five year period. Support was also given to the Cardiff-based charity Race Equality First.

## Honda Motor Europe Limited

470 London Road, Slough, Berkshire SL4 8QY

01753 590500

Website: world.honda.com/community/

Correspondent: Paul Ormond, Sponsorship Manager

Chief officer: S Takagi

| Year end | Turnover | Pre-tax profit |
|---|---|---|
| 31/03/2004 | £3,865,800,000 | £26,800,000 |

Nature of company business
The principal activities of the company are distributing manufactured products of the Honda Group, acting as Honda's European re-invoicing centre and selling and marketing Honda products in the UK.

Main locations: Slough, Swindon

UK employees: 5,409

### Charitable donations
2004: £20,599
2003: £32,808

## Community involvement

Honda in the UK summarises its philanthropic community initiatives under two categories:

- educational – leaders and sponsorships, especially in connection with young people
- community – local festival and event support. Help is also given through the donation of goods/prizes and by supporting its employees in their charitable works.

### Exclusions

No support for animal welfare, appeals from individuals, political appeals, religious appeals and large national charities.

### Applications

In writing to the correspondent.

## Corporate giving

In 2004, cash donations in the UK totalled £21,000. Community contributions previously stood at around £200,000 a year, but we have been unable to confirm if it remains at this level.

Organisations/events benefiting from the company's support included: BEN, the motor industry charity; the Windsor Festival of Art and Music; and, an unnamed breast cancer treatment and research charity.

### In-kind support

The main areas of non-cash support are gifts in kind.

### Employee-led support

Employees at the R&D division near Swindon had their fundraising efforts on behalf of a breast cancer charity matched by the company.

### Commercially-led support

**Sponsorship:** The company undertake sponsorship of educational initiatives.

# Hoover Candy Group Ltd

Pentrebach Factory, Pentrebach, Merthyr Tydfil CF48 4TU

01685 721222

Website: www.hoover.co.uk

Correspondent: Marion Heaffy, Hoover Foundation 01685 721222

| Year end | Turnover | Pre-tax profit |
|----------|----------|----------------|
| 30/11/2006 | | |

Nature of company business
Manufacture of domestic laundry, refrigeration, and vacuuming appliances.

Main locations: Bromborough, Glasgow, Merthyr Tydfil, Bolton

### Charitable donations
2003: £86,687

## Community involvement

The company directs its grant giving through the Hoover Foundation (Charity commission no. 200274). Support is given to strategic UK charities working in education, health and welfare. Small grants are made to local organisations near its main sites in South Wales, Glasgow and Bolton.

Although the income received by the foundation has been steadily decreasing (down from £120,000 in 1999 to £15,000 in 2005), we were advised that it is still in operation.

### Exclusions

No grants to individuals, including students.

### Applications

In writing to the correspondent.

## Corporate giving

In 2005, the Hoover Foundation had an income of £15,028 and a total expenditure of £73,737). No details of beneficiaries were available.

# House of Fraser plc

1 Howick Place, London SW1P 1BH

020 7963 2000; Fax: 020 7828 8885

Website: www.houseoffraser.co.uk

Correspondent: Peter Hearsey, Company Secretary

Chief officer: M Wemms

Chief Executive: J Coleman

| Year end | Turnover | Pre-tax profit |
|----------|----------|----------------|
| 28/01/2006 | £709,100,000 | £22,300,000 |

Nature of company business
Department store operators.

Main locations: Glasgow, Swindon, London

Total employees: 8,074

### Charitable donations
2006: £47,337
2005: £50,183
2003: £54,850

CRM figure: £26,000

## Community involvement

Each year the company chooses three charities to support via covenanted donations. Other donations therefore tend to be given to charities local to company sites and concerned with children and youth, social welfare, medical, environment and heritage, enterprise/training, education and the arts.

**Charity of the Year:** Eve's Appeal; Walk the walk (2005/06).

### Exclusions

Support is not generally given to circular appeals, appeals from individuals, purely denominational (religious or political) appeals, local appeals not in areas of company presence or overseas projects.

### Applications

In writing to the correspondent. Local charities are supported at the discretion of the store managers in their region.

## Corporate giving

In 2006, charitable donations totalled £47,337 (2005: £50,183). No breakdown of this amount was available, but we assume the majority went towards supporting its nominated charities for the year – Eve's Appeal and Walk the Walk.

### In-kind support

The group actively supports Computers for Charity (CFC). CFC is a voluntary, non profit-making organisation, the aim of which is to improve access to IT for community groups which it does by recycling computers. The group has sent some 200 PCs and a large number of laptops and printers to CFC over the last three years.

Additionally the group's information services department in Swindon has donated a small number of computers to a local charity, for the personal home use by disabled persons and those with learning difficulties.

## Employee-led support

In 2005/06, the group organised fund raising activities for two nominated charities raising £34,000. Its nominated charities were 'Walk the Walk', a charity supporting breast cancer research and a support centre in Bristol, and the Eve Appeal, a charity supporting research into ovarian cancer.

The group has previously supported other worthwhile causes such as Cancer Research UK, Action Cancer Research, the NSPCC and the National Autistic Society, raising some £500,000 in the last four years through individual store activities and the sale of pin badges. Each store may also undertake its own fundraising events/activities at its own discretion.

## Commercially-led support

**Cause-related marketing;** Each year the group produces a house-branded teddy bear for sale in its stores in conjunction with the RSPCA and Cancer Research UK.

A portion of the selling price of each bear is donated to both charities. The approximate donation in 2005/06, totalled £26,000.

# HSBC Holdings plc

Level 36, 8 Canada Square, London EC3R 6AE

020 7991 8888; Fax: 020 7992 4880

Website: www.hsbc.com

Correspondent: HSBC in the Community

E-mail: communityaffairs@hsbc.com

Chief officer: Stephen K Green (Group Chairman)

| Year end 31/12/2005 | Turnover | Pre-tax profit |
|---|---|---|

**Nature of company business**
The group provides banking and related financial services.

**Subsidiaries include:** The British Bank of the Middle East, First Direct, Midland Life Ltd, Midland Bank Ltd, East River Savings Bank, Eversholt Holdings Ltd, Samuel Montagu & Co Ltd, HFC Bank, Forward Trust Ltd, James Capel & Co Ltd

Main locations: Leeds, London

UK employees: 55,000

Total employees: 265,285

### Charitable donations

2005: £15,800,000

Total community contributions: £15,800,000

Membership: A & B, BitC, L B Group

## Community involvement

'In its support for communities around the world, HSBC has focused on education and the environment. Although we will consider other causes, we aim to concentrate our funding in these two areas.

'**Education:** HSBC believes that support for primary and secondary education, in particular for the underprivileged, is crucial to the future development and prosperity of every country.

'In addition to funding original education initiatives around the world, HSBC is keen to involve its experienced and supportive staff in building and developing mentoring programmes, and offering career guidance and job internships for talented young people.' Grants were made to schools and colleges in the UK through the HSBC Education Trust (Charity Commission no. 1084542). In February 2005, the trust's deed was updated to enable grants to be made outside the UK, with the trust being renamed the HSBC Global Education Trust in the process. Donations to the trust totalled about £1,000,000 in 2005.

'**Environment:** HSBC is deeply conscious of its responsibility to the environment

'We will always consider support for worthwhile environmental organisations and initiatives.'

### Exclusions

No support for advertising in charity brochures, animal welfare, appeals from individuals, the arts, elderly people, fundraising events, political appeals, religious appeals, science/technology, sickness/disability, or sport.

### Applications

In writing to the correspondent.

## Corporate giving

In 2005, HSBC Holdings plc made global donations totalling around £43,000,000. Donations within the UK totalled around £15,800,000.

## Employee-led support

**Education:** Around 1,000 HSBC employees in the UK work on a voluntary basis with the charity Young Enterprise, advising and encouraging young people to set up their own businesses.

Employees are given time off in which to volunteer, with their fundraising efforts being matched by the bank up to a maximum of £100.

**Payroll giving:** The bank operates the Give As You Earn scheme.

# Hunting plc

3 Cockspur Street, London SW1Y 5BQ

020 7321 0123; Fax: 020 7839 2072

Website: www.hunting.plc.uk

Correspondent: Ms Anna Blundell-Williams, Public Relations Coordinator
E-mail: anna.bw@hunting.plc.uk

Chief officer: R H Hunting

Chief Executive: D L Proctor

| Year end | Turnover | Pre-tax profit |
| --- | --- | --- |
| 31/12/2005 | £1,521,900,000 | £40,900,000 |

**Nature of company business**
The principal activity of the company is oil services.

**Subsidiaries include:** Irvin Group Ltd

**Main locations:** London

**UK employees:** 357

**Total employees:** 2,343

> **Charitable donations**
> 2005: £49,000
> 2004: £26,000
> 2003: £24,000

## Community involvement

Donations are generally made through the Hunting Charitable Trust (not a registered charity), which supports UK charities, both national and local, involved in welfare and medicine.

Local charities are usually only supported by subsidiaries if a member of staff has a particularly close connection with the charity.

### Exclusions

The company does not make political donations.

### Applications

In writing to the correspondent. The trustees of the Hunting Charitable Trust meet once a year, generally in November.

## Corporate giving

In 2005, £49,000 was donated to UK charitable organisations. We have no details of the beneficiaries.

### Commercially-led support
**Sponsorship:** *The arts* – the company sponsors the Hunting Art Prizes Competition. Subsidiaries also have their own sponsorship budgets.

Each year, as part of the Hunting Arts Prizes competition, a charity private view is hosted in order to raise money for good causes. The benefiting charity for 2005 was the Royal Hospital Chelsea and all funds raised at the private view and dinner were donated to its appeal to build a new Infirmary and updated Long Wards for the Pensioners.

# Huntleigh Technology plc

310–312 Dallow Road, Luton, Bedfordshire LU1 1TD

01582 413104; Fax: 01582 402589

Website: www.huntleigh-technology.com

Correspondent: Julian Schild, Chairman

Chief officer: J Schild

Chief Executive: D Schild

Managing Director: G Cox

| Year end | Turnover | Pre-tax profit |
| --- | --- | --- |
| 31/12/2005 | £199,800,000 | £22,200,000 |

**Nature of company business**
The principal activity is the design, manufacture, distribution and rental of equipment, instrumentation and control systems for medical applications.

**Main locations:** Cardiff, Wednesbury, Winsford, Luton

**UK employees:** 1,500

**Total employees:** 2,330

> **Charitable donations**
> 2005: £15,500
> 2004: £12,000
> 2003: £26,000
> Total community contributions: £20,000

## Community involvement

The company prefers to support charities in Bedfordshire and other parts of the UK where it has sites, including South Wales and the West Midlands. It supports charities by advertising in charity brochure, and those involved with: children/youth; elderly people; fundraising events; medical research; sickness/disability; social welfare, and sport.

### Exclusions

No support for animal welfare, appeals from individuals, the arts, education, environment/heritage, overseas projects, political appeals, religious appeals or science/technology.

### Applications

In writing to the correspondent.

## Corporate giving

In 2005, company made global cash donations totalling £42,000 of which £15,500 went to organisations in the UK. An additional £4,500 was given in gifts in kind. Major beneficiaries were: The Pasque Hospice; Arkwright Scholarships; and, Duke of Edinburgh's Award.

### In-kind support
The main area of non-cash support is gifts in kind.

### Employee-led support
**Payroll giving:** Employee donations through this scheme appear to go to the Pasque Hospice, Luton.

### Commercially-led support
**Sponsorship:** The company undertake good-cause sponsorship.

# Huntsman Tioxide

Haverton Hill Road, Billingham TS23 1PS

01642 370300

Website: www.huntsman.com

Correspondent: M Maughan, Company Secretary

| Year end | Turnover | Pre-tax profit |
| --- | --- | --- |
| 31/12/2004 | £2,699,537,000 | £105,385,000 |

**Nature of company business**
The manufacture of titanium oxide and titanium compounds.

## IBM

**Main locations:** Grimsby, London, Teeside

**Total employees:** 5,659

### Charitable donations

2004: £120,646
2003: £307,894

## Community involvement

The company has factories in Teeside and Humberside and support is focused on charities local to these sites.

A wide range of causes in these communities is supported, with the preferred areas being children and youth, social welfare, medical and education.

### Exclusions

No support for circulars, brochure advertising, local appeals not in areas of company presence, large national appeals, fundraising events or appeals from individuals.

### Applications

In writing to the correspondent. Local appeals should be addressed as follows:

Teeside charitable appeals to: Mrs D Hunter, Tioxide Europe Ltd, Haverton Hill Road, Billingham, Stockton on Tees TS23 1PS.

## Corporate giving

During the year 2004 the group made charitable donations totalling £120,646. (2003: £307,894). It is not known the amount donated within the UK and the amount donated worldwide.

## In-kind support

Non-cash support is given in the form of gifts and occasional secondments.

# IBM United Kingdom Ltd

IBM (United Kingdom) Ltd, PO Box 41, North Harbour, Portsmouth, Hampshire PO6 3AU

0870 542 6426; Fax: 0870 542 6329

Website: www.ibm.com

Correspondent: Mark Wakefield, Corporate Community Relations Manager
E-mail: wakefim@uk.ibm.com

| Year end | Turnover | Pre-tax profit |
|----------|----------|----------------|
| 31/12/2005 | £3,732,200,000 | £14,200,000 |

### Nature of company business
IBM United Kingdom Ltd is the UK subsidiary of IBM Corporation. It is involved in the provision of information technology services and solutions, and the development, production and supply of advanced information technology products.

**Main locations:** London, Portsmouth, Glasgow

**Total employees:** 20,288

### Charitable donations

2005: £800,000
2004: £900,000

Membership: BitC

## Community involvement

Community grants are only made to organisations in which an employee (current or retired) has volunteered, for an average of eight hours a month for at least five months.

Organisations that have been supported include: schools providing compulsory education; preschools, nurseries and childcare centres; adult and youth literacy programmes; job training programmes community and family service agencies; museums and other cultural organisations; libraries; children's hospitals; substance abuse programmes; and elderly and disability groups.

### Exclusions

No grants towards capital improvements, running costs, athletic or recreational activities, work that only benefits individuals, third party fundraising events, internet hosting, recurring events or any fundraising initiative such as auctions, raffles and so on.

### Applications

All requests for funding need to be requested by the employee rather than the recipient organisation, as organisations without an IBM employee volunteering cannot be supported. However, it might be worth voluntary groups around company sites advertising voluntary positions on the intranet site to open up this avenue of funding.

We have recently been informed that unsolicited applications from organisations are not considered by the company.

Contact Mark Wakefield, Corporate Community Relations Manager at IBM UK Trust, South Bank, 76 Upper Ground, London SE1 9PZ, telephone no. 020 7202 3608 or e-mail – wakefim@uk.ibm.com.

## Corporate giving

The Directors' Report for 2005 states that the company made donations in the United Kingdom totalling £800,000 (2004: £900,000) for educational, cultural and social welfare activities. We have no information regarding the recipient organisations.

## In-kind support

Most of the company's giving involves in kind donations and product discounts. Eligible groups can apply for equipment (PC, printer or so on).

There is also the IBM MentorPlace programme. MentorPlace teams working on an IBM MentorPlace project may donate a PC or laptop to that school for their use in supporting the programme. To eligible teams must be actively working with an entire class or a designated group of students and their teacher. IBM mentors and the teacher must be fully committed to participating in the programme through to its successful completion. All eligible team members MUST be registered and recording their volunteering hours on the On Demand Community website. Further details from the contact, Mark Wakefield.

## Employee-led support

IBM encourages and supports employees and retirees to undertake voluntary work, organising its community involvement policies to motivate people to volunteer. On the company's intranet site, there is a database of volunteer opportunities which allows staff to find a good cause which matches their interests. The UK Community Grants programme is designed to support the 3,000+ employees and 150+ retirees for the on demand community programme.

**Payroll giving :** The company operates the Give As You Earn scheme.

# ICAP plc

2 Broadgate, London EC2M 7UR

020 7000 5000; Fax: 020 7000 5975

Website: www.icap.com

Correspondent: Nikki Studt, Charity Co-ordinator

Chief officer: Charles Gregson

Chief Executive: Michael Spencer

| Year end | Turnover | Pre-tax profit |
|---|---|---|
| 31/03/2005 | £794,000,000 | £131,700,000 |

**Nature of company business**
The company is the world's largest interdealer broker and is active in the wholesale markets for OTC derivatives, fixed income securities, money market products, foreign exchange, energy, credit and equity derivatives.

**Subsidiaries include:** BrokerTec Europe Limited, Exotix Investments Limited, Garban-Intercapital Systems Limited, Guy Butler Limited, Harlow (London) Limited, T&M Securities Limited

Main locations: London

UK employees: 1,244

Total employees: 2,929

**Charitable donations**
2005: £2,100,000
2004: £2,100,000
2003: £2,000,000

## Community involvement

The company donates to charitable causes the money raised each year during its 'Charity Day'. On this day the group donates its entire revenue, without any cost reductions, to various charities selected by local offices. This unique event includes the commission made by brokers as well as the company's revenue. It appears that employee fundraising efforts also add to the amount raised.

## Applications

In writing to the correspondent.

**Information available**: The company's website has information about its 'Charity Day', including details of some of the organisations to have benefited from it.

## Corporate giving

In 2004/05, the company gave £2,100,000 in the UK (with a further £2,100,000 going overseas). In 2005/06, £5.2 million was raised bringing the worldwide total up to £27,190,000 in 12 years of Charity Day.

As result of these efforts, many charities have received significant donations enabling them to carry on with their valuable work. Amongst these were two charities involved in long-term redevelopment in Asia following the tsunami disaster – CARE International and Medical Aid. Past beneficiaries have included Help the Aged, Barts Cancer Centre of Excellence, The Prostate Project, London Children's Ballet, Lewa, Raynaud's & Scleroderma Association, St Mungo's and the Willow Foundation.

## Employee-led support

**Payroll giving:** The company operates the Give As You Earn scheme.

# IMI plc

Lakeside Solihull Parkway, Birmingham Business Park, Birmingham B37 7XZ

0121 717 3700

Website: www.imiplc.com

Correspondent: Trevor J Slack, Human Resources Director

Chief officer: Norman Askew

Chief Executive: M J Lamb

| Year end | Turnover | Pre-tax profit |
|---|---|---|
| 31/12/2005 | £1,578,000,000 | £169,900,000 |

**Nature of company business**
IMI is a diversified engineering group operating in three areas: Fluid controls; Retail dispense and Building products. It manufactures and sells internationally.

Main locations: Birmingham, Manchester, Liverpool, Yorkshire

Total employees: 17,099

**Charitable donations**
2005: £298,000
2004: £215,000
2003: £231,000
Membership: BitC

## Community involvement

IMI believe that 'successful businesses cannot exist and operate in isolation from the culture in which they operate'. The group therefore supports a range of selected national charities and smaller charitable organisations operating in communities where it has a presence.

'A sizeable proportion of total donations go into education, including establishments in engineering and technology.'

### Exclusions

No support for circular appeals, advertising in charity brochures, appeals from individuals, fundraising events, local appeals not in an area of company presence, political appeals, large national appeals, overseas projects or Christmas cards.

## Applications

In writing to the correspondent. Grant decisions are made by an appeals committee which meets on an ad hoc basis. Local appeals should be sent to the relevant local plant or branch.

**Advice to applicants:** The company welcomes appeals from charities but its appeal mail is getting too large to handle. Applicants should therefore ensure that they can establish some link with the company in order to be considered for support.

Appeals should, where applicable, give details of the total amount to be raised and a description of how the money is to be spent. If possible, the latest statement of accounts should accompany the appeal.

## Corporate giving

In 2005 charitable donations were £298,000. We were previously advised that national grants generally range from £250 to £5,000, and local grants from £25 to £5,000.

During the course of the year IMI has worked closely with Business in the Community on a number of projects. These included:

- Biodiversity with Birmingham & Black Country Wildlife Trust – promoting biodiversity and carrying out a feasibility study.
- Swap & Store – 'Save Waste And Prosper' promotes the need for recycling waste business products for use in the community. It also looked at alternative storage solutions for company waste.
- Earlswood Secure Unit & Kingsmere Remand Unit – conducted a feasibility study to introduce a mentoring scheme in association with the Young Offenders Institute and provided support in personal, social, education and career lessons.

## In-kind support

The main areas of non-cash support are secondments, gifts in kind and allowing charities to use some of the company's office space.

In support of Birmingham Focus on Blindness, Birmingham's biggest charity working with the visually impaired, IMI engineering graduates organised a UK-wide fundraising day. Taking the form of an 'It's a Knockout' event, £4,000 was raised on the charities behalf.

In addition, non-cash support will be provided by many of IMI's subsidiary companies throughout the UK, but this is not quantified.

## Employee-led support

Support for employee charitable activity is provided at subsidiary level and is at the discretion of the management. It is not quantified in the overall company's community contribution.

**Payroll giving:** The company operates the Give As You Earn scheme.

## Commercially-led support

**Sponsorship:** *The arts* – although the company is not a member of Arts & Business the company is a founder patron of Symphony Hall, Birmingham. It also sponsors the City of Birmingham Symphony Orchestra, Birmingham Royal Ballet, and supports the Royal Society of Arts.

Contact: Corporate sponsorship proposals should be addressed to the Corporate Communications Manager.

# Imperial Chemical Industries plc

20 Manchester Square, London W1U 3AN

020 7009 5000; Fax: 020 7009 5703

Website: www.ici.com

Correspondent: Claire Bean, Administrator – Appeals Committee

Chief officer: Peter B Ellwood

Chief Executive: John D G McAdam

| Year end | Turnover | Pre-tax profit |
|---|---|---|
| 31/12/2005 | £5,812,000,000 | £444,000,000 |

**Nature of company business**
The principal activities of the company are research, manufacture and sale of specialty products and paints.

**Subsidiaries include:** Quest International Flavours, Food Ingredients and Fragrances UK Ltd

**Main locations:** Stoke Poges, Stowmarket, Tilbury, Warrington, Wilton, Manningtree, London, Reading, Prudhoe, Runcorn, Slough, Goole, Eastleigh, Heald Green, Hull, Linton, Cannock, Bromborough, Ashford, Birmingham

**UK employees:** 4,520

**Total employees:** 32,530

### Charitable donations

2005: £500,000
2004: £200,000
2003: £500,000

## Community involvement

As previously pointed out, the standard of corporate responsibility reporting presented by a company the size and reputation of Imperial Chemical Industries (ICI) leaves a lot to be desired. To give them their due, however, they at least acknowledge this fact and seem intent on putting the necessary reporting framework in place.

During what ICI refers to as the 'Sustainability Challenge 2010' period, it states it will be reporting against the following community involvement areas: Community involvement; Cash contributions; and volunteer activities. Information regarding these areas is included in the latest 2005 Sustainability Review.

However, somewhat strangely, the figures quoted in the review are then converted into a 'total equivalent value of donations and volunteering'. This measure of 'equivalent hours' is apparently based on local employment costs 'to give a more balanced indication of the real impact of our community involvement in different parts of the world'.

Whilst acknowledging that a £1 donated in Asia has more impact than £1 donated in the UK, is it just coincidence that from a reporting point of view this just happens to boost the overall community investment figure given?

### Exclusions

No donations are given to individuals, political parties, religious bodies or profit-making organisations. An appeal which is the same as, or similar to, one which has been refused within recent years will be not be successful.

## Applications

In writing to the correspondent. Letters of application should include the aims and objectives of the organisation, and outline details of the project requiring funding where appropriate. A current copy of the applicant's annual report and accounts should also be provided.

## Corporate giving

In 2005, ICI made total community contributions worldwide of £2.6 million. Of this, cash donations in the UK accounted for £500,000. We have no details of the beneficiaries.

## In-kind support

**Education:** Employees worldwide are involved in education liaison work with local schools by giving talks, organising visits, and assisting with classroom projects. The group also provides various classroom resources regarding the world of science for use by teachers and pupils, e.g. CD-ROMs.

ICI Paints' global headquarters in Slough organised a Dulux Young Scientist of the Year competition in 2004 involving seven local schools. Teams of pupils completed various experiments and presentations to gain the award.

**Environment:** ICI Paints have also initiated a Community Re-paint scheme to reduce the amount of waste paint going to landfill sites. Under the scheme local householders' unwanted paint is collected and redistributed for use by others in the locality.

Full details of how to apply to the scheme are available at: www.communtyrepaint.org.uk

## Employee-led support

Employees are encouraged to become involved with their local community either through volunteering or fundraising. Additional support may be provided by the company to the benefiting group in recognition of this work.

# Imperial Tobacco Group plc

PO Box 244, Southville, Bristol BS99 7UJ

0117 963 6636; Fax: 0117 988 1492

Website: www.imperial-tobacco.com

Correspondent: Mrs Juliet Hughes, Secretary, Charity Appeals Committee

Chief officer: Derek Bonham

Chief Executive: Gareth Davis

| Year end | Turnover | Pre-tax profit |
|---|---|---|
| 30/09/2005 | £5,191,000,000 | £477,000,000 |

Nature of company business
Tobacco manufacturer.

Subsidiaries include: Sinclair Collis Ltd, Douwe Egberts Van Nelle Tabak

Main locations: Glasgow, Bristol, Liverpool, Nottingham, Ipswich

UK employees: 2,535

Total employees: 14,910

---

### Charitable donations

2005: £984,000
2003: £464,000

Total community contributions: £984,000

Membership: %Club

---

## Community involvement

The vast majority of the company's charitable funding is distributed through the Charities Aid Foundation in accordance with the company's charities policy.

It supports local causes in the communities in which it operates (mainly Bristol, Glasgow, Ipswich, Liverpool and Nottingham) and encourages employee participation in community affairs. There is a preference for supporting causes connected with the arts (sometimes local), education (sometimes local), elderly people, enterprise/training, environment/heritage, medical research, science/technology, sickness/disability charities and social welfare.

### Exclusions

No support for government initiatives, advertising in charity brochures, animal welfare, appeals from individuals, children/youth, fundraising events, overseas projects, religious appeals, or sport.

### Applications

In writing to the correspondent.

## Corporate giving

In 2005 community support totalled £984,000.

## Employee-led support

Employees are encouraged to fundraise and make donations, which are matched by the company.

**Payroll giving:** The company participates in the CAF Give as you Earn scheme.

# In the Pink Leisure Group

44 Queen Street, Blackpool, Lancashire, FY1 2AY

01253 624901; Fax: 01253 649199

Website: www.itpleisure.com

Correspondent: Basil Newby, Managing Director

Managing Director: Basil Newby

| Year end | Turnover | Pre-tax profit |
|---|---|---|
| 30/04/2005 | £813,353 | £7,709 |

Nature of company business
Nightclub and bar ownership.

Main locations: Blackpool

UK employees: 130

Total employees: 130

---

### Charitable donations

2005: £12,549
2004: £23,500

---

## Community involvement

We were advised that there is no set charitable donations policy; all applications are considered on their merit. However, in the past support has been given to Arthritis Care and the Multiple Sclerosis Society. There may also be a preference for animal rescue support and the North West.

### Exclusions

No support for local appeals not in areas of company presence.

### Applications

In writing to the correspondent.

## Corporate giving

The company made charitable donations amounting to £12,549 in 2004/5. (£23,500:2003/04).

# Inchcape plc

22a St James's Square, London SW1Y 5LP

020 7546 0022; Fax: 020 7546 0010

Website: www.inchcape.com

Correspondent: Investor Relations Manager

E-mail: contact@inchcape.com

Chief officer: Peter Johnson

Chief Executive: Andre Lacroix

| Year end | Turnover | Pre-tax profit |
|---|---|---|
| 31/12/2005 | £4,488,100,000 | £177,300,000 |

Nature of company business
Inchcape is a scale automotive retail group operating in Australia, Belgium, Greece, Hong Kong, Singapore and the UK. The group also has operations in a number of other global markets. It represents leading automotive brands and operates either a retail, or a vertically integrated retail model (i.e. exclusive distribution and retail), depending on the market.

Subsidiaries include: Maranello Concessionaires Ltd, Wadham Kenning Motors Group Ltd, Kenning Leaseline Ltd, Autobytel Ltd, Mann Egerton Vehicle Contracts Ltd

Main locations: London, Watford

UK employees: 4,736

Total employees: 10,425

### Charitable donations

2005: £100,000
2003: £100,000

## Community involvement

Inchcape established a corporate social Responsibility (CSR) committee in 2002. The group CSR programme is supplemented locally by a variety of sponsorships, donations and fundraising activities by individual businesses. Wherever possible, the company seeks to involve its employees and business partners in community activities.

### Exclusions

Appeals which do not conform to Inchcape's policy.

### Applications

In writing to the correspondent.

## Corporate giving

In 2005, the company donated £100,000 (2004: £100,000) to charities in the UK, with a further £200,000 (2004: £300,000) being donated globally.

Although we have no details of the beneficiaries, we know that following the tsunami of 2004, Inchcape formed a partnership in 2005 with the charity CARE International (CARE).

### Employee-led support

The company's 2005 annual report states that: 'colleagues are encouraged to become involved in charitable projects at a local level, in order to help the communities in which they operate'.

# Informa plc

4th Floor, 27 Mortimer Street, London W1T 3JF

020 7017 5000

Website: www.informa.com

Correspondent: PA to Keith Brownlie - CR Director

Chief officer: Richard Hooper

Chief Executive: Peter Rigby

Managing Director: David Gilbertson

| Year end | Turnover | Pre-tax profit |
|---|---|---|
| 31/12/2005 | £729,280,000 | £61,045,000 |

Nature of company business
Informa is an international provider of specialist information and services for the academic and scientific, professional and commercial business communities across 40 countries.

Subsidiaries include: IIR, Taylor & Francis Group

Main locations: Weybridge, Colchester, Manchester, Ashford, Glasgow, Abingdon, Victoria, London

Total employees: 7,500

### Charitable donations

2005: £143,000
2004: £24,762
2003: £10,888

## Community involvement

In 2005, Informa formally established a Corporate Responsibility (CR) Committee and have since published a detailed CR report which is available on their website.

They have identified key areas including payroll and company giving; emergency giving for disaster relief; match funding; staff volunteering; community/charity partnerships; and (in conjunction with the Marketplace Committee) providing product discounts for minority and disadvantaged groups. For 2006 the key objectives within the community framework are: To develop a global community initiative and charitable giving policy; and, to explore a number of key partnership opportunities matched to Informa's business competencies and requirements.

The charitable donations made by the company during the year 2005 were principally donated to charities serving the communities in which the group operates. Illustrations of further giving by Informa's staff are given below.

### Exclusions

No support for political appeals.

### Applications

In writing to the correspondent.

## Corporate giving

In 2005, the company made charitable donations of £143,000 (2004: £24,762). We have no information regarding the beneficiaries.

### Employee-led support

As part of the company's CR policy staff are encouraged to volunteer by, for example, participating in the London Triathlon Challenge to raise funds for the 'Run for the Children' initiative. Employees have also entered the UK's Three Peaks Challenge in support of the National Deaf Children's Society, raising £36,000, and organised support for the 2004 tsunami, raising £40,000.

Support has also been given to Book Aid, which provides books to libraries, hospitals and refugee camps and schools in over 40 countries, whilst staff worldwide contribute their time/donations to charities; some case studies are detailed in the company's CR report.

### Commercially-led support

A case study contained in the company's corporate responsibility report for the year ended 31/12/2005 states: 'A charity auction at the Monaco Yacht Show, owned by Informa, ... raised €1,907,000 to fund medical research to help children with Duchenne Muscular Dystrophy. The Monaco Yacht Show hosted the 'Only Watch 05' auction of 34 unique wristwatches with 100% of the funds donated to the charity.'

## Innocent Drinks

Fruit Towers, 3 The Goldhawk Estate, Brakenbury Road, London W6 0BA

Website: www.innocentfoundation.org/

Correspondent: Ms Ailana Kemelmacher, The Innocent Foundation

| Year end | Turnover | Pre-tax profit |
|---|---|---|
| 31/12/2005 | | |

**Nature of company business**
Production of natural fruit drinks.

### Charitable donations

2005: £397,118
2004: £88,704

## Community involvement

The company channels its charitable donations through The Innocent Foundation (Charity Commission no. 1104289), a grant giving charity that works in partnership with community based projects and NGOs. To quote: 'Our vision is to work with local communities to create a sustainable future for people and their environment.'

The company donates 10% of profits to the foundation each year. The majority of the foundation's funding goes to overseas projects. In December 2006, the foundation's website stated that they were not currently giving grants to charities who work within the UK, preferring to send funding to the developing countries it sources its fruit from (at the time of researching this entry the countries were India, Indonesia, Ecuador, Guatemala, Brazil, Colombia and Costa Rica).

### Applications

If you feel that you have a project that might be of interest, please contact the foundation before making a detailed proposal by filling in the short online form.

## Corporate giving

In 2005, charitable donations made by the company to the foundation totalled £397,118 (2004: £88,704). In turn, the foundation made donations of £28,850 in total to six beneficiaries. These included: Send a Cow (£10,000); Find Your Feet (£7,600); and, Groundwork, West London (£1,250).

### Commercially-led support

**Cause-related marketing:** in winter 2006/07, it was hoped that £100,000 would be raised for Age Concern, with 50p donated for every Innocent drink that was sold topped with a special knitted hat.

## Intercontinental Hotels Group plc

67 Alma Road, Windsor, Berkshire SL4 3HD

01753 410100

Website: www.ichotelsgroup.com

Correspondent: Kate Prescott, Charity Sponsorships

Chief officer: David Webster

Managing Director: Richard Hartman

| Year end | Turnover | Pre-tax profit |
|---|---|---|
| 31/12/2005 | £1,910,000,000 | £284,000,000 |

**Nature of company business**
Hospitality chain of hotels, soft drinks and public houses.

**Subsidiaries include:** Britvic Soft Drinks

**Main locations:** Windsor

**Total employees:** 21,986

### Charitable donations

2005: £800,000
2003: £1,420,000

Total community contributions: £936,000

## Community involvement

Intercontinental Hotels focus its charitable giving in the following five areas:

- children
- diversity
- education
- environment
- well-being.

Within this, all donations and sponsorships that the group grants must benefit communities where the company has a presence, and must enhance those communities by providing health and human services, education, arts and culture or community development initiatives.

At corporate level, the group directs all of its annual contributions to a group of carefully selected, major organisations that meet its criteria, and must decline most other requests for funding.

Locally, the group's employees and hotels raise funds and contribute to various organisations through the programmes described elsewhere.

### Exclusions

InterContinental Hotels Group does not direct contributions to: any non-profit organisation that may constitute a conflict of interest for the company or any of its hotel brands; political parties or organisations with political affiliations; individuals seeking personal sponsorships; federal, state or local government organisations; religious organisations, except when the activity being sponsored by a religious organisation is sectarian, such as a food kitchen or shelter.

### Applications

In writing to the correspondent.

Please note that organisations to which the company is asked to contribute must have legal charitable status. Donations must be used for the sole benefit of the eligible institutions and are restricted to the use of the project for which the donation is being made.

## Corporate giving

In 2005, the group made worldwide community contributions of £936,000 of which £800,000 was in cash donations. We do not know what proportion of this was given in the UK.

At corporate level, UNICEF is a major charitable partner of the group.

### In-kind support

The group makes in-kind donations, such as hotel accommodation. As most of the hotels are franchised, such applications should be directed to the general managers of the individual hotels and not to the group.

*Education* – Corporate support for various education-related programmes is also provided, although these appear to be mainly US-based.

### Employee-led support

Employees are encouraged to give their time and skills to a variety of causes. Staff have held 'denim days' with the money raised matched by the company and donated to a charity selected at random from those nominated by the employees taking part.

# Invensys plc

Invensys House, Carlise Place, London SW1P 1BX

020 7834 3848

Website: www.invensys.com

Correspondent: Regina Hitchery, Senior Vice President of Human Resources and Group Services 020 7834 3848

Chief officer: Martin Jay

Chief Executive: Ulf Henriksson

| Year end | Turnover | Pre-tax profit |
|---|---|---|
| 31/03/2005 | £2,923,000,000 | (£500,000,000) |

**Nature of company business**
A leading provider of automation and controls for use in homes, offices and industry.

**Subsidiaries include:** Satchwell Control Systems Ltd, APV UK Limited, Westinghouse Brake & Signal Holdongs Ltd, Eurotherm Limited, Coutant-Lambda Ltd

**Main locations:** London

**Total employees:** 33,987

### Charitable donations

2005: £100,000
2004: £300,000

Membership: BitC

### Exclusions

No support for appeals from individuals, or local appeals not in areas of company presence.

### Applications

In writing to the correspondent.

## Corporate giving

In 2005, the company made cash donations of £100,000 in the UK (£300,000 in 2004). Its donations are reducing each year due to difficult financial circumstances.

### Employee-led support

The company's employees devote time to community fundraising projects in their local community, and receive support from the group wherever possible.

# IPC Media Limited

King's Reach Tower, Stamford Street, London SE1 9LS

0870 444 5000

Website: www.ipcmedia.com

Correspondent: Taryn Barclay, Corporate Responsibility Manager

Chief Executive: Sylvia Auton

| Year end | Turnover | Pre-tax profit |
|---|---|---|
| 31/12/2005 | £412,626,000 | £80,119,000 |

**Nature of company business**
The publication of magazines.

UK employees: 2,120

---

### Charitable donations

2005: £13,403

Membership: L B Group

---

## Community involvement

Following the establishment of the position of corporate responsibility manager in April 2005, IPC Media has looked more closely at its role in the wider community and how it can best be a good corporate citizen.

A member of Business in the Community, the company currently focuses on three areas of activity which involve community engagement, the environment and employee volunteering.

**Charity of the Year:** British Institute for Brain Injured Children.

## Applications

In writing to the correspondent.

## Corporate giving

In 2005, the company declared UK cash donations of £13,403. We do not have a figure for its in-kind support, but believe it to be sufficient to warrant inclusion here.

In keeping with the company's business and its parent company's (Time Warner) focus on youth and arts education, IPC Media's major community initiative is the Schools Design Programme.

Working in association with Creative Partnerships in implementing and managing the programme, local schoolchildren in Southwark benefit from the input of IPC graphic design professionals with the objective of:

- encouraging secondary schoolchildren to view graphic design as a career option
- increasing skills development in the area of graphic design
- providing longer work placements and potential support through higher education
- influencing the skills development of teachers and the way creative arts training is provided in schools
- encouraging the participation of IPC designers in various aspects of the programme.

In 2006, the British Institute for Brain Injured Children (BIBIC) was chosen as IPC's first charity of the year following a company-wide vote. In this inaugural year, BIBIC will be the focus of IPC Media's fundraising efforts for 15 months.

## In-kind support

IPC Media is a key employer in the Roots & Wings Mentoring in the Community Project with which it has been involved since 1995.

IPC staff work with pupils at Northbrook School in Lewisham with the formal relationship between mentor and mentee spanning the full school year.

## Employee-led support

Under the 'Volunteer Release Time' scheme, eligible employees can request up to a maximum of two days' paid time-off per year to participate in voluntary activities.

IPC staff also take part each year in the Time Warner 'Volunteer's Day', which provides the opportunity for staff to help out at a local community organisation.

---

# ITV plc

200 Gray's Inn Road, London WC1X 8XZ

020 7843 8000

**Website:** www.itvplc.com

**Correspondent:** BirgitteTrafford, Communications Director

**Chief officer:** Sir Peter Burt

| Year end | Turnover | Pre-tax profit |
|---|---|---|
| 31/12/2005 | £2,177,000,000 | £311,000,000 |

**Nature of company business**
Independent television company.

**Main locations:** Aberdeen, Bristol, Carlisle, Cardiff, Leeds, Southampton, Plymouth, Glasgow, Norwich, Newcastle, London, Manchester, Birmingham

UK employees: 5,952

---

### Charitable donations

2005: £1,220,000

Total community contributions: £19,580,000
Management costs: £480,000

Membership: BitC, %Club

---

## Community involvement

Formed following the merger between Carlton and Granada television companies, ITV's social investment programme has two strands – airtime donated to good causes, and cash donations made in support of charitable, social and environmental projects.

At regional level, as well as supporting the group's on-air national campaigns, each of the television companies that make up ITV are active in their own communities. The 11 companies comprising ITV plc are: Anglia, Border, Carlton, Central, Granada, HTV, LWT, Meridian, Tyne Tees, West Country and Yorkshire.

With regard to the registered charitable foundations originally established by Carlton and Granada, these still exist, albeit to differing degrees.

The Carlton Television Trust (Charity Commission no. 1019628), was renamed the ITV Trust in August 2005. Formerly reliant upon Carlton Broadcasting Ltd for its income, no donations appear to have been made by the trust since 2004. As at November 2006, we were informed that ITV plc are currently reviewing the situation regarding the trust and that a decision may be taken to wind it up.

The Granada Foundation (Charity Commission no. 241693), although having a distinct preference for supporting the arts, science, education and leisure in the company's North West broadcast region, receives no direct financial or in-kind support from the company. Instead, it is reliant upon income derived from the original donation, made in 1965, and investments made at the discretion of the trustees. As such, it is an independent foundation.

## Applications

Applications for support from the company should be made in writing to the correspondent.

**Information available:** The company produces a corporate social responsibility report.

## Corporate giving

In 2005, the company made total community contributions of £19.6 million of which £1.2 million was in cash. A further £480,000 was expended in management costs. We have no details of the grant beneficiaries.

## In-kind support

Organisations benefiting in 2005 from the company's on-air campaigns/promotions included: The Russell Commission; British Heart Foundation; National Missing Person's Helpline; British Red Cross; and the NSPCC.

## Employee-led support

Staff are encouraged and supported by the company in their volunteering activities.

# Jaguar Cars Ltd

Browns Lane, Allesley, Coventry CV5 9DR

024 7620 2040; Fax: 024 7640 5581

**Website:** www.jaguar.com

**Correspondent:** Les Ratcliffe, Manager, Community Relations
E-mail: lratclif@jaguar.com

| Year end | Turnover | Pre-tax profit |
|----------|----------|----------------|
| 31/12/2004 | | |

**Nature of company business**
The design, development, manufacture and marketing of luxury cars and specialist sports cars.

**Main locations:** Birmingham, Halewood, Merseyside, Coventry

### Charitable donations

2004: £120,318
2003: £108,589

Membership: A & B, BitC, %Club

## Community involvement

The company gives support, through its charitable trust, exclusively for local charities in areas of company presence (Birmingham, Coventry and Halewood – Merseyside) and charities in which a member of staff is involved. Within these geographical constraints, which are strictly adhered to, the company prefers to support organisations concerned with children and youth, education, environment/heritage, sickness/disability, social welfare and sport.

The company will support national charities if they have a local branch, or can in some way benefit the groups' employees and their families.

**Charity of the Year:** The company supports the National Society for the Prevention of Cruelty to Children, the Juvenile Diabetes Research Foundation and BEN (Automotive Benevolent Fund).

## Exclusions

No support is given to fundraising events, advertising in charity brochures, appeals from individuals, purely denominational (religious) appeals, large national appeals or overseas projects.

## Applications

In writing to the correspondent. Decisions are made by a donations committee which meets quarterly.

## Corporate giving

In 2004, the company made donations totalling £120,318.

## In-kind support

The company provides further support through gifts in kind, staff secondments, and joint promotions.

**Education:** The company is involved in local education-business partnerships and operates work experience schemes for pupils.

## Employee-led support

The company allows employees company time off in which to volunteer and provides them with financial help in support of their charitable activities.

**Payroll giving:** The company operates the Jaguar Employee Charities Fund

## Commercially-led support

**Sponsorship:** The group has a preference for prestige sports, arts and similar events. A major objective is to provide hospitality opportunities for dealers, and the group is not necessarily looking for TV exposure or press coverage. Typically, the group will spend up to £5,000 on an event sponsorship, or up to £10,000 on an exhibition. It prefers to be the sole or main sponsor.

Support in previous years has been given to Birmingham Royal Ballet, British Academy of Film & Television Arts, Royal Scottish Opera and the Royal Academy of Arts.

Contact (arts sponsorship): Alan Hodge, Promotions Department. Applicants should note that the group receives up to 15 proposals each day.

# Jardine Lloyd Thompson Group Services

6 Crutched Friars, London EC3N 2HP

020 7528 4444

**Website:** www.jltgroup.com

**Correspondent:** Martin Wakeley

**Chief officer:** Geoffrey Howe

**Chief Executive:** Dominic Burke

| Year end | Turnover | Pre-tax profit |
|----------|----------|----------------|
| 31/12/2005 | | £73,806,000 |

**Nature of company business**
The company is a holding company of an international group of insurance broking companies and a Lloyd's members' agency.

**Subsidiaries include:** Agnew Higgins Pickering & Co Ltd, JIB Group plc

Main locations: London

> **Charitable donations**
>
> 2005: £462,000
> 2004: £430,000
> 2003: £246,000
>
> Membership: BitC

## Community involvement

'Our community programme encourages staff to actively volunteer, to 'get involved' by helping the communities in which we operate.'

### Exclusions

No grants for fundraising events, advertising in charity brochures, appeals from individuals or large national appeals.

### Applications

In writing to the correspondent. The Charities Committee meets four times a year.

## Corporate giving

In 2005 the group made charitable donations of £462,000.

### In-kind support

Each year employees are given a 'Charity Day' during which they can spend company time either directly working with a charity or using their time in helping the local community.

### Employee-led support

The company will match pound for pound any amount raised by employees in fundraising activities they undertake for charity up to a maximum of £5,000.

**Payroll giving:** The company operates a Give as you Earn scheme.

# Jarvis plc

Meridian House, The Crescent, York, YO24 1AW

01904 712712

Website: www.jarvisplc.com

Correspondent: Toni Jackson, Communications Manager
07921 939 031
E-mail: toni.jackson@jarvis-uk.com

Chief officer: Steven Norris

Chief Executive: Richard Entwistle

| Year end | Turnover | Pre-tax profit |
|---|---|---|
| 31/03/2006 | £1,076,000,000 | £23,800,000 |

Nature of company business
The holding company for the Jarvis Group of companies, the principal activities of which are infrastructure services and facilities management; projects and construction; and property development and investment.

Subsidiaries include: Techspan Systems plc, Prismo Ltd, On Track Plant Ltd, Laybond Holdings Ltd

Main locations: York

Total employees: 5,611

> **Charitable donations**
>
> 2004: £57,000
> 2003: £30,000

## Community involvement

The company has previously supported the Prince's Trust and Children Nationwide. Decisions regarding which charities to support are made every 1 to 2 years.

### Exclusions

We are not aware of any exclusions.

### Applications

In writing to the correspondent.

## Corporate giving

In 2005/6, the company's charitable donations amounted to £36,000 (2004/5:£78000). We have no details of the recipient organisation/s.

# JJB Sports plc

Martland Park, Challenge Way, Wigan, Lancashire  WN5 0LD

01942 221400; Fax: 01942 629809

Website: www.jjbcorporate.co.uk

Correspondent: Charity and Sponsorship Requests, Head Office

Chief officer: Roger Lane-Smith

Chief Executive: Tom Knight

| Year end | Turnover | Pre-tax profit |
|---|---|---|
| 29/01/2006 | £745,238,000 | £33,747,000 |

Nature of company business
The principal activity of the group is the retail of sportswear and sports equipment. The group also operates a separate leisure division which operates health clubs and indoor soccer centres.

Main locations: Aberdeen, Luton, Milton Keynes, Wrexham, Blackburn, Truro

Total employees: 11,564

> **Charitable donations**
>
> 2005: £26,000
> 2004: £64,000
> 2003: £9,500

## Community involvement

JJB operates from approximately 430 retail stores nationwide. The group also operates a leisure division which comprises health clubs and soccerdomes. The group's charitable giving centres around commercially led support and their annual Charity Golf Day.

JJB Group plc have produced a social responsibility report which states: 'The Group provides a valuable service to the communities in which it operates by supplying a wide range of competitively priced clothing, footwear and accessories through its retail stores ... '

## Exclusions

We do not know of any specific exclusions.

## Applications

In writing to the contact.

## Corporate giving

The group made charitable donations of £26,000 during the year 2005 (2004: £65,000). We have no details of the beneficiaries.

### In-kind support

JJB's indoor soccer centres are available free of charge to local schools during school hours.

### Employee-led support

The group lends its support to staff taking part in various charitable fundraising activities.

Management and staff from JJB's golf department gave support to the Variety Club Children's Charity appeal through organising an annual charity golf tournament which raised £135,000; this was sufficient to purchase nine Sunshine Coaches. During the last six years that the event has taken place, a total of 31 coaches have been purchased from this fundraising tournament.

### Commercially-led support

**Sponsorship:** *health* The group participated in the Macmillan Cancer Relief football badge campaign. For the year ending 29th January 2006, total donations of around £65,000 were raised by customers and staff.

During the same year the group was associated with the 'Stand Up, Speak Up' campaign, which is an initiative to create a fund which will support anti-racist projects and initiatives across Europe. Approximately £1.24 m was raised by the group through the sale of wrist bands to staff and customers.

The leisure division of the group nominated the British Heart Foundation as its chosen charity partner and to date £18,000 has been raised through the sale of BHF locker tokens within JJB's health clubs.

# S C Johnson Ltd

Frimley Green, Camberley, Surrey GU15 5AJ

01276 852000; Fax: 01276 852412

**Website:** www.scjohnson.co.uk

**Correspondent:** Jan Jewers, Consumer and Community Affairs Manager

| Year end | Turnover | Pre-tax profit |
|---|---|---|
| 30/06/2005 | £135,574,000 | £4,158,000 |

**Nature of company business**
The company manufactures waxes, polishes and cleaning products for the consumer and industrial markets.

**Main locations:** Frimley Green, Egham

**Total employees:** 75

**Charitable donations**
2005: £178,000
2004: £180,000
2003: £210,000

## Community involvement

'SC Johnson believes in contributing to the well being of the countries and communities where we conduct business and here in the UK we involve ourselves with health, education and environmental programmes.'

A request can be made by an organisation or project that:

- is not for profit
- meets a clear social need in the community (local or national)
- has a broad base of support within the community (local or national)
- would reflect favourably on the public image of the company
- has clearly stated, measurable and attainable objectives
- benefits a broad cross-section of the local community, including company employees and their families
- is supported by employees through volunteerism or financial contributions.

Most contributions are directed towards the local communities around its two sites at Frimley Green and Egham, where the majority of its employees and their families live. Smaller amounts go to uk-wide programmes.

The following organisations have recently benefited from the company's charitable giving:

*Health related charities:*

Frimley Park Hospital

Phyllis Tuckwell Hospice, Farnham

Hearing Dogs for Deaf People

Blackwater Valley Alzheimer's Society

Children with Special Needs Foundation

The Beacon Trust

*Schools/education related charities:*

Children's Safety Education Foundation

Resolve & Solve It

Support for pre-schools, infant, primary and secondary in the company's local areas

*Environment related charities:*

Blackwater Valley Countryside Trust

Tongham Wood Improvement Group

Surrey in Bloom

Wildscreen

## Exclusions

'A request falls outside of our corporate guidelines if it:

- benefits a single individual
- is an individual raising money for a charity
- is for another country
- is for attendance at a charity dinner, conference and so on
- is samples for gift bags or other marketing uses
- is payroll giving

- is in conflict with the interests of the company
- duplicates the services of another organisation or project already existing in the community
- duplicates a previous donation made within 12 months.'

## Applications

In writing to the correspondent.

## Corporate giving

In 2004/5, the company donated £178,000 to charitable causes. (2003/04: £180,000).

## In-kind support

Product donations are made, usually in the form of vouchers.

## Employee-led support

The company matches monies raised by employees. The company runs an annual one day event where volunteers from the workforce work on projects in the local community. For the 'Community Day' 2006, 180 volunteers worked at ten local schools helping to create outdoor classrooms and improve outdoor and indoor areas.

# Johnson Matthey plc

40–42 Hatton Garden, London EC1N 8EE

020 7269 8400; Fax: 020 7269 8433

Website: www.matthey.com

Correspondent: I Godwin, Corporate Communications Manager
E-mail: godwini@matthey.com

Chief officer: Sir John Banham

Chief Executive: N A P Carson

| Year end | Turnover | Pre-tax profit |
|---|---|---|
| 31/03/2006 | £4,756,000,000 | £219,800,000 |

Nature of company business
Johnson Matthey is a chemicals company focused on its core skills in catalysts, precious metals and speciality chemicals.

Subsidiaries include: Cascade Biochem Ltd, Avocado Research Chemicals Ltd

Main locations: Enfield, Fenton, Hanley, Clitheroe, Cambridge, Newcastle upon Tyne, London, Heysham, Wallsend, Swindon, Royston, Sheffield, Reading

Total employees: 7,404

## Charitable donations

2005: £340,000
2004: £279,000
2003: £323,000

Membership: BitC

## Community involvement

'Johnson Matthey has a long history of support for charitable causes aligned to issues to which the Johnson Matthey business makes a contribution and issues on which employees are passionate.

'The company's active and wide ranging donations programme encompasses medical research, education, care for the disabled and young people's charities as well as a number of worldwide community action programmes.

'Many employees contribute their own time, effort and money to support local community projects and annually, Johnson Matthey adopts a Charity of the Year which provides a focus for staff support and fundraising.'

### Johnson Matthey plc Educational Trust

The Johnson Matthey plc Educational Trust (Charity Commission no. 313576) and the company appear to be closely linked, with the chairman of the trust being a director of the company. The expenses of the trust are met by Johnson Matthey plc.

The objects of the trust are as follows:

1) provision of financial or other assistance for the education or training of children, students or trainees whose parents are connected to the precious metals industry

2) establishment of professorships, lectureships or other teaching posts

3) promotion of research into any scientific or academic subject

4) general promotion and advancement of education.

Applications are invited for scholarships. Student awards are usually paid for three years. The trust currently makes awards to 50 university students. In 2004/05 the trust had an income of £24,500 and a total expenditure of £43,000.

## Exclusions

No support for advertising in charity brochures, appeals from individuals, political appeals or religious appeals.

## Applications

In writing to the correspondent. A donations committee meets quarterly.

**Note:** Charitable donating is reviewed in March each year to set the programme for the following financial year, beginning in April. Please check for details of current areas of support.

## Corporate giving

In 2005/06 the company donated £340,000 to charitable causes.

## In-kind support

**Enterprise:** The company has supported enterprise agencies in the past. It is also a primary sponsor of the Prince of Wales Business Leaders Forum.

## Employee-led support

**Charity of the Year:** Help the Aged (2006/07).

For its 2005/06 Charity of the Year, Breakthrough Breast Cancer, Johnson Matthey staff raised £35,000.

## Commercially-led support

**Sponsorship:** *The arts* – The company's arts programme has included sponsorship of Glyndebourne Festival Opera, Monteverdi Trust, National Gallery and Royal Opera House.

# Johnson Service Group plc

Mildmay Road, Bootle, Merseyside L20 5EW

0151 933 6161; Fax: 0151 922 8089

Website: www.johnsonplc.com

Correspondent: c/o The Donations Committee

E-mail: enquiries@johnsonplc.com

Chief officer: Simon Sherrrard

Chief Executive: Stuart Graham

| Year end | Turnover | Pre-tax profit |
|---|---|---|
| 27/12/2005 | £431,900,000 | £15,700,000 |

Nature of company business
The company is principally engaged in workwear, towel and linen rental nationwide, corporate hospitality services, garment sourcing and manufacturing and the provision of washroom services, drycleaning and other associated services in Great Britain. The company also offers facilities management services and supplies consumables to the drycleaning and laundry market.

Subsidiaries include: CCM Ltd, Hospitality Services, Workplace Management

Main locations: Bootle

UK employees: 7,767

### Charitable donations

2005: £41,000
2003: £37,902

## Community involvement

Previously the company has informed us that charitable donations are largely arranged at local level through operating subsidiaries. Preference is given to charities in the fields of children and youth, social welfare, environment and heritage.

In May 2006 the company's website stated: 'The Johnson Service Group is acutely aware of its responsibilities to the communities in which it operates, and from which both its customers and employees are drawn. We are committed to progressively embedding corporate social responsibility best practice into every aspect of our operations. The group and its individual operating companies seek to be good neighbours, and work in partnership with our people to help their local communities.'

## Exclusions

No support for circular appeals, appeals from individuals, religious appeals, local appeals not in areas of company presence, large national appeals or overseas projects.

## Applications

In writing to the correspondent.

## Corporate giving

In 2005, the group made charitable donations totalling £41,000. Of this, £19,000 was donated to its major charitable partner, Macmillan Cancer Relief, as a result of the return and re-use of clothes hangers. Other contributions are mainly made to local charities serving the communities in which the group operates.

There is a grant-making trust (The Johnson Group Cleaners' Charity) administered from the same address as the company. It receives most of its income from dividends on shares in the company, but does not appear to receive direct donations. It restricts its giving to the Merseyside area and to local registered charities dedicated to improving the well-being of the sick and the underprivileged.

Further details can be found in *A Guide to Local Trusts in the North of England* published by DSC.

# Jones Lang LaSalle UK

22 Hanover Square, London W1A 2BN

020 7493 6040; Fax: 020 7408 0220

Website: www.joneslanglasalle.co.uk

Correspondent: (see applications section)

| Year end | Turnover | Pre-tax profit |
|---|---|---|
| 31/12/2005 | | |

Nature of company business
Provision of real estate consultancy services.

Main locations: Edinburgh, Glasgow, Leeds, London, Manchester, Norwich, Birmingham

### Charitable donations

Total community contributions: £155,000
Membership: BitC, %Club

## Community involvement

The company has previously stated: 'Jones Lang LaSalle and its employees provide generous financial and other support to many worthwhile community programmes.' Areas of support included children's causes, education, older people's organisations, vocational training, environmental and heritage concerns, medical research, science, welfare, disability and sports. It has offices in Birmingham, Edinburgh, Glasgow, Leeds, Manchester, Norwich and across London and it is likely that preference will be given to these areas.

## Exclusions

No grants for: animal welfare; the arts; overseas projects; religious or political work; or for the benefit of one individual.

## Applications

Contact your nearest office for further information.

## Corporate giving

In 2005 the global figure for charitable contributions was £155,000.

## Employee-led support

**Payroll giving**: The company participates in the Gift Aid Give As You Earn scheme.

## Commercially-led support

The company is prepared to advertise in charity brochures.

# Kaupthing Singer & Friedlander Limited

One Hanover Street, London W1S 1AX

020 3205 5000; Fax: 020 3205 5001

Website: www.singer-friedlander.com

Correspondent: David Griffiths, Personnel Director

Chief officer: S Einarsson

Chief Executive: A Thorvaldsson

| Year end | Turnover | Pre-tax profit |
| --- | --- | --- |
| 31/12/2005 | | £12,856,000 |

Nature of company business
The group companies are involved in merchant banking, investment banking, stockbroking, investment management and property investment.

Subsidiaries include: Hillgrove Developments Ltd, Peninsular Park Developments Ltd, Gilbert Estates Ltd, Quinarius Investments Ltd, Collins Stewart Ltd, Straker Brothers Ltd, Ancomass Ltd, Sinjul Investments Ltd, Peaston Emerson's Green Ltd, Rowan & Co Ltd, Sharepart Ltd, Millwalk Ltd

Main locations: London, Manchester, Nottingham, Isle of Man, Leeds, Glasgow, Dorking, Birmingham

UK employees: 535

### Charitable donations

2005: £52,445
2004: £75,000
2003: £60,000

Membership: BitC

## Community involvement

Singer & Friedlander Group plc were acquired in July 2005 by Kaupthing Holdings UK Limited, a subsidiary of Kaupthing Bank hf, the largest bank in Iceland.

Previously the company had stated that: 'We actively contribute to the well being of the community by seeking to cater for the needs of all groups. We support social, medical, cultural and educational projects that place particular emphasis on supporting the under-privileged within society.'

### Exclusions

No support for local appeals not in areas of company presence.

### Applications

In writing to the correspondent.

## Corporate giving

In 2005, charitable donations totalled £52,445 (2004: £75,000). We have no details of the beneficiaries.

### Employee-led support

Employees are encourages to submit requests for support in which they are involved.

# Kelda Group plc

Western House, Halifax Road, Bradford BD6 2LZ

01274 691111; Fax: 01274 372863

Website: www.keldagroup.com

Correspondent: Anne Reed, Community Affairs Manager
01274 692515; Fax: 01274 372836
E-mail: anne.reed@yorkshirewater.co.uk

Chief officer: John Napier

| Year end | Turnover | Pre-tax profit |
| --- | --- | --- |
| 31/03/2006 | £929,600,000 | £248,200,000 |

Nature of company business
The principal activities of the group are the supply of clean water and the treatment and disposal of waste water.

Subsidiaries include: Ridings Insurance Co Ltd, 3C Waste, WasteNotts Ltd, Arbre Energy Ltd, Yorkshire Environmental Solutions Ltd, Derbyshire Waste Ltd, BDR Waste Disposal Ltd

Main locations: Bradford

UK employees: 2,129

Total employees: 3,669

### Charitable donations

2006: £500,000
2005: £500,000
2004: £500,000
2003: £600,000

Membership: A & B, BitC

## Community involvement

Kelda Group provided the following statement (abridged) regarding its community support:

'The Kelda Group has an extensive community support programme in place. Company policy has moved away from financial donations and towards volunteering, skills sharing, mentoring and gifts in kind, because we believe [these] provide more benefits in terms of building good community relations and staff development opportunities.

'We have a large volunteering programme and, as a formal aspiration of our company vision, aim to be a national role model for volunteering by 2010. [Currently], 31% of our workforce is involved in in-house volunteering programmes.'

The group also funds an independent Yorkshire Water Community Trust (Charity Commission no. 1047923). This trust writes off the water bills of individuals who do not have the means to pay for the services and does not support organisations.

### Applications

In writing to the correspondent.

Information available: The company produce a corporate social responsibility report which is downloadable from its website.

## Corporate giving

In 2005/06, the company made matched donations of £500,000 in support of employees fundraising efforts. Direct grants are no longer given by the group. Yorkshire Water

Community Trust has an income and an expenditure of around £300,000 a year.

## In-kind support

Through in-house volunteering programmes, opportunities exist for staff to take part in: Cares Challenges; GCSE mentoring; primary school mentoring; Halifax Rugby After School Club; Right to Read; Science & Engineering Ambassadors; WaterWheelers; Leeds United Learning Centre; Numbers partners; Business Bridge mentoring; and, Business Dynamics.

*Cool Schools* – A Yorkshire Water campaign, which has provided over 1,000 free water coolers to around 600 primary and secondary schools in Yorkshire at a cost of over £400,000. To encourage the pupils to use the machines, each school has also received educational support material and a visit from a rap artist to encourage them to drink water.

*Cares at Christmas* – This initiative involves employees donating unwanted toys and gifts for distribution throughout the region to groups of deprived individuals.

## Employee-led support

Employees are allowed time off in which to volunteer. The company matches employee fundraising to a maximum of £9,000 a year in respect of WaterAid, a charity which works to provide clean water and sanitation in the under-developed world.

Yorkshire Water employees have founded their own group, WaterWheelers, which organises fundraising events with the income donated to local organisations. The fundraising effort is matched by the company, to a maximum of £5,000. Since it was formed in 1995, over £150,000 has been donated from the fund to local organisations.

Further information on the company's employee volunteering programme is available on request, or by visiting the community pages of Yorkshire Water's website at: www.yorkshirewater.co.uk

**Payroll giving:** The Worlplace Giving UK scheme is operated, to which 6% of the employees subscribe. Although donations are made principally to WaterAid, any registered charity may be nominated by an employee. Up to April 2005, nearly £135,000 had been raised on behalf of over 100 local and national charities. The company covers the associated admin fee normally deducted from employee's donations under the scheme. This equates to around £1,500 a year.

## Commercially-led support

**Sponsorship:** Good-cause sponsorship is undertaken providing it links to the company's current public relations campaign and company vision.

Contact: Anne Reed, Community Affairs Manager.

**Cause-related marketing:** A joint promotion has been run with the Right to Read Campaign.

# Kellogg's

The Kellogg Building, Talbot Road, Manchester M16 0PU

0161 869 2000

Website: www.kelloggs.co.uk

**Correspondent:** Community & Public Affairs Director, Community Affairs Team 0161 869 2226; Fax: 0161 869 2246 E-mail: communityaffairs@kellogg.com

| Year end | Turnover | Pre-tax profit |
|---|---|---|
| 31/12/2005 | £833,074,000 | £63,437,000 |

**Nature of company business**
The principal activity of the group is the manufacture, marketing and sale of cereal-based food products.

**Main locations:** Wrexham, Manchester

**Total employees:** 2,230

### Charitable donations

2005: £548,000
2004: £449,000
2003: £432,132

Total community contributions: £804,000 2003

Membership: BitC, L B Group, %Club

## Community involvement

The company focuses its resources, on local, regional and national organisations that are working in partnership with others to improve the quality of life for those at greatest disadvantage. Details of the company's partnerships and their joint achievements can be found on their website. The Kellogg's Community Affairs programme is primarily delivered by the community affairs team, based at the UK and European headquarters in Trafford, Manchester.

The company is committed to involvement in the communities in which it operates, recognising this as an important element of good corporate citizenship. The focus of its community involvement programme is mainly the areas around its manufacturing sites in Trafford Park and Wrexham, and its European headquarters in Old Trafford, Manchester. The communities of Old Trafford, Moss Side and Hulme, Wythenshawe and Wrexham are the principal beneficiaries of its local commitment.

Kellogg's Active Living Community Fund makes small donations to support activities, projects and organisations that actually promote sustained low cost participation in physical exercise for those people who need it most. A panel of Kellogg employees meets every month to assess applications for funding. The fund is not intended to support the running costs of existing sports clubs or to pay for resources where the panel consider it is the responsibility of statutory providers to pay for those resources. The fund will not support projects or activities that aim to promote sporting excellence.

Kellogg's will make donations of up to £1,000 from this fund but will only fund activities or projects where the donation makes a significant impact. For example they would consider donating £1,000 to a £2,000 project but not £1,000 to a £10,000 project. The priority areas are those local to company presence and those in greatest social need.

Kellogg's excellent community website (www.kelloggs.co.uk/community/) provides wide-ranging information on its programmes, partners, areas of priority and how to apply. There are also details of past beneficiaries and updated news from the Kellogg's Community Team.

### Exclusions

Donations will not normally be given to circular appeals, advertising in charity brochures, animal welfare, appeals from individuals, the arts, fundraising events, medical research, overseas projects, political appeals, religious appeals, science/technology, or able-bodied sport.

## Applications

All applications for support should be addressed to the Kellogg Community Affairs Team at the Talbot Road offices. Applications should be in writing either by e-mail or post. Applications should include the following:

- a brief description of your organisation
- a brief description of how you would spend the donation
- who the donation will benefit, e.g. teenagers, disabled people, elderly people
- where the beneficiaries live, e.g. Manchester, Wrexham or, if applicable, a specific location such as Old Trafford
- who the cheque should be payable to.

*All applicants should read the information on the Community Affairs page of the website before they apply for help.*

The application process for the fund is designed to be quick, simple and applicant friendly. Kellogg's have reduced the need for supporting information to an absolute minimum, and endeavour to reply to all applicants within six weeks. However, due to the large number of applications received, Kellogg's are unable to explain their decisions or provide feedback to unsuccessful applicants. Please refer to the website for further details and advice.

## Corporate giving

Total community contributions in 2005, were £804,000 (2004: £1,256,000) of which cash donations accounted for £548,000 (2004: £449,000).

Although most of the larger sums of money are 'locked up' in relationships with long-term partner organisations, the company will consider new applications for support. For smaller amounts of money the company's Active Living Community Fund is open to local charities and voluntary organisations all year round.

## In-kind support

Kellogg's has a dedicated community affairs team that offers significant time and expertise to partner organisations. Although this time is largely committed to existing partnerships, the company is always happy to consider new requests for support.

Other 'in kind' support includes the expertise and time of other Kellogg's employees, access to facilities and premises, and, occasionally, surplus office equipment and furniture.

## Employee-led support

The group supports charitable activities by employees in their own time. In particular, it operates an employee matching scheme where the company matches pound for pound, to a maximum of £500 (or £1,000 if a group of employees participate) funds raised by employees for charities of their choice.

## Commercially-led support

**Sponsorship:** Kellogg's Nationwide Rice Krispies Multi-Grain Roadshow featuring the KidTribes Hoop Hop Challenge. The Hoop Hop Roadshow was a partnership between Kellogg's, KidTribe (who developed Hoop Hop) and the educational charity Contin You. Kellogg's has also been working with Contin You since 1997 to promote the use of Breakfast Clubs in schools throughout the UK. In 2005 the partnership launched Breakfast Club Movers which helps existing clubs to include physical activity as part of their timetables.

'Personal Best' is a two year partnership between Kellogg's and Manchester City Council to help people become more active. In 2005 over 100 people who were at risk of suffering ill health took part in the programme and completed the Greater Manchester 10k run.

Another Kellogg's partnership, with Wrexham Borough Council encourages young people to take up sports coaching and has won the Local Sports Programme of the year award for 2005. The programme gives young people the chance to gain coaching qualifications in return for volunteering their time.

Kellogg's Corn Flakes Great Walk 2005 which has travelled from John-o-Groats to Lands End to encourage people to walk to get fit. Thousands have taken part, many using the walks to raise money for a variety of charities.

Kellogg's has also announced a £3m partnership with the Amateur Swimming Association which will feature an awards scheme, a Swim Active, (to encourage non-swimmers) and Team Kellogg's which will sponsor 10 young swimmers by providing their coaching and travel fees.

# Kimberly-Clark Europe Ltd

Beech House, 35 London Road, Reigate, Surrey, RH2 9PZ

01737 736000; Fax: 01737 736600

Website: kimberly-clark.com

Correspondent: Joanna Lund

E-mail: joanna.lund@kcc.com

Chief officer: R W Huggins

Managing Director: Ian Jones

| Year end | Turnover | Pre-tax profit |
|---|---|---|
| 31/12/2004 | £577,307,000 | £30,198,000 |

Nature of company business
The principal activity is the manufacture and marketing of tissue products for household, commercial, institutional and industrial uses, and related products.

Main locations: Barrow-in-Furness, Barton-upon-Humber, Northfleet, Flint

UK employees: 1,967

### Charitable donations

Membership: BitC

## Community involvement

No information regarding Kimberly-Clark's UK community support policy was available on its global website. However, we were previously advised that the following causes would normally be considered for support: animal welfare; the arts; children/youth; education; elderly; enterprise/training; environment/heritage; and sickness/disability charities. Appeals will only be considered where there is a company presence, i.e. near office and mill locations.

## Exclusions

No support for circular appeals, advertising in charity brochures, appeals from individuals, fundraising events, large national appeals, medical research, overseas projects, political appeals, religious appeals, science/technology, social welfare or sport.

## Applications

In writing to the correspondent.

# Corporate giving

Kimberly-Clark's community contributions have previously totalled around £350,000. No recent information was available on the current level of financial support to charities. The company's European environmental report does give some examples of organisations supported by the company in the UK, although these are slightly dated. Nevertheless, they include environmental work at Red Pit Wood near the Flint site, the creation of a garden with disabled access at a church local to the Barrow site, and support for the Partners in Leadership scheme.

The Barton facility remained active in the community in 2005. Employees continued to partner with radio station Viking FM's charity committee to raise funds for the charity, For the Kids, an organisation dedicated to helping children in crisis.

## In-kind support

Non-cash support is given through secondments and gifts in kind.

## Employee-led support

Employees have volunteered their time and skills to a variety of organisations, such as the North East Lincolnshire Strategic Leadership Group, a local child centre, and the Common Purpose Programme in Humberside.

Employees' fundraising receives matched funding from the company, which also allows staff time off in which to volunteer.

**Payroll giving:** The Give As You Earn scheme is in operation.

## Commercially-led support

**Sponsorship:** *The arts* – the company undertakes arts sponsorship.

# Kingfisher plc

3 Sheldon Square, Paddington, London, W2 6PX

020 7372 8008; Fax: 0 20 7644 1001

Website: www.kingfisher.co.uk

Correspondent: Ray Baker, Director of Social Responsibilty
E-mail: social.responsibility@kingfisher.com

Chief officer: Sir Francis Mackay

Chief Executive: Gerry Murphy

| Year end | Turnover | Pre-tax profit |
| --- | --- | --- |
| 28/01/2006 | £8,010,100,000 | £231,800,000 |

## Nature of company business
The group trades principally as home improvement, electrical and furniture and general merchandise retailers with stores in the UK, Continental Europe and the rest of the world. In addition, the group has extensive interests in property, which are actively managed in the UK through Chartwell Land.

**Subsidiaries include:** B & Q plc, Chartwell Land plc, MVC Entertainment Ltd, Time Retail Finance Ltd, Superdrug Stores plc, Comet Group plc, Halcyon Finance Ltd, Entertainment UK Ltd, VCI plc

**Main locations:** Middlesex, London, Croydon, Eastleigh, Harrow, Hull, Hayes, Leeds

UK employees: 64,320

## Charitable donations

2006: £300,000
2005: £300,000
2004: £500,000
2003: £700,000

Total community contributions: £1,400,000

Membership: BitC

# Community involvement

The company's website states: 'As a rule, Kingfisher will not consider unregistered UK charities as part of its annual sponsorship programme. This is because charities registered with the Charity Commission work to a set of legal and regulatory standards and requirements which are monitored by the Commission.

'From time to time, Kingfisher may enter in an agreement with an organisation linked to a government department or statutory authority. If this is the case, any funding which we give should not be used to replace that which is provided through public funds and evidence of additional benefits to people or communities must be given.

'Kingfisher will only select a small number of charities to support via our cash fund. These will be approved by the Director of Governance and Corporate Services and/or the Director of Social Responsibility and will be reviewed on an annual basis (Kingfisher financial year) to ensure a broad range of charities and issues are taken into account.

'Kingfisher also supports a selection of charities through its corporate centre fundraising activities. These charities are agreed by the Fundraising Committee (comprising representatives from Social Responsibility, HR & Communications) and are reviewed on an annual basis (Kingfisher financial year) to ensure a broad range of charities and issues are taken into account.

'The only exceptions to this annual review are Poppy Appeal, Children in Need and Comic Relief which are ongoing appeals. Kingfisher Communications also coordinates one-off fundraising activities e.g. for relief for victims of the tsunami.'

In 2005/06, Kingfisher chose the following organisations as its 'charity partners': Save the Children; Motivation; Action for Blind People; Juvenile Diabetes Research Foundation; and, Community Payback.

Donations can be made in cash, or in gift vouchers towards store purchases.

In addition to Kingfisher's giving, its operating companies have their own charity policies and nominated charities. For more information on B&Q UK's charity policies and nominated charities please visit the B&Q UK website.

## Exclusions

As policy, the company will not support the following:

- charity advertising space, unless specifically linked to a Kingfisher-funded project
- arts projects
- expeditions, overseas trips or adventure experiences for individuals
- support for political parties or political causes
- promotion of specific religious ideas or views
- support for religious bodies, except where the project is for the benefit of the general public and wider community
- year end deficits
- support for, or personal appeals by or on behalf of, individuals
- a charity's core costs, including buildings, salaries general running or management costs
- individual overseas projects not linked to our current partners
- anything that would replace funds provided by government or statutory authorities, and that does not bring additional benefits to people or communities.

### Applications

In writing to the correspondent.

For the B&Q 'You Can Do It' scheme, application forms are available from 29 January – 30 March 2007 on B&Q's website www.diy.com/awards or by telephoning the 24 hour application line on 0845 300 1001 (please note that this number is not available to take calls outside of this period).

Further details of how to apply for the 'Better Neighbour Grant Scheme' are also available on B&Q's website. Although there is no closing date, funds are allocated to each store in February, so early application is advised.

## Corporate giving

In 2005/06, community contributions totalled £1.4 million, including £300,000 given in cash donations.

### B&Q

Donations policy: B&Q do not make cash donations, but instead operate a 'Better Neighbour Grant Scheme' through which local organisations can apply directly to their local B&Q store for help (the project must be within a 20-mile radius of the store). This is given in the way of materials to local schools, community groups and charitable organisations. Each of its 325 stores has a budget of £1,000 for such purposes and would normally offer 'grants' of between £50 and £500 (at retail cost) per project.

Further material support is available to projects under the 'You Can Do It' scheme. Only 20 awards are offered each year to the value of £5,000 each.

All stores offer waste materials and unsaleable goods to local projects i.e. off cuts of timber, slightly damaged tins of paint, odd rolls of wallcoverings and so on.

### In-kind support

Kingfisher provides a voucher scheme which is designed to support small requests from local charities and community organisations e.g. requests for raffle prizes.

### Employee-led support

Kingfisher offers various schemes to support personal fundraising. Employees may be involved in personal fundraising activities for charities that do not meet the company guidelines for the charities that it will support.

Volunteering – from February 2007, Kingfisher will allow corporate centre employees to spend one paid day per year volunteering for a charitable organisation.

Through the 'Double It' matched funding scheme, money that Kingfisher employees raise for a charity or good cause can potentially be matched pound for pound by Kingfisher, up to £500.

**Payroll giving:** Employees can choose to contribute to charities of their choice through a pay roll giving scheme. Employees nominate an amount of money to be taken directly from their salary each month, tax free, and paid to their chosen charity.

### Commercially-led support

**Sponsorship:** Sponsorship to encourage young people with the ambition and ability to succeed can be given.

# Kodak Ltd

PO Box 66, Station Road, Hemel Hempstead, Hertfordshire HP1 1JU

01442 261122; Fax: 01442 844623

**Website:** www.kodak.co.uk

**Correspondent:** Barbara O'Halloran, Sponosroship Co-ordinator 020 8950 0815; Fax: 020 8950 7886
E-mail: kodsponsorship@aol.com

| Year end | Turnover | Pre-tax profit |
| --- | --- | --- |
| 31/12/2004 | £438,100,000 | £6,000,000 |

**Nature of company business**
Principal activities are the manufacture, supply and distribution of photographic film, paper, chemicals, digital imaging equipment, together with services associated with these activities. The company is a wholly owned subsidiary of the Eastman Kodak Company.

**Subsidiaries include:** Miller Bros Hall & Co Ltd, Cinesite Ltd, Taylors Developing & Printing Works Ltd

**Main locations:** Hemel Hempstead, Kirkby, Harrow, Annesley

**UK employees:** 4,336

### Charitable donations

2004: £90,707
2003: £210,195

Membership: BitC

## Community involvement

The Directors' Report contained in the 2004 report states: 'Kodak Limited and our parent company Eastman Kodak Company, has always taken an active stance in its approach to charitable programmes and local community support and involvement.

'As well as a major corporate contributor to UNICEF (Save the Children), Breakthrough Cancer and The Prince's Trust, Kodak also supports a wide number of local community programmes and charities. ... Kodak Limited is a member of 'Business in the Community' ... Through this involvement we hope to develop and strengthen our community support programmes even further with greater direct involvement with local communities, not only through direct financial support, but through employee volunteer programmes and effective links with local education and school programmes.'

## Exclusions

Kodak does not support advertising in charity brochures, purely denominational appeals, large national appeals, purely local appeals not in areas of company presence, appeals from individuals, overseas projects or circulars.

## Applications

All appeals, including local appeals, should be sent to the correspondent.

**Advice to applicants:** The company welcomes appeals from charities, but it is receiving a large amount of mail. Applicants should therefore take note of the main areas of interest of the company as stated above.

Whilst this is a fair comment, we believe the provision of fuller and up-to-date information by the company would enable charities to more accurately ascertain if support is likely to be considered in the first place.

## Corporate giving

Charitable donations including those for scientific educational and research purposes in the UK in 2004 were £90,707 (2003: £210,195).

## In-kind support

Kodak may donate products for raffle prizes, provide the use of premises for meetings, or help with graphic reproduction. It has helped UNICEF by donating a range of services including co-branding of picture CD packing and processing envelopes, on-line Christmas card collaboration and photo magic card initiatives.

**Education:** The offices in Harrow and Chalon coordinate at least four research fellowships each year, supporting individuals financially for three years during their PhD studies as well as collaborating between the university staff and group scientists and allowing the beneficiaries to present the results of their studies to the company's research and development centre.

## Employee-led support

Employees are encouraged to fundraise on behalf of charities.

## Commercially-led support

The company has sponsored Breakthrough Breast Cancer's Breakthrough £1,000 Challenge for a number of years. The event challenges individuals, groups and teams to raise £1,000 for the organisation's work a challenge which has been accepted by many of the company's employees.

# KPMG

8 Salisbury Square, London EC4Y 8BB

020 7311 1000; Fax: 020 7311 3311

Website: www.kpmg.co.uk

Correspondent: Jo Clunie, KPMG Foundation 020 7311 4733
E-mail: kpmgfoundation@kpmg.co.uk

Chief officer: John Griffiths-Jones

| Year end | Turnover | Pre-tax profit |
| --- | --- | --- |
| 30/09/2006 | £1,454,000,000 | £374,000,000 |

**Nature of company business**
The provision of professional services through the core functions of assurance, tax, consulting and financial advisory services (covering transaction services, corporate finance, corporate recovery and forensic). Legal services are provided by Klegal, an independent law firm associated with KPMG.

**Main locations:** Birmingham, Bristol, Cardiff, Cambridge, Edinburgh, Gatwick, Glasgow, Ipswich, Leeds, Leicester, Milton Keynes, Newcastle upon Tyne, Liverpool, London, Manchester, Nottingham, Preston, Plymouth, Reading, St Albans, Southampton, Stoke on Trent, Watford, Aberdeen

**Total employees:** 9,815

## Charitable donations

2006: £813,000

Total community contributions: £4,600,000

Membership: A & B, BitC, L B Group, %Club

## Community involvement

There are two strands to KPMG's community involvement activity, namely, employee volunteering and a programme of charitable giving.

KPMG's donations policy states that the primary focus is on community and environment, particularly through education in its broadest sense; to help enhance social inclusion for individuals and communities, especially those that are disadvantaged or underprivileged; and to support charities that maintain and enhance biodiversity and that educate children in the need to live in a sustainable way. The donation budgets are to support the volunteering of KPMG staff.

The range of programmes undertaken is varied and reflects the work needs of staff. There are five main areas: Mentoring; Employability; Enterprise; Leadership and Team Challenges.

KPMG have set up a dedicated contact point for all requests for community help and involvement (see 'Applications' below).

**Charity of the Year:** Help the Hospices.

**The KPMG Foundation**

The KPMG Foundation (Charity Commission no. 1086518) was set up in October 2001. The objects of the foundation are education and social projects for the disadvantaged and underprivileged, with particular emphasis on unlocking the potential of children and young adults (up to 30 years old) who, for primarily social reasons, have not fulfilled their education potential.

The Trustees have chosen to focus funding on four disadvantaged groups:

- refugees
- young offenders
- young people in care
- young people with literacy difficulties.

Care is taken to ensure that, so far as possible, projects supported cover all geographic areas across Great Britain. The Foundation has received £10 million from KPMG. Whilst it is funded by KPMG, it is a separate entity with a Board of Trustees, half of whom have no connection with the company.

## Exclusions

Assistance to private educational establishments, political parties, or primarily evangelical causes and campaigns is not given.

## Applications

For further information on the firm's charitable giving contact the Donations Helpline on 020 7311 1161. The website states that 'the firm is no longer accepting applications from charities to be considered as its next annual charity. However, if you would like to receive an application form for 2007/08 please e-mail csr@kpmg.co.uk'.

For the KPMG Foundation only, contact Jo Clunie at kpmgfoundation@kpmg.co.uk or at KPMG, 8 Salisbury Square, London EC4Y 8BB for an application form and further details.

## Corporate giving

In 2006, KPMG made total community contributions in the UK of £4.6 million, of which £813,000 was in cash donations. One of the main beneficiaries was the staff-selected charity, the Teenage Cancer Trust, for which £420,000 was raised.

It is the firm's policy to give priority to supporting requests from employees. Preference will be given to employee requests in support of sustained personal community involvement, a broader fundraising effort (for example, raising funds by way of a marathon run) or more generally to voluntary/ community groups engaged in areas of high social impact (state education sector, economic regeneration, capacity building).

Each office has its own donation budget to ensure that firm donations support and represent the communities in which staff live and work.

### KPMG Foundation

Established in 2001, the firm has committed £10 million to the KPMG Foundation over five years. The focus of the KPMG Foundation is on education and social projects for people who are disadvantaged, particular emphasis on unlocking the potential of children and young people.

The charities/projects supported by the foundation in 2006 include: Every Child a Reader, Refugee Council, The Dyslexia Institute, DePaul Trust, Devon Youth Association, Fairbridge; Fairbridge is a national youth charity, specialising in the personal development of challenging young people and Tamil Welfare Association.

The foundation capital sum provides an annual income and over £4 million has been used to fund 29 charitable projects. In the year to 30 September 2006, the foundation paid out over £1.85 million to charities, including a new programme through Young Enterprise Scotland to help young women offenders at Corton Vale prison find work on release. A full list of the projects supported can be found at www.kpmg.co.uk/about/foundation/.

## In-kind support

The firm donates PCs and other IT equipment through the national Tools for Schools programme.

From time to time, furniture and other office equipment that is surplus to requirements are made available to community organisations.

## Employee-led support

*Mentoring* – A founding member of the Number Partners, staff support numeracy skills in primary schools.

*Employability* – Employability focuses on fighting exclusion. The 'Ready to Go' programme is a pre-employment training initiative helping ex-homeless people find their way back to work. Volunteers will firstly support an ex-homeless person with letter and CV writing skills, will act as a 'buddy' on a two week work placement and then act as coach for up to a further six months.

*Enterprise* – With the Prince's Trust business mentoring start-up programme, financial and practical support is given to 18–30 year olds with a good business idea rejected by other lenders.

*Leadership* – Partners in Leadership provides senior staff with the opportunity to mentor head teachers.

*Team Challenges* – These are specific challenges where teams of KPMG volunteers help a charity or community group by, for example, building a sensory garden, painting a school or building a bridge. KPMG and its volunteers also benefit through team building and greater involvement in communities.

In 2005 nearly 2,000 KPMG employees volunteered to take part in 83 team challenges. KPMG in the UK are exchanging knowledge developed from these programmes with ENGAGE, an International Employee Community Engagement Campaign. The campaign aims to promote employee community involvement globally to help ensure employee engagement is implemented in the communities and countries where the need is greatest.

In 2005 KPMG also developed the EMA region Corporate Responsibility Network, linking KPMG firms in ten countries together for the first time to help deliver an effective and consistent strategy across the region – the first project will be 'Make a Difference Day'.

**Payroll giving:** Give as You Earn is available nationally and is supported by the firm.

KPMG will match, up to the value of £50,000, employee giving to the staff selected charity via Give As You Earn. Outside of this, individual employee fundraising receives matched funding from the firm up to a maximum of £250.

During 2005, 31% of staff took part in community volunteering schemes.

## Commercially-led support

**Sponsorship:** Minimal sponsorship opportunities exist in relation to the arts and good causes.

# Kraft Foods UK Ltd

St George's House, Bayshill Road, Cheltenham, Gloucester GL50 3AE

01242 236101; Fax: 01242 512084

Website: www.kraftfoods.co.uk

Correspondent: Corporate Affairs Department

Chief officer: Thibaud de Saint-Quentin (VP UK & Ireland)

| Year end | Turnover | Pre-tax profit |
|---|---|---|
| 31/12/2005 | | |

**Nature of company business**
The principal activity of the company is food manufacture.

**Main locations:** Cheltenham, Banbury

**UK employees:** 2,240

---

**Charitable donations**

2005: £97,500

Membership: BitC

---

## Community involvement

Through its Kraft Cares global community involvement programme, the company focuses on two main areas; fighting hunger and advancing healthy lifestyles. In identifying programmes to support that address important local needs and fit within these two areas, Kraft is reliant upon its offices, manufacturing facilities and sales locations worldwide.

Support is also given to communities in other ways through, for example, product donations and the provision of humanitarian aid to victims of natural disasters and other crises around the world.

The company also encourages its employees to support their local communities through various involvement programmes and a matched funding scheme.

### Exclusions

No support for appeals from individuals, or for political or religious appeals.

### Applications

In writing to the correspondent.

## Corporate giving

In 2005, Kraft's global community contributions totalled $84.6 million (£45.9 million) of which $20.7 million (£11.2 million) was in cash donations. No break down of these figures by region was available.

Since September 2004, the Kraft Cares programme in the UK – health 4 schools – has been run successfully in partnership with Business in the Community. The initiative promotes a healthy diet and active play to schoolchildren in Gloucestershire by encouraging them to eat breakfast, grow and cook their own food, and take part in physical play activities. Each school receives a package of support and resources worth nearly £5,000. For their contribution to the programme, Business n the Community received a grant of $179,900 (£97,500) in 2005.

In June 2006, Kraft Cares announced its support for Shape Up, a new programme developed by leading European education specialists as a direct response to the European Union (EU) Platform on Diet, Physical Activity and Health call for action on rising obesity levels in children.

The three-year project will develop, test and evaluate practical in-school and community activities to influence the determinants of a healthy and balanced growing up in 26 cities across the region. This includes helping children investigate food, nutrition and physical activity. A Shape Up Competence Centre has been established at the University of Hull, which will be in charge of developing and implementing the project in the UK.

### In-kind support

The company makes product donations through designated country-specific relief or charitable organisations. The level of product donations can fluctuate significantly from year to year.

### Employee-led support

Employees' fundraising is matched by the company in the US, but we were unable to confirm whether this was also the case here.

---

# Kwik-Fit Holdings plc

216 East Main Street, Broxburn, West Lothian EH52 5AS

01506 856789

**Website:** www.kwik-fit.com

**Correspondent:** PA to the Marketing Director
**E-mail:** info@kwik-fit.com

**Chief officer:** Sir Trevor Chinn

| Year end | Turnover | Pre-tax profit |
|---|---|---|
| 31/12/2004 | £747,300,000 | £37,600,000 |

**Nature of company business**
Principal activity: tyre, exhaust and car repair centres.

**Subsidiaries include:** Apples Ltd, Ecology Tyre Collections Ltd, Tyreplus Autoservice Ltd, Superdrive Motoring Centres Ltd, Town and Country Tyre Services Ltd, Preston Paints Ltd

**Main locations:** Broxburn

**Total employees:** 9,000

---

**Charitable donations**

2004: £100,000
2003: £100,000

---

## Community involvement

The company and its employees continued to support financially and in kind a wide range of charitable activities. In particular, there is an emphasis on initiatives that support children and young people, community development and road safety. In December 2005 Kwik-Fit Financial Services announced NCH Scotland would be their 'Charity of the Year 2005/06'. This would include £25,000 towards NCH's new purpose-built short break and respite centre at Silvertonhill, Hamilton, which provides support to families of children with physical and learning disabilities.

### Exclusions

No response to circular appeals. No grants for advertising in charity brochures or appeals from individuals.

### Applications

In writing to the correspondent.

## Corporate giving

In 2004, the company made charitable donations in the UK totalling £100,000 to national and local charities and community projects. We were unable to obtain any more specific information regarding the beneficiaries. The company has now been acquired by PIA, Paris and we do not know if or how this will affect the level of charitable support the company provides.

## In-kind support

**Education :** The company has been involved in many road safety initiatives, for example, 'Safer Roads for Children' programme. This includes studycards and factsheets for schools, and a 'Kids' Code for the Road' for adults and children.

**Enterprise:** Activities include maintaining links with local schools, colleges and universities through Scottish Business in the Community, and acting as business advisors to students participating in the Young Enterprise Scheme.

**Secondment:** Employees participate in community assignments as part of their training and development, and can spend up to three months on secondment to a range of community based initiatives, through the Prince's Trust – Volunteers scheme. The company is also a Charter Founder Member of the Duke of Edinburgh's Award.

## Employee-led support

Smaller charities also receive support from employees' commitment to the communities in which they operate.

## Commercially-led support

**Sponsorship:** The company undertakes good cause sponsorship of local community events and competitions for local schoolchildren. Examples of this are sponsorship of a local boys' football team in Beverley, a Teenage Pedestrian Road Safety Project and the Kwik Fit Charity Stadium Tour, when staff from Kwik Fit Financial Services set a target to raise £30,000 to purchase a minibus for Mavisbank School in Airdrie. The school caters for children and teenagers who have multiple disabilities and is well known for their expertise in dealing with children who are blind or have an identified visual impairment. The company also regularly sponsor's Tyre Safety Weeks.

# Ladbrokes plc

Imperial House, Imperial Drive, Rayners Lane, Harrow, Middlesex HA2 7JW

020 8868 8899; Fax: 020 8868 8767

Website: www.ladbrokesplc.com

Correspondent: Mike O'Kane, Administrator, LCCT

Chief officer: Sir Ian Robinson

Chief Executive: Christopher Bell

| Year end | Turnover | Pre-tax profit |
|---|---|---|
| 31/12/2005 | £13,354,000,000 | £413,900,000 |

Nature of company business
The group's principal activity is the provision of hotels, health clubs, and a range of betting and gaming services.

Subsidiaries include: Stakis plc, Inter-National Hotel Services Ltd, Ladbrokes Ltd, LivingWell Health & Leisure Ltd, Vernons Pools Ltd

Main locations: Watford, Harlow

UK employees: 50,990

## Charitable donations

2005: £54,000
2003: £152,000
Total community contributions: £261,613
Membership: BitC

## Community involvement

In February 2006, the Hilton Group plc was renamed Ladbrokes plc following the completion of the sale of the Hilton International Hotel division to Hilton Hotel Corporation. Although the Hilton Group of companies made donations in their own right, the majority of support worldwide was made through the Hilton in the Community Foundation (Charity Commission no. 1084220) and the 2004 established Ladbrokes in the Community Charitable Trust (Charity Commission no. 1101804).

The Hilton in the Community Foundation concentrates on three areas: young people and education, employment related schemes in the hospitality sector and disaster relief, when occurring in those areas of the world where Hilton are represented.

Ladbrokes in the Community Charitable Trust seeks to support smaller local charities and groups through its countrywide network of betting shops. Its declared aims are to support causes concerned with education and training, medical/health/sickness issues, and sport and recreation.

### Exclusions

No support is given to appeals for advertising in charity brochures, the arts, appeals from individuals, circular appeals, fundraising events, overseas projects, political appeals, religious appeals, or small, purely local appeals not in an area of company presence.

### Applications

Although Hilton Group plc has now been renamed Ladbrokes plc, the Hilton in the Community Foundation is still operational and receiving funds from Hilton International. All appeals for charitable donations or community involvement should be addressed in writing to: Simon Sheehan, Hilton in the Community Foundation, 179–199 Holland Park Avenue, London W11 4UL.

For Ladbrokes in the Community Charitable Trust, the procedure is to secure the support of your local shop in raising funds on behalf of your cause. Any monies raised are then banked with the trust, with consideration of additional funds being added by Ladbrokes taken by the trust's grants committee which meets every 5–6 weeks.

## Corporate giving

In 2005, Hilton International made financial commitments to the Hilton in the Community Foundation totalling £207,613. Cash donations to other UK charities totalled £54,000.

In 2005, the Ladbrokes in the Community Charitable Trust had an income of £893,427, almost all of which came from 'shop fundraising events', i.e. customers of Ladbrokes betting shops.

### Employee-led support

The group actively encourages its employees to undertake fundraising activities, particularly in support of Ladbrokes in the Community Charitable Trust.

# Lafarge Aggregates Limited

Granite House, PO Box 7388, Watermead Business Park, Syston, Leicester LE7 1WA

0116 264 8000; Fax: 0116 269 8348

Website: www.lafarge-aggregates.co.uk

Correspondent: Communications Manager

Chief officer: Jean Blatz

| Year end | Turnover | Pre-tax profit |
|---|---|---|
| 31/12/2005 | £428,623,000 | £25,231,000 |

**Nature of company business**
Supplier of asphalt, aggregate, concrete products and ready mixed.

Main locations: Leicester

UK employees: 1,883

## Community involvement

Lafarge Aggregates supports a wide variety of charities and other local good causes with employees regularly taking part in fundraising events. The company also hosts and takes part in various events including quarry open days, site visits, village fetes, country shows and so on.

Due to the large number of requests for donations Lafarge receives, it seeks to support community groups close to its sites, particularly those likely to bring long-term benefits; educational and research establishments; charitable activities related to environmental conservation or the construction industry.

The company has over 200 sites around the UK, details of which are available on its website.

### Exclusions

Local appeals not in areas of company presence.

### Applications

In writing to the correspondent.

## Corporate giving

The company's accounts for 2005, did not declare any charitable donations having been made. However, we believe its level of in-kind support to be sufficient to warrant inclusion here.

Grants may also be available under the Landfill Tax Credits Scheme, about which further information can be had by visiting the Entrust website at: www.entrust.org.uk

### In-kind support

*Environment:* Lafarge works in partnership with a number of organisations such as wildlife trusts, national conservation organisations and local community groups on quarry restoration projects.

# The Laird Group plc

3 St James's Square, London SW1Y 4JU

020 7468 4040; Fax: 020 7839 2921

Website: www.laird-plc.com

Correspondent: D Hudson, Company Secretary

Chief officer: Nigel Keen

Chief Executive: Peter Hill

| Year end | Turnover | Pre-tax profit |
|---|---|---|
| 31/12/2005 | £490,300,000 | £34,300,000 |

**Nature of company business**
The principal activities during the year were the design, manufacture and supply of products and services to the electronics, the residential building and the automotive industries.

**Subsidiaries include:** Fullarton Computer Industries (Gourock) Ltd, Verichrome Plating Services Ltd, EWS (Manufacturing) Ltd, Instrument Specialties (Europe) Ltd, ERA Products Ltd, Fullarton Computer Industries Ltd, Feneseal Ltd, Cego Frameware Ltd, Ventrolla Ltd, R H Technical Industries Ltd, Fullarton Computer Industries (Dundee) Ltd, Permacell Finesse Ltd, J K Furnex Ltd, ARC Euro Ltd, Linear Ltd

Main locations: Harrogate, London

Total employees: 8,995

### Charitable donations

2005: £49,000
2004: £116,000
2003: £83,000

## Community involvement

Laird states that the well-being of the communities in which the group operates is important to its long term development and success. In support of this, help is given to national and local charities, both financially and via in-kind support. In addition to this, staff participate in fundraising events on behalf of various good causes.

### Exclusions

No support for political appeals.

### Applications

In writing to the correspondent.

## Corporate giving

During 2005, the group gave £49,000 to national and local charities (2004: £116,000). A number of large UK charities were supported, examples being: Guide Dogs for the Blind; Whizz-Kidz; The Samaritans and Cancer Research. The subsidiaries of the group support a variety of local initiatives.

### In-kind support

Group companies support a variety of local sports teams through the provision of kit and equipment donations. They have also participated in an Annual Toys for Tots campaign through the purchasing of toys, the donation of unwanted Christmas gifts and active promotion of the regional programme which provides toys to needy families in the local community.

Enterprise support days at local schools and the provision of work experience placements are among other forms of in-kind support provided by the company.

## Employee-led support

In instances of major international disasters occurring, e.g. Hurricane Katrina and the Asian tsunami, money raised by employees in support of relief work has been matched by the company.

## Commercially-led support

**Sponsorship:** *Sport* - Several group companies support a variety of local sports teams through the provision of team sponsorships.

*Disability* - At Laird Group head office, through a scheme operated by Guide Dogs for the Blind, staff sponsored a trainee Guide Dog puppy 'Hero' and raised funds for the charity.

# Land Securities Group plc

5 Strand, London WC2N 5AF

020 7413 9000; Fax: 020 7925 0202

Website: www.landsecurities.com

Correspondent: P M Dudgeon, Company Secretary

Chief officer: Peter Birch

Chief Executive: Francis Salway

| Year end | Turnover | Pre-tax profit |
|---|---|---|
| 31/03/2006 | £1,828,700,000 | £2,359,200,000 |

Nature of company business
Land Securities is the largest UK property group, involved in both property development and investment, and property outsourcing.

Subsidiaries include: Ravenside Investments Ltd, Ravenseft Properties Ltd, The City of London Real Property Co. Ltd

Main locations: Birmingham, London, Portsmouth, Sunderland, Cardiff, Gateshead, East Kilbride, Leeds, Glasgow

UK employees: 1,842

## Charitable donations

2006: £559,000
2005: £580,000
2004: £804,000
2003: £774,000

Total community contributions: £1,319,000

Membership: A & B, BitC, L B Group

## Community involvement

The company's website states: 'The group operates a sponsorship & charities committee which acts independently of the board of directors and comprises employees from each business unit. It administers a budget set by the executive directors each year. Support is generally only given for charitable work undertaken in the United Kingdom. Favourable consideration is given to charities carrying out

medical research or those involved in the relief of suffering. Special consideration is also given to appeals from charities located in the areas of the UK where the group has an involvement.'

## Exclusions

No support for advertising in charity brochures, animal welfare, appeals from individuals, overseas projects, political appeals or religious appeals.

## Applications

In writing to the correspondent. The charity committee meets every six weeks to choose the most suitable applications to support.

**Information available:** The company produces a social responsibility report.

## Corporate giving

In 2005/06, the company made total community contributions of £1,319,000. This comprised: Charitable donations of £559,000; Corporate sponsorship of £130,000; £130,000 invested in NGO's and government bodies; and, £500,000 worth of free floor space within the group's shopping centres given to organisations to promote their activities.

In 2007, the group aim to provide a total of £150,000 in small grants to local community and voluntary groups in the Southwark and Westminster areas. These will be made from the Land Securities Capital Commitment Fund.

## In-kind support

The group provides free floor space within its shopping centres to organisations wishing to promote their activities.

## Employee-led support

Through The Land Securities Foundation, the group aims to promote employee volunteering. This will focus on four key themes – education, employability, local enterprise, and personal interest.

A revision of the company's payroll giving schemes is currently in progress.

## Commercially-led support

**Sponsorship:** The company has undertaken the following corporate sponsorships – Christmas Presence, Land Securities Trillium Reading University Fellow of Estate Management, National Gallery, Playtex Moonwalk, Regent's Park Theatre and Times 100 Education case studies.

# Lazard

50 Stratton Street, London, W1J 8LL

020 7187 2000; Fax: 020 7072 6000

Correspondent: The Secretary to the Lazard Charitable Trust

| Year end | Turnover | Pre-tax profit |
|---|---|---|
| 31/12/2005 | £10,008,022,000 | £76,065,000 |

Nature of company business
Banking, capital markets, corporate finance.

Main locations: London

UK employees: 614

Total employees: n/a

## Community involvement

Donations are made through the Lazard Charitable Trust (Charity Commission no. 1048043).

It prefers to support local charities in areas of company presence, charities in which a member of staff is involved and charities in inner cities and areas of deprivation. Preferred areas of support are children and young people, elderly people, social welfare and sickness/disability charities.

### Exclusions

No grants for medical research, overseas charities, large UK/international charities or to individuals.

### Applications

In writing to the correspondent.

## Corporate giving

During 2005 the Charity received total income of £108,908. A total of £140,753 was applied to charitable causes (92 grants).

Beneficiaries included Amnesty International, Anna Trust, British Heart Foundation, Cystic Fibrosis Trust, English Pocket Opera Company, Habitat for Humanity, the Graham Layton Trust, Museum of London, NSPCC, National Society for Epilepsy, Royal Shakespeare Company and Universal Beneficent Society.

### Employee-led support

The trust matches fundraising efforts of staff.

# Leeds Building Society

105 Albion Street, Leeds LS1 5AS

0113 216 7296; Fax: 0113 225 7549

**Website:** www.leedsbuildingsociety.co.uk

**Correspondent:** Sally Smith, Secretary of the Society's Charitable Foundation
E-mail: ssmith@leedsbuildingsociety.co.uk

**Chief officer:** Robert Wade

**Chief Executive:** Ian Ward

| Year end | Turnover | Pre-tax profit |
|---|---|---|
| 31/12/2005 | | £50,200,000 |

**Nature of company business**
The provision, to existing and prospective members, of residential mortgages and retail saving products.

**Main locations:** Leeds

**UK employees:** 847

**Total employees:** 902

## Community involvement

The majority of the society's charitable donations are made through the Leeds Building Society Charitable Foundation (Charity Commission no. 1074429). Requests for donations to community-based projects aiming to 'provide relief of suffering, hardship or poverty, or their direct consequences' are considered. In effect, support is given to registered charities – operating within the area of one of the society's branches – that work with homeless people, adults and children with disabilities, older people, underprivileged families, deaf blind and visually impaired people and projects benefiting local residents.

### Exclusions

There is no support available for:

- projects with religious, political or military purposes
- overseas charities or projects
- individuals, including sponsorship of individuals
- animal welfare projects
- medical research or equipment
- advertising in charity brochures.

It is unlikely that support will be given to the restoration of buildings (including churches), playgroups, Scout & Guide Associations or environmental charities (unless there is a benefit to a disadvantaged community).

### Applications

In writing to the secretary including:

- the name of your project and brief information about it
- a contact name, address and phone number
- your registered charity number
- details of what the donation would be used for and who would benefit from it
- your nearest Leeds Building Society branch.

All applications will be acknowledged. The trustees usually meet quarterly in March, June, September and November. You can also write to the secretary for more information, or visit the society's website (see above).

The foundation's current guidelines can be obtained by writing to the secretary at the above address. Because the foundation operates independently of the building society, local branch staff are unable to answer questions about it.

## Corporate giving

In 2006, the group made a charitable donation to the foundation of £80,000. Grants usually range from £250 to £1,000, with beneficiaries including the 'talking newspaper' in Peterborough, the Citizens Advice Bureau in Kendal, the Motor Neurone Disease Association in Gloucestershire and a hospital radio project in Barnsley.

### Commercially-led support

**Cause-related marketing:** The society offers a number of saver accounts to the public that are linked to a particular charity or community initiative.

The CaringSaver account offers payment by the society to three charities: Help the Aged, Save the Children and Marie

Curie Cancer Care. An amount equal to 1% of the average balances in the account is divided equally between the three charities which, in 2005, totalled £48,306.

The Leeds United Saver account provides support for the Leeds United Youth Academy. A similar account for rugby fans was launched for supporters of Leeds Rhinos Rugby League and Leeds Tykes Rugby Union clubs. The society has made a three-year, £25,000 commitment to support the Leeds Rhinos Study Support Centre, which is used for the benefit of Leeds schoolchildren.

# Legal & General plc

Temple Court, 11 Queen Victoria Street, London EC4N 4TP

020 7528 6200; Fax: 020 7528 6222

Website: www.legalandgeneralgroup.com

Correspondent: Jane Boswell, CSR Manager 020 7528 6215; Fax: 020 7528 6222

Chief officer: Rob Margetts

Chief Executive: Tim Breedon

| Year end | Turnover | Pre-tax profit |
|---|---|---|
| 31/12/2005 | | £1,383,000,000 |

**Nature of company business**
The group's principal activities are: the provision of long-term insurance, investment management and general insurance.

**Subsidiaries include:** Arlington Business Parks Partnership, Gresham Insurance Company Ltd, Trident Componenets Group Ltd

**Main locations:** London, Brighton, Cardiff, Birmingham

**UK employees:** 8,547

## Charitable donations

2005: £2,279,000
2004: £1,100,000
2003: £1,702,000

Total community contributions: £2,435,000 2003
Management costs: £215,000

Membership: A & B, BitC, L B Group, %Club

## Community involvement

Legal & General's policy is to provide support to three principal groups:

- a small number of national charities whose work is directly related to the group's core businesses. These are its 'Major Community Partnerships'
- charities and community groups local to its main offices
- UK employees who commit their own personal time and funds to help a local community or charity.

In addition, the company also operate a 'Young Excellence Scheme' which gives support to young people who have shown outstanding talent in a sporting or creative field.

Contributions take the form of financial support (84%), employees time (4%) and gifts in kind (3%). The remaining 9% was accounted for by management costs.

## Exclusions

Legal & General does not support animal charities, overseas based charities or international projects, religious organisations (except where it can be proven that the project is undertaken on behalf of the community as a whole) or political organisations.

## Applications

Information about national charities which meet the group's guidelines should be sent to the correspondent. Appropriate local appeals should be sent to the relevant local contact.

National decisions are made by the charity committee and approved by the group board on an annual basis; local appeals are considered by individual offices. Overseas grants are handled by the subsidiary company in each country.

## Corporate giving

In 2005, the company made total community contributions of £2,435,000 of which £2,279,000 was in cash donations. This represented 0.5% of UK pre-tax profits. Legal & General calculate the cost of managing its community investment programme to be £215,000.

*Major community pertnerships:* The central themes of this programme are – crime prevention; serious illness prevention; caring for the seriously ill and victims of accidents or crime; caring for the elderly; improving numeracy, financial literacy and awareness; encouraging youth inclusion and helping young people achieve their potential; entrepreneurship.

In 2005, Legal and General worked with British Heart Foundation, Businessdynamics and the Prince's Royal Trust for Carers.

Applications for this programme can be made on-line via the company's website.

*Local community partnerships:* Support for local charities and community groups is centred around its major offices currently located in: Kingswood (Surrey), Hove, Cardiff, Birmingham and London.

Legal & General is the main supporter of the Age Concern Ageing Well programme for the Cardiff and Vale of Glamorgan areas.

*Young Excellence Scheme:* Legal & General are currently supporting 15 young people in their pursuit of excellence in disciplines as varied as chess, opera and fencing.

The following criteria apply

- applicants must be aged between 14 and 27 years of age
- applications from individuals playing team sports will only be considered if the individual is under 18 years of age
- applicants must have already reached a very good standard in their chosen field
- applicants must have a genuine financial need relating to their field of expertise.

If the above criteria are met, applications to the scheme should be addressed to:

Margaret Hall, CSR Assistant, Legal & General Group plc, Temple Court, 11 Queen Victoria Street, London EC4N 4TP.

## In-kind support

This can take the form of gifts in-kind.

## Employee-led support

Employees are encouraged to support charitable activities in their local communities. A 'Community Awards' scheme exists to recognise the good work of its employees in the community. Ten winners are chosen from a list of nominees, each of whom receive £1,000 on behalf of the charity or group supported.

Each year Legal & General donate £500 to every school which has one of its employees as a governor.

The company also matches the first £500 raised over a year by an employee for a charity or community group.

**Payroll giving:** The company offer the Give As You Earn scheme.

## Commercially-led support

**Sponsorship:** *The Arts* – There is an established programme, which means it is difficult to make new commitments.

# Levi Strauss (UK) Ltd

Swann Valley, Northampton NN4 9BA

01604 581501; Fax: 01604 599815

Website: www.levistrauss.com

Correspondent: Margot Mason/ Lucy Fisher, Facilities Manager

Managing Director: Johan Elsner

| Year end | Turnover | Pre-tax profit |
|---|---|---|
| 30/11/2003 | £101,183,000 | (£8,110,000) |

**Nature of company business**
Clothing marketing and sales under the Levi's brand.

**Main locations:** Northampton

**UK employees:** 100

**Total employees:** 10,000

### Charitable donations
2005: £161,300

## Community involvement

The company's website states that the Levi Strauss Foundation has, 'Identified three specific programme areas where we seek to have the most significant impact to alleviate poverty among women and youth. These are building assets; preventing the spread of HIV/AIDS by addressing stigma and discrimination and funding education and harm-reduction programs such as syringe access; and improving the working and living standards of garment workers through a global workers' rights initiative.

'We seek to collaborate with other institutions and to fund innovative programs that will foster positive, long-term social change. We believe that by addressing these issues in the communities where we have a business presence, we can provide people with important tools to help them break the cycle of intergenerational poverty.'

Grants can be made through either the company, or the US-based Levi Strauss Foundation.

### Exclusions

No support is given to: individuals; capital or endowment campaigns; building work; sports teams or competitions; advertising; event sponsorship; sectarian or religious activities; or political campaigns or causes.

### Applications

In writing to the correspondent. However, the company's website states: 'Sorry, we do not accept, nor are we able to respond to, unsolicited grant requests, product donation requests or charitable sponsorship requests.'

## Corporate giving

In 2005, the company supported four UK causes, giving grants totalling US$297,500 (£161,300). These beneficiaries were: Friends of the Music of Leeds Parish Church (£4,050); International HIV/AIDS Alliance, Brighton (£27,100); Charities Aid Foundation (£116,600); and, Prince of Wales International Business Leaders Forum (£13,550).

### In-kind support

The company may occasionally make some of their products (jeans) available to charitable organisations. Donations of furniture, machines, and the like that are no longer in use may also be made to support the work of an organisation.

### Employee-led support

Staff are allowed time off for activity of community benefit and encouraged to become volunteers in their own time. The company operates a matching scheme for employee fundraising.

# John Lewis Partnership plc

171 Victoria Street, London SW1E 5NN

020 7828 1000; Fax: 020 7828 4145

Website: www.johnlewis.co.uk

Correspondent: Marion Goonewardene, Secretary to the Partnership Charities Committee 020 7828 5252

Chief officer: Sir Stuart Hampson

| Year end | Turnover | Pre-tax profit |
|---|---|---|
| 28/01/2006 | £5,149,300,000 | £251,800,000 |

**Nature of company business**
The company operates 26 department stores and 144 Waitrose supermarkets with ancillary manufacturing activities.

The partnership is a retail business run on cooperative principles. All the ordinary share capital is held by a trustee - John Lewis Partnership Trust Ltd - on partners' (employees') behalf. Under irrevocable trusts the balance of profits is available to be shared among all partners after provision for prudent reserves and for interest on loans and fixed dividends on shares held outside. Management is accountable to the general body of partners, in particular through elected councils and through the partnership's journalism.

**Subsidiaries include:** Findlater Mackie Todd & Co Ltd, Herbert Parkinson Ltd, Waitrose Ltd, Stead, McAlpin & Co Ltd, J H Birtwistle & Co Ltd

**Main locations:** Aberdeen, Bluewater, Watford, Welwyn Garden City, Trafford, Windsor, Norwich, Nottingham, London, Liverpool, Newcastle, Milton Keynes, Southsea, Southampton, Reading, Peterborough, Solihull, Sheffeld, Glasgow, Edinburgh, Kingston, High Wycombe, Cheadle, Bristol, Brent Cross

**UK employees:** 59,600

## Charitable donations

2006: £2,040,000
2005: £2,080,000
2004: £1,650,000
2003: £1,700,000

Membership: BitC, L B Group, %Club

## Community involvement

The partnership's Central and Branch Councils are responsible for about half the total donations. Areas of favoured support are care for children, young people and people who are sick, disabled or young, wildlife and conservation, the care and housing of older people, medical research and counselling services. Organisations without charitable status, such as schools, sports clubs and appeals for local amenities can be considered. Organisations at both national and local level are supported, with the councils preferring to give directly to the organisations concerned.

The chairman is responsible for the other half of the giving, and gives to organisations which, in broad terms, fall into the categories of the arts, culture, education and the environment. The funding of musical events which are of a high calibre and can attract a large attendance from a wide geographical spread are particularly supported, with over fifty such projects supported each year.

The company has a charitable trust, John Lewis Partnership General Community Fund (Charity Commission no. 209128).

### Exclusions

The company does not support: individuals; religious, ethnic or political groups; third party fundraising activities; projects overseas; or the purchase of advertising space.

### Applications

For local charities it is best to contact the charities secretary of the local branch as decisions are made locally. For national appeals, there is a separate correspondent for funding from John Lewis Partnership and Waitrose. The John Lewis Partnership correspondent is Marion Goonewardene, as listed above. The Waitrose correspondent is:

Charities Secretary
Waitrose Limited
Doncastle Road
Southern Industrial Area
Bracknell
Berkshire
RG12 8YA

## Corporate giving

In 2005/06, John Lewis gave £2,040,000 (2004/05: £2,080,000) in cash donations, of which £1,580,000 (2005: £1,560,000) was for welfare causes and £460,000 (2005: £520,000) for music and arts, learning and the environment.

In addition, substantial financial and practical support was provided to causes in the communities where the company trade.

### In-kind support

To mark the fiftieth anniversary of the establishment of the John Lewis business as a partnership in 2000, a £5 million trust fund was set up. Through The Golden Jubilee Trust

partners are able to offer their time and expertise to good causes, while still being paid.

Secondments may last from one week to six months at projects with a clear local commitment and a specified objective. The scheme is run on a competitive basis with between 30 and 40 awards being made across the country each year.

The partnership provides additional support to charities through gifts in kind.

### Employee-led support

**Payroll giving**: The company participates in the CAF Give as You Earn scheme.

# Liberty International Holdings plc

40 Broadway, London SW1H 0BT

020 7960 1200; Fax: 020 7960 1333

Website: www.liberty-international.co.uk

Correspondent: Carolyn Kenyon, Public Relations Manager

Chief officer: Sir Robert Finch

Chief Executive: David Fischel

| Year end | Turnover | Pre-tax profit |
|---|---|---|
| 31/12/2005 | £434,300,000 | £109,300,000 |

Nature of company business
The principal activity is that of a property investment company. It is the leading company in the UK regional shopping centre industry.

Subsidiaries include: Portfolio Fund Management Ltd, Capital & Counties plc, Capital Shopping Centres plc

Main locations: London

Total employees: 811

## Charitable donations

2005: £143,000
2003: £84,400

Total community contributions: £500,000

Membership: BitC, L B Group, %Club

## Community involvement

The company has stated some preference for supporting education and youth projects, and has formed a partnership with national charity ICAN to provide facilities for improving literacy skills for the very young, and with Newcastle EBP and local schools to promote retailing as a career. Other projects include Manchester Arndale 4 Youth in association with Crime Concern and the sponsorship of a singing event at the Sage Concert Hall in Gateshead.

It supports both national (UK) charities and charities which are based within the local area of its shopping centres. We do not know whether it accepts unsolicited applications.

### Applications

In writing to the correspondent.

**Information available:** The company produces a corporate social responsibility report.

## Corporate giving

In 2005 the company's charitable donations totalled £143,000. The company's UK shopping centres also contributed £500,000 in community support for various projects and initiatives.

## Employee-led support

In 2005 over 3,600 hours of the company's centre management time was devoted to the company's involvement with the local community. This involvement included a wide range of activities, including working with schools, both with the children and serving as school governors, assisting local community groups and contributing both time and resources to support town centre partnerships.

# Limit Underwriting Ltd

Plantation Place, 30 Fenchurch Street, London EC3M 3BD

020 7105 4000; Fax: 020 7105 4019

**Website:** www.limit.co.uk

**Correspondent:** Chairman
E-mail: info@limit.co.uk

| Year end | Turnover | Pre-tax profit |
|----------|----------|----------------|
| 31/12/2005 | £154,522,000 | £44,871,000 |

**Nature of company business**
Limit Underwriting Limited is the Lloyd's Division of QBE European Operations, offering insurance and reinsurance products across a diverse range of classes.

Limit is a wholly-owned subsidiary of the QBE Insurance Group

**Subsidiaries include:** CUL Holdings, Garwyn, Janson Green Holdings, Bankside Insurance Holdings

**Main locations:** London

**Total employees:** 432

### Charitable donations
2005: £22,775
2004: £12,283

## Community involvement

Unfortunately, we currently have no information on the charitable donations policy of the company.

## Applications

In writing to the correspondent.

## Corporate giving

In 2005, the company donated £22,775 (2004: £12,283) to charity. We have no information regarding the beneficiaries.

# Lincoln Financial Group

Barnett Way, Barnwood, Gloucester GL4 3RZ

01452 374500; Fax: 01452 634300

**Website:** www.lincolnuk.co.uk

**Correspondent:** Claire Maiden, Head of Marketing

**Managing Director:** Michael Tallett-Williams

| Year end | Turnover | Pre-tax profit |
|----------|----------|----------------|
| 31/12/2005 | | £80,600,000 |

**Nature of company business**
Financial service company offering pensions, life assurance, health and disability cover, investment plans, unit trusts and ISAs.

**Main locations:** Gloucester

**Total employees:** 124

### Charitable donations
2005: £117,647

## Community involvement

The group runs a Community Partnership Programme (CPP) which is a scheme for making donations to charities and causes in the field of education, the arts and human services. The aim is to enhance quality of the life to empower and to support people in the communities where Lincoln has a presence.

The CPP has a dedicated committee who meet regularly to consider applications against their award criteria. They aim to make as much of an impact as possible with the donations that they make.

Priority is given to those projects that:

- enable support and service to help people realise their full potential or improve their quality of life
- enable education for disadvantaged people
- enhance quality of life through the arts and culture
- provide evidence that the partner is making a determined effort to help themselves
- provide opportunities for Lincoln to make a significant impact even with a comparatively small sum of money
- preferably give exclusivity for Lincoln
- preferably do not receive funding from elsewhere, e.g., from Lottery monies
- may be supported by employees who are contributing their own time or money.

Lincoln has a strong relationship with The National Star Centre, based near its headquarters, which is a secondary education college for young adults with physical disabilities.

### Exclusions

The following types of projects are not usually supported: capital projects, such as the construction of a village hall or a scout hut; running costs, staffing costs, wages or general operating shortfalls; advertising support; general fundraising where the contribution would be merely a drop in the ocean rather than making a significant difference; schools, playgroups or colleges (except in exceptional circumstances); the services, such as ambulance, police and army; hospitals or health service projects that should normally be funded by the NHS; fraternal, political or religious organisations or activities; projects which are for the benefit of a single individual; travel or sports activities; or ventures partly or wholly outside of the UK.

## Applications

On a form available from the correspondent, or downloadable from the website.

**Information available:** A full list of organisations supported through Lincoln's CPP is available on its website (www.lfg.com).

## Corporate giving

During 2005 the committee has allocated the full funding of £117,647.00 to a range of charities throughout the Gloucestershire area in the areas of education, the arts and human services. The following were included:

### Arts

Cheltenham Festival of Music (£6,000)

Gloucestershire Young Musician of the Year (£3,200)

Gloucester Dance (£5,000)

Everyman Theatre in association with National Star Centre (£6,839)

Gloucestershire Symphony Orchestra (£3,500)

### Education

Cheltenham Festival of Literature (£5,000)

Gloucestershire Wildlife (£5,000)

National Star Centre (£5,600)

Royal National Institute for the Deaf (£2,000)

### Human Services

Holiday Support (£1,350)

Chamwell Holiday Playscheme (£5,000)

Christian Lewis Trust (£2,200)

The Spring Centre (£25,450)

Children's Heart Federation (£6,300)

The Family Haven (£5,450)

## In-kind support

The CPP in the UK has taken an innovative approach to its award giving and decided to help address problems of adult illiteracy highlighted by a national survey carried out in the UK. This showed that one in five adults have problems with reading and/or writing.

With the help of an experienced and acclaimed adult literacy teacher, the CPP commissioned and published two books titled 'Help Yourself to Write a Letter' and 'Help Yourself to Fill in a Form'.

## Employee-led support

The company matches employees' sponsorship efforts to a maximum of £100 per individual or £1,000 for a group.

## Commercially-led support

It has also operated a scheme which gave £10 to the National Star Centre for each new account opened during a month.

# Linklaters

One Silk Street, London EC2Y 8HQ

020 7456 2000

Website: www.linklaters.com

Correspondent: The Community Investment Manager

| Year end 31/12/2005 | Turnover | Pre-tax profit |
|---|---|---|

**Nature of company business**
International law firm.

**Main locations:** London

---

### Charitable donations

Total community contributions: £4,000,000

Membership: A & B, BitC, L B Group, %Club

---

## Community involvement

Linklaters charitable donations budget is based on 0.5% of its global profits. However, Linklaters recognise that there is more to community investment programme than just donating money. As such, it seeks to provide pro bono (i.e. free) legal advice and representation to those unable to afford it, and to tackle social exclusion where it exists in communities close to the firm's offices. The following areas have been identified:

- achievement – empowering emerging talent to achieve its potential
- enterprise – encouraging enterprising and entrepreneurial people
- access to Justice – asserting legal rights and responsibilities.

## Exclusions

No support for appeals from individuals or local appeals not in areas of company presence.

## Applications

In writing to the correspondent.

## Corporate giving

According to the Per Cent Club 2006 report the company's overall contribution was £4 million.

## In-kind support

**Legal:** *Pro bono clients* – this involves providing legal advice and legal services to a range of charities and voluntary organisations at no, or reduced, cost.

More than 15 community programmes are in operation, designed to support non-profit groups, charities, law centres, advice agencies and small businesses in the neighbouring boroughs of Tower Hamlets, Hackney, Newham and Southwark. These range from local school literacy and maths programmes to giving legal advice at law centres, ethnic minority undergraduate mentoring and supporting initiatives to tackle homelessness. Individual, group and firm-wide involvement is encouraged and much of this work is carried out during the working week.

Whenever possible, the firm also makes available meeting rooms for those charities and organisations which require the use of central London facilities.

## Employee-led support

Besides the structured in kind support provided through pro bono work and established volunteering options, staff have raised money for a range of charities. This is matched pound for pound by the firm's community award scheme, up to a maximum of £500 for individuals and £1,000 for teams.

Linklaters LinkAid (Charity Commission no.: 1076058) allows staff to make their own regular personal contribution to charity. The fund is administered by a special committee comprising representatives from across the firm, which assesses requests received from a wide range of organisations and charities that apply for funding. Staff are actively encouraged to promote charities of particular interest to them. In 2004 it had an income and expenditure of £45,000. Beneficiaries have included Action for Kids, Barnardos, Central and Cecil Housing Trust, Childline, Colchester Emergency Night Shelter, London Symphony Orchestra and Lord Mayor's Appeal – Music for Everyone, NCH and NSPCC.

In addition, a large number of staff make monthly fixed amount donations to specific charities of their choice through direct debit arrangements, whilst others create their own personal charity account into which they can place funds and from which they can donate to charities of their choice at a time they consider appropriate.

**Payroll giving:** The Give As You Earn scheme is offered by the firm to enable employees to give tax effectively to a charity/charities of their choice or to the firm's Link Aid Fund.

## Commercially-led support

**Sponsorship:** *The arts* – Around 20% of the firm's annual donations budget goes towards supporting concerts in the City of London and Spitalfields Festivals.

# LINPAC Group Limited

3180 Park Square, Birmingham Business Park, Birmingham B37 7YN

0121 607 6700; Fax: 0121 607 6767

Website: www.linpac.com

Correspondent: Angela Thomas, PA to the Finance Director

| Year end | Turnover | Pre-tax profit |
| --- | --- | --- |
| 31/12/2004 | £1,130,200,000 | £60,300,000 |

Nature of company business
The principle activities of the group are the manufacture and marketing of plastic and paper products for packaging. The principal activity of the company is that of a holding company.

Subsidiaries include: Apex Storage System Ltd, Aquafilm Ltd, Billoway Engineering Ltd, Salter Paper Group Ltd

Main locations: Birmingham

Total employees: 11,673

### Charitable donations

2004: £75,000
2003: £53,000

## Community involvement

The company (previously listed in these pages as Linpac Containers Ltd, a subsidiary which has since been sold) has stated that it does not complete surveys and has not responded to our requests for information on its community support.

We were previously advised that a fund had been set up to support schools, which received all donations made by the company. We do not know if this is still the situation.

### Exclusions

No support for appeals from individuals. No support for local appeals not in areas of company presence.

### Applications

In writing to the correspondent.

## Corporate giving

The group made charitable donations amounting to £75,000 during the year. (£53,000 in 2003).

# Littlewoods Shop Direct Group Ltd

Skyways House, Speke Road, Speke, Liverpool, L70 1AB

Website: www.littlewoods.com

Correspondent: The Head of Corporate Communications

| Year end | Turnover | Pre-tax profit |
| --- | --- | --- |
| 30/04/2005 | £2,634,500,000 | (£56,200,000) |

Nature of company business
Littlewoods is one of the UK's major home shopping organisations. The company was sold to the Barclay brothers in November 2002.

Subsidiaries include: UKCL Ltd, Charities Trust Ltd, J & C Moores Ltd, Old Hall InsuranceServices Ltd, The International Import & Export Co Ltd, CDMS Ltd, Stanley Insurance Services Ltd

Main locations: Preston, Liverpool, Oldham, Sunderland, Bolton

UK employees: 29,110

### Charitable donations

2005: £500,000
2003: £300,000

## Community involvement

The following was taken from the company's website at the end of 2006 under the heading 'Committed to long-term partnerships'.

'We are committed to supporting our local environment and are an active participant within the community.

'We see the value in investing in charitable organisations, to ensure that they receive the full support and benefits that come from working in partnership with a commercial enterprise.

'As part of our ongoing charitable and community support, we actively encourage all employees to join us in helping to make a difference to the charities we have committed to long-term partnerships with.

'Our two charities of choice are Alder Hey Children's Hospital and its Imagine Appeal, and Weston Spirit, a charity working with disadvantaged teenagers.'

### Exclusions

No support for advertising in charity brochures, animal welfare, appeals from individuals, children/youth, elderly people, fundraising events, medical research, overseas projects, political appeals, religious appeals, science/technology, sickness/disability, social welfare or sport.

### Applications

In writing to the correspondent.

## Corporate giving

In 2004/05 the company made charitable donations of £500,000.

### In-kind support

Previously, donations have been made in the form of recycled damaged, returned and surplus items to BDF Newlife and In Kind Direct.

### Employee-led support

Littlewoods continues to be focused and committed in the area of employee involvement. Many of its colleagues actively volunteer in the Merseyside area and nationally.

**Payroll giving:** The company operates the Charities Trust scheme, and match employees' fundraising efforts and giving to limits set for specific campaigns/promotions.

---

# Liverpool Victoria Friendly Society

County Gates, Bournemouth, Dorset BH1 2NF

01202 292333; Fax: 01802 292253

Website: www.liverpoolvictoria.co.uk

Correspondent: Vince Jerrard, Secretary

Chief officer: John Woolhouse

Chief Executive: Mike Rogers

| Year end | Turnover | Pre-tax profit |
|---|---|---|
| 31/12/2005 | | (25,800,000) |

Nature of company business
The society is an incorporated Friendly Society which carries on insurance and financial services business in the UK.

Subsidiaries include: Frizzell Bank, Frizzell Financial Services Limited, Frizzell Life & Financial Planning

Main locations: Bournemouth

UK employees: 1,888

Total employees: 1,888

| Charitable donations |
|---|
| 2005: £32,500 |
| 2004: £38,400 |
| 2003: £27,000 |

## Community involvement

The society did not provide any details of the areas it will or will not support. As such, it is very difficult for charities to make an informed judgement about whether to approach the society regarding its particular needs.

### Applications

In writing to the correspondent.

## Corporate giving

In 2005, the society made cash donations of £32,500 out of the £166,000 donated to its Charities Aid Foundation account. We have no information regarding the beneficiaries.

Liverpool Victoria is involved in Streetwise, a partnership initiative between the emergency services, local authorities and the business community in an aim to raise awareness of everyday safety and good citizenship issues. To date over 30,000 children have benefited from the scheme. Recently Liverpool Victoria, in partnership with Streetwise, has developed a 'home safety game' to promote safety in the home.

---

# Lloyd's of London

One Lime Street, London EC3M 7HA

020 7327 5925

Website: www.lloyds.com

Correspondent: Ms Victoria Mirfin, Trust Secretary

Chief officer: Lord Levene

Chief Executive: Richard Ward

| Year end | Turnover | Pre-tax profit |
|---|---|---|
| 31/12/2005 | | |

Nature of company business
Insurance underwriting market.

Subsidiaries include: LPSO Ltd, LCO Marine Ltd, Lioncover Insurance Co Ltd, Centrewrite Ltd, LCO Non-Marine and Aviation Ltd, Additional Securities Ltd

Main locations: London

| Charitable donations |
|---|
| 2005: £350,000 |
| Membership: BitC, L B Group |

## Community involvement

Lloyd's supports the community through The Lloyd's Charities Trust (Charity Commission no. 207232) and through its community programme.

*The Lloyd's Charities Trust* – Funded mainly by voluntary covenanted subscriptions from members of Lloyd's and by interest on its accumulated endowment. The three nominated charities are supported via the trust through donations, gifts in kind including donations of equipment, and by hosting a meeting/event at Lloyd's for each charity.

*The Lloyd's Community Programme* – This programme was set up in partnership with Business in the Community. It aims to encourage links between Lloyd's and their neighbours in Tower Hamlets. The programme has now become more independent as it has established strong contacts and links with schools and voluntary sector organisations within Tower Hamlets – in particular Tower Hamlets Education Business Partnership.

The programme is supported by subscriptions from Lloyd's firms and firms closely associated with the market.

### Exclusions

No support for advertising in charity brochures, animal welfare, appeals from individuals, the arts, sponsorship, environment/heritage, fundraising events, medical research, political appeals, religious appeals, science/technology, sport or local appeals not in areas of company presence.

### Applications

Due to the current policy, unsolicited applications cannot be supported.

## Corporate giving

In 2005 the company donated around £350,000 to its charitable trust. No other financial details were available.

The company currently supports the following three charities through its charitable trust: Hope & Homes for Children, Macmillan Cancer Relief and St Giles Trust. These charity partners are due to be reviewed in 2007.

In addition to the above, ad hoc income from covenants, bequests and donations is distributed through: Lloyd's Patriotic Fund – established to further research into science, technology and business by way of fellowships and PhD business scholarships, Lloyd's Tercentenary Foundation – established to provide financial assistance to ex-servicemen and women and their widows and dependants; and Lloyd's Community Programme.

### In-kind support

The Community Programme supports schools and local businesses in Tower Hamlets and neighbouring East London boroughs.

### Employee-led support

Although employees of Lloyd's are active volunteers in the communities local to it, we do not know if the company supports charitable activities undertaken by employees in their own time, e.g. by matching funds raised.

### Commercially-led support

Sponsorship is not undertaken.

# Lloyds TSB Group plc

25 Gresham Street, London EC2V 7HN

020 7626 1500

Website: www.lloydstsb.com

Correspondent: Richard Cooper, Head of Corporate Social Responsibility 020 7356 2098
E-mail: richard.cooper@lloydstsb.co.uk

Chief officer: Sir Victor Blank

Chief Executive: J Eric Daniels

| Year end | Turnover | Pre-tax profit |
|---|---|---|
| 31/12/2005 | £10,540,000,000 | £3,820,000,000 |

**Nature of company business**
The Lloyds TSB Group is one of the largest financial services companies in the UK, covering retail banking, commercial and corporate banking, mortgages, life assurance and pensions, general insurance, asset management, leasing, treasury and foreign exchange dealing.

Subsidiaries include: Abbey Life Assurance Co Ltd, Scottish Widows Investment Partnership Group Ltd, Scottish Widows plc, Cheltenham and Gloucester plc, Black Horse Limited, Scottish Widows Annuities Ltd, The Agricultural Mortgage Corpn plc

Main locations: London

UK employees: 77,620

Total employees: 79,594

### Charitable donations

2005: £31,650,000
2004: £31,571,000
2003: £33,800,000

Total community contributions: £36,050,000
Management costs: £500,000
CRM figure: £1,670,000

Membership: A & B, BitC, L B Group, %Club

## Community involvement

Lloyds TSB Group's business is rooted in local communities throughout the UK and the group believes that it has a responsibility to support those communities which it also serves as a business.

Lloyds TSB operates one of the largest community programmes in the UK. Cash donations are made through the four independent Lloyds TSB Foundations, which are grant-making trusts covering England and Wales, Scotland, Northern Ireland and the Channel Islands.

Additional, and not insubstantial, in kind support is provided by the Lloyds TSB Group.

### Exclusions
#### For Lloyds TSB Foundations:

The foundations will not support individuals, including students, or organisations which are not registered charities. There is no support for animal welfare, environment (including geographic/scenic, conservation and protection of flora and fauna), activities which are primarily the responsibility of local or national government or some other responsible body, mainstream schools, universities and colleges (except when benefiting disabled students), hospitals and medical centres, sponsorship and marketing appeals, restoration of buildings, fabric appeals for places of worship, promotion of religion, activities which collect funds for subsequent redistribution to other charities or individuals, endowment funds, general appeals, fundraising events, corporate membership, loans or business finance, expeditions or overseas travel.

## Applications

### For Lloyds TSB Foundations only:

Further details of grant-giving policies and an application form can be obtained by contacting the appropriate Lloyds TSB Foundation for your locality.

- Lloyds TSB Foundation for England and Wales
  PO Box 46156, 3rd Floor, 4 St Dunstan's Hill, London EC3R 8WQ
  0870 411 1223;
  e-mail: guidelines@lloydstsbfoundations.org.uk;
  website: www.lloydstsbfoundations.org.uk
- Lloyds TSB Foundation for Scotland
  Riverside House, 502 Gorgie Road, Edinburgh EH11 3AF
  0870 902 1201;
  e-mail: enquiries@ltsbfoundationforscotland.org.uk;
  website: www.ltsbfoundationforscotland.org.uk
- Lloyds TSB Foundation for Northern Ireland
  The Gate Lodge, 73a Malone Road, Belfast BT9 6SB
  028 9038 2864; e-mail: info@lloydstsbfoundationni.org;
  website: www.lloydstsbfoundationni.org
- Lloyds TSB Foundation for the Channel Islands
  LLoyds TSB House, 25 New Street, St Helier, Jersey, Channel Islands JE4 8RG
  01534 284201;
  e-mail: foundationci@lloydstsb-offshore.com;
  website: www.ltsbfoundationci.org

### For Lloyds TSB Group plc only:

Contact: Richard Cooper, Head of Corporate Responsibility, Lloyds TSB Group plc, 25 Gresham Street, London EC2V 7HN.

## Corporate giving

In 2005, total UK community contributions were £36,550,000 of which £31,650,000 was in cash donations. Management costs amounted to a respectable £500,000. The sum allocated for payment in 2006 to the four Lloyds TSB foundations for distribution in cash grants to registered charities and community groups is £34,450,000 (2004: £31,230,000). This is to be broken down as follows: Scotland will receive £6.7 million, England and Wales £24.8 million, Northern Ireland £1.8 million and the Channel Islands £1.1 million.

### The Lloyds TSB Foundations

The four Lloyds TSB foundations are, in aggregate, one of the UK's largest grant-giving organisations. Since 1996, and the merger of Lloyds Bank and TSB Group, the Lloyds TSB foundations have received around £259 million to distribute to registered charities.

The foundations are shareholders in the Lloyds TSB Group and together they receive, under law, one per cent of the group's pre-tax profits, averaged over three years, instead of the dividend of their shareholding.

The foundations focus their support on social and community needs and education and training. In particular, support is given to recognised charities helping disabled and disadvantaged people to play a fuller role in society. Within this general objective, each of the four foundations support their own areas of special interest. Further details of the foundations proposed activities for 2007 can be had at: www.lloydstsbfoundations.org.uk

## In-kind support

In 2005, the Lloyds TSB Group's corporate community investment totalled £5.4 million.

This included a programme run by Lloyds TSB Scotland which provided an interactive CD-ROM for young people entering work for the first time or starting a course in further education. The Work2 CD-ROM has been issued to every secondary school in Scotland and gives teachers a way of covering a variety of topics relevant to students preparing to leave school.

The Group has a large and dynamic property portfolio and surplus furniture is donated to local groups. Lloyds TSB also provides office space to the charity In-kind Direct.

The Group supports major charity appeals launched by the Disasters Emergency Committee, as well as certain sponsored appeals such as Children in Need, Comic Relief and the Royal British Legion. In addition, the Group runs three nationwide pin badge appeals through its branch network.

Requests for local counter appeal support should be directed to the relevant branch. Please note, however, that no more than one counter appeal will be possible in any branch at any one time.

## Employee-led support

The four independent Lloyds TSB foundations encourage staff of the group to raise funds for community causes through a matched giving scheme. The foundation matches every pound raised, and donates £5 for every hour's voluntary work, to a maximum of £400 per person per year, provided that the charity meets the foundations' broad grant-giving criteria.

In 2005, around £1.3 million was set aside by the foundations to match money raised for, and time given to, charity by staff. Further support is given through:

- Charity of the Year – in 2005, staff raised over £1.6 million for Marie Curie Cancer Care, and in 2004, £1.2 million was raised for NSPCC.
- staff participation in schools as school governors and through mentoring, reading programmes, job hunting and interview skills
- volunteering through the 'Time 2Care' programme which allows employees to donate three working days to support local causes in their community
- staff secondments – currently to Business in the Community.

**Payroll giving:** The group operates the Give As You Earn scheme.

## Commercially-led support

**Sponsorship:** The following is taken from the Group's 'Community Investment Policy' leaflet:

'Sponsorship requests are those that provide a commercial return through exposure of Lloyds TSB's company name or brand.

'You should forward any local requests for sponsorship to your branch who will liaise with their Local Director office where local priorities are determined.

'As a general guide we do not support individuals or overseas activity and would prefer local initiatives to follow the national programme.

'The Group Sponsorship department deals with the national sponsorship programme. Any requests for sponsorship that refers to a specific product should be forwarded to the relevant business unit within Lloyds TSB.'

**Cause-related marketing:** In 2005, a total of £1.67 million was raised on behalf of the company's charity of the year – Marie Curie Cancer Care.

# Lockheed Martin

Manning House, 22 Carlisle Place, London SW1P 1JA

020 7798 2850

Website: www.lockheedmartin.co.uk

Correspondent: Chris Trippick, Director of Communications

Chief Executive: Ian Stopps

**Nature of company business**
Systems integrator and supplier of high technology systems and service to defence and government customers.

**Main locations:** Hertford, Culdrose, Havant, Yeovil, Swindon, London, Malvern, Lincoln, Farnborough, Andover, Ampthill, Whiteley, Aldermaston

UK employees: 1,000

Total employees: 130,000

## Community involvement

Lockheed Martin actively supports over 20 charities in its main operating areas of Hampshire, Somerset and Cornwall. The company also positively encourage its staff to be involved in local community activities.

### Applications

In writing to the correspondent.

## Corporate giving

No UK community contributions figure was available. However, we do know that support has been given to: Charles Dickens Primary School in Portsmouth, for a behavioural unit as well as for trips to Marwell Zoo for high achievers; Culdrose Air Day; Emsworth Food Festival; and, Hawke House Charity in Cornwall.

Lockheed Martin is a charter member of the Duke of Edinburgh's Award, providing financial and practical support to the self-development programme aimed at 14 to 25 year olds. The Prince's Trust is also regularly helped with the company supporting its funding stream for business start-up costs for young people in disadvantaged areas.

### Employee-led support

The company has an annual Lend-a-Hand Day where staff are encouraged to volunteer with Portsmouth Housing Association to undertake tasks such as gardening, DIY and painting. About 10% of the workforce take part in the event.

### Commercially-led support

**Sponsorship:** *The arts* – The company regularly support the Chichester Festival Theatre.

# Lofthouse of Fleetwood Ltd

Maritime Street, Fleetwood, Lancashire FY7 7LP

01253 872435; Fax: 01253 778725

Correspondent: Mrs D W Lofthouse, Trustee, Lofthouse Foundation

Chief officer: Doreen Lofthouse

Managing Director: Tony Lofthouse; Duncan Lofthouse

| Year end | Turnover | Pre-tax profit |
|---|---|---|
| 31/12/2005 | £33,860,248 | £3,881,080 |

**Nature of company business**
Manufacturers of medicated confectionery.

Main locations: Fleetwood

Total employees: 312

**Charitable donations**
2005: £21,712
2004: £350,300

## Community involvement

Manufacturers of the famous 'Fisherman's Friend', most of the company's charitable support is channelled through the Lofthouse Foundation (Charity Commission no. 1038728). In 2005 the company donated £20,000 to the trust. The trust was established in June 1994 with general charitable objects for the benefit of Fleetwood and its environs. There are three trustees, all of whom are members of the Lofthouse family.

### Exclusions

The foundation does not support: advertising in charity brochures, animal welfare, the arts, overseas projects, religious appeals, science/technology or social welfare.

### Applications

In writing to the correspondent.

## Corporate giving

In 2005, the company's annual report states: 'Payments of a charitable nature made during the year amounted to £21,712(2004: £350,300)'. In 2005 the Lofthouse Foundation donated £48,149 to the NHS Trust for Fleetwood Hospital and in 2004 the NHS Trust had benefited from the foundation in the amount of £1,551,851.

# London Stock Exchange

10 Paternoster Square, London EC4M 7LS

020 7797 1000; Fax: 020 7588 3504

Website: www.londonstockexchange.com

Correspondent: Jon Weedon, Internal Communications Manager
020 7797 4330
E-mail: jweedon@londonstockexchange.com

Chief officer: Chris Gibson-Smith

Chief Executive: Clara Furse

| Year end | Turnover | Pre-tax profit |
|----------|----------|----------------|
| 31/03/2005 | £260,000,000 | £89,000,000 |

**Nature of company business**
The London Stock Exchange is one of the world's leading equity exchanges and an international provider of services that facilitate the raising of capital and the trading of shares and debt securities.

**Subsidiaries include:** SE Mutual Reference Ltd, The Birmingham Stock Exchange Buildings Co Ltd

**Main locations:** Birmingham, London

**UK employees:** 519

### Charitable donations
2005: £124,000
2004: £101,000
2003: £108,000

Total community contributions: £167,000

## Community involvement

The London Stock Exchange believes that it has a responsibility towards the wider society in which it conducts its business and to support its staff in their individual and collective efforts to make a contribution to the community. It does this by:

▶ making a positive contribution to the community by adopting a partner charity
▶ encouraging employee involvement in supported community projects and initiatives.

For two years from 2004, the LSE's partner charity has been Brainwave, one of the UK's leading charities supporting children who have brain impairment or injury.

### Exclusions
Political, overseas and purely religious charities are not supported.

### Applications
Applications to be considered as a partner charity should be introduced by e-mail to the named contact. Applications for ad hoc financial support are not encouraged.

## Corporate giving

There is a budget of £100,000 each year for the organisation's charitable support. The budget is split roughly 75% to 25% in favour of the partner charity, with the remaining funds going towards matching employees charitable contributions – around 30 to 40 charities receive small donations in this way. In 2005, cash donations totalled £124,000 with a further £43,000 being raised through the sale of old office equipment.

### In-kind support
Support was given to a number of charities by allowing them the use of the London Stock Exchange event facilities and in-house catering so they could hold business development events at zero cost.

Following an office move and a technology update, the company was able to donate around 800 PCs and screens to Tools For Schools, a charity that matches redundant computers from the business community with schools across the UK who need them most. Similarly, sale of much of the office furniture left behind in the move to staff, small business

start-ups and charities, enabled the £43,000 raised to be donated to the Trident Trust and Brainwave.

### Employee-led support
The London Stock Exchange has a staff matching programme which matches funds raised by staff for any UK registered charity, pound for pound, up to a maximum of £1,000 per employee. 2005 saw a significant increase (over 50%) in staff matching applications on the preceding year. The company also makes 'community awards' to charities to recognise the time spent by members of staff performing voluntary work with them in their own time.

**Payroll giving:** The Give As You Earn scheme is in operation.

# Low & Bonar plc

50 Seymour Street, London W1H 7JG

020 7535 3180; Fax: 020 7535 3181

**Website:** www.lowandbonar.com

**Chief officer:** R D Clegg

**Chief Executive:** P A Forman

| Year end | Turnover | Pre-tax profit |
|----------|----------|----------------|
| 30/11/2005 | £226,986,000 | (£26,563,000) |

**Nature of company business**
Plastics, packaging and specialist material manufacture.

**Subsidiaries include:** Anglo-Danish Fibres Ltd, Fibrin Humberside Ltd

**Main locations:** Ripley, Bamber Bridge, Telford, Dundee, London

**Total employees:** 2,325

### Charitable donations
2005: £20,000
2004: £15,000

## Community involvement

Previously, donations were made through a company trust (the Low & Bonar Charitable Fund – SC010837). However, we have been advised that the assets of this fund have been used to create a new 'independent' charity called the Low & Bonar Charitable Trust (SC031663), which apparently has no connection with the company (name excepted!).

The charitable purposes of the new trust are listed on the Scottish Charity Register as:

▶ relief of poverty
▶ advancement of education
▶ advancement of health
▶ advancement of the arts, heritage, culture or science
▶ relief of those in need through age, ill health, or disability.

There is a preference for supporting smaller charities in the areas of Tayside and north east Fife.

### Exclusions
No support for non-registered charities. No grants for local appeals not in areas of company presence; advertising in charity brochures; animal welfare; appeals from individuals; enterprise/training; fundraising events; political or religious appeals; science/technology; overseas projects, or sport.

## Applications

It is unclear since the transferral of the assets of the company's charitable fund to the new 'independent' trust, whether it accepts unsolicited applications for support. Until clarification can be obtained on this, we suggest applications be addressed to: Nick Barclay, Administrative Secretary, Low & Bonar Charitable Trust, Thortons Law LLP, 50 Castle Street, Dundee DD1 3RU. (Tel: 01382 229111; e-mail: nbarclay@thortons-law.co.uk) Note: Only written applications are accepted by the trust.

The trustees meet quarterly. Support is only given to charities registered with the Charity Commission or, in Scotland, the Inland Revenue.

## Corporate giving

Despite the changes detailed above that have taken place, the company still makes the majority of its donations via this new, unconnected, trust. In 2005, this amounted to £15,000 (substantially down on the average of £65,000 a year made through the company trust), with an additional £5,000 being donated to the Disasters Emergency Committee following the tsunami in south east Asia.

# Lowe & Partners Ltd

60 Sloane Avenue, London SW3 3XB

020 7584 5033; Fax: 020 7823 8429

Website: www.loweuk.com

Correspondent: Amanda Walsh, Chief Executive

Chief Executive: Amanda Walsh

| Year end | Turnover | Pre-tax profit |
|---|---|---|
| 31/12/2004 | £75,352,000 | (£6,621,000) |

Nature of company business
Principal activities: advertising. Subsidiaries are based in 12 European countries, USA and Canada.

Subsidiaries include: Lowe Howard-Spink, Orbit International, Brompton Agency

Main locations: London

UK employees: 225

### Charitable donations

2004: £37,273
2003: £23,304

## Community involvement

Information previously received stated that the company adopted a staff charity voting system whereby their employees decide which charities they would like the company to support in the forthcoming year. Once the charity budget has been allocated in accordance with the staff's wishes, no further support is possible.

### Exclusions

No support for individuals, circular appeals or small purely local appeals not in areas of company presence.

## Applications

In writing to the correspondent, but note the above policy implying that very little support, if any, is available for unsolicited appeals.

## Corporate giving

In 2004, Lowe made charitable contributions in the UK totalling £37,273 (2003: £23,304). We have no details of the beneficiaries.

# Luminar Leisure Limited

Luminar House, Deltic Avenue, Rooksley, Milton Keynes MK13 8LW

Website: www.luminar.co.uk

Correspondent: Stephen Loades, c/o ECHO Trust

Chief officer: Keith Hamill

Chief Executive: Stephen C Thomas

| Year end | Turnover | Pre-tax profit |
|---|---|---|
| 02/03/2006 | £288,100,000 | £24,500,000 |

Nature of company business
The principal activity of the group is as owner, developer and operator of theme bars, nightclubs and restaurants.

Main locations: Milton Keynes

UK employees: 7,870

### Charitable donations

2005: £76,675

## Community involvement

The company established the ECHO (Entertainment Organised for Children's Health) Trust in 2002 to channel its charitable activities to those in need. It aims to ensure the availability of cash for good causes across the country and within the communities in which the company operates. As the trust's acronym indicates, there is a particular preference for causes related to children's health.

The trust's main source of income appears to be from donations made by staff and customers. Although income is also derived directly from the company, this does not currently appear to occur annually.

### Exclusions

No support for advertising in charity brochures, general or circular appeals, political or religious causes.

### Applications

In writing to the correspondent. Letters of application should include: Details of your charity/good cause, details of any current fundraising projects which you would like to have considered for a grant and the cost plan for this.

Please note that applications for essential medical equipment, children's health care projects or new exciting research projects will be favoured more than those for wish fulfilment or upgrading/refurbishment of premises.

Any children's health project wishing to apply for funding can e-mail: contact@echotrust.org

Applications are accepted throughout the year, and considered by trustees in December and January, advising successful applicants in February. The next round of donations will be considered from March 2007.

## Corporate giving

Since its foundation in 2002, the trust has donated money to a number of children's charities, health projects and hospices across the UK. Grants are given towards the costs of specific pieces of specialised equipment. Monies are collected throughout the year and distributed in March.

In 2004/05, the trust had an income of £440,000 mainly from donations, but including £76,675 directly from the company. Grants to about 100 organisations totalled £398,000. Grants were in the range of £60 to £26,000.

Beneficiaries at the end of February 2006 included:

- Children on the Edge, towards building a child friendly space in Banda Ache following the tsunami (£100,000).
- Nordoff Robbins Music Therapy, towards musical equipment including a piano for their new school in Newbury (£13,000).
- The Pace Centre, towards a specialist mobility programme (£8,100).
- British Institute for Brain Injured Children, towards the purchase of equipment for their new centre in Wales (£3,100).
- Brainwave, towards enabling the charity to provide continuous professional development to children with special needs (£7,500).
- East Anglia's Children's Hospices, towards running three hospices and towards general running costs (£7,500).
- Action For Kids, towards the purchase of a powered wheelchair for a child on their waiting list (£7,000).
- Christian Lewis Trust, towards funding for play therapists (£2,300).

# Man Group plc

Sugar Quay, Lower Thames Street, London EC3R 6DU

020 7144 1000; Fax: 020 7144 1923

Website: www.mangroupplc.com

Correspondent: Debbie Styer, Secretary to the Charitable Trust

Chief officer: Harvey McGrath

Chief Executive: Peter Clarke

| Year end | Turnover | Pre-tax profit |
|---|---|---|
| 31/03/2006 | £2,014,000,000 | £712,600,000 |

Nature of company business
The company is a leading global provider of alternative investment products and solutions, as well as one of the world's largest future brokers.

Main locations: London

UK employees: 1,261

Total employees: 4,576

## Charitable donations

2006: £2,455,000
2005: £1,724,596
2004: £506,000

Management costs: £505,000

Membership: A & B, %Club

## Community involvement

The company state in its annual report: 'The group believes that being active in the wider community is an essential part of the way in which we run our business. We seek to do this both through charitable giving, encouragement to staff to become involved in their local communities and through selective sponsorship of the arts.'

The company's donations are mainly made through the Man Group plc Charitable Trust (Charity Commission no. 275386), which was established in 1978.

The company stated that: 'The policy of the trust is spread its donations across a range of medical, educational, social and cultural charities. Donations to selected charities are generally made on the basis of a three year commitment. Members of the charitable trust participate in and visit each selected charity and preference is given to charities where are contribution can make a significant difference.'

**Charity of the year:** The Richard House Children's Hospice (2006/07).

### Applications

In writing to the correspondent.

**Information available:** Besides producing an annual corporate responsibility report, the group also provide online access to its internal 'Corporate Responsibility Manual'. This provides an interesting insight into why the company does what it does for the community and how. Such levels of transparency are to be welcomed.

## Corporate giving

In 2005/06, worldwide cash donations totalled £3,280,000 with a further £505,000 being spent in management costs. Out of the donations, £2,455,000 went to the Man Group plc Charitable Trust.

Beneficiaries during the year included: Whitechapel Art Gallery; London Youth Rowing; and, the pianoMan project which involves international concert pianist, Richard Meyrick, visiting two schools in every county in the UK.

### Employee-led support

All staff are encouraged to become involved in charitable activities. Accordingly, 'In addition to the selected charities the trustees [of the group charitable trust] give preference to charities where a staff member has an involvement and they will generally match any sponsorship raised by staff members for charitable events'.

The trust will match up to £2,500 per person per year, individual employee fundraising efforts. There are no constraints as to which charity may benefit from these donations.

**Payroll giving:** The Give As You Earn scheme is in operation.

## Commercially-led support

**Sponsorship:** *The arts:* Selected arts sponsorship is undertaken. The most significant of these is the Man Booker Prize for Fiction.

# Manchester Airport plc

Wythenshawe, Manchester M90 1QX

0161 489 3000; Fax: 0161 489 3813

Website: www.manchesterairport.co.uk

Correspondent: Mrs Wendy Sinfield, Community Relations Manager
E-mail: community.relations@manairport.co.uk

Chief officer: Alan Jones

Chief Executive: Geoff Muirhead

| Year end 31/03/2006 | Turnover £385,200,000 | Pre-tax profit £60,700,000 |
|---|---|---|

**Nature of company business**
International airport operation.

**Subsidiaries include:** Bainsdown Limited, Ringway Handling Limited, Airport Trading Limited, Airport Advertising Limited, Airport Management Consultants Limited, Worknorth II Limited, Worknorth Limited

**Main locations:** Manchester

**UK employees:** 2,173

### Charitable donations

2006: £100,000
2005: £100,000
2004: £100,000
2003: £100,000

Membership: A & B, BitC

## Community involvement

The airport company established the Manchester Airport Community Trust Fund (Charity Commission no. 1071703) as a community based initiative to promote, enhance, improve, protect and conserve the natural and built environment in areas which are affected by the activities of Manchester Airport.

The trust will support projects which:

- encourage tree planting, forestation, landscaping and other works of environmental improvement or heritage conservation
- promote or advance social welfare for recreation, sport and leisure, with the object of improving the conditions of life for those living or working in, or visitors to, the area of benefit
- provide better appreciation of the natural and urban environment, and ways of better serving, protecting and improving the same. This may include education and training
- promote the use of the natural environment as a safe habitat for flora and fauna of all kinds.

Projects must be for the benefit of the whole local community or a substantial section of it, and not groups of an exclusive nature. Preference will be given to projects that have considered the needs of disabled or elderly people within the community.

Priority will be given to schemes where the trust's grant will be at least matched by funding from other sources, such as an organisation's own fundraising or another grant. The trust will especially welcome partnership schemes or schemes forming part of an agreed overall plan or programme.

Support is only given to organisations within a 20-mile radius of Manchester Airport (i.e. south Manchester, Altrincham, Bramhall, Stockport, Wilmslow, borough of Congleton (excluding the town of Congleton), borough of Macclesfield (excluding the town of Macclesfield), and up to, but not including, the town of Northwich. Exceptionally, local branches of national charities may also receive help.

More information on the trusts activities can be found in the DSC publication *A Guide to Major Trusts in the North of England*.

### Exclusions

No support for appeals from individuals, commercial organisations, organisations which have statutory responsibilities such as hospitals or schools (unless the project is clearly not a statutory responsibility), those working for profit, or for organisations outside of the trust boundary.

### Applications

Policy guidelines are provided on the application form which is available to organisations upon request. Applicants should obtain the fund's brochure to make sure they fit the criteria. The administrator may also visit the project or proposed site or the applicant may be asked to visit the airport, to provide further details. The trust liaises with local environmental organisations such as Cheshire Wildlife Trust, Cheshire Landscape Trust, Manchester Wildlife Trust and the Groundwork Trust Network; their advice may be asked when projects are being evaluated.

If a large grant is being applied for it will be necessary to check whether funding is available from the year's allocation for large projects. All applications must show clear financial records.

Trustees meet quarterly in the first weeks of April, July, October and January. A minimum of one month should be allowed for applications to be processed. Applications must be received by the administrator not later than the first week of the month proceeding the above meeting times. However, early submission of your application will ensure that any queries can be dealt with before passing it to the trustees.

## Corporate giving

Each year the airport will pay £100,000, plus all income from environmental fines imposed on noisy operators, into the trust fund.

The funding is divided between large and small projects as follows: (i) Large projects costing from £5,000 to £25,000 may be funded over a maximum of three years. In any given year, funding for a large-scale project will not be allowed to exceed £50,000. (ii) Small projects may receive grants to a maximum of £5,000. These projects will be for one year only.

Beneficiaries during 2004/05, included: Friends of Woodlands Park; Knutsford Football Club; Parish Church of St Paul; Toft Cricket Club; and, Houghton Green Community Centre.

## Employee-led support

The company has an active employee volunteering scheme and allows employees company time off in which to volunteer.

## Commercially-led support

**Sponsorship:** *The arts* – Initiatives have ranged from support for the Hallé Orchestra World Tour, to local community based arts and drama projects.

Contact: Sue Jones (Tel: 0161 489 3602).

# Marks and Spencer Group plc

Waterside House, 35 North Wharf Street, London W2 1NW

020 7935 4422; Fax: 020 7487 2679

**Website:** www.marksandspencer.com

**Correspondent:** Mike Barry, Corporate Social Responsibility (Secretary)

**Chief officer:** Paul Myners

**Chief Executive:** Stuart Rose

| Year end | Turnover | Pre-tax profit |
|---|---|---|
| 01/04/2006 | £7,797,700,000 | £751,400,000 |

**Nature of company business**
The principal activities are retailing women's wear, men's wear, lingerie, children's wear, beauty products, home products, food and the provision of financial services. Retailing activities are carried out under the Marks & Spencer and King Super Markets brand names.

**Subsidiaries include:** St Michael Finance plc

**Main locations:** London, Chester

**UK employees:** 65,000

---

### Charitable donations

2006: £3,400,000
2005: £3,000,000
2003: £410,000

Total community contributions: £9,300,000
Management costs: £420,000

Membership: BitC, L B Group, %Club

---

## Community involvement

Marks & Spencer's community programme has altered over the last few years as the company seek to reflect its overall philosophy of 'Helping others to help themselves'. Instead of providing small-scale purely charitable donations, emphasis is now being concentrated in four key areas: employability, education, health and community safety.

*Marks & Start:* its flagship community programme helps people (over 3,300 in 2005/06) to prepare for the world of work. In particular it is aimed at: people who are homeless; people with disabilities; the young unemployed; schoolchildren, including those in deprived areas; students who are the first in their family to aim for higher education; and parents wanting to return to work.

## Exclusions

Marks & Spencer is unable to consider appeals that fall within the following categories:

- personal appeals by, or on behalf of, individuals
- fundraising activities and events, except where our employees are responding to appeals to their local budgets, or where they are actively involved as part of the Matching Funds or Individual Award schemes
- advertising, including goodwill messages, except selected opportunities with our community partners
- the Arts, unless specifically for people with disabilities/special needs or where the arts are used as a vehicle to deliver another area of policy
- overseas trips
- capital funding projects
- third party fundraising initiatives on behalf of a charity
- sports, except those that are specifically for people with disabilities/special needs or where they are used to deter young people from getting involved in crime
- support for specialist school status
- multiple year donations
- animal welfare charities
- political parties
- religious bodies, except where the project is for the benefit of the general public and is non-denominational and non-sectarian
- environmental projects, unless they address other areas of policy.

## Applications

Marks & Spencer receives over 50 requests a month for support. Of these about 12% are pursued and 6% accepted. To stand any chance of success, please check that your organisation can help to address key areas of the company's policy before applying.

## Corporate giving

In 2005/06 the company invested a total of £9.3 million in the community. This principally included £3.4 million in cash, including the cost of its flagship community programme 'Marks and Start', £1.3 million of employee time and £4.2 million in gifts-in-kind. The remainder was made up in employee time from UK, Republic of Ireland and Hong Kong operations.

## In-kind support

Donations of stock were made to a variety of charities, including Shelter, Fareshare, Birth Defects Foundation as well as to the local community.

## Employee-led support

Employees give up their spare time to raise cash and volunteer for a wide range of charities and organisations. We are committed to giving them financial support and provide schemes to enable them to become actively involved in their local communities.

## Commercially-led support

**Cause-related marketing :** By donating a percentage of sales of a special range of products, £1.5 million was raised on behalf of Breakthrough Breast Cancer.

# Marsh Ltd

Tower Place, London EC3R 5BU

020 7357 1000; Fax: 020 7929 2705

Website: www.marsh.co.uk

Correspondent: Alexis Swimer, UK Community Relations Executive

Chief officer: Sir Peter Middleton

Chief Executive: Alex Moczarski

| Year end | Turnover | Pre-tax profit |
|---|---|---|
| 31/12/2005 | | |

Nature of company business
Risk management and insurance services company. UK business conducted to identify, value, control, transfer and finance risk for clients that range from multinationals to small commercial and private businesses.

Subsidiaries include: Guy Carpenter & Co Ltd, Global Broking Europe

Main locations: Liverpool, Birmingham, Edinburgh, Glasgow, Leeds, Bristol, Newcastle, London, Southampton

UK employees: 4,100

### Charitable donations

Membership: A & B, BitC, L B Group

## Community involvement

Marsh Limited is an operating unit of Marsh & McLennan Companies Inc. Marsh has had a long and well-established community relations programme in the UK, although its giving programme is currently under review. Once this has been completed, details will be made available on the company's website.

At the moment, its activities in the UK are limited to the following areas:

- employee volunteering
- charity of the year (employee nominated)
- matched funding of payroll donations
- matched funding of employee fundraising and volunteer efforts.

Charity of the Year: The Teenage Cancer Trust (2007/08).

## Exclusions

Donations will not be made (other than in exceptional circumstances) to religious organisations or causes, political parties or causes, advertising in charity brochures, circular appeals, international crisis appeals, overseas causes, appeals for individuals' education, expeditions or recreation, animal welfare or sport.

## Applications

In view of the ongoing review of the company's giving programme, unsolicited applications for funding are not currently being accepted.

Please refer to Marsh's website for updates regarding this.

## Corporate giving

Marsh was unable to provide a figure for its UK community support in 2006. However, it is anticipated that once the above mentioned review process has been completed, figures detailing future levels of support will once again be available.

## Employee-led support
### Employee Volunteering

Marsh's employee volunteering policy entitles every employee to a minimum of one day per year to take part in a programme that supports the community. Activities range from one-day 'Team Challenges' to one-to-one mentoring.

Through the 'Marsh MAGIC' scheme, the fundraising and volunteer efforts of employees, for the communities and charities of their choice, are matched by the company up to a ceiling of £500 per year.

Payroll giving; Marsh adds 10% to employees' payroll donations to charities of their choice via Give As You Earn.

Staff can also choose to donate the odd pennies from their pay slip to the 'Charity of the Year' under the Pennies from Heaven scheme.

# Marshall of Cambridge (Holdings) Ltd

Airport House, Newmarket Road, Cambridge CB5 8RX

01223 373737; Fax: 01223 373562

Website: www.marshallgroup.co.uk

Correspondent: Johnathan Barker, Company Secretary

Chief officer: Michael Marshall

| Year end | Turnover | Pre-tax profit |
|---|---|---|
| 31/12/2005 | £574,042,000 | £1,222,000 |

Nature of company business
The principal activities of the group are car and commercial vehicle sales, distribution, service, hire and associated activities, together with general engineering connected with aircraft and military systems.

Subsidiaries include: Ted Salisbury & Sons Ltd, Tim Brinton Cars Lts, Fellhouse Ltd

Main locations: Ipswich, Huntingdon, Cambridge, Croydon

UK employees: 3,569

### Charitable donations
2005: £29,000
2004: £35,000
2003: £36,000

## Community involvement

A major engineering employee in Cambridge, the company takes an active role in the communities local to its operating sites.

National projects which benefit from the encouragement and help of the Group of Companies include: The Air League Educational Trust, the Air Training Corps, the RAF

Benevolent Fund, the Duke of Edinburgh's Award and BEN, the charity of the Motor Industry.

The company has strong links with Cambridge University (there is a Sir Arthur Marshall Institute within the Engineering Department), along with local schools and colleges and training and enterprise bodies.

### Exclusions

No support for advertising in charity brochures, animal welfare, appeals from individuals, fundraising events, overseas projects, political appeals, religious appeals, or local appeals not in areas of company presence.

### Applications

In writing to the correspondent.

## Corporate giving

In 2005, the company made charitable donations in the UK of £29,000 (2004: £35,000). We have no detailed information as to which organisations benefited from the company's donation/s.

### In-kind support

Help is given through, for example, an adult retraining scheme and headteacher mentoring.

### Employee-led support

The Group of Companies and its employees participate in a wide range of community projects including: wildlife, the arts, sport, healthcare, education and charities.

**Payroll Giving:** The group encourages staff charitable donations under the Give As You Earn scheme.

### Commercially-led support

**Sponsorship:** The company supports a number of local schools and has sponsored four Cambridge Schools, Teversham Church of England Primary School, Bottisham Village College, Coleridge Community College and the Fields Early Years Centre, where dedicated members of staff assist with a wide range of projects, particularly those connected to Science, Technology, Engineering and Mathematics. There is also a diverse programme of visits to the Company's Airport Works premises.

# Bernard Matthews Ltd

Great Witchingham Hall, Norwich NR9 5QD

01603 872611; Fax: 01603 871118

**Website:** www.bernardmatthews.com

**Correspondent:** David M Reger, Company Secretary

**Chief officer:** B T Matthews

**Managing Director:** D J Joll

| Year end | Turnover | Pre-tax profit |
|---|---|---|
| 28/12/2005 | £479,925,000 | £24,371,000 |

**Nature of company business**
The principal activities of the group are the production and marketing of turkey and red meat products, oven-ready turkeys, day-old turkeys, fish products and other poultry products.

**Main locations:** Norwich

Total employees: 7,082

### Charitable donations
2005: £303,611
2004: £463,563
Membership: %Club

## Community involvement

The company has a preference for local charities in the areas where it operates (East Anglia), especially those concerned with children, youth, environment and the arts. As well as cash donations the company donates gifts in kind.

A wide range of small organisations are supported locally, for example local churches, village halls and playgroups.

### Exclusions

No support for circular appeals, advertising in charity brochures, animal welfare, appeals from individuals, overseas projects, political appeals, sport, local appeals not in areas of company presence, or large national appeals.

### Applications

In writing to the correspondent.

## Corporate giving

In 2004/05, the company made donations to charitable causes totalling £303,611. No details of beneficiaries were available, although the company has previously supported the Caister Lifeboat, the Tate in East Anglia Foundation, the Duke of Edinburgh's Award, and the Prince's Trust. Local schools, youth activities and the arts (arts festivals, local museums and exhibitions) have also benefited.

### In-kind support

**Environment:** Support for the environment is a major consideration and a tree planting programme has been ongoing around the East Anglian sites, including a 30-acre future wood.

### Employee-led support

The company supports employees' volunteering/charitable activities through financial support and allowing company time off to volunteer.

# Mazars LLP

24 Bevis Marks, London EC3A 7NR

020 7377 1000

**Website:** www.mazars.co.uk

**Correspondent:** Peter R Hyatt, Partner of Mazars and Chairman of Mazars Charitable Trustee Management Committee
0207 220 3462; Fax: 0207 377 9975
E-mail: peter.hyatt@mazars.co.uk

**Chief officer:** D Evans

**Chief Executive:** D Chapman

**Managing Director:** G Williams

| Year end | Turnover | Pre-tax profit |
|---|---|---|
| 02/09/2005 | £64,884,000 | £14,286,000 |

**Nature of company business**
Accountants and Business Advisers.

**Main locations:** London

**UK employees:** 787

---

### Charitable donations

2005: £165,866
2003: £130,000

Membership: BitC, %Club

---

# Community involvement

Support is given through the Mazars Charitable Trust (Charity Commission no. 287735) whose income is virtually all derived from covenants and Gift Aid donations received from Mazars, which aims to donate 1.75% of its profits. The trust was established by a Trust Deed dated 23 August 1983 for the principal purpose of receiving contributions from the partners of the then firm of Neville Russell, Chartered Accountants and disbursing the same to charitable causes. In the years since, the firm has twice changed its name and, on 1 September 2004, its status also from that of a partnership to Mazars LLP (Accountants and Business Advisors), a limited liability partnership. The name of the charity was also changed to its present form in 2003.

A wide range of charities receive support from the trust in the form of time and money. Resources are committed almost entirely to charities known to the partners and employees of the firm (charities' requests must be authenticated by a recognised agency). Unsolicited appeals are rarely considered.

The trust states it prefers to support specific projects (e.g. capital expenditure, research, an event) rather than normal revenue expenditure, although the latter will be considered provided that the applicant appears to be launching a strategic initiative and is financially sound.

It also: 'supports charities which reflect the corporate ethos of our donor, the UK firm of Mazars. This ethos is being developed over time, but encapsulates the following sorts of charitable activity, associated with organizations which:

▶ will benefit significantly from receipt of a grant (i.e. the trust rarely supports large national charities)
▶ support professionals of whom our team are members (e.g. Chartered Accountants Benevolent Association)
▶ support disadvantaged people in the communities near which our offices are based
▶ seek to place people into employment and assist in housing (essential if a job is to be held down)
▶ seek to relieve hardship in deprived areas of the world in crisis situations
▶ as a firm, we wish to provide active support as a means of encouraging our team's participation in charitable activity (e.g. Business in the Community or Prince's Trust in areas like mentoring, providing time and expertise in lieu of cash, or cash backing for voluntary work)
▶ our clients are encouraging us to support (subject always to careful adherence to independence criteria)'.

'It is hoped that by specifying these varying aims may over time lead to particular focuses in one form of activity in which initiatives are fostered by team members with the active support of the regional reps on the trust management committee and their RMP or other manager reputed to manage the region's pot.'

In addition, applications for smaller amounts, usually between £50 and £500 may be made to one of the company's regions. These do not entail such detailed criteria and information can be obtained from the correspondent's secretary Francoise Dutrieux.

## Exclusions

There is no support available for advertising in charity brochures, fundraising events, political appeals, science/technology or sport.

The company rarely supports large national charities as it prefers to welcome applications where a grant will make a significant impact.

The company will not permit a further application from a particular charity within a three year period of an earlier grant.

Commitment will not be made to on-going funding on the grounds that the future income of the trust is not assured.

The company does not generally support causes that are local to the partner/staff member proposing, as there is a regional allocation for smaller, less strategic applications to be made at the discretion of local managing partners.

## Applications

In writing to any partner or employee of the firm. The trustees operate through a management committee which meets annually to consider applications for major grants which fit with the stated criteria. Some monies are allocated to five regional 'pot' holders who approve minor grant applications from within their own region. Applicants for a national grant must be known to the team members of Mazars LLP. National and Regional criteria are regularly reviewed but, in general, the Trustees consider that the National grant making policy should avoid core funding and other activities that require funding over a number of years. Most National grants are therefore made towards one-off projects. Successful National applicants may not reapply within three years.

A copy of these criteria is available upon request to the Trust Administrator.

From April 2004 onwards, it was determined that grants will be broadly split between those received with a personal commendation of team members of Mazars LLP, the donor firm and those which are aligned to the LLP's corporate ethos.

# Corporate giving

The company donated £165,866 (inclusive of Income Tax recovered) to the trust and its was the largest single donation received. The charity made donations to charitable causes totalling £161,713.

## Employee-led support

Employees are encouraged to get involved with community/charitable projects/fundraising and grants from the trust are available on a meter funding basis. On occasion, match funding may be available for any charitable project/work in which a staff member becomes involved up to a maximum of £250.

**Payroll giving:** The company operates the Give As You Earn scheme.

# MBNA Europe Bank Ltd

Chester Business Park, Chester CH4 9FB

01244 672000; Fax: 01244 673564

Website: www.mbna.com/europe/

Correspondent: Charity Correspondent, MBNA General Foundation 01244 672000

| Year end | Turnover | Pre-tax profit |
|---|---|---|
| 31/12/2005 | £1,372,584,000 | £229,364,000 |

**Nature of company business**
The principal activity of the group is personal lending and ancillary activities in the UK, the Republic of Ireland and Spain.

**Subsidiaries include:** Mainsearch Co Ltd, Chester Property and Services Ltd, Windeluxe Co Ltd, Paneldeluxe Co Ltd

**Main locations:** Chester, London

**UK employees:** 5,388

### Charitable donations

2005: £1,200,000
2004: £1,100,000

Membership: A & B

## Community involvement

The MBNA General Foundation (Charity Commission no. 1065515), which is the recipient of the group's charitable donations, was set up in October 1997 for general charitable purposes. One of its functions is to collect donations from external companies and distribute these to schools, charities and other community groups. Donations are also made by the employees of MBNA Europe Bank Limited and paid over to the charity. The company has contributed a further 50% of the employees' donation for fourteen specified charities and paid these over to the charity.

The Donations Committee and Excellence in Education Grants Committee, subject to approval by the trustees, decide which charities and schools are most suitable based on their assessment of formal applications received.

MBNA and its staff also actively seek to support local charities, the arts and education through volunteering.

### Exclusions

No support for local appeals not in areas of company presence.

### Applications

In writing to the correspondent of the MBNA General Foundation. A donations committee meets monthly to review applications for support.

## Corporate giving

### The MBNA General Charitable Foundation

During the year to 31st December 2005, the group donated £1.2 million to the MBNA General Foundation (2004: £1.1 million) for the purpose of distribution to charities. The foundation also received income from other sources, including the employees of the company. In turn, the foundation distributed £1.2 million (2004: £1.2 million) to charitable causes.

During the period to 31st December 2004, the foundation received £4,174 (2004: £26,365) from the executives of MBNA Europe Bank Limited. These donations were paid directly to schools as recommended by the Excellence in Education Grants Committee and endorsed by the trustees. During this period, the staff of MBNA Europe Bank Limited donated £124,324 (2004: £194,575) and MBNA Europe Bank Limited made a contribution of £49,200 representing 50% of staff contributions to certain charities.

### In-kind support

The company has entered into an agreement with the MBNA General Foundation under which it provides certain administrative, accounting, professional and support services without charge. This agreement cannot be terminated by the company on less than nine months notice.

### Employee-led support

Staff are encouraged to give their time in support of the local community.

**Payroll giving:** The company operates a scheme, People for People, on behalf of its employees. The company match funds 50% of employees' charitable contributions.

### Commercially-led support

MBNA Europe Bank Limited operates a charity card scheme. There are various charities that can be supported in this way. An example is Breakthrough Breast Cancer. When the charity card is first used, MBNA pay a contribution of £5 to Breakthrough Breast Cancer. MBNA will then pay £2 for every year the card is in use and make contributions to the charity every time a purchase is made with the card (0.25% of the value of the purchase).

MBNA's contribution to Breakthrough through this Scheme has now reached over £1,000,000.

# Robert McAlpine Ltd

Eaton Court, Maylands Avenue, Hemel Hempstead, Hertfordshire HP2 7TR

01442 233444; Fax: 01422 230024

Website: www.sir-robert-mcalpine.com

Correspondent: Graham Prain, Charity Co-ordinator

Chief officer: Sir John Hedley Greenborough

| Year end | Turnover | Pre-tax profit |
|---|---|---|
| 31/10/2004 | £681,324,000 | (£43,869,000) |

**Nature of company business**
Principal activities: construction, property and investment.

**Main locations:** Hemel Hempstead

**UK employees:** 1,939

## Community involvement

The company has a preference for local charities in areas where it operates and charities in which a member of the company is involved. Preferred areas for support are children and youth, and education.

There are two charitable trusts associated with the company – The Robert McAlpine Foundation and the McAlpine Educational Endowment. Details of each are given below.

## Exclusions

No support for local appeals not in areas of company presence.

## Applications

In writing to the correspondent.

## Corporate giving

In 2005, the total given in grants by the funds was £360,000.

### The Robert McAlpine Foundation

This gives to organisations supporting children, and people who are deaf or elderly. Support is also given for education, hospices, medical research and social welfare. The foundation receives about 1,000 applications each year, but we are not sure how many are successful or of the size of the grants given. The trustees meet in July and November; successful applicants are informed at the end of the year. Applications should be addressed to the Secretary of the Trustees of the Robert McAlpine Foundation, at the address above.

### The McAlpine Educational Endowment

This trust is for 13 to 18 year olds, who have sound academic ability, show leadership potential and are facing financial hardship. The trust favours ten particular schools, with referrals coming from the headmasters. Applications should be addressed to the Secretary of the Trustees of the McAlpine Educational Endowment, at the address above.

# McCain Foods (GB) Ltd

Havers Hill, Scarborough, North Yorkshire YO11 3BS

01723 584141; Fax: 01723 581230

Website: www.mccain.co.uk

Correspondent: Nicola Loobey, Secretary to the Charities Committee

Managing Director: Nick Vermont

| Year end | Turnover | Pre-tax profit |
|---|---|---|
| 30/06/2005 | £302,601,000 | £33,240,000 |

Nature of company business
The main activities are the manufacture and selling of frozen foods and dry goods, buying and selling of agricultural and industrial handling equipment, operation of cold stores and selling of dairy products.

Subsidiaries include: SSHP Holdings Ltd, Everest Foods plc, Dansco Dairy Products Ltd, PAS Ltd, Britfish Ltd, Tolona Pizza Products Ltd, Everest Frozen Foods Ltd

Main locations: Scarborough, Peterborough, Montrose, Wolverhampton, Teddington

UK employees: 1,790

### Charitable donations

2005: £80,806
2004: £75,406
2003: £20,000

## Community involvement

The company prefers to give all cash donations locally (mainly in Yorkshire and particularly Scarborough). Large national charities are supported through local fundraising events. There is a preference for appeals relevant to company business. Preferred areas of support: children and youth; medical; education; recreation/sport; environment and heritage; the arts; enterprise/training.

### Exclusions

Generally no support for: circular appeals; fundraising events; advertising in charity brochures; appeals from individuals; purely denominational (religious) appeals or local appeals not in areas of company presence.

### Applications

In writing to the correspondent.

## Corporate giving

The contributions made by the company during the year for charitable purposes amounted to £80,806 (2004: £75,406). We have no details regarding the beneficiary charities/groups.

### In-kind support

Additional support is provided through gifts in kind. Although not explicitly stated, we believe this to be in the form of product donations.

# McDonald's UK

11–59 High Road, East Finchley, London N2 8AW

0870 241 3300

Website: www.mcdonalds.co.uk

Correspondent: Joe Zammuto, Corporate Affairs
E-mail: joe.zammuto@uk.mcd.com

| Year end | Turnover | Pre-tax profit |
|---|---|---|
| 31/12/2005 | £1,103,436,000 | £36,949,000 |

Nature of company business
The activity of the company is quick service restaurants.

Main locations: London

Total employees: 47,868

### Charitable donations

2005: £2,197,000
2004: £531,000

Membership: BitC

## Community involvement

Most funding is given through its charitable trust, Ronald McDonald House Charities (UK) formerly Ronald McDonald Children's Charities (Charity Commission no. 802047). The bulk of the trust's work is the creation of 'home away from home' accommodation for the families of children requiring in-patient care in hospitals or hospices. The only other funding available is through the Equipment Grants award programme, which purchases equipment for registered charities, hospitals and schools which will directly support children with special need. There is a preference for specialist play equipment for children who are wheelchair users.

### Exclusions

No support for animal welfare charities, appeals from individuals, the arts, elderly people, medical research, overseas projects, political appeals, religious appeals, or science/technology.

### Applications

In writing to the correspondent, preferably by e-mail.

## Corporate giving

McDonald's Restaurants Ltd, made charitable contributions totalling £2,197,000 (2004: £531,000). £2,110,000 was donated to Ronald McDonald House Charities (UK) and £87,000 to the Tsunami Appeal. It has not been possible to breakdown the company's charitable giving figure further.

Collection box gross income in the year 2005, for the charity, increased to £1,928,614 (2004: £1,653,618), as a result of more targeted approach to fundraising by McDonald's operations. The combined donation from McDonald's Restaurants Limited and individual owner operators of £465,276 (2004: £481,210) covered the cost of the charity's combined administrative and fundraising expenditure.

This meant that all the money donated by the charity's supporters was used for fulfilling the charity's mission without deduction. The charity expended £1,628,843 (2004: £2,162,201) on the establishment of two new Ronald McDonald Houses and six new Ronald McDonald Family Room complexes.

### Employee-led support

McDonald's has an employee volunteering scheme and allows staff company time off in which to carry out charitable activities. Please note, however, that staff are encouraged to participant in fundraising events for the company's own charity.

### Commercially-led support

**Sponsorship:** *Sports* – the company supports a football coaching qualification provided by the national football associations of England, Northern Ireland, Scotland and Wales.

---

# McKesson Information Solutions UK Ltd

European Headquarters, Warwick Technology Park, Warwick CV34 6NZ

0870 600 0426; Fax: 01926 475444

Website: www.uk.mckesson.com

Correspondent: The Marketing Department

Nature of company business
Provider of healthcare IT and technology services.

Main locations: Newcastle, Southwark, Romford, Sheffield, Warwick

UK employees: 400

Total employees: 25,000

## Community involvement

The company supports youth causes, particularly health services for disadvantaged communities.

### Exclusions

No grants are made towards endowment appeals, individuals, religious purposes, political causes, research or health organisations concentrating on just one disease. It does not advertise in charity publications.

### Applications

In writing to the correspondent.

**Information available:** In January 2006, the company published its first corporate social responsibility report.

## Corporate giving

The group has a worldwide giving figure of US$4 million, with most of the funds given in the US. In the US grants range from US$5,000 to US$25,000 each.

## Employee-led support

Employees are encouraged to volunteer. There is a matched funding scheme for employees' volunteering, donations and fundraising.

---

# Medtronic Ltd

Suite One, Sherbourne House, Croxley Business Centre, Watford WD18 8WW

01923 212213

Website: www.medtronic.co.uk

Correspondent: Claire Miles, Office Services

| Year end | Turnover | Pre-tax profit |
|----------|----------|----------------|
| 29/04/2005 | £97,262,000 | £4,741,000 |

Nature of company business
Producer of medical technology to treat and manage conditions such as heart disease, neurological disorders, vascular illnesses and diabetes.

Main locations: Watford

### Charitable donations
2005: £170,842

## Community involvement

Areas of support are: community health; education and training opportunities; welfare; patient associations; and science education for children. Its two main programmes for UK applicants are as follows:

**Patient Link**

The programme aims to improve the lives of people with chronic diseases and conditions by partnering with patient associations that educate, support and advocate on behalf of patients. Grants are awarded for specific projects, programmes or capacity building activities.

### Heart Rescue Grant Programme

These grants support education, awareness and training efforts concerned with sudden cardiac arrest (SCA) and early defibrillation programmes in local communities. Priority is given to projects that demonstrate or are striving to implement eight key components as recommended by the National Center for Early Defibrillation (in the USA) or offer an educational component for survivors of SCA which addresses risk factors for future episodes and follow-up therapy options.

### Applications

All appeals from Europe, the Middle East and Africa are processed centrally by:

Marija Sepic Fraefel
Medtronic Foundation
Medtronic Europe
Route du Molliau 31
Case postale
CH-1131
Tolochenaz
Switzerland
e-mail: marija.sepic.fraefel@medtronic.com

Application forms are available at www.medtronic.com.

## Corporate giving

In 2004/05 the company made charitable donations of £170,842. The largest donation was £17,000 to the Pain Relief Foundation.

## In-kind support

Products are available to international medical relief organisations.

## Employee-led support

Employees are encouraged to carry out community work.

---

# John Menzies plc

108 Princes Street, Edinburgh EH2 3AA

0131 225 8555

Website: www.johnmenziesplc.com

Correspondent: Gordon McVinnie, Charity Funds Administrator
0131 459 8005; Fax: 0131 459 8164
E-mail: gordon.mcvinnie@johnmenziesplc.com

Chief officer: William Thomson

Chief Executive: Patrick Macdonald

| Year end | Turnover | Pre-tax profit |
|---|---|---|
| 31/12/2005 | £1,362,100,000 | £36,100,000 |

Nature of company business
Logistics support services group.

Main locations: Edinburgh, Hounslow

UK employees: 5,732

Total employees: 11,692

### Charitable donations

2005: £125,000
2004: £94,000
2003: £100,000

## Community involvement

The company prefers to support charities in the fields of health/welfare, youth/sport, the arts, the services and environmental charities. Preference is given to charities in areas of company presence.

Consideration may also be given to organisations involved with children/youth, education, older people, environment/heritage, fundraising events, medical research and overseas projects (only if they are based near to a Menzies Aviation Business).

### Exclusions

Generally, no support for appeals from individuals, political appeals or enterprise/ training.

### Applications

In writing to the correspondent. No formal application form is required. Advice on policy guidelines and so on can be given verbally or in letter form. Queries via e-mail will be answered, but contact by post is preferred.

## Corporate giving

In 2005, the company donated £125,000 worldwide to various charitable, community and arts organisations. Donations vary between £250 and £1,000. Recent beneficiaries have included: SSAFA Forces Help; Newstraid; Association for International Cancer Care; The Scuba Trust.

Around 50% of donations in 2005 have been made to Scottish-based charities or UK charities with a Scottish connection. However, this may reduce in future given that a greater proportion of the company's staff are employed in England and overseas and that preference is given to applications from charities close to its business operations.

### Employee-led support

The John Maxwell Menzies Community Fund distributes funds to organisations in which company staff are directly involved. Every employee (retired and present) receives *The Reporter*, the group's magazine, which gives details of employees' community activities.

Employees' fundraising and giving initiatives each may receive funding from the company to a maximum of £350 for individuals or £700 for teams.

**Payroll giving:** The company introduced the Give As You Earn scheme in 2006, for which they meet the administration costs.

### Commercially-led support

**Sponsorship:** The company may donate to good-cause charities and events if trade related.

# MEPC Ltd

8 Cedarwood, Crockford Lane, Basingstoke, RG24 8WD

01256 486 680; Fax: 01256 486 681

Website: www.mepc.com

Correspondent: See Below

Chief Executive: Rick de Blaby

Managing Director: John Bateman

| Year end | Turnover | Pre-tax profit |
|---|---|---|
| 30/09/2004 | £71,900,000 | £44,900,000 |

**Nature of company business**
Property investment, development and trading.

**Subsidiaries include:** Caledonian Land Properties Ltd, Birchwood Park Estates Ltd, Threadneedle Property Co Ltd, PSIT Limited, The Metropolitan Railway Surplus Lands Co Ltd, Iceni Estates Ltd, English Property Corporation plc

Main locations: London

UK employees: 32

Total employees: 32

### Charitable donations

2004: £2,337
2003: £39,844

## Community involvement

The company supports a range of charities. Each application is considered on its merit. Preferred areas of support are children/youth, education, older people, enterprise/training, sickness/disability and social welfare.

### Exclusions

No support for advertising in charity brochures, animal welfare, appeals from individuals, the arts, environment/heritage, fundraising events, medical research, overseas projects, political or religious appeals, science/technology and sport.

### Applications

In writing to the correspondent. The charities committee meets quarterly.

## Corporate giving

Charitable donations fell by over £37,500 in 2004 to £2,337. Although this is below the minimum level required for inclusion, this may well be a one-off. We will, however, continue to monitor the situation.

# Merck Sharp & Dohme Ltd

Hertford Road, Hoddesdon, Hertfordshire EN11 9BU

01992 467272; Fax: 01992 467270

Website: www.msd-uk.co.uk

Correspondent: External Affairs Manager

Managing Director: Vincent Lawton

| Year end | Turnover | Pre-tax profit |
|---|---|---|
| 31/12/2005 | £373,904,000 | (£193,654,000) |

**Nature of company business**
Merck Sharp & Dohme Ltd is the UK subsidiary of Merck & Co. Inc., a research-driven pharmaceutical and services company. It discovers, manufactures and markets a broad range of innovative products to improve human and animal health.

Main locations: Hoddesdon, Cramlington

UK employees: 1,929

### Charitable donations

2005: £51,089
2004: £69,580

Membership: BitC

## Community involvement

Merck, Sharp & Dohme states on its UK website that it: 'Aims to make a positive contribution to its local communities by supporting a wide range of charitable, educational and environmental initiatives worldwide [and] strives to be a "Neighbour of Choice" in the local communities where it is based.'

The company has two sites in the UK: headquarters and pharmaceutical research and development laboratories in Hoddesdon, Hertfordshire; and manufacturing at Cramlington in Northumberland. The main thrust of the company's community support at these sites involves education and the environment.

### Applications

In writing to the correspondent.

**Information Available:** Further information regarding any of the initiatives listed is available via the company website.

## Corporate giving

In 2005, the company made charitable donations of £51,089 (2004: £69,580). Although we have no specific details of the beneficiaries we do know that the company's support around Cramlington has included the following:

- organisation of lectures/site tours/workshops for students promoting the study of science
- donation of equipment to partner schools and community groups
- support in establishing the local Science College (£18,000 in cash and donations) as well as on-going participation on the science college board of governors
- providing school science clubs for Years 9 and 10 to spark an interest in budding scientists
- training and supporting the site's Science & Engineering Ambassadors in their activities with schools
- creating Merck Champions for the Environment projects for MSD volunteers and local environmental groups to work on together for the benefit of the community.

### In-kind support

At Hoddeston, the company is supporting eight local primary schools with digital microscopes and associated software and training. The scheme has been organised in conjunction with SETPOINT, an educational charity.

### Employee-led support

Employees are involved in educational and environmental projects within the local community.

# Michelin Tyre Public Limited Company

Campbell Road, Stoke-on-Trent ST4 4EY

01782 402000; Fax: 01782 402011

Website: www.michelin.co.uk

Correspondent: Christine Reynolds, Corporate Image Assistant 01782 402083; Fax: 01782 401751
E-mail: christine.reynolds@uk.michelin.com

Chief officer: M Caron

Managing Director: J Rickard

| Year end | Turnover | Pre-tax profit |
| --- | --- | --- |
| 31/12/2004 | £611,658,000 | £12,126,000 |

Nature of company business
The manufacture and sale of tyres, tubes, wheels and accessories, maps and guides, and mobility support services.

Subsidiaries include: ATS (Investment) Ltd

Main locations: Ballymena, Stoke-on-Trent, Dundee

UK employees: 3,489

### Charitable donations

2004: £57,713
2003: £99,020

## Community involvement

The company has a usual preference for:

- national and local initiatives dedicated to improve mobility (road safety, environment and accessibility)
- local initiatives (Ballymena, Dundee and Stoke-on-Trent) concerned mainly with the progress of mobility, training and youth development schemes and other local development programmes.

### Exclusions

No support for circular appeals, advertising in charity brochures, animal welfare, appeals from individuals, political appeals, religious appeals, or local appeals not in areas of company presence.

### Applications

In writing to the correspondent.

## Corporate giving

In 2004, the company made donations of £57,713. We have no details of the beneficiaries.

### In-kind support

**Education:** The company is involved in local education/ business partnerships and links have been developed through the provision of educational assistance for schools, including work experience.

**Enterprise:** The company gives support to local enterprise agencies.

**Environment:** The company is involved in local schemes to improve wasteland and works with local business networks providing environmental expertise and training.

**Other:** The company also provides its sports and social facilities free of charge for local school sports events and training for local organisations such as the police and fire brigade.

### Employee-led support

As well as preference being given to charities in which a member of staff is involved, employees are encouraged to become involved in the local community through acting as volunteers in both their own time and business hours when appropriate. The company provides matched funding to certain activities by its employees.

**Payroll giving:** The Give As You Earn scheme is operated by the company.

### Commercially-led support

**Sponsorship:** The company is committed to improve the quality of mobility and may support various initiatives in road safety or environmentally friendly mobility issues.

# Microsoft Limited

Microsoft Campus, Thames Valley Park, Reading RG6 1WG

0870 601 0100; Fax: 0870 60 20 100

Website: www.microsoft.com/uk/

Correspondent: Liz Harding, UK Community Affairs Project Manager

| Year end | Turnover | Pre-tax profit |
| --- | --- | --- |
| | £413,256,000 | £36,298,000 |

Nature of company business
Computer software manufacturer and supplier.

Main locations: Edinburgh, London, Manchester, Reading

Total employees: 1,826

### Charitable donations

2005: £223,142
2004: £373,888

Membership: BitC, L B Group

## Community involvement

Microsoft has established an extensive network of non-profit partners who they work with to support community-based programmes and local projects which enable more people to have access to technology. The company gives to a range of major charity projects both financially and through gifts in kind.

Launched in 2003 'Unlimited Potential' is a Microsoft global community investment programme. Unlimited Potential is focused on improving lifelong learning for disadvantaged young people and adults by providing access to IT training and skills. In the UK, Microsoft works with and through charity partnerships to deliver the Unlimited Potential programme. Microsoft currently has Unlimited Potential partnerships with the following organisations in the UK:

- Age Concern
- Citizens Online
- Fairbridge
- Leonard Cheshire
- NCH
- Scarman Trust
- The 'Karrot Bus' Project.

Through these partnerships support can be given to those in greatest need.

In May 2006, Microsoft received the Living Legends award in recognition of its work in tackling the issue of digital exclusion among older people.

In addition to Unlimited Potential programme, Microsoft also works with a number of other charities including the NSPCC and Ability Net and runs other programmes to aid communities in the UK.

The NSPCC and Microsoft have been in partnership for 11 years.

Microsoft has been in partnership with Ability Net for the past seven years and has provided funding for trainers in Ability Net centres across the UK.

### Exclusions

Microsoft is only able to donate cash to selected major charity projects. They do not supply PC hardware, but do support a scheme to recycle PCs. No support is given, in any form, for political, religious or racially motivated projects.

### Applications

In writing to the correspondent.

## Corporate giving

During the period 2004/2005, Microsoft Limited donated £223,142 for charitable purposes. (2003/2004: £373,888).

Microsoft's community affairs website contains extensive information on, and examples of, its community support in the UK. The information below covers the major components of its community investment.

- Community Learning Awards 2004 – The awards seek to support groups and charities across the UK who are tackling the 'digital divide'. Organisations providing opportunities for disadvantaged young people and adults to learn about IT through community-based technology and learning centres can apply for one of 25 awards of £2,000 each.

- Improving the life of children – Microsoft has been supporting the NSPCC since 1994 and during this time has contributed over £5.5 million in direct donations by working together on a variety of different initiatives to raise both funds and awareness for the NSPCC. In addition to the direct donations, Microsoft sponsored the NSPCC FULL STOP launch advertising in 1999, and other advertising campaigns including 'Babies and Toddlers' in 2000 and 'Someone To Turn To' in 2002. Microsoft also sponsored NSPCC schools fundraising materials for seven years, helping to raise a further £11 million.

- Supporting disabled people – by developing more accessible software and providing a range of activities to help people develop their skills. Support has been given to projects run by Leonard Cheshire and AbilityNet.

- Bringing IT to later life – by working in partnership with Age Concern on projects aimed at helping older people use new technology. Over the past five years the partnership has provided over 20,000 internet taster sessions.

- Supporting education and IT skills – through public sector programmes and its own initiatives, Microsoft aim to ensure access for all to IT equipment and training.

Whilst the 2004/2005 Annual Report of Microsoft Limited gives a figure for charitable donations of £223,142, we do not have any details about which specific charities benefited. It is clear from the information on the company's website that the company gives considerable support in kind, including equipment, staff time, and so on, but it is not possible to calculate a figure for this.

### In-kind support

The Microsoft Giving programme provides in-kind support to charities and community groups each year by donating software for use in fundraising or helping to run voluntary organisations.

Microsoft Authorised Refurbisher (MAR) and Fresh Start programmes are specifically designed to make it easier for charities and schools to use donated computers and to acquire low cost, second use, refurbished PCs, using properly licensed software.

Microsoft Community Affairs is working with Charity Technology Trust (CTT) a UK registered charity, to take over the management of the UK Microsoft product philanthropy programme. Effective from the 1st July 2006, CTT will be taking over the existing UK product donation programme and full details are available on the company's website.

In July 2006, Microsoft's UK local and regional government team joined the Shoreditch Trust's new 'Digital Divide' programme to provide low cost access to Microsoft Office tools with the aim of providing access for 70,000 residents and small businesses in the East London neighbourhood.

### Employee-led support

The company encourages its staff to contribute to the community with their time and skills. A formalised Employee Volunteering Programme was introduced in 2003. The UK programme enables employees to get involved in various ways – e.g. helping out on a one-off key skills workshop or making a long-term commitment to mentor a young person.

The staff volunteering is delivered through a number of external partners including The Prince's Trust, Central Berkshire Education Business Partnership, IT4Communities, The Prince's Scottish Youth Business Trust among others.

In addition the company aims to build volunteering opportunities into the Unlimited Potential Partnerships. Microsoft runs a matched giving scheme to encourage individual fundraising activities. The scheme matches staff fundraising up to £7,500 per annum, per employee. In 2005, Microsoft matched over £180,000 to help support over 55 organisations.

**Payroll giving:** The company runs the Give As You Earn scheme for its employees.

# The Midcounties Co-operative

New Barclay House, 234 Botley Road, Oxford OX2 0HP

01865 249241

Website: www.osg.coop

**Correspondent:** Sarah Buy, Membership & Corporate Marketing Department
E-mail: contact@osg.coop

**Chief officer:** Vivien Woodell (President)

**Chief Executive:** Steve Allsopp (Vice President)

| Year end | Turnover | Pre-tax profit |
|----------|----------|----------------|
| 24/01/2006 | | |

**Nature of company business**
The society has a number of diverse trading activities covering food, motor, property, travel childcare and funeral services.

**Subsidiaries include:** Oxford Garage Group Ltd, A W Bruce Ltd, North Oxfordshire Stores Ltd

**Main locations:** Gloucester, Oxford, Swindon

**UK employees:** 4,000

### Charitable donations

2006: £300,000
2004: £212,000

Membership: %Club

## Community involvement

In 2005, the Oxford, Swindon & Gloucester Co-operative Society Ltd merged with the West Midlands Co-operative Society to form the Midcounties Co-operative. The society has pledged to raise £150,000 for the Oxford Children's Hospital Campaign by 2007.

The society also offers support for community events through Co-operative Community Festival Support, which offers grants, selected publicity and a presence by the Midcounties Co-operative at events that are organised by the community and take place for all of the community to enjoy. It aims to support events with a wide appeal to benefit as many people as possible across its trading area. For further details e-mail: communityfestivals@midcounties.coop or telephone Jasmine Turner on 01865 256272.

### Exclusions

Applications from outside the operating area of the Midcounties Co-operative Society, i.e. Oxfordshire, Gloucestershire, Swindon, parts of Buckinghamshire and the West Midlands.

No support for advertising in charity brochures, appeals from individuals, enterprise/training, fundraising events, medical research, overseas projects, political appeals, religious appeals, or science/technology.

### Applications

Further details regarding the method of application and the Community Dividend Scheme guidelines can be found by writing in the first instance to the correspondent. Alternatively, contact Sarah Buy (tel: 01865 249241).

## Corporate giving

Since the merger of the two societies in 2005, no financial information is available on the new society. In previous years community contributions have totalled around £300,000.

### In-kind support

The company gave gifts in kind in the form of partnership work on regeneration schemes.

### Employee-led support

The company supports employees' volunteering/charitable activities by giving them time off work.

# Misys plc

125 Kensington High Street, London W8 5SF

020 7368 2300; Fax: 020 7368 2400

Website: www.misys.co.uk

**Correspondent:** Nigel Talbot-Rice, Director, Mysis Charitable Foundation

**Chief officer:** Sir Dominic Cadbury

**Chief Executive:** Kevin Lomax

| Year end | Turnover | Pre-tax profit |
|----------|----------|----------------|
| 31/05/2006 | £953,300,000 | £39,500,000 |

**Nature of company business**
The development and licensing of application software products to customers in well-defined vertical markets within the financial services and healthcare sectors, together with transaction processing and professional services.

**Main locations:** London

**Total employees:** 6,148

### Charitable donations

2006: £100,000
2005: £124,453
2004: £120,000
2003: £505,000

## Community involvement

The following information is taken from the company's website.

'As a global information technology leader with operations spanning five continents, Misys plc makes its broader contribution to society through the activities of the Misys Charitable Foundation (Charity Commission no. 1065678). The foundation was formed in November 1997, with the aim of supporting the advancement of education in information and communications technology worldwide.'

The foundation offers support in three distinct areas:

### Scholarships

'Scholarships at university level represent the core support activity of the foundation and it aims to establish scholarship funding with leading educational institutions, to enable exceptional students, particularly from less privileged backgrounds, to undertake undergraduate and postgraduate studies.

### Purchase of equipment

'Grants are occasionally given towards the purchase of equipment for use in teaching information technology in educational institutions that have limited funds for IT resources, usually in an area where there is a Misys presence.

### General grants

'In certain cases, the foundation is prepared to support special projects where there is a broader contribution towards the enhancement of information technology education.'

In addition to its support for the Misys Foundation, the company donates to many other charities and causes, and supports employee giving and involvement.

### Exclusions

Appeals from local community organisations not in areas of company presence. Direct appeals from individuals outside of 'linked' schools or universities.

### Applications

In writing to the correspondent. Only student referrals from 'linked' schools and universities will be considered.

## Corporate giving

### Misys Charitable Foundation

'The foundation is funded directly through donations from Misys, whose board is firmly committed to the foundation's aims. One of these aims is to strengthen ties with the company's own 6,500 employees worldwide – many of whom are personally involved in local community and charitable activities

'In addition to the £1.1m that the company has already put into the foundation, the board has further agreed to provide minimum funding of £100,000 per annum for five years from 2003.'

In 2005/06, the company donated £100,000 (2004: £124,453) to the foundation, in line with its above stated commitment. In total the foundation has funded 267 students at university from 1998 through to 2007, with 65 of these scholarships awarded this year.

The foundation has donated more than £1m since it was established and in 2005/6 gave grants totalling £238,000. This comprised £170,000 of funding to scholarships and a further £67,500 to nine schools, five of which were nominated for support by Misys employees. Support was also given to Voluntary Service Organisation for the provision of funding for a teacher from the United Kingdom to develop the IT curriculum in secondary schools in Ethiopia. Further donations totalling £500 were made to a number of causes.

### In-kind support

Misys donated redundant IT hardware to Digital Links International, a charity that arranges the refurbishment and dispatch of equipment to needy schools in Africa. The transport and training costs involved were covered by the foundation.

### Employee-led support

**Payroll giving:** The company's 2006 Annual Report states that the company will re-launch its 'Give as You Earn' scheme in the UK during 2006, and will make funds of up to £100,000 in total available for matched giving to specified charities designated by the company.

# Mitchells & Butlers plc

27 Fleet Street, Birmingham B3 1JP

0870 609 3000; Fax: 0121 233 2246

Website: www.mbplc.com

**Correspondent:** Becky Davies, Communications Assistant

**Chief officer:** Roger Carr

**Chief Executive:** Tim Clarke

| Year end | Turnover | Pre-tax profit |
|---|---|---|
| 30/09/2005 | £1,662,000,000 | £192,000,000 |

**Nature of company business**
Operator of managed pubs, bars and restaurants.

**Main locations:** Birmingham

**UK employees:** 37,411

**Total employees:** 37,411

> ### Charitable donations
> 2005: £143,000
> 2003: £71,000
>
> Total community contributions: £520,000

## Community involvement

Donations of £100 each are available as a one-off donation. Larger grants can be made at the company's discretion. Support is given throughout the UK, although there is an interest around the Birmingham area. Applicants must be: a registered charity or an organisation with charitable objectives; based in the UK and meet the needs of local communities; financially sound; and able to show their projects meet a local need and/or have a relationship with one of its venues.

It has previously assisted 120 projects applying to become a Millennium Green by matching the donation made by the Millennium Commission.

### Exclusions

No grants are made to: provide expeditions or adventure travel for individuals; fund advertising space; restore historic buildings; support political causes; sponsor sporting events; promote religious ideas or views; or fund year-end deficits.

### Applications
In writing to the correspondent.

## Corporate giving

In 2004/05 cash donations totalled £143,000. In-kind donations and employee volunteering time are estimated by the company to total around £500,000.

Barnardos was chosen in 2005 to be the company's official charity partner. 'In addition to an initial company donation of £50,000, Mitchells & Butlers supports Barnardos by encouraging employee-based fundraising through events. Over £7,000 had been raised by corporate staff for Barnardos in the six months to the end of the financial year.'

## Employee-led support

It operates an Employee Community Award Scheme which enables employees who actively support a charity through fundraising or voluntary work to apply for a company donation.

## Commercially-led support

Pubs, bars and restaurants owned by the group often have their own charity days to raise funds for local good causes. These have included golf days, sponsored silences and sponsored walks within a restaurant.

### Sponsorship

It has sponsored City of Birmingham Orchestra for over 20 years, as well as Birmingham Repertory Theatre.

# J P Morgan Chase

10 Aldermanbury, London EC2V 7RF

Website: www.jpmorgan.com

Correspondent: Duncan Grant, Director 020 7325 1308; Fax: 020 7325 8195
E-mail: duncan.grant@jpmorgan.com

| Year end | Turnover | Pre-tax profit |
|---|---|---|
| 31/12/2004 | | |

Nature of company business
Financial services organisation.

Main locations: London

---

### Charitable donations

2004: £629,000

Membership: A & B

---

## Community involvement

This company was created in July 2004 following a merger between J P Morgan Fleming, Chase & Co and Bank One Corporation.

The company organises its giving through The J P Morgan Educational Trust (Charity Commission no. 325103). It was initially established as part of a tax-avoiding school fees planning service, although this practice has now been stopped by the Inland Revenue and this trust will cease to exist by 2014. However, another trust will gradually be built up to replace this trust; J P Morgan Foundation (Charity Commission no. 291617). However, at present both trusts are effectively being administered together with the same policies and procedures with only the budgets differing.

Both the The J P Morgan Fleming Educational Trust and J P Morgan Fleming Foundation fund three major areas of social need.

▶ community asset development – to encourage, sustain and develop economic self-reliance

▶ youth education – to help young people succeed in life and in work

▶ community life – to enrich communities with sponsorships and events focused on arts and culture.

Funding is targeted to support the development of communities local to J P Morgan offices. In 2004 these location included London (43%), Bournemouth (28%), Edinburgh (6%), Glasgow (2%), Havering (14%) and a few UK-wide projects (7%).

## Exclusions

Projects that are not usually supported include: open appeals from national charities; direct appeals by individuals; charity gala nights and similar events; and medical charities.

## Applications

In writing to the correspondent on two sides of A4. There are no application forms. Please set out your reasons for applying along with an indication of the amount of funding required. There are no specific closing dates for initial enquiries.

Applications are always acknowledged. Trustees meet in March, May, July, September and December. If your application is unsuccessful we suggest you wait at least a year before re-applying.

## Corporate giving

In 2004 the sum of £629,000 was awarded to 89 organisations. Those based in London and Bournemouth received over 71% of grants, reflecting the fact that over 90% of UK J P Morgan employees work in these two locations.

Beneficiaries included Streetwise (£29,000), Almedia Theatre and KIDS (£20,000 each), Create (£18,000), Fryent Primary School (£17,000), Young Vic Theatre (£15,000), Changing Faces, Hackney City Farm, Network for Teaching Entrepreneurship, Roundhouse Trust, St Francis Hospice and the Who Cares? Trust (£10,000 each), Linwood School and Wicheslea School (£8,300 each), Brunswick Club (£7,500), Magic Lantern (£3,000), Museum of Fulham Palace and UK Youth (£2,500 each), 198 Gallery, Freightliners City Farm, Hackney City Farm, Havering Youth Games, Kith and Kids, Scotts Project Trust and Waldorf School of South West London (£2,000 each), Kaimes Special School (£1,800) and Northwold Junior School (£1,500).

## Employee-led support

**Payroll giving:** employees are able to donate money to charities of their choice, through monthly donations.

**Matched giving scheme:** the company matches donations that employees give to charities of their choice.

---

# Morgan Crucible Company plc

Quadrant, 55–57 High Street, Windsor, Berkshire SL4 1LP

01753 837000; Fax: 01753 850872

Website: www.morgancrucible.com

Correspondent: David Coker, Company Secretary
01753 837000; Fax: 01753 850872

Chief officer: Lars Kylberg

Chief Executive: Mark Robertshaw

| Year end | Turnover | Pre-tax profit |
|---|---|---|
| 04/01/2006 | £745,700,000 | £20,400,000 |

Nature of company business
The Morgan Crucible Company plc is the ultimate holding company of a group of subsidiary undertakings engaged in the manufacture and marketing of carbon and ceramic components for application in a wide range of industries and services.

Subsidiaries include: Morgan Matroc Ltd, Thermal Ceramics UK Ltd

Main locations: Windsor, Wirral, Worcester, Leeds

UK employees: 1,442

Total employees: 11,629

### Charitable donations

2006: £171,057
2005: £168,882
2004: £89,257
2003: £51,563

## Community involvement

The company states that its main support goes to relatively small 'niche' charities in the fields of medical care and research. Some limited support is given to the arts in areas of company presence. Grants are distributed by the Morgan Crucible Company plc Charitable Trust (Charity Commission no. 273507) which has categorised its donations as follows:

Medical development & research; care (including holidays) of people physically or mentally disabled; care (including holidays) of young people in deprived or undesirable circumstances; adventure or training holidays or courses for character development ; local (Windsor area) good causes; character reform; arts; education; community services; and director sponsored.

### Exclusions

No support for: animal welfare; appeals from individuals; overseas projects; political appeals; religious appeals; science/technology; or sport.

### Applications

In writing to the correspondent. Grant decisions are made by a donations committee which meets quarterly.

## Corporate giving

In 2005/06, the company made charitable contributions totalling £171,057 of which £65,385 was donated to the associated charity. We have no details of the beneficiaries.

Grants of between £100 and £500 are made nationally, but primarily in Wirral, Leeds, South Wales, South London, Worcester and Thames Valley. Subsidiary companies do have their own budgets for appeals, but no figures are available.

# Morgan Stanley International Limited

25 Cabot Square, Canary Wharf, London E14 4QA

020 7425 8000; Fax: 020 7425 8984

Website: www.morganstanley.co.uk

Correspondent: Louise Ellison, Morgan Stanley International Foundation

Chief officer: J C S Chenevix-Trench

| Year end | Turnover | Pre-tax profit |
|----------|----------|----------------|
| 30/11/2005 | | £1,041,755,000 |

Nature of company business
Principal activities: the provision of financial services to corporations, governments, financial institutions and individual investors.

Main locations: London

UK employees: 4645

### Charitable donations

2005: £2,610,256

Membership: BitC, L B Group

## Community involvement

The company makes a proportion of its charitable donations through the Morgan Stanley International Foundation (Charity Commission no. 1042671). The following guidelines for making charitable donations apply:

'The Morgan Stanley International Foundation (MSIF) is funded by Morgan Stanley International Limited. It makes contributions to non-profit educational, health care and social service organisations which provide a benefit to our local communities. In London, this is primarily focused on the boroughs of Tower Hamlets and Newham; in Scotland on Cumbernauld and Glasgow and in continental Europe on the cities in which our offices are based.

'The foundation's grants are made to registered charities and state-funded schools which provide benefit to the communities local to our offices across Europe. The main thematic focuses are as follows:

- education and employability – particular emphasis is given to the provision of services to schools with which Morgan Stanley has an established relationship.

'In addition, but to a lesser extent, projects that provide support in the following areas will be considered:

- job training/remedial education/handicapped and homeless support – for adults and young people in order to prepare these people to become self-supporting.

- hospitals/health – support for hospitals and innovative healthcare projects in the East End of London. As a rule, the foundation does not support organisations involved in the research of specific diseases.

'As a rule, the foundation will give, consistent with the above guidelines, preferential treatment to those organisations which are actively supported through volunteer work or board representation by Morgan Stanley employees.'

The foundation also runs a 'Charity of the Year' programme in London and Glasgow. Employees are able to select a local charity to which all funds raised through company initiatives are donated.

**Charity of the Year:** Age Concern (2005/06).

### Exclusions

'As a rule, grants will not be made to either national or international charitable organisations unless they have a project in one of these areas. In addition, grants will not be made to either political or evangelistic organisations, pressure groups or individuals outside the firm who are seeking sponsorship either for themselves (e.g. to help pay for education) or for onward transmission to a charitable organisation.'

## Applications

All initial funding enquiries should be directed to Louise Ellison at the Morgan Stanley International Foundation (MSIF): louise.ellison@morganstanley.com

There is no pro forma for grant applications. Please send details of the project for which you are seeking funding, along with a copy of your latest report and accounts, to the correspondent.

Grant applications are considered quarterly in March, June, September and December by the MSIF trustees. The trustees are senior representatives from across the firm's divisions.

Please note that the MSIF takes a proactive approach to grant making and rarely responds to unsolicited requests.

## Corporate giving

During 2005, subsidiaries of the company made donations to various charities of over £3.9 million (2004: £2.3 million). Of this, around £2.6 million was paid to the Morgan Stanley International Foundation for the foundation's financial years 2005 and 2006.

### Morgan Stanley International Foundation

In 2005, the foundation had assets of £2.76 million and an income of just over £2.69 million most of which came from a donation from Morgan Stanley and Co. International Limited. Just over £1.78 million was distributed or committed in grants.

The largest grant of £155,521 was made to the foundation's 'charity of the year', Age Concern There were a further 135 grants made of over £1,000 each including: Save the Children (£100,000); Community Links (£75,769); London Bomb Appeal (£50,000); East Side Educational Trust and Tower Hamlets Summer University (£25,000 each); Trees for Cities (£16,500); and, Crime Concern (£12,500).

### In-kind support

*Education* – As part of the Tower Hamlets Education Business Partnership's 'Take Our Students to Work Day' programme, 30 local students, aged 13–14 spent a day in the Cabot Square offices.

Morgan Stanley also provided paid summer internships to two local 'A' Level students as part of the Corporation of London's Business Traineeship Program.

### Employee-led support

The company encourages its employees to get involved with the local community and the chosen 'charity of the year'. Fundraising efforts by staff on behalf of Age Concern raised over £150,000 in 2005/06.

Staff contributions to charities of their own choice are matched by the foundation up to a maximum of £2,000 per employee, per event. Additionally, employees can apply to the foundation for matching of their time in volunteering. The size of the grant is dependent upon the employee's length of service with both Morgan Stanley and the benefiting organisation.

### Commercially-led support

**Sponsorship:** The company are sponsors of the 'Great Britons' Awards in partnership with The Daily Telegraph. Members of the public have been invited each year since 2004, to nominate individuals who have achieved success in a particularly 'British' way.

Nominations are made across seven categories: arts; business; campaigning; creative industries; public life; science and innovation; and, sport.

To complement Morgan Stanley's recent sponsorship of The Old Vic Theatre, the company funded 'Soapbox', an innovative pilot project created by The Old Vic Education Department. The programme harnesses the skills of actors, writers, producers, directors, education facilitators and Morgan Stanley employees in order to help children communicate more effectively.

Involving 250 pupils over two summer months, the workshop was converted into a curriculum insert aimed at primary schools across London. Following the success of the pilot project, Morgan Stanley funded an expanded 'Soapbox' program in 2006.

# Wm Morrison Supermarkets plc

Hillmore House, Gain Lane, Bradford BD3 7DL

0845 611 5000

Website: www.morrisons.co.uk

Correspondent: Susanna Corbelli, Charities Administrator
0845 611 5360

Chief officer: Sir Kenneth D Morrison

Chief Executive: Marc Bolland

Managing Director: Marie M. Melnyk

| Year end | Turnover | Pre-tax profit |
| --- | --- | --- |
| 29/01/2006 | £12,114,800,000 | (£312,900,000) |

Nature of company business
Retail distribution of goods through the medium of supermarkets.

Subsidiaries include: Erith Pier Co Ltd, Farmers Boy Ltd, Returnvital Ltd, Lifestyle Wholesale Distribution Ltd, Nathanspire Ltd, Farock Insurance Co Ltd, M1 Discount Stores Ltd

Main locations: Bradford

Total employees: 134,337

### Charitable donations

2006: £200,000
2005: £153,000
2004: £130,000
2003: £117,000

## Community involvement

Each year a single (usually national) charity is nominated as the company's 'Charity of the Year' and supported throughout the stores through fundraising and collection points. One of the main criteria for selection is that the money raised in a particular area, is used by the charity in that area. The company also contributes to this cause.

Other appeals are supported through the Wm Morrison Supermarkets plc Charitable Trust (Charity Commission no. 1007857). Support is given to a wide range of charities within the definition of 'general charitable purposes'.

**Charity of the Year:** Breast Cancer Campaign (2005/06).

## Exclusions

No response to circular appeals or support for the arts, overseas projects, or political appeals.

## Applications

In writing to the correspondent.

## Corporate giving

In 2005/06, the company made charitable donations of £200,000 (2004/05: £153,000). As in previous year the majority of this was donated to the company's charitable trust. We have no details of the beneficiaries for the year.

### Wm Morrison Supermarkets plc Charitable Trust

For the year ending 30 January 2005, the trust exceptionally had an income of just over £3 million of which £142,000 came from the company and the balance from money raised by staff and customers on behalf of the Tsunami Appeal. 69 grants totalling £3,030,205 were made during the year of which those greater than £1,000 went to: the Tsunami Appeal (£3,008,000); the Lord Mayor of Bradford's Appeal (£5,000); and, the Lord Mayor of Leeds Appeal (£5,000).

## In-kind support

Main areas of non-cash support are gifts in kind, joint promotions and training schemes.

## Employee-led support

Employees and customers raised over £1.5 million for Morrison's Charity of the Year, Breast Cancer Campaign (BCC). It was the largest single donation to the BCC. Staff and customers raised £65,000 for the Asian Earthquake Appeal which was donated to Shelterbox Trust and over £197,000 was raised for Children in Need.

# Mothercare plc

Cherry Tree Road, Watford, Hertfordshire WD24 6SH

01923 241000

Website: www.mothercare.com

Correspondent: Charity Administrator, The Mothercare Charitable Foundation 01923 206077; Fax: 01923 206376
E-mail: simone.spencer-ahmed@mothercare.co.uk

Chief officer: Ian R Peacock

Chief Executive: Ben Gordon

| Year end | Turnover | Pre-tax profit |
|---|---|---|
| 01/04/2006 | £482,700,000 | £24,200,000 |

Nature of company business
Principal activities: selling, by retail and mail order, clothing, household goods, furniture and furnishing. The company operates mainly in the UK, US and Europe.

Subsidiaries include: Storehouse Finance plc, Mothercare UK Ltd

Main locations: Watford

UK employees: 5,255

---

| Charitable donations |
|---|
| 2006: £100,000 |
| 2005: £250,000 |
| 2004: £150,000 |
| 2003: £85,000 |

## Community involvement

In order that Mothercare could have a more focused approach to charitable activities, the Mothercare Charitable Foundation (Charity Commission no. 1104386) was created and registered with the Charity Commission on 16th June 2004.

### The Mothercare Charitable Foundation

The foundation aims to help parents in the UK and worldwide meet their needs and aspirations for their children and to give their children the very best chance of good health, education, well-being and a secure start in life. Specifically, the foundation welcomes applications from registered charities and research organisations associated with the following criteria:

- ensuring the good health and well-being of mums-to-be, new mums and their children
- special baby-care needs and premature births
- other parenting initiatives relating to family well-being.

## Exclusions

Previous information stated that unsolicited appeals are unlikely to be successful. No response to circular appeals. Support is not given to: animal welfare, appeals from individuals, the arts, elderly people, environment/heritage, religious appeals, political appeals, or sport.

## Applications

In writing to the correspondent. Requests for donations will only be considered when made in writing on the application form that can be printed from the company's website. Applications are welcomed from registered charities whose objectives match those of The Mothercare Charitable Foundation. Applications should be accompanied by details of your charity's financial status.

If your cause does not match those of The Mothercare Charitable Foundation please do not make an application. All applications received that do not meet the criteria will automatically be rejected.

Please note that meetings of the foundation that consider applications for support normally take place on a quarterly basis. Whilst successful applicants will be notified, the process may take several weeks. If you have not heard from them within six months of submitting your application you should assume that your application has been rejected and should not reapply within six months.

**Information available:** The company produces a social responsibility report. Policy guidelines are available for those considering applying to the foundation.

## Corporate giving

In 2005/06, the group made a donation of £100,000 to the Mothercare Charitable Foundation.

During the year donations from the foundation primarily focused on three areas: medical research, information resources, and education. Beneficiaries included: Action Medical Research – 'Touching Tiny Lives' campaign

(£40,700); BLISS (£30,000); and, WellBeing of Women (£5,000);

## In-kind support

The company undertake joint promotions and may offer gifts in kind.

## Employee-led support

Past information suggested that employees are encouraged to fundraise on behalf of selected charities.

# Mott MacDonald Group Limited

St Anne House, 20–26 Wellesley Road, Croydon, Surrey CR9 2UL

020 8774 2000; Fax: 020 8681 5706

Website: www.mottmac.com

Correspondent: Rachel Mason

Chief officer: Mike Blackburn

Managing Director: Keith Howells

| Year end | Turnover | Pre-tax profit |
|---|---|---|
| 31/12/2004 | £485,493,000 | £11,463,000 |

**Nature of company business**
The company is one of the world's leading engineering, management and development consultancies.

**Main locations:** Aberdeen, Belfast, Colwyn Bay, Glasgow, Liverpool, Preston

**Total employees:** 7,029

### Charitable donations

2004: £156,185
2003: £89,463

Membership: BitC, %Club

## Community involvement

The majority of the company's financial support for charitable activities appears to be channelled through the Mott McDonald Charitable Trust (Charity Commission no. 275040). Support is mainly given for education and training purposes in the fields of civil, structural, mechanical, electrical and allied engineering.

Employees are encouraged to get involved with their local communities and to raise funds on behalf of their chosen charity.

Through its not-for-profit arm, the Cambridge Education Foundation, the company supports lectures, research and publications in education focusing on learning and development.

Having recently joined Business in the Community, the company has agreed to set aside 1% of pre-tax profit towards charitable and community initiatives.

## Applications

In writing to the correspondent.

## Corporate giving

In 2004, the company declared donations 'to recognised charities' totalling £156,185 including a donation of £9,000 to RedR (Registered Engineers for Disaster Relief). During the same year, the trust had an income of £152,480, mainly as a result of a donation from the company. Grants totalling £157,712 were made and were broken down into the following categories:

- scholarships £90,000
- bursaries £54,000
- Milne award £3,330
- best paper award £3,085
- chairman's award £4,264
- project manager of the year £3,033.

## In-kind support

In helping develop the Global School Partnership, Cambridge Education Foundation has been able to support teachers in the UK and in developing countries to share their knowledge.

## Employee-led support

UK staff have engaged in a variety of fundraising activities on behalf of numerous charities including: British Heart Foundation; WaterAid; and Children in Need.

# MyTravel Group plc

Holiday House, Sandbrook Park, Sandbrook Way, Rochdale, Lancashire, OL11 1SA

01706 742000

Website: www.mytravelgroup.com

Correspondent: (See 'Applications')

Chief officer: Michael Beckett

Chief Executive: Peter McHugh

| Year end | Turnover | Pre-tax profit |
|---|---|---|
| 31/10/2005 | £2,928,900,000 | (£18,300,000) |

**Nature of company business**
The principal activity is the operation of leisure travel industry businesses in the UK, Ireland, mainland Europe, Scandinavia, Australia, Canada, Mexico and the USA. The group distributes through a range of retail outlets, telephone and e-commerce channels; operates tours for a range of customers to destinations worldwide; has its own fleet of aircraft and cruise ships; and operates a portfolio of hotels and other resort properties.

**Subsidiaries include:** Going Place Leisure Travel Ltd, Late Escapes Ltd, The BTN Finance Company, Carousel Holidays Ltd, Sun International (UK) Ltd, Blue Sea Overseas Investments Ltd, The Travelworld Group Ltd, Blue Sea Investments Ltd, UKLG Ltd

**Main locations:** Rochdale

**UK employees:** 10,473

**Total employees:** 14,597

### Charitable donations

2005: £15,000
2003: £76,000

## Community involvement

The dramatic decrease in charitable donations from the high of 2002, has been justified by the company to some extent with reference to its poor financial performance in the interim period (total losses of around £300 million). As a consequence of this, donations have been restricted to honouring pre-existing commitments, although some support may still be given in-kind and through the associated MyTravel Charitable Trust (Charity Commission no. 1091673).

They were briefly a member of Business in the Community (BitC); this is no longer the case.

### Exclusions

Generally no support for projects outside of health, children and families.

### Applications

All requests for charitable support within the stated guidelines should be addressed to The MyTravel Group Charitable Trust, 80 Croydon Road, Elmers End, Beckenham, Kent BR3 4DE.

## Corporate giving

Charitable donations in 2005 stood at £15,000, down from a high of £638,000 in 2002. We have no details of the beneficiaries.

#### MyTravel Charitable Trust

Currently, the trustees state that they will look more favourably on support for causes or projects aimed at assisting children, families and health-related issues. Any requests for charitable support falling outside of this should be directed towards the management at the relevant business unit.

Given the already limited funds available from the company and the fact that the last available accounts for the trust at the Charity Commission show a total expenditure in 2004 of £69, successful applications are likely to be limited.

### In-kind support

This takes the form of gifts in kind.

# N M Rothschild & Sons Ltd

New Court, St Swithin's Lane, London EC4P 4DU

020 7280 5000; Fax: 020 7929 1643

Website: www.nmrothschild.com

Correspondent: Secretary to the Charities Committee

Chief officer: David de Rothschild

| Year end | Turnover | Pre-tax profit |
|---|---|---|
| 31/03/2006 | £296,972,000 | £101,584,000 |

Nature of company business
The company and its subsidiaries carry on the business of merchants and bankers. The parent company is Rothschild Continuation Ltd and the ultimate holding company is Rothschild Concordia A G, incorporated in Switzerland.

Main locations: London

Total employees: 662

---

Charitable donations
2006: £709,000
2005: £862,000
2004: £717,000
2003: £901,000
Membership: BitC, L B Group, %Club

## Community involvement

The group is committed to supporting charities both in the areas in which it operates and those in the wider community. A charities committee was established in 1975 to consider the requests received every year from charities seeking financial support. Typical beneficiaries include organisations concerned with elderly people, healthcare, social welfare and education.

The company's subsidiaries around the world support causes in their areas of operation.

### Exclusions

Donations are not normally made to local groups. No response to circular appeals. No grants for advertising in charity brochures; animal welfare; appeals from individuals; fundraising events; overseas projects; political appeals; religious appeals or sport.

### Applications

In writing to the Secretary to the Charities Committee, which meets quarterly to make grant decisions.

## Corporate giving

The sum of £709,000 (2005: £862,000) was charged against the profits of the group during the year in respect of gifts for charitable purposes.

### Employee-led support

Requests for support from staff in respect of charitable causes with which they are associated, or have an involvement, are actively encouraged.

Apart from making financial donations, the group also provides charitable support in the form of the involvement of members of staff in various community programmes. In particular, it is a supporter of The Specialist Schools Trust (promoting a dialogue between educators and financial institutions) and The Prince's Trust (several members of staff being engaged as business mentors to trust-sponsored businesses).

### Commercially-led support

**Sponsorship:** Proposals should be addressed to the Group Corporate Affairs Department.

# National Express Group plc

75 Davies Street, London W1K 5HT

020 7529 2000; Fax: 020 7529 2100

Website: www.nationalexpressgroup.com

Correspondent: Jo Harrison, Group Communications Secretary

Chief officer: David Ross

Chief Executive: Phil White

| Year end | Turnover | Pre-tax profit |
|---|---|---|
| 31/12/2005 | £2,216,000,000 | £89,300,000 |

**Nature of company business**
The principal activities of the group are the provision of passenger transport services in coaches, buses, airports and trains in the UK, USA and Australia.

**Subsidiaries include:** Eurolines (UK) Ltd, one, Gatwick Express Ltd, Wagn, Airlinks The Airport Coach Company Ltd, Stansted Express, c2c Rail Ltd, Travel West Midlands, Central Trains, Midland Main Line Ltd, Wessex Trains, Travel MidlandMetro, Silverlink Train Services Ltd

**Main locations:** London

**Total employees:** 39,508

### Charitable donations

2005: £286,000
2004: £210,000

## Community involvement

The National Express Group's Charity Policy states that it seeks to form partnerships with a range of charities who meet the following criteria.

Charities should ideally be:

- registered (local groups such as football clubs should be encouraged to contact the company's local operators who have more flexible policies)
- national with local branches that connect with the group's local and regional operations
- promoting public transport
- minimal on their administration costs
- involved in one or more of the following areas: education, environment, the arts.

The group has also indicated that within the above criteria, support would be considered for organisations concerned with advertising in charity brochures, children/youth, the older people, enterprise/training and environment/heritage.

### Exclusions

The group does not support political or religious organisations and is unlikely to provide corporate assistance to high profile charities with significant existing corporate support.

### Applications

Further information is available in writing to the correspondent. All charitable applications are reviewed on a quarterly basis with the Charity Committee providing a regular input.

**Information Available:** The company produces a social responsibility report.

## Corporate giving

The company made cash donations of £286,000. We have no details of the beneficiaries.

Previously, information regarding some of the beneficiaries was as follows:

- Long term financial support from the company has helped Birmingham-based regional publisher, Tindall Street Press, publish the books of local authors. Over the last three years they have donated £15,000.

- 2003 was the fifth year of Operation Safer Travel (OST), a unique partnership between the company and West Midlands Police (with a similar project duplicated in Dundee, Scotland). OST aims to reduce and detect crime and anti-social behaviour in and around the company's bus networks.

- In partnership with The Wildlife Trust, the company hopes to raise awareness of biodiversity initiatives, an issue it finds significant due to it being a public transport provider.

- To mark 2003 the Year of the Disabled, the company developed an association with Candoco which develops dance amongst both the able and less able.

- In addition to sponsoring a case manager at the National Missing Persons Helpline, the company actively promotes the charity's telephone number and website wherever possible.

### In-kind support

The company also gives support in the form of gifts in kind and joint promotions. No further details of this were available.

### Employee-led support

The company supports its staff in their charitable activities where practical. It also matches employee fundraising to an amount which varies.

**Payroll giving:** A payroll giving scheme is in operation.

### Commercially-led support

The company also provides arts and good-cause sponsorship, an example being the sponsorship of a case worker at the National Missing Person's Helpline in 2003.

# National Grid plc

1–3 The Strand, London WC2N 5EH

020 7004 3000; Fax: 020 7004 3004

**Website:** www.nationalgrid.com

**Correspondent:** Dr Maeve Chappell, Head of Communications & Social Policy 020 7001 3000; Fax: 020 7004 3004
E-mail: csrinfo@nationalgrid.com

**Chief officer:** Sir John Parker

**Chief Executive:** Roger Urwin

| Year end | Turnover | Pre-tax profit |
|---|---|---|
| 31/03/2005 | £8,521,000,000 | £1,852,000,000 |

**Nature of company business**
The principal UK activities of the group are the operation of the electricity transmission system in England and Wales, matching national electricity supply and demand, and the operation of interconnectors with Scotland and France.

**Subsidiaries include:** Utility Metering Services Ltd, SecondSite Property, Advantica, Fulcrum Connections, Network Mapping Limited

**Main locations:** London

**UK employees:** 15,841

**Total employees:** 24,527

> **Charitable donations**
>
> 2005: £1,352,000
>
> Total community contributions: £5,449,000
>
> Membership: A & B, BitC, L B Group, %Club

## Community involvement

The National Grid Company has an extensive community involvement programme, focused on:

- regenerating communities – by seeking to minimise social disadvantage and regenerate local communities by supporting projects which help people turn their communities into safer, more prosperous places
- improving local environments – by seeking to make economically disadvantaged areas better places to live through: funding projects that improving living conditions in rural or urban areas; and promoting energy efficiency and projects to reduce energy use, especially amongst low-income groups
- encourage lifelong learning and skills training – by seeking to develop people continuously and increase their skills by supporting projects which develop abilities, unlock potential and build confidence in people of all ages.

There are three types of funding available:

- flagship projects are major projects requiring between £10,000 and £1,000,000 of help, with opportunities for employee involvement
- innovation projects are put forward by group companies and can receive cash grants of £10,000 to £100,000 per project per year, plus use of employees' skills and time (to a maximum of £300,000 value a year)
- charitable giving can be made on a local or regional basis. The main focus of these grants are for support for people who are socially excluded, disenfranchised or marginalised, such as low-income groups and people who are elderly, unemployed or have learning difficulties.

### Exclusions

Support is not given to circular appeals, advertising in charity brochures, appeals from individuals, overseas projects, political appeals, religious appeals, and local appeals not in areas of company presence.

### Applications

In writing to the correspondent. For innovative grants, applications must be submitted on a form by a senior manager of one of the group's businesses rather than the applicant charity.

**Information available:** A leaflet on National Grid's sponsorship and donations policy is available on request. The company is in the process of producing a social and environmental report.

## Corporate giving

In 2004/05, total community contributions amounted to £5,449,000 of which cash donations comprised £1,352,000.

Beneficiaries included: tsunami victims; fuel poor; environmental education centres; and, employee supported charities.

## In-kind support

**Education:** National Grid Company is involved in a number of liaison activities with schools and universities. It also supports educational materials for schools through the Electricity Association's 'Understanding Energy' service.

**Environment:** National Grid supports beneficial environmental initiatives, both on its own land and elsewhere. The company has established a major network of environmental education centres, with the active involvement of local education authorities.

## Employee-led support

The company matches pound for pound employees' fundraising up to £400 per year and employee giving up to £100 per year.

**Payroll giving:** The company operates the Give As You Earn scheme.

## Commercially-led support

**Sponsorship:** The company has two national sponsorships, in partnership with the Improvement & Development Agency (National Grid Community 21 Awards Scheme), and the Tree Council (National Grid Tree Warden Scheme).

Contact: Trevor Seeley, Head of Community Involvement.

# National Magazine Co Ltd

National Magazine House, 72 Broadwick Street, London W1F 9EP

020 7439 5000; Fax: 020 7439 6886

**Website:** www.natmags.co.uk

**Correspondent:** Kate Kingsmill, Team Secretary, MD's office

**Chief officer:** F A Bennack

**Managing Director:** J D Edwards

| Year end | Turnover | Pre-tax profit |
|---|---|---|
| 31/12/2005 | £355,165,000 | £12,433,000 |

**Nature of company business**
The main activities are the publishing and distribution of magazines and periodicals.

**Main locations:** London

**UK employees:** 968

> **Charitable donations**
>
> 2005: £44,770
> 2004: £30,768

## Community involvement

The National Magazine Company states that 'each year The National Magazine Company offers The Soho Family Centre financial support and also assists and works together on a number of projects to further the aims of the Centre'.

The company also states that it does not make ad hoc donations to charities, but that it is able to offer a number of annual subscriptions on request. Outside of this, support appears only to be given to the community local to its offices in Soho.

## Exclusions

Local appeals not in areas of company presence.

## Applications

In writing to the correspondent.

## Corporate giving

In 2005, the company made charitable donations of £44,770 (2004: £30,768).

## In-kind support

NatMag staff have assisted the Soho Family Centre through writing and designing its annual report, redesigning and equipping a new kitchen and playroom, donating equipment and resources, and raising extra funds.

## Employee-led support

The company supports employees' volunteering/charitable activities with financial help.

# Nationwide Building Society

Nationwide House, Pipers Way, Swindon SN38 2SN

01793 583000

Website: www.nationwide.co.uk

Correspondent: Michelle Leighton, Community Affairs Manager 01793 583000

Chief officer: Jonathan Agnew

Chief Executive: Philip Williamson

| Year end | Turnover | Pre-tax profit |
|---|---|---|
| 04/04/2006 | £1,173,900,000 | £325,700,000 |

Nature of company business
The group provides a comprehensive range of personal financial services.

UK employees: 14,521

Total employees: n/a

### Charitable donations

2006: £2,324,287
2005: £1,343,009
2004: £1,296,965
2003: £2,645,239

Membership: BitC, L B Group

## Community involvement

The society has made the following statement: 'Nationwide has a strong history of involvement in community projects and is firmly committed to supporting the communities from which it has grown. Through sponsorship, fundraising and other activities, Nationwide supports hundreds of events and initiatives across the country each year.

'The Community Affairs team are responsible for co-ordinating charitable activity and making decisions on requests for sponsorship and funding made to Nationwide.'

The following information refers to the donations made by the Nationwide Foundation (Charity Commission no.

1065552). As a separate legal entity the foundation is not part of the Nationwide Group and is controlled by an independent Board of Trustees which determines the policies. However, as requests for charitable donations made to the society are referred to the foundation, we include it here.

**The Nationwide Foundation:**

The Nationwide Foundation was set up in 1998 by the society from which, as its main benefactor, it receives an annual donation (£1 million in 2004).

The foundation previously had two areas of support – (i) Volunteering programmes, which also had a focus on projects concerning children and young people leaving care; and crime and justice. (ii) Rural communities.

However, in August 2005, it was involved in a strategic review of its grant making activity and criteria and since then has not been accepting new applications for funding.

New funding criteria are in the process of being agreed by the trustees and these will be announced on its website (www.nationwidefoundation.org.uk) in due course.

## Exclusions

No response to circular appeals. No support for advertising in charity brochures, animal welfare, appeals from individuals, medical research, overseas projects, political appeals, religious appeals, or for commercial (as opposed to community related) sponsorship.

## Applications

Applications to the company for donations or sponsorship should be sent to the correspondent named above.

For applications to the Nationwide Foundation, further information can be obtained from Lisa Parker at the foundation's office (Tel: 01793 655113).

On a local basis, giving depends on the local area managers, who have small budgets for local community projects.

## Corporate giving

In 2005/06, the society made charitable donations of £2,324,287 of which £2 million went to the Nationwide Foundation.

The Nationwide makes an annual donation of £150,000 to Macmillan, its flagship charity since 1993.

## In-kind support

Non-cash support in the form of equipment, consultancy, furniture, prizes/merchandise, and print/design is provided. In 2004, Nationwide helped launch two initiatives focusing on child safety.

*Cats' Eyes for Kids* – Since October 2001, Nationwide has distributed almost 6 million reflectors throughout the United Kingdom – one for every primary school child. It has now re-pledged to give every new intake child a reflector until 2006.

*Tag your Tots* In conjunction with GMTV, Nationwide launched a child safety scheme, 'Tag your Tots', and will give away one million child identity wrist bands, aiming to cut down the time a lost child spends apart from its parents.

## Employee-led support

**Payroll giving:** Nationwide operates the Give As You Earn payroll giving scheme and supports employee fundraising in various ways.

# NEC (UK) Ltd

NEC House, 1 Victoria Road, London W3 6BL

020 8993 8111; Fax: 020 8992 7161

Website: www.nec.co.uk

Correspondent: The Marketing Department

| Year end | Turnover | Pre-tax profit |
|---|---|---|
| 31/03/2004 | £223,962,000 | £3,650,000 |

**Nature of company business**
Principal activities: IT, communications and display technologies.

**Subsidiaries include:** Telecom MODUS Ltd

**Main locations:** Slough, London

**UK employees:** 192

## Community involvement

We were unable to find out whether NEC makes cash donations directly to UK-based organisations. However, its level of in-kind support and matched funding programme is sufficient for it to be included here.

## Exclusions

No support for local appeals not in areas of company presence.

## Applications

In writing to the correspondent.

## Corporate giving

Beneficiaries in the UK have included Dunstable Town Youth FC Under 9's team, which received a collection of waterproof jackets for match days.

## In-kind support

The company recently donated a second portable projector to the Great Ormond Street Children's Hospital School. Refurbished equipment may also be donated to charitable organisations.

## Employee-led support

Employee volunteering, donating and fundraising is encouraged. Fundraising activities can be match funded to a maximum of £500.

The global parent company organises an annual NEC Make a Difference Day which encourages employees to take part in a voluntary activity.

## Commercially-led support

**Sponsorship:** *Disabled sport* – The company is heavily involved in the promotion of wheelchair tennis and sponsors the annual NEC Wheelchair Tennis Camps at Nottingham Tennis Centre.

# Nestlé UK Ltd

PO Box 207, York YO91 1XY

01904 604 604; Fax: 01904 603461

Website: www.nestle.co.uk

Correspondent: Mrs Lesley Lee, Consumer Services

Chief officer: A Sykes

| Year end | Turnover | Pre-tax profit |
|---|---|---|
| 31/12/2005 | £1,390,700,000 | £100,100,000 |

**Nature of company business**
Manufacture and sale of food products and associated activities.

**Main locations:** Hayes, Castleford, Cuddington, Croydon, Dalston, Fawdon, Girvan, Halifax, York, Tutbury, Staverton, Mallow

**Total employees:** 5,781

### Charitable donations

2005: £1,700,000
2004: £1,900,000

Membership: BitC, L B Group, %Club

## Community involvement

The company supports young people (aged 11 to 18) in the following areas:

- out of school childcare and education
- arts and culture
- sport
- nutrition, health and well-being.

In 2000 Nestle joined the Prince of Wales International Business Leaders Forum, an international educational charity dedicated to promoting responsible business practice that benefits society and helps to achieve sustainable development.

The company's key charity partners are 4Children (formerly Kids' Club Network), Institute of Youth Sport, London Mozart Players and Book Trust. The single largest charity partner is 4Children with whom the company have worked since 1996 and have supported them in their campaign for safe out of school clubs. The partnership created the Nestle Music Days workshop programme with the London Mozart Players, and the Nestle Kids' Clubs Tennis Scheme with the Lawn Tennis Association. Nestle has worked with the Institute of Youth Sport since 2000. The organisation was set up to improve sporting provision for children by developing ad implementing quality physical education and sports programmes for young people. The company's leading arts sponsorship is the support for the London Mozart Players with which the company has been involved since 1989. Nestle has also worked with the Book Trust for 20 years, an independent educational charity working to bring books and people together.

On a local level, requests are considered much more widely, including community development, environmental concerns and medical activities. It is likely that this support is centred on the areas it operates.

## Exclusions

No support is given towards student expeditions, individuals, political causes, third-party fundraising events or the purchase of advertising space in charity programmes.

## Applications

Applications for support of local good causes should be made to the manager of the nearest Nestle location, but for large-scale donations or national charities the request should be made by writing to the correspondent.

## Corporate giving

The company made charitable donations totalling £1.7m during 2005 (2004: £1.9m). Details of the specific amounts given to the company's key partners and/or other organisations were not available.

## In-kind support

Nestlé's main area of non-cash support is gifts in kind – the company providing product, furniture and equipment donations to local good causes.

## Employee-led support

Employees involved with local voluntary groups may apply for a grant of up to £1,500. Employee Volunteer Awards to a total of £50,000 a year are given to those actively involved in their local community, with more than 1,000 causes benefiting since 1992.

A couple of the sites have their own employee charitable trusts, which raise funds from employees and are donated in small grants to local organisations in which employees hold an interest. These are The Nestlé Rowntree York Employees Community Fund Trust (Charity Commission no. 516702) and Nestlé Employees Community Fund Trust – Halifax (Charity Commission no. 327799); please contact Miss Vivien Tweddell at the York site or Miss Rosanne Jackson at the Halifax site respectively for further information.

**Payroll giving:** A scheme is operated through an 'internal' company community fund.

## Commercially-led support

**Sponsorship:** *The arts* – support has been given to London Mozart Players, and York Early Music Festival. It has sponsored a children's book prize in partnership with Book Trust for a number of years. Each year involves around 42,000 children in choosing the nation's favourite children's books.

*Sport* – support has been given to junior tennis for over forty years to encourage more young people to play the game.

# Newcastle Building Society

Portland House, New Bridge Street,
Newcastle upon Tyne NE1 8AL

0191 244 2000; Fax: 0191 244 2002

Website: www.newcastle.co.uk

Correspondent: Corporate Communications Manager

Chief officer: Chris Hilton

Chief Executive: Colin Seccombe

| Year end | Turnover | Pre-tax profit |
|---|---|---|
| 31/12/2005 | £188,400,000 | £14,800,000 |

Nature of company business
Building society.

**Subsidiaries include:** NBS Financial Services Ltd, Newton Facilities Computer Leasing Ltd, Newton Facilities Management Ltd, Newton Facilities Computer Purchasing Ltd

**Main locations:** Newcastle upon Tyne

Total employees: 796

### Charitable donations

2005: £100,000
2004: £90,000
2003: £98,625

Membership: A & B

## Community involvement

All charitable requests to the society are redirected to the Community Foundation serving Tyne & Wear and Northumberland (Charity Commission no.: 700510), which manages the society's fund on its behalf. The society supports community groups and organisations through their sponsorship programmes and the Newcastle Building Society Community Fund. The fund was set up in 1992 by the society to provide financial support to grass roots charities and voluntary organisations in areas where the society has a branch presence.

The fund is managed by The Community Foundation serving Tyne & Wear and Northumberland. The foundation is established for the support or promotion of any charitable purpose, relief of poverty, advancement of education, advancement of religion or any charitable purpose for the benefit of the community in the area of Tyne & Wear and its immediate neighbourhood

Community foundations operate throughout the country and this particular community foundation provides a service to families, individuals and companies in Tyne & Wear and Northumberland who want to make a lasting difference to the communities where they live and work. Grants made by the Newcastle Building Society Community Fund are reviewed as part of the foundation's overall grants programme which now totals over £7 million a year.

The predominant activity is grant making but the community foundation also devotes resources to development and donor education which aim to increase local philanthropy. It also manages a small number of projects that contribute to tackling urgent social needs such as Youth Homelessness and Men's Health as part of a commitment to play a wider role in the community.

Since the community fund began, the society has helped hundreds of voluntary projects and charities in the areas in which it has branches.

### Exclusions

No grants for: sponsorship and fundraising events; small contributions to major appeals; large capital projects; endowments; political or religious groups; or work which should be funded by health and local authorities, or government grant aid.

### Applications

Applications should be sent to: Newcastle Building Society Community Fund at the Community Foundation, Cale Cross, 156 Pilgrim Street, Newcastle upon Tyne NE1 6SU (0191 222

0945; Fax: 0191 230 0689; e-mail: grants@communityfoundation.org.uk).

Applications should include background information and a full explanation of how any grant will be used. Applications can be received at any time and are acknowledged.

Full grant guidelines can be obtained from the society's website.

## Corporate giving

### Newcastle Building Society Community Fund

'The Newcastle Building Society Community Fund was set up in 1992 and has increased its commitment significantly over the past few years. Each year the Newcastle donates around £100,000 to worthwhile charities and individual causes.' The society has also established the Members' Community Fund (for details see below).

Considerable in-kind support is also given.

### In-kind support

In addition to charitable donations, support is given through gifts in kind, joint promotions, and advice and mentoring.

### Commercially-led support

**Sponsorship:** The Newcastle has been involved in several key sponsorship projects that have benefited the communities in which it operates. For a whole season in 2003 the Society sponsored The NABC Football League, the North-East's premier junior football league, recognising and developing footballing talent in the region.

Throughout 2003 until 2006 they have lent their support as sponsors to the North of England Cadet Force with the benefits going to support air, sea and army forces throughout Northumberland, Tyneside, Cleveland and County Durham.

Previously they have also supported projects such as Northumbria in Bloom, promoting community spirit and the Scottish Community Police Awards, encouraging local communities to vote for their 'Top Cop' and reward exceptional work by local police.

### The Members' Community Fund

In 2003 the society launched The Members' Community Fund which allows members to make an annual donation from one of their Newcastle Building Society savings accounts.

The society selects three charitable themes aimed at covering a wide cross section of people and activities, including:

 ▷ children's education
 ▷ adult literacy and numeracy
 ▷ IT schemes for the over 55s.

The money raised is then divided among these themes so that if 30% of respondents choose to support children's education, 30% of the funds will go to causes related to this.

Places such as Cleadon Park in South Sheilds have benefited from money from this fund with a £5,000 donation to assist with various projects including an After School Club and an Innovation Week for young people to develop their skills with dance and music.

As with the community fund, the funds are also held and distributed by The Community Foundation serving Tyne & Wear and Northumberland.

# News International plc

1 Virginia Street, London E98 1XY

020 7782 6000

Website: www.newscorp.com

Correspondent: Peter Rimmer, Community Affairs Manager 020 7782 6641

Chief officer: K R Murdoch

Chief Executive: L Hinton

| Year end | Turnover | Pre-tax profit |
|---|---|---|
| 30/06/2006 | | £118,100,000 |

Nature of company business
Main activity: the printing and publishing of national newspapers. Other activities include newsprint storage and distribution.

Subsidiaries include: News Group Newspapers, British Sky Broadcasting (40%), Times Newspapers Holdings, The Times Supplements, Broadsystem, Convoys

Main locations: Glasgow, Knowsley, London, Peterborough

UK employees: 3,000

### Charitable donations

2005: £1,200,000
2004: £900,000

## Community involvement

We have been unable to obtain any up-to-date policy information for the company, but confirm the contact to be correct.

*Subsidiary companies:* Local appeals are dealt with by the company's plants in Glasgow, Knowsley, and Peterborough which are encouraged to pursue their own community affairs programmes. Unfortunately, no details were available regarding what this might cover.

### Exclusions

No support for advertising in charity brochures, appeals from individuals, fundraising events, medical research, overseas projects, religious/political appeals, science/technology, sport or local appeals not in areas of company presence. As a general rule the company does not make contributions to capital building projects.

### Applications

In writing to the correspondent. A charities committee meets regularly. Unsuccessful applicants are given reasons and the corporate policy is explained.

Appeals to subsidiary companies should be made to managing directors, managing editors or editors.

## Corporate giving

According to the company accounts for 2004/05 filed at Companies House, charitable contributions for the year amounted to £1.2 million (2003/04: £900,000). No details of the beneficiaries were available.

## Employee-led support

Previously, we were advised that there is a preference for supporting charities in which a member of staff is involved. Staff are encouraged to become volunteers in their own time and to become school governors.

**Payroll giving:** A scheme is operated by the company.

# Next plc

Desford Road, Enderby, Leicester LE19 4AT

0845 456 7777

Website: www.next.co.uk

Correspondent: Jeanette Cooper-Hudson, Charities Co-ordinator

Chief officer: David Jones

Chief Executive: Simon Wolfson

| Year end | Turnover | Pre-tax profit |
|---|---|---|
| 28/01/2006 | £3,106,200,000 | £449,100,000 |

### Nature of company business
The principal activities of the group are high-street retailing, home shopping, customer services management and financial services.

**Subsidiaries include:** First Retail Finance Ltd, Club 24 Ltd, Vetura, Callscan Ltd

**Main locations:** Bradford, Leeds, Leicester

**UK employees:** 45,360

**Total employees:** 57,454

### Charitable donations
2006: £350,000
2005: £708,000

Membership: BitC

## Community involvement

The company states in its 2006 Corporate Social Responsibility Report that: 'Next believes it is important to maintain healthy relationships with the communities we operate in by contributing money, goods or the time and expertise of our employees. We focus our resources on projects that support communities and offer sponsorship to a wide variety of organisations and charities. One of the ways charitable organisations can make a huge difference to the lives of the people they help is by forming partnerships with businesses and through fundraising events organised by Next additional monies are raised that help the charities we support.

'Our charity and sponsorship programme is made up of three categories:

- charitable support – we gave charitable donations to 13 registered charities comprising of 10 health charities, 2 youth charities and 1 animal welfare charity. We also support a range of other charities in response to individual requests

- community support – we are a member of Business in the Community, Leicestershire Cares and The Duke of Edinburgh's Award Scheme

- commercial support – we sponsor a number of fashion and sports organisations which offers the benefit of supporting them with funds as well as helping to raise awareness of our brand.'

Help may also be given in the form of product donations, charity Christmas cards, and supporting staff fundraising efforts.

### Exclusions

It does not second staff to voluntary organisations. No support is given to political causes and the company prefers not to give for adverts in publications and/or sponsorship of an event or individual – the company's involvement in these areas is limited.

Although a member of Business in the Community, the company does not support enterprise agencies, nor is it involved in any local economic development initiatives.

### Applications

All donation requests should be sent to the personnel department where they will be carefully considered, with priority being given to local charities, i.e. local to Leicester and Leeds (this is where the majority of employees are based). A budget has been specifically allocated for this purpose. As such, **all letters and telephone requests** should be directed to the Charities Co-ordinator and she will reply.

Full details of the company's involvement are carefully recorded by and further information can be obtained from the correspondent. Details of charitable donations will be presented to the board and be available for all members of the charity committee.

## Corporate giving

Next made cash donations in 2005/06, totalling just under £350,000. This was broken down by the company as follows: charitable support £313,377; community support £34,397. We have no details of the beneficiaries.

Although the company provides in-kind support, no figure regarding the value of this was available.

### In-kind support

*Product donations* – Next make use of damaged stock by donating it to charities for them to either sell in their shops, help individuals, or recycle and make into new product to sell on. The British Red Cross raised over £100,000 in their shops by selling this stock.

*Charity Christmas cards* – by donating 25p from each pack Next raised £211,521 which was shared equally between British Heart Foundation, Macmillan Cancer Relief and Barnados. Stores in Ireland raised £4,219 which was equally divided between Barnados and the Irish Heart Foundation.

### Employee-led support

The staff at Next have a charity committee which raises money. The committee has decided, after discussion with the different staff councils (and through them with employees), to have two social events a year to raise money for local organisations. The sports & social committee will run the events with the charity committee providing support.

Future events will raise funds for local charities suggested by staff. Employees' wishes will be taken into consideration following the results of a questionnaire distributed to staff.

Next are also considering opening up this opportunity to store managers to volunteer their own time, with projects initiated by themselves in their own communities.

### Commercially-led support

**Sponsorship:** *Sport* – Next were the main sponsors of the British Transplant Games which took place in August 2005 at Loughborough University.

The company also gives support to local sporting teams, particularly where there is employee involvement. The value of commercial sponsorship in total was £247,093. We do not know what proportion of this was in aid of local organisations involving employees.

*Health* – Next sponsored Breast Cancer Care's annual fashion show by donating additional funding.

# Nike (UK) Limited

One Victory Way, Doxford International Business Park, Sunderland, Tyne & Wear SR3 3XF

0191 401 6453; Fax: 0191 401 2012

Website: www.nike.com

Correspondent: Carole Ewart

Managing Director: Dan Loeb

| Year end | Turnover | Pre-tax profit |
| --- | --- | --- |
| 31/05/2003 | £53,344,000 | £9,367,000 |

**Nature of company business**
Multi-national manufacturer of sports clothing and equipment.

**Main locations:** Sunderland

**UK employees:** 192

### Charitable donations

Total community contributions: £100,000

## Community involvement

The company supports projects which help children get active and become involved in teamwork through sport.

### Exclusions

Only registered charities can be supported. No grants are made to individuals, sports teams, non-registered charities, for-profit groups, religious groups, capital campaigns, endowment funds, memorials or political activities.

### Applications

The following application guidelines are taken from Nike's corporate website (www.nikebiz.com) to which you should refer for fuller information.

#### Cash grants

'For those seeking cash support, we invite proposals from non-profit organisations or collaborations among organisations. Before preparing your proposal, please ensure that your non-profit or NGO organisation meets the eligibility criteria outlined in these guidelines. Proposals should include the following information in this order:

- description of the organisation, including its mission, major accomplishments, governance, area, and population served
- detailed description of the project or activity for which support is being requested, including the amount of the grant request
- operating budget for the current fiscal year
- identification of funding sources for the current fiscal year and amounts received (include foundation, corporate, individual, and public support)
- list of any previous funding received from Nike, Inc. or the Nike Foundation and short project description
- project budget
- list of current board members and key staff
- most recent financial statement
- copy of the organisation's tax-exempt notification letter from the IRS or equivalent documentation.'

**Product donations**

'Each year, Nike proactively donates product to non-profit organisations and NGOs dedicated to youth physical activity, and disaster relief efforts around the world. In 2005, Nike donated more than $23 million in footwear, apparel and equipment to non-profit organisations.

'Nike will not provide product donations to individual sports teams in order to clearly separate our philanthropy from our marketing efforts.

'Product donations are made based upon availability. If you are requesting product in support of an event, Nike must receive your request at least 12 weeks before the event date.

'Requests for product should include the following information:

- description of the organisation, including its mission, major accomplishments, governance, area, and population served
- detailed description of the project or activity and those benefiting for which product is being requested
- specific purpose for product, type of product, quantity and size run
- method of distribution, and accountability for delivery and utilization of product
- project budget
- list of any previous product support received from Nike, Inc. and short project description
- copy of the organisation's tax-exempt notification letter from the IRS or equivalent documentation.

'Nike may request additional information. Proposal materials, including photographs, videos, CDs, and special binders cannot be returned.

'E-mail or fax proposals will not be accepted.'

All applications are processed centrally from its US office. The address is: Global Community Affairs, Nike Inc, PO Box 4027, Beaverton, OR 97076, USA.

Applicants are generally notified of a decision within eight weeks (although as this probably means a reply is sent within eight weeks of it receiving a request, transatlantic applications may extend slightly beyond this barrier).

## Corporate giving

In 2005, Nike contributed $46.1 million (around £25 million) in cash and products to non-profit partners around the world.

Nike's major programme in the UK is Zoneparcs. Working with the Youth Sport Trust, the UK Department for Education and Skills, Nike set out to radically transform recess and lunchtime at schools. The intent was to promote physical and mental activities that were creative, positive and sporting. What started as a pilot programme in one school in east London has spread out to 300 schools across the UK. Nike has committed more than £500,000 since the scheme started in 2000.

NikeGO – Sport for Social Change, is an initiative that seeks to effect positive change through sport in excluded young people's lives. In its EMEA (Europe, the Middle East and Africa) Community Book, the following organisations are listed as having received support under the scheme either through grants, volunteer time or product donations: Community Service Volunteers, London; Youth Sport Trust (Girls in Sport); Northumbria Police & Gateshead MBC (Offbeat); Sunderland Youth Development Group (Young Achievers); Hoop Dreams; Hylton Redhouse Primary School; St Aloysius R.C. School, London; Richard Cobden Primary School, London; and, Ecclesbourne Primary School.

Support is also provided through the Nike Foundation which currently contributes to poverty alleviation through investments in adolescent girls in Bangladesh, Brazil, China, Ethiopia and Zambia.

### In-kind support

Much of Nike's community work involves the donation of its products.

### Employee-led support

Employee activism is encouraged through Nike's Sport4ACause Fund. Employees engaged in charitable sporting events have the funds they raise matched by the company.

Nike's "EXTRA TIME" programme gives employees six days per year for volunteer activities.

# Northern Foods plc

2180 Century Way, Thorpe Park, Leeds, LS15 8ZB

0113 390 0110; Fax: 0113 390 0211

Website: www.northern-foods.co.uk

Correspondent: Fran Pilling, Corporate Social Responsibility Officer

Chief officer: Anthony Hobson

Chief Executive: Pat O'Driscoll

| Year end | Turnover | Pre-tax profit |
|---|---|---|
| 01/04/2006 | £1,438,200,000 | £16,100,000 |

### Nature of company business
A leading supplier of high-quality chilled foods under the own labels of the major multiple retailers, with strong brands of its own in premium quality biscuits, fresh chilled dairy products, frozen food and savoury pastry products. The company has a strong operating presence in Nottingham, Sheffield, Greater Manchester, Batley and Lancashire.

Subsidiaries include: Cavaghan & Gray Group Ltd, Cavaghan & Gray Ltd, Fletchers Bakeries Ltd, F W Farnsworth Ltd, Convenience Foods Ltd, NFT Distribution Ltd

Main locations: Accrington, Bolton, Batley, Sheffield, Nottingham, Oldham, Market Drayton, Manchester, Worksop, Wakefield, Corby, Carlisle, Hull

Total employees: 20,231

### Charitable donations

2006: £89,000
2005: £273,000
2004: £291,000
2003: £266,000

Membership: BitC

## Community involvement

Following the completion of a comprehensive review of its corporate social responsibility commitments in 2006, the company is to concentrate on supporting the promotion of healthy balanced lifestyles. One aspect of this will be through a pilot health and nutritional education programme called Phunky Foods. The programme has been introduced to 55 primary schools across the Yorkshire region.

Progress on this new focus will be reported on during 2007.

### Exclusions

The company does not generally support the larger national charities, religious or political bodies. Support given to health charities and the arts is extremely limited. No grants for circular appeals, advertising in charity brochures, animal welfare, appeals from individuals, elderly people, environment/heritage, fundraising events, medical appeals, science/technology, sickness charities or sport.

### Applications

In writing to the committee, including supporting information. Applications are considered by a committee comprising Directors and Executives which meets on a quarterly basis.

## Corporate giving

In 2005/06, the company made cash donations of £89,000.

The following is a sample of the charities listed as major grant beneficiaries in the company's 2003/04 social responsibility report: Samaritans; Wybourn Youth Trust, Sheffield; Fairbridge, Greater Manchester; Youth at Risk, Nottingham; Opera North Community Education; Sobriety Projects, Yorkshire; Parents at Work; The Warren, Hull; Fair Play, Batley; First Data, Nottingham; and Hope for the Homeless, Worksop.

In addition to the regions highlighted below, Northern Foods supports charities across the UK, matching the spread of its locations.

*Yorkshire* – Because of its Hull roots, Northern Foods has many local community links with the city. One such link is with the Warren, a drop-in centre for young people who may be unemployed, victims of violence or harassment, homeless, single parents or involved with drugs. The Warren aims to empower young people by helping them develop the skills necessary for them to take greater control over their own lives. Northern Foods' support has been through direct funding and also through sponsoring a brochure to help The Warren with fundraising and public relations.

*East Midlands* – The company has championed Race for Opportunity, an initiative targeting ethnic minorities, in the campaign in this area. Support for an entrepreneurial businesswoman in Nottingham has helped her to develop her food manufacturing company, Original Eastern Foods, to the point where she now has around thirty, mainly ethnic minority, employees.

*Greater Manchester* – Support for Fairbridge, a charity focusing on inner-city youth, have funded a two-year pilot project for thirty 14- and 15-year olds who were failing to attend Windsor High School in Salford. The scheme aimed to develop a broad range of personal and social skills and reintegrate participants back into mainstream education. An alternative curriculum is offered, including safety awareness, arts and crafts, navigation and a community or business based project.

*Overseas* – The company's links with the Third World go back over many years. It has consistently supported Oxfam since the 1950s, and also supports One World Action and VSO.

## In-kind support

**Education:** In addition to financial support, support for education includes: gifts in kind to schools and universities, particularly those close to its companies or from which it recruits staff. It is also involved with a number of industry-education links including Compacts and support for CRAC and UBI.

**Enterprise:** The company supports enterprise agencies.

In kind support is also given in the form of stock or equipment and the provision of professional services free of charge.

## Employee-led support

The Northern Foods Association covers all employees. Though primarily a sports and social club its activities include fundraising for charities, which is encouraged by the company. Employees at many of the companies are involved in charitable and community activities and a number have participated in short assignments or longer-term secondments to community projects. A number of directors and senior managers serve as trustees, advisers or non-executive directors of these groups.

**Payroll giving:** The Give As You Earn scheme is operated.

# Northern Rock plc

Northern Rock House, Gosforth, Newcastle upon Tyne NE3 4PL

0191 285 7191; Fax: 0191 284 8470

**Website:** www.northernrock.co.uk

**Correspondent:** Colin Taylor, Group Secretary

**Chief officer:** Dr M W Ridley

**Chief Executive:** Adam Applegarth

| Year end | Turnover | Pre-tax profit |
|---|---|---|
| 31/12/2005 | | £494,200,000 |

**Nature of company business**
The main purpose of the group is the provision of housing finance, savings and a range of related personal financial and banking services.

**Subsidiaries include:** Indemnity Company Ltd

**Main locations:** Newcastle upon Tyne

**UK employees:** 4,569

**Charitable donations**
2005: £24,700,000
2003: £19,300,000
Total community contributions: £24,840,000
Membership: A & B, L B Group, %Club

## Community involvement

The conversion of Northern Rock Building Society into a public company was completed on 1 October 1997. An integral part of this was the formation of a charitable body, the Northern Rock Foundation (Charity Commission no. 1063906). This was launched in January 1998 and is entitled to receive a covenant of about five per cent of annual pre-tax profits of Northern Rock plc.

The foundation holds a special category of shares which are non-dividend bearing and non-voting. In the event of a change of control of the company the covenant would cease, and the shares held by the foundation would be converted into 15% of the company's ordinary shares, thus creating an endowment to enable it to fulfil its purpose in perpetuity.

The foundation is an independent grant-making trust supporting charitable causes in the North East of England and Cumbria. Its primary aim is to help improve the conditions of those disadvantaged in society due to:

- age – for example, young people and older people
- disability
- displacement – for example, refugees, asylum seekers, survivors of domestic violence
- a lack of employment opportunities
- geography – where people live may affect their ability to get basic services, to work together for mutual benefit or to enjoy a healthy and fulfilled life
- crime – for example, victims of domestic abuse
- prejudice and discrimination, for example, against gay men and lesbians or black and minority ethnic people.

Support is also given to cultural activities that benefit everyone, without a specific focus on disadvantage.

### Exclusions

'There are certain organisations, projects and proposals that we will not consider for grants. You should be aware that it costs the equivalent of several small grants to administer ineligible applications each year. If your organisation or your project falls into one of the categories below please do not apply to us for a grant.

'Activities which are not recognised as charitable in law; Applications for under £1,000; Charities which appear to us to have excessive unrestricted or free reserves (up to 12 months' expenditure is normally acceptable), or are in serious deficit; National charities which do not have a regional office or other representation in North East England or Cumbria; Grant-making bodies seeking to distribute grants on our behalf; Open-ended funding agreements; General appeals, sponsorship and marketing appeals; Corporate applications for founder membership of a charity; Retrospective grants; Replacement of statutory funding; Activities primarily the responsibility of central or local government or health authorities; Individuals and organisations that distribute funds to individuals; Animal welfare; Mainstream educational activity, schools and educational establishments; Medical research, hospitals, hospices and medical centres; Medical treatments and therapies including art therapy; Fabric appeals for places of worship; Promotion of religion; Expeditions or overseas travel; Minibuses, other vehicles and transport schemes except where they are a small and integral part of a larger scheme; Holidays and outings; Playgrounds and play equipment; Private clubs or those with such restricted membership as to make them not charitable; Capital bids purely towards compliance with the Disability Discrimination Act; Amateur arts organisations; Musical instruments; Sports kit and equipment.'

## Applications

The foundation has different grant application processes: one for requests from £1,000 to £20,000; the other for requests over £20,000. Please make sure you complete the correct application form.

Applications can be made online, or by downloading the appropriate form from the foundation's website at: www.nr-foundation.org.uk which also contains all the information you will need to assess your eligibility.

Alternatively, application forms can be obtained by writing to the Grants Manager, The Northern Rock Foundation, The Old Chapel, Woodbine Road, Gosforth, Newcastle upon Tyne NE3 1DD.

(Tel: 0191 284 8412; Fax: 0191 284 8413; E-mail: generaloffice@nr-foundation.org.uk)

The pack contains comprehensive information on how to apply and on the foundation's current policy. It is important to be aware of the latter as the criteria can change from year to year.

The foundation will acknowledge all applications and let you know straight away whether or not it is eligible. If it is eligible, you will be told which staff manager will assess it. They will be your main contact should there be any queries. They will usually visit your organisation, but sometimes assessment interviews are carried out by telephone. Others may be asked about your organisation or proposal, so let the foundation know if there is anything confidential about your plans or situation which should not be divulged.

Trustees make their decisions based on the staff manager's assessment. They meet five times a year to make decisions on grants over £20,000. For grants over £20,000, the aim is to give a decision within six months of receiving the application, though sometimes it necessarily takes longer. For grants under £20,000 there are more regular meetings, and a response within two to four months can be expected, though, once again, some applications take longer.

**Please avoid telephoning to enquire about progress.**

# Corporate giving

The company's contribution for 2005 to the foundation was £24.7 million.

### The Northern Rock Foundation

During 2005, the foundation awarded 313 grants totalling £20.2 million under its main grant programmes for capital and/or revenue grants which were for a term of between one and five years. Within this, grants were distributed as follows:

Prevention (£4,987,000); Basics (£3,237,000); Money & jobs (£2,791,000); Aspiration (£2,984,000); Exploration (£720,000); Better sector (£2,153,000); Capital (£2,775,000); and, Exceptional (£550,000).

Out of the 902 grant applications received in 2005, 23% were ineligible.

### Grant programmes for 2007

- money and jobs – helping disadvantaged people and communities to increase their assets, income and economic activity. 2007 budget: £4 million

- independence and choice – giving people with mental health problems, people with learning disabilities, older people and carers a choice of excellent services that help them to become or remain independent. 2007 budget: £4 million

- strong and healthy communities – strengthening people's well-being through community and physical activities, improving local environments and by helping them get healthy, fresh food. 2007 budget: £2 million

- building positive lives – helping people who lack self-confidence or motivation, or who face discrimination, to have the individual support they need to lead more positive and fulfilling lives. 2007 budget: £3 million

- safety and justice – reducing the incidence and impact of domestic abuse, sexual violence, prostitution, child abuse and hate crimes, by investing in better support for victims. 2007 budget: £3 million

- culture and heritage – inspiring, enjoyable and diverse culture programmes and events that raise our region's profile and make it a better place for everyone to live and enjoy life. 2007 budget: £3 million

- better buildings – investing in improved buildings for cultural organisations and for voluntary and community groups. 2007 budget: £4 million.

To obtain fuller and more up to date details of the above grants programmes, please refer to the information given in 'Applications' section, above.

The foundation also offers loans in certain instances as they are a way of providing funding to worthy projects or organisations which might not necessarily be eligible to apply for a grant.

## In-kind support

Northern Rock, through its link with the Calvert Trust, gave prior trained staff paid leave from work to help with and organise an annual weekend event at Keilder Centre on behalf of local Leonard Cheshire residents. The event provided people with disabilities with the chance to take part in a range of outdoor activities including: sailing, canoeing, abseiling, zip winding and archery.

Northern Rock valued the input of staff time to support corporate giving in 2005 at £140,000.

## Employee-led support

The foundation runs a scheme to match pound for pound money donated by employees to charity. Some of the money came from the Give as You Earn payroll giving scheme, but the majority of money donated by staff came from their own fundraising efforts.

**Payroll giving:** The Give As You Earn scheme is in operation.

# Northern Trust Group Ltd

Lynton House, Ackhurst Business Park, Foxhole Road, Chorley PR7 1NY

01257 269400; Fax: 01257 238701

Correspondent: J C Kay, Trustee of the TJH Foundation

Chief officer: T J Hemmings

| Year end | Turnover | Pre-tax profit |
|---|---|---|
| 31/03/2005 | £107,501,000 | £14,443,000 |

Nature of company business
Property, leisure and investment.

Main locations: Chorley

Total employees: 2,031

## Charitable donations
2004: £650,500
2003: £1,150,500

## Community involvement

Support is given to a number of nominated charities each year through the TJH Foundation (Charity Commission no: 1077311). Outside of this, general requests for support are considered on their merit. The foundation aims to support existing national and north-west based charitable organisation by means of donation. We have been informed (December 2005) that the trustees tend to fund organisations for a couple of years or so and there is nothing available for new applicants 'within the foreseeable future'.

### Applications

In writing to the correspondent at: The TJH Foundation, Gleadhill House, Dawbers Lane, Euxton, Chorley PR7 6EA.

## Corporate giving

In 2004 the company donated £650,000 to the foundation (2003: £1,150,500). The foundation made 44 grants to 29 organisations which totalled £443,800.

By far the largest grant was £301,350 to British Red Cross.

Other beneficiaries included The Prince's Royal Trust for Carers North West (£97,150), Royal Lancashire Agricultural Society (£10,000 each), University of Central Lancashire Foundation (£9,000), Great Ormond Street Hospital (£5,100 each) and NSPCC (£3,000).

No charitable donations were made by the company for the year ending 31st March 2005.

# Northumbrian Water

Abbey Road, Pity Me, Durham DH1 5FJ

08457 171 100; Fax: 0191 384 1920

Website: www.nwl.co.uk

Correspondent: The Community Relations Manager

Chief officer: Sir Derek Wanless

Managing Director: J A Cuthbert

| Year end | Turnover | Pre-tax profit |
|---|---|---|
| 31/03/2006 | £550,500,000 | £96,600,000 |

Nature of company business
Northumbrian Water Group plc is one of the UK's ten water and sewerage businesses. The company and its subsidiaries work in three related areas: the supply of water and waste water services within the UK; international water management; and a range of supporting technical and consultancy services.

Subsidiaries include: ULG Northumbrian Limited, Fastflow Pipeline Services Limited, Entec UK Ltd

Main locations: Durham

UK employees: 2,553

## Charitable donations
2006: £122,411
2005: £89,369
2004: £33,084
2003: £56,827

Membership: A & B, BitC, %Club

## Community involvement

The company stated that is moving its emphasis of community activity away from cash donations towards a greater involvement with community issues. It supports local charities in its area of operation (i.e. North East, Essex and Suffolk) and appeals relevant to company business.

### Exclusions

No support for circular appeals, local appeals not in areas of company presence, large national appeals or overseas projects (other than support for WaterAid).

### Applications
In writing to the correspondent.

## Corporate giving

During 2005/06 the company made charitable donations of £122,411.

### In-kind support

The company gives additional support through gifts in kind, joint promotions and encouraging employee volunteering.

### Employee-led support

An employee volunteering scheme launched in 2002, Just an Hour, encourages employees to spend an hour of work time a month providing support to community or environmental initiatives.

### Commercially-led support

**Sponsorship:** *The arts* – in recent years the company has sponsored the RSC.

# Norwich & Peterborough Building Society

Peterborough Business Park, Lynch Wood, Peterborough PE2 6ZA

01733 372372

Website: www.npbs.co.uk

Correspondent: Pat Turner, General Manager – HR

Chief officer: Keith Bedell-Pearce

Chief Executive: Matthew Bullock

| Year end | Turnover | Pre-tax profit |
|---|---|---|
| 31/12/2005 | | £15,800,000 |

**Nature of company business**
Independent building society offering a range of financial products and services.

**Subsidiaries include:** Hockleys Professional Surveyors and Valuers

**Main locations:** Lowestoft, Norwich, Great Yarmouth, Peterborough, Stamford, Southwold, King's Lynn, Ipswich, Lincoln, Bury St Edmunds, Cambridge

**UK employees:** 1,000

### Charitable donations

2005: £89,000
2003: £147,000

Total community contributions: £147,000

Membership: BitC

## Community involvement

The society only supports organisations based in East Anglia and Lincolnshire and prefers to support those that focus on housing-related issues, family debt, social and financial exclusion, and young people. It also gives support to cathedrals, churches and other places of worship, including other faiths.

As a mutual building society it was decided to draw up an agreement requiring customers opening new savings accounts to assign any windfall benefits to charity. Although certain exemptions apply to this, any eligible windfalls will go to the Charities Aid Foundation.

### Exclusions

No support for overseas projects, political appeals, religious appeals or sport.

### Applications

In writing to the correspondent.

## Corporate giving

In 2005, the society made total community contributions of £147,000 of which £89,000 was in cash donations. No details of the beneficiaries were provided, but in the past support has been given to organisations such as Shelter, Citizens Advice, Cambridge Association of Youth Clubs and Peterborough Cathedral.

Society members are encouraged to put forward their ideas for charity and community support.

### Employee-led support

In arrangement with the society, employees are allowed company time off in which to volunteer. Money raised by employees is matched up to a maximum of £500, while employees giving receives a 10% top up from the society.

**Payroll giving:** The society operates the Give As You Earn scheme.

### Commercially-led support

**Sponsorship:** The society undertakes good-cause sponsorship.

# Nottingham Building Society

5–13 Upper Parliament Street, Nottingham NG1 2BX

0115 948 1444; Fax: 0115 948 3948

Website: www.thenottingham.com

Correspondent: Will Howell, Senior Public Relations Assistant
0115 956 4289; Fax: 0115 950 2314
E-mail: william.howell@thenottingham.com

Chief officer: David Thompson

Chief Executive: Ian Rowling

| Year end | Turnover | Pre-tax profit |
|---|---|---|
| 31/12/2005 | | £8,655,000 |

**Nature of company business**
Independent building society offering a range of financial products and services.

**Main locations:** Nottingham

**UK employees:** 538

### Charitable donations

2005: £45,630
2003: £55,538

## Community involvement

The following statement is taken from the Society's annual report:

'The Society's community schemes aim to support causes which help to protect people's homes and communities. In the autumn, we joined forces with regional press to launch the 'Safe As Houses' awards, which seek to reward groups and organisations with funding for projects which help to make their communities safer. We also gave community awards to numerous groups and organisations as we helped to make a difference to the quality of life in our communities.'

A wide variety of groups are supported, including large and small registered and non-registered charities. Only groups in areas of society presence are supported, i.e. Nottinghamshire, Lincolnshire, Derbyshire and South Yorkshire.

### Exclusions

No support for advertising in charity brochures, appeals from individuals, children/youth, education, elderly people enterprise/training, overseas projects, political appeals, part funding of a larger project, travel expenses, rent or property maintenance, staffing costs or projects which are the responsibility of statutory organisations.

## Applications

For an application form for the awards scheme you can e-mail the society at: marketinggroup@thenottingham.com; tel. 0115 956 4378; or go to your local branch. Alternatively, an application form can be downloaded from the society's website.

**Advice for applicants:** The awards panel meet four times a year in February, May, August and November. Successful applicants must: spend the money within three months of receiving the cheque; have a receipt available if the society asks to see it; be prepared to take part in publicity; spend the money on the items agreed with the society.

The society stated: 'Everyone who applies, whether they get one of our Community Awards or not, will be helping others by applying, because we will donate £1 to a registered charity for every application we get.'

## Corporate giving

In 2005, the society made cash donations of over £45,000 primarily through its Community Spirit Awards scheme which makes grants every year in March, June, September and December. Donations of up to £1,000 are available under three categories:

(i) *Crime Reduction and Security* – Helping to keep people safe in their homes and whilst they are out and about.

(ii) *Health and Quality of Life* – Helping to promote health and improving the quality of life of those living with illness or disability.

(iii) *Education and New Talent* – Helping to provide opportunities to learn and to encourage new talent.

In addition to the above, charitable donations are made on an ad hoc basis in response to written appeals received from groups or organisations based in an area in which the society has a presence.

# Nottingham East Midlands Airport

Building 34, Nottingham East Midlands Airport, Castle Donnington, Derby DE74 2SA

01332 852801; Fax: 01332 852959

**Website:** www.nottinghamema.com

**Correspondent:** Anna Thomson, Community Relations Executive 01332 852801
E-mail: community@nottinghamema.com

**Managing Director:** Penny Coates

| Year end | Turnover | Pre-tax profit |
| --- | --- | --- |
| 31/03/2005 | £50,000,000 | £2,900,000 |

**Nature of company business**
Principal activity: Airport operator.

**Main locations:** Derby

**UK employees:** 250

---

| Charitable donations |
| --- |
| 2005: £40,000 |
| 2004: £40,000 |
| 2003: £40,000 |
| Membership: BitC |

## Community involvement

Nottingham East Midlands Airport (NEMA) supports local communities within a ten-mile radius of the airport, although in practice, those benefiting appear mainly to be within a five-mile radius. Donations are made through the East Midlands Airport Community Fund which is funded by an annual donation from the company and the surcharges it levies on those airlines generating too much noise during night flights. Projects must meet one of the following criteria:

- bringing the community closer together through facilities for sport, recreational or other leisure-time activities
- environmental improvement and heritage conservation
- improving awareness of environmental issues through environmental education
- encouraging and protecting wildlife.

### Exclusions

No support for local appeals not within ten miles of the airport boundary.

### Applications

On a form available by writing to the Secretary of the East Midlands Airport Community Fund. On-line applications can be submitted through the websites. Applications must be accompanied by a constitution, annual report, financial statements, press cutting, written estimates and photographs, as appropriate. The committee meets four times a year.

## Corporate giving

East Midlands Airport Community Fund has a budget of over £40,000 a year. It supports around 50 local groups each year, giving between £50 and £10,000 each. Recent recipients have included: Nottinghamshire and Leicestershire Youth Games; the East Midlands-based charity 'When You Wish Upon a Star'; and, Mantile Arts. Past beneficiaries have included: Walton-on-the-Wolds Village Hall (installation of disabled toilets); Shepshed Disabled Swimming Group (specialised sports equipment); Breaston Elder Citizens Club (chairs and tables); e-motion Dance Academy (show costumes); and Erewash Valley Gymnastics Club (gym equipment for pre-school participants).

**Environment:** Support has also been provided for environmental projects, most noticeably in partnership with Groundwork Erewash Valley. Two projects have received support from the fund:

i) Community Orchards Project – An initiative designed to involve local school children in educational tree-based activities, e.g. woodland visits, and seed and berry collections.

ii) Footpaths Project – Following on from the success of the above, this new two-year project focuses on encouraging people to become more aware of the accessibility of the countryside on the outskirts of the airport. Groundwork and the airport will together produce a leaflet featuring two guided walks that will highlight existing rights of way and the Airport Trail, which circles the entire site. The leaflet will contain information about the local history and wildlife and also illustrate the health benefits of walking in the countryside.

## In-kind support

In cooperation with South Derbyshire Environmental Education, NEMA has produced an on-site educational programme for children aged seven to ten. Supplied activity boxes contain the various pieces of equipment necessary for the children to carry out a series of challenges covering subjects such as flight, sound, creatures, weather and landscape.

The airport is also a major supporter of Derby Playhouse's 'Hot Tickets' initiative. Working together with local companies and charitable trusts, thousands of theatre tickets will be distributed across Derbyshire to benefit people who have never had the opportunity to experience live theatre before.

## Commercially-led support

**Sponsorship:** NEMA has provided £300 scholarships to two talented sporting youngsters from Leicestershire. These are awarded to those with outstanding ability and potential and are designed to help with the ongoing costs associated with training and competing at the highest level.

# NTL UK Limited

NTL House, Bartley Wood Business Park, Bartley Way, Hook, RG27 9UP

01256 752 000

**Website:** www.ntl.com

**Correspondent:** Lucy Atabey

**E-mail:** lucy.atabey@virginmobile.com

**Chief officer:** James Mooney

**Nature of company business**
Communications and content distribution company offering digital TV, telephone and internet services for the home.

**Main locations:** Hook, Middlesbrough, Huddersfield, Winchester, Bournemouth, Norwich

### Charitable donations

2005: £50,000

## Community involvement

NTL's head office advised that there is a preference for organisations based near company operations (Scotland, Middlesbrough, Norwich, the Midlands and Bournemouth).

The types of initiatives supported included: education, information technology, health, older people, and communication/design technology.

## Exclusions

No support for local appeals outside areas of company presence.

## Applications

In writing to the correspondent who should be contacted by e-mail only.

## Corporate giving

In 2005, donations exceeded £50,000. No further details were provided by the company

# O2 plc

Wellington Street, Slough SL1 1YP

0113 272 2000

**Website:** www.o2.com

**Correspondent:** CR, Legal & Corporate Affairs

**E-mail:** cr@o2.com

**Chief officer:** David Arcuilus

**Chief Executive:** Peter Erskine

| Year end | Turnover | Pre-tax profit |
|---|---|---|
| 31/03/2005 | £6,683,000,000 | £309,000,000 |

**Nature of company business**
O2 is a group of companies providing mobile phones and other mobile communication equipment throughout Europe.

**Main locations:** Braddan, Bury, Hammersmith, Douglas, Leeds, Runcorn, Slough

**UK employees:** 7,854

**Total employees:** 12,905

### Charitable donations

2005: £636,266
2004: £427,000
2003: £444,000

Membership: BitC, L B Group, %Club

## Community involvement

In considering applications for support, the company is currently looking for projects that:

▸ 'use mobile or other wireless technology to address a social need in new ways

▸ are based in, and supportive of, a community in a country and regional location in which we operate (for our purposes, the UK, Ireland, and the Isle of Man)

▸ involve our employees, who are central to our community investment activity

▸ enable those supported through the project to achieve self-generated sustainable improvements in their lives

▸ link with our business ethos to build positive relationships and foster learning, particularly for young people

▸ enable people to make real improvements to where they live'.

## Exclusions

No support for religious organisations; political organisations; individuals; expeditions; general appeals; and, those intending to buy advertising or promotion.

## Applications

The company provided the following guidance for applicants:

▸ firstly, read the funding policy carefully to assess whether your organisation or project would be eligible for funding

- to become O2's 'charity of choice' download and complete an application form and application form guidance which will offer advice to help you complete the form

- include the completed form with your funding or partnership proposal

- include your latest set of report and accounts if you have one, and any other relevant supporting documents

- include supporting letters from partner organisations.

To apply for O2's Community Fund download and complete the application form from the company's website. For any further information about the fund contact:

Libby Symon, The Conservation Foundation, 1 Kensington Gore, London SW7 2AR

Tel: 020 7591 3111);
e-mail: LibbySymon@ConservationFoundation.co.uk

## Corporate giving

In 2004/05, the company made worldwide community contributions of £2,239,795. Of this, £636,266 was made in donations in the UK.

Among the many and diverse charities and causes O2 have supported are:

*Youth* – Child Victims of Crime (CVOC, tackling safety); Me, myself and Eye; Suzy Lamplugh Trust; Weston Spirit; and Prison, Me – No Way!

*Education* – SCHOLA-21, Reading Buddies, Career Mentoring in the UK and Ireland, Telecomputer Bus for children on the Isle of Man, and pfeg (personal finance education group: an education resource programme).

*Health* – Asthma and cystic fibrosis remote monitoring trials, trials with the British Lung Foundation, Irish Autism Action, Aisling Foundation (which supports disability in the workplace), and fitness and wellbeing programmes for all O2 staff.

*Environment* – Blue/Green, an employee run scheme, to engage O2 people in green and ethical activity, such as handset recycling.

## In-kind support

Equipment is available which would be of use to voluntary projects. O2 has looked at integrating its technology with disability access equipment (with DisabledGo!) and asthma monitors.

## Employee-led support

To support employees fundraising and giving efforts O2 run two formal employee schemes: 'Can Do Matching' and 'Can Do Giving'.

Can Do Matching promises to donate an equal sum to that raised by an individual or team up to a maximum of £350. Over 150 applications have been received so far and, to date, O2 and its employees have donated more than £256,000 to charities. £82,000 of which was matched by O2.

**Payroll giving:** In the UK, Ireland and the Isle of Man, Can Do Giving is an easy way for employees to support their favourite charities regularly. Their contributions are automatically donated through the payroll, are exempt from tax (in the UK) and then are boosted by the company by an additional 20%.

## Commercially-led support

**Sponsorship:** O2 will not consider commercial sponsorships for funding within the 'Can Do in the Community' programme unless the key objective is to address a charitable or social cause.

The marketing teams within the O2 operating businesses deal with commercial sponsorships (such as sports, art or cultural projects). Enquiries can be made through the Interactive Partnerships department by e-mailing: sponsorship@o2.com

# Old Mutual plc

5th Floor, Old Mutual Place, 2 Lambeth Hill, London EC4V 4GG

020 7002 7000

Website: www.oldmutual.com

Correspondent: Helen Wilson, Head of Corporate Social Responsibility

Chief officer: Christopher Collins

Chief Executive: Jim Sutcliffe

| Year end | Turnover | Pre-tax profit |
|---|---|---|
| 31/12/2005 | £14,352,000,000 | £1,606,000,000 |

Nature of company business
Provision of financial services.

Main locations: London

Total employees: 42,950

### Charitable donations

2005: £382,000
2004: £234,000
2003: £222,000

Membership: %Club

## Community involvement

Grants in the UK are made through its non-registered Old Mutual (Bermuda) Foundation Limited. It is intended that the foundation support several 'flagship' projects each year, with the remaining funds used for smaller donations and ad hoc appeals up to a maximum of £5,000 each. Grants are one-off and projects must have the potential to continue when the support from the company ceases. Areas of support included:

- the arts – supporting a production, exhibition or event for one or more of the national arts organisations (although international tours are not supported)

- welfare – relating to global social issues such as food or housing

- education – increasing awareness and knowledge of financial matters or promoting understanding of international development

- environmental – relating to global environmental issues, such as conservation, pollution and recycling

- medical – work with disease or health promotion which could benefit a significant number of people.

'Projects that received support in 2005 included the fund established to help the victims of the London bombs and African Footprint, a dance troupe who were invited to perform at St James's Palace for the Duke of Edinburgh Trust. Staff also chose three charities, Marie Curie Cancer Care, ChildLine and WWF-UK to receive £10,000 each from the Old Mutual Bermuda Foundation. Proceeds from the Christmas party and money saved through the use of electronic, instead of paper, Christmas cards, totalling nearly £10,000, was donated to the NSPCC, to support its work with children.'

## Exclusions

No grants towards: sports; religious organisations; capital projects; non-registered charities; organisations without published, audited accounts for the last three years; or organisations whose total administrative and marketing expenses exceed 12% of the income.

## Applications

In writing to the correspondent.

## Corporate giving

In 2005 grants totalling £382,000 were given to groups in the UK.

## In-kind support

Applications for gifts in kind are considered on a case-by-case basis.

## Employee-led support

The company stated: 'The involvement of our employees with charitable activities is important to Old Mutual and we try to support our employees' involvement. We do that through matching sponsorship money they raise (up to a pre-arranged amount, this amount is set on a case-by-case basis), giving them time to be involved in volunteering projects (e.g. the schools project, taking maths into primary schools in Southwark) and matching funds donated by staff when an office charitable event is run such as Jeans for Genes day or Children in Need.'

# Oracle UK

Oracle Parkway, Thames Valley Park, Reading, Berkshire RG6 1RA

0118 924 0000; Fax: 0118 924 3000

Website: www.oracle.com/uk

Correspondent: Stacey Torman, Corporate/Community Senior Director 0118 924 6468
E-mail: stacey.torman@oracle.com

Managing Director: Ian Smith

Nature of company business
Producer of IT solutions and database software.

Main locations: Manchester, London, Reading, Edinburgh, Bristol, Birmingham, Belfast

## Community involvement

Oracle focuses its efforts in three primary areas across the UK – advancing education, protecting the environment and enriching the community. In order to achieve meaningful change in each of these areas it has four key programmes, namely:

- education initiatives
- hands-on support/enriching the community
- green programmes
- charitable giving.

## Applications

In writing to the correspondent.

## Corporate giving

In 2003, Oracle Corporation (of which the UK subsidiary is a part) made worldwide contributions totalling US$8.5 million with a further US$91 million of in-kind software donations. Although figures for the UK were not available, the following examples of support were drawn from the company's website.

### Advancing education:

Oracle UK has made a million pound pledge to the government to support 'Specialist' schools.

### Hands-on activities/enriching the local community:

In conjunction with Central Berkshire Education Business Partnership, the company sponsored the first 'Leadership Challenge' for sixth-form students from five reading area schools. The programme gave 17–18 year old students the opportunity to deal with real-world business challenges.

### Green programme:

Oracle UK donated four high-spec bicycles to the police force.

### Charitable giving:

Oracle UK has chosen three charities (ChildLine, Shelter and Comic Relief) to support both financially and technologically.

## In-kind support

The Oracle Internet Initiative provides software and resources to educational establishments for use in degree programmes. In June 2003 it began a four-year, £1 million programme to support 40 specialist schools in creating and delivering maths, science and IT lessons.

The company has helped Berkshire schools create materials to enhance financial coursework in business studies programmes and has established a number of resources, such as Think.com and Oracle Internet Academy, which provide free educational information for teachers and students alike.

## Employee-led support

All employees are encouraged to participate in renovation projects in disadvantaged areas. Examples of such work have included the management team renovating the art room and garden area of a Leonard Cheshire Centre in Battersea, sales representatives participating in a clean-up of two Hackney community centres and the entire Scottish workforce taking part in an environmental clean-up activity.

In addition to this work, its global parent company organises global volunteering days each year when all employees are encouraged to participate in community work during a fortnight. In 2002 this led to work by over 2,000 employees on 95 projects in 26 countries. Those in the UK were a donor registration drive for Anthony Nolan Bone Marrow Trust in Reading, an environmental preservation project in Caversham, a beach clean in Swanage and support to ChildLine centres in London and Manchester.

## Commercially-led support

The company has sponsored a programme operated by Wokingham District Council to teach business skills to 'non-professional' staff (such as caterers, cleaners and so on) and, in 2004, a Bicycle Helmet Initiative Trust bike ride from Brands Hatch to Monaco to raise awareness of bicycle safety.

# Orange

Great Park Road, Almondsbury Park, Bradley Stoke, Bristol BS12 4QJ

0870 376 8888

Website: www.orange.co.uk

Correspondent: Head of Charities

**Nature of company business**
The company was acquired by France Telecom in August 2000. Main activity is the provision of wirefree personal communications services.

Subsidiaries include: Hutchinson Ltd

Main locations: Bristol

Total employees: 13,289

### Charitable donations

Membership: A & B, BitC

## Community involvement

Orange intend to support local projects around the UK that are working to make a difference to people with sensory disabilities. Orange's support for the community is channelled through partnerships, employee fundraising and volunteering, regional initiatives, and sponsorship. There is some preference for supporting children/youth, education, music, culture and sport. The support is provided through a framework called Community Futures, which is about enabling people to participate more fully in society.

### Exclusions

Orange do not support applications for projects:

- for work that does not primarily benefit those with sensory disabilities
- for the benefit of individuals rather than a group
- for beneficiaries outside the UK
- for work that has already taken place
- for core funding (operational running costs such as staff salaries or administration costs)
- for fundraising events, receptions or trips
- for the promotion of religion or politics.

### Applications

In writing to the correspondent.

## Corporate giving

Through the provision of awards, Orange seek to recognise and reward innovative community projects that use communication to enable people with sensory disabilities to participate more fully in society.

In a two year period (2001 – April 2003), Orange employees have raised a total of £400,000 in support of NCH Action for Children. Its charity partnership with RNIB (Royal National

Institute for The Blind) and the BDA (British Deaf Association), ended in June 2005, raising over £160,000. It also participates in national fundraising events such as Comic Relief.

In 2006 employees were helping to raise funding for Sense.

### In-kind support

**Education:** Orange has established a number of initiatives in this area of which the most important are: Orange Chatterbooks, which helps children develop an interest in books; Open for Business, a free resource for teachers and post-16 students of business courses; 'you, your phone and staying safe', a free resource to help raise awareness and educate 14–16 year olds about how to stay safe with their mobile phones.

Through the Computers for Classrooms scheme, Orange has donated hundreds of refurbished computers to schools and charitable organisations around the UK.

**Academic Research:** Orange have commissioned independent academic research relating to the issue of sensory disability, which impairs one or more of the five senses. This research helped Orange to identify areas where support is particularly needed and to raise awareness of the issue itself. In support of this, Orange have established a joint charity partnership with the Royal National Institute of the Blind (RNIB) and the British Deaf Association (BDA).

### Employee-led support

Besides raising money each year for the staff-nominated charity, employees at Orange sites throughout the UK hold fundraising events.

Staff also volunteer their time and skills in support of community regeneration schemes around Orange's major sites.

**Payroll Giving:** Orange operate a payroll giving scheme, which allows employees to make contributions directly from their salary before tax is deducted. Employees can choose to contribute to up to 12 different registered charitable organisations.

### Commercially-led support

**Sponsorship:** Orange sponsors a variety of events nationwide in music, culture, and sport. These range from regional free festivals to grassroots music projects and writing initiatives.

# Osborne & Little

Riverside House, 26 Osiers Road, London SW18 1NH

020 8812 3000; Fax: 020 8877 7500

Website: www.osborneandlittle.com

Correspondent: Samantha Millar

Chief officer: Sir Peter Osborne

| Year end | Turnover | Pre-tax profit |
|---|---|---|
| 31/03/2000 | £39,325,000 | £5,529,000 |

**Nature of company business**
The main activities are the design and distribution of fine furnishing fabrics and wallpapers.

Subsidiaries include: Tamesa Fabrics Ltd

Main locations: London

UK employees: 248

## Community involvement

The company prefers to support local charities where it operates, appeals relevant to its business and those where an employee is involved. Preferred areas of support are children and youth, education (design) and arts (design).

### Exclusions

The company does not advertise in charity brochures.

### Applications

In writing to the correspondent.

## Corporate giving

We were advised by the company that they did not wish to be included in our guide, even though they continue to support good causes. In line with our policy of including all relevant companies we repeat the information previously published with a few additions.

In 2000, the company's donations to charity more than doubled to over £92,000.

In 2005, the company supported U Can Do I.T., a charity which provides computer training for blind, deaf and disabled people in their own homes, and gave £3,500 to the Campaign for Museums of which Sir Peter Osborne, chairman, is a trustee.

### Employee-led support

Employees' charitable activities may be supported by the company.

## Otis Limited

The Otis Building, 187 Twyford Abbey Road, London NW10 7DG

020 8955 3000; Fax: 020 8955 3001

Website: www.otis.com

Correspondent: Fiona Spelman, Buildings Factilities Manager

Managing Director: D Michaud

Nature of company business
Manufacturer of lifts, escalators, travelators and other horizontal transportation systems.

Main locations: Southampton, Wokingham, Liverpool, Lleicester, Norwich, Bristol, Burgess Hill, Cardiff, Stockport, Jersey, Leeds, Guernsey, Gateshead, Glasgow, Dundee, Edinburgh, Aberdeen, Birmingham

## Community involvement

The company's community support is dedicated to supporting the Special Olympics.

### Applications

It is very unlikely that this company would assist voluntary groups other than the Special Olympics.

### Employee-led support

It has established Team Otis which is a worldwide volunteering group of employees consisting of 1,600 members in 35 different countries including the United Kingdom.

## Oxford Instruments plc

Old Station Way, Eynsham, Witney OX29 4TL

01865 881437; Fax: 01865 881944

Website: www.oxford-instruments.com

Correspondent: Jonathan Flint, Chief Executive

Chief officer: Nigel Keen

Chief Executive: Jonathan Flint

| Year end | Turnover | Pre-tax profit |
|---|---|---|
| 31/03/2005 | £187,100,000 | £3,600,000 |

Nature of company business
The company is the ultimate holding company of a group of subsidiary and associated undertakings engaged in the research, development, manufacture and sale of advanced instrumentation.

Main locations: Witney

UK employees: 691

Total employees: 1,295

### Charitable donations
2005: £30,000
2004: £23,000
2003: £29,000

## Community involvement

Community contributions made by the company include charitable donations and student sponsorship.

Previous information provided suggested the company mainly supports local initiatives in the fields of education, children/youth, elderly people, enterprise and training, science and technology, medical research, social welfare and healthcare in the Oxford area. Decisions to fund projects are made both by head office and by individual business units.

### Exclusions

Group policy prohibits donations to any political party or similar organisation.

### Applications

In writing to the correspondent.

## Corporate giving

In 2005, charitable donations amounted to £30,000 with a variety of community organisations benefiting.

As far as we are aware the company continues to support the 'Education plus' programme at Peers School and Bartholomew School. Support has also been given to New Century which works to bring Japanese scholars to study at Oxford University.

## In-kind support

The group provides work placement experience for students.

## Employee-led support

**Payroll giving:** The Give As You Earn (GAYE) scheme is in operation.

Employees are encouraged to contribute to local charities using the GAYE scheme, with the company making an additional donation to the chosen charities.

Employees are also encouraged to take participate in the Business In The Community scheme.

## Commercially-led support

**Sponsorship:** In 2005, the group spent £47,000 providing student sponsorship in the UK.

# Palmer & Harvey McLane Ltd

P&H House, 106–112 Davigdor Road, Hove,
East Sussex BN3 1RE

01273 222100; Fax: 01273 222101

Website: www.palmerharvey.co.uk

Correspondent: Joe Currey, Charities Administrator

Chief officer: Christopher Adams

Managing Director: Graham McPherson

| Year end | Turnover | Pre-tax profit |
|---|---|---|
| 04/04/2004 | £6,445,100,000 | |

Nature of company business
The main activity of the company is tobacco and confectionery distribution.

Subsidiaries include: Snowking Ltd

Main locations: Tonbridge, Coventry, Hove, Haydock

Total employees: 4,000

## Charitable donations

2004: £40,000

## Community involvement

The company holds an annual Charity Greyhound Evening in order to raise money for the Confectioner's Benevolent Fund, a charity dedicated to caring for people who have worked in the confectionary industry.

Previous information suggested that other than support for certain trade charities, the company has no set policy, although it prefers to support 'people charities' local to its branches.

## Exclusions

Past information suggested the company provides no support for local appeals outside areas of company presence.

## Applications

In writing to the correspondent.

## Corporate giving

Despite not being able to obtain an updated donations figure, the appointment of a 'Charities Administrator' indicates the company's continued commitment towards its communities. However, we cannot be sure whether donations remain at around £40,000 a year as previously advised.

# Panasonic UK Ltd

Panasonic House, Willoughby Road, Bracknell RG12 8FP

01344 862444

Website: www.panasonic.co.uk

Correspondent: Katherine Lomas, Assistant PA to Managing Director

| Year end | Turnover | Pre-tax profit |
|---|---|---|
| 31/03/2005 | £659,074,000 | £3,779,000 |

Nature of company business
The ultimate holding company is Matsushita Electric Industrial whose main businesses are video equipment, audio equipment, home appliances, communication and individual equipment, electronic components, kitchen-related products, and others.

Main locations: Bracknell, Northampton

UK employees: 435

## Charitable donations

2005: £134,050
2004: £56,057
2003: £47,000

## Community involvement

We understand that each office/site has its own budget to support local charities in its area. Panasonic predominately supports causes local to its main office in Bracknell and its other regional site in Northampton.

The company's charitable giving has been directed towards the following categories:

(i) *General* – charities and groups which assist those in need, particularly people who are disadvantaged, disabled, sick or elderly people, plus local schools and playgroups.

(ii) *Cause related* – charities with a theme chosen by staff.

(iii) *Key project* – support for one or two major projects per year within the immediate local area.

The company is patron of the Berkshire Community Foundation, an independent community foundation serving the wider community where it is based. The Berkshire Community Foundation seeks to address the changing needs within the county of Berkshire.

The Panasonic Trust (Charity Commission no. 290652), administered by the Royal Academy of Engineering, funds the updating and retraining of qualified engineers, particularly in new engineering developments and new technologies. Since its inception in 1984 the Panasonic Trust has awarded grants to more than 800 engineers. The majority of these grants have been awarded to enable the engineers to undertake part time modular MSc courses, the structures of which appeal to both the individual and the employer.

Globally Panasonic's Corporate Outreach Programme concentrates its resources in three strategic areas: education, civic and social welfare and arts and cultural. Within each of these strategic areas Panasonic has particular interest in projects that are targeted to address the needs of women and diverse populations. Applications are only considered through proposals submitted on-line.

## Exclusions

The company does not normally respond favourably to unsolicited requests. No support for advertising in charity brochures, animal charities, appeals from individuals, overseas projects, political appeals, religious appeals or sport.

## Applications

In writing to the correspondent.

# Corporate giving

In 2005, the company's charitable contributions totalled £134,050 (2004: £56,057).

## In-kind support

The company prefers to donate equipment for either office use or fundraising purposes wherever possible and responds to requests received accordingly.

## Employee-led support

The company runs a scheme to encourage employees to take an active part in volunteer activities. Established in 1998 the Volunteer Activity Financial Support Programme provides financial support to non profit organisations in which employees, their families and retired former employees are actively involved.

Employees' giving is matched by the company to a maximum of £100. Employees' fundraising may be matched, but this is considered on a case by case basis.

# The Peacock Group

Atlantic House, Tyndall Street, Cardiff CF10 4PS

029 2027 0000

Website: www.peacocks.co.uk

Correspondent: Mark Holley, Customer Services Manager

Chief Executive: Richard S. Kirk

| Year end | Turnover | Pre-tax profit |
|---|---|---|
| 31/03/2004 | £490,396,000 | £32,436,000 |

Nature of company business
National fashion, footwear and accessories retailer.

Main locations: Cardiff

UK employees: 10,187

### Charitable donations
2004: £26,000

## Community involvement

Peacocks operate over 430 stores nationwide. Following a management buyout in 2005, the company have been de-listed from the stock exchange and, therefore, the last financial figures we have are for 2004.

The annual report for that year states that whilst the company believes in supporting its local communities, it has a clear policy of not making any charitable or political donations. Any financial help that is given appears to be in support of employees fundraising activities for the nominated charity.

**Charity of the year:** Cancer Research UK (2005/06).

## Exclusions

No support for general or circular appeals, political or religious causes, or local appeals not in areas of company presence.

## Applications

In writing to the correspondent or contact the nearest local store.

Please note, however, that cash donations appear to be limited to supporting employees fundraising endeavours on behalf of the company's chosen charity.

# Corporate giving

In 2004, the company declared charitable donations of £26,000. No details of how this was distributed were available.

For the past two years (2005/06) the company has been actively supporting Cancer Research UK through staff fundraising activities, the sale of Pink Party products and customer contributions. To the end of January 2006, £344,000 had been raised on the charity's behalf.

## Commercially-led support

**Cause-related marketing:** In 2005, the company raised £80,000 on behalf on Cancer Research UK through the sale of its Pink Party products.

# Pearson plc

80 Strand, London WC2R ORL

020 7010 2000

Website: www.pearson.com

Correspondent: Thomasina Coombe, Communications Co-ordinator 020 7010 2319
E-mail: thomasina.coombe@pearson.com

Chief officer: Glen Moreno

Chief Executive: Marjorie Scardino

| Year end | Turnover | Pre-tax profit |
|---|---|---|
| 31/12/2005 | £4,100,000,000 | £466,000,000 |

Nature of company business
The company is an international media group.

Subsidiaries include: Pearson Education, The Penguin Group, Financial Times Group Ltd

Main locations: London

Total employees: 33,000

## Community involvement

Pearson responds to causes at national level where it concentrates on activities that are in some way linked to its own, and to which it can make contributions at a sufficiently high level to produce lasting benefits. Preference is also given to projects where there is a possibility of monitoring the benefits and where there is scope for personal involvement of the company's staff. Most support is given in the field of education.

The majority of Pearson's giving is in the US. Overseas projects are also supported in France, Spain and South Africa.

The company has a comprehensive 'Our Business and Society' report detailing its corporate and social responsibilities and how it works towards its aims.

The latest figure above is the worldwide figure, compared to earlier figures, which relate to UK giving.

### Exclusions

No support for advertising in charity brochures, animal welfare, appeals from individuals, enterprise/training, environment/heritage, fundraising events, medical research, political/religious appeals, science/technology, sickness/disability charities, social welfare or sport.

### Applications

Appeals should be addressed to the correspondent. Local and trade appeals should be sent directly to the relevant subsidiary company.

## Corporate giving

In 2005, the company's worldwide community contributions totalled £6.2 million. Of this, cash donations to charity totalled £3.4 million and gifts in-kind/staff time £2.8 million. Management costs stood at £260,000. We have no details of the beneficiaries.

### In-kind support

The operating companies also respond to trade and local causes through in kind donations. The main area of non-cash support is via gifts in kind.

### Employee-led support

Wherever possible, employees are encouraged to become involved in charitable work in their local communities. Pearson matches employee fundraising to a maximum of £1,000. There is also an awards scheme where six of its employees around the world are rewarded for their charitable work by a donation of US$2,000 being made to their charity.

**Payroll giving:** The company runs and matches the Give As You Earn scheme up to £500 per employee.

### Commercially-led support

**Sponsorship:** Support of the arts is undertaken. The Pearson Gallery of Living Words was opened at the British Library in 1998. It is one of three galleries open free to the public and reflects the diversity of the Library's collection through a series of special exhibitions. The Pearson Playwrights' Scheme offers bursaries to writers working in the theatre and awards to the authors of plays that are staged.

# Pennon Group plc

Peninsula House, Rydon Lane, Exeter EX2 7HR

01392 446688; Fax: 01392 434966

**Website:** www.pennon-group.co.uk

**Correspondent:** Ms Lorna Shearman, Communications Manager
01392 443022; Fax: 01392 443018
E-mail: lshearman@southwestwater.co.uk

**Chief officer:** Kenneth George Harvey

**Chief Executive:** Robert Baty/ Colin Drummond

| Year end | Turnover | Pre-tax profit |
|---|---|---|
| 31/03/2006 | £645,700,000 | £110,900,000 |

**Nature of company business**
The provision of water, sewerage services and waste management.

**Subsidiaries include:** South West Water Ltd, Orbisphere UK Ltd, Viridor Ltd, Viridor Waste Ltd, Viridor Instrumentation Ltd, Exe Continental Ltd, ELE International Ltd, T J Brent Ltd, GLI International Ltd, Viridor Contracting Ltd, VWM (Scotland) Ltd

**Main locations:** Exeter

**UK employees:** 3,000

**Total employees:** 3,000

## Community involvement

Formerly South West Water plc, the company is now known as Pennon Group plc. Its main subsidiaries are South West Water Ltd and Viridor Waste Ltd.

The Group's financial involvement in the community is channelled through a number of initiatives:
- charitable donations
- community sponsorship programme
- Landfill Tax Credit Scheme (LTCS)
- environmental fund committee
- special assistance fund.

The company website states that the group recognises its responsibilities by providing financial and other support to assist those communities and organisations in which it operates, i.e. Devon and Cornwall, to enhance their local environment.

Areas considered for support are advertising in charity brochures, animal welfare, appeals from individuals, the arts, children/youth, education, elderly people, enterprise/training, environment/heritage, fundraising events, science/technology, sickness/disability, social welfare and sport.

**Charity of the Year (2005):** WaterAid (South West Water); Scope and Primary Immunodeficiency Association (Viridor Waste).

## Exclusions

No support for circular appeals, medical research, political appeals, religious appeals, local appeals not in areas of company presence, large national appeals or overseas projects.

## Applications

In writing to the correspondent.

**Information available:** The company produces an annual social responsibility report.

## Corporate giving

In 2005/06, the group made cash donations totalling £131,000 to charities operating in Devon and Cornwall. The main beneficiaries of this were Plymouth Young Peoples' Agenda 21, Treleigh Harmony Senior Citizens Club, Drugs Awareness in Schools, Dartmoor Search & Rescue, Lympstone Young People's Society, Klimington Playing Fields Trustees, Callington Young Farmers Club, Carn Brae Leisure Centre and Vranch House School and Centre.

Initiatives the company are involved with (as mentioned above) are detailed here:

- charitable donations by Pennon Group plc are primarily to charities operating in Devon and Cornwall, the average donation being around £500
- South West Water Community Sponsorship Programmes are delivered across a wide range of activities and totalled £73,000 during the year
- Landfill Tax Credit Scheme (LTCS) enables Viridor Waste to deliver lasting environmental and social benefits for communities in the vicinity of its landfill operations. £3.9 million was awarded during 2004/05
- Pennon – Environmental Fund Committee was formed with the specific aim of bringing environmental and social benefits to the communities within South West Water's operating area by utilising some of the Viridor Waste's landfill tax credits
- South West Water Special Assistance Fund was established to provide help to customers trying pay their water and sewerage bills but, for reasons of severe financial or personal difficulties, were having problems paying the full amount.

## In-kind support

**Education:** Group companies provide advice and support ranging from organising site visits relating to waste and recycling process for school pupils and students, to providing a training service to plumbers and ground workers under the Water Industry Approved Plumbers Scheme.

Students at Plymouth University have also been provided with work placements through the 'Year in Industry' scheme.

## Employee-led support

The company supports employees in their volunteering and fundraising efforts. For example, employees carrying out charitable/community work are given time off during working hours in which to do so. Whilst the company matches pound for pound individual employees fundraising (up to £1,000) and charitable giving (also up to £1,000). An example of this is Viridor Waste's employees support for the company's two 'adopted' charities – Scope and Primary Immunodeficiency Association.

## Commercially-led support

**Sponsorship:** The company undertakes both arts and good-cause sponsorships. In 2004/05, the South West Water Community Sponsorship programme made awards totalling £73,000. Examples of beneficiaries include: Surf Life Saving Association; St Breward Primary School; Devon & Exeter Spastics Society; and, Great Torrington Horticultural Society.

Contact: Mr H Weatherley on 01392 443035.

# Pentland Group plc

The Pentland Centre, Lakeside, Squires Lane, London N3 2QL

020 8346 2600; Fax: 020 8970 2387

Website: www.pentland.com

Correspondent: Community Involvement Officer

Chief officer: R S Rubin

Chief Executive: A K Rubin

| Year end | Turnover | Pre-tax profit |
|---|---|---|
| 31/12/2005 | £735,300,000 | £47,400,000 |

**Nature of company business**
The main activities of the subsidiary companies are footwear, clothing and sports, consumer products and international trading.

**Subsidiaries include:** Ellesse Ltd, Pony UK Sports Ltd, Brasher Boot Co Ltd, Pony International Ltd, Airborne Footwear Ltd, Sportsflair Ltd, Kangaroos International Ltd, Speedo International Ltd, Red or Dead Ltd, Berghaus Ltd, Airborne Leisure Ltd

**Main locations:** Sunderland, London, Nottingham

**UK employees:** 10,415

**Total employees:** 12,018

### Charitable donations
2005: £1,859,000
2004: £253,000

## Community involvement

The company states on its website that: 'We work with many different organisations around the globe to support programmes that care for those in need. We are always amazed at how much our employees are prepared to dedicate their time, skills and energy to support a number of meaningful causes.'

Under the heading of 'Making a Difference', Pentland list four areas within which they give support. These are: people; health; environment; and, education.

There is a preference for charitable and community projects associated with the group's products and business activities and local to its offices and factories. The group is also particularly keen to provide seed corn funding for projects that have a multiplier effect in generating money for a charity from other sources.

## Exclusions

No support for local appeals not in areas of company presence.

## Applications

In writing to the correspondent.

## Corporate giving

In 2005, the group declared worldwide charitable donations of £1,859,000 'of which £1,232,000 was made directly by the company'. It also states in its annual report and accounts for the year that 'donations were primarily made to the Ruben Foundation'.

The Ruben Foundation (Charity Commission no. 327062) is closely linked to the company, which it primarily relies on for its income. In 2003, the foundation received £130,000 from the company, but nothing the following year. Unfortunately, as the 2005 accounts were not available at the Charity Commission, we do not know what proportion of the £1.86 million donated by the group went to the foundation.

In 2004, grants made by the foundation totalled £428,050, most of which went to the same set of recipients as in the previous year. The main exception was a grant of £100,000 (the largest grant made that year) which went to The Artsdepot Trust. Fuller details are available in *Guide to the Major Trusts volume 1*, also published by the Directory of Social Change.

The Pentland Group's website lists a number of UK charities it has supported, but it is unclear if this is solely during 2005. Under the four areas previously noted, the charities were:

- people – In Kind Direct; Rays of Sunshine; Sport Relief; Outward Bound Trust; The Wishes and Dreams Trust; and, the Jack Brown Appeal
- health – World Swim for Malaria; Cancer Research UK; and, Marie Curie Cancer Care
- environment – WaterAid; John Muir Trust; WWF for Nature; and, The College Farm Trust
- education – The Greenhouse Schools Project; Capital Kids Cricket; London Schools Cricket Association; and Barnet Education Business Partnership.

## Employee-led support

Employees are encouraged to support local good causes.

# PepsiCo Holdings

1600 Arlington Business Park, Theale, Reading, Berkshire, RG7 4SA

**Website:** walkers.corpex.com

**Correspondent:** The Corporate Affairs Department

**E-mail:** www.pepsicowiderworld.co.uk

| Year end | Turnover | Pre-tax profit |
|---|---|---|
| 25/12/2004 | £349,647,000 | £8,222,000 |

**Nature of company business**
The group's activities include the manufacture, warehousing, marketing, distribution and sale of snack foods, the bottling and distribution of soft drinks and the supply of services on behalf of group companies.

**Main locations:** Reading, East Durham, Warrington, Leicester

**UK employees:** 5480

---

**Charitable donations**

Membership: BitC

## Community involvement

Support has been given to the Peterlee Learning Centre – East Durham, a community learning centre that caters for self-development and business needs and the Peepul Centre – Leicester which provides a range of learning, health and creative resources to the area.

## Applications

It is unclear as to whether this company accepts applications from charities.

## Corporate giving

No figure was available for the company's total giving for the year. Its website shows that its charitable activities are extensive.

## Employee-led support

PepsiCo employees have the opportunity to make donations from their pay packet to a registered charity of their choice. Employees have also been involved with various fundraising activities for Comic Relief.

In the field of education/schools, volunteers take part in the Reading Buddies scheme in 20 schools across the country. Support is also given in the form of materials and funding for books at the beginning of each school year. Other activities include fundraising to more hands-on projects, such as painting a classroom or creating a garden area. The company encourages employees to volunteer as school governors and works in partnership with School Governors' One-Stop Shop.

## Commercially-led support

As official Red Nose Day sponsors in both 2003 and 2005, the PepsiCo business has now contributed over £1.5 million to the charity.

# Persimmon plc

Persimmon House, Fulford, York YO19 4FE

01904 642199; Fax: 01904 610014

**Website:** www.persimmonhomes.com

**Correspondent:** G N Francis, Company Secretary 01904 642199

**Chief officer:** Duncan Davidson

**Chief Executive:** John White

| Year end | Turnover | Pre-tax profit |
|---|---|---|
| 31/12/2005 | £2,230,000,000 | £495,400,000 |

**Nature of company business**
Principal activities: residential building and development. Persimmon Homes is based in Anglia, Midlands, North East, North West, Scotland, South Coast, South East, South West, Thames Valley, Wales, Wessex, and Yorkshire.

**Main locations:** Leigh, Leicester, Peterborough, Exeter, Fareham (Hampshire), Gerrards Cross (Buckinghamshire), Hamilton, York, Weybridge, Northampton, Llantrisant (Mid-Glamorgan),

Lowestoft, Malmesbury (Wiltshire), Norwich, Beverley, Blaydon-on-Tyne

**UK employees:** 4,273

---

### Charitable donations

2005: £203,000

Total community contributions: £490,000

---

## Community involvement

Persimmon supports charitable and community initiatives at both a group and regional operating business level.

### Applications

In writing only to the correspondent. Each application is considered on its merits.

**Information available:** The company produce a corporate social responsibility report.

## Corporate giving

In 2005, community contributions totalled £490,000 (generated by the group, its employees and suppliers) of which cash donations amounted to £203,000. Beneficiaries included; Marie Curie Cancer Care; York Minster; Samaritans; St Leonard's Hospice; and, Tsunami Appeal.

Over the next ten years the group will donate over £700,000 to help train apprentices in the ancient craft skills which will be used to repair and conserve the east front of York Minster.

It is also involved in two educational initiatives entitled 'Homing in on Opportunity' which aims to promote the education of young people and advise them of the career opportunities within the house building sector and the 'Surveyors Committee' which amongst other things has looked at ways to encourage young people to join the business and train to become qualified quantity surveyors.

## In-kind support

The company provides gifts in kind by providing labour, material and, where appropriate, staff time. However, donations of gifts in kind and time made by individual businesses are not collated centrally.

---

# Peugeot Motor Company plc

Aldermoor House, PO Box 227, Aldermoor Lane, Coventry CV3 1LT

0247 688 4000

**Website:** www.peugeot.co.uk

**Correspondent:** Glenda Gilkes, Secretary to the Charitable Trust 0247 688 4368

**Managing Director:** Pierre Louis Colin

| Year end | Turnover | Pre-tax profit |
|---|---|---|
| 31/12/2004 | £1,978,700,000 | |

**Nature of company business**
Motor vehicle manufacture.

**Subsidiaries include:** Robin & Day Ltd, Talbot Exports Ltd

**Main locations:** Coventry

**UK employees:** 829

---

### Charitable donations

2005: £30,450

Total community contributions: £30,827

Membership: BitC

---

## Community involvement

Peugeot Motors are part of PSA Peugeot Citroen which, through its industrial sites and commercial subsidiaries, seeks to support local communities. To implement the group's social policy worldwide, the sites are able to set up Local Sponsorship Plans (LSPs) which aim to contribute to progress in educational systems, meet the needs of local communities and foster local development.

Unfortunately, no examples of how this policy is being put into practice are given and, as such, the rest of this entry details the charitable support given via the PSA Peugeot Citroen Charity Trust (Charity Commission no. 266182).

### Applications

In writing to the correspondent.

**Information available:** The company reports on its community activity in its annual report and in staff newsletters.

## Corporate giving

### PSA Peugeot Citroen Charity Trust

Towards the end of 2005, a decision was taken by the trustees to bring the trust's charitable giving policy in line with company policy. Essentially, this means that the trust will now only support company employees in their charitable and community work. Any applications received outside of this will be past over to the Heart of England Community Foundation to establish whether the application fits the criteria for any other funds it administers.

The most recent grants information available is for 2004/05, when grants totalling £30,450 were distributed amongst 108 local organisations. Beneficiaries included: Peugeot Talbot Charitable Fund for Employees (£2,850); Heart of England Revival Church (£500); Life Education Centres (Heart of England) Ltd (£400); Breakaway Holiday Project (£300); Tea and Talk Club (£200); and, Warwickshire Wildlife Trust (£50).

## In-kind support

Raffle gifts may be provided to local groups in the Coventry and Warwickshire area.

## Employee-led support

The company supports employees in their volunteering and fundraising activities.

**Payroll giving:** The company runs the BEN scheme.

## Commercially-led support

**Sponsorship:** *Good-cause sponsorship* – In support of its employees community work events may be sponsored.

# Pfizer Limited

Walton Oaks, Dorking Road, Tadworth, Surrey KT20 7NS

Website: www.pfizer.co.uk

Correspondent: Corporate Affairs

Managing Director: Olivier Brandicourt

| Year end | Turnover | Pre-tax profit |
|---|---|---|
| 30/11/2005 | | £149,333,000 |

**Nature of company business**
Pfizer Inc is a worldwide, research-based company with businesses in healthcare, agriculture, speciality chemicals, materials science and consumer products all trading under the Pfizer name.

**Subsidiaries include:** Howmedica International Ltd, Unicliffe Ltd, Shiley Ltd

**Main locations:** Sandwich, Morpeth, Tadworth

## Community involvement

Pfizer's main sites at Sandwich, Kent and Walton Oaks, Surrey, seek to work closely with many diverse charitable, local organisations and statutory agencies.

The Pfizer UK Foundation 'focuses exclusively on tackling the social, economic and demographic factors that contribute to health inequalities in communities in England, Scotland, Northern Ireland and Wales, by offering grants and/or additional resources such as Pfizer staff on a volunteer basis. In responding to these challenges, its aim is to provide tailored, modest, local solutions to needs defined by local healthcare experts, social care experts, community groups and charities in areas of deprivation across the UK'. The foundation supports projects which:

▶ are community based in an area of deprivation in the UK

▶ address local health inequality issues

▶ have measurable health related outcomes.

**Education:** The company runs an Academic Liaison Programme, mainly in East Kent, to encourage schools and colleges to adopt innovative approaches to the teaching of science. Currently, over 200 schools in Kent are supported by the programme through cash grants for science projects, work experience programmes curriculum-based visits and special events.

### Applications

Applications to the Pfizer UK Foundation can only be made by completing an application form only – e-mail: pfizerukfoundation@pfizer.com to receive a copy.

Please note that Pfizer receive many more applications than it is able to fund, so not all applications that fall within its guidelines will receive support.

## Corporate giving

In 2003 Pfizer donated £6 million to a wide range of local and national charities, educational establishments and a variety of scientific projects. In 2004 the Sandwich site gave £300,000 in donations to local community projects and charities in the East Kent area. Grants made from the Pfizer UK Foundation in February 2006 totalled £338,000.

### In-kind support

The company cites two examples of 'gifts in kind' – the use of premises and the use of equipment, e.g. use of projector and/or screens and photocopying. Such contributions, although small, are recognised as being able to 'make all the difference to voluntary sector organisations that may approach us [Pfizer] from time to time'.

### Employee-led support

The company encourages volunteering in support of its community values. Staff may seek to undertake an activity which is compatible with the company's business plan and the individual's personal development plan. Paid leave is offered to staff willing to volunteer their time to local charitable organisations.

**Payroll giving:** The company operates the Give As You Earn scheme. 'Staff make regular monthly payments direct from their salary to the charities of their choice. The company matches an employee's gross donation.' Currently the combined annual donation is nearly £400,000.

# Philips Electronics UK Ltd

Guildford Business Park, Guildford, Surrey GU2 8HX

01293 776675

Website: www.philips.co.uk

Correspondent: David Charlesworth, Corporate Communications Director

| Year end | Turnover | Pre-tax profit |
|---|---|---|
| 31/12/2003 | £850,000,000 | £244,000,000 |

**Nature of company business**
Production and sale of electrical goods.

**Main locations:** Guildford, Reigate, Redhill, Manchester, Colchester, Hamilton - Lanarkshire

**UK employees:** 3,100

**Total employees:** 164,438

> ### Charitable donations
>
> Membership: BitC

## Community involvement

Philips has never provided detailed information or figures to show whether its level of community support is in line with other large multi-nationals. It has, however, provided the following statement:

'Philips aims to act as a responsible member of the local communities within which it operates. Donations are therefore targeted at the regions which have operating units and that reflect local priorities. All unsolicited requests are reviewed, but only a small proportion are considered.'

Referring to the company's 2005 Sustainability Report, there appears to be a focus on supporting initiatives working with children/youth, especially in the areas of education and HIV health issues.

## Applications

All applications must be forwarded to Philips in writing, outlining the nature and purpose of the request. These will then be reviewed and a decision will be made as to any donation which might be forthcoming. However, due to a high demand on limited resources, less than 10% of all enquiries end in a donation.

All applications will be acknowledged and should be addressed to the correspondent.

## Corporate giving

In its 2005 Sustainability Report, Philips quote an annual global social investment figure of €9 million (around £6.1 million). We do not know what proportion of this was given to UK-based organisations.

### In-kind support

In 2003, the company's in-kind support included working with the Croydon Education Business Partnership in providing mentors, reading partners and curriculum develop materials to local schools.

### Employee-led support

Employees around the world are cited as having been engaged in fundraising and volunteering activities, although though no UK-specific examples are given.

# Pilkington plc

Prescot Road, St Helens, Merseyside WA10 3TT

01744 28882; Fax: 01744 692660

Website: www.pilkington.com

Correspondent: Julie Woodward, Public Relations

Chief officer: Katsuji Fujimoto

Chief Executive: Stuart Chambers

| Year end | Turnover | Pre-tax profit |
|---|---|---|
| 31/03/2005 | £2,694,000,000 | £165,000,000 |

Nature of company business
Producer of glass and related products worldwide.

Subsidiaries include: Triplex Safety Glass Ltd

Main locations: Doncaster, St Helens, St Asaph, Kings Norton

UK employees: 4,200

Total employees: 24,100

> ### Charitable donations
> 2005: £199,000
> 2004: £204,000
> 2003: £235,000
>
> Membership: BitC

## Community involvement

In June 2006, Pilkington was acquired by NSG UK Enterprises Ltd and became a member of the NSG Group, a wholly-owned subsidiary of Nippon Sheet Glass Co Limited of Japan.

Previously, we were advised that: 'The group and its employees also work closely with non-profit organisations through a wide range of voluntary work programmes and charitable contributions covering education, arts, medicine, welfare and young people and programmes that help create jobs and promote urban renewal. In total, the group's direct charitable and non-charitable contributions around the world amounted to £638,000, complementing the significant inputs of the time and skills of employees.'

However, we do not know at present how the above acquisition may affect this policy.

### Exclusions

No support for appeals from individuals, enterprise/training, overseas projects, political appeals or religious appeals.

### Applications

In writing to the correspondent.

## Corporate giving

In 2004/05, donations to charitable organisations in the UK totalled £199,000. An additional £166,000 was donated overseas. We have no detail concerning the beneficiaries, but can confirm the contact to be correct as at December 2006.

### In-kind support

The company provides non-cash support through gifts in kind.

Pilkington management time is given in support of young people in St Helens running their own business under the Young Enterprise scheme.

### Employee-led support

UK employees and retirees regularly give their time to a variety of educational projects, including helping children with their reading, the twinning of managers with head teachers and employment and career advice.

**Payroll giving:** The Give As You Earn scheme is in operation.

### Commercially-led support

**Sponsorship:** *Education* – In November 2006, the company announced its sponsorship of two Arkwright Scholarships.

Founded in 1991, the Arkwright scheme identifies young innovators and encourages the top engineers of the future

Each scholarship consists of an award of £950 over two years, which is divided between the successful scholar – to support their sixth form studies – and the Technology Department at his or her school.

# PKF

Pannell House, Park Street, Guildford, Surrey GU1 4HN

01483 564646

Website: www.pkf.co.uk

Correspondent: Bob Durham

Chief officer: John Wosner

| Year end | Turnover | Pre-tax profit |
|---|---|---|
| 30/04/2006 | | |

**Nature of company business**
Principal activities: chartered accountants and management consultants.

**Main locations:** Bristol, Cardiff, Coatbridge, Derby, Lancaster, Ipswich, Leeds, Leicester, Edinburgh, Glasgow, Great Yarmouth, Sheffield, St Asaph, Liverpool, London, Northampton, Manchester, Lowestoft, Nottingham, Norwich, Stoke, Birmingham

**UK employees:** 1,500

**Total employees:** 12,600

### Charitable donations

Membership: BitC

## Community involvement

Previously we were advised that the company supports national charities and local charities near regional offices; also, that many PKF offices throughout the country contribute to their local communities by way of cash donations and the provision of employees' time and skills to local community initiatives.

The company is actively involved in Business in the Community initiatives.

### Exclusions

No support for circular appeals, fundraising events, advertising in charity brochures, individuals, purely denominational (religious) appeals, local appeals not in areas of company presence, large national appeals or overseas projects.

### Applications

In writing to the correspondent.

## Corporate giving

As with all professional firms, there is no legal obligation on PKF to make publicly known any charitable donations they may have made. For this reason we are unable to provide a figure for 2005. Information in this entry is repeated from the last edition.

### In-kind support

The firm may provide professional advice to charitable and community groups on a pro bono basis.

### Commercially-led support

**Sponsorship:** *The arts* – Support has been given to Royal National Theatre and Millstream Touring.

# The Port of Liverpool

Maritime Centre, Port of Liverpool, Liverpool L21 1LA

0151 949 6000; Fax: 0151 949 6300

**Website:** www.merseydocks.co.uk

**Correspondent:** W J Bowley, Secretary to the Dock Charitable Fund

**Chief officer:** G H Waddell

**Chief Executive:** P A Jones

| Year end | Turnover | Pre-tax profit |
|---|---|---|
| 31/12/2003 | £297,400,000 | £55,200,000 |

**Nature of company business**
The principal activities of the group are the operation and maintenance of port facilities on the Rivers Mersey and Medway, provision of cargo handling and associated services, and the conservancy and pilotage of the Ports of Liverpool and Medway and their approaches and the development of their respective dock estates.

**Subsidiaries include:** Woodside Business Park Ltd, Concorde Container Line Ltd, Marine Terminals Ltd, Link Transport Services Ltd, Spade Lane Cool Store Ltd, Roadferry Ltd, Portia Management Services Ltd, Portia World Travel Ltd, Medway Ports Ltd, Seawing International Ltd, Heysham Port Ltd, Coastal Container Line Ltd, Tankspeed Ltd, Sheerness Produce Terminal Ltd, Imar Ltd

**Main locations:** Sheerness, Liverpool, Heysham, Birkenhead

### Charitable donations

2004: £126,425
2003: £133,913

## Community involvement

Previously known as The Mersey Docks and Harbour Company and acquired by Peel Ports Investments Limited in July 2005, the majority of the company's donations are made through The Mersey Docks and Harbour Charitable Fund (Charity Commission no. 206913). There is a preference for local charities in the areas of company presence and appeals relevant to company business. Preferred areas of support are the arts, children/youth, education, elderly people, medical research, sickness/disability, social welfare and sport.

### Exclusions

No support for circular appeals, advertising in charity brochures, appeals from individuals, fundraising events, religious appeals, local appeals not in areas of company presence, large national appeals or overseas projects.

### Applications

In writing to the correspondent.

## Corporate giving

### The Mersey Docks and Harbour Charitable Fund

The fund gives grants annually to certain local charities. The trust was set up with three objectives:

- reward of people assisting in the preservation of the life of the crew of any ship wrecked in the port of Liverpool or in the preservation of the ship or cargo or in the preserving or endeavouring to preserve people from drowning
- relief of sick, disabled or superannuated men in the dock service or the families of such men who were killed in service
- benefit of charities in the town or port of Liverpool.

In the year to 31 December 2004, the fund had an income of £126,425 (2003: £117,500) and a total expenditure of £131,171 (2003: £113,589). Grants made during 2004 included The Weston Spirit (£3,202), Aintree Clinical Services Centre Fund (£10,000), Mersey Mission to Seafarers (£5,450) and Community Foundation for Merseyside (£19,800). Other donations included awards of £2,000 to Liverpool Personal

Services Society, Apostleship of the Sea, Royal Liverpool Seamen's Orphans Trust and Jubilee Sailing Trust.

A new website is at present (December 2006) under construction and financial figures for the former company, The Mersey Docks and Harbour Company are for the year 2003.

# Portman Building Society

Portman House, Richmond Hill, Bournemouth BH2 6EP

01202 292 444

Website: www.portman.co.uk

Correspondent: Group Communications Dept.

Chief officer: John Roques

Chief Executive: Robert Sharpe

| Year end | Turnover | Pre-tax profit |
|---|---|---|
| 31/12/2005 | £210,900,000 | £85,000,000 |

Nature of company business
Building society.

Main locations: Bournemouth, Wolverhampton

UK employees: 2,362

## Charitable donations

2005: £245,000
2003: £113,000

## Community involvement

The society continues to run a comprehensive community programme rotating support for local, regional and national charities and sponsoring a number of local organisations. Portman's Community Fund supports:

- community projects
- educational projects
- sponsorship projects
- sporting projects
- the arts.

Portman will only support projects and initiatives if they are for a registered charity.

### Exclusions

Portman will only support projects and initiatives if they are for a registered charity. Funding for the following falls outside of their contribution guidelines:

- fundraising activities for the benefit of an individual
- expeditions and overseas projects
- projects outside the Group's operating region covered by our branches, Portman and Staffordshire House
- party political activities
- promotion of religious causes
- causes that should receive statutory funding
- rent/maintenance of property.

### Applications

In writing to the correspondent.

## Corporate giving

In 2005, £245,000 was donated by the society which supported nine community and charitable events. The Directors' Report states that direct support was given to the raising of a further £465,000. We do not have any specific details regarding the company's contribution to the raising of this money or who it was raised by.

Various donations were made in 2005 through the Portman Community Support Programme, including:

Sussex Snow Drop Trust (£1,000)

League of Friends of St Leonards Hospital (£250)

Neil Heritage Fund (£200)

Hereford Carers Support Ltd (£500)

Save the Children (£1,000)

Wolverhampton Boys Brigade (£250)

So far in 2006, Portman has made donations to several charities/organisations including:

St Johns School (£150)

St Peter's CE Primary School (£150)

NSPCC (£1,000)

Forever Friends Appeal (£4,700)

### Commercially-led support

**Sponsorship:** Portman sponsors various charities, organisations and events including:

Bournemouth Symphony Orchestra

U15's National Club Cricket Championship

Wessex Volleyball

Bournemouth Dolphins

Plymouth Armada Cup

Plumpton Raceday in aid of Spinal Research

Somerly Fun Run in aid of Wessex Autistic Society

2CR FM Community Champion Award

Staffordshire County Show

Avonbourne School Business Enterprise Initiative

Portman donates 10p to charity for every vote that is received. In 2005 members votes raised £18,786. The charities to benefit were:

Sussex Association for Spina Bifida and Hydrocephalus (SASBAH)

Wiltshire Blind Association

Lewis Manning House Cancer Trust

North Devon Hospice

County Air Ambulance

The charities selected to benefit from the 2006 AGM fall under the chosen theme of the year as voted by Portman staff, 'Body and Soul' (Cancer Related Charities):

Compton Hospice

Tenovus Cancer Charity

London Prostate Cancer Charity

Force Cancer Charity

Berkshire Cancer Centre

# PricewaterhouseCoopers

1 Embankment Place, London WC2N 6RH

020 7583 5000; Fax: 020 7822 4652

Website: www.pwc.com/uk

Correspondent: Tavia Bentley, Community Affairs Assistant
E-mail: community.affairs@uk.pwc.com

Chief officer: Kieran Poynter

| Year end | Turnover | Pre-tax profit |
|---|---|---|
| 30/06/2006 | £1,980,000,000 | £700,000,000 |

Nature of company business
Professional services firm.

Main locations: Leeds, Bristol, Southampton, Manchester, London, Birmingham

Total employees: 14,302

### Charitable donations

2006: £1,500,000
2004: £1,107,914

Total community contributions: £4,200,000

Membership: A & B, BitC, L B Group, %Club

## Community involvement

Price Waterhouse Cooper (PwC) has this year introduced a PwC in the Community Annual Report which gives details of their charitable giving. For the 19th year in a row it met the Business in the Community PerCent Standard.

Generally the firm is proactive in selecting initiatives in the following fields:

▶ raising educational achievement in primary and secondary schools and encouraging citizenship

▶ developing employability schemes, encouraging enterprise and overcoming social exclusion in its local communities.

Support is given nationwide, but particularly where the firm has offices, i.e. Southwark and Westminster in London, Birmingham, Bristol, Leeds, Manchester and Southampton.

### Exclusions

No support for circular appeals, advertising in charity brochures, animal welfare, appeals from individuals, the arts, elderly people, environment/heritage, fundraising events, medical research, overseas projects, political or religious appeals, science/technology, sickness/disability, social welfare, sport, or local appeals not in areas of company presence.

### Applications

In writing to the correspondent. Donations are approved after consideration by a charities committee.

**Information available:** A corporate social responsibility report can be downloaded from the firm's website (www.pwc.com/uk) along with further information for applicants.

## Corporate giving

In 2005/06, the firm made total community contributions in the UK of over £4 million in cash donations, gifts in kind and staff time. Beneficiaries included: The Prince's Trust, Shakespeare's Globe, several local community foundations and Wings of Hope, which offers support to orphaned and poor children by providing free education.

### In-kind support

The firm runs a secondment programme for a small number of staff each year. Secondments are usually for three months to existing community partners.

Gifts in kind and training schemes are also provided in support of the community.

### Employee-led support

The firm operates a Volunteering Awards scheme and an employee matched giving programme up to a maximum of £250 per person per year. In 2005/06, Awards totalling £75,000 were made to 176 charities through the scheme, which is now in its ninth year. The awards recognise those PwC people who give their time and skills to charities outside office hours.

**Payroll giving:** The Give As You Earn scheme is operated. During 2005/06, more than 2,000 of the firm's staff gave more than 21,000 working hours to a wide range of volunteering activities sharing their skills and expertise. Staff also raised over £365,000 for the Red Cross and UNICEF relief efforts for the Asian tsunami as part of the firm's match funding programme.

### Commercially-led support

**Partnerships:** *the Artist* – In London 'Our Theatre' is the result of a nine year partnership between PwC, Shakespeare's Globed Education and Southwark Council. More than 2,300 local schoolchildren have benefited from in-school workshops. In Birmingham, the 'Perform, Write and Create' project involved PwC volunteers and musicians working with children from local primary schools to develop their own musical compositions. Young artists from inner-city schools in Southward and Westminster have been given the opportunity to work with professional artists at The Prince's Drawing School. In April 2005 they exhibited a selection of their work at PwC's Embankment Place office in London.

# Principality Building Society

PO Box 89, Principality Buildings, Queen Street, Cardiff CF10 1UA

029 2038 2000; Fax: 029 2037 4567

Website: www.principality.co.uk

Correspondent: Coporate Communications Manager, Corporate Communications Team 029 2038 2000; Fax: 029 2037 4567

Chief officer: D Peter L Davies

Chief Executive: Peter Griffiths

| Year end | Turnover | Pre-tax profit |
|---|---|---|
| 31/12/2005 | £228,400,000 | £22,600,000 |

Nature of company business
The provision of housing finance and a range of insurance and financial services.

Main locations: Cardiff

Total employees: 754

## Charitable donations

2005: £10,674
2004: £8,528

## Community involvement

The Principality supports a number of initiatives such as cultural events, sport at various levels and the volunteering and fundraising efforts of its staff.

### Applications

In writing to the correspondent.

## Corporate giving

In 2005, the group made charitable donations of £10,674. We have no information regarding the specific recipient organisation(s).

### Employee-led support

Staff members have been involved in various community projects and these have included:

A team undertaking the Welsh Three Peaks Challenge to raise money for a children's hospice, Ty Hafan, in Sully, near Cardiff.

A donation of £500 from staff in Pwllheli to Ysgol Hafod Lon to pay for transport and accommodation for the pupils competing at a three day Welsh sporting event for pupils with learning difficulties.

A team from the Llanelli branch re-building a garden in a primary school which had been vandalised. The team paid for paints, brushes, plants, wooden benches and pots and through the sponsorship package and gave their time to complete the work.

### Commercially-led support

**Sponsorship:** *The arts* – For over 25 years the society has sponsored the National Eisteddfod of Wales.

The group were runner up in the Arts and Business Cymru Awards 2004 with the Live Music Now programme for children. The group state that the partnership with Live Music Now proved the ideal way to work with young people, whom the Society had not specifically reached before. 'Both Live Music Now and ourselves wanted to get involved in the communities of Wales at grass roots level and we both felt strongly that we should try to do something that allowed children who would normally never get the chance to enjoy a new experience – live music in a theatre setting. We also wanted the project to be something that would benefit as many children as possible.

The partnership fulfilled these objectives by taking live music into theatres across Wales – we reached Newport, Swansea, Wrexham, Pwllheli, Aberystwyth and Pontypridd.'

The society has also sponsored various events, such as National Science Week at the Techniquest Centre in Cardiff Bay.

The group recently announced a £50,000 sponsorship package through its 51 branches based throughout Wales and the borders, to support schools, local groups and community projects.

# Procter & Gamble UK

The Heights, Brooklands, Weybridge, Surrey KT13 0XP

01932 896073; Fax: 01932 896233

Website: www.uk.pg.com

**Correspondent:** Mrs J S Butler, Community Matters Co-ordinator, UK & Ireland
E-mail: butler.js@pg.com

**Chief officer:** A G Lafley

**Chief Executive:** A G Lafley

| Year end 30/06/2006 | Turnover | Pre-tax profit |
|---|---|---|

**Nature of company business**
Procter & Gamble UK is a wholly owned subsidiary of The Procter & Gamble Company, USA. The principal activities of the company and its subsidiaries are the manufacture and marketing of innovative consumer products, with associated research and development services.

**Main locations:** Seaton Delaval, Skelmersdale, Weybridge, Manchester, Newcastle upon Tyne, West Thurrock, Egham, Harrogate, Bournemouth

**UK employees:** 5,000

## Charitable donations

2004: £150,118

Total community contributions: £3,686,297

Membership: A & B, BitC, L B Group, %Club

## Community involvement

The company only supports local charities in areas of company presence (Weybridge and Egham in Surrey; Newcastle upon Tyne; Bournemouth in Dorset; Harrogate in Yorkshire; West Thurrock in Essex; Skelmersdale in Lancashire; Manchester; Dublin and Nenagh in Ireland; across a wide range of causes covering education (ED), economic well-being (E/WB), and leisure/social welfare (L/SW).

Support for certain groups is only considered if the project is concerned with the indicated cause. These groups are: children/youth (ED), elderly people (L/SW), enterprise/training (ED), and environment/heritage (E/WB).

### Exclusions

No support is given to circular appeals, advertising in charity brochures, appeals from individuals, fundraising events, medical research, overseas projects, political or religious appeals, or local appeals not in areas of company presence.

### Applications

Applications should be by letter only and addressed to the correspondent.

For financial grants in Tyne & Wear, and Northumberland only, call the 'P&G Fund' at The Community Foundation (0191 222 0945) and ask for Joe Galletley, who will be pleased to discuss your application. Alternatively, write to: The P&G Fund, The Community Foundation, Cale Cross, 156 Pilgrim Street, Newcastle-upon-Tyne NE1 6SU.

It is advisable to apply to the P&G Fund before the closing dates at the end of February and August. Panel meetings award grants twice each year in April and October. Applicants are sent an acknowledgement letter and are contacted again in writing following the meeting.

**Information available:** The company produces a social responsibility report and provides policy guidelines for applicants. The company also produces a newsletter entitled Community Matters.

## Corporate giving

In 2005, the company made donations totalling almost £3,700,000 in the UK, according to Business in the Community's PerCent Club figures. No figures for 2006 were available in the company's literature for 2006.

### P&G Fund

The Community Foundation for Tyne & Wear and Northumberland, manages the above fund on behalf of Procter & Gamble to support the company's charitable giving. Procter & Gamble have pledged to build a £1 million fund over ten years to support charitable groups in the North East.

Applications are welcomed:

▷ from charitable groups in Tyne & Wear and Northumberland

▷ from projects requiring £500–£5,000 with the majority of grants around £1,000

▷ for capital purposes for equipment, or revenue support for running costs.

Procter & Gamble aims to improve the quality of life for local people and grants are made in a broad field of activity to spread support across the community. Support is offered to:

▷ organisations which deliver sustained benefit to the community in areas of education, cultural and leisure amenities, and social well-being.

Procter & Gamble will target support at those groups which can demonstrate a sustained and long-term benefit to the communities they work with.

### In-kind support

The company also contributes through gifts in kind, training schemes and provision of employee time/expertise, for example, marketing, finance etc. to community projects. Company employee skills and expertise are used by many community projects in the areas of education, economic well-being, leisure and social welfare projects.

### Employee-led support

Employees undertake voluntary work in both company time their own time can request funds to support the project, when appropriate.

**Payroll giving:** The company operates an Employee Charitable Fund scheme, matching employee giving on a pound for pound basis.

### Commercially-led support

**Sponsorship:** The company undertakes local arts and good-cause support.

Contact: (P&G Fund) The Community Foundation (tel: 0191 222 0945).

**Cause-related marketing:** Procter & Gamble has run joint promotions on behalf of Race for Life; Wellbeing; Breast Cancer Care; ERIC; NSPCC; Children in Need; Marie Curie Cancer Care; Lawn Tennis Association; Association of Children's Hospices; Make a Wish Foundation; Everyman; The Animal Health Trust; Pets as Therapy; Hearing Dogs;

Manchester Dogs Home; Caravan and P&G's Schools Programme. These promotions have raised over £5 million for these good causes.

## Provident Financial plc

Colonnade, Sunbridge Road, Bradford, West Yorkshire BD1 2LQ

01274 731111; Fax: 01274 727300

Website: www.providentfinancial.co.uk

Correspondent: Brent Shackleton, Community Affairs Manager

Chief officer: John van Kuffeler

Chief Executive: Robert Ashton

| Year end | Turnover | Pre-tax profit |
|---|---|---|
| 31/12/2005 | £751,400,000 | £144,700,000 |

Nature of company business
Personal credit and insurance.

Subsidiaries include: Colonnade Insurance Brokers Ltd, Greenwood Personal Credit Ltd

Main locations: Bradford

UK employees: 8,547

### Charitable donations

2005: £677,751
2004: £450,083
2003: £270,820

Total community contributions: £2,077,883

Membership: A & B, BitC, L B Group, %Club

## Community involvement

The company states on its website that: 'Our community programme aims to help people who live and work in the areas in which we operate – our customers, agents, employees and the local community. We work with local partners to offer new opportunities and to play our part in the development of neighbourhoods and communities.

'The aim of our programmes is to create new opportunities for young people, but other themes are developed by businesses according to the needs of their local communities. The projects and associations we support are wide-ranging and varied.'

Currently there are two major strands to the company's community programme: (i) community partnerships; (ii) money advice and financial education.

Further details of each of these are given below.

Additionally, through the 'Provident in the Community' programme, support and encouragement is given to employees and agents to initiate and take part in fundraising activities within the communities in which they live and work.

### Exclusions

No support for advertising in charity brochures, animal welfare, appeals from individuals, elderly people, medical research, overseas projects, political appeals, religious appeals, or sickness/disability charities.

## Applications

In writing to the correspondent.

## Corporate giving

Total community contributions by the company in 2005 were £2,077,883 of which £677,751 were in cash donations. Examples of some of the organisations benefiting from this are given below.

### Community partnerships

*Spark* – 'Spark embraces a spread of art forms from singing to circus skills and will involve around 50 schools and 6,000 children a year.

'Our partners in the project will be the West Yorkshire Playhouse and seven other local theatres. As well as rooting the programme in the community, this type of joint initiative offers our partners the opportunity to apply for matched funding, helping our money go further.

'Spark was piloted at seven schools in Bradford at the start of 2006 and opens at its first main venue in Birmingham in the summer term.'

*L'Ouverture* – 'For the past six years, we have supported L'Ouverture – a not for profit organisation that provides unique opportunities for young people to learn about the arts and the media. Attention is focused on young people unlikely to find such opportunities elsewhere, including those from deprived inner city areas and those who have fallen between the cracks of the formal education system.

'L'Ouverture teaches young people about the traditional arts, including drama, dance, singing, drawing and creative writing, as well as the media industry – both about how it works, and about the relevant skills such as design, web building and video making.'

*PACK (Provident Action for Creative Kids)* – 'Working with the Youth Hostels Association (YHA) in England and Wales, Scotland and Ireland, we have set up a programme called 'PACK' – Provident Action for Creative Kids. The aim of 'PACK' is to provide new opportunities for young people to take part in outdoor activities and so increase their confidence and self-esteem.

'The breaks take the form of a two-day stay in a youth hostel with a focus on activity-based breaks. The aim is to introduce young people from schools and community groups to new activities and environments. For many of the children taking part, this is their first time away from home. Provident provides extra support with employees and agents attending the breaks wherever possible.'

### Money advice

'Under the Gateway initiative, the UK government is encouraging debt advice organisations to come together and adopt a more coherent approach to the task with a common phone number for help and common standards of advice. Provident supports the move as a way of offering better support to those in difficulty.

'We also support financial education providers who focus on building individuals' financial literacy and budgeting skills. These include the Bradford-based Christians Against Poverty along with Credit Action, Debt Cred, Citizens' Advice, Money Advice, National Debtline, and Advice UK.'

## Employee-led support

*Provident in the Community* – This is a nationwide programme which provides practical support to small community projects identified by the company's agents and employees. Requests for support should be submitted through an employee or agent of the group.

Recent examples include employees and agents of the home credit division in Rhondda Cynon in Wales, raising £3,000 for children's cancer charity LATCH, which supports Welsh children and their families and is based at the Children's Hospital for Wales in Cardiff.

Meanwhile, employees at Provident Insurance also raised £14,000 for a special needs school in Calderdale through themed days at work, competitions and raffles.

# Prudential plc

Laurence Pountney Hill, London EC4R 0HH

020 7220 7588; Fax: 020 7548 3528

**Website:** www.prudential.co.uk

**Correspondent:** Tina Christou, Head of Corporate Responsibilty
E-mail: tina.christou@prudential.co.uk

**Chief officer:** Sir David Clementi

**Chief Executive:** Mark Tucker

| Year end | Turnover | Pre-tax profit |
|---|---|---|
| 31/12/2005 | | £2,145,000,000 |

**Nature of company business**
Prudential plc, through its businesses in Europe, the US and Asia, provides retail financial products and services.

**Subsidiaries include:** Scottish Amicable Life plc, M&G Investment Management Ltd, Jackson National Life

**Main locations:** Belfast, Chelmsford, Reading, Nottingham, London, Stirling

### Charitable donations

2005: £3,500,000
2003: £2,800,000

Total community contributions: £4,700,000 (global)
Management costs: £40,000

Membership: A & B, BitC, L B Group, %Club

## Community involvement

Prudential's corporate community involvement is part of its wider commitment to corporate social responsibility. Each business within the group has its own community investment plan in place. However, identified as a key issue across all locations is the need to improve financial literacy within communities. This is therefore dealt with at group level.

National (UK) and local charities are supported in areas where the company has offices.

### Exclusions

No support for appeals for sponsorship of individuals or groups, fundraising events, advertising in charity brochures, circular appeals, political organisations, purely denominational (religious) appeals, local arts or drama groups, animal welfare, heritage and building projects, medical research, or science/technology.

## Applications

Further information can be sought from the corporate social responsibility team at the above number.

## Corporate giving

In 2005 the group made total community contributions worldwide of £4.7 million. Within this, direct donations to charitable organisations amounted to £3.5 million, of which £2.3 million came from European Union (EU) operations. This is broken down as follows: Education (£1,068,000); Social and Welfare (£1,039,000); Environment and Regeneration (£91,000); Cultural (£84,000) and Staff Volunteering (£56,000).

## In-kind support

A range of in kind support is offered to organisations on a local basis. This includes employees' time and skills, office space, meeting rooms, computers and office furniture.

## Employee-led support

A new international employee volunteering programme, The Chairman's Award, was launched across the group in December 2005. The initiative encourages employees to volunteer with charities within their local communities.

**Payroll giving:** The company operate the Give As You Earn scheme.

# Psion plc

Alexander House, 85 Frampton Street, London NW8 8NQ

020 7535 4253; Fax: 020 7535 4226

Website: www.psionteklogix.com

Correspondent: Group Communications

Chief officer: Dr David Potter

Chief Executive: Jacky Lecuivre

| Year end | Turnover | Pre-tax profit |
|---|---|---|
| 31/12/2005 | £168,643,000 | £10,539,000 |

Nature of company business
Development, manufacture and supply of mobile, digital communication and computing technology.

Subsidiaries include: Trivanti Ltd, Symbian Ltd

Main locations: High Wycombe, Didcot, Milton Keynes, London

UK employees: 1,055

Total employees: 1,055

### Charitable donations
2005: £20,293
2003: £41,000

## Community involvement

Previous information suggested that Psion focuses its support principally on activities closely related to mobile computing and communications, southern African education and development. Psion also supports organisations local to its production sites in Didcot, Milton Keynes and High Wycombe.

## Exclusions

No support for appeals from individuals or local appeals not in areas of company presence. The company does not provide support for political parties.

## Applications

In writing to the correspondent.

## Corporate giving

In 2005, Psion made charitable donations totalling £20,293. We have no details of the beneficiaries.

# QinetiQ Group plc

Cody Technology Park, Ively Road, Farnborough, Hampshire, GU14 0LX

08700 100 942

Website: www.qinetiq.com

Correspondent: Brenda Jones

Chief officer: Sir John Chisholm

Chief Executive: Graham Love

| Year end | Turnover | Pre-tax profit |
|---|---|---|
| 31/03/2006 | £1,053,100,000 | £72,500,000 |

Nature of company business
The group's principal activity is the supply of scientific and technical solutions and services.

Main locations: Farnborough

UK employees: 11,024

### Charitable donations
2006: £54,000
2005: £57,000

## Community involvement

The company states in the corporate responsibility section of its 2006 annual report and accounts that: 'QinetiQ recognises its responsibility to manage its impact on local communities in respect of the 54 sites on which it operates across the UK.

'This year it has continued to work in partnership with local stakeholders in helping to address sensitive and important local issues. QinetiQ has focused its corporate giving around a number of priority charities. An emphasis has been placed on supporting science and technology in education.'

## Applications

In writing to the correspondent.

## Corporate giving

In 2005/05, global cash donations amounted to £136,000 of which £54,000 was given in the UK. Beneficiaries included: The National Trust for Scotland, whom it helped secure St Kilda's dual world heritage status; St Richard's Hospice in Malvern; and, support for two schools in attaining specialist science status – St Augustine's, Malvern and Cove, Farnborough.

Through the Community Foundation for Wiltshire and Swindon, the company established the QinetiQ Boscombe Down Fund which is designed to improve the life of disadvantaged people through education and science.

## In-kind support

To increase awareness of science and technology in local schools, the company is piloting the use of 'Lab in a Lorry' in Boscombe Down. In addition, a particular emphasis has been placed on investigating ways to make a contribution through technology support for the Royal National Lifeboat Institute (RNLI) and Cancer Research UK.

## Employee-led support

In support of 'charities that matter to our staff', QinetiQ has implemented a match-funding arrangement through which certain identified charities are given funding priority. These charities include: Cancer Research UK, St Richard's Hospice, NSPCC, RNLI, Royal British Legion and SSAFA. As a result of this over £15,000 was provided by the group.

**Payroll giving:** The company funds a payroll giving scheme.

## Commercially-led support

**Sponsorship:** *Education* – QinetiQ sponsor the following events: the Schools Aerospace Challenge, the Stockholm Prize at the BA Crest Science Fair, the Cheltenham Science Festival, Generation Science as part of the Edinburgh Science Festival, and the Engineering Education Scheme.

# The Rank Group plc

6 Connaught Place, London W2 2EZ

020 7706 1111; Fax: 020 7262 9886

Website: www.rank.com

Correspondent: Pamela Coles, Company Secretary

Chief officer: Alun Cathcart

Chief Executive: Mike Smith

| Year end | Turnover | Pre-tax profit |
|---|---|---|
| 31/12/2005 | £810,300,000 | £50,700,000 |

Nature of company business
The Rank Group is one of the UK's leading leisure and entertainment companies and an international provider of services to the film industry. Leisure and entertainment activities include Hard Rock Cafés and global rights to the Hard Rock brand, casinos, bingo clubs, pub restaurants and holiday resorts. Rank also owns film processing and video and DVD duplication and distribution facilities. Rank operates primarily in the UK and North America, although it has activities in Continental Europe and other parts of the world.

Subsidiaries include: Deluxe Laboratories Ltd, Deluxe Video Services Ltd, Grosvenor Casinos Ltd, Mecca Bingo Ltd

Main locations: London

UK employees: 11,453

Total employees: 29,167

## Charitable donations

2005: £269,000
2004: £233,000
2003: £275,000

## Community involvement

The company supports local and national charities with major support going to industry related trusts.

### Exclusions

No response is given to circular appeals. No support for individuals is granted – students, expeditions and so on. No grants for advertising in charity brochures, animal welfare, the arts, fundraising events, overseas projects, political appeals, religious appeals, science/technology, sport, or local appeals not in areas of company presence.

### Applications

In writing to the correspondent.

## Corporate giving

In 2005, charitable donations made in the UK amounted to £269,000. The largest donation was to BCA Gaming Industry Trust

Subsidiary companies support a variety of local and national charities and, in particular, Hard Rock Café International Inc. which continues its focus on humanitarian and environmental causes.

# Ravensale Ltd

115 Wembley Commercial Centre, East Lane, North Wembley, Middlesex HA9 7UR

020 8908 4655

Correspondent: Bruce D G Jarvis, Charity Correspondent

| Year end | Turnover | Pre-tax profit |
|---|---|---|
| 30/06/2005 | £19,728,614 | (£853,171) |

Nature of company business
The principal activity of Ravensale Ltd is property development and investment, and the design and manufacture of ballpoint pen components.

Total employees: 54

## Charitable donations

2005: £1,903,000
2004: £959,471

## Community involvement

Ravensale Ltd directs all its charitable giving, which is substantial, through the registered charity, The Jordon Charitable Trust (Charity Commission no. 1062547). The trust is established for general charitable purposes and makes grants to registered charities in various fields where it can be demonstrated that the grants will be used effectively. There is no formal grant application procedure and the trustees retain the services of a charitable grants advisor and take advice when deciding on grants. The trustees of the charity are members of the Jarvis family.

## Exclusions

No support for political organisations.

## Applications

There is no formal grant application procedure. Apply to the contact in writing.

## Corporate giving

During the year ending 30 June 2005 the company donated £1,903,000 (2004: £959,471) to The Joron Charitable Trust. The trust, during the year 31 March 2005 made grants and donations totalling £1,361,550 (2004: £1,000,040).

Grants/donations included the following:

Christopher's Hospice – to establish the post of Nurse Lecturer-Practitioner (£50,000)

Barts Cancer Centre of Excellence – to purchase equipment for a new cancer centre (£473,100)

Norwood – to support children and their families with learning difficulties (£2,600)

British Heart Foundation – for research (£25,000)

Royal Opera House Foundation – for restoration work (£1,500)

The Battle of Britain Monument Fund – to help underprivileged youths (£50,000)

DELTA – for educational purposes (£5,000)

CIS Development Fund – towards saving lives of Jewish families in Eastern Europe (£10,000)

The Michael Palin Centre for Stammering Children – to support their work (£15,000)

The Women's Interfaith Network – to assist in their work of bringing all faiths together (£10,000)

The Chicken Shed Theatre – to support the performing arts for children who are disabled (£100,00)

Animal Care Trust – to purchase equipment for an animal hospital (£2,500)

JAMI – to support the work of the Jewish Association for Mental Illness (£5,000)

RAFT – for research into reconstructive plastic surgery (£110,000)

The Chemical Dependency Centre – towards alcohol and drug dependency projects (£5,000)

# Reckitt Benckiser plc

103–105 Bath Road, Slough, Berkshire SL1 3UH

01753 217800

Website: www.reckittbenckiser.com

Correspondent: Corporate Communications Department
01753 446534
E-mail: corpcomms@reckittbenckiser.com

Chief officer: Adrian Bellamy

Chief Executive: Bart Becht

| Year end | Turnover | Pre-tax profit |
|---|---|---|
| 31/12/2005 | £4,179,000,000 | £876,000,000 |

**Nature of company business**
Principal activities: The manufacture and sale of household and healthcare products.

**Main locations:** Derby, Hull, Slough, Windsor, Swindon

**Total employees:** 20,300

### Charitable donations

2005: £568,000
2004: £496,000
2003: £367,000

Membership: BitC

## Community involvement

Reckitt Benckiser operates a community involvement policy executed through its Community Involvement Committee (CIC) which consists of senior executives from the company.

The company provided the following guidelines which are applied in deciding which projects it will seek to be involved with:

- 'Relevance to the company's core business, which is about cleaning, health and protection in the family home. This relates our community involvement to the consumers of our brands in the place of consumption.
- Relevance to the company's locations. In the UK this means a specific responsibility in Hull, Derby, Swindon and Windsor/Slough. This relates to our employees' local communities, our ability to recruit and retain a motivated workforce.
- Relevance to the learning of the members of the company of the future through support for education.
- Support for our employees' community/charity involvement through matched giving or support activities, or support for their preferred causes.'

In relation to the above guidelines the CIC allocates its resources into four areas:

- 'A single major project in which Reckitt Benckiser can make a meaningful difference related to its core business, that will involve company employees at the company's sites in the programme, and that will raise the company's profile in the area of community involvement.
- Specific support for the localities in which the company operates. In particular the company recognises a responsibility to the community in Hull.
- A support for educational work which has specific relevance to recruitment and training of the management of tomorrow.
- Support for employees own efforts in fundraising and for other small scale projects that are judged by the CIC to be worth supporting.'

### Exclusions

No grants for animal welfare charities, the arts, elderly people, political appeals, religious appeals, science/technology, sickness/disability or sport.

### Applications

In writing to the correspondent. Applications are considered by the Community Involvement Committee which meets four times a year. In addition to authorising donations, the committee is concerned with the implementation of policy relating to the company's community programme.

**Information available:** An application form and policy guidelines are available to applicants. The company published its first corporate social responsibility report at the end of 2004.

## Corporate giving

Donations to charitable organisations in the UK in 2005 were £568,000 (2004: £496,000). Beneficiaries have included: Home Start; Crisis; and Weston Spirit.

### In-kind support

Additional support may be given through gifts in kind.

**Education:** In Hull, projects in the area involving children/ young people receive support, such as the purchase of books for schools and equipment for an allotment to be used by young disabled people. Help has also been given to local primary schools to attend a one-day safety education course, which covered drugs, fires, and health and safety.

### Employee-led support

The company matches employee fundraising.

---

# Redrow Group plc

Redrow House, St David's Park, Flintshire CH5 3RX

01244 520044; Fax: 01244 520720

Website: www.redrowcsr.co.uk

Correspondent: Simon Bennett, Marketing Director
01244 520044; Fax: 01244 520580

Chief officer: Robert Jones

Chief Executive: Neil Fitzsimmons

| Year end | Turnover | Pre-tax profit |
|---|---|---|
| 30/06/2006 | £770,100,000 | £120,500,000 |

**Nature of company business**
The principal activities are housebuilding and commercial development.

**Subsidiaries include:** Bates Business Centre, Poche Interior Design, Harwood Homes

**Main locations:** Barnsley, Bexhill on Sea, Liverpool, Flintshire, Leek, Falkirk, Aberdare, Preston Brook, High Wycombe, Leigh, Cardiff, Launceston

Total employees: 1,369

> ### Charitable donations
>
> 2006: £304,000
> 2004: £96,000
> 2003: £15,000
>
> Membership: BitC, %Club

## Community involvement

Following a steady decline in the company's charitable donations during the early part of this century, they have now risen to in excess of the high of 2000. During 2006, the company established a charitable trust – the Redrow Foundation (Charity Commission no. 1113073) – and launched a dedicated corporate community support website (see above). The foundation will focus particularly on providing accommodation and related assistance, such as respite care, for vulnerable groups including children in need, the elderly, the sick, or the infirm.

The company and its employees also support educational initiatives, arts, craft, sport and small charities at a local level.

### Exclusions

No support for circular appeals, advertising in charity brochures, purely denominational (religious) appeals, large national appeals, overseas projects or local appeals not in areas of company presence.

### Applications

In writing to the correspondent, or, via e-mail to: foundation@redrow.co.uk. You will then be informed of the foundation's full criteria, together with the next date when the trustees are to meet to discuss the merits of each submission.

In considering each request, the trustees will be looking for evidence of leverage on the funds. Please state, therefore, how you intend to match or increase any donation you may receive in your application.

## Corporate giving

In 2006, the group made charitable donations in the UK totalling £304,000. Of this, £246,000 was paid to national charities (including £218,000 to the Redrow Foundation) and £58,000 to local charities. A recent beneficiary has been the National Trust's Schools Partnership programme to which Redrow has donated £150,000 over the last few years.

### The Redrow Foundation

Redrow has made an initial donation to the foundation of £100,000 and, thereafter, will contribute £50 for every Redrow home purchased. It is estimated that this will amount to around £250,000 a year.

### In-kind support

In-kind help may be given through the donation of furniture to needy causes such as care homes, or the development of curriculum resource packs for primary school children. Suitable IT equipment may also be donated to local schools as the company updates its hardware.

### Employee-led support

All employees are encouraged to take part in fundraising on behalf of their local community. Each of Redrow's regional companies is encouraged to adopt a local charity and fundraise on its behalf.

For example, staff, suppliers and sub-contractors in South Wales raise funds annually for the Ty Hafan Children's Hospice.

---

# Renishaw plc

New Mills, Wotton-under-Edge, Gloucestershire GL12 8JR

01453 524524; Fax: 01453 524401

Website: www.renishaw.com

Correspondent: David Champion, Chairman, Charities Committee
E-mail: genenq@renishaw.com

Chief officer: Sir D R McMurtry

Chief Executive: Sir D R McMurtry

| Year end | Turnover | Pre-tax profit |
|---|---|---|
| 30/06/2006 | £175,835,000 | £38,102,000 |

**Nature of company business**
The main activities are the design, manufacture and sale of advanced precision metrology and inspection equipment, and computer aided design and manufacturing systems.

**Subsidiaries include:** Wotton Travel Ltd

**Main locations:** Stonehouse, Woodchester, Wotton-under-Edge

**Total employees:** 2,004

### Charitable donations

2006: £104,532
2005: £62,541
2004: £49,758

## Community involvement

The company gives priority to local appeals (in areas immediate to company locations – Wotton-under-Edge, Stonehouse and Woodchester), involving young people, and to local branches of national charities concerned with children/youth. Other preferred causes include: animal welfare, the arts, education, older people, enterprise/training, environment/heritage, fundraising events, medical research, religious appeals, science/technology, sickness/disability charities and sport.

The group organises its charitable donations by two methods: firstly, by allocating a fund of money to its charities committee; and secondly, through direct grants decided by the board.

### Exclusions

No support for advertising in charity brochures, appeals from individuals, fundraising events for third parties, overseas projects or political appeals. No sponsorship is undertaken.

### Applications

Written appeals only, to David Champion, Chairman of the Charities Committee at the above address. The committee meets at least four times a year to consider all applications for donations from local (Gloucestershire) groups.

## Corporate giving

In 2005/06, the company made charitable donations of £104,532 (2004/05: £62,541). We have no details regarding the beneficiaries.

## In-kind support

In-kind support is given by, for example, hosting community/charitable events at its premises.

# Rentokil Initial plc

Belgrave House, 76 Buckingham Palace Road, London SW1W 9RF

020 7866 3000; Fax: 020 7866 3800

Website: www.rentokil-initial.com

Correspondent: Paul Griffiths, Director, Group Secretariat

Chief officer: B D McGowan

Chief Executive: D Flynn

| Year end | Turnover | Pre-tax profit |
|---|---|---|
| 31/12/2005 | £2,301,200,000 | £190,100,000 |

**Nature of company business**
Principal activity: international company providing services to businesses including, pest control, package delivery, interior landscaping, catering, electronic security, cleaning.

**Subsidiaries include:** Dudley Industries Ltd

**Main locations:** East Grinstead, Orpington

**Total employees:** 90,096

### Charitable donations

2005: £254,000
2004: £130,000
2003: £115,000

Membership: BitC

## Community involvement

Previously we were advised that the company is only prepared to consider supporting registered charities or non-profit making organisations which raise funds for charitable causes. There exists a local charities budget which supports organisations local to its East Grinstead and Orpington offices. Assistance is also given to employees in their fundraising efforts.

The company is a member of Business in the Community.

### Exclusions

Consideration will not be given to any charity or sponsorship related proposal from any organisation unless a company employee or employees are involved.

### Applications

In writing to the correspondent, but note 'exclusions' above.

**Other information:** The company produces an annual corporate social responsibility report.

## Corporate giving

In 2005, donations for UK charitable purposes totalled £254,000 with a further £45,000 donated in other countries. We have no details of the beneficiaries.

## In-kind support

In the UK, Initial catering has developed two websites which provide healthy eating guidelines for schoolchildren (www.coolmeals.co.uk and www.feedyourminds.co.uk), along with healthy eating education packs for teachers to support classroom education and workshops.

## Employee-led support

The company operates a staff matched-giving scheme for all its employees worldwide. This means Rentokil Initial will match any amount raised by staff member(s) who take part in an event for a charitable cause. However, only funds raised by employees who actively participate in fundraising events themselves will be matched by the company.

**Payroll giving:** The company operate the Give As You Earn scheme.

# Resolution plc

Juxon House, 100 St Paul's Churchyard, London EC4M 8BU

020 7489 4880; Fax: 020 7489 4860

Website: www.resolutionplc.com

Correspondent: Sue Regan, The Resolution Foundation
020 7489 4880
E-mail: sue.regan@resolutionfoundation.org

Chief officer: Clive Cowdery

Chief Executive: P Thompson

| Year end | Turnover | Pre-tax profit |
|---|---|---|
| 31/12/2005 | | 354,000,000 |

**Nature of company business**
Resolution plc (formerly Britannic Group plc) and Resolution Life Group Limited merged on 6th September 2005. Resolution plc is the holding company of the Group that specialises in the ownership and administration of closed life funds.

Subsidiaries include: Alba Life

Main locations: Glasgow, Wythall

Total employees: 1,545

### Charitable donations

2005: £447,235
2004: £65,058
2003: £62,363

## Community involvement

In September 2005, Britannic Group plc merged with Resolution Life Group Ltd to form Resolution plc.

Although the details below presently refer to Britannic's community support policy, the new company has also established a charity – The Resolution Foundation (Charity Commission no. 1114839). Resolution plc is to make an annual payment of £400,000 to the foundation; further information on which can be found at: www.resolutionfoundation.org.

The following extract is taken from the company's website: 'During the year Resolution also made a £400,000 charitable donation to the not-for-profit organisation, The Resolution Foundation. The purpose of the Foundation, which was established by Resolution chairman Clive Cowdery, is to carry out research into the financial decisions made by, and the financial advice available to, people on limited incomes, and to provide education on financial matters and the making of responsible financial decisions.'

The foundation was registered as a charity on 24th June 2006 and accounts are not as yet available to enable us to provide information regarding the distribution of the foundation's income.

## Exclusions

No information was available regarding causes the group would not support.

## Applications

In writing to the correspondent.

## Corporate giving

During the year £47,235 (2004: £65,058) was donated by Resolution companies for charitable purposes. A significant proportion of this sum was given to national charities involved in medical research into life threatening diseases. No further breakdown of this amount was available. In addition the company made a charitable donation of £400,000 to The Resolution Foundation.

## Employee-led support

The group allows employees to take time off work to support charitable initiatives. During 2005 Employee Charity Consultative Groups were established with responsibility for co-ordinating employee fundraising and reviewing requests from employees to support specific charities.

Such fundraising events organised by staff have included raffles, dress down days and various competitions. During the year 2005 a total of £19,521 was raised by employees around the Group. In addition, on the evening of 15 March 2005, the Life division's call centre at Wythall was used to take donations to Comic Relief with staff volunteers manning the phones.

The following text taken from Resolution plc Report and Accounts 2005: 'At the life division's Wythall office efforts continued to build on involvement with the local community. A specific partnership approach has been developed with two secondary schools whereby assistance is given in the form of carrying out mock interviews and contributing generally to the transition from school to working life. Resolution also participates in the Young Enterprise programme in which volunteers from the local business community act as mentors to a group of sixth formers who set up and run a real business for an academic year. In addition, Resolution has provided work experience placements to schools, including Queen Alexandra College in Birmingham which is a college for people with visual impairment and other disabilities.'

## Commercially-led support

**Sponsorship:** 2005 was the ninth successive year that Britannic Asset Management was the main sponsor of the Glasgow Women's 10k Road Race. The 2005 race saw 12,500 runners raise £1 million for worthy causes. Britannic Asset Management state they will continue to sponsor the event for a further three years from 2006 through to 2008.

Project Ability is a community based initiative established in 1984. The Glasgow based scheme aims to encourage and develop the artistic talents of those with special needs, assisting them in taking an active part in local and international arts events. Britannic Asset Management has now sponsored this project for 6 consecutive years and has committed to fund it through to 2006.

# Reuters Limited

The Reuters Building, South Colonnade, Canary Wharf, London E14 5EP

020 7250 1122; Fax: 020 7353 3002

Website: www.foundation.reuters.com

Correspondent: Julia Fuller, Corporate Responsibility Manager
E-mail: www.about.reuters.com

Chief officer: Niall FitzGerald

Chief Executive: Thomas Glocer

| Year end | Turnover | Pre-tax profit |
|---|---|---|
| 31/12/2005 | £2,409,000,000 | £238,000,000 |

Nature of company business
The group's principal activity is the provision of information and software applications tailored for professionals in the financial services, media and corporate markets.

Main locations: London, Nottingham, Tiverton

UK employees: 3,332

Total employees: 15,018

## Charitable donations

2005: £1,200,000
2004: £1,500,000
2003: £2,500,000

Total community contributions: £1,497,566 (global)

Membership: BitC, L B Group

## Community involvement

### Reuters Foundation

Support for charitable causes and community initiatives continues mainly through the Reuters Foundation (Charity Commission no. 1082139), the group's charitable trust. Reuters Foundation has been established with very broad objects, which enables the charity to undertake purposes which are exclusively charitable according to the laws of England and Wales. However, the trustees have decided to focus on programmes of a humanitarian and educational purpose. The foundation receives an annual, unrestricted grant from Reuters, the global news and information group.

The work of the foundation reflects the values and concerns of Reuters and its employees, focusing in particular on areas where Reuters' skills and expertise in information gathering and communications can be put to use in ways which will benefit the communities in which Reuters works worldwide.

In 2005 the Reuter Foundation's charitable expenditure was broken down as follows:

| | |
|---|---|
| Journalism | 50% |
| Humanitarian Aid | 46% |
| Health & Community | 1% |
| Environment & Other | 1% |
| Management & Admin | 2% |

Other foundation programmes include:

### Reuters AlertNet

A website offering rapid news and communications services for the international disaster relief community.

### The Reuters Foundation Fellowship Programme at Green College, Oxford University

In 2005, the twenty-second year of the Oxford Fellowship, the Reuters Foundation programme enabled 29 mid-career journalists to study at Green College, Oxford University. Fellowships for ten of these journalists, mainly from developing countries have been directly funded by Reuters Foundation. In all, 16 of the journalists came from developing countries or countries in transition.

In 2005, the foundation offered training opportunities to journalists from all over the world, providing short training courses to 391 journalists from 86 countries including participants from Togo, Kyrgyzstan and Turkmenistan.

Amongst the courses was a workshop held in New York on HIV/AIDS reporting, coinciding with World Aids Day and attracting 22 journalists from 18 countries.

### Reuters Institute for the Study of Journalism

In January 2006, Oxford University and Reuters Foundation announced the creation of the Reuters Institute for the Study of Journalism. The foundation will provide funding of £1.75m over five years to establish and develop a research centre of excellence in the study of journalism. The Institute will build on Oxford's already wide-ranging engagement with media issues and the long-standing Reuters Foundation Journalists Fellowship Programme at Green College, Oxford. The programme for visiting journalists will continue as a key component of the new institute. The institute will have a distinct focus: it will analyse the practice of journalism worldwide and examine the basis for reliable and accurate reporting in the digital age.

### Exclusions

No support for circulars, unsolicited appeals or advertising in charity brochures. No grants for: animal welfare charities; political appeals; religious appeals; or sport (unless fundraising for other causes).

### Applications

Reuters Foundation no longer gives cash grants to community-based charities or concerns outside the range of core programmes described in this report. Reuters Foundation instead supports local causes by donating small cash sums for the provision of materials and resources to enable Reuters' employees to engage in community involvement programmes on a voluntary basis. In line with Reuters Foundation's guidelines projects associated with political, religious or militant causes, animal welfare causes or sports events are not supported.

Reuters Foundation does not consider unsolicited requests for support.

## Corporate giving

A substantial proportion of the donations received by Reuters Foundation is made up of an annual grant from Reuters Limited, a wholly owned subsidiary of Reuters Group plc. In 2005, this grant was £1,200,000 (2004: £1,500,000). In addition, Reuters Foundation received £132,529 in unrestricted income to fund journalism and media training and AlertNet development work. Reuters Foundation received £790,242 of restricted income from various organisations to fund fellowships, programmes, developments or co-sponsored events. (2004: £238,589).

Reuters Foundation Consultants Limited made a profit of £50,034 in the year (2004: £40,452). Of this amount £48,545 is to be passed to the foundation under Gift Aid, with the payment to be made in 2006. The balance will be retained in the trading subsidiary as working capital. In addition to the above donations and income, the foundation received £105,448 in bank interest (2004: £100,657).

## In-kind support

Gifts in kind of £297,566 were donated by Reuters Limited (2004: £177,749). Services provided to AlertNet by other external partners are valued at £188,500 (2004: £108,500). In total, Gifts in Kind of £486,066 (2004: £286,249) were received by Reuters Foundation in the year.

## Employee-led support

In May 2004, Reuters Foundation launched its first annual Community Events Week. The worldwide volunteering programme gives Reuters' employees an opportunity to use a workday to become involved in community activities. Community Events Week gives Reuters' staff a chance to support the communities in which they operate and also aims to improve employee productivity by encouraging teamwork and the development of skills which can also be used at work. Examples of staff participation range from building houses with Habitat for Humanity around the world to holding a computer carnival for 150 senior citizens in Hong Kong. Building on the enthusiasm shown by employees for house building projects, the company are now looking at offering employees further opportunities to build in areas of New Orleans affected by Hurricane Katrina, and KwaZulu Natal, South Africa, as part of a programme to provide housing to families devastated by AIDS.

In 2005, 1,856 employees from 42 countries (12% of employees) participated in the scheme, undertaking a range of challenges. The projects ranged from hosted school visits, children's events and fundraising to conservation work.

During May 2005, the company held a second programme of community volunteering and involvement and have noted an increasing level of participation. 1,856 staff (12%) from 42 locations took part in 164 projects. Comparative data from 2004 reported 1,796 volunteers (12%) from 36 locations taking part in 120 projects.

Having moved the company's head quarters to Canary Wharf in 2005, London based staff were invited to a 'Know Your Neighbours' event which helped to introduce them to local community groups and organisations in need of their support. Following this session, many staff have been able to share their skills with local groups including business mentoring, office design work, IT skills training and website development.

In addition, Reuters operate programmes in the US and UK which match the donations and fundraising efforts of employees. 2006 will see the launch of a similar scheme for employees across Asia.

# Rexam plc

4 Millbank, London SW1P 3XR

020 7227 4100; Fax: 020 7227 4109

Website: www.rexam.com

Correspondent: Kate Trumper, PA to Director of Corporate Communications

Chief officer: Rolf Borjesson

Chief Executive: Lars Emilson

| Year end | Turnover | Pre-tax profit |
|---|---|---|
| 31/12/2005 | £3,237,000,000 | £331,000,000 |

**Nature of company business**
Rexam plc is an international consumer packaging company and beverage can maker.

**Subsidiaries include:** Bowater Security Products Ltd, W H S Halo, Business Printing Group, Staybrite Windows, McCorquodale Card Technology, Cox and Wyman, McCorquodale Engineering Ltd, Cartham Papers, Broadprint Ltd, Bowater Windows Ltd, Bowater Business Forms Ltd, TBS, Laser Image Ltd, Essex Business Forms, Zenith Windows

**Main locations:** Stevenage, Wakefield, Milton Keynes, Deeside, Luton, London, Tonbridge

**Total employees:** 25,500

## Charitable donations

2005: £68,000
2004: £98,000
2003: £98,000

## Community involvement

The company's annual report states: 'Management teams are encouraged to invest in local charities, voluntary groups and other suitable initiatives. Instead of a centralised sponsorship programme, the company encourages its staff to participate in whatever activities local people consider most important. This may include work with local charities, voluntary groups and other initiatives.'

### Exclusions

Previous information stated that there is no support available for: advertising in charity brochures; animal welfare; appeals from individuals; overseas projects; political appeals; religious appeals; or sport. Sponsorships are not usually undertaken.

### Applications

In writing to the correspondent.

**Other information:** The company produce a corporate environmental and social report. Copies can be downloaded from its website.

## Corporate giving

In 2005, the company's UK cash donations amounted to £68,000 (2004: £98,000). The two main recipients were the Prince's Trust and the British Occupational Health Research Foundation.

Worldwide donations, including the above, totalled £790,000 (2004: £257,000). The significant rise is mainly accounted for by support given to the relief efforts following the earthquake and tsunami in Asia and the hurricane in the United States.

## In-kind support

The Rexam Healthcare Flexibles plant at Winterbourne in the UK has established a 'Business Partnership with Education' with the local high school to support students in a wide range of business practice and work experience.

## Employee-led support

The company matches employees' fundraising efforts on behalf of charities of their choice.

**Payroll giving:** The company operates the Give As You Earn scheme.

# Richer Sounds plc

Unit 3/4, Richer House, Gallery Court, Hankey Place, London SE1 4BB

020 7357 9298; Fax: 020 7357 8685

Website: www.persula.org

Correspondent: Ed Gates, Projects Manager Persula Foundation
E-mail: info@persula.org

| Year end | Turnover | Pre-tax profit |
|---|---|---|
| 29/04/2006 | £81,834,000 | £3,636,000 |

Nature of company business
Hi-fi retail.

Main locations: London

UK employees: 349

Total employees: 349

## Community involvement

The Persula Foundation was initiated by the founder of Richer Sounds plc. It is a registered charity (Charity Commission no. 1044174), established in 1994 as an independent grant-giving foundation. The main objects of the foundation are to support charitable organisations and develop original charitable projects. The foundation's current priorities are the homeless, disablement, human rights and animal welfare. The following is an extract from the charity's financial statements for the year 2005:

'The Persula Foundation is not only committed to straightforward donations, but we aim to add value to original and the most needed areas of communitywide and nationwide projects, and the majority of our funds are set aside for this purpose. Through supporting our own research groups to develop creative projects, our aim is achieved. Our main priorities have been in the areas of human welfare focusing on such areas as the homeless, the disabled and the victimised, as well as animal welfare. In our priority areas we can offer commercial advice in many ways, such as business and marketing advice.'

### Exclusions

No support for circular appeals, advertising in charity brochures, appeals from individuals, the arts, education, enterprise/training, fundraising events, medical research, overseas projects, political/religious appeals, science/ technology, sport or large national appeals.

Money for core costs, buildings/building work or to statutory bodies is not given.

Sponsorship is not undertaken.

### Applications

In writing to the correspondent.

## Corporate giving

In 2005, the foundation had a total income of £780,723 (2004: £1,440,074). All incoming resources were unrestricted funds. Donations from individuals were £564,200 (2004: £1,369,812) and from corporate donors £216,523 (2004: £70,262). Charitable expenditure for 2005 totalled £351,387 (2004: £246,512).

The following extract is again taken from the foundation's financial statement for 2005:

'During the 12 months ended 30 April 2005 the generic research groups of The Persula Foundation continued their work and support of various projects established within the previous year as well as supporting new projects such as support for Action Against ME for their unique counselling service across the UK; support for Spinal Research with design work for their 'Runners Network'; assisting the Apex Trust with support for their Job-Check helpline ; and support for Amnesty International for their new Human Rights Action Centre.

'Ongoing projects which continued to run successfully in 2004/2005 included the 'On The Right Track Project' providing free touch-screen computerised kiosks for homeless people and young runaways and 'Tapesense' our mail-order service which offers subsidised, brand new blank audio cassettes, and popular hi fi accessories including the revolutionary Pure Digital Sonus 1 XT Talking Digital Radio' to Blind and Visually Impaired people (over 5,000 products sent out every week).

'We have continued to develop our 'Storytelling Tour' project giving over 430 free sessions of wonderful storytelling and music to visually impaired, disabled children and adults including the elderly throughout the UK and expenditure increased from £25,678 to over £38,424 in the last 12 months which was due to us holding more sessions within each tour and expanding our 'troop' of professional Storytellers working on the project.

'Our prospective future work will continue to be through out generic research groups which will continue to research and offer support and commercial advice to existing charities across the UK. There are also plans to extend regional projects to a nationwide level for greater impact.'

Past beneficiaries have included: Bridge Housing Association; Kidscape; League Against Cruel Sports; National Missing Persons Helpline; and Royal National Institute for the Deaf.

### In-kind support

The foundation also has access to many resources from the company, such as marketing, design and strategic consultation. It prefers to use these resources to provide an added value aspect to its collaboration with organisations. It also offers support in the form of time and resources. 'Tapesense', the foundation's mail-order service, offers subsidised, brand new blank audio cassettes, and popular hi fi accessories to blind and visually impaired people.

### Employee-led support

The company supports employee volunteering, allowing paid time off work to volunteers and matching employee fundraising.

# Rio Tinto plc

6 St James's Square, London SW1Y 4LD

020 7930 2399; Fax: 020 7930 3429

Website: www.riotinto.com

Correspondent: External Affairs

Chief officer: Paul Skinner

**Chief Executive:** Leigh Clifford

| Year end | Turnover | Pre-tax profit |
|---|---|---|
| 31/12/2005 | £10,460,565,000 | £3,021,709,000 |

**Nature of company business**
Rio Tinto is one of the world's largest mining companies. Based in the UK, Rio Tinto has substantial worldwide interests in metals and industrial minerals with major assets in Australia, South America, Asia, Europe and Southern Africa.

**Subsidiaries include:** Anglesey Aluminium Ltd

**Main locations:** London

**UK employees:** 1,000

**Total employees:** 28,000

### Charitable donations
2005: £2,700,000
2004: £2,100,000
2003: £400,000

Membership: BitC, L B Group

## Community involvement

Rio Tinto group companies around the world give active support to their local communities, both directly and through independently managed foundations.

We were previously informed that following a review of its community support programme in the UK, Rio Tinto has restated its objectives to align with those of its statement of business practice *The way we work*. Support will now be concentrated on communities in close proximity to its group businesses. The 2005 annual report states: 'Rio Tinto sets out to build enduring relationships with its neighbours that are characterised by mutual respect, active partnership, and long term commitment.

Every business unit is required to have rolling five year community plans which are updated annually. In 2004, a series of pilot studies were completed aimed at achieving a deeper level of understanding of the linkages between mining activities and the economies in which they take place.

All group businesses produce their own reports for their local communities and other audiences. Community assurance of the quality and content of these reports is increasing. This provides an opportunity for engagement with the community on their views of programmes sponsored by the operations.

### Exclusions
No support is given, directly or indirectly, to any sectarian, religious or political activity. No funding is provided for building projects or general running costs, nor for advertising in charity brochures. Support is not given to individuals, animal welfare or any sporting events.

### Applications
In writing to the correspondent.

## Corporate giving

Donations in the UK during 2005 amounted to £2.7 million (2004: £2.1 million) of which £0.5 million (2004: £0.4 million) was for charitable purposes as defined by the Companies Act 1985 and £2.2 million (2004: £1.7 million) for other community purposes.

Worldwide, businesses managed by Rio Tinto contributed US$93.4 million to community programmes in 2005 (2004: US$87.8 million) calculated on the basis of the London Benchmarking Group model. Of the total contributions, US$37.3 million was community investment and US$29 million in direct payments made under legislation or an agreement with a local community.

# RM plc

New Mill House, 183 Milton Park, Abingdon, Oxfordshire OX14 4SE

01235 826000; Fax: 01235 826999

Website: www.rm.com

**Correspondent:** Claire Mann, HR Officer

**Chief officer:** John Leighfield

**Chief Executive:** Tim Pearson

| Year end | Turnover | Pre-tax profit |
|---|---|---|
| 30/09/2005 | £263,000,000 | £12,800,000 |

**Nature of company business**
The main activities are the supply of IT solutions to educational markets, based upon PC technology and incorporating networking, software and services.

**Subsidiaries include:** Softease, Helicon, Sentinel Products, TTS (Technology Teaching Systems), Forvus, 3T Productions Ltd

**Main locations:** Glasgow, Cheadle, Otley, Sheffield, Abingdon

**UK employees:** 2,137

**Total employees:** 2,137

### Charitable donations
2005: £35,000
2004: £59,000
2003: £35,000

## Community involvement

Support is mainly focused on the two charities chosen by staff, one of which is nominated as the 'Charity of the Year'. Some smaller support is available for locally-based community projects in which staff have a personal interest or involvement. To serve as a focal point for the company's charitable fundraising activities, a foundation has been established.

**Charity of the Year:** Marie Curie Cancer Care (2005).

### Exclusions
No support for local appeals not in areas of company presence, general or circular appeals and individuals.

### Applications
In writing to the correspondent.

## Corporate giving

During 2005 the company made various charitable donations totalling £33,000. A further £2,000 was given in locally-based community support projects.

**The RM Charitable Foundation**

Through the foundation (which is not registered with the Charity Commission), the company supports two charities chosen by RM staff: Volunteer Reading Help, an educational charity, with which the company is building a long-term relationship; and a charity of the year (see above). The foundation also 'tops-up' money raised by staff for these charities.

### In-kind support

In 2005, the Dudley Grid for Learning project replaced 7,000 computers. The RM project team worked in partnership with the charity Digital Links International to send these computers to schools in Africa, playing an important part in improving the life chances of thousands of children across Africa.

### Employee-led support

The company adds 33% of any money raised by staff to The RM Charitable Foundation. The foundation runs a community-support programme which allows staff to apply for charitable donations to support causes and projects in which they are personally interested in or involved with.

Every employee can choose to devote a small amount of work time each year to support one of RM's two chosen charities.

RM staff are also encouraged to serve as local school governors.

# Roche Products Ltd

Hexagon Place, 6 Falcon Way, Shire Park, Welwyn Garden City, Hertfordshire AL7 1TW

01707 366000; Fax: 01707 338297

Website: www.rocheuk.com

Correspondent: Corporate Affairs
E-mail: welwyn.corporate_affairs@roche.com

| Year end | Turnover | Pre-tax profit |
|---|---|---|
| 31/12/2005 | £345,789,000 | £14,940,000 |

**Nature of company business**
Principal activity: the manufacture and sale of pharmaceutical products used in human health care.

**Subsidiaries include:** Bohringer Products Ltd, De Puy Inc

**Main locations:** Welwyn Garden City, Lewes

**Total employees:** 1,285

### Charitable donations

2005: £61,000
2004: £99,000
2003: £10,000

## Community involvement

'Each year, Roche in the UK supports a corporate charity as well as a wide range of charities and organisations, primarily based in our local communities but some at a national level where we can support efforts to raise awareness of important health issues.

Roche's relationship with patient organisations and healthcare charities is governed by the Association of the British Pharmaceutical Industry Code of Practice, which requires that our involvement with voluntary healthcare organisations must be made clear.'

A list of the patient organisations who work collaboratively with Roche can be found on the company's website.

### Applications

In writing to the correspondent.

## Corporate giving

In the year 2005 the company donated £61,000 for charitable purposes. (£99,000 in 2004).

### Employee-led support

Employees are encouraged to contribute to their community.

# Rolls–Royce plc

65 Buckingham Gate, London SW1E 6AT

020 7222 9020

Website: www.rolls-royce.com

Correspondent: Charles E Blundell, Company Secretary

Chief officer: Simon Robertson

Chief Executive: Sir John E V Rose

| Year end | Turnover | Pre-tax profit |
|---|---|---|
| 31/12/2005 | £6,603,000,000 | £477,000,000 |

**Nature of company business**
Rolls-Royce is a global company providing power on land, sea and air.

**Subsidiaries include:** Vickers plc, NEI Overseas Holdings Ltd, Vickers Engineering plc, Sourcerer Ltd

**Main locations:** Bristol, Derby, Dounreay, East Kilbride, Hucknall, Hillington, Newcastle, London, Sunderland, Barnoldswick, Ansty

**Total employees:** 35,214

### Charitable donations

2005: £671,000
2003: £397,000

Total community contributions: £5,124,000
Management costs: £430,000

Membership: A & B, BitC, L B Group

## Community involvement

The company established the Group Community Investment Committee (Group CIC) in 2003 to oversee the implementation and operation of a new, group-wide policy on charitable donations. The Group CIC is supported by a series of national committees which operate within the policy established by the Group CIC. The policy is as follows:

'The company's policy on donations is to direct its support primarily to causes with educational, engineering and scientific objectives, as well as to social objectives connected with the company's business and place in the wider community.'

### Exclusions

No support for advertising in charity brochures, political appeals, religious appeals, or local appeals not in areas of company presence.

### Applications

In writing to the correspondent.

## Corporate giving

In 2005, total worldwide community contributions were £5.12 million. Of this, charitable donations amounted to £1.48 million, arts and education sponsorship to £1.7 million, staff time/gifts in kind to £1.94 million, and management costs to £430,000.

Charitable donations in the UK amounted to £671,000 and included support for The Prince's Trust, Community Foundations, SS Great Britain, The Industrial Trust and Duxford AirSpace.

A list of the principal donations made in the year is available on written request to the Company Secretary.

In response to the tsunami disaster in south east Asia, the group contributed £250,000 in 2004 and an additional £250,000 in 2005 to match employee donations. Funding is being used to support a number of projects in the affected areas, including the construction of a primary care clinic in Aceh, Indonesia, the construction of a school in India and other projects in Thailand.

### In-kind support

The group offers support in-kind to local initiatives including providing places on in-house training programmes; donating surplus computer equipment and furniture; and offering the free use of meeting rooms and premises.

### Employee-led support

The company supports employees' volunteering/charitable activities by allowing time off in which to volunteer and through financial support.

**Payroll giving:** The company operates the Sharing the Caring payroll giving scheme. In 2005, the scheme helped employees make donations of over £396,000 to over 200 charities of their choice. 16% of employees participate.

### Commercially-led support

**Sponsorship:** In addition to charitable donations, contributions of £1,700,000 were made by the group's sponsorship committee and individual business groups, primarily to support arts and educational programmes.

# Royal & Sun Alliance Insurance Group plc

Level 6, Leadenhall Court, Leadenhall Street, London EC3V 1PP

Website: www.royalsunalliance.com

Correspondent: Paul Pritchard, Corporate Responsibility Manager

Chief officer: John Napier

Chief Executive: Andy Haste

| Year end | Turnover | Pre-tax profit |
|---|---|---|
| 31/12/2005 | £5,400,000,000 | £865,000,000 |

### Nature of company business

The company's principal activity is the transaction of personal and commercial general insurance business.

**Subsidiaries include:** The London Assurance, Phoenix Assurance plc, Royal Insurance Holdings plc, Swinton (Holdings) Ltd, RSA E-Holdings Ltd, The Marine Insurance Co Ltd, Sun Insurance Office Ltd, Legal Protection Goup Holdings Ltd, FirstAssist Group Ltd, Royal International Insurance Holdings Ltd, The Globe Insurance Co Ltd

**Main locations:** Belfast, Birmingham, Glasgow, Horsham, Leeds, Bristol, Manchester, Liverpool, London

UK employees: 13,045

Total employees: 39,157

### Charitable donations

2005: £530,000
2003: £793,000

Total community contributions: £540,000
Management costs: £90,000

Membership: BitC, L B Group

## Community involvement

Royal & Sun Alliance's 2005 Corporate Responsibility Report stated: 'Throughout 2005 we continued to support local UK communities through our network of regional community investment committees. Employees participated in a wide range of activities from volunteering through to sponsored runs and dress down days in support of local causes, including our second National Charity Day. We celebrated the Year of the Volunteer in 2005 through a National Volunteer Initiative. This involved a number of team events across the region where employees spent time out of the office working on local community projects, including a three day project to landscape a care home garden and several school projects where classrooms and outside facilities were renovated.

'We have continued to rollout our partnership with Samaritans, focusing on emotional health promotion. Samaritans are aiming to provide coping skills and to change societal attitudes towards emotional health. We have worked with them to develop material for both school and workplace projects with the aim of enabling Samaritans to develop a secure, long term source of potential funding.'

### Exclusions

There are few circumstances in which the company is able to provide support outside this policy framework. Therefore, applicants such as political, religious appeals, social or animal welfare, overseas projects or environment/heritage are not considered, nor can charities whose work mainly benefits people overseas or individuals seeking personal or professional sponsorship. Requests received by circular are not actioned.

### Applications

Generally applications should be in writing to the correspondent above. However, given the decision to focus on supporting the education of young people through a three year partnership with the Samaritans, successful unsolicited applications are likely to be limited.

## Corporate giving

In 2005, the company made worldwide charitable donations of £744,412. In the UK, according to figures published by the London Benchmarking Group, cash donations totalled £530,000 of which the largest donation was £250,000 to the Samaritans. A further £10,000 was given in gifts in kind, with £90,000 spent in management costs.

The company has also been working with the UK environmental charity, Trees for Cities (www.treesforcities.org), to raise awareness of more appropriate tree planting to help reduce subsidence incidents.

### In-kind support

Non-cash support includes staff involvement, gifts in kind, training schemes, and use of resources (premises and equipment).

### Employee-led support

As well as corporate support, company employees raised an additional £70,000 for the Samaritans at a local and national level, with a number of employees having trained to become Samaritans volunteers.

The company has been working with Business in the Community on a site by site basis to identify opportunities for increasing employee involvement in volunteering, drawing on their extensive network of contacts to identify appropriate local activities.

**Payroll giving:** Through the company payroll, the Give As You Earn scheme enables staff and pensioners to make tax-efficient donations to any charity of their choice. The company matches this to a value of £100 per donor per month.

# The Royal Bank of Scotland Group plc

Business House F, PO Box 1000, Gogarburn, Edinburgh, United Kingdom, EH12 1 HQ

0131 626 3660; Fax: 0131 626 3074

**Website:** www.rbs.com/community

**Correspondent:** Stephen Moir, Head of Community Investment
0131 626 4190; Fax: 0131 626 0742
E-mail: corporate.responsibility@rbs.co.uk

**Chief officer:** Sir Tom McKillop

**Chief Executive:** Sir Fred Goodwin

| Year end | Turnover | Pre-tax profit |
|----------|----------|----------------|
| 31/12/2005 | £25,569,000,000 | £7,936,000,000 |

**Nature of company business**
The Royal Bank of Scotland is one of the world's largest financial services organisations and is engaged in a wide range of banking, insurance and financial services.

**Subsidiaries include:** Direct Line Insurance Group, RBS Insurance Group Limited, NatWest Bank plc, Ulster Bank plc

**Main locations:** Edinburgh

**UK employees:** 103,000

---

**Charitable donations**

2005: £38,999,064
2004: £20,100,000
2003: £14,700,000

Total community contributions: £53,833,487
Management costs: £2,371,045

Membership: A & B, BitC, L B Group, %Club

---

## Community involvement

In the UK, the group's community investment programme is focused in two areas: business-led activity and employee-led activity.

The business driven programme focuses on issues central to the group's business: helping people to access financial services and money advice, helping people to better understand and effectively manage their money and helping to stimulate and support enterprise.

The employee-led programme supports the group employees who are active in the community as volunteers, fundraisers and payroll givers.

Donations and support of charities, community groups and local organisations are through employee-led involvement.

### Exclusions

In backing the fundraising and volunteer efforts of employees the group does not support charities direct with grants, general funding contributions, core costs, charity advertising, sponsorships of events in aid of charity, individuals/team fundraising for charities

### Applications

Applications forms are not used. Please apply in writing to the correspondent for your initiative to be considered.

## Corporate giving

In 2005, the group made global community contributions of £56.2 million, of which £39 million was in cash, £12.8 million in gifts in kind, £1.9 million in employee time and £2.3 million in management costs.

It is not known how much of this support was to the benefit of UK-based organisations. Management costs (i.e. the cost of administering the group's community support programme) have risen significantly – up from £1.72 million in 2004.

**Business-led activity**

Face to face money advice – A £1.8 million partnership with money advice organisations such as Citizens Advice to improve the quality of free, independent money advice for people facing serious problems with debt.

Supergrounds – A £3 million, three-year community programme funded by RBS Group. Helping 450 primary schools from around the UK, the Supergrounds programme, in partnership with the charities Learning through Landscapes and Groundwork UK aims to transform school grounds into more fun and creativity play areas. Schools are nominated through local staff.

The Prince's Trust – A £5 million partnership which helps disadvantaged 14 to 25 years old realise their potential and transform lives by offering training, mentoring and financial assistance.

Face 2 Face with finance – a unique programme delivers personal finance lessons to young people. Group staff work with teachers to deliver lessons and interactive activities.

In addition, through the RBS Financial Inclusion Innovation Fund, grants totalling over £100,000 were awarded in 2005 to a variety of voluntary and charitable organisations working in this area. Administered by Transact, the national forum for financial inclusion, further details and an application form can be found at www.transact.org.uk

Beneficiaries in 2005 included: Addaction (£25,000); Golden Gates Housing (£23,500); Fair Finance (£20,000); Mind (£20,000); My Time (£20,000); and, West Somerset Advice Bureaux (£15,000).

## In-kind support

Group employees are encouraged to get involved in projects funded from the Community programme and in 2005 over 650 employees volunteered with the Prince's Trust. Staff in the Group spent 123,469 hours on community activities during work hours.

## Employee-led support

### Employee-led activity

Charities and community groups are supported through the employee-led programme. The programme generated £12m for 8,500 good causes in 2005 through the direct involvement of 25,000 employees helping as fundraisers, volunteers or payroll gives.

RBS group is the only employer to double match employees' donations to charity made through Give As You Earn. For every £1 donated directly by staff, from their pay, the Group donates a further £2. Over 14,000 employees currently take part in the scheme.

Employees who help good causes with their time, effort and skills can apply for a Community Cashback Award for their organisation. In 2005, the Group made 7,000 awards ranging from £100 to £1,000.

## Commercially-led support

**Sponsorship:** The bank has three main areas of sponsorship – sports, the arts and agriculture.

*The arts* – Support is usually focused on national, quality non-profit making organisations, such as the Edinburgh International Book Festival. Other events recently sponsored include: Edinburgh Military Tattoo, Royal Highland Show, Royal Bank Street Party, Kelvingrove Art Gallery and many more.

*Sport* – 'Our main sports sponsorships are in Rugby (RBS 6 Nations), F1 (Williams F1), Golf (Open Golf, Jack Nicklaus and other RBS players) and Tennis (Andrew Murray).

For further details of our sponsorships please look at our website www.RBS.com'

Please note that sponsorship is not generally undertaken with respect to: individuals; teams, clubs or societies; fundraising events; publications, videos, films, recordings or website development.

Contact: Proposals should be addressed to David Webb, Head of Sponsorship (tel: 0131 626 3886).

# The Royal London Mutual Insurance Society Ltd

Royal London House, Alderley Road, Wilmslow SK9 1PF

01625 605416; Fax: 01625 605406

Website: www.royallondongroup.com

Correspondent: Jane Relf, Head of Internal Communications

Chief officer: Tim Melville-Ross

| Year end | Turnover | Pre-tax profit |
|---|---|---|
| 31/12/2005 | £4,430,000,000 | |

**Nature of company business**
Principal activities: the group's businesses offer pensions, life assurance, savings and investment products, protection insurance and provide investment management.

**Subsidiaries include:** Scottish Life, Bright Grey, Scottish Life International

**Main locations:** London, Wilmslow, Edinburgh, Douglas

UK employees: 2,854

Total employees: 2,854

### Charitable donations
2005: £70,128
2004: £88,803
2003: £46,099
Membership: BitC

## Community involvement

Royal London's policy of adding value to community wherever possible is delivered through its Helping Hand initiative. The policy has three main elements: (i) a national charity partner; (ii) grass roots involvement with local community initiatives around the main offices in London, Edinburgh, Wilmslow and Douglas as well as branch offices; and, (iii) employee matched donation scheme.

**Charity of the Year:** Marie Curie Cancer Care (2006).

### Exclusions

No support for advertising in charity brochures, animal welfare, appeals from individuals, environment/heritage, overseas projects, political appeals, or religious appeals.

### Applications

In writing to the correspondent to whom sponsorship proposals should also be addressed. Further information on the company's donations policy and how to apply are available.

## Corporate giving

In 2005, the society made donations of over £70,000 to charities and community organisations. Some of the organisations supported include Child Victim Support, Northwest Air Ambulance, Institute for Neuro-physiological Psychology, St Colombas Hospice, The Treloar Trust and Blackfriars Settlement.

## Employee-led support

An employee-matched donation scheme exists – matching employees' fundraising for individual charities up to £250 per person, per year.

During 2005, employees received over £29,000 in matched donations. Charities benefiting from this included: National Children's Home, Maggies Scotland, World Vision UK, British Heart Foundation, Cancer Research UK, Francis House Children's hospice and Alzheimer's Society.

**Payroll giving:** The company operates a payroll giving scheme.

## Commercially-led support

**Sponsorship:** Arts and good-cause sponsorship are undertaken by the company.

# Royal Mail Group plc

148 Old Street, London EC1V 9HQ

020 7250 2243; Fax: 020 7250 2729

Website: www.royalmailgroup.com

Correspondent: The Charities Committee

Chief Executive: Adam Crozier

| Year end | Turnover | Pre-tax profit |
|---|---|---|
| 28/03/2005 | £8,956,000,000 | £207,000,000 |

**Nature of company business**
This is the parent company of Royal Mail, Parcelforce and the Post Office.

Main locations: London

UK employees: 193,000

> **Charitable donations**
> 2005: £2,000,000
> 2004: £600,000
>
> Membership: A & B, BitC, L B Group

## Community involvement

The company's charity partner is Help the Hospices, and its objectives in this relationship are stated as follows:

- to raise at least £1,000,000 from the campaign, including the £250,000 contribution from Royal Mail Group;
- to recruit 2,500 new payroll giving donors for Help the Hospices or local hospices during the course of the partnership;
- to have 20,000 of our people involved in volunteering activities with hospices by the end of the campaign;
- to explore opportunities for Cause Related Marketing activities.

## Applications

In writing to the correspondent. It appears that local organisations can also apply directly to their regional office for support.

## Corporate giving

In 2004/05 the company gave £2,000,000 in cash donations and in-kind support.

### In-kind support

**Education:** Resources have been created to teach primary school children, including educational packs concerning the role of Post Offices and how letters are delivered.

### Employee-led support

Staff are encouraged to volunteer and employees are available for secondments. A small financial contribution is made to chosen causes, including for fundraising efforts.

**Payroll giving:** The company operates a scheme managed on its behalf by the Charities Trust. Currently around 40,000 employees donate over £2.3 million a year. These donations are supported by the company by additional donations (£50,000 in 2004).

# RWE npower

Trigonos, Windmill Hill Business Park, Whitehill Way, Swindon, Wiltshire SN5 6PB

01793 877777; Fax: 01793 892781

Website: www.rwenpower.com

Correspondent: Carol Hart, Corporate Charity Officer

Chief Executive: Harry Roels

| Year end | Turnover | Pre-tax profit |
|---|---|---|
| 31/12/2005 | | |

**Nature of company business**
Electricity generation and supply; water supply.

Main locations: Worcester, Swindon

> **Charitable donations**
> 2005: £496,000
> 2003: £280,000
>
> Membership: BitC, %Club

## Community involvement

Following a successful two-year partnership with Macmillan Cancer Relief, during which time £1 million was raised for the charity, employee feedback has led to the partnership being extended until the end of 2007.

### Exclusions

Support is NOT given to: advertising in charity brochures, animal welfare, appeals from individuals, the arts, heritage, fundraising events, political appeals, religious appeals, science/technology or sport.

### Applications

In writing to the correspondent.

## Corporate giving

In 2005 the company made donations to 67 charities totalling £496,000.

## In-kind support

In partnership with the charity National Energy Action and the NHS, the company has been involved in the 'Health Through Warmth' scheme, which identifies people at risk through cold and damp homes.

## Employee-led support

**Payroll giving:** The company operates the Give As You Earn scheme. The company also matched employees' charitable donations to a total of £154,000.

## Commercially-led support

**Sponsorship:** The company undertakes good-cause sponsorship.

*Contact:* Proposals should be addressed to the Sponsorship Manager, Corporate Communications.

# Saga Leisure Ltd

Saga Building, Enbrook Park, Sandgate, Folkestone, Kent CT20 3SE

01303 771111; Fax: 01303 256676

Website: www.saga.co.uk

Correspondent: Helen Hall, PA to Janice Lee, Director Saga Charitable Trust

Nature of company business
Tour operators and financial services.

Subsidiaries include: MetroMail Ltd, Inter-Church Travel Ltd

Main locations: Folkstone

## Charitable donations

Membership: A & B, BitC

## Community involvement

The Saga Charitable Trust (Charity Commission no. 291991) is constituted by Trust Deed dated 1st May 1985 and is funded by the Saga Group of companies, its customers and staff, with the objective of funding worthy projects at destinations that feature in tour programmes operated by Saga Holidays Ltd.

The trust supports projects that will empower and benefit under-privileged local communities at destinations in developing countries that host Saga holidaymakers. Primarily, this covers the Far East, the Indian sub-continent, South Africa and South America.

A director and PA are employed by the trust and those costs are met by Saga Group Limited.

The trust reports further expansion and growth in 2004/05 with the opening of the Himaljyoti Community School in Nepal, the La Paz nursery in Peru, and a school library in Sri Lanka. The trust has embarked on its first project in India, by helping to set up a shelter for street children at New Delhi Railway Station and a mentorship programme in South Africa is having a significant impact on childcare in the region. The Indian Ocean Reconstruction Appeal, launched in January 2005, raised funds to help communities affected by the tsunami to rebuild their lives. The trust's objective was to help with the reconstruction process, once the relief phase was over, by identifying and supporting sustainable grassroots projects that would benefit those most in need.

The trust is expecting to take on more new projects in the forthcoming year and we have been informed by the trust that they will consider applications from UK registered charities where the proposals are 'small scale' and for causes in the developing world as described above.

## Exclusions

No support for advertising in charity brochures; animal welfare; the arts; enterprise/training; fundraising events; medical research; political appeals; religious appeals; science/ technology; or sport.

## Applications

We are advised that The Saga Charitable Trust will consider small-scale proposals from UK registered charities operating in the developing world. For further information apply in writing to the correspondent.

## Corporate giving

Unfortunately we have been unable to obtain financial information regarding Saga Group; however, the following information has been taken from the Financial Statements of The Saga Charitable Trust for the year ending 5th April 2005.

For the year ending 5th April 2005 the trust reports that the unrestricted incoming resources £83,881. During the year £155,123 was expended for direct charitable purposes. A donation of £70,000 was made by Saga Group Ltd on 12th April 2005.

The designated fund set up as an appeal for donations to help the victims of the Asian tsunami crisis of 26th December 2004 had incoming resources of £125,173.

Since the year end a number of projects have already been funded to help affected communities in Sri Lanka and Thailand.

A Christmas appeal in the Saga Magazine generated £8,966 and customers and crew aboard the 2004 Saga Rose World cruise raised £13,886 to establish and support a market garden project in South Africa.

## In-kind support

The Saga Group Limited has provided donations-in-kind of facilities, staff time and the trust's overheads and administrative costs.

## Employee-led support

Local fundraising events supported by Saga staff have included a 70's night, a book sale and a quiz evening and the Saga Charitable Trust continues to receive donations from Saga customers who have visited projects whilst on holiday.

# J Sainsbury plc

33 Holborn, London EC1N 2HT

0845 074 2618

Website: www.j-sainsbury.co.uk/csr

Correspondent: Sainsbury's Community Affairs Helpline 0845 074 2618

Chief officer: Philip Hampton

Chief Executive: Justin King

| Year end | Turnover | Pre-tax profit |
|---|---|---|
| 25/03/2006 | £16,061,000,000 | £104,000,000 |

**Nature of company business**
The group's principal activities are food retailing, financial services and property development. The group is composed of Sainsbury's Supermarkets, Shaws Supermarkets and Sainsbury's Bank. It has a total of 683 stores operating in the United Kingdom and the United States.

**Main locations:** London

**UK employees:** 153,300

---

**Charitable donations**

2005: £2,340,000
2004: £1,600,000

Total community contributions: £5,600,000

CRM figure: £12,500,000

Membership: BitC, L B Group, %Club

---

## Community involvement

J Sainsbury's community investment focuses on two areas: support for charities and other organisations promoting healthy eating and active living, particularly with children, and donating food to homeless hostels and other charities to provide nutritious meals for people in need.

### Exclusions

No response to circulars. No support for advertising in charity brochures, individuals, enterprise/training, environment/ heritage, medical research, science/technology, social welfare, restoration/fabric of buildings, National Health projects, overseas projects, local appeals not in areas of company presence, political or religious causes, core or pump priming.

### Applications

Appeals to the head office should be addressed to the correspondent. Applications can be received at any time, and should include details of aims and objectives, target audience and PR opportunities. Local appeals should be sent to local stores who will then approach the donations committee. This meets quarterly, but a sub-committee meets as and when necessary.

A separate budget exists for small donations to local charities/ voluntary groups, administered at store level, in the form of vouchers (see below).

There are also a number of Sainsbury Family Trusts with major grant-making programmes. These are administered separately (see *A Guide to the Major Trusts*), although close contact is maintained with the company's donations programme.

**Information available:** The company publishes its social report on the 'Responsibility' section of its website.

**Advice to applicants:** Sainsbury's advises applicants to try to avoid stereotyped circulars. All appeals are responded to, but charities often underestimate the time required for consideration of their appeals. So, applicants should be patient!

## Corporate giving

UK community contributions to charitable organisations and other community projects totalled £5.6 million in 2005/06. Unfortunately, this was not broken down between cash and in-kind support. A further £12.5 million (at cost) was donated through the 'Active Kids' cause-related marketing scheme.

**Education:** *Taste of Success* – Sainsbury's Taste of Success promotes food education in schools with food awards for pupils aged 5–16, teacher training sessions and an educational website. The emphasis is on recognising and rewarding the good work already going on in schools. The initiative is run in partnership with the British Nutrition Foundation and the Design & Technology Association. Sainsbury's provided £100,000 in funding in 2005/06.

### In-kind support

Sainsbury provides in-kind support in a number of ways, including:

*Food donations* – These are made to charities, such as the Salvation Army, FareShare and the Nehemiah drug rehabilitation project. In 2005/06, the value of food donated was £3.3 million.

*Charity donation boxes* – All stores have a charity donation box for customers' 'loose change', with the money being given to local registered charities.

*Store door collections* – Registered charities can hold cash collections outside our stores by applying in writing to the Store Manager. £3.2 million was raised in 2005/06.

*Gift vouchers* – Stores are allocated small budgets for charitable donations. These are usually in the form of gift vouchers for local groups and charities for use as raffle prizes. The vouchers can be used as a prize themselves or exchanged at any Sainsbury's for suitable goods.

### Employee-led support

'Our stores support local and national charities with their fundraising efforts and help customers and colleagues raise money for good causes. Store colleagues are supported via our Local Heroes awards to make a valuable contribution to causes in their local community.'

Through the Local Heroes awards Sainsbury's recognises the efforts of its staff in supporting local charities and good causes, by giving a donation of £200 to the charities they support.

Local Heroes also provides match funding of up to £500 to support fundraising events at Sainsbury's stores, depots and business centres. Over £250,000 was given in 2005/06.

**Payroll giving:** The company operates the Give As You Earn payroll giving scheme.

### Commercially-led support

**Sponsorship:** Corporate sponsorship requests should also be addressed to Sainsbury's Marketing Department.

**Cause-related marketing:** 'Active Kids' is a nationwide initiative launched in 2005 to encourage schoolchildren to take more exercise through non-traditional activities. Customers earn one 'Active Kids' voucher for every £10 spent. These are then collected and redeemed by schools for activity and sports equipment.

For 2006/07, the scheme has been extended to nursery and special schools, whilst the vouchers can now be used to buy coaching from trained specialists in addition to sports and activity equipment.

Sainsbury's continue to be the national retail partner for Comic Relief's Red Nose Day. Money is raised by selling Red Noses in its stores and through Sainsbury's to You (online shopping). It also works with suppliers to stock products that promote the campaign and include a donation in their price.

# Samsung Electronics (UK) Ltd

1000 Hillswood Drive, Chertsey, Surrey KT16 0PS

01932 455000; Fax: 01932 455400

Website: www.samsung.com/uk/

Correspondent: Keith Donald, HR General Manager, UK

Managing Director: J Park

| Year end | Turnover | Pre-tax profit |
|----------|----------|----------------|
| 31/12/1998 | | |

**Nature of company business**
Samsung Electronics manufacture and distribute electronic and electrical goods. In the UK it manufactures fax machines and colour televisions and designs and develops microwave ovens.

**Main locations:** London, Manchester, Telford, Chertsey, Wynard

**UK employees:** 1,200

**Total employees:** 230,000

## Community involvement

Although the company's global website is quite comprehensive in its reporting of Samsung's community support programmes, coverage is mainly restricted to Korea and the US.

In general, however, the company supports causes concerned with: social welfare; culture and the arts; academia and education; and environmental preservation. However, we understand that financial support in the UK tends to be directed towards the charity/charities 'adopted' by the workforce.

### Applications
In writing to the correspondent.

## Corporate giving

In 2001, Samsung had a worldwide contributions figure of $1,070 million, including the costs of over 10,000 employees' volunteering efforts. Although no UK charitable donation figures were available, we believe its in-kind contributions to be sufficiently high to warrant inclusion.

### Employee-led support

According to the company's website, it has set up more than 300 central offices for Samsung community relations worldwide. Strong encouragement and support is given to employees to actively volunteer for social improvement projects. No UK examples were available.

### Commercially-led support

The company sponsors community events, such as educational projects for young people and environmental volunteering initiatives. It also sponsors sporting and similar events, including an equestrian meeting and the Crufts Dog Show. The Victoria and Albert Museum in London houses the Samsung Gallery.

# Sara Lee UK Holdings Limited

225 Bath Road, Slough, Berkshire SL1 4AU

Website: www.saralee.com

Correspondent: The Charity Manager

Managing Director: Antonious Van. Bilson

**Nature of company business**
Principal activities are: food and beverage; branded apparel; and household products. It operates in 55 countries and has nearly 150,000 employees worldwide.

**Main locations:** Nottingham, Worksop, Slough, Belper

## Community involvement

The company has a structured policy for its grantmaking. Much information is available on the grantmaking activities of The Sara Lee Foundation, which provides grants around its headquarters in Chicago. The foundation's website states that grant policies outside of Chicago are at the discretion of the regional departments (presumably the UK headquarters).

### Applications
In writing to the correspondent.

## Corporate giving

The group donated £45,000 to charities during the year. No details were available on the size or number of grants in this year.

# Savills plc

20 Grosvenor Hill, Berkeley Square, London W1K 3HQ

020 7499 8644; Fax: 020 7495 3773

Website: www.savills.com

Correspondent: Ruth Michelson-Carr, Company Secretary E-mail: rmcarr@savills.com

Chief officer: Peter Smith

Chief Executive: Aubrey Adams

| Year end | Turnover | Pre-tax profit |
|----------|----------|----------------|
| 31/12/2005 | £373,866,000 | £58,579,000 |

**Nature of company business**
Savills plc is a holding company. Its principal subsidiaries' activities are advising on matters affecting commercial, agricultural and residential property, and providing corporate finance advice, property and venture capital funding and a range of property related financial services.

**Subsidiaries include:** NetMortgage Ltd, CMI Project Services Ltd, GHV (Sale) Ltd, Batley Mills Ltd, Grosvenor Hill Ventures Ltd, Grosvenor Hill Properties Ltd, Grosvenor Hill (Southampton) Ltd

**Main locations:** Banbury, Birmingham, Bishop's Storford, Bath, Perth, Salisbury, Solihull, Sevenoaks, Stamford, Southampton, Windsor, Winchester, Wimbourne, Wilmslow, Esher, Harpenden, Cirencester, Canford Cliffs, Beaconsfield, York, London, Manchester, Oxford, Norwich, Nottingham, Chelmsford, Cranbrook, Bristol, Brechin, Cambridge, Telford, Ipswich, Henley,

Lincoln, Glasgow, Exeter, Farnham, Edinburgh, Guildford, Sunningdale

UK employees: 2414

Total employees: 14,516

## Charitable donations

2005: £64,007
2004: £77,000
2003: £41,669

Membership: BitC

## Community involvement

Previous information has suggested the company has a preference for local charities in the areas of operation, appeals relevant to company business and charities in which a member of staff is involved. Preferred areas of support are projects involving medicine, enterprise/training and overseas aid/development.

## Exclusions

Previous information suggested generally no support for advertising in charity brochures, appeals from individuals, purely denominational (religious) appeals or local appeals not in areas of company presence. Unsolicited appeals are unwelcome.

## Applications

In writing to the correspondent who is based at Savills plc, 4th Floor, Landsdowne Road East, 27 Berkeley Square, London W1J 6ER. Local appeals should be addressed to the nearest Savills office, not the head office.

## Corporate giving

In 2005, the group made UK cash donations totalling £64,007 (2004: £77,000). Savills also made additional charitable donations equivalent to 10% of waived annual staff bonus payments. We do not know how much this totalled

No information regarding the beneficiaries was available. However, past beneficiaries have included Mencap, British Heart Foundation, Macmillan Cancer Relief, NSPCC, British Red Cross and Haven Trust.

## Employee-led support

The group offers a bonus waiver whereby employees may elect to waive an element of annual bonus to registered charities of their own choice upon which the group augments the donation to the chosen charity by 10%.

**Payroll giving:** The group operates the Give As You Earn (GAYE) payroll scheme.

These additional group contributions totalled £33,100 (2004 – £13,724) during 2005. No breakdown of this figure was available.

# Schroders plc

31 Gresham Street, London EC2V 7QA

020 7658 6000; Fax: 020 7658 6965

Website: www.schroders.com

**Correspondent:** Caroline Davis, Charity Co-ordinator

**Chief officer:** Michael Miles

**Chief Executive:** Michael Dobson

| Year end | Turnover | Pre-tax profit |
|---|---|---|
| 31/12/2005 | £808,000,000 | £250,700,000 |

**Nature of company business**
Schroders plc is the holding company of an international asset management group. The group is organised into three principal operating divisions on a worldwide basis: Institutional, Retail/Unit Trusts and Private Banking.

**Subsidiaries include:** Milk Street Investments Ltd

**Main locations:** London

**Total employees:** 6,156

## Charitable donations

2005: £271,000
2004: £543,000
2003: £290,000

Membership: %Club

## Community involvement

The company has ceased all its reactive grant-making programmes and now only supports those charitable causes chosen by its employees. The number of charities supported through this is, however, 'significant'.

**Charity of the Year:** Macmillan Cancer Relief (2005).

## Applications

As the company only supports the community involvement of its employees, applications from charities cannot be considered.

**Information available:** The company produce an annual corporate responsibility report.

## Corporate giving

The company stated that all its funds are committed in the matching of employee's donations. In 2005, Schroders made global charitable contributions of £541,000 (2004: £894,000) of which £271,000 (2004: £543,000) was donated in the UK.

## Employee-led support

Employees are encouraged to volunteer, with financial rewards being given to the charity they are involved with. From June 2005, every employee has been given the opportunity to take up to 15 hours paid leave per year to provide volunteer services to the community.

**Payroll giving:** The company operates the Give As You Earn scheme, matching all donations up to certain limits.

Currently, 16% of staff participate in the scheme, making donations totalling £242,000 in 2005.

## Commercially-led support

**Sponsorship:** *The arts* – the company is a corporate member of the Royal Liverpool Philharmonic Orchestra, Royal Opera House and Glyndebourne Festival Society.

# Scottish & Newcastle plc

28 St Andrew Square, Edinburgh EH2 1AF

0131 203 2000

Website: www.scottish-newcastle.com

Correspondent: Eleanor Cannon, Corporate Affairs Manager

Chief officer: Sir Brian Stewart

Chief Executive: Tony G Froggatt

| Year end | Turnover | Pre-tax profit |
|---|---|---|
| 31/12/2005 | £3,260,000,000 | £280,000,000 |

Nature of company business
The group's principal activity is the operation of breweries in 14 countries in Europe and Central Asia.

Main locations: Nottingham, Manchester, Newcastle, Hereford, Edinburgh, Blackburn

UK employees: 7,023

Total employees: 15,600

### Charitable donations

2005: £1,061,648
2004: £528,000
2003: £536,000

Total community contributions: £1,071,648
Management costs: £80,000

Membership: L B Group, %Club

## Community involvement

At the end of 2005 the company produced its first Group Community Policy:

'We have undertaken a comprehensive review of the Group's community investment (CI) activity and this has enabled us to agree a coherent, integrated strategy. This is underpinned by a robust measurement system that will enable the Group to evaluate the benefits of its community investment. The strategy brings all of S&N's community involvement activities – donations, gifts in kind and employee volunteering – within a framework that supports core business priorities. This strategic approach will ensure that S&N is using community involvement to gain maximum benefit for the communities in which it operates, its staff and the business.'

The full impact of this review was due to be analysed in the 2006 annual report.

### Exclusions

Previously, no grants for advertising in charity brochures, appeals from individuals, under-18 age group, fundraising events, medical research, political appeals, religious appeals, or local appeals not in areas of company presence.

Sponsorship of individuals, other than company employees, is not undertaken.

### Applications

In light of the review of community investment taking place within the group, please check the current situation with the company before making an appeal.

Information available: In 2005 the company produced its first Group Community Policy, which outlines its 'Community Investment' policy as follows:

'We aim to support the stakeholders identified above through our community investment policy. This has evolved from our 2004 strategic review, and we have committed to:

- The development of a core strategic programme focused on our core business impact of responsible drinking. We will work in partnership with specialist organisations to develop a programme to support education and prevention in relation to responsible drinking.

- A more streamlined business level programme focused on "Bringing Communities Together". Individual business units will continue to support local community initiatives but under a more focused theme.

- An employee involvement programme to enable employees to volunteer within their own communities and to support their commitments to charitable causes.'

## Corporate giving

In 2005 cash donations by the company totalled £1,061,648 in the UK. In previous years donations were channelled through the Scottish & Newcastle Foundation, although this now seems to have been wound up following a review of the company's community support programme.

### Employee-led support

The company supports staff fundraising through the 'Helping Hand' initiative. The company valued employee volunteering time in the UK at around £5,000 in 2005.

# Scottish and Southern Energy plc

Inveralmond House, 200 Dunkeld Road, Perth PH1 3AQ

01738 456000; Fax: 01738 457005

Website: www.scottish-southern.co.uk

Correspondent: Alan Young, Director of Corporate Communications

Chief officer: Sir Robert Smith

Chief Executive: Ian Marchant

| Year end | Turnover | Pre-tax profit |
|---|---|---|
| 31/03/2006 | £10,145,000,000 | £896,900,000 |

Nature of company business
The group's main business is: the generation, transmission, distribution and supply of electricity to industrial, commercial and domestic customers; electrical and utility contracting; and gas marketing. The group holds the generation, transmission and public supply licence for the north of Scotland, and, through its subsidiary Southern Electric plc, the public supply licence for the south of England, as well as a Gas Supplier's licence.

Subsidiaries include: Scottish Hydro Electricity, SSE Network Solutions, Generation, SSE Power Distribution, Southern Electric Contracting Ltd, Swalec, Neos, hienergyshop, SSE Telecom

Main locations: Perth

UK employees: 12,287

> **Charitable donations**
> 2006: £496,000
> 2005: £400,000
> 2004: £300,000
> 2003: £300,000

## Community involvement

This company was formed by the merger at the end of 1998 of Scottish Hydro-Electric and Southern Electric. We were previously advised that the company prefers to support community projects which have a strong focus on young people and creating opportunities for them.

### Exclusions

The company does not support individuals, teams or organisations which have political affiliations. It also excludes advertising in charity brochures, research projects including medical research, overseas projects, animal welfare and religious appeals.

### Applications

In writing to the correspondent.

## Corporate giving

In 2005/06, the company made charitable donations totalling £496,000.

### In-kind support

The company website states:

'We support educational initiatives through the provision of materials aimed at 7–11 year olds. These comprise a comic and associated activity sheet, and an interactive website which cover topics including safety and energy efficiency.

We also have a Museum of Electricity in Christchurch, Dorset, and Visitors' Centres at our Fiddler's Ferry Power Station and at Pitlochry Dam and Power Station in Perthshire. These facilities are free to schools organising visits.'

### Employee-led support

The company has introduced a scheme by which funds raised by employees for charitable and community causes are matched by SSE, up to a limit of £500 per employee.

'From time to time, we select a 'partner' charity or charities (currently a number of children's hospices) which we will encourage staff to support through payroll giving. Under the 'Quids In' scheme 20% of the money raised by staff is used to fund a prize draw. The balance – which is matched by the company – is donated to the 'partner' charity.'

# Scottish Media Group plc

200 Renfield Street, Glasgow G2 3PR

0141 300 3300; Fax: 0141 332 6982

Website: www.smg.plc.uk

Correspondent: Callum Spring, Director of Corporate Affairs

Chief officer: Chris Masters

| Year end | Turnover | Pre-tax profit |
|---|---|---|
| 31/12/2005 | £210,000,000 | £20,000,000 |

**Nature of company business**
The main companies in the group are Scottish Television Ltd and Grampian Television Ltd which provide Channel 3 services to central Scotland and north Scotland respectively, Scottish Television Enterprises Ltd which produces and sells television programmes internationally, Scottish Media Newspapers Ltd which publishes The Herald and Evening Times and Scottish Media publishing Ltd which publishes the Sunday Herald, all newspapers which circulate principally in west and central Scotland, and Primesight plc which constructs poster panels on which it sells advertising space.

**Subsidiaries include:** Pearl & Dean Cinemas Ltd, Ginger Television Productions Ltd, Grampian Television Ltd, Scottish Television Ltd, Scottish Television Enterprises Ltd, Caledonian Publishing Ltd, Primesight Ltd, Virgin Radio Holdings Ltd

**Main locations:** Glasgow

**UK employees:** 892

> **Charitable donations**
> 2005: £328,000
> 2004: £307,000
> 2003: £346,000

## Community involvement

The group has a policy of providing assistance to professional, community and amateur organisations and individuals concerned with theatrical and musical performances. It will also consider charitable or social organisations undertaking new or special activities. There is a preference for Scottish-based appeals, especially local charities in central Scotland and particularly those providing an element of training. In kind support is also given.

### Exclusions

Sponsorship is not undertaken. No support for fundraising events, advertising in charity brochures, purely denominational (religious) appeals, local appeals not in areas of company presence, large national appeals or overseas projects.

### Applications

In writing to the correspondent. The Community Programmes Co-ordinator should be contacted regarding Social Action broadcasting.

## Corporate giving

In 2005, the group made cash donations of £328,000. Grants usually range from £100 to £15,000. Major recipients in previous years have included Scottish Opera, Scottish Ballet, Edinburgh International Television Festival, Drambuie Edinburgh Film Festival, Celtic Film Festival, Museum of Scotland Projects, National Television Archive, various community festivals, support for young trainee film-makers and Comunn Na Gaidhlig.

### In-kind support

**Social action:** The Social Action Broadcast service gives local charities the opportunity to describe their activities and to appeal for volunteers. These last for 40 seconds and receive six transmissions. The *Scottish Action* programme has won awards for work in this field.

In addition, support may be given in the form of equipment and the use of facilities free of charge.

## Employee-led support

Staff are allowed time off for activities of community benefit and are encouraged to become volunteers in their own time.

# ScottishPower plc

Dealain House, Napier Road, Wardpark North, Cumbernauld, G68 0DF

Website: www.scottishpower.com

Correspondent: Paul McKelvie, Corporate Responsibility Director
E-mail: paul.mckelvie@scottishpower.com

Chief officer: Charles W Smith

Chief Executive: Philip Bowman

| Year end | Turnover | Pre-tax profit |
|---|---|---|
| 31/03/2006 | £5,446,100,000 | £625,100,000 |

Nature of company business
Principal activities: the generation, transmission, distribution and supply of electricity in the UK and USA.

Main locations: Warrington, Glasgow, Rhostylien

UK employees: 8,892

Total employees: 9,793

### Charitable donations

2006: £2,610,000

Total community contributions: £3,330,000 2005
Management costs: £500,000

Membership: A & B, BitC, L B Group

## Community involvement

ScottishPower plc concentrates its community support in the UK in six main areas: the arts, charity, community, education, employability, and environment.

In addition to the long established ScottishPower Learning Programme, which is split between school-based, community-based and work-based programmes, the other main areas of support are:

- public safety
- science
- energy efficiency
- arts sponsorship.

## Exclusions

No support is given to appeals from individuals, national charities (unless the fund is used solely for a local project), preservation of historic buildings, research, expeditions, political or military organisations, circular appeals, advertising in charity brochures, animal welfare charities, religious appeals, local appeals not in areas of company presence or overseas projects.

Sponsorship for sporting events and advertisements in publications etc., will normally only be considered commercially, in terms of potential advertising benefits.

## Applications

In writing to the correspondent.

## Corporate giving

In 2005/06, the company made UK total community contributions of £33,830,000. Of this amount, cash donations comprised £2,610,000, in-kind support £720,000, and management costs £500,000.

Further information about ScottishPower's range of community investment is available on its website.

### In-kind support

The company gives many gifts in kind:

**Community:** The ScottishPower Community Champions Awards are run in conjunction with the Chronicle series of newspapers and North Wales Independent Press. Recognition is given to the significant contributions of the Cheshire and North Wales community.

**Education:** Committed to the principle of lifelong learning, ScottishPower works in partnership with Trade Unions and external agencies to deliver training to people of different ages and abilities and so enable them to make a greater contribution to society.

Further information about ScottishPower's learning programme is available on its website or by e-mailing: scottishpowerlearning@scottishpower.com

**Environment:** The Cockenzie Community in Bloom Project in East Lothian was given use of facilities and equipment at the nearby power station.

**Sport:** The company supports the Warrington Wolves Primary Link scheme. Wolves players visit primary schools giving talks on healthy living and undertaking coaching assistance. With additional backing from Sportsmatch, the main aim is to encourage children to take part in a healthy activity through playing rugby. Nearly 20,000 youngsters have been through the scheme so far.

### Employee-led support

The company matches fundraising by employees and employee giving.

**Payroll giving:** The company operate the Give As You Earn scheme in the UK. Contributions for 2003/04 amounted to £68,366.

### Commercially-led support

**Sponsorship:** *The arts* – Sponsorship is limited and planned well in advance. Recent beneficiaries of ScottishPower's support include: ScottishPower Pipe Band; Edinburgh International Book Festival; National Theatre for Scotland; and, Ballet Central.

The company also undertakes good cause sponsorship.

# Serco Group plc

Serco House, 16 Bartley Wood Business Park, Bartley Way, Hook, Hampshire RG27 9UY

01256 745900; Fax: 01256 744111

Website: www.serco.com

Correspondent: Gail Johnson, Head of Corporate
Responsibilities and Charities

Chief officer: Kevin Beeston

Chief Executive: Christopher Hyman

| Year end | Turnover | Pre-tax profit |
|---|---|---|
| 31/12/2005 | £2,260,300,000 | £77,900,000 |

Nature of company business
The provision of a range of facilities management and systems
engineering services.

Subsidiaries include: Community Leisure Management Ltd, NPL
Management Ltd, Rakmulti Technology Ltd

Main locations: London, Oldbury, Sunbury-on-Thames,
Southampton, Wolverhampton, Hook, Glasgow, Lincoln,
Leicester

Total employees: 37,253

### Charitable donations

2005: £586,324
2004: £333,965
2003: £322,349

Total community contributions: £850,619
Management costs: £166,511

Membership: BitC, L B Group

## Community involvement

The company prefers to support local appeals relevant to the
business. As such, requests for support should be made to the
local operating site. Support is given to children and youth,
education, medical, overseas aid and development, and forces
charities.

### Exclusions

No support for large national appeals, circular appeals or
purely denominational (religious) appeals.

### Applications

In writing to the correspondent.

## Corporate giving

In previous years the groups fundraising activities has focused
on a single charity, such as Save the Children which was
supported in 2002. A review of charitable giving in 2003 led to
more of an emphasis on supporting local charities and
communities and the subsequent launch of the Serco
Foundation, about which the website states: '[it] provides
additional financial resources to our employees and businesses
to undertake community projects'.

In 2003, cash donations to charity totalled £159,395.
Beneficiaries included £10,000 to Doncaster Prison and Reed
in Partnership. Donations to community projects and
sponsorships totalled £162,954.

### In-kind support

Gifts in kind, including facilities and assets amounted to
£141,811 in 2003.

### Employee-led support

Serco encourages its employees to volunteer their time to local
projects and in 2003 employee time, including professional

expertise and volunteering in company time amounted to
£102,849.

# Severn Trent plc

2297 Coventry Road, Birmingham B26 3PU

0121 722 4000; Fax: 0121 722 4800

Website: www.severn-trent.com

Correspondent: Corporate Community Affairs Manager
0121 722 4000; Fax: 0121 722 4800
E-mail: corporateresponsibilty@stplc.com

Chief officer: Sir John Egan

Chief Executive: Colin Matthews

| Year end | Turnover | Pre-tax profit |
|---|---|---|
| 31/03/2006 | £2,295,000,000 | £488,200,000 |

Nature of company business
The group's principal activities are the supply of water and
sewerage services, waste management and the provision of
environmental services.

Subsidiaries include: Capital Controls Ltd, UK Waste
Management Ltd, Derwent Insurance Ltd, Daventry International
Rail Freight Terminal Ltd, Biffa plc, Fusion Meters Ltd, Charles
Haswell and Partners Ltd

Main locations: Birmingham

UK employees: 11,522

Total employees: 16,312

### Charitable donations

2006: £487,422
2005: £378,825
2004: £276,121

Management costs: £110,000

Membership: BitC, L B Group

## Community involvement

Severn Trent's community investment programme focuses on
the development of long term partnerships and supports
projects in the environmental area, whilst also addressing
issues concerned with social exclusion, young people and
education. It focuses on three key areas:

- environmental education – developing environmental
  awareness and responsibility amongst young people
- the built environment – addressing social exclusion issues
  such as homelessness, deprivation and disability
- the natural environment – ensuring its preservation and
  enhancement.

In 2005/06 the company worked with nine partner charities:
WaterAid, Birmingham Cares, Leicester Cares, Cromford
Venture Centre, Bridlegate, Stonebridge City Farm, VSO,
Crash-IT and Ackers.

Severn Trent Water has its own education team committed to
promoting environmental education in schools, and it has a
network of five custom built education centres across its
region. Severn Trent Water's education team also produces a
range of resources for teachers which link into the National
Curriculum.

Severn Trent is one of the founder members and leading corporate supporters of WaterAid. This non-governmental organisation was set up by the water industry 25 years ago in the belief that everyone should have access to clean water and effective sanitation. Severn Trent supports WaterAid in a variety of ways ranging from an annual corporate donation to corporate events, employee fundraising activities and awareness initiatives.

In the main, support is given to appeals from within the area of Severn Trent Group operations. National charities are included if they have a branch close to where the company has a business presence. This support may be financial in-kind or through the employee volunteering.

The company has made significant contributions to The Severn Trent Water Charitable Trust Fund. This charity was established in 1997 (Charity Commission no. 1064005).

In 2005 the Trustees resolved to establish a subsidiary trading company (Auriga Services Limited) and to convert the charity to a company limited by guarantee. As part of the re-structuring a new charity has been incorporated, Severn Trent Water Charitable Trust Fund (Charity Commission no. 1108278), which will continue to provide assistance for people in need. The fixed assets owned by the Charity were sold at fair market value to Auriga Services Limited and all its remaining assets and liabilities transferred to the successor Severn Trent Water Charitable Trust Fund. The new charity has taken over all operations with effect from l April 2005. Each year around 8,000 people in Severn Trent Water's region apply for the Trust's help with paying water and other utility bills and over 70% of those applicants receive financial assistance. In the year 2005/06 the Trust's Income was £3,491,000 and total charitable expenditure £2,822,807.

## Exclusions

No support for advertising in charity brochures, appeals from individuals, local appeals not in areas of company presence, medical research, fundraising events, political or religious appeals, expeditions, study tours and cultural exchanges or third party organisations fundraising on behalf of national charities.

## Applications

In writing to the correspondent. Your application to the company should include:

- a summary of the aims and objectives of your charity
- a summary of the project for which the donation is required
- an explanation of how the money will be spent
- a copy of your latest annual report and accounts.

Applications to the trust should be made on a form available from: The Severn Trent Water Charitable Trust Fund, Emmanuel Court, 12–14 Mill Street, Sutton Coalfield, West Midlands B72 1TJ. Alternatively, telephone 0121 355 7766.

# Corporate giving

Donations to charitable organisations during the year amounted to £487,422 (2005: £378,825)

The company focuses on the development of long term partnerships with charities close to its major sites and which reflect the company's value of environmental leadership. The work focuses on environmental education, the preservation and enhancement of the natural environment or addressing social exclusion issues in the built environment.

Substantial support is also given to WaterAid.

## The Severn Trent Water Charitable Trust Fund

'The independent trustees have adopted a policy of giving grants to individuals and families to (a) help them overcome immediate crisis and (b) to encourage financial stability. The majority of grants provide help toward insurmountable water debt but, in addition, help is given with other priority urgent bills and household needs.

The trust supports money advice and debt counselling work and has funded advice work in 28 agencies spread throughout the region. Over half of these in Citizens Advice Bureaus. We missed our target of maintaining community investment at 1% of pre-tax profits or above. This was primarily caused by a reduction in the management costs contribution, whilst pre-tax profits increased. In 2006/07 we will be reviewing our community strategy to ensure that communities receive best value from our activities.'

## In-kind support

The company receives many requests for a charitable donation in order that a vital piece of equipment can be purchased. In such cases, attempts are made to locate similar surplus equipment within the group of companies and then to donate it as a gift in-kind.

## Employee-led support

Severn Trent Water encourages employees to engage with the local community. Many staff work with partner charities, while some support other community initiatives. In 2005/06 Severn Trent Water donated almost 5,000 hours of staff time to community projects. Around 950 staff took part in volunteering activities.

The company's Self Managed Career Development (SMCD) programme brings together teams of eight staff from across Severn Trent Water to take on challenges in the community, in turn, the teams can learn about their interpersonal and team-building skills. Each SMCD team chooses its own project, and is responsible for its own planning, performance and feedback. SMCD challenges are arranged through the charity Birmingham Cares.

Volunteer rangers play an important role at many of Severn Trent Water's reservoirs, carrying out conservation tasks, maintenance work, wildlife surveys, and health and safety checks. In return, staff receive benefits such as a uniform, staff discounts at its shops, free parking at its countryside sides, and annual dinners.

**Payroll giving:** The Give As You Earn scheme is promoted throughout the group companies.

## Commercially-led support

Severn Trent Water has launched a new 'Be Smart Award' to recognise schools that demonstrate a commitment to the wise use of water. Schools are assigned a Severn Trent Water mentor to support them throughout the scheme which has been designed to meet the organisational and curriculum needs of schools. The interactive CD on waste has won two prestigious communications awards. Full details of the required criteria can be found on the company's website.

The company also encourages suppliers and contractors in their volunteering initiatives. For example, ECS Engineering, one of Severn Trent Water's main contractors, has adopted one of their partner charities, Bridle Gate, as one of its own partnership charities.

Biffa's landfill tax credit scheme, Biffaward, distributed almost £8.6 million in 2005/06 to over 200 individual projects. They included, urban regeneration projects, a project to double the population of the brown hare and a grant for the Roald Dahl Museum and Story Centre.

# Shell

Shell Centre, York Road, Waterloo, London SE1 7NA

020 7934 1234

Website: www.shell.com

Correspondent: Louise Johnson, Head of Social Investment 020 7934 3199; Fax: 020 7934 7039 E-mail: susan.s.saloom@si.shell.com

Chief officer: James Smith

| Year end | Turnover | Pre-tax profit |
|---|---|---|
| 31/12/2005 | £162,000,000,000 | £23,604,000,000 |

Nature of company business
Shell is a global group of energy and petrochemicals companies. Most people know Shell for its retail stations, and its exploration and production of oil and natural gas. However, its activities also include: marketing, transporting and trading oil and gas; generating electricity (including wind power); providing oil products for industrial uses; producing petrochemicals used for plastics, coatings and detergents; and developing technology for hydrogen vehicles.

Main locations: Aberdeen, Bacton, London, Lowestoft, Stanlow (Merseyside), St Fergus, Wythenshawe, Chester, Cowdenbeath

UK employees: 8,363

## Charitable donations

2005: £7,730,000

Membership: A & B, BitC, L B Group

## Community involvement

Shell's community contributions in the UK are channelled in two ways.

Firstly, support is managed by key Shell plants or offices at a local level for causes in their neighbouring communities. Examples of activities supported at this level include engineering training colleges, arts and sports events, local charities and schools.

Secondly, Shell is the driving force behind five UK-wide programmes, which focus on entrepreneurship, skills and training, and science education:

Shell Education Service: provides practical science workshops in primary schools, as well as after-school science clubs and family science days.

Shell LiveWIRE: offers year-round help and advice to young entrepreneurs, and an annual awards scheme.

Shell Technology Enterprise Programme (STEP): creates summer work placements in small businesses for penultimate-year students.

Shell Connections: the country's largest youth theatre programme, run in partnership with the National Theatre.

Shell Environment: A successor programme to Shell Better Britain is currently under development.

With the majority of resources channelled in these two ways, Shell does not commonly award grants at UK level to charities or voluntary organisations.

### Exclusions

Shell is unable to support appeals from individuals, political or religious groups, or for building projects.

### Applications

In writing to the community relations teams at Shell plants or offices for enquiries about local support.

Shell does not commonly award grants outside neighbourhoods surrounding Shell plants and offices. However, applications should be addressed to: UK Social Investment, Shell Centre, York Road, London, SE1 7NA.

Individual programme websites give application details and more information for LiveWIRE, STEP and Connections: (www.shell-livewire.org), (www.step.org.uk), (www.shellconnections.org).

For international initiatives (overseas beneficiaries), applications in writing to Eli de Castro, Shell Centre, York Road, London, SE1 7NA.

Also, there is the Shell Foundation, a registered charity. Please see the Shell Foundation website for its areas of focus, themes covered and positioning (www.shellfoundation.org).

## Corporate giving

In 2005, a donation of $14.6 million (£7.73 million) was made to The Shell Foundation (Charity Commission no. 1080999).

### In-kind support

Shell in the UK leases its computer equipment, so does not donate redundant hardware. Shell does offer facilities at its key UK plants and offices to community organisations by prior arrangement. Please contact local community relations teams to discuss this.

### Employee-led support

Shell employees and pensioners in the UK are very active in their local communities. Many employees get involved in local community activities through initiatives run by local Shell sites. For example, Shell's North West plant runs the Save 'n' Score scheme, linking safe workplace operations by employees to the size of a monthly grant to local good causes. While in London, Shell employees take part in volunteer reading and mentoring at local secondary schools. Shell supports its employees and pensioners in their work with local organisations by making small grants available.

The Project Better World volunteering programme was initiated by Shell employees. Employees volunteer to develop and maintain local initiatives that work towards sustainable development.

Payroll giving: Shell operates the Give as You Earn scheme.

# Shepherd Building Group Ltd

Huntington House, Jockey Lane, York YO32 9XW

01904 650700; Fax: 01904 650701

Website: www.shepherd-buildinggroup.com

Correspondent: Chris Mason 01904 650721; Fax: 01904 650746

E-mail: chris.mason@shepherd-building-group.com

Chief officer: Alan T Fletcher

| Year end | Turnover | Pre-tax profit |
|---|---|---|
| 30/06/2005 | £655,900,000 | £35,000,000 |

**Nature of company business**
The company is a holding company with subsidiaries engaged in building and ancillary activities.

**Subsidiaries include:** Portasilo Ltd, Yorkon Ltd, Mechplant Ltd, Portakabin Ltd, Paton Plant Ltd, Computer Skills Ltd

**Main locations:** York, Manchester, London, Northampton, Langley, Leeds, Darlington, Birmingham

**UK employees:** 3,400

---

**Charitable donations**

2005: £98,000

---

## Community involvement

The company's policy is to concentrate support in York and Yorkshire and to avoid contributing to more than one charity or organisation operating in the same field. The main areas of support are the arts, children and youth, community/social welfare, education, elderly people, enterprise and training, environment, fundraising events, heritage, medical research, science/technology, sickness/disability and sport.

### Exclusions

No support for telephone appeals, circular appeals, fundraising events, advertising in charity brochures, appeals from individuals, purely denominational appeals, local appeals not in areas of company presence, large national appeals or overseas projects.

### Applications

In writing to the correspondent.

## Corporate giving

In 2005, the company made UK charitable donations totalling £98,000. Beneficiaries included: York Minster Restoration Fund (£50,000); York Museums Trust (£25,000); York, City Knights Foundation (£15,000); University of York Outreach Programme (£7,500); and, Shepherd Building Group Brass Band (£5,000).

### In-kind support

In October 2001, the group launched the Shepherd School Challenge. Competing schools, nationwide, have to research, develop and present a bid to the company, outlining how their school could be improved via a new project build, e.g. a classroom makeover or a playground revamp, to the value of £10,000. The winning school will have their project built, with four additional schools receiving regional runners-up prizes related to their projects.

The challenge makes up part of Shepherd's strategic Educational Liaison and Career Development programme. The objective of this is to encourage young people to consider and enter construction as a career. Other aspects of the programme include work experience placements, careers presentations, site visits and assistance with life skills such as interview techniques.

### Employee-led support

In support of its employees volunteering/charitable activities, approved company time off for volunteering is allowed and employees fundraising matched.

**Payroll giving:** The company operates the Charity Service scheme.

### Commercially-led support

**Sponsorship:** Arts and good-cause sponsorship are undertaken.

Contact: Chris Mason (Tel: 01904 650721).

---

# Shire Pharmaceuticals

Hampshire International Business Park, Chineham, Basingstoke, Hampshire RG24 8EP

01256 894000; Fax: 01256 894708

Website: www.shire.com

Chief officer: Dr James Cavanaugh

Chief Executive: Matthew Emmens

| Year end | Turnover | Pre-tax profit |
|---|---|---|
| 31/12/2005 | £1,599,316 | (£141,993) |

**Nature of company business**
Speciality pharmaceutical company.

**Main locations:** Basingstoke

**UK employees:** 377

**Total employees:** 2,403

---

**Charitable donations**

2005: £154,933
2004: £42,319
2003: £66,627

Membership: BitC, %Club

---

## Community involvement

Shire's corporate responsibility report states: 'We have long-standing relationships with a number of charities working in our specialist areas, including CHADD (Children and Adults with ADHD), the Alzheimer's Society, National Osteoporosis Society and the Society for Mucopolysaccharide Diseases.

In many cases time is even more valuable than cash donations and our specialists have worked with a wide variety of organizations, giving their time and expertise. This doesn't just benefit the charity, but gives us real insights that help us with our own work for patients.'

The Company's Community strategy and plan of activities is led and implemented by Shire's Corporate Communications department in conjunction with HR Business Partners, Country or Site Managers and local groups of employees where relevant.

The Corporate Giving program is also led by Corporate Communications and funded from the Corporate Communications budget; however, a charity committee or activities committee involving representative employees is usually involved to ensure that nomination of a 'Charity of the Year' or dissemination of major matched donations is agreed with input from all parts of Shire's organization.

Key stakeholders in the company's communities include patient groups and medical/healthcare education bodies as well as established not-for-profit organisations that are linked with the company's therapy areas of focus (for example CHADD, Alzheimer's Society, MPS Society) and related research bodies.

Shire also engages with and supports local schools and support groups that offer advice to young people who experience behaviour disorders, learning difficulties or social problems. It also supports organisations and community initiatives that provide help for senior citizens.

### Exclusions

No support is given which merely benefits one person.

### Applications

In writing to the company. The company would not give a name, or department to which applications should be addressed.

## Corporate giving

UK charitable donations for 2005 were £154,933 (2004: £42,319).

### In-kind support

Shire does not send seasonal greetings cards to customers or suppliers. Instead, a group of employees at each site nominates a not-for-profit beneficiary and a one-off donation is made. This organisation is then publicised via Shire's outgoing e-mails during the month of December.

### Employee-led support

The Corporate Communications department in consultation with Human Resources manages requests from individual employee fund-raising matching. Shire will consider matching or providing a donation to an employee's own raised amount.

Employee volunteering activities are agreed and arranged with line managers in consultation with Human Resources. Shire provides one fully paid day off per year to spend working for a not-for-profit organisation. In addition, the company supports community-related activities by its employees including involvement in helping schools, homes for senior citizens and counselling services through the provision of paid time off.

*Give As You Earn* – Where possible, Shire provides a payroll deduction program for its employees to enable ongoing individual donations to a charity of their choice.

Corporate fundraising campaigns are launched at both global and local levels. On these occasions, Shire invites employees to make personal one-off donations to a topical high-profile cause; the Company agrees to make a matching donation to the total raised by all employees.

## Siemens plc

Siemens House, Oldbury, Bracknell RG12 8FZ

01344 396000

Website: www.siemens.co.uk

**Correspondent:** Corporate Communications Department

**Chief Executive:** Alan Wood

| Year end | Turnover | Pre-tax profit |
|---|---|---|
| 30/12/2005 | £3,048,000,000 | £96,200,000 |

**Nature of company business**
Siemen's principal activities in the UK cover: information & communication, automation & control, transportation, power, and medical businesses. The company are also engaged in the supply of lighting, commercial research and development, and financial services.

**Main locations:** Birmingham, Banbury, Basildon, Bracknell, Swindon, Telford, Wellingborough, Worcester, Congelton, Cirencester, Manchester, London, Newcastle, Milton Keynes, Nottingham, Oxford, Reading, Poole, Harrogate, Harrow, Ipswich, Hayes, Langley, Hitchin, Hinckley, Lincoln, Crawley, Staines, Ramsey, Walton on Thames

**UK employees:** 20,314

### Charitable donations

Membership: BitC, %Club

## Community involvement

Siemens businesses and employees alike support their local communities through charity fundraisng events and sponsorship of various educational and community programmes. In particular the company's community activities concentrate on helping young people take advantage of the educational opportunities available to them and so achieve their potential. In support of this, many of the company's businesses have close links with local schools, colleges and universities, particularly in subjects such as science and engineering.

In addition to the above, other UK charities outside of the corporate focus on education are supported through the efforts of Siemens' employees. These include Mencap, NSPCC, Children in Need, the Imperial Cancer Research Foundation, the Motor Neurone Disease Association and the British Heart Foundation.

### Applications

In writing to the correspondent.

## Corporate giving

Although we are unable to give a figure for the company's total community contributions, it is clear from the range of support referred to on its website (www.siemens.co.uk) that it is fairly substantial. Examples of this include support for various educational projects and initiatives, such as development of an MSc course targeted at software engineers at Nottingham Trent University. Activities in this area focus on Generation21 – supporting education and initiatives that foster the development of young people; and Caring Hands – social and charitable work in the communities in which it operates. Futher details on this and other areas of support can be found on the aforementioned website.

### Employee-led support

Siemens encourages and supports its employees to be active on behalf of their local communities, whether this be through volunteering or fundraising. Charities recently benefiting from this include: British Heart Foundation and the Motor Neurone Disease Association.

Every month, through the Employee in the Community Award scheme, a cheque for £500 is given to an employee on behalf of the charity/organisation they support.

The company's three main sites in Manchester, Poole and Bracknell have a community fund to which employees can choose to make monthly donations. These are then matched by the company. An employees charity committee meets monthly to decide how to allocate the donations to local charities and community groups.

### Commercially-led support

**Sponsorship:** *The Arts* – In 2006 it was sponsoring the Antenna Gallery at the Science Museum in London for the next three years.

# SIG plc

Hillsborough Works, Langsett Road, Sheffield, South Yorkshire S6 2LW

0114 285 6300; Fax: 0114 285 6385

Website: www.sigplc.co.uk

Correspondent: Les Tench, Chairman
E-mail: info@sigplc.co.uk

Chief officer: Leslie Tench

Chief Executive: David Williams

| Year end | Turnover | Pre-tax profit |
|---|---|---|
| 31/12/2005 | £1,581,142,000 | £86,811,000 |

**Nature of company business**
International multi-site distributor. It has three core business sectors: insulation, roofing commercial interiors and specialist construction and safety products.

**Subsidiaries include:** Miller Pattison Ltd, Leaderflush and Shapland Ltd

**Main locations:** Sheffield, Southampton, Barking, Littleborough, Leominster, Leicester, London, Maidstone, Crawley, Cardiff, Wednesbury, Hyde, St Ives

### Charitable donations

2005: £98,000
2004: £53,000
2003: £47,000

Membership: BitC

## Community involvement

The company supports local as well as national and international charities.

## Exclusions

No political donations are made. No support to local appeals not in areas of company presence.

## Applications

In writing to the correspondent.

## Corporate giving

In 2005 donations totalled £98,000.

In 2005 it introduced a new policy. In addition to supporting local causes where employees are involved, they will support three main charities for a period of three years. Five visually impaired students from Henshaws College, an education facility offering independent living skills training to around 65 young people aged between 16 and 23, will be supported. A number of wildlife projects will be sponsored through Yorkshire Wildlife Trust and Hope and Homes for Children, an international charity providing homes for children in the third world, will also receive support.

### Employee-led support

The company encourages employees to take an interest in social and community activities outside the workplace. It also provides financial support for employees undertaking charity work overseas.

It is currently in the process of introducing a Payroll Giving Scheme.

# SigmaKalon UK & Ireland

Huddersfield Road, Birstall, Batley, West Yorkshire WF17 9XA

01924 354000; Fax: 01924 354001

Website: www.sigmakalon.co.uk

Correspondent: Phil Evans, Managing Director
E-mail: enquiries@kalon.co.uk

Chief officer: Rt Hon. Lord Wakeham

Managing Director: M J W Hennessy

| Year end | Turnover | Pre-tax profit |
|---|---|---|
| 31/12/1998 | £474,300,000 | £37,000,000 |

**Nature of company business**
The Group is a worldwide leader in decorative, marine, protective and industrial paints. Its main activities are the manufacture and distribution of branded and own-label decorative paints.

**Subsidiaries include:** Deco UK, SPL, Sigmakalon UK Ltd

**Main locations:** Leeds, Morley, Batley

UK employees: 4,683

### Charitable donations

Membership: BitC

## Community involvement

Formerly part of TotalFinaElf, the group was acquired by Bain Capital in 2003, but continues trading under the SigmaKalon name in this country. The company takes part in the life of local communities, in particular, involvement with schools and practical support for charities and community programmes.

## Exclusions

No support for local appeals not in areas of company presence.

## Applications

In writing to the correspondent.

## Corporate giving

In 1997, the company donated nearly £42,000 to charity. We have neither details of the beneficiaries, nor confirmation that this level of support continues.

## In-kind support

The company offered material help to victims of the 2004 tsunami by purchasing and repairing fishing boats and equipment. SigmaKalon is also involved in the life of local communities, in particular, involvement with schools and practical support for charities and community programmes.

## Employee-led support

Group employees acted as a relay in the areas affected by the 2004 tsunami. In 2005, £117,000 was collected within the company in gifts to the 'SigmaKalon Tsunami Aid Programme'.

# Simmons & Simmons

Citypoint, 1 Ropemaker Street, London EC2Y 9SS

020 7628 2020

Website: www.simmons-simmons.co.uk

Correspondent: Belinda Lodge

**Nature of company business**
Law firm.

Main locations: London

## Community involvement

Simmons & Simmons undertakes pro bono and community work within the communities in which it operates, actively encouraging its staff to become involved in the provision of legal and non-legal services.

**Charity of the Year:** World Wildlife Fund (2006).

## Applications

In writing to the correspondent.

## Corporate giving

The most up-to-date contributions total is from 2000, when giving totalled £171,436.

## In-kind support

A variety of schemes are organised by the firm's pro bono coordinator, including mentoring under-privileged children at two Inner London primary schools, and giving free legal advice at an evening surgery at the Battersea Legal Advice Centre.

As members of Lawyers in the Community, a number of the firm's solicitors sit on the management boards of charities and charitable organisations, providing their expertise and advice. The firm also provides help through the ProHelp scheme assisting, for example, the Borough Community Centre, a Southwark-based charity.

Through the British Executive Overseas, the firm sponsors individual legal specialists to travel to developing countries requiring law-related assistance.

## Employee-led support

Employees are encouraged to volunteer, in tasks not connected with the legal profession, including mentoring schemes.

In recent year the company took part in Stepney Children's Fund scheme to purchase and wrap gifts of around £10 each to young children in disadvantaged areas of London's East End. Over 200 staff donated to this cause.

# Slough Estates plc

234 Bath Road, Slough, Berkshire SL1 4EE

01753 537171; Fax: 01753 820585

Website: www.sloughestates.com

Correspondent: Air Commodore N Hamilton (Retired), Manager External Affairs
E-mail: nick.hamilton@sloughestates.com

Chief officer: P D Orchard-Lisle

Chief Executive: Ian Coull

| Year end | Turnover | Pre-tax profit |
|---|---|---|
| 31/12/2005 | | £582,300,000 |

**Nature of company business**
Industrial and commercial property development, construction and investment, supply of utility services and the provision of services associated with such activities.

**Subsidiaries include:** Pentagon Developments (Chatham) Ltd, Cambridge Research Park Ltd, Bilton plc, Bredero Properties plc, Kingswood Ascot Properties Investments Ltd, Shopping Centres Ltd, Howard Centre Properties Ltd, The Buchanan Partnership, Real Estate and Commercial Trust Ltd, Lewisham Investment Partnership Ltd, The Bishop Centre Ltd, Allnatt London Properties plc, Farnborough Business Park Ltd

Main locations: Slough

### Charitable donations

2005: £627,914
2003: £539,557

Membership: BitC

## Community involvement

'We continue to recognise our responsibilities towards the local community, and believe in the mutual benefits of improving quality of life in communities where we invest. Due to our strong presence in the Slough area, we are particularly keen to contribute to projects in this area. Our ongoing efforts to support young people in Slough continued with major contributions to the Prince's Trust and the Outward Bound Trust and we also helped a local school, Westgate achieve specialist status with a donation of £10,000.'

### Exclusions

No grants for non-charities, circular appeals, local appeals not in areas of company presence, appeals from individuals, or overseas projects.

## Applications

Decisions are made by a committee which meets quarterly. Air Commodore Nick Hamilton should be contacted for donations.

## Corporate giving

In 2005 charitable donations made by the company totalled £627,914.

## In-kind support

In addition to donations to charities, the main area of support is gifts in kind. Equipment and material, professional services and the use of in-house facilities have been donated free of charge for specific purposes.

## Employee-led support

The company allows each staff member one day of company time to participate in a community project or a company-wide community initiative.

**Payroll giving:** The company operates a payroll giving scheme.

---

# Smith & Nephew plc

15 Adam Street, London WC2R 6LA

020 7401 7646; Fax: 020 7930 3353

Website: www.smith-nephew.com

Correspondent: Corporate Affairs

Chief officer: John Buchanan

Chief Executive: Sir Christopher O'Donnell

| Year end | Turnover | Pre-tax profit |
|---|---|---|
| 31/12/2005 | £1,407,000,000 | £240,000,000 |

Nature of company business
A global medical devices company manufacturing and marketing clinical products principally in orthopaedics, endoscopy, wound management and rehabilitation.

Main locations: Cambridge, Hull, Huntingdon, Gilberdyke, York

UK employees: 1,750

Total employees: 8,618

### Charitable donations

2005: £325,000
2003: £470,000

Total community contributions: £1,379,000

Membership: A & B, BitC, %Club

## Community involvement

Most of the company's UK charitable donations are channelled through the Smith & Nephew Foundation (Charity Commission no. 267061), which supports education and research for individuals in the medical and nursing professions. The funding policy is to invite individuals to apply to advertisements (see 'Applications' below).

## Exclusions

All awards are advertised in the relevant medical and nursing journals. Applications are not considered at any other time. Physicians and/or surgeons must be resident and working in the UK. Nurses, midwives and health visitors must hold an active UKCC number.

## Applications

All awards are advertised in relevant medical or nursing journals. Any correspondence should be addressed to the Foundation Administrator, Smith & Nephew Foundation. Applications are not considered except in response to advertisements for the various awards.

## Corporate giving

In 2005, Smith & Nephew made total community contributions of £1,379,000 of which £325,000 was in cash donations.

### Doctoral Nursing Research Fellowship

This is offered once a year to nurses, midwives and health visitors, working in the UK, who are at the beginning of their career. It is advertised in the *Nursing Standard, The Nursing Times*, and other nursing journals, and posted on the Smith & Nephew Foundation's website (www.snfoundation.org.uk) at the beginning of March: 'It provides financial support to work with an established UK research team, based in a university, school/faculty or department of nursing, which has a proven track record of research and development in the field of skin or tissue damage and vulnerability.' The award is worth up to £90,000 over three years.

### Post-Doctoral Nursing Research Fellowships:

These are offered once a year to nurses, midwives and health visitors, working in the UK, who are undertaking research as part of a PhD programme. These awards are advertised in the *Nursing Standard, The Nursing Times*, and other nursing journals, and posted on the foundation's website (www.snfoundation.org.uk) at the beginning of March. 'This award will support an outstanding career nurse researcher and seeks to enhance nursing post-doctoral research capacity. It provides financial support to work with an established UK research team, based in a University School/Faculty or Department of Nursing, which has a proven track record of research and development in the field of skin or tissue damage and vulnerability. The award is open to members of the nursing and midwifery professions, working in the United Kingdom, who hold active registration with the Nursing & Midwifery Council.' The award is worth up to £120,000 over three years.

Applicants should check that the focus of their research meets the criteria as it may change each year.

## In-kind support

In addition to support given through the foundation, the company supports links with educational facilities in areas where its main operations are situated, provides gifts in kind and seconds staff.

## Employee-led support

The company supports employees' volunteering/charitable activities by allowing time off in which to volunteer, and matching employee fundraising and giving.

# D S Smith Holdings plc

4–16 Artillery Row, London SW1P 1RZ

020 7932 5000; Fax: 020 7932 5003

**Website:** www.dssmith.uk.com

**Correspondent:** Peter Aubusson, Group Communications Manager

**Chief officer:** A P Hichens

**Chief Executive:** A D Thorne

| Year end | Turnover | Pre-tax profit |
|---|---|---|
| 30/04/2006 | £1,652,700,000 | £11,000,000 |

**Nature of company business**
Production of corrugated and plastic packaging, primarily from recycled waste, and the distribution of office products.

**Subsidiaries include:** St Regis Paper Company Ltd, Spicers Ltd, A A Griggs & Co Ltd

**Main locations:** London, Maidenhead, Rugby, Windsor, Cambridge

**UK employees:** 6,900

**Total employees:** 11,653

### Charitable donations

2006: £84,000
2005: £128,000
2004: £109,000
2003: £112,000

Membership: BitC

## Community involvement

The corporate social responsibility review contained in the company's annual report 2006 states: 'Our individual businesses support their local communities through a range of activities such as sponsorship of community projects or sport teams; helping local schools with project work, training, mentoring or provision of work experience opportunities; and provision of adult training skills or facilities.

'The group supports charitable fundraising activities through cash contributions and in the form of product and services or staff time. The majority of the modest amount of money donated by the group is given by individual operating units, principally to causes in their local communities. Donations by the group headquarters are focused on a small number of educational training and support causes that help young people become involved in business and working life.'

The group is a member of Business in the Community.

### Exclusions

No support for advertising in charity brochures, animal welfare, appeals from individuals, the arts, fundraising events, overseas projects, political or religious appeals.

### Applications

In writing to the correspondent.

**Information available:** The company includes a social responsibility report as part of its annual report and accounts.

## Corporate giving

In 2005/06, the company made charitable donations totalling £84,000. We have no details of the beneficiaries.

### In-kind support

In addition to cash donations, the company provides gifts in kind.

### Employee-led support

Donations made through employee fundraising and giving is matched by the company.

**Payroll giving:** The company operates the Charities Trust scheme.

### Commercially-led support

**Cause-related marketing:** Prior to its sale in July 2005, John Dickinson Stationery contributed a substantial donation to a charity as a result of a cause-related marketing campaign. No figure relating to this was available.

# WH Smith plc

Nation's House, 103 Wigmore Street, London W1U 1WH

020 7409 3222; Fax: 020 7514 9635

**Website:** www.whsmithplc.com

**Correspondent:** Melissa Duncan, Head of Communications

**Chief officer:** Robert Walker

**Chief Executive:** Kate Swann

| Year end | Turnover | Pre-tax profit |
|---|---|---|
| 28/06/2006 | £2,508,000,000 | £73,000,000 |

**Nature of company business**
The group's principal activities are the retail, publishing and news distribution.

**Subsidiaries include:** Hodder Headline Ltd

**Main locations:** London

**UK employees:** 23,120

### Charitable donations

2005: £781,000
2003: £96,000

Total community contributions: £891,000 –2000
Management costs: £136,000

Membership: BitC, L B Group, %Club

## Community involvement

As a member of Business in the Community and a founder member of the PerCent Club, WH Smith is committed to investing a minimum of one percent of its UK pre-tax profits in support of the community. Over the last few years it has refocused its efforts towards education, with particular emphasis on improving young people's literacy skills.

The company's donations programme is entirely proactive.

### Exclusions

Unsolicited requests are not supported. No support for advertising in charity brochures, animal welfare, appeals from individuals, the arts, older people, enterprise/training, environment/heritage, fundraising events, medical research, overseas projects, political appeals, religious appeals, science/technology, sickness/disability, social welfare or sport.

## Applications

The group is proactive in identifying potential partners for its community programme. Unsolicited requests, therefore, are not considered.

## Corporate giving

WH Smith's first stand-alone corporate responsibility report, produced in 2006, states that the company's community contributions amounted to £781,000 in cash, however the 2005 annual report of WH Smith plc states that charitable donations during that year amounted to just £1,000. Recent annual reports for the WH Smith Trust indicate that it receives donations of less than £100,000 each year, including monies from staff fundraising activities. It would seem that recent consistent figures are unavailable for the company.

## In-kind support

2006 saw the second year of the Summer Read initiative, a partnership between WH Smith plc, the WH Smith Trust and the National Literacy Trust's Reading is Fundamental initiative. During the year, more than 2,700 children took part in the event in 15 locations around the country. The company provided books and goody bags for the initiative.

It also supported the Quick Reads adult literacy initiative by funding promotional materials to be distributed to adult literacy classes and further education colleges.

## Employee-led support

The company encourages employee volunteering, matching the time committed by staff volunteers to 'reading initiatives'. It also actively encourages staff to raise funds for its own trust – The WH Smith Trust (Charity Commission no. 1013782). The funds raised each year are split, with two-thirds of the net proceeds going to the staff's chosen charity of the year. The remaining third is allocated to support the efforts of employees who are directly involved in local charities or schools. In addition, support is provided to a smaller number of selected trade/allied charities such as the Newsvendors Benevolent Fund. Grants can be for up to £3,000.

In recognition of the ambassadorial role staff volunteers play, WH Smith established Community Awards in May 2006 to spotlight their efforts.

**Payroll giving:** The group operates the Give As You Earn scheme.

The company puts the value of staff time and costs at £136,000.

## Commercially-led support

**Sponsorship:** The group does not undertake sponsorship.

# Smiths Group plc

765 Finchley Road, Childs Hill, London NW11 8DS

020 8458 3232; Fax: 020 8457 8346

Website: www.smiths-group.com

Correspondent: Guy Norris, Company Secretary

**Chief officer:** Donald Brydon

**Chief Executive:** Keith Butler-Wheelhouse

| Year end | Turnover | Pre-tax profit |
|---|---|---|
| 31/07/2005 | £3,016,800,000 | £309,800,000 |

**Nature of company business**
The company is involved in the medical, industrial, aerospace and sealing solutions industries.

**Subsidiaries include:** Hypertac Ltd, John Crane, Chartco Ltd, Specac Ltd, Dowty Propellors, Graseby Medical Ltd, Hamble Structures, Microcircuit Engineering, Beagle Aircraft, Kelvin Hughes Ltd, Trak Microwave, Portex Ltd, Reynolds Rings Ltd, Flexible Ducting Ltd, Pneupac Ltd, Mixing Solutions Ltd, Performance Plus

**Main locations:** Birmingham, Dundee, Eastleigh, Gloucester, Hounslow, Burnley, Crawley, Tewkesbury, Watford, Croyden, Christchhurch, Glalsgow, Wolverhampton, Hythe, Ilford, Orpington, Nelson, Onchan, Newmarket, Newbury, Manchester, Luton, Slough, Southampton

**Total employees:** 28,509

### Charitable donations

2005: £635,000
2004: £602,000
2003: £708,000

Membership: BitC

## Community involvement

Smiths seek to contribute to the communities in which it operates by participation in, and support for, community and charitable initiatives. The company's support of charities is wide-ranging covering everything from the local village fete to national causes. Appeals are considered on their merits and their relevance to the company's business (i.e. medical, industrial, aerospace and sealing solutions) and geographical interests.

Smiths make donations, in cash and kind, to schools, community institutions and projects and it sponsors charities, communities and arts organisations worldwide.

Individual group businesses review and approve local requests, while a charity & donations committee administers a central budget supporting national and international charitable organisations.

### Exclusions

No support for advertising in charity brochures, animal welfare, appeals from individuals, the arts, fundraising events, overseas projects, political appeals, religious appeals or sport.

### Applications

In writing to the correspondent. Charities should give their appeals reasonable time to be processed as the company receives about ten appeals a week and all are considered. A donations committee decides appeals and meets fairly regularly. Applications should be concise, not too scruffy or glossy, and should briefly set out what is wanted and why.

## Corporate giving

In 2004/05, global community contributions amounted to £635,000. Of this, £300,000 went to support the Portex Chair of Paediatric Anaesthesia and £8,000 to charities with selected medical objectives. Other donations were made by the company's businesses worldwide to miscellaneous charities. No political donations were made.

### In-kind support

Support such as gifts in kind and secondments may be provided at a local level by subsidiaries. Education and enterprise initiative support is also carried out at a local level.

### Commercially-led support

**Sponsorship:** The subsidiary Portex Ltd sponsor the Chair of Paediatric Anaesthesia at the Institute of Child Health at Great Ormond Street Hospital.

# Sodexho Ltd

Communications Department, Capital House, 2nd Floor, 25 Chapel Street, London, NW1 5DH

Website: www.sodexho.co.uk

Correspondent: Tim Lucas, Corporate Responsibility Manager

| Year end | Turnover | Pre-tax profit |
|---|---|---|
| 15/12/2005 | £387,245,000 | £5,261,000 |

**Nature of company business**
The provision of catering management services to clients in commercial, industrial, educational, healthcare and other establishments. Activities also include catering at special events, sporting, leisure and public locations, vending services, supply of catering equipment, facilities management, design and allied services.

**Subsidiaries include:** Town & County Catering Ltd, Kelvin International Services Ltd, Gilmour & Pether Ltd, Ring & Brymer Holdings Ltd, Wheatsheaf Catering Ltd

**Main locations:** Kenley, Hitchin, Abertillery, Aberdeen, Alperton, Aldershot

**UK employees:** 50,000

> ### Charitable donations
>
> 2005: £55,229
> 2004: £145,875
> 2003: £100,000
>
> Membership: BitC, %Club

### Applications

In writing to the correspondent.

Organisations wishing to apply to become a charity partner for the STOP Hunger campaign should e-mail a one page summary (stophunger@sodexho-uk.com).

## Corporate giving

In 2005 the company launched the STOP Hunger campaign in the UK and Ireland, with clear aims to both combat poor nutrition in our local communities and provide a central focus for community related activities. The campaign is managed through the Sodexho Foundation (Charity Commission no. 1110266). Its objectives are to educate and provide relief from financial hardship in relation to health, nutrition and well-being through the provision of grants, goods and services.

STOP Hunger supports a number of charities but is insistent that each are involved in one or more of the following activities:

- healthy eating and healthy lifestyle education
- healthy food provision to those in need
- basic life skills education to those in need, for example cooking on a budget, basic cooking skills, basic food hygiene and health and safety.

In 2004/05 the company made charitable donation totalling £55,229.

### Employee-led support

'Sodexho employees are involved in the following three ways; financial donations through employee fundraising, employee volunteering and the sharing of Sodexho knowledge and expertise with charity partners (beneficiary charities).'

**Payroll giving:** The company operates a giving scheme.

### Commercially-led support

Sedexho supports a variety of causes that reflect business and community interests, forging partnerships with a number of organisations.

# Sony United Kingdom Limited

The Heights, Brooklands, Weybridge, Surrey KT13 0XW

01932 816000; Fax: 01932 817000

Website: www.sony.net

Correspondent: Deborah Dymott, Business Development

| Year end | Turnover | Pre-tax profit |
|---|---|---|
| 31/03/2005 | £2,667,249,000 | (£29,404,000) |

**Nature of company business**
The company is the distributor in the United Kingdom of Sony and AIWA branded products which are principally electronic goods for the domestic, leisure, business and professional markets. The company distributes Sony branded video and audio systems for commercial and professional use, and computer peripheral and component products, including semiconductor products, for use throughout Europe, Africa and the Middle East. Sony colour televisions, television tubes and other key components for the domestic and export markets are manufactured at factories which are operated by the company in South Wales.

**Subsidiaries include:** Specialized Electonics Services (Glasgow) Ltd

**Main locations:** Bridgend, Thatcham, Pencoed, Weybridge, Basingstoke

**UK employees:** 3,132

**Total employees:** 3,236

> ### Charitable donations
>
> 2005: £94,385
> 2004: £154,056
>
> Membership: BitC

## Community involvement

Sony prefers to support local charities in areas of company presence (Weybridge, Basingstoke, Thatcham, Pencoed and Bridgend), appeals relevant to company business, and charities in which a member of staff is involved. There is a preference for children/youth, education, sickness/disability charities and social welfare. The Sony Group publish an annual corporate social responsibility report. The Report states 'Sony undertakes a wide variety of social contribution activities in fields in which it is best able to do so, to help address the needs of communities in regions around the world where Sony conducts business.' Expenditure is largely in the areas of education, particularly science education, as well as the arts, music and culture.

### Exclusions

No support for advertising in charity brochures.

### Applications

Appeals should be addressed to the correspondent.

## Corporate giving

In 2005, donations to charitable organisations totalled £94,385 (2004: £154,056). These donations relate primarily to support for local charities and events. We have no information regarding the recipient organisations.

### Employee-led support

Sony's Global Volunteer Day is when Sony employees can take an active part in their local community and are encouraged to cooperate with colleagues all over the world to build on Sony's team spirit through sponsorship of coordinated volunteer activities. Two projects were undertaken by Sony UK in Weybridge. Project one was a conservation project, carried out at the Elmbridge Commons area. The Sony party undertook work to ensure that the habitat at West End Common would encourage the growth of wild plants and flowers as well as creating an attractive environment for visitors. The second project was a general clean up of the riding for the disabled facilities in Thatcham. 12 Sony volunteers participated.

**Payroll giving:** Sony operates the Give As You Earn scheme.

### Commercially-led support

**Sponsorship:** *The arts* – Local organisations to have received support include Brooklands Museum and the Newbury Spring Festival.

# Spar (UK) Limited

Mezzanine Floor, Hygeia Building, 66–68 College Road, Harrow, HA3 1BE

020 8426 3700; Fax: 020 8426 3701

Website: www.spar.co.uk

Correspondent: Susan Darbyshire, Marketing Director

Managing Director: Jerry Marwood

| Year end | Turnover | Pre-tax profit |
|---|---|---|
| 30/04/2005 | £51,000,000 | |

**Nature of company business**
Independently-owned nationwide convenience stores operating under the SPAR banner.

### Charitable donations

Membership: BitC

## Community involvement

SPAR states that its role within the community is an integral part of the way it does business and because of this is a subscribed member of Business in the Community (BitC). As part of this involvement, SPAR is developing a framework in which it can support those issues that are important to the communities local to its stores. This could include the local rugby team, a charitable event or, as part of the BitC Rural Campaign, the local Post Office.

In addition to the above, national organisations can also receive support with those involved with children and sport being particularly favoured.

SPAR also has an associated charitable trust – The SPAR Charitable Fund (Charity Commission No. 236252) administered from the address given above.

### Applications

Please contact your local store manager, unless stated otherwise above.

## Corporate giving

Quantifying SPAR's community investment in monetary terms has proved elusive. However, we believe its cash and in-kind support to be sufficient to warrant inclusion here.

In 2006, SPAR announced the beginning of its partnership with the NSPCC, Childline and Children 1st (Scotland). Due to last until 2008, SPAR's support will enable, amongst other positives, the continued availability of child telephone helplines for adults or children requiring advice and support.

**The SPAR Charitable Trust:** In 2005, the trust had income of £54,632 and made donations of £45,031 to related trade benevolent funds and Macmillan Cancer Relief. Support outside of this is unlikely, but further details can be found in *A Guide to the Major Trusts Volume 2*, published by the Directory of Social Change.

### In-kind support

Some local SPAR stores are donating special athletics kits to local schools and youth sports teams (over 70% of SPAR retailers already support their local schools in some way or another). If you haven't been approached yet please DON'T contact you local store directly, but send an e-mail to Simon Fisher (sportsdaykits@spar.co.uk). SPAR will then ask your local store if they would like to donate a kit to your school.

# Spirax Sarco Engineering plc

Charlton House, Cirencester Road, Cheltenham,
Gloucestershire GL53 8ER

01242 521361; Fax: 01242 581470

Website: www.spiraxsarcoengineering.com

Correspondent: Jane Husband, Secretary to the Chief Executive

Chief officer: M Townsend

Chief Executive: M J D Steel

| Year end | Turnover | Pre-tax profit |
| --- | --- | --- |
| 31/12/2005 | £349,100,000 | £56,959,000 |

**Nature of company business**
The provision of knowledge, service and products worldwide for the control and efficient use of steam and other industrial fluids.

Subsidiaries include: Watson-Marlow Ltd

Main locations: Glasgow, Cheltenham

UK employees: 1,133

Total employees: 3,899

### Charitable donations
2005: £59,400
2004: £47,982
2003: £49,910

## Community involvement

The company's 2005 Annual Report states: 'The group has a charitable trust which donates to registered charities and additional donations are made to appropriate requests for support from bodies which are not registered charities.

'The operating companies in the group are encouraged to provide support to local communities through company donations, employee organised charitable activities, donation of equipment no longer required and through the provision of information.'

### Exclusions

Previous information collated suggested that the company will make no response to circular appeals, and no grants for advertising in charity brochures, religious appeals, local appeals not in areas of company presence and large national appeals.

### Applications

In writing to the correspondent.

## Corporate giving

In 2005, the company made cash donations totalling £59,400, primarily through the Spirax-Sarco Engineering plc Group Charitable Trust (Charity Commission No. 1082534). Beneficiaries included: British Red Cross – Tsunami Appeal (£10,000); National Star Centre (£3,000); Lillian Faithful Homes (£2,000); Seven Springs Play and Support Centre (£1,000); Gloucestershire Wildlife Fund (£750); and, SS Great Britain (£500).

### In-kind support

In addition to cash donations, the company donates equipment that is no longer required to the local community.

### Employee-led support

Employees are encouraged to organise charitable activities.

# Spirent plc

Spirent House, Crawley Business Centre, Fleming Road, Crawley, West Sussex RH10 9QL

01293 767676; Fax: 01293 767677

Website: www.spirent.com

Correspondent: Company Secretary

Chief officer: John Weston

Chief Executive: Anders Gustafsson

| Year end | Turnover | Pre-tax profit |
| --- | --- | --- |
| 31/12/2005 | £259,300,000 | (£41,700,000) |

**Nature of company business**
An international technology group focused on the design, development, manufacture and marketing of specialist electronic products.

Subsidiaries include: Hellermann Tyton UK, Staeng Ltd, PG Drives Technology Ltd

Main locations: Aldridge, Glasgow, Crawley, Christchurch, Plymouth, Paignton, Northampton, Manchester

Total employees: 4,378

### Charitable donations
2005: £96,000
2004: £63,000
2003: £63,000

## Community involvement

The company made the following statement in its 2005 annual report. 'Spirent recognises the significance of local communities and through our Charitable Donations Policy we strive to be a responsible partner in the communities in which we operate. We encourage all our businesses to support the particular needs of their communities by contributing to local charities and community initiatives. Support takes the form of employee time and skills, gifts in kind and cash donations.'

### Exclusions

No support for appeals from individuals, or for local appeals not in areas of company presence.

### Applications

In writing to the correspondent.

## Corporate giving

In 2005, the company declared worldwide charitable cash donations of £96,000 (2004: £63,000). This excludes operating units support and participation in local community activities. We have no details of the beneficiaries.

## In-kind support

Spirent continues to support education in its local communities by offering internships and work experience programmes. The company also donate materials and equipment to local causes throughout the world. During 2005, donations included computers to those affected by the Asian tsunami, computer screens and furniture to local schools and mobile phones to a women's shelter.

## Employee-led support

Spirent continues to support and encourage all its employees and businesses to find new ways of helping their communities. As a result, employees may become involved in fundraising activities or give their time in support of local concerns and community initiatives.

# SSL International plc

Head Office, 35 New Bridge Street, London EC4V 6BW

020 7367 5760; Fax: 020 7367 5790

Website: www.ssl-international.com

Correspondent: Garry Watts, Chief Executive

Chief officer: Gerald Corbett

Chief Executive: Garry Watts

| Year end | Turnover | Pre-tax profit |
|---|---|---|
| 31/03/2006 | £458,800,000 | £33,500,000 |

Nature of company business
The manufacture and distribution of healthcare products.

Subsidiaries include: London International Group plc, Scholl Consumer Products Ltd, Scholl Ltd, LRC Products Ltd

Main locations: Manchester, London

Total employees: 5,095

### Charitable donations

2004: £100,000
2003: £100,000

## Community involvement

Grants are apparently made through the Stoller Charitable Trust which is based at the same address. During 2004/05 the trust received a £500,000 donation which was not attributed, but is likely to have come from the company – there was no such donation in 2005/06. Information on this trust can be found in *A Guide to the Major Trusts Volume 2*, published by Directory of Social Change.

## Exclusions

No support for local appeals not in areas of company presence.

## Applications

In writing to the correspondent.

## Corporate giving

Figures for the company's community support were unavailable, as in previous years.

# St James's Place plc

St James's Place House, Dollar Street, Cirencester, Gloucestershire, GL7 2AQ

020 7493 8111

Website: www.sjp.co.uk

Correspondent: Mrs Gail Mitchell-Briggs, Secretary, St James's Place Foundation 01285 640302
E-mail: gail.mitchell-briggs@sjpc.co.uk

Chief officer: Sir Mark Weinberg

Chief Executive: Mike Wilson

| Year end | Turnover | Pre-tax profit |
|---|---|---|
| 31/12/2005 | | 127,100,000 |

Nature of company business
St James's Place plc is a financial services group involved in the provision of wealth management services.

Subsidiaries include: J Rothschild Assurance plc

Main locations: London

Total employees: 549

### Charitable donations

2005: £765,380
2003: £500,000

Membership: %Club

## Community involvement

St James's Place channels its cash contributions to charity through the St James's Place Foundation (Charity Commission no. 1031456). All administrative and management costs are met by St James's Place plc.

The objective of the foundation is to raise money for distribution to organisations that meet its main current theme of 'Cherishing the Children'. This theme is aimed at children and young people who are mentally and/or physically disabled, or have a life threatening or degenerative illness up to the age of 25. The foundation now also supports the Hospice Movement.

## Exclusions

No response to circular appeals, and no grants for advertising in charity brochures sponsorship or individuals.

## Applications

The foundation will only consider applications from established charities or special needs schools for projects that meet the funding criteria.

The management committee of the St James's Place Foundation considers applications at its quarterly meetings. An application form should be requested from the secretary at the following address:

St James's Place Foundation
St James's Place House
Dollar Street
Cirencester
Gloucestershire
GL7 2AQ

## Corporate giving

St James's Place plc matches, on a pound for pound basis, all the money raised by the foundation up to an increased maximum of £800,000 in 2005. During 2005 the company donated £765,380 to the foundation.

The corporate donation is distributed differently from the other funds raised. It was agreed between the management committee and the trustees, that the corporate donation should be used to fund larger projects not necessarily in keeping with the foundation's theme.

Full details of the foundation can be found in *A Guide to the Major Trusts Volume 1*, published by the Directory of Social Change.

# Stagecoach Group plc

10 Dunkeld Road, Perth PH1 5TW

01738 442111

Website: www.stagecoachgroup.com

Correspondent: Stagecoach Group Community Fund
01738 442111

Chief officer: Robert Speirs

Chief Executive: Brian Souter

| Year end | Turnover | Pre-tax profit |
|---|---|---|
| 30/04/2005 | £1,479,500,000 | £108,300,000 |

**Nature of company business**
Principal activity: The provision of public transport services in the UK and overseas.

**Subsidiaries include:** East Kent Road Car Co Ltd, East London Bus & Coach Co Ltd, National Transport Tokens Ltd, Stagecoach Scotland Ltd, PSV Claims Bureau Ltd, Cleveland Transit Ltd, South East London & Kent Bus Co Ltd, Greater Manchester Buses South Ltd, East Midland Motor Services Ltd, Busways Travel Services Ltd, Cambus Ltd

**Main locations:** Ilford, Chichester, Isle of Wight, Exteter, Gwent, Norhampton, Perth, Sheffield, Rugby, Sunderland, Oxford, Manchester, London, Liverpool, Cowdenbeath, Cambridge, Chesterfield, Carlisle, Gloucester, Ayr

UK employees: 29,163

Total employees: 29,657

### Charitable donations

2004: £300,000
2003: £700,000

## Community involvement

The company referred us to its website from where the following information was taken.

Stagecoach support the work of local, national and international charities, particularly those concerned with health, education, young people and communities local to its business activities.

### Applications

In writing to the Stagecoach Group Community Fund at the above address.

## Corporate giving

In 2004/05, the company made cash donations of £300,000. Much of this was focused on education and young people. Stagecoach work closely with schools and police on local crime prevention initiatives and education of youngsters about the dangers and consequences of anti-social behaviour. The company also assists many local initiatives that help provide opportunities for young people. Its bus company in Warwickshire, for example, is a partner in an innovative "text2talk" anti-bullying initiative with the police and other agencies. It is also a key partner in Kent People's Trust, a police and business initiative in the county targeted at reducing youth crime. In Strathclyde, Stagecoach has two information and training vehicles, which are used by the police to work with youngsters in housing estates in Glasgow and Ayrshire to cut crime and vandalism. At South West Trains, there is a focus on projects designed to give young people alternatives to antisocial behaviour, particularly highlighting the dangers of trespassing on railway lines.

Stagecoach is also helping promote social inclusion with its communities and help those who are the most vulnerable. A national agreement exists with Guide Dogs for the Blind that allows the dog trainers free travel on its buses.

The company also pledged £100,000 towards the Asian Tsunami Appeal which was distributed via four charities – Save the Children, British Red Cross, Tearfund and World Vision. A further £40,000 was added to this to match pound for pound employees fundraising efforts for the relief fund.

### In-kind support

Although not disclosed, further non-cash support (estimated to be at least an additional 0.2% of pre-tax profits) was made through joint promotions, and training schemes.

For example, hundreds of Stagecoach employees devote their own time every day to local projects that make a real difference in their area. Its businesses provide much-needed in-kind support, while its people also give charities the benefit of their expertise during secondments. Earlier this year, for example, Stagecoach provided transport for a group of children from Beslan in Russia who were on a month-long stay in Scotland following the terrorist siege at a school in their homeland.

### Employee-led support

The company also supports employees' volunteering/charitable activities by considering, where appropriate, financial help, allowing time off to volunteer, and matching employee fundraising.

In 2005, for example, employees raised £40,000 for the Asian tsunami disaster; a figure matched by the company.

### Commercially-led support

**Sponsorship:** *The Arts* – Support continued for a number of arts initiatives with 2005 marking the 10th anniversary of the groups support for the Mari Markus Gomori children's concerts.

**Cause-related marketing:** The group undertook a number of joint promotional campaigns with Understanding Industry (now Business Dynamics), New Deal and the Kent Police.

# Standard Chartered plc

1 Aldermanbury Square, London EC2V 7SB

020 7280 7500; Fax: 020 7280 7791

**Website:** www.standardchartered.com/uk/

**Correspondent:** Community Relations Manager 020 7280 7247

**Chief officer:** Bryan Sanderson

**Chief Executive:** Evan M Davies

| Year end | Turnover | Pre-tax profit |
|---|---|---|
| 31/12/2005 | £4,809,013 | £1,473,482 |

**Nature of company business**
The group's principal activity is the provision of banking and other financial services.

**Main locations:** London

**UK employees:** 1,276

**Total employees:** 44,000

### Charitable donations

2005: £71,448
2003: £780,000

Membership: L B Group, %Club

## Community involvement

The group's donations policy is focused on those countries in Asia, Africa, the Middle East and Latin America where it has operations. It concentrates on projects that assist children, particularly in the areas of health and education. Environmental projects are occasionally considered.

The following criteria must be met before Standard Chartered can consider making a donation. All donations must:

- reflect the group's focus on youth, health and education
- assist those in the community who are most in need
- support the national aspirations of the country
- be environmentally sound
- support non-governmental organisations involved in charitable or community activities but not political or religious projects, or individuals other than staff.

Priority is given to those projects which: allow Standard Chartered and its staff the opportunity to become involved, generate mutually beneficial publicity, have clear and agreed objectives, and are readily applicable to measurement and audit.

**Note:** Although some support is given to UK registered charities, this is only given to those focusing on supporting work outside the United Kingdom.

## Exclusions

Generally no support for charities working to the benefit of communities in the UK, circular appeals, advertising in charity brochures, appeals from individuals, purely denominational (religious) appeals, local appeals not in areas of company presence or large national appeals. Donations are not made to political parties.

## Applications

Please note the following points:

- Ensure that the project for which you are seeking support fits the criteria set out.
- Write a short summary of the project (not more than one page of A4 paper). It should then be sent to the Standard Chartered corporate affairs manager of the country where the project is taking place. Should the group then be able to consider supporting the project a more detailed proposal will be required. The company has operations in over 40 countries in Africa, Asia, the Middle East, and Latin America.
- As donation plans for the year are usually agreed at the end of the year, it is advisable to submit a proposal no later than the third quarter of a given year.
- It is group practice to support a limited number of charities and, where possible, to support them for a period of up to three years. The opportunity for involvement of Standard Chartered and direct support by our people is a key element in gaining funding.

## Corporate giving

In 2005, the Group gave over £4 million to fund the work of non-governmental organisations (of which £71,448 was given to United Kingdom registered charities, focusing on supporting their work outside the United Kingdom).

### In-kind support

The company also supports a range of fundraising events, provides advice, secondments and scholarships.

### Employee-led support

Standard Chartered encourages its people to become involved in the communities in which they work. Many participate in a wide range of charitable and community support programmes.

# Standard Life

Standard Life House, 30 Lothian Road, Edinburgh EH1 2DH

0131 225 2552

**Website:** www.standardlife.com

**Correspondent:** Andrew Marshall-Roberts, Corporate Social Responsibility Manager

**Chief officer:** Sir Brian Stewart

**Chief Executive:** Sandy Crombie

| Year end | Turnover | Pre-tax profit |
|---|---|---|
| 31/12/2005 | | |

**Nature of company business**
Life assurance, pensions, health insurance, investment management and banking.

**Subsidiaries include:** STLM Ltd

**Main locations:** Edinburgh

**UK employees:** 8,324

**Total employees:** 11,320

## Community involvement

The Standard Life UK Group actively supports local communities and educational institutions where it works and where its employees live. The group focuses its activities in the following five areas:

- education and training
- homelessness
- older people – promote a good quality of life
- environment local to its offices.

The group prefers to work in partnership with charitable and voluntary organisations and educational establishments so that it is able to give largely in kind as opposed to giving cash.

However, on rare occasions cash is given and specific events and activities are sponsored from time to time.

The group gives priority to activities which maximise the inclusion of minorities into mainstream society.

Much of the activity takes place in Edinburgh where the majority of its staff are employed. There is, however, limited activity in its area offices across the UK.

**Charities of the Year:** Association of International Cancer Research and Wellchild (2006).

### Exclusions

In order for the company to concentrate its energies on the five main areas stated above, the following are excluded: political or religious activities, animal welfare, buildings and heritage, or sports clubs.

Further, the group does not sponsor individuals, nor get involved with third party funding activities, nor buy charity advertising space.

### Applications

In writing to the correspondent.

## Corporate giving

In 2005 cash donations totalled £342,364, which included £246,000 donated to the Standard Life Charity Fund.

### In-kind support

Services provided to charities have included use of its design, print and copying facilities, meeting room space in its buildings, provision of old computer equipment and even the donation of an unused forklift truck.

**Education:** Liaison activities have included producing 6,000 packs for a Junior Road Safety Officers Scheme in conjunction with Lothian and Borders Police

Work placements – Standard Life offers work experience to around 100 school students a year.

Mock interviews – a programme for those about to enter or re-enter the world of work.

**The homeless:** The Pathfinders Project assists young homeless people into employment through six-month placements with Standard Life. The group aims to take on four to six people per year through this route.

**Secondments:** The group also sends up to 14 employees at a time out on secondment to organisations for periods of three months to undertake specific projects.

### Employee-led support

Staff are encouraged to raise funds for charities chosen by staff, with limited time off (one hour a week) given to encourage staff to volunteer. It advertises events its staff are involved in, as well as having a section on its intranet site advertising voluntary placements to staff.

**Payroll giving:** The Give As You Earn scheme is in operation.

### Commercially-led support

**Sponsorship:** Standard Life undertakes arts sponsorship. It has also sponsored the printing of publicity materials and helped to publicise those events.

# Stanley Leisure plc

Stanley House, 151 Dale Street, Liverpool L2 2JW

0151 237 6000; Fax: 0151 237 6197

Website: www.stanleyleisure.com

Correspondent: Lord L Steinberg, Chairman

Chief officer: Lord Steinberg

Chief Executive: Bob Wiper

| Year end | Turnover | Pre-tax profit |
|---|---|---|
| 30/04/2006 | £224,800,000 | £19,100,000 |

Nature of company business
The main activity of the company is that of betting office and casino operators.

Subsidiaries include: Pakm Beach Club Ltd, B J O'Connor Ltd

Main locations: Liverpool

UK employees: 4,559

## Community involvement

The company prefers to support local charities in Northern Ireland and the North West of England, especially Merseyside. Preferred areas of support are advertising in charity brochures; animal welfare charities; children/youth; education; elderly people; sickness/disability charities; and sport.

A donations committee was established in June 2003 and meets at least twice a year to consider and monitor donations that are made to charitable causes.

### Exclusions

No support for appeals from individuals; the arts; environment/heritage; fundraising events; overseas projects; political appeals; religious appeals; or science/technology.

### Applications

In writing to the correspondent.

## Corporate giving

In 2004, cash donations totalled £300,000 although no details of beneficiaries were available.

Past beneficiaries have included children's hospitals, Salford University, Children in Need, Forth AM Help a Child and Thoroughbred Rehabilitation Centre.

## Employee-led support

Employees are encouraged to participate in charitable events, such as the BBC Children in Need Appeal.

# Starbucks Coffee Company

11 Heathmans Road, London SW6 4TJ

020 7878 4900

Website: www.starbucks.co.uk

Correspondent: Jim Curtis, Community Affairs Specialist
020 7878 4900

| Year end | Turnover | Pre-tax profit |
|---|---|---|
| | £244,216,333 | (£8,105,680) |

**Nature of company business**
A worldwide chain of coffee houses, with over 360 branches in the UK.

Main locations: London

UK employees: 6,092

### Charitable donations

Membership: BitC

## Community involvement

The company provides support in the areas around its stores, which now covers most of the UK. It provides cash grants and other support to local causes, as well as supporting causes in the developing world.

### Applications

In writing to the correspondent.

## Corporate giving

In 2005 the company had worldwide giving figures of $30.3 million in corporate donations including in kind contributions and gave the number of hours volunteered by partners and customers as 299,000. In 1997 Starbucks founder, Howard Schultz established The Starbucks Foundation. Since then, the Foundation has provided more than $11 million to approximately 700 organisations primarily in the areas of literacy and youth education in underserved communities in the USA and Canada. The Foundation receives the majority of its funding from the Starbucks Corporation.

Beneficiaries in the UK have included All Books for Children, Birmingham Arts Council for support for local artists, Bolton Fairtrade Town towards printing 10,000 fairtrade guides to the town, Book Drop, Business in the Community for a district-manager-coordinated two-day course for 14 to 15 year olds in Manchester, Macmillan Cancer Relief, Royal Free Hospital for a coffee morning, RSA Coffee House Challenge

and Workwise an initiative to improve the employability of young people. The UK company also has a long-term commitment to creating opportunities in the arts and have supported two projects during 2005, one in partnership with The Old Vic Theatre and the second in partnership with the Hayward Gallery. Unfortunately, no figures are available from the 2005 Accounts.

## In-kind support

The company can donate its products to coffee mornings and so on. It has also allowed its premises to be used for similar activities.

## Employee-led support

Staff (partners) are encouraged to volunteer, either for voluntary organisations of their own selection or through initiatives supported by the company such as Timebank, the national volunteering charity. In some circumstances, cash donations have been linked to volunteering, with the organisation affected receiving a payment similar to the employee's wages for the work performed. The UK company has established a Parnters in Education programme comprising three initiatives, all of which provide help to children in their educational development. The initiatives are: All Books for Children, The Starbucks Bookdrive and Workwise.

# J Stobart and Sons Ltd

Newlands Mill, Hesket Newmarket, Wigton, Cumbria CA7 8HP

01697 478261

Correspondent: (See 'Applications')

Managing Director: P J Stobart

| Year end | Turnover | Pre-tax profit |
|---|---|---|
| 31/12/2005 | | £568,698 |

**Nature of company business**
The manufacture and retail of animal feeding stuffs.

Main locations: Carlisle

UK employees: 21

### Charitable donations

2005: £700,000
2004: £700,000

## Community involvement

No doubt much to the chagrin of Eddie Stobart 'spotters', we have decided to replace that company's entry with information about a perhaps less well known Stobart family business. The main reason for this is that despite the company having a high and recognisable profile, information about what it did in support of local charities and good causes has remained very sketchy. The company's acquisition by W A Developments Limited has further muddied the water, although according to the 2006 accounts, it does still make very limited charitable donations.

On the other hand, J Stobart and Sons Limited provide substantial charitable support through the Stobart Newlands Charitable Trust (Charity Commission no. 328464), although this is mainly in aid of Christian causes.

## Exclusions

No grants for individuals.

## Applications

In writing to: Mrs M Stobart, Trustee, The Stobart Newlands Charitable Trust, Mill Croft, Newlands, Hesket Newmarket, Wigton, Cumbria CA7 8HP. Please note, however, that unsolicited causes are unlikely to succeed.

## Corporate giving

In 2005, the company made charitable donations of £700,000 (2004: £700,000), all of which went to the associated family trust of which the directors of the company are also trustees.

### The Stobart Newlands Charitable Trust

For the year ended 31 December 2004, the trust made around 50 grants to various charities totalling nearly £1.3 million, the majority to Christian, religious and missionary bodies. The major beneficiaries were: Logos Ministries (£324,700); Mission Aviation Fellowship (£200,000); and, World Vision (£191,644). However, support was also given to Help the Aged (£8,000).

# J Swire & Sons Ltd

Swire House, 59 Buckingham Gate, London SW1E 6AJ

020 7834 7717; Fax: 020 7630 0353

Website: www.swire.com

Correspondent: J R Adams, Secretary

Chief officer: J W J Hughes-Hallett

| Year end | Turnover | Pre-tax profit |
|---|---|---|
| 31/12/2005 | £2,290,000,000 | £772,000,000 |

Nature of company business
Principal activities: marine including shipowning and operating, aviation (via Cathay Pacific Airways which is 44% owned by Swire Pacific), cold storage and road transport, industrial and trading activities, plantations and property. The company owns a 30% stake in the tea trader, James Finlay.

Subsidiaries include: James Finlay, Cathay Pacific

Main locations: London

Total employees: 76,034

> ### Charitable donations
> 2005: £508,000
> 2004: £1,187,000

## Community involvement

Worldwide, the main thrust of the company's charitable support programme is education and assisting those individuals who are least able to help themselves. Support may also be given to the arts, sport and a range of community activities.

In the UK, John Swire & Sons provide support for a variety of charities, particularly those in the medical and educational fields.

There are also several trusts with connections to the company. These are: the John Swire (1989) Charitable Trust (Charity Commission no. 802142) and the Swire Charitable Trust (Charity Commission no. 270726). The former has substantial assets from which it derives its income, however it appears that latter receives almost all of its income from the company. There is also the Swire Educational Trust (see below).

## Applications

In writing to the correspondent. All the above mentioned trusts are also based at the company's address.

## Corporate giving

Worldwide, the company donates several million pounds each year in areas in which it operates (in 2005, for example, the worldwide figure was £3,494,000). The company's website details the company's activities in communities around the world where it has a presence or business connection, such as mainland China and Hong Kong. In 2005 the Swire Charitable Trust received an income of £400,000 from the company. Beneficiaries of the trust include the Motor Neurone Disease Association (£75,000), Wantage Nursing Home Charitable Trust (£50,000), Book Aid International (£10,000), Brooklands Museum Trust Limited (£5,000) and St John Ambulance (£1,000), amongst many other health and social welfare organisations.

**Education:** The Swire Educational Trust (Charity Commission no. 328366) funds graduate and postgraduate places in the UK for scholars around the world, especially those from countries where the group does business. In 2004/05 this trust received a donation of £600,000 towards its total income from the company, as it did in the previous year. The Swire Educational Trust's income also included a transfer of funds from the James Henry Scott Educational Trust to the value of £2,659,963. This trust was also supported by the company and now appears to have wound up.

# Tate & Lyle plc

Sugar Quay, Lower Thames Street, London EC3R 6DQ

020 7626 6525; Fax: 020 7623 5213

Website: www.tate-lyle.co.uk

Correspondent: Mike Grier, Corporate Social Responsibility Manager

Chief officer: Sir David Lees

Chief Executive: Iain Ferguson

| Year end | Turnover | Pre-tax profit |
|---|---|---|
| 31/03/2006 | £3,720,000,000 | £42,000,000 |

Nature of company business
Principal activities are: the processing of carbohydrates to provide a range of sweetener and starch products and animal feed; and bulk storage. The company's UK sugar refinery is in London.

Subsidiaries include: The Molasses Trading Co Ltd, Greenwich Distillers Ltd, Amylum UK Limited, Redpath (UK) Limited, FSL Bells, Speciality Sweeteners

Main locations: Avonmouth, Burton-on-Trent, Hull, Newham, Merseyside, Selby

UK employees: 1,240

Total employees: 6,646

> ### Charitable donations
> 2006: £386,000
> 2005: £317,000
> 2004: £297,000
>
> Membership: BitC

## Community involvement

Tate & Lyle's main areas of charitable support are education and causes close to where the company operates or those in which an employee is involved. Main locations are Newham, Merseyside, Avonmouth, Hull, Burton-on-Trent and Selby.

The company is a founder member of the PerCent Club and allocates around 0.7% of profit before tax worldwide and 1% of UK pre-tax profits to community projects. Within these overall targets the company aims to contribute to the following sectors:

- education and youth (50%)
- civic and environment (25%)
- health and welfare (15%)
- arts (10%).

### Exclusions

No support is given to circular appeals, advertising in charity brochures, individuals, purely denominational (religious) appeals, local appeals not in areas of company presence, animal welfare, political appeals, sport or large national appeals.

### Applications

In writing to the correspondent.

## Corporate giving

In 2005/06, worldwide charitable donations totalled £766,000 (2005: £778,000), of which £386,000 (2005: £317,000) was donated in the UK.

In the UK, the top three supported charities in 2005/06 were: Tate Britain, London Bombings Relief Charitable Fund, and Community Links.

### In-kind support

**Education:** The company's main education activities are the major literacy programmes, Reading is Fundamental and the Newham Literacy Programme.

Non-cash support has also been given to education business partnerships.

**Enterprise:** The company supports Business in the Community and the East London Partnership.

**Secondments:** Applications for secondments to enterprise agencies are considered, and executives throughout the group are encouraged to participate in local educational systems.

### Employee-led support

The company operates an employee volunteering scheme and provides some matching to employee giving.

**Education:** Links are developed with local schools and colleges offering work experience and work shadowing.

**Payroll giving:** The company operates the Give As You Earn scheme.

### Commercially-led support

**Sponsorship:** Arts and good cause sponsorship are undertaken.

# Taylor Woodrow plc

2 Princes Way, Solihull, West Midlands B91 3ES

0121 600 8000; Fax: 0121 600 8001

Website: www.taywood.co.uk

Correspondent: Kate Booth, Communications Assistant

Chief officer: Norman Askew

Chief Executive: Iain Napier

| Year end | Turnover | Pre-tax profit |
|---|---|---|
| 31/12/2005 | £3,476,900,000 | £411,000,000 |

**Nature of company business**
The group is engaged in construction, property, housing and trading activities.

**Subsidiaries include:** Taywood Homes Ltd, Greenham Trading Ltd

**Main locations:** Solihull, Livingston, Leeds, Birchwood, Leicester, Welwyn Garden City, Newbury, Crawley, Chipping Sodbury, Newmarket

**UK employees:** 4,472

**Total employees:** 8,132

> ### Charitable donations
> 2005: £96,000
> 2004: £113,000
> 2003: £98,000

## Community involvement

The company declined to participate in our survey and requested we delete their entry. However, in line with our policy of including all relevant companies, we have updated the previously published information using material available in the public domain.

### Exclusions

No support for appeals from individuals, fundraising events, political or religious appeals.

### Applications

In writing to the correspondent.

## Corporate giving

In 2005, the company made total community contributions worldwide of £363,000. Of this, £96,000 was given in support of charities in the UK.

Through its 'Building Futures' partnership with Barnardo's, the company helps fund skills and training programmes for disadvantaged young people.

**Education:** In 2005, the company launched a new community initiative to further strengthen its ties with those communities in which it operates. Entitled 'Community in the Curriculum', the scheme is being piloted with three schools in different parts of the country.

## Employee-led support

Through the company's 'Support the Team' programme, employees' fundraising efforts are matched.

**Payroll giving:** Employees are encourage to participate in 'give as you earn' programmes.

# TDG plc

25 Victoria Street, London, SW1H 0EX

020 7222 7411; Fax: 020 7222 2806

Website: www.tdg.eu.com

Correspondent: Neil Swan, Group Secretary

Chief officer: Charles Mackay

Chief Executive: David Garman

| Year end | Turnover | Pre-tax profit |
|---|---|---|
| 31/12/2005 | £510,500,000 | £8,100,000 |

Nature of company business
Road transport, warehousing and logistics.

Subsidiaries include: Scio Solutions Limited

Main locations: London

UK employees: 5,869

Total employees: 7,080

### Charitable donations
2005: £32,856
2003: £36,500

## Community involvement

In 2006 the company was actively supporting two charities, the transport charity, Transaid and the road safety charity, Brake.

## Exclusions

No donations for political, circular or general appeals. No assistance is given to individuals.

## Applications

Although not clear from the information available, it would appear that until new policy guidelines are established, unsolicited applications will not be considered.

## Corporate giving

In 2005 the company made charitable donations totalling £32,856.

## Employee-led support

The company actively encourages employees to raise money for charities and matches, pound for pound, any money raised up to a maximum of £500. Charities that benefited from the support of TDG employees in 2005 were Ambergate Special Needs School, Macmillan Cancer Relief and Children in Need.

# Telegraph Group Ltd

1 Canada Square, Canary Wharf, London E14 5DT

020 7538 5000

Website: www.telegraph.co.uk

Correspondent: Public Relations Department

Chief officer: A S Barclay

Chief Executive: Murdoch MacLennan

| Year end | Turnover | Pre-tax profit |
|---|---|---|
| 01/01/2006 | £322,800,000 | £34,000,000 |

Nature of company business
Publication of national newspapers. Within the UK the company publishes the Daily Telegraph, Sunday Telegraph, Weekly Telegraph, Electronic Telegraph and the Spectator.

Subsidiaries include: The Spectator Ltd

Main locations: London

Total employees: 1,071

### Charitable donations
2005: £164,375
2004: £162,520

## Community involvement

The company supports UK charities working in the fields of children/youth, education, elderly people, medical research, sickness/disability, ex-servicemen appeals, and newspaper printing and publishing charities. There is a preference for East London.

The company previously made donations through the Daily Telegraph Charitable Trust (Charity Commission no. 205296), although this trust was wound up in October 2003. Grants presumably are now made directly by the company to the beneficiary organisations rather than through a trust.

## Exclusions

No support for activities outside of the trust's remit.

## Applications

In writing to the correspondent. The appeal committee usually meets quarterly to decide on donations, and these will generally only be made to organisations with recognised charitable status.

## Corporate giving

In 2005 £164,375 was donated, principally to charities associated with the newspapers and their employees.

Previous beneficiaries have included Royal Opera House, Royal Free Hospital, Newspaper Education Trust (£20,000 each), The AoC Charitable Trust (£15,000), Business for Sterling (£12,500), Almeida Theatre Company (£11,000), and North London Collegiate and Royal Free Hospital – Sclerodermn Laboratory (£10,000 each). Smaller grants of between £1,000 and £6,000 were made to a variety of causes falling within the support criteria e.g. Children's Aid Direct, Politeia, Remembering for the Future, and the Voices Foundation.

## Employee-led support

Financial help is given in support of employees' volunteering/charitable activities.

**Payroll giving:** The Give As You Earn scheme is operated by the company.

# Tesco plc

Tesco House, Delamare Road, Cheshunt, Hertfordshire EN8 9SL

01992 632222

Website: www.tesco.com/everylittlehelps

Correspondent: Linda Marsh, Charities Manager 01992 644143;
Fax: 01992 646794
E-mail: linda.marsh@uk.tesco.com

Chief officer: David Reid

Chief Executive: Sir Terry Leahy

| Year end | Turnover | Pre-tax profit |
|---|---|---|
| 25/02/2006 | £43,137,000,000 | £2,235,000,000 |

Nature of company business
Tesco is a multiple retailer with superstores and supermarkets in England, Scotland, Wales and Northern Ireland.

Subsidiaries include: Spen Hill Properties Ltd

Main locations: Cheshunt

UK employees: 261,578

Total employees: 368,213

### Charitable donations

2006: £15,047,768
2005: £4,576,210
2004: £3,953,582
2003: £3,509,398

Total community contributions: £41,768,741 (global)
Management costs: £360,000

Membership: BitC, L B Group, %Club

## Community involvement

Each year the company gives financial and practical help to hundreds of charities and projects which support children, education, people with disabilities and the elderly in areas local to stores.

Support is given to projects and initiatives whose work falls within the following criteria:

- organisations and projects concerned with children, particularly in the areas of welfare and education
- organisations and projects which support the elderly and people with disabilities.

There is a central committee team in head office who manage national charity and sponsorship activity and set the guidelines for the company's community support. Community Co-ordinators have responsibility for coordinating and managing the community awards and sponsorship funds for the Tesco stores in their region.

The company differentiates between donations and sponsorship (although not between donations and cause-related marketing). The former are made through the Tesco Charity Trust (Charity Commission no. 297126), which supports registered charities only, or organisations recognised by the Inland Revenue as having charitable status.

**Charity of the Year:** British Red Cross (2007).

## Exclusions

No support for circular appeals, advertising in charity brochures, animal welfare, appeals from individuals, the arts, enterprise/training, environment/heritage, fundraising events, medical research, overseas projects (outside of help given through the British Red Cross), political appeals, religious appeals, science/technology, or sport.

The trust will not give grants to other trusts or charities acting as intermediaries.

## Applications

In writing to the correspondent.

**Other information:** The company's Retired Staff Association maintains links with retired employees and through it can offer support and assistance to those in retirement who need it.

Details of the company's community support is given in the text of its annual report and on its website at: www.tesco.com/everylittlehelps

## Corporate giving

In 2005/06, the company made total contributions to community projects and to charities worldwide of £41,768,741 of which cash donations accounted for £15,047,768.

**Tesco Charitable Trust**

Support is given to national charities and local community projects in areas of company presence. In 2005/06, the trust gave a total of £1,584,298 to local and national charities in the UK. In addition, £400,000 was granted through the Community Awards Scheme to local community charities. Grants generally range between £1,500 and £5,000.

Tesco Charity Trust donations are primarily targeted towards educational projects and charities working for the welfare of children, elderly people and people with disabilities.

Guidelines for the Tesco Charity Trust Community Award Scheme can be downloaded from the company's website, or obtained by writing to Tesco Charity Trust, Tesco Stores Ltd, Delamare Road, Cheshunt EN8 9SL.

**Community vouchers**

In addition to the above, stores receive an allocation of community vouchers to support requests for raffle prizes and so on. The vouchers may be redeemed at checkouts in the store. A maximum donation of £50 can be made to local organisations through this scheme. Over £600,000 is donated in this way.

## In-kind support

**Education:** Local schools are supported through visits and work experience placements for pupils. Training schemes are also set up where new stores are built in regeneration areas.

**Facilitated giving:** Charity collections at stores are balanced between national charities and local community appeals. One two-day collection is allocated each month. Details of how bookings may be made to secure a place can be found on Tesco's website at: 'About Us' > 'Corporate Responsibility' > 'Charities & Fundraising'.

Alternatively, for further details write to: Community Sponsorship, CSR Dept., Tesco Stores Ltd, Delamare Road, Cheshunt EN8 9SL.

### Employee-led support

A considerable amount of staff fundraising is organised in company time, with the Tesco Charity Trust adding 20% to all money raised for charity by Tesco employees.

Through the Tesco Time to Care Appeal, staff, customers and supporters aim to raise £3 million on behalf of the 2004 'Charity of the Year' – Help the Hospices.

**Payroll giving:** The company operates the Give As You Earn and Sharing the Caring payroll giving schemes. Around 12,250 employees have donated over £1,520,000 in the past two years.

### Commercially-led support

**Sponsorship:** Tesco defines its sponsorship as the payment of money to a business, charity, local voluntary organisation, school or local council to support a specific project. In return, and unlike donations, the company gets brand recognition as the sponsor. Projects which are supported through Tesco's community sponsorship programme could include an education project for a local school, a children's Christmas party, a local fun day or carnival, or a scheme to benefit elderly people.

**Cause-related marketing:** The Computers for Schools scheme runs for a ten-week period each year.

In total, Computers for Schools had donated over £100 million worth of computer equipment by the end of 2005.

# Tetra Pak Ltd

Bedwell Road, Cross Lanes, Wrexham LL13 0UT

0870 442 6000; Fax: 0870 442 6001

Website: www.tetrapak.com/uk/

Correspondent: Gayle Petite, Communications Officer

Managing Director: P Knutsson

| Year end | Turnover | Pre-tax profit |
|---|---|---|
| 31/12/2004 | £131,292,000 | £10,150,000 |

Nature of company business
The sale and lease of machines for liquid packaging and supply of related packaging materials.

Subsidiaries include: Choicebond Ltd, Maxicrop International Ltd, Beckswift Ltd, PakcentreLtd

Main locations: East Kilbride, Nantwich, Reading, Wrexham

UK employees: 273

| Charitable donations |
|---|
| 2004: £7,604 |
| 2003: £20,000 |
| Membership: A & B |

## Community involvement

Whilst there is no geographical restriction, the company stated that it now tends to concentrate its support in the North Wales area. It has a preference for appeals relating to children, youth and education, health and the arts. Support ranges from charitable donations to offering work experience to local students.

Although the company declares rather minor charitable donations, this belies the enormous financial contributions of the Rausing family – the Tetra Pak heirs. Their independent charitable trusts, give millions of pounds each year to various causes, both in the UK and worldwide. Full details of the Rausing family trusts can be found in *A Guide to the Major Trusts Volume 1*, published by the Directory of Social Change.

### Exclusions

No support for local appeals from outside areas of company presence.

### Applications

In writing to the correspondent.

## Corporate giving

In 2004, the company made global community contributions of €20 million (around £13.5 million), of which the largest single donation of US$1.5 million (around £820,000) went in aid of the Asian tsunami disaster.

The company declared charitable donations of £7,604 in 2004, down from £20,000 in the previous year. Although this is below our threshold for inclusion here, we believe the level of in-kind support to be sufficient to warrant doing so.

### In-kind support

**The arts:** Tetra Pak is a member of Arts & Business and continues to support its educational activities. These have included work with primary school and deprived children at Wrexham Print Centre, Theatre Clwyd Cymru Music and Wrexham Music Festival. The company also continues its long-term support for the International Eisteddfod in Llangollen.

**Education:** Every year a selection of Year 10 students from the local community are given work placement experience with the company. To demonstrate their learning, all students are expected to prepare a project linked to an aspect of the company's business. Practical training and advice is also given on preparing for interviews and writing a CV.

**Environment:** Since 2004, the company has been working closely with Groundwork Wrexham & Flintshire on a three year plan to introduce new wetland habitats and the construction of a footpath and boardwalk system.

Tetra Pak has also promoted environmental awareness through its Europe-wide Eco-Schools programme.

### Employee-led support

Tetra Pak matches the funds raised by its staff for charitable purposes 'according to set guidelines'. During 2005, three main charitable events were supported in this way: Children in Need Appeal; Race for Life; and, Hope House and Nightingale House Hospices, in North Wales.

# Thales UK Limited

2 Dashwood Lang Road, The Bourne Business Park, Addlestone, Surrey KT15 2NX

01932 824800; Fax: 01932 824887

Website: www.thalesgroup.co.uk

Correspondent: Corporate Services

| Year end | Turnover | Pre-tax profit |
|---|---|---|
| 31/12/2004 | £211,239,000 | £4,526,000 |

**Nature of company business**
Principal activities: The design, manufacture and sale of defence electronic products, encompassing electronic warfare, radar, displays, defence radio and command information systems.

**Main locations:** Belfast, Birmingham, Bury St Edmunds, Glasgow, Doncaster, Stockport, Addlestone

**UK employees:** 2,161

### Charitable donations
2005: £130,000
2004: £130,000
2003: £131,000

Membership: BitC

## Community involvement

The company state on its website that: 'Thales UK is committed to conducting its business activities in a socially responsible way to achieve business growth. Its business is built upon strong values which embrace our responsibilities to customers, employees, suppliers, local communities and the environment.'

Donations by the company are primarily made through the Thales Charitable Trust (Charity Commission no. 1000162). The trust's policy is to relieve poor, needy, sick and disabled people, and to support those who are engaged in work, including research, to this end. Thus 70% of the budget is spent on health and medical care, 20% on social welfare and 5% on community services.

### Exclusions
No support for circulars, individuals, expeditions, advertising in charity brochures, fundraising events or small purely local events in areas of company presence. Unless there are exceptional reasons, the trustees prefer to deal directly with a charity rather than with intermediaries.

### Applications
All appeals for charitable donations should be sent in writing to the correspondent. Grant decisions are made by a donations committee which meets quarterly. No appeals are considered independently of head office as subsidiaries have no authority to respond.

The company has previously stated that it welcomes appeals from charities, but that the volume of mail is getting too large to handle. Thus, applicants should consider the nature and relevance of their appeal and the following advice from the charitable trust. Applicants are advised to apply at the same time every year. No reply is sent to unsuccessful applicants, and it is seldom worth repeating an appeal regularly if it has been rejected.

## Corporate giving

In 2005, as in the previous year, £130,000 was donated to charity via the Thales Charitable Trust. Major beneficiaries included: Childnet International (£40,000); National Deaf Children's Society (£20,000); Armed Forces Memorial Trust and Richard House Trust (£10,000 each); and, grants of £5,000 each to ten organisations including, EDT Headstart and Young Engineers.

## Commercially-led support

**Sponsorship:** *Education* – Thales sponsors the annual Schools Aerospace Challenge.

# Thistle Hotels Ltd

London Corporate Office, PO Box 909, Bath Road, West Drayton UB7 0EQ

020 7138 0000

Website: www.thistlehotels.com

Correspondent: The Secretariat

**Nature of company business**
The ownership and operation of hotels in the UK.

**Subsidiaries include:** Kingsmead Hotels Ltd, Pinewood Hotel Ltd, LPH Grand Ltd, Castle Ross Hotels Ltd, Highlife Value Breaks Ltd, London Park Hotels plc, LPH Angus Ltd, Arden Hotel (Stratford upon Avon) Ltd, LPH London Park Ltd, Mount Charlotte Hotels Ltd

**Main locations:** Leeds

## Community involvement

Thistle Hotels are now part of BIL International Limited, an investment company.

It appears that Thistle select one or two charities each year towards which their fundraising activities are directed.

### Applications
In writing to the correspondent.

## Corporate giving

We were previously informed in 2004, that the company's chosen charities were the Muscular Dystrophy Campaign and BLISS – the premature baby charity.

Although the wording on the company's website suggests that different charities are picked to receive support each year, the above named remain those listed. Furthermore, it is unclear whether this constitutes the extent of the company's involvement in charitable activity as no figures or reference to other charitable support was available.

## Employee-led support

The selected charities are the recipients of monies from the fundraising activities of Thistle employees. No information was available as to whether the company matches this.

# The Thomson Corporation plc

The Quadrangle, PO Box 4YG, 180 Wardour Street, London W1A 4YG

Website: www.thomson.com

Correspondent: Sue Jenner, Company Secretary

| Year end | Turnover | Pre-tax profit |
|---|---|---|
| 31/12/2005 | £517,900,000 | (£40,100,000) |

**Nature of company business**
The Thomson Corporation plc (the company) is the parent company for a group of companies whose principal businesses are providing integrated information solutions to business and professional markets.

Subsidiaries include: Crossaig, Gee Publishing Ltd, Legal Information Resources Ltd, Jane's Information Group, Thomas Nelson UK, Institute for Scientific Information, Derwent Information, W Green & Son Ltd, Primary Source Media, Sweet & Maxwell Ltd

Main locations: London

Total employees: 4,868

### Charitable donations
2005: £200,000
2004: £25,000

## Community involvement

The company is currently only supporting charities connected with literacy and lifelong learning. Recipient organisations must be registered charities. Some preference is given to national and local charities in the London area.

### Exclusions

Generally no support for fundraising events, appeals from individuals, purely denominational (religious) appeals or political appeals, animal welfare, overseas, environment/heritage, local appeals not in areas of company presence, or advertising in charity brochures. No sponsorships or advertising.

### Applications

In writing to the correspondent. Only registered charities need apply. Applications must include audited accounts and any other relevant information before they will be considered by the appeals committee.

## Corporate giving

Support has previously been channelled through The Thomson Corporation Charitable Trust, which received around £100,000 a year from Thomson Corporation plc. However, the trust was wound up in 2003.

In 2005 the group has made charitable contributions amounting to £200,000; we have no information regarding amounts given in the UK or worldwide. In addition to match-funding, charitable donations are made to literacy and life-long learning charities at the discretion of the group's charities committee.

### Employee-led support

It is the group's policy to match all charitable donations from employees in its corporate offices subject to a maximum of £3,300 per employee per year.

# Thorntons plc

Thornton Park, Somercotes, Alfreton, Derby DE55 4XJ

0845 075 7585; Fax: 01773 540842

Website: www.thorntons.co.uk

Correspondent: Customer Services Department

Chief officer: John von Spreckelsen

Chief Executive: Peter Burdon

| Year end | Turnover | Pre-tax profit |
|---|---|---|
| 30/06/2005 | £187,704,000 | £8,154,000 |

**Nature of company business**
Principal activity: confectionery manufacture and retailing.

Main locations: Derby

UK employees: 4,224

Total employees: 4,224

### Charitable donations
2005: £32,000
2004: £3,000
2003: £20,000

## Community involvement

The following statement was taken from the company's website.

'Due to the very large number of requests for assistance that we receive, and our limited resources, we decided some time ago to concentrate our support with a single charity.'

### Exclusions

No support is given for circular appeals, advertising in charity brochures, animal welfare, appeals from individuals, the arts, older people, enterprise/training, medical research, overseas projects, political or religious appeals, science/technology, sickness/disability charities, social welfare or sport.

### Applications

In view of the company's commitment to their chosen charity, they regret that they are unable to help with any other requests for donations or sponsorship.

## Corporate giving

In 2005, the company made charitable contributions to Childline (£22,000) and The Tsunami Earthquake Appeal (£10,000). No donations were made to local causes.

# TK Maxx

50 Clarendon Road, Watford, Hertfordshire WD17 1TX

01923 473000

Website: www.tkmaxx.com

Correspondent: Marketing Department

| Year end | Turnover | Pre-tax profit |
|----------|----------|----------------|
| 28/01/2006 | £788,446,800 | £23,785,700 |

**Nature of company business**
A nationwide chain of stores selling clothing, gifts and homeware below recommended retail prices.

Main locations: Watford

Total employees: 11,127

> **Charitable donations**
>
> 2006: £750,824
> 2005: £590,161
> 2003: £350,000

## Community involvement

The company has five nominated charities which receive cash support. These are Cancer Research UK, Comic Relief, Enable Ireland, Northern Ireland Hospice Care and NCH Action for Children.

### Applications

In writing to the correspondent.

## Corporate giving

In 2005/06 donations made directly to the nominated charities by the company totalled £750,824; this figure includes administration costs.

### Commercially-led support

In 2005/06 the company generated £1,176,840 for its five nominated charities through various fundraising activities.

# TNT UK Limited

TNT Express House, Holly Lane Industrial Estate, Atherstone, CV9 2RY

01827 303030; Fax: 01827 720215

Website: www.tnt.co.uk

Correspondent: Steve Doig, Marketing Director

| Year end | Turnover | Pre-tax profit |
|----------|----------|----------------|
| 31/12/2005 | £699,856,000 | £61,624,000 |

**Nature of company business**
Transportation and logistics holding company.

Main locations: Atherstone, Stubbins

Total employees: 10,169

> **Charitable donations**
>
> 2005: £160,000
> 2004: £148,000
>
> Membership: BitC, %Club

## Community involvement

The Company's strategy is '... to develop mutually beneficial partnerships with charitable organisations that focus on the personal development of young people whose success depends on efficient transport networks'. In the UK, TNT Express Services is a major supporter of Wooden Spoon, a charity for children and young people who are physically, mentally or socially disadvantaged. Also in the UK, TNT supports The Duke of Edinburgh's Award and Young Enterprise, a national educational charity which delivers hands-on business experience to young people in full-time education. TNT is also instrumental in supporting Crucial Crew events raising road safety awareness for schoolchildren around the UK. TNT also gives logistical help to the No Way Trust, a charity that seeks to dissuade young people from crime. On a global level, since 2002, TNT has been an active partner of, and provided skills and resources to, the United Nations World Food Programme (WFP), the world's largest humanitarian aid agency. The group also supports Transaid.

### Exclusions

No support for motor sports or appeals from individuals.

### Applications

In writing to the correspondent.

## Corporate giving

For 2005, TNT UK Ltd, declared charitable donations in the UK of £160,000. We have no details as to how this was distributed, but know that support in the UK is given to the following: The Wooden Spoon Society, Young Enterprise, The Duke of Edinburgh's Award, Brake and Crucial Crew events.

### In-kind support

TNT provides in-kind support to Wooden Spoon events across the UK through distribution and transport services and also supports Crucial Crew events, raising road safety awareness. TNT supports Transaid, an organisation which contributes transport and logistics support to help the development of poorer countries.

### Employee-led support

TNT fully encourages staff at all levels to become involved in the support of local community and charitable projects.

# Tomkins plc

East Putney House, 84 Upper Richmond Road, London SW15 2ST

020 8871 4544; Fax: 020 8877 5053

Website: www.tomkins.co.uk

Correspondent: Sharon Haliburton, Charitable Fund Administrator & Secretary to the Chairman

Chief officer: David Newlands

Chief Executive: James Nicol

| Year end | Turnover | Pre-tax profit |
|---|---|---|
| 31/12/2005 | £3,182,400,000 | £257,700,000 |

**Nature of company business**
Tomkins plc is an international engineering business. The company is organised into two business segments – Industrial & Automotive and Building Products, consisting of various business areas which operate in a variety of end markets.

**Subsidiaries include:** Gates (UK) Ltd, Schrader Electronics Ltd

**Main locations:** London

**Total employees:** 37,324

> **Charitable donations**
> 2005: £165,483
> 2004: £68,424
> 2003: £110,090

## Community involvement

According to the company's 2005 annual report, 'The board's policy on charitable giving was reviewed during the year and whilst no changes were made to the underlying policies, donations of an exceptional nature were included in the policy framework.

'Tomkins has well-established guidelines that determine the nature of organisations to which support is given. Tomkins recognises its responsibilities to the wider community in which its businesses operate to provide balanced and targeted charitable assistance.

'The charities given assistance cover a wide range of activities including health and welfare, education, civic and community projects, culture and the arts. Tomkins prefers to spread its charitable giving over many smaller local charities.

'Each year donations are made to hundreds of charities. Tomkins makes further donations through advertising, sponsorship, products for prizes and volunteers or other in-kind support.'

### Exclusions
No support for overseas projects.

### Applications
Applications should be made in writing to the correspondent.

## Corporate giving

The total charitable donations made by the company in 2005 were £836,348. This comprised £165,483 in the UK, £571,253 in the United States (including £394,477 came from a Tomkins funded charitable trust), with the remaining £99,612 given by other overseas companies.

During the year the board approved a donation of £100,000 to Seeability (formerly known as the Royal School for the Blind).

### In-kind support
The company's UK employees have an annual vote to select a community project and in 2005 the choice was property maintenance at a local school.

The company and its subsidiaries may also provide products for prizes and advertising.

### Employee-led support
In 2005, the Company and its employees continued with their support for The Aplastic Anaemia Trust through donations and participation in a London to Paris Triathlon.

### Commercially-led support
**Sponsorship:** The company does undertake sponsorship, but we have no details of the areas supported.

# Topps Tiles plc

Rushworth House, Wilmslow Road, Handforth, Wilmslow SK9 3HJ

01625 446700; Fax: 01625 446800

Website: www.toppstiles.co.uk

Correspondent: Andy Liggett, Financial Director

Chief officer: B F J Bester

Chief Executive: N D Ounstead

| Year end | Turnover | Pre-tax profit |
|---|---|---|
| 27/10/2005 | £173,300,000 | £39,200,000 |

**Nature of company business**
The principal activity of the company is the retail and wholesale distribution of ceramic tiles, wood flooring and related products.

**Main locations:** Wilmslow

**UK employees:** 1,672

> **Charitable donations**
> 2005: £20,000
> 2003: £32,000

## Community involvement

Each year support is given to a particular cause such as asthma charities, and appeals from areas in which the company has a presence. Only a limited number of appeals can be assisted in any one year.

**Charity of the Year:** Asthma UK.

### Exclusions
The company will not make political contributions.

### Applications
In writing to the correspondent.

## Corporate giving

In 2004/05 the company made charitable donations of £10,000 to the Tsunami Appeal and £10,000 to Asthma UK.

### In-kind support
In addition to cash donations, the company provides support through a scheme via its product catalogue where schools can win valuable computer equipment. Since the scheme started, over 30 schools have benefited nationwide.

### Employee-led support
The company encourages employees to take an interest in social and community activities. Staff fundraising events have

helped support Primary Care Trusts in North Kirklees, Yorkshire, and Haringey in north London.

## Commercially-led support

**Sponsorship:** *Sport* – The company's 2004/05 annual report stated: 'Topps is one of the biggest supporters of youth football in the UK, providing new kits and equipment to junior teams local to our stores.

'We have a policy of building local brand awareness of Topps Tiles and Tile Clearing House through involvement with young people.

'Probably our most well-known community project is our youth sports sponsorship, providing new kits and equipment to juniors in each town where we have an outlet. This has made Topps one of the biggest supporters of youth football in Britain and we now have over 225 teams playing regularly in our colours.'

# Toshiba Information Systems (UK) Ltd

Toshiba Court, Weybridge Business Park, Addlestone Road, Weybridge, Surrey KT15 2UL

01932 841600; Fax: 01932 847240

Website: www.toshiba.co.uk

Correspondent: Helen Downey, Corporate Sponsorship E-mail: communications@toshiba.co.uk

Managing Director: A Thompson

| Year end | Turnover | Pre-tax profit |
|---|---|---|
| 31/03/2005 | £574,541,875 | £15,939,641 |

Nature of company business
The sale, marketing and distribution of photocopiers, fax machines, computers and telephone systems.

Main locations: Weybridge, Weybridge, Bristol, Cambridge

UK employees: 733

### Charitable donations

2005: £37,406

Total community contributions: £42,206

## Community involvement

After many years of not providing information, Toshiba kindly participated in our 2006 survey.

The company has a preference for local charities in Surrey, particularly those working in the fields of children and youth, elderly people, education, sport and the arts. It also undertakes significant sponsorship in the field of education.

National charities are not generally supported.

**Charity of the Year:** The Duke of Edinburgh's Award (2006).

## Exclusions

The company does not support appeals from individuals, enterprise/training, medical research, purely denominational appeals, political appeals, local appeals not in areas of company presence, large national appeals, overseas projects, or science/technology.

## Applications

In writing to the correspondent.

**Information available:** The company produces a corporate social responsibility report.

## Corporate giving

In 2005, Toshiba made total UK community contributions of £42,206 of which £37,406 was in cash donations. Organisations benefiting from this included: Duke of Edinburgh's Award; Disability Challengers; Weybridge Male Voice Choir; The Science Museum; and, the Surrey Herald Sports Awards.

## In-kind support

The main area of non-cash support is gifts in-kind.

## Employee-led support

Depending on the activity, the company may match employees fundraising and/or giving on behalf of charitable causes.

**Payroll giving:** The Give As You Earn scheme is in operation.

## Commercially-led support

**Sponsorship:** *Education* – Toshiba has sponsored the Science Museum in London since 1997 as part of its commitment to furthering the understanding and enjoyment of science in the UK. The sponsorship includes: support for The Wellcome Wing – a leading centre for the presentation of contemporary science and technology through six galleries, a 3D IMAX cinema and simulator; the provision of state-of-the-art touch screen terminals displaying up-to-the-minute details of exhibitions, events and visitor facilities; and the STEM (Students' and Teachers' Educational Materials) Project Awards – an Internet-driven competition requiring students and teachers, either individually or in groups of up to three, to design educational websites based on a visit, real or virtual, to the Science Museum or one of its affiliates (National Railway Museum or National Museum of Film, Photography & Television).

# Total Holdings UK Ltd

33 Cavendish Square, London W1G 0PW

020 7416 4377; Fax: 020 7416 4497

Website: www.uk.total.com

Correspondent: Andrew Hogg, Public Affairs and Corporate Communications Manager 020 7416 4376; Fax: 020 7416 4497

Chief officer: Michel Contie

| Year end | Turnover | Pre-tax profit |
|---|---|---|
| 31/12/2005 | £15,619,000,000 | |

Nature of company business
Oil and gas exploration and production.

Main locations: Milford Haven, London, Watford, Redhill, Immingham, Stalybridge, Aberdeen

UK employees: 7,130

## Charitable donations

2005: £280,000

Total community contributions: £350,000

Membership: A & B

## Community involvement

Formerly having entries under Total Oil Marine plc and Elf Exploration UK plc, the company was formed through the merger of Total, Petrofina and Elf. The company supports national charities (see below), while at a local level, regional offices, refineries and service stations organise 'Fun Days' on behalf of a chosen charity.

We were previously advised that the company had a preference for: local charities in areas of company presence (i.e. Aberdeen, Watford, Immingham, Milford Haven, Redhill and Stalybridge), appeals relevant to company business, or those which have a member of company staff involved. Preferred areas of support are: the arts, youth, education, enterprise/training, environment/heritage, medical research and science/technology.

**Charity of the Year:** CLIC Sargent (Caring for Children with Cancer and Leukaemia).

## Exclusions

No support for circular appeals, advertising in charity brochures, animal welfare, appeals from individuals, elderly people, fundraising events, overseas projects, political appeals, religious appeals, sickness/disability, social welfare or sport.

## Applications

In writing only to the correspondent for those organisations located near to Total refining and marketing facilities (please refer to the list of 'preferred locations'). For organisations based near to Total's exploration and production facilities in Aberdeen, please contact: Sandra McIntosh, Public Affairs & Communications Department, Total E&P plc, Crawpeel Road, Altens, Aberdeen AB12 3FG.

**Information available:** The company produce a corporate social responsibility report.

## Corporate giving

Total community contributions in 2005 amounted to £350,000 of which £280,000 was in cash donations. Beneficiaries included: Royal Scottish National Orchestra; National Galleries of Scotland; Young People's Trust for the Environment; Disaster Emergency Committee; and, CLIC Sargent.

**Education:** Through the Total Bursary Awards Scheme awards of £1,000 each are available to up to six local students who will be taking up a university course immediately after their A-levels. Some bursaries are reserved for students with disabilities, for those who have suffered illness or experienced a family bereavement, or for whom English is not their first language. Gap year students are not eligible to apply.

Application forms are available from the schools in the scheme (we do not have a list) or from: Eleanor Brooks, TOTAL UK, 40 Clarendon Road, Watford WD17 1TQ (e-mail: eleanor.brooks@total.co.uk). Applications must be submitted before the end of January in the year in which the student will be commencing university.

## In-kind support

The company provides the use of facilities such as postage/photocopying.

## Employee-led support

**Payroll giving:** The company operates the Give As You Earn Scheme.

## Commercially-led support

**Sponsorship:** *The arts* – sponsorship is undertaken.

# Toyota Motor Manufacturing (UK) Ltd

Burnaston, Derbyshire DE1 9TA

01332 282121

Website: www.toyotauk.com

Correspondent: Susan Wilkinson, External Affairs Department

Managing Director: Hein Van Gerwen

**Nature of company business**
Car and engine manufacture.

Main locations: Burnaston, Deeside

UK employees: 5,156

## Charitable donations

Membership: BitC

## Community involvement

Priority is given to projects which add to the welfare of local communities and support or enhance community life. Projects must have some long-term tangible benefit for the wider community. The current focus is environment, children, education and health.

## Exclusions

No support for advertising in charity brochures, animal welfare, appeals from individuals, the arts, enterprise/training, fundraising events, overseas projects, political or religious appeals, science/technology, social welfare, sport, or local appeals not in areas of company presence. No response to circular appeals.

## Applications

A self-screening eligibility form and an application form are posted on the company's website. If your organisation meets the eligibility criteria, please forward your completed application form to the correspondent.

## Corporate giving

Since the start of vehicle production in the UK at the end of 1992, Toyota has contributed more than £1.5 million to various charities and foundations, half a million pounds of which has gone to good causes local to the Burnaston and Deeside plants.

Unfortunately, no precise information regarding the company's level of giving was available. However, we understand that recent beneficiaries include: Conkers, NSPCC, and Hope House Children's Hospice in North Wales.

## Employee-led support

Employee involvement in the community is encouraged, and where suitable, the company will offer financial support to member fundraising activities or to local community organisations in which members play an active role. For example, a major fundraising initiative on behalf of the NSPCC in Derbyshire and Deeside raised more than £25,000 in a month.

Employee fundraising efforts are matched by the company up to a maximum of £250 per activity.

**Payroll giving:** A payroll giving scheme is in operation.

---

# Travelex Holdings Limited

65 Kingsway, London WC2B 6TD

020 7400 4000; Fax: 020 7400 4001

Website: www.travelex.co.uk

Correspondent: PA to the Chairman 020 7400 4000

Chief officer: Lloyd Dorfman

| Year end | Turnover | Pre-tax profit |
|---|---|---|
| 28/11/2006 | £503,269,000 | £13,791,000 |

Nature of company business
The Group's principal activities are the provision of travel money services, funds transfer services, issuance of travellers' cheques, dealing in foreign bank notes and the provision of other travel and financial related services. The Group operates through its subsidiaries in the United Kingdom, North America, Asia Pacific, Continental Europe and Africa.

UK employees: 2,473

Total employees: 5,553

### Charitable donations
2004: £103,000
2003: £105,000

## Community involvement

Very little information was available concerning the charitable giving of this company, other than the amount given for charitable purposes for the years 2003 and 2004 and brief details of their current sponsorships.

## Exclusions

No support for advertising in charity brochures, local appeals not in areas of company presence.

## Applications

In writing to the correspondent.

## Corporate giving

During the year 2004 the group made donations in the UK for charitable purposes amounting to £103,000 (2003: £105,000). Unfortunately we have no information regarding the recipient organisations.

## Commercially-led support

**Sponsorship:** *The arts* – Travelex have sponsored the 'Travelex £10 Season' at the National Theatre and following its success have launched 'Travelex £10 Mondays' at London's Royal Opera House.

---

# Travis Perkins plc

Lodge Way House, Harlestone Road, Northampton NN5 7UG

01604 752424; Fax: 01604 587244

Website: www.travisperkins.co.uk

Correspondent: Linda Doughty, Marketing Director
E-mail: linda-doughty@travisperkins.co.uk

Chief officer: Tim E P Stevenson

Chief Executive: Geoff Cooper

| Year end | Turnover | Pre-tax profit |
|---|---|---|
| 31/12/2005 | £2,640,800,000 | £206,700,000 |

Nature of company business
The marketing and distribution of timber, building and plumbing materials and the hiring of tools to the building trade and industry generally.

Subsidiaries include: Keyline Builders Merchants Ltd, D W Archer Ltd

Main locations: Northampton

UK employees: 15000

### Charitable donations
2005: £281,000
2004: £312,000
2003: £105,310
Total community contributions: £334,794

## Community involvement

With 1,000 branches throughout the UK, the group encourages each branch to support their local community through involvement in local affairs such as by sponsoring organisations or donating materials to projects. Local appeals should be made to the appropriate regional office.

**Charity of the Year:** NSPCC, Macmillan Cancer Relief and Children 1st (Scotland).

## Exclusions

No support for advertising in charity brochures, animal welfare, appeals from individuals, the arts, children/youth, education, elderly people, enterprise/training, environment, heritage, medical research, overseas projects, political appeals, religious appeals science/technology, sickness/disability, social welfare, sport, local appeals not in areas of company presence or large national appeals.

## Applications

In writing to the correspondent.

## Corporate giving

In 2005, the company made total community contributions of £334,794 of which cash donations amounted to £281,000 (see below). Beneficiaries included the NSPCC and Macmilllan Cancer Relief, no further breakdown was available.

During 2005, £281,000 was raised through charity fundraising in which staff in conjunction with customers and suppliers took part in a variety of activities to support the NSPCC, Macmillan Cancer Relief and Children 1st (Scotland).

### In-kind support

The company may occasionally donate materials.

### Employee-led support

The company have an employee volunteering scheme towards which it provides financial support. The company also matches employee giving.

**Payroll giving:** In 2003, staff raised £19,833 through a payroll-giving scheme to support the chosen charities the NSPCC and Macmillan Cancer Relief.

# Trinity Mirror plc

One Canada Square, Canary Wharf, London E14 5AP

020 7293 3000; Fax: 020 7510 3000

Website: www.trinitymirror.com

Correspondent: Paul Vickers, Secretary & Group Legal Director

Chief officer: Sir Ian Gibson

Chief Executive: Sly Bailey

| Year end | Turnover | Pre-tax profit |
|---|---|---|
| 02/01/2005 | £1,122,000,000 | £209,500,000 |

Nature of company business
The main activity of the group is the publication and printing of newspapers both in the UK and overseas.

Subsidiaries include: Century Press and Publishing Ltd, Midland Newspapers Ltd, Inside Communications Ltd, Examiner News & Information Ltd, The Derry Journal Ltd, Southnews plc, Western Mail & Echo Ltd, The Chester Chronicle and Associated Newpapers Ltd, Ethnic Media Group Ltd, Gazette Media Co Ltd, Scottish Daily Record and Sunday Mail Ltd, Yellow Advertiser Newspaper Group Ltd, Newcastle Chronicle and Journal Ltd, Middlesex County Press Ltd, Raceform Ltd, Midland Independent Newspapers Ltd, The Liverpool Daily Post and Echo Ltd, Mediaserve Ltd, Scottish and Universal Newspapers Ltd, MGN Ltd

Main locations: Chester, Liverpool

Total employees: 11,065

### Charitable donations

2005: £60,000
2004: £287,000
2003: £181,000

Membership: BitC

## Community involvement

The company's policy with regard to charitable donations is as follows:

'Trinity Mirror believes that it can best support charities through the pages of its newspapers. This support will either be through appeals to readers for donations or through editorial content, describing the aims and activities of various charities. In every case the decision as to whether or not to support a charity appeal, or whether to run an editorial comment, will be one for the editor of each newspaper.

'Trinity Mirror plc will make direct cash donations to charities in certain limited circumstances. The company will, at a group level, support various charities connected or associated with the newspaper, printing or advertising industries.

'A second category of direct cash support will be to charities operating in the communities immediately surrounding Trinity Mirror's offices and print sites. The charities that are likely to receive support are smaller community-based charities where a modest donation will make a big impact. It is unlikely that a major national charity that just happens to be based very close to one of our offices will receive a donation.

'There will be a further limited general pool of funds out of which donations will be made to legitimate and supportable causes that fall outside the above two criteria. There will, however, need in each case to be a demonstrable business/commercial reason why such support should be given.

'Each of our regional newspaper companies will have a small budget out of which they will make direct cash donations to charities working in the community in which the newspaper is based. Scottish Daily Record and Sunday Mail Limited will similarly make a number of donations to appropriate charities based in Scotland.

'The national titles of The Mirror, Sunday Mirror and Sunday People are most unlikely to make direct cash donations. They will do so only where they are asked to make a payment to a charity in lieu of a fee for an interview or some form of support. Any corporate donations requested from the national titles are likely to be redirected to the group as the company's headquarters share the same location as that of the national titles'.

### Exclusions

No support for local appeals not in areas of company presence.

### Applications

Applications at group level should be made in writing to the correspondent, but only where one of the following applies:

▶ charities connected with or associated with the newspaper, printing or advertising industries

▶ charities operating in the communities immediately surrounding Trinity Mirror's offices and print sites

▶ legitimate and supportable causes falling outside the above two criteria, but with a demonstrable business/commercial reason why such support should be given.

Applications at regional level should be addressed to the editor or manager of the newspaper/print site based in your community. Prior agreement of the relevant managing director will be required before a donation can be made.

## Corporate giving

In 2004/05, contributions to charities totalled £60,000; a substantial fall compared to the previous year when £287,000 was contributed. No explanation for this was given.

Donations were made 'principally to various charities connected or associated with the newspaper, printing or advertising industries and local charities serving the communities in which the group operates'.

## In-kind support

In addition to cash donations, the company is active in making donations in kind, in the form of used computer equipment, furniture, books and so on. Through its community involvement programmes the company makes available members of its staff for volunteering and mentoring programmes.

## Employee-led support

**Payroll giving:** 'The company is actively investigating the introduction of a payroll giving programme.'

# TT Electronics plc

Clive House, 12–18 Queens Road, Weybridge, Surrey KT13 9XB

01932 841310; Fax: 01932 836450

Website: www.ttelectronicsplc.com/

Correspondent: John Newman, Chairman

Chief officer: John W Newman

Chief Executive: Neil Rodgers

| Year end | Turnover | Pre-tax profit |
|---|---|---|
| 31/12/2005 | £565,300,000 | £26,800,000 |

Nature of company business
The main activities of the company are in two business divisions: electronic components and industrial engineering.

Subsidiaries include: AEI Compounds Limited, Welwyn Components limited, AB Connectors Limited, Prestwick Circuits Limited, Erskine Systems Limited, MMG Neosid Limited, BAS Components Limited, Welwyn Systems Limited, Linton and Hirst Limited, BI Technologies, AB Automotive Electronics Limited, W T Henley Limited, Genergy plc, Houchin Aerospace Limited, AEI Cables Limited, AB Electronic Assemblies Limited

Main locations: Havant, Edenbridge, Gravesend, Filey, Letchworth, Hinckley, Haverhill, Lancing, Cardiff, Cowes, Colnbrook, Coalville, Cleckheaton, Chester-le-Street, Tipton, Swindon, Wolverhampton, Mountain Ash, Newport, Manchester, Skelmersdale, Sevenoaks, Scarborough, Rotherham, Romford, Ramsbottom, Bedlington, Ashford, Blyth, Bootle

Total employees: 8,430

### Charitable donations

2005: £50,000
2004: £50,000
2003: £50,000

## Community involvement

We currently have no information on the charitable donations policy of the company.

## Exclusions

The company does not make political contributions.

## Applications

In writing to the correspondent.

## Corporate giving

In 2005, the company made cash donations to charity of £50,000. No breakdown of this amount was available.

# TUI UK Limited

Columbus House, Westwood Way, Westwood Business Park, Coventry CV4 8TT

02476 282 828

Website: www.tui.com

Correspondent: Phil White, Operations Manager

Managing Director: Peter Rothwell

| Year end | Turnover | Pre-tax profit |
|---|---|---|
| 31/12/2005 | £2,507,432,000 | (£50,156,000) |

Nature of company business
Since 2000, Thomson Travel has been part of Preussag AG, the largest tourism and travel group in the world.

The principal activities of the company comprise the provision of inclusive holidays and the sale of other related travel services, including the sale of foreign currencies.

Subsidiaries include: Simply Travel Ltd, Crystal International Travel Group Ltd, TTG Independent Holidays Group Ltd, Manchester Flights Ltd, Port Philip Group Ltd, Robert Sibbald Travel Agents Ltd, Britannia Airways Ltd, The Original Travel House Ltd, Digital Travel Group Ltd, Team Lincoln Ltd, Magic Travel Group Ltd, Lunn Poly Ltd

Main locations: London

Total employees: 9,589

### Charitable donations

2005: £87,499
2004: £65,245

## Community involvement

Since the company's integration into the Preussag AG group, we have been unable to obtain updated information other than to confirm the contact details. We therefore reproduce the following information from the company's website.

'TUI UK has a particular fundraising focus on supporting Macmillan Cancer Relief.

'As a company, we receive many individual requests for support, all for very worthwhile causes. However our fundraising programme and partnership with Macmillan unfortunately means we are unable to support other charities at this time.'

## Applications

Please see above.

## Corporate giving

During the year the company contributed £87,499 to charities (2004: £65,245). We have no information regarding the recipient charities.

### Employee-led support

Staff fundraising efforts are acknowledged by the company through matched funding, on which there is a relatively low cap.

# Tullis Russell Group Ltd

Rothersfield, Markinch Glenrothes, Fife KY7 6PB

01592 753311; Fax: 01592 755872

Website: www.trg.co.uk

Correspondent: Lisa Bradley, Secretary, Charities Committee

| Year end | Turnover | Pre-tax profit |
|---|---|---|
| 31/03/2006 | £138,417,000 | £4,157,000 |

### Nature of company business

Tullis Russell Group Limited is an employee-owned industrial holding company, providing management services. The principal subsidiary companies are involved in the manufacture of papers and boards for clients world-wide.

Main locations: Bollington, Hanley, Glenrothes

UK employees: 806

### Charitable donations

2006: £29,000
2005: £37,000

## Community involvement

Past information suggested that the company decides how to distribute funds via a charity/donations committee and that support is only given to local appeals in areas of company presence, covering a wide range of causes.

### Exclusions

No grants for local appeals not in areas of company presence, large national appeals, enterprise/training, medical research, overseas projects, political appeals, science/technology or sport.

### Applications

In writing to the correspondent.

## Corporate giving

In 2005/06, the company reported they made cash donations to 'charitable and public organisations' of £29,000 (2004: £37,000). We have no information regarding specific recipient public organisations/charities.

### In-kind support

The main area of non-cash support is gifts in kind such as donations of paper to schools and local organisations. Larger amounts have also been supplied for the production of posters, guides and catalogues for arts events.

### Employee-led support

A group of employees based in Fife raised £2,500 for Rachel House, a children's hospice in Kinross. The five strong team set themselves the target of raising £2,500 for Rachel House. Through a variety of fundraising activities, including a

10-mile hike in the Lomond Hills, the team successfully reached their target in 2001.

Group companies are involved in local schools, colleges and universities through individual employees and the Paper Federation of Great Britain Schools Link Programme.

### Commercially-led support

**Education:** Under the Paper Federation of Great Britain Schools Link programme, three-year sponsorships at university (TR Scholarships) are available.

# UBS

100 Liverpool Street, London EC2M 2RH

020 7568 2365; Fax: 020 7567 3364

Website: www.ubs.com

Correspondent: Nick Wright, Executive Director, Community Affairs

| Year end | Turnover | Pre-tax profit |
|---|---|---|
| 31/12/2005 | | |

### Nature of company business
International banking.

Main locations: Taunton, Worthing, Eastbourne, Manchester, London, Newcastle, Edinburgh, Bury St Edmunds, Birmingham

### Charitable donations

2005: £2,000,000

Membership: BitC, L B Group

## Community involvement

UBS is a leading international bank, and states: 'Successful companies need successful communities. A truly successful company is sensitive to the concerns of all those on whom it depends and that's why UBS Warburg is committed to being a good corporate citizen.'

UBS also enables its clients the opportunity of engaging in charitable causes. The UBS Optimus Foundation invests donations from clients into a number of programmes and organisations that focus particularly on children.

### Applications

In writing to the correspondent.

## Corporate giving

Although we were unable to obtain a full figure for the company's community support, the breadth of its work in the community suggests substantial investment in terms of time and money.

UBS was the first financial firm to sponsor a new secondary school under the UK government's 'Academy' program, making a financial contribution of £2 million to the project.

### In-kind support

Staff use their business expertise and specialist skills to help small voluntary groups with activities that range from marketing and HR to general management, IT and accounts. A mentoring scheme in operation, linking employees with teenagers from local schools. UBS Warburg also works with charitable and voluntary organisations in the redistribution of mobile phones, business clothes, spectacles, office equipment, toys and foreign coins.

### Employee-led support

Employees of UBS are active fundraisers and, in many cases, volunteer their own time and efforts to these and other organisations. Staff are strongly encouraged to participate in volunteering projects and are given two days a year to do so. Current initiatives, in which employees are currently participating, include business mentoring, student mentoring, community challenges, and work experience projects.

By way of further encouragement the bank has put in place a number of schemes to facilitate employees' community and charitable involvement. These include matched giving which entitles each employee to have the funds they raise for charity matched by the company to certain annual limits.

**Payroll giving:** The Give As You Earn scheme is in operation, which in most instances is matched by the company pound for pound.

# UGC Ltd Unipart Group of Companies

Unipart House, Garsington House, Cowley, Oxford OX4 2PG

01865 778966; Fax: 01865 383763

**Correspondent:** Jane Magé, Communications Officer

**Chief officer:** Lord Shepherd

**Chief Executive:** J M Neill

| Year end | Turnover | Pre-tax profit |
|----------|----------|----------------|
| 31/12/2005 | £1,305,479,000 | £75,174,000 |

**Nature of company business**
Principal activity: marketing, sale and distribution of parts, components and accessories for the automotive, computer and rail industries and in the design and manufacture of original equipment components for the automotive industry.

**Subsidiaries include:** Surestock Health Services Ltd, Advanced Engineering Systems Ltd, H Burden Ltd, Partco International Ltd, Partco Group Ltd, Surepart Ltd, Railpart (UK) Ltd, EW (Holdings) Ltd, Serck Ltd, Partco Ltd, SVG Ltd

**Main locations:** Oxford, Paddockwood (Kent), Coventry, Birmingham

**Total employees:** 8,786

### Charitable donations

Total community contributions: £380,500

Membership: BitC

## Community involvement

The following information is taken from the company's website. 'The Unipart Group will encourage and support its employees in participating in activities which benefit the community at large ...

For this purpose 'the community' is defined as one or more of the following: Charities; Not-for-profit organisations representing economically and socially disadvantaged groups;

Schools and youth organisations; Environmental, developmental and cultural organisations which aid economic or social regeneration; Campaigns addressing specific community needs.'

### Applications

In writing to the correspondent.

## Corporate giving

During the year the company contributed £11,300 to charities (2004: £7,300). £3,700 was for health and well-being, £4,000 for child welfare and youth development and £3,600 to other charitable purposes in support of employees in their fund-raising activities.

### In-kind support

In addition to cash donations the company contributes through gifts in kind, management and employee time and expertise, and the free use of company facilities and premises.

### Employee-led support

Unipart actively encourages all employees to become involved in community service and charitable activity. The company provides matched funding for employees' fundraising efforts.

### Commercially-led support

**Sponsorship:** *Culture* – Unipart sponsored the StoryQuest 2004 Festival in Oxfordshire. StoryQuest is a festival of stories and storytelling to inspire reading and writing in children at the beginning of secondary school.

# UIA (Insurance) Limited

King's Court, London Road, Stevenage, Herts SG1 2NG

01438 761761; Fax: 01438 761762

**Website:** www.uia.co.uk

**Correspondent:** Andrew Gay, Charity Administrator, UIA Charitable Foundation
E-mail: info@uia.co.uk

**Managing Director:** Ian Templeton

| Year end | Turnover | Pre-tax profit |
|----------|----------|----------------|
| 31/12/2005 | | £2,867,000 |

**Nature of company business**
Insurance company.

**Main locations:** Stevenage

### Charitable donations

2005: £28,000
2004: £28,000
2003: £74,000

## Community involvement

UIA is a mutual insurance company that provides services to UNISON, other trade unions and similar organisations. Its community support programme is directed through a charitable foundation, details of which are available on UIA's website (www.uia.co.uk) and from where much of the following was taken.

## UIA Charitable Foundation

Set up in 1999, the UIA Charitable Foundation (Charity Commission no. 1079982) funds registered charities working to help 'the disadvantaged in society'. Funded entirely by donations from UIA (Insurance) Ltd, UNISON's insurance company, the foundation focuses its support on lesser known groups that take positive action on important social issues that might not otherwise be addressed.

Grants are given both nationally and internationally, with the preferred areas of support being: support of people living in poverty; promotion of human rights; provision of humanitarian aid; provision for oversees development; support for the victims of drug and alcohol addiction; support for people who are elderly and/or people with disability; support for people who are homeless. This list is not exclusive and may change from time to time.

The trustees are drawn from UNISON and UIA ensuring that charities benefit from the strong links between both organisations. The foundation endeavours to focus its support on groups that fit with the ethos of the trade union movement, but is also happy to look at supporting 'unpopular' causes which may not always fall neatly into one of the programme areas listed above.

### Exclusions

Formerly, grants were not available for: (i) work in larger, older national charities which have an established constituency of supporters; (ii) work which the trustees believe should be funded by the state, or which has been in the recent past; (iii) the personal support of individuals in need; (iv) the arts, except where they are used in the context of the kind of work the foundation does support; (v) work in mainstream education, including schools and academic research in the UK; (vi) environment and conservation, animal welfare, heritage and sporting projects; (vii) work with bias towards a particular religion.

### Applications

In writing to the correspondent. Applications are considered at least four times a year.

*Please note that the application form and criteria for grants from the foundation are being up-dated and applicants are advised to visit the UIA website in January 2007 for up-dated application details.*

## Corporate giving

In the year ending 31st December 2005, the foundation received an income of £27,740 (2004: £28,788) in donations from UIA (Insurance) Limited and sundry income of £1,251 (2004: £977).

In 2005 the foundation made 47 grants totalling £40,816 which included:

*Children And Families:* Carmarthen Breakthrough; Shooting Star Children's Hospice; Friendship Project for Children; CHICKS.

*Disability:* Rochdale Special Needs Cycling Club; Baswich & Bromley Sensory Garden; Northampton Society for Autism; Open Minds.

*Drug and Alcohol Addiction:* Alcohol Support; Scottish Communities Against Drugs; Lifeline.

*Elderly:* North Tamar Community Transport Association; Grandparents Association.

*Homelessness and Housing:* Luton Accommodation & Move-on Project Limited; Derbyshire WISH; Broadgreen Breakfast Club; Streatham Streetlink.

*Humanitarian Aid:* Anti Slavery International; Kurdish Humanitarian Rights Project; Oxfam.

*Overseas Development:* Exeter-Ethiopia Link; HUGS.

*Poverty:* Newham Bengali Trust; The Northampton Soup Kitchen; The Connection at St Martins.

# UK Coal plc

Harworth Park, Blyth Road, Harworth, Doncaster, South Yorkshire DN11 8DB

01302 751751; Fax: 01302 752420

**Website:** www.ukcoal.com

**Correspondent:** Laura Heath, PA to the Chief Executive

**Chief officer:** David Jones

**Chief Executive:** Gerry Spindler

| Year end | Turnover | Pre-tax profit |
|---|---|---|
| 31/12/2005 | £341,214,000 | (£62,094,000) |

**Nature of company business**
The principal activities of the group are coal mining, opencast and underground, and associated activities.

**Subsidiaries include:** CIM Resources Ltd, Harworth Insurance Co Ltd, Harworth Power Ltd, The Monckton Coke & Chemical Co Ltd, Coal Supplies (UK) Ltd

**Main locations:** Doncaster

**UK employees:** 4,320

| Charitable donations |
|---|
| 2005: £30,000 |
| 2004: £39,000 |
| 2003: £27,000 |

## Community involvement

The company has a preference for supporting charities and associations involved with the coal industry and local communities.

### Exclusions

No support for local appeals outside areas of company presence.

### Applications

In writing to the correspondent.

## Corporate giving

In 2005, charitable donations totalled £30,000 and the directors expect this level to be sustained in 2006. The group has for many years provided sponsorship to Grimethorpe Colliery Band and this support will continue in 2006.

# Ulster Carpet Mills Limited

Castleisland Factory, Garvaghy Road, Portadown,
Co. Armagh BT62 1EE

028 3833 4433; Fax: 028 3835 1021

Website: www.ulstercarpets.co.uk

Correspondent: Edward Wilson, Chairman

Chief officer: Edward Wilson

Chief Executive: Nicky Coburn

| Year end | Turnover | Pre-tax profit |
|---|---|---|
| 31/03/2006 | £50,000,000 | £3,000,000 |

Nature of company business
Design and manufacture of carpets

Subsidiaries include: Riverstone Spinning Ltd

Main locations: Portadown, Dewsbbury

UK employees: 750

### Charitable donations

Total community contributions: £110,700
Management costs: £1,000

Membership: BitC, %Club

## Community involvement

Information about the company's work with charities is outlined in the publication *Ulster Carpets – Another Side of Business*. Support is given both in cash and in kind, with employees at all levels taking an active role in supporting various charities.

### Exclusions

No support for advertising in charity brochures, animal welfare, appeals from individuals, overseas projects, political appeals, religious appeals or local appeals not in areas of company presence.

### Applications

In writing to the correspondent.

## Corporate giving

Although Ulster Carpets updated its year end figures, no new information was provided regarding the company's donations to charity. We can only assume the amounts involved are similar to those previously provided, which we repeat below.

In 1999/2000, the company made total community contributions of over £110,000. Of this, some £37,000 consisted of cash donations. We have no details of the grant recipients for this year, but understand that over 70 different charities received help.

Decisions regarding which charities to support are made every 12 months by an employee charity committee.

### In-kind support

Donations of carpets have been made to a variety of charity and community groups. In addition, the Craigavon Talking Newspaper operated from the company's Seagoe factory, where facilities were provided to the charity at no cost.

### Employee-led support

In 2002, employees raised more than £20,000 for local causes which was matched pound for pound by the company. Some of those organisations benefiting from this included: Northern Ireland Mother & Baby Appeal; National Asthma Campaign; Action Cancer; Save the Children; Meningitis Research; and, Oxfam.

Employees are also actively encouraged to get involved in charitable work, with their fundraising efforts occasionally receiving sponsorship from the company.

**Payroll giving:** The Give As You Earn scheme is in operation.

# Unilever UK

Walton Court, Station Avenue, Walton on Thames,
Surrey KT12 1UP

Website: www.unilever.co.uk

Correspondent: Community Affairs Team

Chief officer: A Burgmans

Chief Executive: P Cescau

| Year end | Turnover | Pre-tax profit |
|---|---|---|
| 31/12/2005 | £27,260,000,000 | £3,248,000,000 |

Nature of company business
Unilever is one of the world's leading suppliers of fast moving consumer goods in foods, household and personal care products. Its brands include Knorr, Hellmans, PG Tips, Birds Eye, Wall's Ice Cream, Sure, Persil, Comfort, Cif, Dove, Lynx and Colman's.

Unilever UK is based in a number of sites around the UK. The head office is in Walton on Thames, and it is from here that UK Community Involvement is managed.

Subsidiaries include: Diversey Lever, Ben & Jerry's Ice Cream, Birds Eye Wall's, Lever Fabergé, Slimfast, Unipath

Main locations: Bedford, Walton on Thames, Lowestoft, Purfleet, London, Manchester, Port Sunlight, Windsor, Kingston on Thames, Burton on Trent, Crumlin, Bebington, Warrington, Crawley, Leeds, Hull, Ipswich, Gloucester

UK employees: 11,000

Total employees: 212,000

### Charitable donations

2005: £2,800,000
2003: £7,600,000

Total community contributions: £6,700,000
Management costs: £700,000

Membership: A & B, BitC, L B Group, %Club

## Community involvement

The link between Unilever's products and people, business and community goes back over 100 years to William Hesketh Lever, who built Port Sunlight village to provide his employees with decent living conditions. His vision lives on today in Unilever UK's commitment to making a positive impact on society as a whole.

Unilever is present in over 100 countries around the world. Their approach is to manage community involvement locally, so Unilever UK would normally only fund projects in the UK, as decisions concerning overseas projects would be made in the relevant countries.

Community involvement takes place in many forms, from direct funding for national projects to employee volunteering support for local community initiatives.

Unilever is increasingly focusing on longer term partnerships, in some cases lasting up to 25 years. This means that while Unilever invests a great deal in Community involvement, budgets are often fully committed years in advance, with funding for major projects only becoming available when an existing project comes to an end.

In order to maximise the impact of Unilever UK's community investment programme its efforts are focused on the following key areas:

▷ education – in the form of school governance and leadership

▷ sustainable development – in the areas of water, agriculture and fisheries

▷ the arts – focused on visual arts

▷ health – focused on nutrition and healthy lifestyles.

## Exclusions

Under no circumstances is support given to political parties or to organisations with primarily political aims. Unilever makes a declaration to this effect in the Annual Report and Accounts that binds Unilever and all its operating units. Support is not given to churches or denominational charities. This does not exclude support for charities with a religious connection whose work is ecumenical. Support is not given to individuals to undertake studies, gap year trips, social work or for any other purposes.

## Applications

Projects supported by Unilever's community investment programme are mostly researched and identified by its in-house community investment team.

Unsolicited applications are not therefore encouraged as less than 1% of unsolicited applications sent to the UK head office generally receive support.

Unilever asks that you use the 'Contact Us' section of the Unilever UK website to ensure that your request is directed to the correct person.

**Information Available:** Unilever UK has an internet site www.unilever.co.uk which contains information about its community involvement activities as well as more general information on its approach to managing corporate responsibility issues.

# Corporate giving

Unilever UK measures the cost of its community involvement using the London Benchmarking Group (LBG) model. Unilever helped to develop this model and are represented on the LBG's steering group.

In 2005, Unilever made total community contributions in the UK of £6,700,000. Usefully, and in line with the LBG recommendations, this was broken down as follows:

▷ charitable donations: £1.5 million

▷ community investment: £1.3 million

▷ commercial initiatives in the community: £3.9 million

▷ management costs: £0.7 million.

## In-kind support

The main areas of non-cash support are secondments, employee time and occasional donations of stock (although these are normally made to In-Kind Direct, please see the 'Sponsorship' section, below).

**Education:** Education is a key area of support, particularly for employee volunteering, and a number of sites participate in reading and number partner schemes. Unilever has moved away from the funding and provision of curriculum based educational resources, although selected resources such as From Field to Fork (a KS 3&4 resource focused on plant science, nutrition and sustainability) continue to be funded on an ongoing basis. Unilever also invests heavily in supporting current and retired staff who volunteer as school governors, with a monthly e-mail briefing, regional seminars and a high profile annual conference which attracts leading figures from the world of education.

**Sustainable development:** Unilever is committed to sustainable development and this is reflected in the UK by the significant support provided to a number of key organisations and campaigns. Unilever has a 25 year commitment to providing support to the Mersey Basin Campaign and is a Foundation Corporate Partner of the Forum for the Future, the UK's leading sustainable development charity.

**Health & nutrition:** Unilever provides significant funding to both the British Nutrition Foundation and the British Skin Foundation. It has also worked with the Anaphylaxis Campaign to raise the awareness of food allergy issues.

## Employee-led support

Numerous Unilever employees give time in assisting local schoolchildren with their reading and writing skills. Whilst since 1990, through the Unilever Governors' network, support has been given to employees who volunteer to be school governors.

**Payroll giving:** The company operates the Give As You Earn scheme.

## Commercially-led support

**Sponsorship:** *The arts* – Unilever sponsors 'The Unilever Series at Tate Modern'. Unilever began this sponsorship in 2000 and has recently announced a new three year extension (at a cost of £1m between 2005 and 2008). As a result it is not looking to fund other major arts sponsorships during this time.

Locally, Unilever has a number of local sites around the UK. Each of these sites are encouraged to develop partnerships with key local organisations to address local issues. Again, many of these partnerships are with long term established community partners. Decisions about local programmes are made locally at the relevant site.

Requests for product donations, advertising or brand sponsorship (e.g. Flora London Marathon) should be addressed directly to the brand concerned at the following address: Unilever UK Corporate Affairs Team, Freepost NATE 139, Milton Keynes MK9 1BR.

# Uniq plc

No 1 Chalfont Park, Gerrards Cross, Buckinghamshire SL9 0UN

01753 276000; Fax: 01753 276071

Website: www.uniq.com

Correspondent: JF Burkitt, Company Secretary

Chief officer: Nigel Stapleton

| Year end | Turnover | Pre-tax profit |
|---|---|---|
| 31/03/2005 | £879,000,000 | £22,500,000 |

**Nature of company business**
Formerly trading as Unigate plc, the group is principally engaged in food processing and logistics.

Subsidiaries include: Wincanton Holdings Ltd, Toft Foods Ltd

Main locations: Gerrards Cross

UK employees: 8,741

### Charitable donations

2005: £52,000
2004: £30,000

## Community involvement

Support is given to a limited range of charitable causes on a selective basis with most donations committed long term to national charities.

In addition, there is a strong preference for local charities in areas of company presence and appeals relevant to the company's business. We were previously advised that areas likely to be considered for support include the arts, children/youth, education and elderly people.

### Exclusions

No support for brochure advertising, individuals, local appeals not in areas of company presence, overseas projects or political appeals.

### Applications

Appeals, where relevant, should be addressed to the correspondent. However, unsolicited requests outside the criteria listed will not succeed.

## Corporate giving

In 2004/05 the company made donations to charitable causes totalling £52,000 and support was focused primarily on Caravan, the grocery industry charity.

The company also contributes financial support and practical assistance to many different local initiatives.

### In-kind support

Non-cash support is given in the form of gifts in kind, secretarial and administrative support, and advice and consultation.

### Employee-led support

The company encourages employees to contribute directly to community initiatives; allowing them time away from work to serve as magistrates, school governors, local councillors, trade union officials or representatives of professional bodies.

A great many Uniq employees serve on charitable committees or have worked together to organise and participate in fundraising events. These have included sponsored mountain climbs, rowing events and other activities.

# Unisys Ltd

Bakers Court, Bakers Road, Uxbridge UB8 1RG

01895 237137; Fax: 01895 862093

Website: www.unisys.co.uk

Correspondent: Ian Ryder

Managing Director: Nick Wilson

| Year end | Turnover | Pre-tax profit |
|---|---|---|
| 31/12/2005 | £266,877,000 | £27,273,000 |

**Nature of company business**
The development, manufacture, supply and maintenance of information technology systems and related services and supplies.

Main locations: Altrincham, Birmingham, Bristol, Glasgow, Leeds, Slough, Milton Keynes, Liverpool, Uxbridge

UK employees: 1,661

### Charitable donations

2005: £101,036
2004: £166,404

Membership: BitC

## Community involvement

Unisys prefers to invest in those communities in which it has a presence. These investments take the form of:

- technology and business education
- health and human services
- arts, cultural and civic organisations
- global diversity.

### Exclusions

Charitable causes operating outside of community focused employee-led initiatives.

### Applications

In writing to the correspondent; but in view of support being directed towards matching employee fundraising initiatives, unsolicited applications are unlikely to be successful.

## Corporate giving

In 2005, Unisys Limited made cash donations to charitable organisations amounting to £101,036. We have no details of the beneficiaries.

### In-kind support

This mainly comprises of gifts in kind.

### Employee-led support

Staff are encouraged to become involved in the local community through becoming volunteers and school governors and through fundraising which the company matches pound for pound up to a maximum of £500.

## Commercially-led support

**Sponsorship:** *The arts* – Support is again focused in those places where the company has a major presence, and which can also be used for client entertainment and public relations. The company has concentrated on music with support given to City of Birmingham Symphony Orchestra, Leeds Festival Chorus, Milton Keynes Chamber Orchestra and The Stables, Milton Keynes.

# United Airlines

United House Building, 451 Southern Perimeter Road, Hounslow, Middlesex TW6 3LP

0845 844 4777

Website: www.unitedairlines.co.uk

Nature of company business
Airline.

Main locations: Hounslow

## Community involvement

The company states on its website that: 'Our commitment to corporate philanthropy, community sponsorships and promotions, extends around the globe'. Philanthropic support is mostly given via the United Airlines Foundation, which focuses on education, health, arts and culture, volunteerism and diversity. However, being an American airline, it is likely that only a small percentage of its support is given in the UK.

### Exclusions

No support for matching gifts, or air transportation for fundraising events or individuals. No philanthropic support for the following: capital and building grants, development campaigns, individuals, political or fraternal organisations, religious institutions, or individual public or private schools.

### Applications

As at September 2006, the foundation was no longer accepting new or unsolicited proposals whilst new guidelines were being drafted. However, examples of the information typically required for an application to be considered are still available on the company's website.

## Corporate giving

Past beneficiaries have included Habitat for Humanity, towards building affordable subsidised homes in Banbury, Eastbourne, Liverpool and Southwark.

## Employee-led support

The company has created a United We Care scheme which both encourages payroll giving and matches employees with volunteer opportunities.

# United Biscuits Ltd

Hayes Park, Hayes End Road, Hayes, Middlesex UB4 8EE

020 8234 5000; Fax: 020 8234 5555

Website: www.unitedbiscuits.co.uk

**Correspondent:** Alison Harper, Communications Department

**Chief officer:** David Fish

**Chief Executive:** Malcolm Ritchie

**Managing Director:** Benoit Testard

| Year end | Turnover | Pre-tax profit |
|---|---|---|
| 31/12/2005 | £1,266,900,000 | (£95,500,000) |

**Nature of company business**
The principal activity of the group is the manufacture and sale of a wide range of food products, including biscuits and savoury snacks.

In October 2006, an agreement was reached to sell United Biscuits in its entirety to a consortium comprising The Blackstone Group and PAI. No further details were available at the time.

**Subsidiaries include:** McVities Group, KP Snacks, UK Foods

**Main locations:** Glasgow, Harlesden, Halifax, Hayes, High Wycombe, Carlisle, Manchester, Liverpool, Consett, Rotherham, Billingham, Ashby-de-la-Zouch

**UK employees:** 7,318

**Total employees:** 10,639

### Charitable donations

2005: £50,000
2004: £30,000

Membership: BitC

## Community involvement

United Biscuits' (UB) community affairs programme is divided into two main areas: community investment and charitable giving.

The company has published a 'Charitable Affairs Policy' which states that: 'As a general rule, it is recommended that priority be given to local charities or schools, where the emphasis is on health (e.g. Macmillan), education and children, since these are causes which tend to appeal to people across the board. However, it is ultimately up to individual sites to determine how they prefer to spend their allocated budget.

'Support to charities/schools can be offered in the form of product, vouchers or cash, at the discretion of the site.

'UB is happy for sites/factories to encourage their employees to take part in national fundraising initiatives such as Jeans for Genes, Red Nose Day etc. where appropriate.'

### Exclusions

No response to circular appeals. No grants for animal charities, political appeals, or religious appeals.

### Applications

For appeals from organisations local to Hayes Park, please apply in writing to the correspondent.

Please note that there is no central charitable budget. The charitable policy across the company is operated on the basis of decentralisation. Individual sites are therefore responsible for decisions regarding the budget they allocate to charitable causes and the charities they support (within the guidelines already noted).

**Other information available:** The company publish an annual 'Community Affairs Review'.

## Corporate giving

In 2005, the group made charitable cash donations of £50,000 (2004: £30,000). We have no details of the beneficiaries.

### In-kind support

**Education:** Support is given to employees who are school governors and the company works in partnership with the School Governors' One Stop Shop to encourage more employees to become governors with inner city schools.

### Employee-led support

United Biscuits is happy for sites/factories to encourage their employees to take part in national fundraising initiatives such as Jeans for Genes, Red Nose Day and so on, where appropriate. It also appears that 'much of [the company's] fundraising is done through employees'.

Employees have also become involved with the Reading and Numeracy Partnership scheme. Visits are made by employees to local schools in the Hayes and Harlesden area to assist those children needing extra help in these subjects.

**Payroll giving:** The group is registered with the Give As You Earn scheme.

### Commercially-led support

**Sponsorship:** Requests regarding sponsorship, or use of a particular brand (such as Penguin or Hula Hoops), should be forwarded to the relevant brand managers. United Biscuits does not have a central sponsorship budget as all sponsorship should be done by a brand recognised by consumers.

An example of the above is the use of the Jaffa Cakes brand in the sponsorship of an under-7's football team in Hayes.

# United Business Media

Ludgate House, 245 Blackfriars Road, London SE1 9UY

020 7921 5000; Fax: 020 7928 2728

Website: www.unm.com

Correspondent: Nigel Main, Head of Marketing

Chief officer: Geoff Unwin

Chief Executive: David Levin

| Year end | Turnover | Pre-tax profit |
|---|---|---|
| 31/12/2005 | £675,800,000 | £232,200,000 |

**Nature of company business**
UBM is an international media and business information company.

**Subsidiaries include:** NOP Research Group Ltd, CMP Europe Ltd, PR Newswire Europe Ltd, United Advertising Publications plc

Main locations: London

UK employees: 2,094

Total employees: 6,175

### Charitable donations

2005: £434,300

Total community contributions: £434,300

## Community involvement

A charitable donation committee was established which makes central donations as well as allocating funds to divisions for disbursement.

As a media and information group, UBM particularly supports projects which promote communications, education and literacy. It also seeks to assist in relieving poverty and homelessness and promoting healthcare.

### Exclusions

No support is given to circular appeals, fundraising events, purely denominational (religious) appeals, local appeals not in areas of company presence or overseas projects.

### Applications

In writing to the correspondent.

## Corporate giving

The group supports communities through financial contributions, donations in kind and employee volunteering. In 2005 the total charitable contribution was £434,000. Donations made from central funds included those to the Asian Tsunami Relief Fund, London Bombings Fund and Hurricane Katrina Relief Fund. At a divisional level, support was given to over 40 organisations nominated by employees around the world.

### In-kind support

In 2005 hundreds of computers were donated through Digital Links International for reuse in developing countries, together with a financial donation to cover shipping, installation and training.

### Employee-led support

UBM encourages employees to support the community through employee volunteering programmes. 'We operate a matching scheme whereby employees can apply for corporate donations to match their own fundraising efforts, and we offer employees a tax-efficient way of contributing to charities of their choice through payroll giving.'

**Payroll giving:** The company operates the Give As You Earn scheme.

# United Utilities plc

Dawson House, Liverpool Road, Great Sankey, Warrington WA5 3LW

01925 234000

Website: www.unitedutilities.com

Correspondent: Pat Houghton, Community Partnership Assistant
01925 237018; Fax: 01925 233028
E-mail: pat.houghton@uuplc.co.uk

Chief officer: Sir Richard Evans

Chief Executive: Phillip Green

| Year end | Turnover | Pre-tax profit |
|---|---|---|
| 31/03/2005 | £2,368,200,000 | £370,400,000 |

**Nature of company business**
A multi-utility supplying water/waste water services, electricity, gas and telecommunications worldwide.

Subsidiaries include: Norweb Gas Ltd, NORWEB plc, Vertex Data Science Ltd, Norweb Telecom Ltd

Main locations: Warrington

UK employees: 15,774

## Charitable donations

2005: £1,432,000
2004: £1,335,759
2003: £1,015,310

Total community contributions: £1,948,452
Management costs: £780,476

Membership: BitC, L B Group, %Club

## Community involvement

The company's policy for community support was arrived at following consultation with stakeholders. It focuses on the following main areas:

- environment
- social exclusion
- education and training
- children/youth.

### Exclusions

No support for appeals from individuals, religious appeals or political appeals.

### Applications

In writing to the correspondent.

**Information available:** The group publishes a social and environmental impact report.

## Corporate giving

Total community contributions in 2004/05, were £1.95 million of which £1,432,000 was in the form of cash donations to UK charitable organisations.

The majority of the UK donations went towards supporting the company's official community partners. These are: Thorncross Young Offenders Unit; WaterAid; Young Enterprise; Prince's Trust; Groundwork; and a number of projects involving the visually and sensory impaired.

Support is also given through the United Utilities Trust Fund (Charity Commission no. 1108296). This 'independent' grant-making trust was established in 2005 to help people out of poverty and debt. Funded by United Utilities, the day to day management and administration is carried out by Auriga Services Ltd in line with the policy set by the trustees.

As with similar trusts established by other utility companies, the people it primarily assists are customers of United Utilities who are unable to pay their water bills. As at 24 April 2006, 2,346 households had received assistance totalling £1.9 million. Although small grants (up to £1,500) and Project Funding (up to £30,000 per year for a maximum of two years) are available to organisations providing money advice and debt counselling services, no total grant figure was available regarding this.

Further details on how to apply are available at: www.uutf.org.uk

## In-kind support

**Education:** Schoolchildren in the North West are able to attend one of the group's six purpose-built environmental education centres.

**Environment:** The group has developed a green commuter plan in partnership with Warrington Borough Council. This provides employees at its two main offices in the town with the opportunity to use environmentally-friendly modes of transport between their workplace and the town centre; for example, through bike loan, car-sharing and free bus travel schemes.

**Enterprise:** In cooperation with the Manchester University based Campus Ventures, the group has helped with the start-up of over 60 new ventures.

**Recreation:** As a major landowner in the North West, the group makes available its various properties and estates for a range of water and land based recreation and conservation activities.

## Employee-led support

United Utilities match funds employees' fundraising efforts on behalf of charitable organisations up to a maximum of £250 per application.

Since the scheme started in September 2002, 339 employees have made applications and received £74,000 in matched funding on behalf of over 140 local and national charities. In total, these charities received over £200,000 when the actual amounts raised by staff on their behalf are included.

**Payroll giving:** The company offer its employees the Charities Trust payroll giving scheme. 757 donors give a total of nearly £8,600 per month to just under 200 different charities.

# UnumProvident

Milton Court, Dorking, Surrey RH4 3LZ

01306 887766; Fax: 01306 881394

Website: www.unum.co.uk

Correspondent: Inderpal Sokhy, Head of Community Affairs

Chief officer: Susan Ring

Managing Director: Susan Ring

| Year end | Turnover | Pre-tax profit |
|---|---|---|
| 31/12/2005 | | £109,798,000 |

Nature of company business
Income protection insurance.

Main locations: Dorking

Total employees: 887

## Charitable donations

2004: £499,118
2003: £427,427

Total community contributions: £703,350

Membership: BitC, L B Group, %Club

## Community involvement

'UnumProvident's corporate responsibility programme seeks to ensure that we achieve high standards in how the business is led and in our behaviour in the marketplace, among our workforce, in the communities where we have a presence and in the environment more widely.'

Volunteering constitutes a major part of the company's community involvement.

The company along with other stakeholders from various sectors, is involved in the 'New Beginnings' (now 'Beginnings') programme. The programme seeks to develop and implement integrated welfare solutions to the employment issues affecting people who are disabled.

### Exclusions

No support for local appeals outside areas of company presence.

### Applications

In writing to the correspondent.

## Corporate giving

In 2005, total community contributions were £703,350, in the form of contributions to 'Beginnings', cash donations, social sponsorships and the value of staff volunteering days. The major beneficiary, 'Beginnings', is an organisation with notable success in raising the profile of disability and rehabilitation in the policy arena.

### In-kind support

During 2005, days taken up with staff volunteering were numbered at 842 (notional salary costs were valued at £109,500).

### Employee-led support

Employees are encouraged and supported in their volunteering activities.

### Commercially-led support

**Sponsorship:** The company was a major sponsor of the Disabled and Able-bodied British Sports Initiative Area project in Boston, Lincolnshire.

---

# UPS

Forest Road, Feltham, Middlesex TW13 7DY

08457 877877; Fax: 020 8844 2815

Website: www.ups.com

Correspondent: Marketing & Communications

Managing Director: Jim Barber

| Year end 31/12/2005 | Turnover | Pre-tax profit |
|---|---|---|

Nature of company business
Carrier and package delivery company providing specialist transportation, logistics, capital and e-commerce services.

Main locations: Feltham

UK employees: 3,700

---

Charitable donations
2004: £148,600
2003: £34,450

## Community involvement

Grants in the UK are made through the US-based UPS Foundation. However, these may be initiated by the company proactively seeking potential beneficiaries whose work ties in with the interests of the foundation. The principal interest of the foundation is in supporting projects concerned with literacy, hunger and volunteerism.

### Exclusions

The UPS Foundation does not award grants to individuals, religious organisations or theological functions, or church-sponsored programmes limited to church members.

Grants supporting capital campaigns, endowments or operating expenses are seldom approved.

### Applications

In writing to: Grant Proposals, The UPS Foundation, 55 Glenlake Parkway NE, Atlanta GA 30328, USA. Your application should include a current budget and audited financial statement, an annual report, and proof of charitable status. A concise covering letter (no more than two pages in length) should address the following:

- description and mission of the organisation
- description of the specific programme/project for which funding is requested
- statement of programme/project goals will be attained and evaluated
- total costs of the programme/project
- list of committed alternative funding sources and dollar amounts for the programme/project
- total amount requested for The UPS Foundation.

Requests for grants can be submitted at anytime. However, proposals received during the final quarter of the year may not be considered until the following year.

Further guidelines are available at: www.communty.ups.com/philanthropy/grant.html

## Corporate giving

In 2004, global giving through the foundation totalled nearly $40 million. Of this, the foundation's annual report shows that £148,600 was donated to six organisations in the UK. The beneficiaries were: Express Link Up, Volunteer Reading Help and The Who Cares? Trust (£41,000 each); Groundwork, Erewash and Age Concern, Suffolk (£9,800 each); and, Gloucestershire Emergency Accommodation Resource (£6,000).

In the case of Express Link Up, who provide computer hardware and software, internet links and teaching resources for use by hospitalised children, the grant enabled the purchase of much needed multi-lingual software. This will be used at hospitals in the main immigration cities in the UK to assist non-English speaking children learn the language.

### Employee-led support

Staff at the head office in Middlesex have taken part in a joint project with Volunteer Reading Help (VRH) and the National Literacy Trust, called 'Reading is Fundamental'. 18 employees were trained by VRH to help children at a local primary school with their reading, with each child being seen for 30 minutes twice a week on a one-to-one basis. UPS hope to set up similar schemes in other parts of the country.

# Reg Vardy plc

Newway House, Little Oak Drive, Annersely, Notts. NG15 0PR

0191 525 3000; Fax: 0191 525 3030

Website: www.regvardy.com

Correspondent: Eleanor Delahaye, Corporate and Events Manager

Chief officer: John F Standen

Chief Executive: Sir P Vardy

| Year end | Turnover | Pre-tax profit |
|----------|----------|----------------|
| 30/04/2005 | £1,717,921,000 | £43,787,000 |

Nature of company business
The main activity is motor vehicle distribution.

Subsidiaries include: Victoria (Bavaria) Ltd

Main locations: Sunderland

Total employees: 5,551

### Charitable donations

2005: £258,700
2004: £195,410
2003: £117,137

## Community involvement

The group is committed to making a positive contribution to the communities in which it operates and supporting the involvement of colleagues in their local communities. This commitment in fulfilled in the operations across the UK, in group initiatives at national level and in supporting individual colleagues involved in local activities. The group is involved in a wide range of initiatives for the benefit of local communities.

Support is also given through the independent family trust, The Vardy Foundation (Charity Commission no. 328415), which augments the company's charitable and community work.

## Exclusions

No support for circular appeals, local appeals not in areas of company presence or political appeals.

## Applications

In writing to the correspondent.

## Corporate giving

In 2004/05, the company made charitable donations of £258,700. The following examples are an indication of some of initiatives in which the company is involved.

Reg Vardy Limited is an official partner of the BBC's annual Children in Need appeal. As a group, Reg Vardy Limited donated £10 for every car sold across its expanding dealership network and hosted an online Intranet auction which was accessed by its colleagues across the UK.

The group is also a long-term supporter of BEN, the motor industry benevolent fund.

**The Vardy Foundation**

The foundation supports the City Academies programme in the North of England – an initiative that aims to drive the highest standards of education and increase access to the best academic facilities in areas of high disadvantage.

Through the Emmanuel Schools Foundation (ESF) the Vardy Foundation is currently the main sponsor of two schools, Emmanuel College in Gateshead and the King's Academy in Middlesbrough. The ESF will open a third school, Trinity Academy in Doncaster, in September 2005. The foundation has also helped to finance schools in Ethiopia, Bolivia and South Africa and supports Mercy Ships.

The foundation pledged to match fund the total raised by the group in support of Children in Need.

## Employee-led support

Reg Vardy is an official partner of the BBC's annual Children in Need appeal. The company has supported the appeal for the last three years and raised around £200,000 during this period through fundraising activities organised by colleagues with support from customers, suppliers and other donors.

**Payroll giving:** The company operates the BEN (motor industry) scheme.

## Commercially-led support

**Sponsorship:** 'In 2004, the group signed a 5-year sponsorship arrangement with the Ever Ready Brass Band. The Reg Vardy (Ever Ready) Band is the new name for the 28-musician band, which was formed in 1910 at Craghead Colliery, near Stanley, in County Durham. For the last 12 years the former Ever Ready Band had been self-supporting but is still recognised as one of the leading bands in the country and it is the reigning Northern Area Champion.

'The support from Reg Vardy will allow the band, which is based at Stanley, to update their uniforms, commission new music, upgrade the band room and to subsidise travel and accommodation costs.'

# Vauxhall Motors Ltd

Public Affairs, Griffin House, Osborne Road, Luton LU1 3YT

Website: www.vauxhall.co.uk

Correspondent: Paul Patten, Community Affairs & Charities Coordinator

| Year end | Turnover | Pre-tax profit |
|----------|----------|----------------|
| 31/12/2003 | £3,574,800,000 | (£115,100,000) |

Nature of company business
The company manufactures, markets and services passenger cars, recreational vehicles and light vans.

Main locations: Ellesmere Port, Luton

UK employees: 5,158

### Charitable donations
2003: £264,432

Membership: BitC

## Community involvement

Vauxhall Motors' community support programme aims to support voluntary activities which benefit the local communities in the catchment areas of the company's Luton, Bedfordshire and Ellesmere Port plants. Particular emphasis is given to supporting causes concerned with education, health and the environment.

In 2001 the company introduced The Griffin Community Award Scheme. In each region, Bedfordshire and the Wirral, a £10,000 first prize and three runner-up prizes of £1,000 are donated to those organisations that are judged to meet the criteria that the judging panel believe will bring most benefit to the local community. Also, one organisation in each region can win the use of a Vauxhall vehicle, which they can use to support their charitable projects.

### Exclusions

No grants for circular appeals, advertising in charity brochures, appeals from individuals, fundraising events, medical research, overseas projects, political appeals, religious appeals, science/technology, or local appeals not in areas of company presence. The company does not give raffle prizes or vehicle donations.

### Applications

In writing to the correspondent at: CCAS, 80 Croydon Road, Beckenham, Kent BR3 4DF.

Application forms for the Griffin Award can be downloaded from the Vauxhall website.

## Corporate giving

In 2003 Vauxhall donated a total of £264,432 to charities. Over £100,000 was given to local charities in Bedfordshire and Cheshire.

### In-kind support

The company provide additional support through gifts in kind and joint promotions. For example, the Ellesmere Port plant has donated materials such as scrap wood and over 40 car engines to schools, colleges and universities for educational use.

### Employee-led support

In the past, employees have helped local youngsters develop their business skills.

### Commercially-led support

**Commercially-led support:** BEN – Motor & Allied Trades Benevolent Fund, received over £166,000 as part of a per Vauxhall vehicle sold donation.

# Vodafone Group

Vodaphone House, The Connection, Newbury, Berkshire RG14 2FN

01635 33251; Fax: 01635 45713

Website: www.vodafone.com

Correspondent: Sarah Shillito, Senior Manager Vodafone UK Foundation

Chief officer: Lord MacLaurin of Knebworth

Chief Executive: Arun Sarin

| Year end | Turnover | Pre-tax profit |
|---|---|---|
| 31/03/2006 | £34,133,000,000 | (£4,702,000,000) |

**Nature of company business**
Mobile telecommunications.

**Main locations:** Banbury, Gloucester, Warrington, Welwyn Garden City, Theale, Trowbridge, Croydon, Newbury, Abingdon

**UK employees:** 10,620

**Total employees:** 61,672

### Charitable donations

2006: £7,820,000

Total community contributions: £7,820,000

Membership: BitC, L B Group, %Club

## Community involvement

Much of its support is given through the Vodafone UK Foundation, formerly known as The Vodafone Group Charitable Trust (registration no. 1013850).

'Our aim is to make social investments to help the people of the UK to have fuller lives by:

▷ enabling access to information and opportunities primarily via mobile technology (for example laptops, websites, outreach work)

▷ supporting the local communities in which Vodafone has a significant physical presence

▷ supporting Vodafone employees in their engagement in community activities.

We focus on the age group of 16–25 whose lives are on the cusp of change and where we believe there is the potential to make long-lasting change for the better. We particularly aim to prevent exclusion in this age-group.

And the areas where the UK foundation seeks to invest – with the emphasis on enabling access via communications technology – are where we can call upon the skills and expertise of the Vodafone business and its employees to add lasting value to our programmes. In this way we will achieve more benefit for communities than we could alone.'

### Applications

An application form can be downloaded from the Vodafone UK Foundation's website (www.vodafoneukfoundation.org). Alternatively, e-mail a proposal to: thevodafoneukfoundation@vodafone.co.uk

## Corporate giving

In 2005/06 the company gave £7.82 million to charity, over £5.39 million of which was given through the Vodafone UK Foundation.

### Employee-led support

**Payroll giving:** Vodafone employees in the UK donate through this channel.

In 2005/06 employees in the UK took part in 530 separate fundraising events and succeeded in raising a total of £482,289 for 300 different charities and community projects across the UK. With £375,736 then provided by the UK foundation in matched funding, the total for fundraising reached £858,025.

Employees can claim up to 24 hours paid leave per year for volunteering activities in the local community.

# VT Group plc

V T House, Grange Drive, Hedge End, Southampton SO30 2DQ

023 8083 9001; Fax: 023 8083 9002

Website: www.vvtplc.com

Correspondent: M Jowett, Company Secretary

Chief officer: M Jefferies

Chief Executive: P Lester

| Year end | Turnover | Pre-tax profit |
|---|---|---|
| 31/03/2005 | £744,000,000 | £43,000,000 |

**Nature of company business**
Support services, shipbuilding and marine products.

**Subsidiaries include:** Flagship Training Ltd, Airwork Limited, Fleet Support Limited, Careers Enterprise Limited

**Main locations:** Bournemouth, Chichester, Bordon, Watford, Portsmouth, Reading, Southampton, London, Hove, Leatherhead

**UK employees:** 8,360

### Charitable donations

2005: £86,000
2004: £77,000
2003: £67,000

Membership: BitC

## Community involvement

The company has a central group charity committee made up of employees' representative of the main areas of the group. The committee meets regularly throughout the year and distributes funds to charities with preference given to those local to the group's principal places of business and which relate to education, health, community and the arts.

### Exclusions

No support for advertising in charity brochures, animal welfare, appeals from individuals, the arts, enterprise/training, environment/heritage, overseas projects, political appeals, social welfare or sport.

### Applications

In writing to the correspondent.

## Corporate giving

In 2004/05, the group contributed a total of £86,000 to charitable organisations including £25,000 to the Tsunami Appeal. Other beneficiaries included: Wessex Cancer Trust; Trustee Armed Forces Memorial Appeal; Gosport/Fareham HomeStart; Canine Partners for Independence, and Age Concern (Hampshire).

## In-kind support

In addition to cash donations, the company provides in kind support to its local communities in the form of manual work for schools and old people's residences providing members for

charitable fundraising committees, school bodies and local authorities.

### Employee-led support

Employees are positively encouraged to undertake fundraising activities for their chosen charity and are assisted in this by financial support from the company.

In 2005, £25,000 was raised by employees in aid of the Tsunami Appeal; a figure matched by the company.

# Warburtons Ltd

Back O'th' Bank House, Hereford Street, Bolton, Lancashire BL1 8HJ

01204 531004; Fax: 01204 523361

Website: www.warburtons.co.uk

Correspondent: Jill Kippax, Corporate Affairs Manager
01204 556600; Fax: 01204 532283

Chief officer: Jonathan Warburton

Managing Director: W Brett Warburton

| Year end | Turnover | Pre-tax profit |
|---|---|---|
| 24/09/2005 | £321,852,000 | £48,605,000 |

**Nature of company business**
Bakers.

**Main locations:** Wakefield, Bolton, Enfield, North London

**UK employees:** 3,791

**Total employees:** 3,791

### Charitable donations

2005: £219,000
2004: £149,000
2003: £15,625

Membership: BitC

## Community involvement

The company has established a community giving programme which focuses on charities, organisations and initiatives that improve the quality of family life. Therefore, the programme supports projects that have a positive impact on the health and wellbeing of the whole family, especially in the areas of diet, fitness, safety and education, as well as caring initiatives that improve the quality of life for the sick, elderly or disabled.

The company has a facility on its website for applications from organisations requesting support, either financial or in kind donations.

The company prefers to support appeals from local charities in areas of company presence, especially projects concerned with education and health (young socially disadvantaged groups in particular), the arts and environment. Examples of giving during the year are: the provision of high visibility safety jackets for pupils of a Kirkby primary school in Merseyside, supporting a junior school at Perry Beeches by making a donation towards the continuance of an after-school activities club and the donation of goods for their 'Celebration Day', a donation towards new football kits for

College High School, Erdington and a donation to the Clissold Swimming Club for children in Hackney and the surrounding area.

'Warburtons is committed to operating in a socially responsible manner within its local communities. As a family business, the company has a strong track record of charitable giving and active involvement and recognises the positive effect of community partnerships.'

## Exclusions

No support for: advertising in charity brochures; animal welfare; appeals from individuals; medical research; overseas projects; political appeals; religious appeals; or science/technology.

## Applications

In writing to the correspondent.

## Corporate giving

During the year 2005 the company contributed £219,000 (2004: £149,000).

Over the past twelve months approximately 250 charities and organisations have been helped by Warburtons, either through financial support, product donations and the employees' match-funding programme.

Family members of the company spearhead Warburtons Community Giving Programme and the company is a member of Business in the Community. Warburtons provides support in three ways: financial support, product donations and the personal involvement of individuals (both employees and family members).

The company supports its employees in their fundraising initiatives through a match-funding programme.

## In-kind support

Help is given in time, donations of products and equipment.

## Employee-led support

A matched funding scheme is operated for employees' fundraising.

## Commercially-led support

**Sponsorship:** *Education* – Warburtons sponsored Crime Packs, a school initiative including information on how to give first aid, the dangers of smoking, alcohol abuse and guidelines on how to deal with day-to-day issues, such as bullying and teasing in the school environment.

The company has also supported children at Colfes Prep School in Greenwich by arranging a visit by James McGranahan, Commonwealth Games gymnast, to motivate and inspire young children into getting fit through sport. Warburtons also provided nutritional information and healthy recipes along with bread samples.

# Josiah Wedgwood & Sons Limited

Barlaston, Stoke-on-Trent, Staffordshire ST12 9ES

01782 204141; Fax: 01782 204402

Website: www.wedgwood.com

Correspondent: Andrew Stanistreet, External Communications Manager

**Chief officer:** Sir Anthony O'Reilly

| Year end | Turnover | Pre-tax profit |
|---|---|---|
| 31/03/2005 | £499,386,500 | (£101,704,150) |

**Nature of company business**
Manufacture, distribution and retailing of high quality crystal products, including giftware, stemware and lighting products, fine bone china, porcelain, earthenware and ceramics.

**Subsidiaries include:** Josiah Wedgwood & Sons Ltd, Stuart & Sons Ltd, Royal Doulton (UK) Ltd

**Main locations:** Stoke-on-Trent

**Total employees:** 8,536

## Charitable donations

2005: £187,457

## Community involvement

We were requested not to publish details of the company's charitable activities on the grounds that: 'We currently have a full portfolio of sponsorship and community activities and feel that publicising the company's extensive good works in the directory will only lead to disappointment for new applicants in the near future. Rest assured we will continue to support the community and charitable organisations as a matter of course.'

Although it was pointed out to us that information previously held about the company was incorrect, we have checked and updated this as far as is possible without its direct input. At the most basic level of policy, we believe there is still some preference for local charities in areas of company presence.

## Applications

In writing to the correspondent. Please note, however, that we were advised in May 2006, that cuts were being made to the community support budget.

## Corporate giving

In 2004/05, the company declared worldwide cash donations of €275,000 (around £187,000). We have no further information regarding the beneficiaries.

## In-kind support

Gifts in kind may be made to local or industry-related charities.

## Employee-led support

In 2004, workers at Wedgwood again chose to support the North Staffordshire Hospital Charitable Fund from money raised through their staff lottery. A percentage of the takings are put into a charitable fund and each year this is presented to a chosen charity. This year staff presented £13,000 towards cancer research.

## Commercially-led support

**Sponsorship:** 'A full portfolio' exists.

# Weetabix Ltd

Weetabix Mills, Burton Latimer, Kettering NN15 5JR

01536 722181; Fax: 01536 726148

Website: www.weetabix.co.uk

Correspondent: Hilary Bull, PA to Cheif Executive

Chief officer: Sir Richard W George

Chief Executive: K L Wood

| Year end | Turnover | Pre-tax profit |
|---|---|---|
| 25/12/2005 | £259,660,000 | £55,922,000 |

Nature of company business
Manufacture of cereal foods.

Subsidiaries include: Ryecroft Foods Ltd, Vibixa Ltd, B L Marketing Ltd

Main locations: Ashton under Lyne, Burton Latimer, Hastings, Corby

Total employees: 1,612

> ### Charitable donations
> 2005: £115,193
> 2004: £584,256

## Community involvement

Weetabix have supported a wide range of groups and activities in the county of Northamptonshire. These have ranged from making donations to local schools, to sponsoring a variety of projects involving local charities. The company has also been keen to support local sports groups.

There exists an associated trust through which the company appears to make the majority of its charitable donations. This is The Weetabix Charitable Trust (Charity Commission no. 1044949).

## Exclusions

No support for local appeals not in areas of company presence, or appeals from individuals.

## Applications

In writing to the correspondent.

## Corporate giving

The company donated £115,193 (2004: £584,256) for charitable purposes. Unfortunately we have no information regarding the beneficiaries of these donations although it is likely that the Weetabix Charitable Trust benefited.

### The Weetabix Charitable Trust

In 2004/5 the trust had an income of £4,194 compared with an income of £705,835 in the year 2003/04.

Again, we do not have access to the charity's accounts for the year ending April 2005 and no information regarding the recipients of the grants made for this year.

## Commercially-led support

Sponsorship: *Sport* – In association with The Golf Foundation, the company has for fourteen years supported 'grassroots' competition for young boys and girls through the Weetabix Age Group Championships. The Golf Foundation

reports that the company has decided to withdraw its sponsorship as part of a review of their sponsorship strategy generally. The company has also sponsored the Weetabix Youth Football League in Northamptonshire.

# The Weir Group plc

149 Newlands Road, Cathcart, Glasgow G44 4EX

0141 637 7111; Fax: 0141 221 9789

Website: www.weir.co.uk

Correspondent: Alan Mitchelson, Company Secretary
E-mail: alan.mitchelson@weir.co.uk

Chief officer: Sir Robert Smith

Chief Executive: Mark Selway

| Year end | Turnover | Pre-tax profit |
|---|---|---|
| 30/12/2005 | £789,384,000 | £37,488,000 |

Nature of company business
Principal activities: engineering services and specialist engineering products.

Subsidiaries include: Neyrfor-Weir Ltd, Tooling Products Holdings Ltd, Hopkinsons Ltd, Girdlestone Pumps Ltd, Liquid Gas Equipment Ltd, Flowguard Ltd, Strachan & Henshaw Ltd, G Perry & Sons Ltd, Warman International Ltd

Main locations: Aylestone, Altens, Bristol, Cathcart, Glasgow, Newton Heath, Huddersfield, Stockton on Tees, South Gyle, Petersfield

Total employees: 7,642

> ### Charitable donations
> 2005: £101,757
> 2003: £118,516

## Community involvement

'Causes, events and charities are often nominated and driven by our employees, reflecting their own interests and social engagement.'

## Applications

In writing to the correspondent. The main decisions are made by a board committee.

## Corporate giving

In 2005 community contributions totalled £101,757.

# Wellington Underwriting

88 Leadenhall Street, London EC3A 3BA

020 7337 2000; Fax: 020 7337 2001

Website: www.wellington.co.uk

Correspondent: The Marketing Department

Chief officer: John Barton

Chief Executive: Preben Prebenson

| Year end | Turnover | Pre-tax profit |
|---|---|---|
| 31/12/2005 | | |

**Nature of company business**
The principal activity is insurance underwriting.

**Main locations:** London

**UK employees:** 302

**Total employees:** 400

### Charitable donations

2006: £80,000

## Applications

In writing to the correspondent.

## Corporate giving

The company made charitable donations during the year of £80,000 including £15,000 to the Tsunami Appeal. The group's charitable activities in the UK and US are co-ordinated by local committees which make donations to a number of causes.

The UK Charities Committee was asked by the board to nominate a major partner from amongst charities supporting the young, disadvantaged, predominantly inner-city youth in Tower Hamlets and the surrounding area. The committee selected the Stepney Children's Fund, donating £15,000 in 2005, with fundraising by staff amounting to a further £2,500.

Previous beneficiaries of cash donations have included Age Concern, Cancer Research UK and NSPCC.

### In-kind support

The group donated surplus furniture and computers for use by the Stepney Children's Fund.

### Employee-led support

The group provides employees with the facility of supporting charities through the Give as You Earn scheme.

Fundraising by employees in encouraged, with sums raised matched by the company.

Volunteering is also encouraged with staff helping schoolchildren with their reading at the local Thomas Buxton Infant School.

### Commercially-led support

Longstanding support has been given to the National Maritime Museum through their corporate loan scheme.

# Wessex Water plc

Claverton Down Road, Claverton Down, Bath BA2 7WW

01225 526000; Fax: 01225 528000

**Website:** www.wessexwater.co.uk

**Correspondent:** Marilyn Smith, Head of Stakeholder Relations
E-mail: info@wessexwater.co.uk

**Chief officer:** Colin Skellett

| Year end | Turnover | Pre-tax profit |
|---|---|---|
| 31/03/2005 | £303,600,000 | £57,100,000 |

**Nature of company business**
Principal activity: water and sewerage services.

**Main locations:** Bath

**UK employees:** 1,396

**Total employees:** 1,396

### Charitable donations

2005: £56,000
2004: £37,000
2003: £55,000

Membership: BitC

## Community involvement

Grants are given to registered charities operating in the area administered by Wessex Water, i.e. South Gloucestershire, Wiltshire, Dorset, and Somerset.

The company's 2004/05 report stated: 'It is important to us to make a difference within the communities we serve and we have invested in a number of areas that directly benefit our customers. These include providing a range of additional services to customers who require extra care, providing an extensive education service to schools and making grants to help fund environmental projects in our area.'

### Exclusions

No support for national charities, advertising in charity brochures, animal welfare, the arts, enterprise/training, political appeals, religious appeals or science/technology.

### Applications

In writing to the correspondent. The Community Involvement Committee meets monthly.

**Information available:** The company produces a booklet detailing its work in the community.

## Corporate giving

In 2004/05, the company donated a total of £56,000 to UK charities.

Launched in 1993, Wessex Watermark is a grant scheme set up by the company to help fund environmental projects in the region. Organised by the Conservation Foundation, grants from £100 to £2,500 were awarded to numerous environmental projects throughout the region.

Local charities based within the region also receive support through the company's community involvement committee which awards small grants every month.

Since its creation in 1981, Wessex Water has supported WaterAid, the international water and sanitation charity by organising fundraising events and raising money through customers and staff. A new initiative, Business 4 Life, gives graduates from local businesses an opportunity to develop new skills and raise money for WaterAid at the same time. With support and training from the company, ten graduates from local firms set up their 'own business' with the objective of raising £20,000 for WaterAid. A partnership between WaterAid, Wessex Water and local firms, Business 4 Life contributed to the record £750,000 raised in the region for WaterAid during 2004/05.

## In-kind support

**Education:** Wessex Water offers an education service catering for 5 to 15 year olds. There are now nine education centres in the Wessex Water region. Services include:

- primary and secondary education packs
- education advisers
- visits to schools
- tailor-made lessons (water cycle, river & pond studies, WaterAid and practical sessions)
- education centres (nine in total – details on website)
- site visits.

**Special needs:** Customer Care Plus is a special programme for those customers with special needs, including older and disabled people. A register of such customers is held, in order that the company can identify and respond to their requirements.

Help includes: a text telephone service for people with impaired hearing; Braille or audio bills; a doorstep security password system; and advance warning of interruptions to water supply.

## Employee-led support

The company supports employee volunteering through giving time off to volunteers and by matching employee fundraising by up to £250 through the Community Plus Fund.

**Payroll giving:** The company operates the Give As You Earn scheme.

## Commercially-led support

**Sponsorship:** *The environment* – The company sponsors local, environmental and water-related activities.

# West Bromwich Building Society

374 High Street, West Bromwich, West Midlands B70 8LR

0845 33 00 611

Website: www.westbrom.co.uk

Correspondent: Brian Seymour-Smith, Public Relations Manager

Chief officer: Brian Woods-Scarwen

Chief Executive: Andrew Messenger

| Year end | Turnover | Pre-tax profit |
|---|---|---|
| 31/03/2006 | | £38,500,000 |

Nature of company business
Building society.

Main locations: West Bromwich

UK employees: 800

### Charitable donations

2006: £500,000
2005: £500,000

Total community contributions: £500,000

## Community involvement

The society does not make direct contributions to charities, but supports many community-based activities and local projects, especially those involving young people.

**Charity of the Year:** British Heart Foundation (2005/06).

### Exclusions

No support for local appeals not in areas of company presence.

### Applications

In writing to the correspondent.

## Corporate giving

In 2005/06, the society, through sponsorship and in kind donations made contributions to its local communities of £500,000.

### Employee-led support

The society encourages its staff to fundraise. In 2005/06, staff raised £20,000 on behalf of the society's 'Charity of the Year', the British Heart Foundation.

### Commercially-led support

**Cause-related marketing:** The society runs an affinity savings account for local charities and a Community Counts scheme which gives new mortgage customers the chance to donate £100 to a local charity or good cause of their choice. We have no figure regarding how much this has raised on behalf of local charities.

# Western Power Distribution

Avonbank, Feeder Road, Bristol BS2 0TB

0117 933 2005; Fax: 0117 933 2366

Website: www.westernpower.co.uk

Correspondent: Sharon Cross, Corporate Communications
0117 933 2005
E-mail: scross@westernpower.co.uk

Chief Executive: R A Symons

| Year end | Turnover | Pre-tax profit |
|---|---|---|
| 31/03/2006 | £234,200,000 | £95,900,000 |

Nature of company business
Distribution of electricity.

Main locations: Bristol

UK employees: 1,654

### Charitable donations

2006: £55,000
2004: £186,000

## Community involvement

The company has established a foundation, administered by the Charities Aid Foundation, under which registered charities may receive grants from the company. The foundation enables WPD to support those good causes, which may otherwise fall outside the company's sponsorship activities.

Each year the company sets a community support policy. In 2006 the themes were education, safety and environment. The company will consider offering support to projects or events in the South West and Wales region that fall under these banners.

The following extract is taken from the company's website:

'Western Power Distribution, the electricity company serving south west England and south Wales, has been awarded £500,000 from energy regulator OFGEM for its work in the community. The energy regulator made two awards with WPD being the only UK company to receive a £200,000 reward for social corporate responsibility initiatives and a 50% share of an award for its work with vulnerable customers.

Run for the first time this year, OFGEM's initiative set out to recognise and reward those companies whom it felt demonstrated best practice. In its application WPD demonstrated that corporate citizenship is integral to its wider business strategy and the difference that grass roots support for local projects can make. OFGEM commended WPD for its 'breadth, depth and holistic approach' to community support.

Among the initiatives highlighted were:

- 'An anti bullying booklet for new secondary school children in Bath, Bristol and parts of north Somerset. This was developed in conjunction with Wansdyke MP Dan Norris and national children's charity, Kidscape and was distributed to more than 180,000 homes in the area.

- An annual apprentice challenge project where new apprentice employees at the company spend three days in their local community improving the environment. The example used was a special school near Haverfordwest where an outdoor classroom was created and access to the school grounds was improved.

- The use of a paper recycling rebate gained by the company to make awards to primary schools in Exeter who wanted to improve their grounds and create wildlife gardens.

Chief Executive, Robert Symons, said: 'We take our role as a corporate citizen very seriously and believe it is the role of every company to put something back into the community its serves. However, to have our efforts recognised by an independent panel, and subsequently rewarded in this way is very satisfying.

'We will continue to be an active member of the community and these funds will be reinvested in our community support activities for the benefit of local organisations and groups in the future.'

In WPD's other reward, the company was praised for its work with vulnerable customers including the development of a Priority Services Register for electricity dependent customers and a partnership with the WRVS in times of emergency'.

### Exclusions

No support for local appeals not in areas of company presence, advertising in charity brochures, animal welfare, appeals from individuals, overseas appeals, religious appeals, political appeals, or sport.

### Applications

In writing to the correspondent.

## Corporate giving

In 2005/06, the company made cash donations of £55,000, of which £47,000 went to registered charities. In addition to this the WPD Foundation donated £65,000. We have no details of the beneficiaries other than that the donations were made to organisations in the South West.

### In-kind support

This was estimated to have been in excess of £100,000.

### Employee-led support

The company encourages its employees to support their communities in practical as well as monetary terms. This may be through the Leading Lights initiative – an employee volunteer scheme – or by fundraising for their favourite charity, which WPD acknowledges by matching the funds raised pound for pound.

### Commercially-led support

**Sponsorship:** Young women cricketers from Gwent will benefit from a new sponsorship deal secured between the Welsh Women's Cricket Association (WWCA) and Western Power Distribution (WPD).

In 2006 St John Ambulance in Somerset joined forces with Western Power Distribution to sponsor a 2006–7 competition in road safety for 'Badger' groups across the county.

Badgers are between five-ten years' old and members of the St John's Ambulance service, who receive training in up to 15 subjects aimed at helping them develop social and citizenship skills. They take part in an active programme to earn badges that includes caring, safety, first aid and being healthy. Badgers can go on to join the Cadets and hopefully will progress to becoming adult members of the charity.

## Whitbread Group plc

Whitbread Court, Houghton Hall Business Park, Porz Avenue, Dunstable, LU5 5XE

01582 424200

Website: www.whitbread.co.uk

Correspondent: The Community Investment Director

E-mail: communityinvestment@whitbread.com

Chief officer: A Habgood

Chief Executive: A Parker

| Year end | Turnover | Pre-tax profit |
|---|---|---|
| 04/03/2006 | £1,450,500,000 | £160,100,000 |

Nature of company business
The company's principal activities are the operation of hotels, restaurants and racquets, health and fitness clubs.

Subsidiaries include: David Lloyd Leisure plc, The Pelican Group plc

Main locations: London

UK employees: 45,000

### Charitable donations

2004: £1,380,000

Total community contributions: £22,000,000

Membership: A & B, BitC

## Community involvement

Whitbread underwent a major transformation at the beginning of this century by concentrating on the lodging, eating-out and active leisure markets. This resulted in a major review of its community investment policy which, on completion, saw the new programme more closely aligned to 'New Whitbread' business priorities. The focus is now on enabling young people (14–28) to achieve their potential. The great majority of available budget will support a limited number of projects, linked closely to main business divisions and brands, through long-term partnerships with young people's charities and organisations at national level. Initiatives will continue to exploit Whitbread's experience and track record in the fields of volunteering and education.

**Charity of the Year:** Support has been given to a number of national charities through brand partnerships, for example Brewers Fayre supporting Whizz-Kidz and TGI Friday supporting KidsOut.

### Exclusions

The following are not usually supported: advertising in charity brochures, animal welfare, the arts, elderly people, enterprise/training, ticket purchases for charity events, appeals from religious bodies (unless for the benefit of the community as a whole), political organisations, medical research, charitable organisations operating overseas, science/technology, sickness/disability, social welfare or appeals from individuals.

### Applications

Corporate responsibility is led by Angie Risley, Group HR Director and member of the main board and is supported by a small specialist team. The team works through four steering groups, which are sponsored by the appropriate member of the group's executive council, and reports twice a year to the full executive committee and the board.

## Corporate giving

In 2006, the company's website stated 'Currently, our community investment contribution totals more than £2.2 million annually, made up of direct cash contributions, donated employee time and recycled furniture and equipment. This figure includes around £500,000 raised through the company's payroll giving scheme, as well as Whitbread's employees and customers raising a further £1.3 million through charitable activities.'

The Whitbread 1988 Charitable Trust (Charity Commission no.: 800501) was established in 1988, the trust has supported many projects that assist young people in achieving their potential.

### In-kind support

**Volunteering:** Whitbread has supported the volunteering activity of other young people via the annual Whitbread Young Achievers Awards.

**Environment:** Through its CARE (Community Action by Recycling Equipment) programme the company donates furniture and equipment to voluntary organisations and community groups.

### Employee-led support

Employees are encouraged to get actively involved in local community projects. The company matches employee giving and fundraising.

**Payroll giving:** The company promotes and administers its own payroll giving scheme. In 2005, 15% of the workforce participated.

### Commercially-led support

**Sponsorship:** Whitbread's main commercial sponsorship covers national sport and literary awards. Community sponsorship is generally of a local nature covering a wide range of issues.

# Whittard of Chelsea plc

Unit 3b Union Court, 22 Union Road, London SW4 6JP

020 7819 6400; Fax: 020 7627 8850

Website: www.whittard.com

Correspondent: Yvonne Johnson, Secretary
E-mail: info@whittard.co.uk

Chief Executive: Nicholas Shutts

| Year end | Turnover | Pre-tax profit |
|---|---|---|
| 30/09/2005 | £46,079,000 | £2,354,000 |

Nature of company business
Retailers of fine teas and coffees.

Main locations: London

UK employees: 584

Total employees: 584

> **Charitable donations**
> 2004: £18,586

## Community involvement

Whittard tends to choose a single charity (usually cancer related) to support throughout the year and due to this focus, support outside of it is unlikely.

### Applications

In writing to the correspondent. But note comments above.

## Corporate giving

Since 2002, Whittard of Chelsea has been involved in fundraising for Macmillan Cancer Relief primarily through their support for 'The World's Biggest Coffee Morning'. In 2004 the company raised a total of £18,586.

### In-kind support

Past information suggested that where possible, the company also gives in kind support, usually in the form of products. This may be the donation of post-expiry date tea or coffee to charities to help run coffee mornings, or the donation of promotional ceramics (cups, saucers, teapots, and so on) to charity shops to sell. The company has also run children's art competitions and engineered as much activity as possible in-store to raise the profile of the Macmillan charity.

### Employee-led support

The company encourages employees to take part in activities that aim to 'give something back' to the community or environment in which it operates. Members of the team collect customer donations, make personal pledges and undertake a variety of sponsored events such as head shaving, sponsored silences and participating in the Peak District challenge.

# Wilkinson Hardware Stores Ltd

J K House, Roebuck Way, Manton Wood, Worksop, Nottinghamshire S80 3YY

01909 505505; Fax: 01909 505777

Website: www.wilko.co.uk

Correspondent: Lynn Eadie, Charity Coordinator

Managing Director: G R S Brown

| Year end | Turnover | Pre-tax profit |
|---|---|---|
| 27/01/2006 | £1,135,409,000 | £24,102,000 |

Nature of company business
Principal activity: sale of domestic hardware and other related goods.

Subsidiaries include: L M Cooper & Co Ltd, Wilkinson Bros (Handsworth) Ltd, S C Hardwares Ltd

Main locations: Worksop

UK employees: 21,277

### Charitable donations
2005: £565,290
2003: £426,432

Membership: BitC

## Community involvement

The company has over 200 stores throughout the UK and tends to support charities local to those stores. Each year a contribution is made from company profits to community initiatives within the company's trading areas and usually supporting education, the family, sports and arts.

Schemes supported range from education projects in partnership with the BBC Orchestra of Wales to sponsorship of the Best Kept Village Competition in Nottinghamshire.

For many years the company has been a core supporter and sponsor of DARE (Drug Abuse Resistance Education). DARE works within schools to raise awareness of drug abuse and teach self-confidence. There is a dedicated committee to consider applications from groups for charitable donations.

The company aims to make modest contributions to as many organisations as possible. The company is a member of Business in the Community.

## Exclusions

No support for local appeals not in areas of company presence.

## Applications

In writing to the correspondent.

## Corporate giving

The company made cash donations to charitable organisations in 2005 of £565,290. We have no specific details of the beneficiaries other than the information given above.

## In-kind support

At new store locations the company's Helping Hand scheme offers product and financial support to local groups, charities and organisations within the store's catchment area. A recent Helping Hand project involved 12 volunteers from the company's Andover store using products donated by the store to redecorate a family centre on the outskirts of the town.

## Employee-led support

Each year team members select a national charity to fundraise for. In 2005/06 the chosen charity was Cancer Research UK and through a year long programme of events £250,000 was raised for that charity. Team members have chosen to fundraise for the NSPCC in the year 2006/07. Staff are actively encouraged to raise funds for the year's national charity and for annual events such as Comic Relief and Children in Need. Staff have also raised funds for the Tsunami Appeal and the Pakistan Earthquake.

For the past two years, staff at the company's head office have been involved with the Volunteer Reading Scheme at a local school to improve children's reading abilities.

# Willmott Dixon Ltd

Spirella, 2 Icknield Way, Letchworth, Hertfordshire SG6 4GY

01462 671852; Fax: 01462 681852

Website: www.willmottdixon.co.uk

Correspondent: Rick Willmott, Chief Executive Officer

| Year end | Turnover | Pre-tax profit |
|---|---|---|
| 31/12/2005 | £412,671,000 | £10,506,000 |

Nature of company business
A holding company for a group engaged in all sectors of the building industry.

Subsidiaries include: Widacre Homes, Inspace, Camtec

Main locations: Letchworth

Total employees: 863

### Charitable donations
2005: £52,750
2003: £72,041

Membership: A & B

## Community involvement

There was no information available regarding the company's policy, however, previous information has suggested that strong emphasis is placed on involvement by staff with their favoured charities, coupled with a commitment to support clients' preferred causes wherever possible. We have been informed that the directors choose one charity per year to donate to.

## Exclusions

General and unsolicited appeals are not considered. No grants for local appeals not in areas of company presence or for overseas projects.

## Applications

In writing to the correspondent.

## Corporate giving

In 2005, the company made cash donations to charity of £52,750. We have no details of the beneficiaries.

# Wilson Bowden plc

Wilson Bowden House, 207 Leicester Road, Ibstock, Leicester LE67 6WB

01530 260777; Fax: 01530 262805

Website: www.wilsonbowden.plc.uk

Correspondent: Ian Webb, Marketing Director

Chief officer: D W Wilson

Chief Executive: I Robertson

| Year end | Turnover | Pre-tax profit |
|---|---|---|
| 31/12/2005 | £1,230,800,000 | £216,400,000 |

Nature of company business
The main activities are house building, and property development and investment.

Subsidiaries include: David Wilson Homes Ltd, Trenchwood Commercial Ltd, David Wilson Estates Ltd

Main locations: Ibstock

Total employees: 2,464

> **Charitable donations**
> 2005: £26,400
> 2004: £72,700
> 2003: £49,800

## Community involvement

In the past the company has stated that it has no set policy; both national and local appeals are considered. However, a returned questionnaire indicated the following areas would be considered for support: advertising in charity brochures, appeals from individuals, the arts, children/youth, education, enterprise/training, environment/heritage, fundraising events, medical research, overseas projects, science/technology, sickness/disability charities, social welfare and sport.

## Exclusions

Information provided in the past has stated that the company provides no support for animal welfare, elderly people, political appeals or religious appeals.

## Applications

In writing to the correspondent.

## Corporate giving

In 2005, the company declared charitable donations of £26,400. One beneficiary of this was the Rhodes Project in Bishop's Stortford.

Although in-kind support is provided in various forms (see below), the company does not appear to attribute a value to this.

## In-kind support

The following information is taken from the company's Social Responsibility Policy document.

**Education:** 'Schools are seen as an important focus for us and we work alongside teaching staff in a number of ways from assisting with design and technology projects, through to providing equipment.

'Similarly, safety on building sites is a major issue, especially during school holidays, so we work with schools to teach children at an early age about the dangers of playing on sites. Our booklet 'Stay off Building Sites' illustrates the potential dangers of straying onto a site and our staff go into local schools to reinforce the message. Furthermore Wilson Bowden Developments, in conjunction with David Wilson Homes, are now working with the charity 'Warning Zone', which is a children's safety education centre for Leicester, Leicestershire and Rutland. During 2006, the company will construct a permanent building site 'safety scenario' with the aim of getting twelve to thirteen thousand children visiting it each year.'

## Employee-led support

During late 2005, the company joined the 'Leicestershire Cares' charity which will enable its employees to undertake teaching and mentoring roles within the local community.

**Payroll giving:** The company operates a scheme to allow its employees to make charitable donations from their salary.

# Robert Wiseman Dairies plc

159 Glasgow Road, East Kilbride, Glasgow G74 4PA

01355 244261; Fax: 01355 230352

Website: www.wiseman-dairies.co.uk

Correspondent: Joanne Rae, Marketing Manager
E-mail: care@wiseman-dairies.co.uk

Chief officer: Alan W Wiseman

Chief Executive: Robert T Wiseman

| Year end | Turnover | Pre-tax profit |
|---|---|---|
| 01/04/2006 | £489,168,000 | £24,684,000 |

Nature of company business
The processing and distribution of milk and associated products.

Main locations: Glasgow

UK employees: 3,340

> **Charitable donations**
> 2006: £10,000
> 2005: £10,000
> 2004: £32,000
> 2003: £25,000

## Community involvement

With a customer base extending from the north of Scotland through to the Midlands and into parts of London, the company is aware of its responsibility to assist charities and fundraising events in whatever way is practical. Various initiatives are undertaken throughout the year guided by the three principal elements of its community investment programme, namely: education, designated charity and community involvement.

**Charity of the Year:** The Variety Club (currently receives year on year support from the company as its 'designated' charity).

### Exclusions

Local appeals not in areas of company presence. No support for appeals from individuals.

### Applications

In writing to the correspondent.

## Corporate giving

In 2005/06, the company declared UK cash donations of £10,000 principally to the benefit of local charities serving the communities in which it operates. Although this figure in below the threshold for inclusion here, we consider the company's education bursaries, good-cause sponsorship and in-kind support to be at a level which justifies this. Some examples are given below.

**Education:** The company has created a bursary which provides funds over three years to students from Droitwich Spa High School to assist them in their studies at university.

**Designated charity:** A successful partnership with The Variety Club continues with the company pledging its seventh Robert Wiseman Dairies Sunshine Coach to Wren Spinney School in Kettering, near to its new depot in Northampton.

**Community involvement:** Locally, support has been given to the Prince and Princess of Wales Hospice in Glasgow to enable its Go Yellow Walk event for Primary 7 children in the city to take place.

### In-kind support

**Disability:** In support of the 2005 Glasgow Special Olympics, the company provided vehicles, refrigeration and product to assist in the running of the event.

**Local charities:** In 2004, the company ran a specific promotion called Charity Month which focused on six smaller and regional charities in order to raise their profile and the work they do. One such charity was Send A Cow, an organisation that raises funds to send livestock to families in the developing world.

### Commercially-led support

**Sponsorship:** *The Arts* – The company have agreed to sponsor the Vale of Athol Pipe Band over a three year period. This will enable the band to attend events and competitions throughout the year.

# John Wood Group plc

John Wood House, Greenwell Road, East Tullos, Aberdeen AB12 3AX

01224 851000; Fax: 01224 851474

Website: www.woodgroup.com

Correspondent: Carolyn Smith, Corporate Communications Manager 01224 851099
E-mail: carolyn.smith@woodgroup.com

Chief officer: Sir I C Wood

Chief Executive: Sir I C Wood

| Year end | Turnover | Pre-tax profit |
|----------|----------|----------------|
| 31/12/2005 | £1,497,400,000 | £67,600,000 |

**Nature of company business**
Engineering services to the oil and gas, petrochemical and power-related industries.

**Subsidiaries include:** Frontier Engineering Solutions Ltd, IONIK Consulting, J P Kenny Engineering Ltd, Mustang Engineering Ltd, ODL, Sulzer Wood Ltd, TransCanada Turbines UK Ltd, Woodhill Frontier, Northern Integrated Services Ltd, Rolls Wood Group Ltd

**Main locations:** Staines, Surrey, Ellon, Glasgow, Liverpool, Dundee, Aberdeen

**UK employees:** 2,858

**Total employees:** 16,587

> **Charitable donations**
> 2005: £184,000
> 2003: £45,000

## Community involvement

The Wood Group believes in supporting the communities in which it operates. In particular, the company supports projects involving the young, older people, medical research, education, the arts and the disabled. The Wood Group recognises the importance of providing in-kind support as well as financial help. Each company within the Wood Group has the freedom to choose which charities and projects they would like to support.

The company only supports local community projects in areas of company presence and projects in which employees are directly involved. National charities are generally not supported except in special circumstances, in which case the donation must receive approval from Sir Ian Wood. Unlike many major companies, the Wood Group does not select one charity each year, but prefers to distribute their budget across as many worthwhile causes as possible.

### Exclusions

The following causes are not likely to receive support: specific religious groups, political organisations, sports organisations with no Wood Group employee involvement, organisations without charitable status.

### Applications

In writing to the correspondent. All requests for donations are reviewed monthly by the charity and community relations committee.

## Corporate giving

In 2005 about £184,000 was given in donations to UK-based charitable organisations.

Long-term financial support in the UK includes £45,000 to ARCHIE Foundation; £10,000 each to Princess Royal Trust for Carers, Macmillan Caner, Sue Ryder Care, Prince's Scottish Youth Business Trust, Aberdeen Cyrenians and Gordon Highlanders Museum; £6,000 to Cornerstone Charity; £4,000 each to CLAN and Cloverfield Appeal; £3,000 each to Aberdeen Youth Festival and Scottish Business in the Community and £2,000 to Epilepsy Appeals Committee. The company has also made a recent commitment of £50,000 over four years to UCAN for research into urological cancers.

One-off payments have been given to The Friends of Royal Cornhill Hospital, DEBRA, Breast Cancer Research, The Scottish Society of Autism, Voluntary Service Aberdeen and The Stars of Light Concert.

The company also offers support to Scottish Business in the Community (SBC), of which it is a member.

### In-kind support

The group believes in 'building bridges' in the community; it provides ongoing support to local schools, universities and charitable organisations. For instance, young engineers from Wood Group Engineering North Sea volunteered to run an after-school science club at Tullos Primary School in Aberdeen to encourage children to take an interest in science and engineering.

### Employee-led support

The company runs an Employee Community Fund to encourage employees to support a charity/sponsorship of their choice, up to a maximum of £250 per employee. The group gives an average of £10,000 a year through the scheme. Organisations supported include Roxburghe House Support Group, Denman Preschool Playgroup, Aberdeen University Rollerhockey Club, Stonehaven and District Lions Club, Culter Boys Club and Millie's Campaign.

# Woolworths Group plc

Woolworths House, 242–246 Marylebone Road, London NW1 6JL

020 7262 1222

Website: www.woolworthsgroupplc.com

Correspondent: Trevor Dahl, Community Affairs 020 7262 1222; Fax: 020 7706 5416

Chief officer: Gerald Corbett

Chief Executive: Trevor Bish-Jones

| Year end | Turnover | Pre-tax profit |
|---|---|---|
| 28/01/2006 | £2,630,700,000 | £61,500,000 |

Nature of company business
Retailer focused on the family, home and entertainment.

Main locations: London

Total employees: 31,754

| Charitable donations |
|---|
| 2006: £151,000 |
| 2005: £156,000 |
| 2004: £204,000 |
| 2003: £264,000 |
| Membership: BitC, L B Group |

## Community involvement

The company has a charitable trust: Woolworths Kids First (Charity Commission no. 1073947). This was launched in 1999 to enable Woolworths' employees to support children's causes through their fundraising efforts. Its income derives from donations from employees, customers and suppliers, as well as a block grant from the company. Certain products are also sold in stores with all profits going to the trust. It has also Golden Bond places for the London Marathon, has an annual Ball and has organised golf days.

Grants can go to individuals, children's hospices, Home-Start schemes, schools, educational establishments, disability groups and children's sports clubs and teams.

The trust also runs a specific programme called Playground Partnerships, which provides £1 million a year in grants of £1,000 to £10,000 to enable primary schools to develop their playgrounds. This programme was initially piloted in Essex and Kent and has now been extended UK-wide. The aims of the programme are to:

- produce a resource that stands alone and offers practical and useful advice that is of educational value to pupils, teachers and other members of the school community
- empower pupils to make decisions about their school environment
- involve pupils in every stage of the development – from consultation, through to the creation and design stages to the implementation and maintenance of the playground
- recognise the potential for transforming playgrounds by schools as well as the absolute need of schools (that is the focus will not just be on disadvantaged areas).

### Applications

Teams in stores, offices and distribution centres select local initiatives they would like to see supported. These are all forwarded to the trustees who make their decisions on which ones to support. Therefore unsolicited applications are not accepted.

## Corporate giving

In 2005/06, community contributions totalled around £350,000 of which cash donations accounted for £151,000. Organisations supported by the group during the year included: Nordoff-Robbins; Childline; Liam Drew Trust for Autism; and, Northholt Junior Football Team.

The Woolworths Kids First charity made record grants of £746,000 in 2005/06 to children's causes in the UK. £493,000 was given to UK primary and special schools through the Playground Partnerships scheme.

### Commercially-led support

The company is a supporter of Nordoff-Robbins, a charity devoted to music therapy.

# WPP Group plc

27 Farm Street, London W1J 5RJ

020 7408 2204; Fax: 020 7493 6819

Website: www.wpp.com

Correspondent: JanetSmith, Executive PA
E-mail: jsmith@wpp.com

Chief officer: Philip Lader

Chief Executive: Sir Martin Sorrell

| Year end | Turnover | Pre-tax profit |
|---|---|---|
| 31/12/2005 | £26,673,700,000 | £592,000,000 |

Nature of company business
Principal activity: the provision of communications services worldwide.

**Subsidiaries include:** The Gepetto Group, Banner MacBride, Goldfarb Consultants, IMRB International, PRISM Group, Tempus Group plc, Carl Byoir & Associates, The Food Group, Management Ventures, A Eicoff & Co, Mando Marketing, The Farm, RTCdirect, Walker Group/CNI, MindShare, Coley Porter Bell, Millward Brown, SCPF, Pace, The Henley Centre, Portland Outdoor, BDG McColl, International Presentations, The Market Segment Group, Lambie-Nairn, Buchanan Communications, EWA, Addison, P Four Consultancy, The Grass Roots Group, Ogilvy Public Relations, CommonHealth, RMG International, The Wexler Group, Y & R Advertising, Clever Media, Research International, Shire Hall Group, Savatar, Einson Freeman, J Walter Thompson, The Media Partnership, Timmons and Company, Ogilvy & Mather, Oakley Young, Metro Group, Media Insight/Maximize, Brierley & Partners, Chime Communications plc, ROCQM, Equus, Quadra Advisory, Enterprise IG

**Main locations:** London

### Charitable donations

2005: £3,400,000
2003: £120,000

Total community contributions: £17,300,000

Membership: BitC, %Club

## Community involvement

The following policy relates to donations and support provided by the UK parent company. Support is also provided by the operating companies, particularly from the UK advertising agencies, J Walter Thompson and Ogilvy & Mather.

The company focuses its support on education and the arts. Other areas supported included health, local community, environment and drugs/alcohol. No geographical area is given preference; each application is considered on merit.

### Applications

In writing to the correspondent.

**Information available:** Further details of the company's charitable support can be found in the Corporate Social Responsibility section of its annual report.

## Corporate giving

In 2005, the group made worldwide community contributions of £17.3 million, much of which was given through pro bono work. Cash donations totalled £3.4 million, but we do not know what proportion of this went to UK organisations.

### Commercially-led support

**Sponsorship:** *Arts and education* – sponsorship is undertaken. In the UK, WWP sponsorship support includes that to Charles Edward Brooke Girls' School, which specialises in media arts; the Royal College of Art; and two bursary awards for D&AD, the professional association for design and advertising. The company is the corporate patron of the National Portrait Gallery in London.

# Wragge & Co LLP

55 Colmore Row, Birmingham B3 2AS

0121 233 1000; Fax: 0121 233 1099

Website: www.wragge.com

Correspondent: Peter Barber

| Year end | Turnover | Pre-tax profit |
|---|---|---|
| 30/12/2005 | £88,500,000 | |

**Nature of company business**
Legal firm.

**Main locations:** London, Birmingham

**UK employees:** 1100

**Total employees:** 1,100

### Charitable donations

Membership: BitC

## Community involvement

Most of the firm's giving is channelled through The Wragge & Co Charitable Trust (Charity Commission no. 803009). Support is given to registered charities across the West Midlands, with a slight preference for health organisations. A large number of arts organisations have also been supported in the past. Grants are generally in the range of £100 to £500 each, although larger amounts (of up to £2,500) have been given. It appears that more than one grant can be made to an organisation each year, and it is not uncommon for more than one local branch of a national organisation to be funded.

### Applications

In writing to the correspondent, enclosing a copy of the most recent accounts.

### Exclusions

No grants for individuals or for local appeals not in the area of company presence.

## Corporate giving

In 2001/02 the firm donated £65,000 to its trust, which gave 82 grants totalling £37,000. (The surplus of £25,000 was presumably in response to the £54,000 deficit it had in the previous year.) More up-to-date financial information was not available.

In 2003/04 the trust gave a total of £48,304 in grants.

Amongst the beneficiaries were Acorn Children's Hospice, Autism West Midlands, Birmingham Civic Society, Birmingham Royal Ballet Trust, Breakthrough Breast Cancer, Children Nationwide, County Air Ambulance, Coventry Cathedral Development Trust, Endeavour Training, Fireside Day Centre, Jericho Community Project, Leukaemia Research Fund, MIND, National Star College, Prisoners Abroad, RNLI, Saving Faces, Shelter and Volunteer Reading Help. Many of these charities have been supported in previous years.

### In-kind support

The firm provides pro bono work to a number of organisations, such as providing legal support to Birmingham College of Law students and their clients at a legal advice centre, working with Pension Advisory Service and advising local not-for-profit groups on a variety of matters. Its in-house design team has provided its services for free to client charities.

## Employee-led support

The company has annual fundraising event for its employees. In 2003 over £100,000 was raised for Sense by a trek across the Pyrenees. The 2004 event took place in Morocco. Employees have also taken part in other events, including five people who ran the London Marathon for NSPCC and Samaritans.

# WSP Group plc

24–30 Buchanan House, London EC1N 2HS

020 7314 5000

Website: wspgroup.com

Correspondent: MIke O'Brien, Managing Director (WSP UK)
E-mail: info@wspgroup.com

Chief officer: David Turner

Chief Executive: Christopher Cole

| Year end | Turnover | Pre-tax profit |
|---|---|---|
| 31/12/2005 | £394,074,000 | £19,822,000 |

Nature of company business
An international business supplying specialist management and integrated services in the built and natural environment.

Main locations: London

UK employees: 1,928

### Charitable donations

2005: £237,556
2004: £31,127

## Community involvement

The company's policy is to contribute to the economic, social and sustainable development of the communities in which it operates.

## Exclusions

No support for general or circular appeals, individuals, political or religious causes, or local appeals not in areas of company presence.

## Applications

In writing to the correspondent.

## Corporate giving

In 2005, the company declared charitable donations of just under £238,000 (2004: £31,000). Although the UK is the company's largest market, we believe this latest figure to be a global one. Not only because of the increase over 2004, but also because the examples of support provided in the company's CSR report cover the USA, South Africa, Nepal and Bangladesh.

References to the UK include support for victims of the London bombings and involvement with a road safety scheme in Birmingham.

## Employee-led support

On an informal basis the company makes donations to support charities with which its staff are involved.

# Wyevale Garden Centres Limited

Kings Acre Road, Hereford HR4 0SE

01432 276568; Fax: 01432 263289

Website: www.wyevale.co.uk

Chief Executive: Robert Hewitt

| Year end | Turnover | Pre-tax profit |
|---|---|---|
| 31/12/2005 | £187,600,000 | |

Nature of company business
Garden centres.

Subsidiaries include: Wyevale (Leisure Centres) Ltd, Great Gardens of England Investments Ltd, Country Gardens plc

Main locations: Hereford

Total employees: 1,666

### Charitable donations

2003: £109,000

## Community involvement

Wyevale Garden Centres plc was acquired in 2006 by WCC Hortis, a takeover company promoted by millionaire retail entrepreneur Tom Hunter's TBH Trading and Icelandic investment group Baugur. As a result, it has been delisted from the Stock Exchange and is now a privately-owned company.

Previously, we were advised that there was a preference for supporting causes local to its garden centres (which are throughout England and Wales), such as schools, gardening related organisations and sports associations. We do not know at present if this will continue under the new owners.

## Exclusions

No support for local appeals not in areas of company presence.

## Applications

Due to the recent change in company ownership, no clear community support policy was available.

For small scale donations at a local level, it is suggested contact is made with the nearest Wyevale Garden Centre rather than head office.

## Corporate giving

In 2003, the company made donations to charity of £109,000. We have no information on the beneficiaries.

### Commercially-led support

**Cause-related marketing:** The company is currently supporting Breast Cancer Care through its 'Plant Pink' initiative. For every purchase of one of Wyedale's special pink flowering plants, fifty pence is donated to the charity with the aim of raising over £60,000.

# Xansa Group plc

420 Thames Valley Park, Thames Valley Park Drive, Reading RG6 1PU

08702 416181; Fax: 08702 426282

Website: www.xansa.com

Correspondent: Sarah Massingham, Corporate Relations

Chief officer: Bill Alexander

Chief Executive: Alistair Cox

| Year end | Turnover | Pre-tax profit |
|---|---|---|
| 30/04/2006 | £357,300,000 | £9,000,000 |

Nature of company business
Formerly known as the FI Group, the company is engaged in the supply of computer software services.

Subsidiaries include: Druid Group plc, First Banking Systems Limited, ASL Information Services Limited, OSI Group Holdings Limited

Main locations: Bedford, Birminham, Manchester, Northampton, Southampton, Reading, Edinburgh, Leeds, Holborn

UK employees: 3,156

Total employees: 6,580

## Charitable donations

2006: £68,307
2005: £102,882
2004: £66,605
2003: £64,835

Total community contributions: £98,970

## Community involvement

The company states that its community policy commits it to:

- give priority to activities that will help young people maximise their potential to lead successful working lives, particularly through the medium of information technology
- focus its resources on the young unemployed homeless and on education
- promote, encourage and support employees to become involved in the community and charitable activities through volunteering
- encourage employees to look for personal and professional development opportunities for themselves and their team members through involvement in Xansa's community programme
- support issues which are of international importance but are also relevant to Xansa's national and local communities.

## Applications

In writing to the correspondent.

## Corporate giving

In 2005/06, the company made total community contributions of £98,970 (2004/05: £214,500) of which cash donations accounted for £68,307 (2004/05: £102,882). This reflects the company's emphasis on applying the skills and energies of its employees rather than providing just cash donations and/or sponsorship.

Previous beneficiaries include Fairbridge, SIYPA in Skelmersdale and St Basil's Centre in Birmingham.

The company also has the Xansa Employee Trust, which benefit current and former employees of Xansa and their families.

# Xerox (UK) Ltd

Bridge House, Oxford Road, Uxbridge UB8 1HS

01895 251133; Fax: 01895 254095

Website: www.xerox.com

Correspondent: Paula Childs, Xerox (UK) Trust

Managing Director: R Peacock

| Year end | Turnover | Pre-tax profit |
|---|---|---|
| 31/12/2005 | | |

Nature of company business
The marketing of Xerox products and services in the UK. Products range from small desk top plain paper copiers, printers and fax machines, to large volume document production and publishing systems. It also has a Supplies Business (Xerox Office Supplies) and a Facilities Management and Copy Centre Business (Xerox Business Services).

Main locations: Mitcheldean, Cambridge, Welwyn Garden City

UK employees: 3,535

## Charitable donations

2004: £60,000
2003: £60,000

## Community involvement

The company makes donations through an associated trust – The Xerox (UK) Trust (Charity Commission no. 284698) – the application policy for which has recently been simplified. Only registered charities need apply, with special consideration being given to applications supported by a Xerox employee. Further details are given in the 'Applications' section.

### Exclusions

Strictly no support for non-registered charities, or charities concerned with 'non-UK' activities or causes.

Applications for overseas projects, and such like, MUST be addressed to the local Rank Xerox operation in the country concerned.

### Applications

Information about the trust's grantmaking criteria can be obtained by calling the telephone helpline on: 01895 843 288.

If you meet the conditions that apply, you should then send a letter of application containing the requested information to the above named contact. All applications are considered, but only those that are successful will receive a response. Trustees meet in April and October to consider grants payable in June and December (these dates may be subject to change).

Please note that there is no application form and that you should not try ringing the company to check on your application's progress.

## Corporate giving

### The Xerox (UK) Trust

The trust, unsurprisingly, 'has a very close relationship' with the company, from which it receives a yearly donation of £60,000 under deed of covenant. This was, however, suspended for the years 2005 and 2006, but is due to recommence at the same level in 2007. During the interim period the trust still made grants using its reserve funds.

The latest set of accounts available at the Charity Commission as at October 2006, were those for year ending 31 December 2004. During the period, the trust generated an income of £63,540 and made charitable donations totalling £64,240. Beneficiaries included: The Free Spirit Trust and Maggie's Centre (£5,000 each); The Mulberry Centre (£4,000); St Raphael's Hospice (£3,000); The Panathlan Charity (£2,500); Music Alive (£2,000); and, Get Kids Going (£1,000).

### In-kind support

Please note that the company does NOT make donations of equipment or consumables no matter how worthy the cause.

# Yattendon Investment Trust plc

Barn Close, Yattendon, Thatcham, Berkshire RG18 0UX

01635 203929; Fax: 01635 203921

Website: www.yattendoninvestmenttrust.co.uk

Correspondent: (See 'Applications', below.)

Chief officer: R P R Iliffe

| Year end | Turnover | Pre-tax profit |
|---|---|---|
| 31/12/2005 | £98,500,000 | £16,593,000 |

### Nature of company business
Yattendon Investment Trust is a private company owned by the Iliffe family, with operations in the UK and Canada, and interests in newspaper publishing, television, electronic media, marinas and property.

Subsidiaries include: Hartridge Investments Ltd, Stafforshire Newsletter Ltd, Dean & Dyball Ltd, MDL Management plc, Staffordshire Newspapers Ltd, The Advertiser, Herts & Essex Newspapers Ltd, Cambridge Newspapers Ltd, Marina Developments Ltd, Burton Daily Mail Ltd

Main locations: Thatcham

Total employees: 1,331

### Charitable donations

2005: £150,000
2004: £120,000

## Community involvement

Charitable giving is made through The Iliffe Family Charitable Trust (Charity Commission no. 273437). The trust was established in February 1977 for 'such exclusively charitable objects and purposes in the United Kingdom or in any other part of the world as the trustees ... think fit'. In 2005 the company donated £150,000 to the trust and the trust in turn donated funds to charities operating in the areas of education, medicine, welfare, religion, conservation and heritage.

### Exclusions

We are not aware of any exclusions.

### Applications

The trust is administered from the same address as the company. Applications should be addressed to the charity correspondent, Mr G A Bremner. Only successful applications are acknowledged.

## Corporate giving

In 2005, The Iliffe Family Charitable Trust received a total income of £193,263 and awarded grants totalling £195,032. Some of the donations are listed below:

Bradfield Greek Theatre Project – £10,000

Life Education Centres – £5,000

King Edward V11 Hospital and Sister Agnes – £1,500

Cystic Fibrosis Trust – £25,000

Yattendon and Frilsham Christian Stewardship – £3,000

Mousehole Methodist Church – £150

Marine Society & Cadets – £1,000

Save The Children Fund – £1,000

Game Conservancy – £15,000

Save the Rhino International – £10,000

Royal Horticultural Society – £10,000

National Maritime Museum – £12,500

# Yorkshire Bank plc

20 Merrion Way, Leeds LS2 8NZ

0113 247 2000; Fax: 0113 242 0733

Website: www.ybonline.co.uk

Correspondent: Nicola Ashcroft, Secretary to the Yorkshire Bank Charitable Trust

Chief officer: Sir Hugh Sykes

Chief Executive: Ross Pinney

### Nature of company business
The Group provides a comprehensive banking system in the North and Midlands.

The Bank is a member of the National Australia Bank Group.

Subsidiaries include: Northern and General Finance Limited, Allerton House Properties Limited, YB Lease Limited, Storecard Limited, Yorkshire International Finance B.V

Main locations: Leeds

# Community involvement

The bank has an excellent community programme being involved with charity partners, providing sponsorships, giving in-kind support and donating to the Yorkshire Bank Charitable Trust (Charity Commission no. 326269). The bank's charitable cash donation is made directly by the bank to the trust.

The trust was set up in 1982 and the objectives of the trust are very wide being established for such exclusively charitable purposes as the trustees see fit. The following extracts are taken from the trust's 2005 financial statements and give more of an indication of how the trustees currently apply funds:

The main 'objective of the trust is to provide charitable donations to support, those engaged in youth work, facilities for the less able-bodied and mentally handicapped, counselling and community work in depressed areas and arts and education.

'The trustees are unlikely to make more than one donation to a given charity within any 12 month period. The beneficial area is that area covered by branches of Yorkshire Bank i.e. in England from the north of the Thames Valley to Newcastle upon Tyne. Donations are usually for a specific project or part thereof and are made to registered charities working in the fields outlined above.'

Yorkshire Bank currently has community partnerships which include:

British Heart Foundation

Count Me In (a pre-school numeracy initiative delivered through libraries nationwide. The project is now being expanded to include primary schools and material is also being developed for young people with special needs)

Count & Grow (educating 6–8 yr olds in maths by innovative methods)

The bank also has a very good community section on its website giving full details of their community policies and involvement and providing information on how organisations can apply to benefit from their programmes.

## Exclusions

Applications from individuals, including students, are ineligible, as are appeals for advertising in charity brochures, animal welfare, environment/heritage, medical research, overseas projects, political appeals, religious appeals and science/technology. No grants for general appeals from national organisations.

## Applications

Requests for donations should be addressed to the correspondent of the Yorkshire Bank Charitable Trust; for community partnership proposals to Jacqui Atkinson, Community Affairs Manager, Corporate Affairs at Yorkshire Bank plc; and for sponsorship proposals to Janet Myers, Brand & Sponsorships at the same address. All programmes have policies and restrictions in place and applicants are advised to visit the Bank's website.

# Corporate giving

We have been unable to obtain financial details of the Bank itself but the following information was available from the financial statements (y/e 31/12/2005) of The Yorkshire Bank Charitable Trust.

£57,655 (2004: £115,000) was received from Clydesdale Bank, trading as Yorkshire Bank and the following donations were then made by the trust:

British Heart Foundation (£16,312)

Business in the Community (£13,513)

Childline (£3,000)

Johnston Publishing (North) (£8,000)

Opera North and Leeds Grand Theatre Development Trust (£100,000)

St George's Crypt (£1,200)

Unsuccessful charity partners (£3,000).

## In-kind support

The bank runs a School Bank Savings Scheme which aims to introduce schoolchildren to financial management, through manual or computer-based systems, and can also be used for National Curriculum project work in secondary schools. The bank also helps schools to stimulate interest in extra-curricular activities through a conservation grants award scheme administered by the British Trust for Conservation Volunteers. This scheme is available to all schools operating a Yorkshire Bank Savings Scheme. Schools involved in environmental or conservation projects undertaken on school premises may apply for grants of up to £100 and additional special cash awards are made for projects of particular merit.

## Employee-led support

The following extract is taken from the bank's website:

'As members of the communities they serve, Yorkshire Bank's own staff are encouraged to take part in charitable work.

We also recognise that many of our staff volunteer in their own time to support their local community. We have therefore recently introduced the Staff Volunteer Grants Programme to reward and recognise the personal contribution of staff by providing grants to charitable organisations with which they volunteer their own time. Grants of up to £500 each are awarded quarterly.'

The bank also match-funds money raised by staff.

## Commercially-led support

**Sponsorship:** *The arts* – The bank sponsors organisations and events throughout the UK. It has sponsored the Leeds International Festival, Harrogate International Festival, Oldham Girls Choir and the Faure Festival and York Singing Day.

*Education* – The bank has sponsored a BA Hons Financial Course and Professor of Financial Services at Sheffield Hallam University.

Yorkshire Bank currently supports high profile sponsorships including – the Leeds Grand Theatre/Opera North, the Twenty20 Cup, (the domestic cricket competition), The Commonwealth Games Council for Scotland and The Enterprising Scotland Award.

Yorkshire Bank states that it pursues sponsorship opportunities that clearly enhance the brand and a detailed list of the required criteria for sponsorship is given on the bank's website.

# Yorkshire Building Society

Yorkshire House, Yorkshire Drive, Bradford BD5 8LJ

08451 200100

Website: www.ybs.co.uk

Correspondent: Mrs A L Fitzpatrick, Trust Secretary

Chief officer: Christopher Sheridan

Chief Executive: Iain Cornish

| Year end | Turnover | Pre-tax profit |
|---|---|---|
| 31/12/2005 | | |

Nature of company business
Building society.

Subsidiaries include: Yorkshire Gurnsey, Accord Mortgages

Main locations: Bradford

UK employees: 2,000

## Charitable donations

2004: £75,000
2003: £326,000

CRM figure: £187,546

Membership: A & B

## Community involvement

The Yorkshire Building Society Charitable Foundation (YBSCF) was set up in April 1998, and is the focal point of the Yorkshire Building Society's charitable giving. Its purpose is to support good causes where the society's members and staff live and work, helping to demonstrate the value and support that the Yorkshire provides to local communities throughout the UK.

All requests made to the society are therefore referred to the foundation (which is based at the same address). There are five trustees, three of which are independent of the society.

The foundation's priorities are to support registered charities or good causes involving the elderly, anyone who is vulnerable (particularly children or people with special needs) and people suffering hardship. However, consideration will be given to other local charities and good causes suggested by society members or staff.

The foundation's geographical area of operation is limited to the UK and preference is given to specific items rather than donate to a general fund or expenses.

The following (non-exhaustive) list provides examples of projects or activities which the foundation would consider as likely to fall within its main areas of focus:

- Anything specifically to help priority cases of vulnerable people, people who are in need such as children, the elderly, or anyone with special needs, or people who are suffering hardship.
- Help to be given to those who are sick, or with special needs, or learning difficulties and/or who are physically disabled.
- Provision towards the welfare of sick and neglected animals and the prevention of cruelty to animals.
- The resettlement and rehabilitation of offenders and drug abusers.

- The provision of relief for victims of natural and civil disasters.
- Help to be given to an individual beneficiary e.g. special equipment for a disabled person or for a child in need.
- Help given to particular geographic or social areas of benefit, or groups of people where it can be shown that such areas or groups are in need. Examples would be groups of people suffering hardship, pupils at a special school, and residents of a particular community or an individual within a community.

### Exclusions

The society does not support any activity which is not carried out by a registered charity or which does not otherwise count as being a good cause. Additionally, there may be projects or activities which could be considered as registered charities or good causes but which the society feels do not fall within its priorities or meet other criteria. Examples of these are:

- Fundraising for the purposes of pursuing political or propagandist activities.
- The support of religious activities or the advancement of religion (although this would not prevent consideration for support to members of a group or community that was otherwise in need).
- Any fundraising or activity under which those organising the fundraising activity would or could have a personal benefit.
- Provision of support for a person or people who do not come within the priority of the foundation or are not in genuine need.
- Applications from national charitable organisations for general ongoing funding (although this would not prevent consideration of specific items for local initiatives/branches).
- Any organisation considered to be illegal or which may act illegally, or where funds are raised from, or for immoral purposes.
- Provision of sport generally or seeking to achieve excellence or professionalism in sport. For example this would exclude any sponsorship activities, or the provision of equipment for sports teams. The only exception to this would be, for example, some sporting activity for children who are in need, or disabled people, or other people suffering hardship.
- Support for individuals or groups engaged in expeditions or projects requiring them to raise funds to enable them to participate.
- Proposals which are purely concerned with raising funds for other organisations or charities and/or where such funds are likely to go to the administration expenses of such organisations; e.g. provision of sponsorship to an individual or individuals participating in another charitable or good cause event.
- Carnivals or shows which are concerned with mainly entertaining the public and where there is no control over the eventual destination of funds raised.
- Any purposes concerned with the promotion of friendship or international friendship; e.g. town twinning associations.
- Support for a person or persons who do not come within the priority of the foundation, or are not thought to be in genuine need.
- Support of activities in or equipment for mainstream schools. The only exception to this would be activities or equipment to help children with special needs.
- Provision of equipment for hospitals or other health

establishments which are the responsibility of a statutory body. Equipment to be provided by a charity or good cause supporting a hospital/establishment may be considered.

## Applications

Applications are usually received from members of the society or through the society's branches or head office departments. This helps ensure support is given to local charities and good causes in areas important to members and staff.

To apply, contact your local branch to discuss your application. Staff there will be pleased to help and provide you with a copy of the foundation guidelines. If you don't have a local branch apply in writing to the above named correspondent.

## Corporate giving

In 2005, the Yorkshire Building Society made a cash donation of £75,000 to the foundation. During the year foundation donated £348,000 to 615 good causes. The main beneficiary was the Marie Curie Xmas Appeal, which received £95,500.

The foundation also received £187,546 from the society's Small Change, Big Difference scheme, which is 'promoted by Yorkshire Building Society under which the holders of society savings or loan accounts agree to the transfer to the foundation of an amount equivalent to the pence earned (or charged) on their accounts.'

The maximum size of grant given is usually £5,000 as the foundation wants to spread its funds (received from the society, members, staff and public) 'to help as many people in as many areas as possible'.

## In-kind support

The society has previously made donations of equipment.

## Employee-led support

The society runs an employee volunteering scheme with staff allowed time of in which to volunteer. Funding from YBSCF is given in support of this.

Staff were involved in various initiatives including: Right to Read, Bradford Cares and general fundraising. Examples of the latter are:

- halesowen's Easter events bought an essential heart-monitoring machine for the Children's Heart Federation
- alloa's raffle helped their local community centre buy new equipment for many different activities
- lancaster's fundraising enabled the purchase of a special bed for the local St John's Hospice
- bolton's efforts supported their local special needs school with keyboards to develop hand and easy listening skills.

Donations made by staff through fundraising is matched by the foundation to a maximum of £2,000.

**Payroll giving:** The Charities Trust, 'Caring Together', payroll giving scheme is in operation.

# Yule Catto & Co plc

Central Road, Temple Fields, Harlow, Essex CM20 2BH

01279 442791; Fax: 01279 641360

Website: www.yulecatto.com

Correspondent: Richard Atkinson, Company Secretary

Chief officer: A E Richmond-Watson

Chief Executive: A Walker

| Year end | Turnover | Pre-tax profit |
|---|---|---|
| 31/12/2005 | £556,051,000 | £32,031,000 |

**Nature of company business**
The principal activities of the company are in the areas of speciality chemicals, pharmaceuticals and building products.

**Subsidiaries include:** Autoclenz Ltd, William Blythe Ltd, Oxford Chemicals Ltd, Arrow Direct, Reabrook Ltd, Uquifa, Synthomer Ltd, Revertex Finewaters, PFW, Holliday Pigments Ltd, Arrow Chemicals, James Robinson Ltd, Brencliffe Ltd, Nielsen Chemical

**Main locations:** Harlow

**Total employees:** 3,051

### Charitable donations
2006: £93,000
2005: £93,000
2004: £116,000
2003: £78,000

## Community involvement

The company supports an established list of charities, mainly in the fields of children and youth, elderly people, medical research, and sickness/disability charities. Both local and national charities (in the Harlow area) are supported.

### Exclusions

No support for overseas projects, political appeals, or religious appeals.

### Applications

In writing to the correspondent, but please note that as the company has charities which it supports regularly, unsolicited applications are unlikely to be successful.

## Corporate giving

In 2005, the company made cash donations of £93,000. We have no details of the recipients, but know that support has been given in the past to: Harlow Community Trust, St Clare Hospice Care Trust, Help the Aged, Age Concern – England, and Barnardo's.

# Zurich Financial Services (UKISA) Ltd

PO Box 1288, Swindon, Wiltshire SN1 1FL

01793 514514

Website: www.zurich.co.uk

**Correspondent:** Kate Hodges, Community Affairs 01793 514514

**E-mail:** communityaffairs@uk.zurich.com

**Chief Executive:** David Sims

| Year end | Turnover | Pre-tax profit |
|---|---|---|
| 31/12/2005 | | |

**Nature of company business**
Zurich Financial Services (UKISA) is part of the Zurich Financial Services Group and comprises the group's operations in the UK, Ireland and South Africa.

**Main locations:** Swindon

**UK employees:** 13,500

**Total employees:** 55,000

### Charitable donations

2005: £1,900,000

Membership: BitC, L B Group

## Community involvement

The Zurich Community Trust (Charity Commission no. 266983) provides the umbrella for all the company's community work in the UK.

The trust gives time, money and skills to help disadvantaged people achieve an independent future for themselves. Zurich encourages and support its employees to do their part to make a better world and get involved with their communities.

The trust supports over 600 charities each year and works in partnership for three to five years with around 30 of those. Local, national and overseas charities are supported.

There are two strands to the trust's work in the UK:

**Community Trust programmes**

- breaking the generational cycle of drug abuse
- vulnerable older people
- inclusion
- the India programme.

**Employee and Financial Adviser Involvement programmes**

- Zurich Cares – for Zurich UK business staff
- Openwork Foundation – for members of Zurich's new multi-tie distribution network and their support staff across the UK.

December 2006 – A new programme was announced by Zurich's Community Trust in the UK that will give support to families dealing with a mental health issue.

The first phase of this will be in partnership with The Observer's Christmas Appeal, with a commitment to match public donations to the appeal of up to £100,000 (the figure raised by last year's appeal).

The public donations from the appeal, together with matching from Zurich's Community Trust, will benefit the Family Welfare Association, Place2Be and Rethink

### Exclusions

No grants to individuals, research, animal welfare, emergency or disaster appeals or to political, religious or mainstream educational institutions – unless directly benefiting people with disabilities, political or religious organisations.

## Applications

**Trust programmes** – potential partners are researched, identified and selected by the Community Affairs team.

**Zurich Cares** – you can check your eligibility for these grants by looking at the Zurich Cares section of the company's website.

**Openwork Foundation** – further advice can be obtained about this scheme by calling 0870 608 2550.

## Corporate giving

In 2005, Zurich UK businesses donated £1.9 million to the Zurich Community Trust.

### Zurich Community Trust

In 2005, the trust made grants totalling £2.6 million. The trust's policy is to focus on areas that are less popular and where support can be difficult to obtain. Typically, the trust allocates large amounts of money (around £1 million) to a limited number of issues.

Within the charitable activities already identified, beneficiaries included: Addaction (£188,000); Weston Spirit (£107,500); The Calvert Trust (£57,500); Hopes and Homes (£42,251); Swindon Carers (£20,000); CALM (£15,434); TWIGS (£13,375); The Acorn Children's Hospice Trust (£12,550); Devon Youth Association (£12,300); and, Winston's Wish (£11,266).

### Employee-led support

Staff are encouraged to support charitable causes through contributions of time as well as money. Two funds exist to facilitate this:

### Zurich Cares

Supported by staff of the UK businesses, sharing time and money with local communities. They do this through:

- payroll giving scheme
- active volunteering
- challenge programmes
- matching schemes for staff and their children for fundraising for charity (50% to £500 maximum per event)
- donation of gifts – for example, at Christmas and Easter time
- partnerships with 17 local, national and overseas voluntary
- a local grant programme awarding grants to local and overseas projects – all selected by employees.

Local grant programmes are active in Wiltshire, Hampshire, Gloucestershire and a few other locations where Zurich have large offices. Grants range from £100–£10,000 and support disadvantaged people to live a more independent lifestyle. Support has also been given for carers, special needs children, people with disabilities, counselling, homeless people, teenage pregnancy, and ethnic minorities.

Grants are sometimes given for core costs such as salaries, premises, transport and food costs, whilst a number of one-off purchases, e.g. IT equipment, training, access and equipment for people with disabilities, have also been made.

### Openwork Foundation

Formerly called the Zurich Advice Network Foundation, support is given to some of the most disadvantaged people in society and enables them to lead more independent lives. Around 3,500 financial advisers and sales support staff support the foundation to raise money, agree policy and then decide which charities to assist.

The current £2 million programme is called Kids 2 Care 4 and supports disadvantaged children up to the age of 18.

The foundation supports capital projects and awards grants of £10 to £20,000. Up to 25% of the grant can be used for revenue funding.

**Payroll giving:** The company runs the Give As You Earn scheme. Employees' giving is matched in full by the company, without limit.

20% of employees donate to the Zurich community Trust through this scheme.

## Commercially-led support

**Sponsorship:** Arts and good-cause sponsorship is undertaken.

Arts & Business exists to promote and encourage partnerships between the private sector and the arts, to their mutual benefit and to that of the community at large. Its priority is to provide a service for its members but a number of its services are of value to arts organisations as well.

Among its activities are: annual award ceremonies; New Partners (a government-funded incentive for businesses to support the arts); and Arts and Business, aiming to improve the quality of management in the arts through business involvement in schemes such as the Skills Bank (for business people to volunteer to support specific projects), and training courses.

Arts & Business produces a quarterly bulletin and an annual report and are online at: www.aandb.org.uk.

## Contacts

### Arts & Business Head Office (London)
Nutmeg House
60 Gainsford Street
Butlers Wharf
London
SE1 2NY
Tel: 020 7378 8143
Email: head.office@AandB.org.uk

### Scotland
6 Randolph Crescent
Edinburgh
EH3 7TH
Tel: 0131 220 2499
Email: scotland@AandB.org.uk

### Northern Ireland
Bridge House
Paulett Avenue
Belfast
BT5 4HD
Northern Ireland
Tel: 028 9073 5150
Email: northern.ireland@AandB.org.uk

### Wales
16 Museum Place
Cardiff
CF10 3BH
Tel: 029 2030 3023
Email: cymru@AandB.org.uk

### North Wales
Room 40
The Town Hall
Lloyd Street
Llandudno
LL30 2UP
Tel: 01492 574 003
Email: lorraine.hopkins@AandB.org.uk

### North East
9th Floor, Cale Cross
156 Pilgrim Street
Newcastle upon Tyne
NE1 6SU
Tel: 0191 222 0945
Email: sg@communityfoundation.org.uk

### North West
Portland Buildings
127–129 Portland Street
Manchester
M1 4PZ
Tel: 0161 236 2058
Email: north.west@AandB.org.uk

### North West – Cumbria
Cumbria Office
Community Foundation
Dovenby Hall
Dovenby
Cockermouth
Cumbria
CA13 0PN
Tel: 01900 825760
Email: wiseelaine.hotmail.co.uk

### Yorkshire
Dean Clough
Halifax
West Yorkshire
HX3 5AX
Tel: 01422 367 860
Email: yorkshire@AandB.org.uk

### East Midlands
Martindale House
The Green
Ruddington
Nottingham
NG11 6HH
Tel: 0115 921 6950
Email: nottingham@AandB.org.uk

### West Midlands
Suite 16–18
21 Bennetts Hill
Birmingham
B2 5QP
Tel: 0121 248 1200
Email: midlands@AandB.org.uk

### East
67 Regent Street
Cambridge
CB2 1AB
Tel: 01223 321 421
Email: east@AandB.org.uk

### South East – Brighton
Frederick Terrace
Frederick Place
Brighton
East Sussex
BN1 1AX
Tel: 01273 738 333
Email: south.east@AandB.org.uk

### South East – Eastleigh
The Point
Leigh Road
Eastleigh
Hampshire
SO50 9DE
Tel: 023 8061 9172
Email: south.east@AandB.org.uk

### South West
61 Park Street
Bristol
BS1 5NU
Tel: 0117 929 0522
Email: south.west@AandB.org.uk

## Corporate Members

### CYMRU
33 Park Place
Aaron & Partners Solicitors
Admiral Group
Alchemy Wealth Management Ltd
Architen Landrell Associates
Arriva Trains Wales
Arts Council of Wales
Arup
Atradius
Barclays plc
BHP Billiton Petroleum
Black Sheep
Cardiff Audi
Cardiff Council
Carrick Design & Print
CBI Wales
City & County of Swansea
Confused.com
Conwy County Borough Council
Daily Post
Deloitte
DeVine Wines
Ethnic Business Support Programme
Eversheds

G W Consulting
Geldards LLP
Grant Thornton UK LLP
Heritage Hardwood Conservatories
HSBC Bank plc
Hugh James
ITV Wales
Konica Minolta Business Solutions
KTS Owens Thomas Ltd
Legal & General (Wales)
Leo Abse & Cohen
Lloyds TSB Bank plc
Maskreys Ltd
Nolan UPVC Ltd
Royal Mail Group plc
Royal Oak Hotel
S4C
Thames Water Services
The Co-operative Group – Wales &
Borders
Tipyn Bach Chocolate Company
University Of Glamorgan
View Creative
Warwick International Group
WD Turner
Welsh Slate
West Coast Energy
Williams Medical Supplies

## EAST

Anglian Water
Arndale Centre Luton
Ashwell Developments Ltd
Autoglass Ltd
BAA Stansted
Barclays Bank plc
BT Research & Venturing
Cambridge City Council
Cambridge University Press
Chasestead Engineering Ltd
Deloitte
Essex & Suffolk Water
Essex County Council
Granta Park Ltd
Harlow District Council
Healeys Printers
Hertfordshire County Council
James Blake Associates
Jarrold & Sons Ltd
Land Securities Properties Ltd
Luton Borough Council
Marsh
MLA East of England
One Railway
Robert Sayle Partnership
Slough Estates (Cambridge Research Park)
South Cambridgeshire District Council
Southend-on-Sea Borough Council
Stagecoach
Stevenage Borough Council
The Grafton Centre
The Howard Centre
The Technology Partnership plc
Thurrock Council
Whitbread Group plc
Wrenbridge Land Ltd

## EAST MIDLANDS

AstraZeneca
Berryman
BioCity
Egg Banking plc

Experian Ltd
First Enterprise
Geldards LLP
Hart Hambleton plc
Leicestershire County Council
Museums, Libraries & Archives East
Midlands
Nottingham City Council
Nottinghamshire County Council
Pro Active Accounting
Rolls-Royce plc
Savills
Simons Group Ltd

## LONDON

Agnès b. UK
Aviva plc
AXA Art Insurance Ltd
BAFTA
Baker & McKenzie
Barclays Bank plc
Bloomberg
BMW UK Ltd
BNP Paribas
BOX
BP plc
British Airways London Eye
British Airways plc
British Council
British Land Company plc
British Sky Broadcasting Group plc
BT Global Services
Business in the Community
Cadwalader, Wickersham & Taft LLP
Capitalize
Carat Sponsorship
Capitalize
Carat Sponsorship
CGI
Chrysalis Group plc
Circle Anglia
City Inn Westminster
City of London
Clifford Chance
CMS Cameron McKenna
Confederation of British Industry
Coutts & Co
Deloitte
Deutsche Bank
Diageo GB
DMW
EDF Energy
Entara Ltd
Ernst & Young
Four Communications plc
GlaxoSmithKline plc
Great Eastern Hotel
Habitat UK
Herbert Smith LLP
Heritage Lottery Fund
Hermès (GB) Ltd
HIT Entertainment plc
HS Projects
HSBC Holdings plc
Hunter Rubber Company
Icon Display
innocent drinks
Institute of Physics
JPMorgan
Kallaway Ltd
Land Securities Group plc
Legal & General Group plc

Lehman Brothers Ltd
Linklaters
Live Nation
Lloyd Northover
Lloyd's of London
London Borough of Haringey
London Borough of Southwark
London Calling Arts Ltd
London Underground Ltd
Man Group plc
Marsh & McLennan Companies
Merrill Lynch
MTV Networks UK & Ireland
National Australia Bank
Ogilvy & Mather Ltd
Orange PCS Ltd
Parker Harris
Pentland Group plc
Pretzel Films Ltd
PricewaterhouseCoopers
ProbusBNW Ltd
Prudential Ltd
Re-Solve
Richard Lynam Partnership
Richemont International Ltd
Royal Bank of Scotland
Sage Publications
Shell International Ltd
Shiseido Co. Ltd
Singer & Friedlander Group plc
Sponsorship Consulting Limited
Strategic Real Estate Advisors Ltd
The Phoenix Consultancy
The Principle Partnership
The World Famous
Turner Broadcasting System Europe
UBS
Unilever UK
UNISON
United Business Media plc
WCRS
Wolff Olins
YSC Limited

## NORTH EAST

Admast Advertising
Browne Smith Baker
Dickinson Dees
EDF Energy
Eversheds
ITV Tyne Tees
MLA (North East)
ncj Media Ltd
Newcastle Building Society
Newcastle College
North East Times
Northern Rock
Northumbria University
Northumbrian Water Group
One North East
Orange
Parabola Estates
Polar Productions
Procter & Gamble
Robert Muckle LLP
Samuel Philips
Silverlink
The Community Foundation serving Tyne
& Wear and Northumberland
The Copthorne Hotel
The Gate
UBS Wealth Management

UK Land Estates
Universal Building Society
University of Durham
University of Newcastle
Ward Hadaway

## NORTH WEST

Addleshaw Goddard
Argent Estates Ltd
Arrk Ltd
AstraZeneca
Blackburn with Darwen Borough Council
Bruntwood Estates Ltd
Castle Green Hotel
City Inn Manchester
CN Group Ltd
Consort Healthcare
Creative Lancashire
Cumbria Community Foundation
Cumbria County Council
Deloitte
Gilbraith (ts) Ltd
Groundwork Blackburn
Haden Freeman Ltd
Hill Dickinson
Institute of Directors
Lanternhouse International
LDC (Lloyds TSB Development Capital Ltd)
Liverpool John Moores University
Manchester Airport Group plc
Mawdsleys
Museums, Libraries And Archives
North West
Nynas Bitumen
Portfolio Art & Design
Rossetti Hotel
Royal Bank of Scotland
Selfridges & Co – Manchester
Showing Off Ltd
Specialist Search Ltd
St Helens Borough Council
Stockport Holdings Ltd (Merseyway)
T Shirts & Suits Ltd
The Circle Club
The Co-operative Group (CWS) Ltd
The Creative Branch
The Mersey Partnership
Yorkshire Bank

## NORTHERN IRELAND

Allianz Nothern Ireland
Andersonstown News Group
Andor Technology
Angela Connolly
Autoline Insurance Group
B&Q
Bank Of Ireland
Belfast Visitor & Convention Bureau
Bell Lawrie
Blu Zebra
Bombardier Aerospace
Botanic Inns Ltd
BT Northern Ireland
Business In The Community Northern Ireland
Canvas
Carson McDowell
Circle Creative Communications
Clear Channel NI Ltd
Coca Cola Bottlers (Ulster) Ltd
Coolkeeragh ESB
Cunningham Coates Stockbrokers

Diageo Northern Ireland
Donnelly Neary & Donnelly
DWS Group
Finbrook Investments Ltd
First Trust Bank plc
Gaelic Gear
Harrison Photography
HURSON
IAS SMARTS
Inbev
Lagan Boat Company
Laganside Corporation
Legal & General Partnership Services Ltd
Lomac Tiles
M&D Financial Management
Marcus Musical Instruments
Marsh UK Ltd
McGimpsey Brothers (Removals) Limited
McKinty & Wright
Nicholson & Bass Ltd
Northern Bank
Orange PCS Ltd
Ovation Group
Paperjam Design
Patton Group
Paul Monaghan Chartered Architects
Potato Bred Ltd
PricewaterhouseCoopers
Project Planning International
Richard O'Rawe Associates
Robinson McIlwaine
Royal Mail Group plc
Sheridan Group
Stratagem
Tandem Design
Templeton Robinson
3rd Source Media
Translink
Ulster Bank Ltd
Ulster Journals Ltd
Viacom Outdoor Ltd
Whitenoise Design Ltd
Wooden Floor Company
Yellow Moon Post Production

## SCOTLAND

AAMCI Consulting Ltd
Aberdeen City Council
Aeolus Group
Andy McAlpine Associates
AOC Archaeology Group
AXA Art Insurance Ltd
BBMC Goodword
Black Light
Bonhams
Bright People Ltd
Burness
CB Richard Ellis Ltd
City Inn Glasgow
City of Edinburgh Council
Clydesdale Bank
Constantine Ltd
D8
Davis Duncan Architects
Deloitte
Diageo Scotland
Dunfermline Building Society
Edinburgh Chamber of Commerce
Elphinstone Group Ltd
Eskmills (Isertal)
Fairway Forklifts Ltd
Freight Design Ltd

Glasgow Chamber of Commerce
Glasgow City Council
Great Circle Communications
Bank of Scotland (part of the HBOS Group)
Henzteeth
Inglis Allen Printers
Inverness Chamber of Commerce
JMA Associates
John Dewar & Sons Ltd
Kingscavil Consulting
Liddell Thomson
Lloyds TSB Scotland
Loch Lomond Shores Management
Material Marketing & Communications Ltd
McFadden Associates Ltd
MRUK
Orange PCS Ltd
Parallel 56
Peoplematters
Peopletree
Print 2000 Ltd
Quality Scotland
Quirk & Co
Rare
Royal Bank of Scotland
Royal Mail Group plc
SATV
Scotch Malt Whisky Society
Scottish Borders Chamber of Commerce
Scottish Executive Health Department
Scottish Leadership Foundation
Scottish Widows
ScottishPower
ScottishPower Learning
Standard Life
Strathclyde Fire & Rescue
Suio Water
The List
The Town House Company
Third Eye Design
TOTAL E&P UK plc
TSYS Europe
Tullibardine Distillery
Turcan Connell
University of Strathclyde
VisitScotland
Various Creative
Weber Shandwick Worldwide
William Grant & Sons Distillers Ltd
Wolffe and Co
YSC Scotland

## SOUTH EAST

Advanced Media Associates
American Express Europe Ltd
American Express Technologies Division
Arora International Hotel
AXA PPP
Blake Lapthorn Linnell
Brighton & Hove Chamber of Commerce
CADIA
Christopher Gull Dental Practice
Click Netherfield Ltd
County Mall Shopping Centre
Crawley Chamber of Commerce
DMH Stallard
Drallim Industries Ltd
East Sussex County Council
EEF South
Ferrari GB Ltd

Folkestone Enterprise Gateway
Gifford and Partners Ltd
Gunwharf Quays Management Ltd
Holiday Extras
Hot Horse Ltd
Isle of Wight Chamber of Commerce,
Tourism & Industry
John Packer Associates
Kingsley Smith Solicitors LLP
Kingston Smith Chartered Accountants
(LLP)
KPMG
Legal & General Assurance Society Ltd
Liberty Property Trust UK Ltd
Lime Marketing
MLA South East
Nominet UK
SEOS Ltd
Slough Estates plc
Store 2 Limited
Surrey Chambers of Commerce
Thames Valley Chamber of Commerce
Group
The Royal Bank of Scotland
Toshiba Information Systems UK Ltd
Unilever Ice Cream & Frozen Food
Unilever UK
UPSO
West Sussex County Council Library
Service
Wilson & Scott (Highways) Ltd
Women in Business Crawley
Yamaha-Kemble Music (UK) Ltd

## SOUTH WEST

Aedas
Arts Council England, South West
Barclays Bank plc
Bart Spices Ltd
Bath Spa University
Batt Broadbent Solicitors
Beachcroft LLP
Bristol East Side Traders (BEST)
Bristol Institute for Research in
Humanities & Art
Business West
Byzantium Restaurants Limited
Chelsea Building Society
City Inn Bristol
Clydesdale Bank plc
Coutts UK
Crest Nicholson (South West) Ltd
Devon & Cornwall Business Council
Dorset Business
Dorset County Council
Dorset Echo
Edis Partnerships
Ernst & Young LLP
Eyegaze Limited
Feilden Clegg Bradley Architects
Hark Solutions
Hulbert Press
Humphries Kirk
Hunter-Fleming Ltd
HW Chartered Accountants
Iconography Ltd
Institute of Physics Publishing

Kdesign Group
Lyons Davidson
Minster Press
Museums Libraries & Archives South West
(MLA)
Northcroft
Olives Et Al
Orange PCS Ltd
Redlynch Leisure Installations Ltd
Respect Organics
Richmond Solicitors
Rickerbys
Rolls Royce – Naval Marine
Roper Rhodes Ltd
RWE npower
Scolarest-Pace
Solomon Hare
Southwell Business Park Ltd
Steele Raymond LLP
Swindon Borough Council
Target Consulting Group
The Arts Institute at Bournemouth
The Financial Training Company
The Loop Communication Agency
TLT Solicitors
Tuffin Ferraby Taylor
University of Gloucestershire
University of the West of England
V&S Plymouth Limited
Wessex Water plc
Western Newspapers Ltd
Willmott Dixon Construction
Wilsons
WOW Creative
Wykeham Group Limited

## WEST MIDLANDS

3i
Acme Whistles
Baker Tilly
Bentley Jennison
Bfm – Business & Finance
Midlands Magazines
Birmingham & Solihull Chamber
Birmingham City Council
Birmingham International Airport
CBI West Midlands
Centro
City Inn Birmingham
Complex Development Projects
Deloitte & Touche
Dynamo Marketing Communication
EDS
Ernst & Young
Fired Earth Ltd
Heartlands Hospital
Hortons' Estate Ltd
Irwin Mitchell Solicitors
Jaguar & Land Rover
Kent Jones & Done
Lois Burley Public Relations
Macdonald Burlington Hotel
MADE – Midlands Architecture &
Designed Environment
Museums, Libraries and Archives – West
Midlands
Nurture Systems

Parenthesis Design and Marketing
Pinsent Masons
PMD Group Ltd
Ro St Bernards Ltd
Ross Labels Limited
Rsm Robson Rhodes
Rubery Owen Holdings Limited
Shrewsbury & Atcham Borough Council
The Mailbox
Trans4mation
University of Birmingham
University of Central England
University of Worcester
Worcester City Council

## YORKSHIRE

Addleshaw Goddard
Asda
Balance Consulting
Barclays
Bogacki Project
Boxwood
Bradford & Bingley plc
Bradford Urban Regeneration
Company
Calderdale MBC
City of York Council
Cobbetts
Dean Clough Limited
Deloitte
designSmiths
Emsleys Solicitors
Eon Visual Media
Elspeth Consulting
Ernst & Young
FeONICS
Foundation Ltd
Great North Eastern Railway
Hepher Dixon
Homeloan Management Ltd
Hull College
IT Help & Training
JDA Group
Jackson Coles
Jenko Graphics
Last Cawthra Feather
Leeds Grammar School
Lilian Black
Lupton Fawcett Solicitors
Now Consulting
Provident Financial plc
Richmonds Solicitors
Sheffield City Council
Skipton Building Society
SMC Gower Architects
Smith & Nephew plc
St James Securities
Stephen Mason Solicitors
Tennants Auctioneers
The Firm Consultancy
The Osmosis Agency
The White Rose Centre
Walker Morris
Yorkshire Bank
Yorkshire Building Society
Yorkshire Forward
Yorkshire Water

# Business in the Community members

Business in the Community aims to make community involvement a natural part of successful business practice, and to increase the quality and extent of business activity in the community. It exists to work with companies to mobilise resources (skills, expertise, influence, products and profits) to promote social and economic regeneration. The PerCent Club and ProHelp (see separate listings in this guide) are initiatives of Business in the Community.

## Contacts

### Business in the Community Head Office (covering London and South East)
137 Shepherdess Walk
London
N1 7RQ
Tel: 0870 600 2482
Web: www.bitc.org.uk

### Northern Ireland
Bridge House
Paulett Avenue
Belfast
BT5 4HD
Tel: 028 9046 0606
Email: info@bitcni.org.uk

### Wales
4th Floor, Empire House
Mount Stuart Sq
Cardiff
CF10 5FN
Tel: 029 2048 3348
Email: wales@bitc.org.uk

### North East
4 & 6 Kingsway House
Kingsway
Team Valley Trading Estate
Gateshead
NE11 0HW
Tel: 0191 487 7799
Email: anne.dutton@bitc.org.uk

### North West
2nd Floor
Amazon House
3 Brazil Street
Manchester
M1 3PJ
Tel: 0161 233 7750
Email: northwest@bitc.org.uk

### Yorkshire & Humberside
Kingswood House
80 Richardshaw Lane
Pudsey
Leeds
West Yorkshire
LS28 6BN
Tel: 0113 205 8200
Email: yorkshire@bitc.org.uk

### East Midlands
3rd Floor
30-34 Hounds Gate
Nottingham
NG1 7AB
Tel: 0115 911 6666
Email: eastmidlands@bitc.org.uk

### West Midlands
83 Bournville Lane
Birmingham
B30 2HP
Tel: 0121 451 2227
Email: purvy.patel@bitc.org.uk

### East
Bank House
58 High Street
P O Box 93
Newmarket
CB8 8ZN
Tel: 0163 866 3272
Email: mike.brophy@bitc.org.uk

### South East
Organisations based in Kent, Surrey, Sussex, Buckinghamshire, Hampshire, Oxfordshire and the Isle of Wight should contact the head office above.

### West
Royal Oak House
Royal Oak Avenue
Bristol
BS1 4GB
Tel: 0117 989 7749
Email: westofengland@bitc.org.uk

### South West
2nd Floor
Alliance House
161 Armada Way
Plymouth
PL1 1HZ
Tel: 0175 251 0410
Email: kdamarell@bitc.org.uk

## Corporate members

3i Group
3M UK Holdings plc
ABB
ACAS
Accenture

Accord plc
AES Kilroot
A F Blakemore & Son Ltd
Alcoa Flat Rolled Products
Almanac Gallery
Altnagelvin Hospitals H & SS Trust
AMEC
Anglia Regional Co-operative Society Ltd
Archant
ARM Holdings plc
Arriva plc
Arthur D Little
Ashton Morton Slack
AstraZeneca
AWG plc
Axis Europe plc

Balfour Beatty
Bank of Ireland
Barques Design Limited
Barratt Developments plc
Belfast Harbour Commissioners
Belfast Telegraph
Bernard Matthews Ltd
BHP Billiton plc
BNFL
Boots the chemists Northern Ireland
Bourne Leisure
British Gas Wales
British Transport Police
Brother UK Ltd
Bruntwood Estates
Burnley Football Club

Cambridge University Press
Camelot Group plc
Carillion plc
Castle Leisure
Cattles plc
Center Parcs
CGI
Cheshire Building Society
Compass Group plc Northern Ireland
Co-operative Financial Services
Co-operative Group
Corporate Culture Ltd

Dillon Bass Ltd
Direct Rail Services Limited
Down Lisburn Trust
Driver & Vehicle Licensing NI
DVLA

Dwr Cymru Welsh Water

Eason & Son (NI) Ltd
East of England Development Agency
EDF Energy
E H Booth & Co Ltd
Enterprise plc
Environment Agency

FG Wilson
FIRE IMC Ltd
Flag
Ford Motor Company Ltd
Foyle Food Group
FPM Accountants LLP
Fujitsu Services
Funeral Services NI Ltd

George Best Belfast City Airport
GMAC plc
Greggs plc

Haldane Fisher
HBOS
Hendre Housing Association
HM Revenue & Customs

IMI plc
Impact Development Training Group
Inbev
Inter Link Foods plc

Jaguar
J Sainsbury plc

Kainos Software Ltd

Kerry Foods
Kilwaughter Chemical Company
KPMG

Lafarge Cement
Lancashire County Developments Ltd
Lancaster University
Leekes Retail and Leisure Group of
Companies
Leyland Trucks Ltd
Liverpool City Council
Loans.co.uk

Manchester Airports Group
Marsh
Merck Sharp & Dohme Ltd
Merseyside Fire & Rescue Service
Mills & Reeve
MK Electric

Northumbrian Water Ltd
North Wales Police
Northwest Regional Development Agency
Nuclear Decommissioning Authority

Orange

Paymentshield Ltd
Pilkington plc

Reed Elsevier
Royal Liver Assurance
Royal London Group

Sage (UK) Ltd
Severn Trent plc

Shere Khan Foods Ltd
Speedy Hire plc
Sperrin Lakeland Health & Social Care
Trust
SPP Group
Styles & Wood Ltd
Syngenta

TATA Consultancy Services
TESCO plc
TNT UK Limited
Total UK
Training Services Wales
Trinity Expert Systems

Unisys
University of Central Lancashire
University of Warwick

Voca
Vodafone Group

Wales & West Utilities
Warburtons Ltd
Ward Hadaway
Warwick International
Westmorland Limited
Williams Medical Supplies plc
Wilson James
Wrengate Limited

YMCA Lakeside

Zurich Assurance Limited

# Scottish Business in the Community

Scottish Business in the Community (SBC) is Scotland's lead organisation in the field of Corporate Social Responsibility (CSR). SBC act as a broker between business and communities, providing support and advice as well as channelling resources to deliver sustainable community investment.

SBC promotes CSR as a mark of sound business practice. This is achieved through an integrated mix of national programmes and contributions, to genuine effective local partnerships.

SBC's programmes and activities are designed to offer companies a practical means of engaging in community investment.

## Contact:

*Scottish Business in the Community*
Livingstone House
First Floor (East)
43 Discovery Terrace
Heriott-Watt Research Park
Edinburgh
EH14 4AP
Tel: 0131 451 1100
Fax: 0131 451 1127
Email: info@sbcscot.com

## Corporate members

| | | |
|---|---|---|
| Amey | First | RBS Group |
| Aramark | George Wimpey | Reed in Partnership |
| BAA Scotland | Glasgow Housing Association | Royal Mail |
| Blackhorse | GlaxoSmithKline | Sainsbury's |
| Boots | Greggs | Scotmid |
| BT Scotland | HBOS | Scottish & Southern Energy |
| BP | Holyrood Communications | Scottish Enterprise |
| BrightHouse | HSBC | Scottish Gas |
| British Energy | John Lewis | ScottishPower |
| Buccleuch Group | Johnson & Johnson | Scottish Water |
| Cala | Johnson Press | Scottish Widows |
| Calor Gas | KPMG | Shell |
| Cisco Systems | Kwik Fit | Sodexho |
| Clydesdale Bank | Laing O'Rourke Scotland | Standard Life |
| Cunninghame Housing Association | Lloyds TSB Scotland | Student Loans |
| DC Thomson | Marks & Spencer | Tesco |
| DLA Piper Rudnick Gray Cary | McGrigors | United Utilities |
| Diageo | Morgan Stanley | VisitScotland |
| Dunfermline Building Society | Oracle | Weir Group |
| Enterprise rent-a-car | PriceWaterhouseCoopers | WH Smith |
| Johnson and Johnson | Prudential | Wood Group |

# London Benchmarking Group members

In 1994 six leading UK based international companies came together to form the London Benchmarking Group (LBG), to better manage, measure and understand corporate community involvement.

Companies' foremost contribution to society is in providing goods and services and thereby creating wealth, generating jobs and paying taxes. Traditionally many have also made an additional voluntary, usually charitable, contribution. As companies' relationship with the community becomes more complex, the motivations for involvement are more diverse. These include:

▶ a sense of moral and social responsibility, also responding to expectations from society

▶ a belief that companies have a long term interest in fostering a healthy community, sometimes known as enlightened self-interest

▶ the knowledge that community interventions involving employees, customers and suppliers can have direct benefits, through increased profitability, stronger company image, reduced costs, better employee morale and improved customer loyalty.

The original members used these three motivations as the basis to understand how each managed and measured its community involvement programmes.

Since then, the group has grown to number 109, with many more applying the techniques independently.

All members recognise that companies are expected to get involved in the community and are often judged on the amount they contribute. This involvement often goes beyond straightforward donations to charity – and if a comprehensive account is not produced, key groups such as staff, local communities, opinion formers and the media might easily form the wrong impression.

The challenge facing the founding members of the LBG was how to effectively report their community activities to demonstrate that they are indeed responsible corporate citizens. Effective reporting is best based on solid measures of performance, but in the 'soft' area of social reporting hard measures are still in their infancy.

Their solution was to devise a tool with which to manage, measure and compare their relationship with the community – The London Benchmarking Model. Further information about the group and its benchmarking model may be found at www.lbg-online.net.

## Members

| | | | |
|---|---|---|---|
| Abbey | CMS Cameron McKenna | Lloyds of London | Sainsburys |
| ABN AMRO | Credit Suisse First Boston | Lloyds TSB | Scottish & Newcastle |
| Airbus | Deloitte & Touche | Marks & Spencer | ScottishPower |
| Altria | Deutsche Bank AG London | Marsh | Serco |
| Alliance Boots | Diageo | Microsoft UK | Severn Trent |
| Anglo American | DLA Piper | Morgan Stanley | Shell International |
| ANZ | DSG International | National Grid | Standard Chartered |
| AOL UK | E.ON UK | Nationwide | Standard Life |
| ASDA | EDF Energy | Nestlé UK | Telecom Italia |
| AstraZeneca | EMI Group | Nokia | Tesco Stores |
| BAA | Ernst & Young | Northern Rock | The Body Shop International |
| BAE Systems | Freshfields Bruckhaus Deringer | npower | The Boots Group |
| Barclays | Friends Provident | O2 | The Co-operative Group |
| BBC | FSA | OMV | Trader Media Group |
| BG Group | Gallaher | Pearson | Turner Broadcasting |
| BNFL | GlaxoSmithKline | PricewaterhouseCoopers | UBS |
| Bradford & Bingley | HBOS | Procter & Gamble UK | Unilever |
| British Airways | Herbert Smith | Provident Financial | United Utilities |
| British American Tobacco | Home Retail Group | Prudential | UnumProvident |
| BSkyB | HSBC | Reed Elsevier | VISA Europe |
| BT | IPC Media | Reuters | Vodafone in the UK |
| BUPA | John Lewis Partnership | Rio Tinto | Wates Group |
| Capita Group | Kelloggs | Rolls-Royce | WH Smith |
| Cadbury Schweppes | KPMG | Rothschild | Woolworths |
| Camelot Group | Land Securities | Royal & Sun Alliance | Yell |
| Centrica | Legal & General | Royal Bank of Scotland Group | Zurich |
| Cheshire Building Society | Liberty Global Europe | Royal Mail | |
| CitiFinancial Europe | Linklaters | SABMiller | |

# PerCent Club members

The PerCent Club has traditionally consisted of a group of companies committed to contributing at least 0.5% of pre-tax profits (or 1.0% of dividends) in contributions to the community. As of 1 January 2001, this threshold was raised to 1% to mark the millennium; so establishing the PerCent Club Millennium Standard. Contributions can include cash donations as well as investment in the form of staff time and skills, gifts in kind and the use of facilities. The aim of the club is to promote increased levels of support by the private sector both for charities generally, and for social issues which most concern businesses and the communities in which they operate. The PerCent Club also seeks to be the leading benchmark for corporate community investment and helps companies to measure their programmes.

It should not be assumed that these companies are necessarily the best to approach when seeking support. They should already be giving the required amount for membership, and will not necessarily have extra resources to give away.

## Members

3M United Kingdom plc
AF Blakemore and Sons
Accord plc
Adnams
Allen & Overy LLP
Alliance & Leicester
Alliance Boots
Alpheus Solutions Ltd
Anglian Water
Anglo American
Arco
AstraZeneca plc
Aviva plc
Axis Europe plc

Barchester Healthcare
Barclays
BBC
Ben Bailey Homes
Bernard Matthews Ltd
BG Group
BHP Billiton
Birkett Long Solicitors
BOC Group plc
Body Shop International
Bradford & Bingley
Bridge Economics
British Airways
British American Tobacco
British Nuclear Fuels
BSkyB
BT Group
Bunzl
BUPA

C. Hoare & Co
Cadbury Schweppes
Calor Gas Ltd
Capita Group plc
Camelot
Capital One
Cardiff Bus
Care Circle

Carillion plc
Centrica
Charis Limited
Clarendon Executive
CM Works
Coca-Cola Bottlers (Ulster) Ltd.
Coca-Cola Great Britain
Colliers CRE plc
Co-operative Group
Compass Group UK & Ireland
Customer Interpreter Ltd

Deloitte & Touche
Deutsche Bank AG London
Derbyshire Building Society
Diageo
Dollond & Aitchison
DSG international plc

Eaga Partnership Ltd
East of Eng Co-operative Soc.
EMI Group
EDF Energy
Ernst & Young
Eversheds LLP
FA Premier League
fabcats
Faber Maunsell Ltd
Financial Services Authority
First Trust Bank
Force-techie Limited
Ford
Freshfields Bruckhaus Deringer
Foyle Food Group Ltd
Funeral Services N Ireland

GCap Media plc
get2thepoint
GKN plc
GlaxoSmithKline
Greggs plc
GUS plc

Happy
HBOS plc
Herbert Smith LLP
Hughes Christensen Co

Imperial Tobacco Ltd
innocent
International Training Service
ITV plc

Jaguar Cars
Jarrold and Sons Ltd
John Day Marketing Associates
John Laing plc
Jones Lang LaSalle
John Lewis Partnership

Kelloggs
KPMG

Lafarge Cement Ireland
Leadership Talks
Legal & General
Linklaters
Liberty IT
Lincolnshire Co-operative
Lloyds TSB
London Communications
LSI Architects LLP

Man Group plc
Marks & Spencer
Maybin Support Services NI
Mazars LLP
Mears Group
Mills & Reeve
Mott MacDonald
Moy Park

National Grid
Nestle
N M Rothschild & Sons
Newbury Building Society

Norfolk County Services
Nortel
Northern Rock
Northumbrian Water
NPS Group
NRG Group UK Ltd

Old Mutual

Pearson plc
Positve Media Consultancy
Premier Farnell plc
Premier Rugby
PricewaterhouseCoopers
Procter & Gamble

Reed Elsevier
Royal Bank of Scotland
RWE npower
Provident Financial
Prudential plc

Redrow plc

SABMiller plc
Sainsburys
Samworth Brothers
Schroders plc
Scott Bader
Scottish & Newcastle
Screenprint Plus
sf group
Shaftesbury plc
Shire plc
Siemens Ind. Turbomachinery
SMG plc
Smith & Nephew plc
Sodexho
St James's Place Capital plc
Standard Chartered Bank

TATA Consultancy Services Ltd
Tesco Stores
The Big Oxford Computer Co
The British Land Company
The Design Conspiracy
The Marshall Group

The Midcounties Co-operative
The Phone Co-op
The Tussauds Group
The-Pink-Pig.Co.Uk Ltd
TNT UK Ltd
Turner Broadcasting

Ulster Carpets
Unilever
United Co-operatives
United Utilities
UnumProvident
Vodafone Group
UTV

We Research It Ltd
WH Smith
Workspace Group
WPP

XMA Limited
Xstrata

# ProHelp

## What is ProHelp?

Formerly the Professional Firms Group, ProHelp is a national network of around 1,000 firms across the UK who volunteer their time and expertise for the benefit of the local community. It is a Business in the Community initiative whose member firms have committed over £15 million worth of support. ProHelp was established over 15 years ago.

Participating professional firms include Lawyers, Accountants, IT Consultants, Architects, Surveyors, Marketing Specialists and Engineers. Community Groups that receive support from ProHelp are non-profit making, locally based and cannot afford to pay for professional services. Firms can contribute towards a single project or give longer-term strategic support such as becoming a trustee.

## What help can they provide?

The professional firms take undertake short assignments which include feasibility studies, structural surveys, marketing and business plans, legal and accountancy advice and property valuations.

## Will my project be eligible?

You must be a community-based not-for-profit organisation working for the social and economic regeneration of your local area and should fit within the following criteria:

- you must have a track record of working successfully with the local community

- you must not have the funding for the specific piece of work to be done nor be retaining paid advisors to do the work

- if you are a branch of a national organisation, you must be locally constituted and prove that neither the expertise nor the funding to pay for the work is available centrally

- your project must be realistic and viable

- your governing body must authorise the involvement of ProHelp.

## When will a project not qualify?

- applications for assistance with litigation will not be considered;

- help is generally not given to animal welfare organisations whose primary focus is overseas aid

- assistance to religious groups will only be offered if the project benefits the wider community.

## What do I do now?

If you have a project in mind which could benefit from help from ProHelp, please get in touch. Local group contacts are listed below.

## What will happen then?

If your project is appropriate, you will be asked to fill in a standard questionnaire. It may also be necessary for you to meet with a representative from ProHelp to develop a fuller brief for the assignment. A summary of your project will then be taken to a group who will decide whether or not your project meets the eligibility criteria and if there is a firm available to do the work. A meeting will then be arranged between yourself and the interested professional firm.

### The National Prohelp Manager

Nicki Della-Porter
Tel: 020 7566 6611
Email: nicki.della-porta@bitc.org.uk

## Local group contacts

### East of England

**Cambridge**
Celia Johns
Cambridge ProHelp Manager
c/o Anglia Water (awg) plc
Anglia House, Ambury Rd
Huntingdon, Cambs
PE29 3NZ
Tel: 0148 043 5362
Email: celia.johns@bitc.org.uk

**Colchester**
Russ Cottee
PO Box 184
Benslett
Essex
SS7 9BQ
Tel: 0170 255 8192
Email: russ.cottee@bitc.org.uk

**Norfolk**
Gary Towers
BITC
PO Box 543
Norwich
NR4 7SR
Tel: 0160 350 8438
Email: gary.towers@bitc.org.uk

**Peterborough**
Celia Johns
Cambridge ProHelp Manager
c/o Anglia Water (awg) plc
Anglia House
Ambury Rd
Huntingdon
Cambs
PE29 3NZ
Tel: 0148 043 5362
Email: celia.johns@bitc.org.uk

**Suffolk**
Crawford Gillan
PO Box 559
Ipswich
Suffolk
IP1 3YB
Tel: 0147 340 1117
Email: c.gillan@ntlworld.com

## East Midlands

**Derbyshire**
Ann Hilton
BITC
30-34 Hounds Gate
Nottingham
NG1 78B
Tel: 0115 924 7408
Email: ann.Hilton@bitc.org.uk

**High Peak and Derbyshire Dales**
High Peak CVS
1a Bingswood Trading Estate
Whaley Bridge
High Peak
SK23 7LY
Tel: 0166 373 6430
Email: chris@highpeakcvs.org.uk

**Leicestershire**
Rosie Colls
Community Development Co-ordinator
42 Towers Street
Leicestershire
LE1 6WT
Tel: 0116 275 6469
Email: Rosie@leicestershirecares.co.uk

**Lincolnshire & Rutland**
Shona Welberry
Care of Business in the Community
Po Box 33
Boston
PE22 0YT
Tel: 0778 965 1530
Email: shona.welberry@bitc.org.uk

**Northhamptonshire**
Ann Hilton
BITC
30-34 Hounds Gate
Nottingham
NG1 78B
Tel: 0115 924 7408
Email: ann.hilton@bitc.org.uk

**Nottinghamshire**
Ann Hilton
BITC
30-34 Hounds Gate
Nottingham
NG1 78B
Tel: 0115 924 7408
Email: ann.hilton@bitc.org.uk

## London and the South East

**Brighton & Hove**
Oliver Maxwell
Brighton & Hove Business Community
Partnership
Office 2A
11 Jew Street
Brighton
BN1 7UT
Tel: 0127 377 0075
Email: oliver.maxwell@bhcp.org.uk

**London**
Emma Price Thomas
ProHelp Manager
Business in the Community
137 Shepherdess Walk
London
N1 7RQ
Tel: 020 7566 8652
Email: emma.thomas@bitc.org.uk

**Surrey**
Edward Baker
Surrey Voluntary Service Council
Astolat
Coniers Way
New Inn Lane
Burpham
Surrey
GU4 7HL
Tel: 0148 345 9292 (x204)
Email: edwardb@surreyca.org.uk

**North East**
Stephen Linney
BITC
Units 4 & 6 Kingsway House
Kingsway
Team Valley
Gateshead
NE11 0HW
Tel: 0191 487 7799
Email: stephen.linney@bitc.org.uk

## North West

**Cumbria**
Lynn Macnaughton
The Office Building
Mardale Road
Penrith
CA11 9EH
Tel: 0176 886 8940
Email: lynn.macnaughton@bitc.org.uk

**Greater Manchester**
Chris Gopal
ProHelp Manager
BITC
2nd Floor
Amazon House
3 Brazil Street
Manchester
M1 3PJ
Tel: 0161 233 7750
Email: chris.gopal@bitc.org.uk

**Merseyside**
Chris Gopal
ProHelp Manager
Room 301
39 Fleet Street
Liverpool
L1 4AR
Tel: 0151 706 9500
Email: chris.gopal@bitc.org.uk

**Wirral**
Tranmere Alliance
225 Church Road
Tranmere
Wirrall
CH42 0LD
Tel: 0151 644 1100
Email:
justine.burns@tranmerealliance.org.uk

**Northern Ireland**
Rosin McVickeri
Bridge House
Paulett Avenue
Belfast
BT5 4HD
Tel: 028 9046 0606
Email: roisin.mcvicker@bitcni.org.uk

## South West

**Cornwall**
Ann Davies
BITC
2nd Floor
Alliance House
161 Armada Way
Plymouth
PL1 1HZ
Tel: 01752 510410
Email: ann.davies@bitc.org.uk

**Devon**
Bob Northey
BITC
2nd Floor
Alliance House
161 Armada Way
Plymouth
PL1 1HZ
Tel: 0175 251 0410
Email: bob.northey@bitc.org.uk

## Wales
**Cardiff**
Roger Jones
BITC
9th Floor
Empire House
Mount Stuart Square
Cardiff
CF10 5FN
Tel: 029 2043 6919
Email: roger.jones@bitc.org.uk

**North Wales**
David Collins
BITC
2nd Floor
12-14 Hall Square
Denbigh
Denbighshire
LL16 3NU
Tel: 0174 581 7325
Email: david.collins@bitc.org.uk

**South West Wales**
Martyn Bannister
William Knox House
Suite D
Brittanic Way
Llandarcy
Neath
SA10 6EL
Tel: 0179 232 3689
Email: martyn.bannister@bitc.org.uk

## West of England
**Bristol**
Marie Smith
Care of ITV West
Bath Road
Brislington
Bristol
BSF4 3HG
Tel: 0117 972 2111
Email: marie.smith@bitc.org.uk

**Gloucestershire**
Kieran Daly
Tel: 0166 683 8581
Email: kierandaly@btinternet.com

**Swindon**
Kieran Daly
Tel: 0166 683 8581
Email: kierandaly@btinternet.com

## West Midlands
**Birmingham**
John Guilford
c/o Trinity Systems
The Oaks
Westwood Park
Coventry
CV4 8JB
Tel: 024 7642 0115
Email: john.guilford@bitc.org.uk

## Yorkshire & Humber
**Hull & Humber**
Anthony Wallis
Melton Cart
North Ferrebe
East Yorkshire
HU14 3HH
Tel: 0148 263 8610
Email: antony.wallis@bitc.org.uk

**North Yorkshire**
Rebecca Addy
Kingswood House
80 Richardshaw Lane
Pudsey
Leeds
LS28 6BN
Tel: 0113 205 8200
Email: rebecca.addy@bitc.org.uk

**South Yorkshire**
Helen Sims
Albion House
Savile Street
Sheffield
S4 7UD
Tel: 0114 201 8983
Email: helen.sims@bitc.org.uk

**West Yorkshire**
Rebecca Addy
Kingswood House
80 Richardshaw Lane
Pudsey
Leeds
LS28 6BN
Tel: 0113 205 8200
Email: rebecca.addy@bitc.org.uk

In this section we list national agencies which may be helpful in the context of company giving, under the general headings employees, sponsorship, enterprise and training, education, donations, promoting good practice, media, general and informal contacts.

## Employees/professional advice

### Business Community Connections
Gainsborough House, 2 Sheen Road, Richmond upon Thames, Surrey TW9 1AE. Tel: 020 8973 2390 Fax: 020 8973 2396 Web: www.bcconnections.org.uk

### Business in the Community
137 Shepherdess Walk, London N1 7RQ. Tel: 0870 600 2482 Web: www.bitc.org.uk

### Chartered Surveyors Voluntary Service
RICS Contact Centre, Surveyor Court, Westwood Business Park, Westwood Way, Coventry CV4 8JE. Tel: 0870 333 1600 Web: www.rics.org.uk

### Community Service Volunteers (CSV)
237 Pentonville Road, London N1 9NJ. Tel: 020 7278 6601 Web: www.csv.org.uk

### Life Academy
9 Chesham Road, Guildford, Surrey GU1 3LS. Tel: 01483 301 170 Web: www.life-academy.co.uk

### ProHelp
c/o Business in the Community, 137 Shepherdess Walk, London N1 7RQ. Tel: 0870 600 2482 Web: www.bitc.org.uk

### REACH (Retired Executives Action Clearing House)
89 Albert Embankment, London SE1 7TP. Tel: 020 7582 6543 Web: www.volwork.org.uk

### The Retirement Trust
Tulip House, 70 Borough High Street, London SE1 1XF. Tel: 020 7864 9908 Web: www.theretirementtrust.org.uk

### Volunteering England
London Office, Regents Wharf, 8 All Saints Street, London N1 9RL. Tel: 0845 305 6979 Web: www.volunteering.org.uk

## Sponsorship

### Arts and Business
Nutmeg House, 0 Gainsford Street, Butlers Wharf, London SE1 2NY. Tel: 020 7378 8143 Web: www.AandB.org.uk

### Community Links
Canning Town Public Hall, 105 Barking Road, Canning Town, London E16 4HQ. Tel: 020 7473 2270 Web: www.community-links.org

### Groundwork UK
Lockside, 5 Scotland Street, Birmingham, B1 2RR. Tel: 0121 236 8565 Web: www.groundwork.org.uk

## Enterprise & Training

### Common Purpose UK
Common Purpose, Discovery House, 28–42 Banner Street, London EC1Y 8QE. Tel: 020 7608 8100 Web: www.commonpurpose.org.uk There are regional offices throughout the UK.

### Community Development Foundation (CDF)
Headquarters, Unit 5, Angel Gate, 320–326 City Road, London EC1V 2PT. Tel: 020 7833 1772 Web: www.cdf.org.uk

### National Federation of Enterprise Agencies
12 Stephenson Court, Fraser Road, Priory Business Park, Bedford MK44 3WH. Tel: 0123 483 1623 Web: www.nfea.com

## Education

### Confederation of British Industry (CBI)
Centre Point, 103 New Oxford Street, London WC1A 1DU. Tel: 020 7379 7400 Web: www.cbi.org.uk

### Council for Industry and Higher Education (CIHE)
Studio 11, Tiger House, Burton Street, London WC1H 9BY. Tel: 020 7383 7667 Web: www.cihe-uk.com

### The Work Foundation
Peter Runge House, 3 Carlton House, London SW1Y 5DG. Tel: 020 7004 7200 Web: www.theworkfoundation.com

## Donations

### Charities Aid Foundation (CAF)
25 Kings Hill Avenue, Kings Hill, West Malling, Kent ME19 4TA. Tel: 0173 252 0000 Web: www.cafonline.org

### Charities Trust
Suite 22, Century Building, Brunswick Business Park, Tower Street, Liverpool L3 4BJ. Tel: 0151 286 5129 Web: www.charitiestrust.org

### Charity Commission
London
Harmsworth House, 13–15 Bouverie Street, London EC4Y 8DP. Main Contact Centre: 0845 300 0218 Web: www.charitycommission.gov.uk
Liverpool
12 Princes Dock, Princes Parade, Liverpool L3 1DE
Taunton
Woodfield House, Tangier, Taunton, Somerset TA1 4BL
Newport
8th Floor, Clarence House, Clarence Place, Newport, South Wales NP19 7AA

### In Kind Direct
5th Floor, 11–15 Monument Street, London EC3R 8JU.
Tel: 020 7714 3930 Web: www.inkinddirect.org

### ShareGift
5 Lower Grosvenor Place, London SW1W 0EJ.
Tel: 020 7828 1151 Web: www.sharegift.org

### Workplace Giving UK Ltd
2nd Floor, Cavendish House, 369 Burnt Oak Broadway, Edgware,
Middlesex HA8 5AW. Tel: 020 8731 5125
Web: www.workplacegiving-uk.com

## Promoting Good Practice

### Business in the Community
137 Shepherdess Walk, London N1 7RQ. Tel: 0870 600 2482
Web: www.bitc.org.uk

### Scottish Business in the Community
Livingstone House, First Floor (East), 43 Discovery Terrace,
Heriott-Watt Research Park, Edinburgh, EH14 4AP.
Tel: 0131 451 1100 Web: www.sbcscot.com

### Charities Tax Reform Group (CTRG)
1 Millbank, London SW1P 3JZ. Tel: 020 7222 1265
Web: www.charitytax.info

### The Corporate Responsibility Group
87–91 Newman Street, London W1T 3EY. Tel: 020 7299 8744
Web: www.crguk.org

### Directory of Social Change
London
24 Stephenson Way, London NW1 2DP. Tel: 08450 77 77 07
Liverpool
Federation House, Hope Street, Liverpool L1 9BW.
Tel: 0151 708 0136

### Ethical Investment Research Services (EIRIS)
The Ethical Investment Research Service, 80–84 Bondway,
London SW8 1SF. Tel: 020 7840 5700 Web: www.eiris.org

### Out of This World
106 High Street, Gosforth, Newcastle upon Tyne NE3 1HB.
Tel: 0191 213 5377 Web: www.ootw.co.uk

### The Corporate Citizenship Company
Ground Floor South, Cottons Centre, London Bridge City, London
SE1 2QG. Tel: 020 7940 5610
Web: www.corporate-citizenship.co.uk

### The London Benchmarking Group
c/o The Corporate Citizenship Company, Ground Floor South,
Cottons Centre, London Bridge City, London SE1 2QG.
Tel: 020 7940 5610 Web: www.corporate-citizenship.co.uk

### The PerCent Club
c/o Business in the Community, 137 Shepherdess Walk, London
N1 7RQ. Tel: 0870 600 2482 Web: www.bitc.org.uk

### The Prince of Wales International Business Leaders Forum (IBLF)
15–16 Cornwall Terrace, Regent's Park, London NW1 4QP.
Tel: 020 7467 3600 Web: www.iblf.org

## Media

### BBC Appeals Office
MC3D3 Media Centre, Media Village, 201 Wood Lane, London
W12 7TQ. Tel: 020 8008 1198
Web: www.bbc.co.uk/info/policies/charities

### Campaign for Press & Broadcasting Freedom
2nd Floor, Vi & Garner Smith House, 23 Orford Road,
Walthamstow, London E17 9NL. Tel: 020 8521 5932
Web: www.cpbf.org.uk

### Channel Four Television Company
124 Horseferry Road, London SW1P 2TX. Tel: 020 7396 4444
Web: www.channel4.com

### CSV Media
237 Pentonville Road, London N1 9NJ. Tel: 0800 525 165
Web: www.csv.org.uk

### ITV Network Centre
200 Gray's Inn Road, London WC1X 8HF. Tel: 020 7843 8000
Web: www.itv.com

### Media Trust
3–7 Euston Centre, Regent's Place, London NW1 3JG.
Tel: 020 7874 7600 Web: www.mediatrust.org

## General Company Information

### Companies House
Crown Way, Cardiff CF14 3UZ. Tel: 0870 333 3636
Web: www.companieshouse.gov.uk

### Trades Union Congress (TUC)
Congress House, Great Russell Street, London WC1B 3LS.
Tel: 020 7636 4030 Web: www.tuc.org.uk

### Industrial Common Ownership Finance Ltd (ICOF)
Brunswick Court, Brunswick Square, Bristol BS2 8PE.
Tel: 01179 166750 Web: www.icof.co.uk

### Industrial Common Ownership Movement Ltd (ICOM)
Brunswick Court, Brunswick Square, Bristol BS2 8PE.
Tel: 01179 166750 Web: www.icof.co.uk

### British Urban Regeneration Association
63–66 Hatton Garden, London EC1N 8LE.
Freephone: 0800 0181 260 Tel: 020 7539 4030
Web: www.bura.org.uk

### Urban and Economic Development Ltd
26 Gray's Inn Road, London WC1X 8HP. Tel: 020 7831 9986
Web: www.urbed.com

### Young Enterprise UK
Peterley House, Peterley Road, Oxford OX4 2TZ.
Tel. 0186 577 6845 Web: www.young-enterprise.org.uk

## Informal Contacts

### Association of Inner Wheel Clubs in Great Britain & Ireland
51 Warwick Square, London SW1V 2AT. Tel: 020 7834 4600
Web: www.association-innerwheel.org.uk

### Rotary International in Great Britain & Ireland
Kinwarton Road, Alcester, Warwickshire B49 6PB.
Tel: 01789 765 411 Web: www.rotary-ribi.org

# Index